ENVIRONMENTAL ADMINISTRATION

McGRAW-HILL SERIES IN POPULATION BIOLOGY

Consulting Editors
Paul R. Ehrlich, Stanford University
Richard W. Holm, Stanford University

ENVIRONMENTAL ADMINISTRATION

STAHRL EDMUNDS

Dean, Graduate School of Administration
University of California, Riverside

JOHN LETEY

Professor of Soil Physics
Chairman, Environmental Sciences Division
University of California, Riverside

McGRAW-HILL BOOK COMPANY

New York   St. Louis   San Francisco   Düsseldorf   Johannesburg
Kuala Lumpur   London   Mexico   Montreal   New Delhi   Panama
Rio de Janeiro   Singapore   Sydney   Toronto

ENVIRONMENTAL ADMINISTRATION

1 2 3 4 5 6 7 8 9 0 K P K P 7 9 8 7 6 5 4 3 2

This book was set in Times Roman by Black Dot, Inc. The editors
were Richard F. Dojny and Annette Hall; the designer was Rolando
Morales; and the production supervisor was Ted Agrillo. The
drawings were done by Anco Technical Services.
The printer and binder was Kingsport Press, Inc.

Library of Congress Cataloging in Publication Data

Edmunds, Stahrl.
Environmental administration.

(McGraw-Hill series in population biology)
(McGraw-Hill management series)
1. Environmental policy.   2.   Decision-making.
I. Letey, John, 1933–   joint author. II. Title.
HC79.E5E325   301.31   72-10054
ISBN 0-07-019023-2

To Amy

CONTENTS

FOREWORD

It has now become clear that the first phase of a program to turn humanity in the direction of ecological sanity is over—at least in the United States. The mule has been hit between the eyes with a two-by-four, and its attention attracted. Even the most Neanderthal politicians have heard of the environmental crisis, and at least give lip service to doing something about it.

Now phase two is beginning. People are starting to realize that the kinds of societal transformations which survival requires will be neither cheap nor easy. On one hand this has produced a "backlash"—a concerted effort to keep mankind on the road to oblivion—mounted by those with a strong financial or emotional interest in the preservation of the status quo. On the other hand serious people in all parts of society have begun a dialogue on the ways and means of meeting the growing crisis. In this book Edmunds and Letey have made an extensive and important contribution to that dialogue.

PAUL R. EHRLICH
Stanford University

PREFACE

The deep concern shown by consumers and the public over the quality of the environment, the passage of the National Environmental Quality Act of 1969, and the numerous governmental regulations to control pollution and environmental quality have, by now, made it abundantly clear that a new level of involvement with ecological effects is required of any administrator in business or government who makes decisions about products and residuals which end up in land, air, or water—as most materials do. That is to say, the outputs of the economic system have had their impact upon environmental degradation, and now the environment will have its impact upon management decisions.

The questions then are: How will administrative decision making be altered to take environmental effects into account? What biological data will influence the decision process? How will the new decision model work? What will be the consequences of a new decision structure for present managerial actions?

Questions such as these are of significant interest to business executives who will be affected by changes in decision making, to governmental administrators who are initiating the changes, and to students and faculties concerned with the teaching of administrative processes to new generations of executives. This book on environmental administration is addressed to the crucial questions of how environmental side effects occur from present decision processes and how the decision structure may be altered to improve environmental quality. As such, the discussion should concern the business executive, the government administrator, the scholar, and the students who are interested in the environment and its impact on management.

The purpose of the book, then, is to trace the environmental effects of our economic activity in the past, to show how they affect the ecological system, and to inquire how these actions and decisions might be changed to lessen their adverse impact. The central theme of the inquiry is to see how ecological diversity, balance, and well-being can be maintained consistent with the satisfaction of human economic needs. The idea of "consistent with" implies some form of tradeoff; that is, a choice or tradeoff between economic objectives and environmental quality may be required. The issue then becomes what degree of environmental quality, or what rate of economic growth, is sufficient? To such a question there is, of course, only an individual subjective answer which reflects each person's individual preferences and value scheme. Therefore, each person is a part of a larger decision process in the making; but that new decision process cannot come into being without the pertinent information being available and structured into a set of choices. The book attempts to show what information is pertinent for an administrative decision affecting the environment and how that information should be structured for intelligent choices.

The organization of the contents reflects this purpose. The first section deals with the emerging problems of the environment and how the problems resulted from our present mode of making decisions. The second section describes the natural processes in the ecological system, their limits and tolerances, and the effects of human actions on the health of species or biological communities (including human). The third section describes how these biological processes can be observed, measured, and related to economic decision making. The fourth, and last, section shows how programs to improve the environment might be implemented. The whole is intended to demonstrate how alternatives in decisions, human actions, and environmental consequences may be examined so that choices can be made between economic actions and environmental quality.

A book which covers ecology, economics, administration, information handling, choice making, and political science is ambitious in seeking to integrate a wide range of knowledge, especially since we are all specialized by training in one or few disciplines. We are grateful to Henry Vaux, Ralph d'Arge, Thomas Crocker, and Guy L. Zahn for their valuable suggestions regarding Section Three, and to Peggy Darlington and Sandra Lesh for their secretarial help. Most of all we are grateful for the environmental interest of campuses and youth. Whatever else the youthful counterculture may bring to the future, nothing can be more significant than their awareness of the need to change our decision processes in order that we may live as human beings in, of, and compatible with our environment. And so this book is dedicated to the youth who helped us perceive something that we did not formerly see. We hope that the contribution of administrative skills to their vision will make the quality of their lives and the quality of their environment what they wish it to be; and we wish them well.

STAHRL EDMUNDS

JOHN LETEY

ENVIRONMENTAL ADMINISTRATION

Section One

The Emerging Problem of Environmental Administration

The rapid urbanization of the United States in recent decades and the increasing technology have concentrated populations and wastes in very limited land areas. More than half the population is crowded into 1 percent of the land, and wasteloads in these crowded areas approximate 15 tons per person. Such concentrated wasteloads are more than the surrounding land, air, and water can assimilate without deterioration in quality. As environmental quality has deteriorated, biological damage to many species, including man, has become apparent. The President of the United States has warned that, unless we arrest the depredations inflicted on nature, we face the prospect of ecological disaster.

This section describes the emerging problems in environmental administration in terms of their origins, history, and causes. From such a background, some alternative solutions are explored, especially in changing decision processes which adversely affect the environment. Chapter 1 discusses the critical nature of the environmental problems and issues, along with their historic origin in industrialization and Western thought.

Industrialization and economic growth lead to changes in natural cycles, mainly through residuals and wastes altering streams, air, and land, and reducing their biological productivity. These relationships are explored in Chapter 2 on human interaction with the environment.

Much of our environmental damage is inadvertent due to lack of attention to ecological effects, which have little part in current decisions. Current decisions are based upon land-use practices, market mechanisms, and industrial organization derived from the past. These decision practices, and their effects, are dealt with in Chapter 3.

The government is a factor in how decisions are made because legislation establishes most of the contractual, regulatory, and incentive parameters in the decision structure. The role of government as conservationist, developer, and monitor is explored in Chapters 4 and 5.

Finally, in Chapter 6 an expanded view of environmental decision making, which would be more consistent with maintaining environmental quality, is suggested, as a framework for the balance of the book.

Chapter 1

The Concept of Environmental Administration

Environmental administration is a concept of managing human affairs in such a way that biological health, diversity, and ecological balance will be preserved. In other words, environmental administration is concerned with providing a congruous and workable interface between men's activity and nature. *Nature* is all the biological processes making up the interrelations of organisms with their environment. The totality of these interactions between organisms and their environment is referred to as ecology, or the *ecosystem*.

Why should anyone be interested in environmental administration? Man, too, is an organism living in the environment and depending upon it for energy, resources, habitat, and, above all, for sustenance from the same food chain from which all other organisms subsist. That is, the human organism has its being in nature, depends on the environment, is part of the ecosystem. Yet human beings often take actions and behave as though they were apart from the ecosystem. This is seen in the notion of "the conquest of nature," which has been a technological pursuit for three centuries. The separation of the human organism from the base of its being in nature is seen even more clearly in high wasteloads which are disposed by an urban, technological society upon the ecosystem. These wasteloads are greater than the natural processes of the ecosystem can assimilate, with the result that oxygen is depleted from the streams, toxic chemicals enter the waterways and the oceans, and air pollutants cause damaging photochemical reactions in the atmosphere.

The result of these wastes and residuals from human activity is that the environment loses some of its life support capability. Species die and man himself suffers biological damage. The depletion of species populations reduces diversity in the environment, impairs the food chain, and causes ecological imbalances which in the end are felt as health damage to human beings. Environmental administration is, then, a concept concerning itself with the long-run biological well-being of the human species.

What does not concern environmental administration? It is not primarily concerned with economic growth, the optimization of production, or the conquest of nature. Economic growth and maximizing output are short-run goals directed at the early satisfaction of human wants. The short-run satisfaction of wants has been the concern of industrialization, economics, and technology for three centuries.

Unfortunately, the output of usable goods is accompanied by about an equal quantity of unwanted wastes. This wasteload has become so great that there is biological damage to human beings and the environment. In these circumstances, environmental administration takes a long-run view of human priorities and assumes that human affairs should so be managed that human health, diversity, and ecological balance will be preserved. Environmental administration does not ignore the need of human beings for consumption and early satisfaction of wants; rather, it seeks the balanced view that satiation of wants should be met within the constraints of natural laws, and that short-run satisfactions must take account of long-run ecological survival.

ABSTRACT OF CONTENT

The content of this book deals with the tradeoff between short-run satisfactions and long-run ecological balance. Section One is concerned with defining the emerging problems in the environment, particularly the biological hazards from pollution and chemicalization of the environment. The history and decision processes which cause these residuals to degrade the environment are examined, with a view to seeking alternatives. These alternative decision processes are explored in Chapter 6 and

Section Three. Meantime, Section Two delineates the biological process which acts as a constraint on man's decision structures.

The general proposition is advanced in Section Three that the quality of the environment can be affected, for better or worse, by the cost structure and incentives which pertain to "common goods," which are the allegedly "free goods" like air and water that have no (or minimal) prices in the market structure. The lack of pricing of these common goods leads to their overuse and to environmental degradation. That is, the overuse of free resources results in "external," or social, costs to the society at large, either in expenditures to clean up the environment or in health damage to the populace. A methodology for examining these external, or social, costs is provided in Chapters 10 through 17 with the purpose of creating the foundation for decisions on how to improve environmental quality.

A workable decision process for improving the environment being available, the next step is how to manage projects and organizations to achieve better environmental quality. The managerial methods for organizing and implementing environmental improvement are dealt with in Section Four. In a sense, then, the entire book is a commentary and an analysis of how we arrive at decisions today and how we might change the decision structure for the purpose of enhancing the quality of life. As such, we necessarily must examine the historical origin of present ideas and practices, as well as alternatives open to us. The balance of this chapter describes briefly the nature of the present ecological crisis and the historical origins of contemporary ideas regarding nature which have brought us near to disaster. The following headings outline the chapter's content:

1 The potential for ecological disaster
2 Health hazards
3 Basic causes of environmental troubles
4 Learning to manage ourselves
5 Some deeply embedded assumptions underlying technology
6 Some origins of thought on natural science and the environment
7 The scientific views of Francis Bacon
8 Giordano Bruno—precursor of the conquest of nature
9 The conquest of nature
10 Concept of environmental administration

THE POTENTIAL FOR ECOLOGICAL DISASTER

The President of the United States reported to the Congress: "The recent upsurge of public concern over environmental questions reflects a belated recognition that man has been too cavalier in his relations with nature. Unless we arrest the depredations that have been inflicted so carelessly on our natural systems—which exist in an intricate set of balances—we face the prospect of ecological disaster."[1]

If the prospect of ecological disaster is, as the President says, before us, obviously very serious thought is needed to avert it. The need to avoid a disaster also implies that some very deep and pervasive assumptions must underlie the way we have been doing things in the past to have come upon this disaster in the first place.

Economic progress and rising living standards have been dominant goals in the Western world since the industrial revolution. The United States has the goal of economic stability and progress written into the Employment Act of 1946. The federal government also fosters the goal of progress through technological means by heavy funding of research and development; and, institutionally, the tax regulations encourage technological development through the allowance of research and development expense, depreciation on new equipment, and capital gains as reductions to ordinary income tax. What we have, then, is a closely articulated series of institutional arrangements to foster economic progress through technological development, and it is technological development which has the impact on the environment.

The Administrator of the Environmental Health Service in the U.S. Department of Health, Education, and Welfare has testified before the Senate on this point:

> The almost incredible advances in science and technology during recent history have produced tremendous benefits to human life. These benefits, however, have been accompanied by frightening changes in the balance of the ecological system of which man is an integral part but to which he has been complacent. Deterioration of the quality of the environment has brought this generation to an awareness that its own health and well-being and the fate of future generations depend on action to avert environmental catastrophe.
>
> We are at a point when death, injury, and disease are measures of the pollution of our air, land and water. We have not yet passed the point of no return. The natural systems and renewable resources which support all life can be restored. The physical and mental health of our children and grandchildren can be protected—but only if our Nation acts now.[2]

---

[1] *Environmental Quality*, First Annual Report of the Council of Environmental Quality, August 1970, Washington, p. v.

[2] *Senate Hearings before the Committee on Appropriations*, Department of HEW Appropriations, H.R. 18515, 91st Cong., 2d Sess., Fiscal Year 1971, Part IV, p. 2090.

Considering the proclivity of government officials toward cautious statements, one is a bit startled to find that the head of the Environmental Health Service speaks so strongly; that the survival of human life itself may soon be in jeopardy; and that death, injury, and disease are measures of the pollution of our air, land, and water.

HEALTH HAZARDS

Some of the specific environmental health hazards to which people are exposed are described by a medical task force report made for the Public Health Service and the National Institutes of Health. Among their findings are the following:

1   Deleterious health effects are well established for acute episodes of air pollution associated with specific meteorological conditions, certain industrial exposures, and cigarette smoking. It is impossible, however, to specify a level of air pollution that is safe for all elements of the community. Children and adults with respiratory ailments are more sensitive than others. Increasing precision of the dose-response relations is the only valid way to establish acceptable levels. An important need is a "personal" sampling device to measure concentrations of pollution at the breathing zone where the individual performs his daily work.

2   Earlier successes in controlling food and waterborne diseases have led to a dangerous complacency. New foods, new processes, new methods of preservation, new packaging, new industrial chemical wastes, increasing use of fertilizers and pesticides, and deteriorating water quality make increased research efforts imperative to assure the safety of food and water.

3   The evaluation of the toxic hazards of consumer products stands out as a pressing public health need.

4   Old problems of exposure to heat and cold, community noise, and crowded living spaces are still of major consequence. The Task Force noted for example, that some community noise levels are beginning to reach the intensities which have been associated with hearing defects in occupational groups.

5   Among new hazards, it has been estimated that nearly half of the United States population lives in a measurable microwave environment. Microwave exposure standards for occupational hazard in the United States are set on the basis of thermal effects. Standards developed in the Soviet Union and Eastern Europe are based on nonthermal, biological effects. Quite significant, in the opinion of the Task Force, is the fact that the permissible level of microwave exposure in these countries is one-thousandth the value acceptable in the United States.

6   Cancer is one of the major causes of death and as such is a public health problem of the first rank. Many environmental causes have been identified, both from specific occupations and from cigarette smoking. Research has identified additional potent agents from natural sources. There is, in fact, a growing view that environmental factors may be responsible for the great majority of all human cancers.

7   Among the potential effects from chemicals released into the environment, three are of particular concern. These are cancer, mutation of genes, and birth defects. Contributing to the complexity of scientific investigations of these effects are the following features: their insidious nature, the relatively long time span between exposure and overt effect, the irreversible nature of the resulting disease, the relatively greater susceptibility of immature or developing tissue, and the aggravation of effects from synergistic interactions. As a result of these complexities, reliable tests for the evaluation of products from new technologies are not available, and, in fact, new products are being introduced into our society faster than their safety can be ascertained.[3]

BASIC CAUSES OF ENVIRONMENTAL TROUBLES

According to these reports, then, we are at a point where death, injury, and disease are measures of the pollution of air, land, and water; and, yet, new products are introduced into society faster than their safety can be ascertained. Some ecologists think the time is already too late to avoid ecological disaster, because there are too many people already born, too many pesticides in the soils, too much toxicity already in the cells of marine life and in the food chain, too much residue, and too little time.

The hopeful side is that such a prospect can be avoided. Recognition of the danger has come late, but forcefully. Large gaps exist in our environmental knowledge, but a great deal of what needs to be done can be identified.

The basic causes of environmental problems are complex and deeply embedded. They include: the past tendency to emphasize quantitative growth at the expense of qualitative growth; the failure of the economy to provide full accounting for the social costs of environmental pollution; the failure to take environmental factors into account as a normal and necessary part of our planning and decision making; the inadequacy of our institutions for dealing with problems that cut across traditional political boundaries; the dependence on conveniences, without regard for their impact on the environment; and more fundamentally, the failure to perceive the environment as a totality and to understand and to

[3]"Man's Health and the Environment," *Report of the Task Force on Research Planning in Environmental Health Science,* U.S. Public Health Service, March 1970, pp. 11–15.

recognize the fundamental interdependence of all its parts, including man himself.

> Such deep-rooted causes cannot be corrected overnight, nor can they be simply legislated away. New knowledge, new perceptions, new attitudes must extend to government, to industry, to the professions, to each citizen. Nothing less than basic reform in the way society looks at problems and makes decisions is required to improve environmental quality.
>
> In dealing with the environment we must learn not how to master nature but how to master ourselves, our institutions, and our technology. We must achieve a new awareness of our dependence on our surroundings and on the natural systems which support all life, but awareness must be coupled with a full realization of our enormous capability to alter these surroundings. This country must lead the way in showing that our human and technological resources can be devoted to a better life and an improved environment for ourselves and our inheritors on this planet.[4]

LEARNING TO MANAGE OURSELVES

Why does the President say in his report that we must learn, not how to manage nature, but how to manage ourselves? The implications of this statement are that the problem is a managerial one, that there are constraints on our decision making imposed by life-limiting conditions in ecology, and therefore that the decisions we can make are principally as to our own behavior. An example of this may be found in our preferences for amenities in life which require high electric power consumption, perhaps at rates which the environment cannot sustain.

The electric power industry is growing at a rate of 8 percent per year, or doubling every ten years. The population increase of only 1 percent per year is clearly but a small factor in the expanding power demand. Rather the power requirements come from consumers' desires for increasing conveniences, as well as from the expansion in industrial production of 3 to 4 percent per year.

The high energy demands raise serious questions about the capacity of the environment to absorb the waste, heat, and air pollutants emitted in power production. Energy production, doubling every ten years, will soon exhaust the physical space available for power plants at sites where air, land, and water quality can be maintained. Indeed, the search for new power sites is already pressing, and each new location tends to bring controversy over environmental effects.

If we are running out of appropriate power plant sites, the other

---

[4]*Environmental Quality*, op. cit., pp. v–xiv.

question to be asked is whether all the power is needed. About 40 percent of the new power needs are for industry, and the balance is evenly divided between residential and commercial use for air conditioning, appliances, or business machinery.[5] The possibility exists that electric power is underpriced if full account is taken for the social cost of its environmental effects. However, a reduction in the rate of power growth would have clear implications in lowering the economic growth rate as well. Presumably the public would only concur in reducing economic growth rates if it felt compensated by an equal improvement in environmental quality.

The fact that electric power consumption increases nearly eight times as fast as the population, when the population itself is increasing fast enough, according to Ehrlich,[6] to threaten other species as well as ecological balances, provides a significant index of our demands on the environment. Power usage is the means for materials conversion, and thus it measures the processing of resources which we demand to fill our wants. These wants include conveniences and amenities of living, as well as consumable products.

Power generation itself requires a high materials input in the form of fossil or nuclear fuels; and the output, besides electric energy, includes wastes in the form of air pollutants (principally particulates, oxides of nitrogen, and sulfur dioxide), heat dissipated through cooling towers into water sources, and solid waste residues of the fuel. These wastes are growing so fast that we are running out of sites for new power plants, because the capacity of the environment to absorb the wastes is being exceeded. Los Angeles ruled against a new power plant in its airshed on the grounds that the atmosphere would be oversaturated with pollutants. In New York State, the siting of a nuclear plant was held up for several years to study the possible effects of the heat dissipation on the eutrophication (aging) of a lake. These are not isolated examples. They are becoming so typical that electric power companies are deeply concerned about their future ability to locate enough plants to provide sufficient power.

But generally the question is not asked: Do we really need all this power? Certainly the power is needed, if we are to extrapolate the quantitative growth in living standards into the future and continue to place the same demands on the environment for more products and services. But do we need to continue to expand the use of power, for example, for electric heating and air conditioning? The peak power requirements, and the power failures, frequently come in summer when

---

[5]Committee for Environmental Information, "The Space Available; A Report," *Environment 12:* *2–9,* March 1970.

[6]Paul R. Ehrlich, *The Population Bomb,* Ballantine Books, Inc., New York, 1968, pp. 46–47.

air conditioning demands coincide with high industrial or residential use. The peak power requirements could be avoided by less comfort or less products, and this would alleviate the enormous demands for increased power generation. The question of whether we need all this power is, then, closely related to whether we need all the comforts and products which we have.

With our ingrained assumptions about high and rising living standards, it may seem absurd to ask if we want all the power, goods, and comforts which we have? Of course we want them. Why should we even consider giving them up or moderating our demands?

Some possible answers to this question may be the following:

1 *For the sake of our own health and survival*   The environmental health consequences previously cited by the U.S. Public Health Service and its medical task forces might be evidence that we would be better off in physical well-being if we moderated our demands for goods and power and thus diminished the pollutants which are toxic to us.

2 *For the reason of practicality*   It is physically impossible for two geometric ratios to continue indefinitely at such disparate rates as a 1 percent annual increase in population and an 8 percent annual increase in energy requirements. A 1 percent annual growth rate will cause the population to double in seventy years. In seventy years, the 8 percent annual increase in energy requirements will mean that power usage will have increased about 220-fold. That is, energy needs will be about 220 times what they are now. Is it reasonable to expect that so much fuel, waste, heat, and residues can be dissipated then, when we are already having trouble with such pollution now?

3 *For the sake of understanding and managing ourselves*   Aristotle speaks of the beginnings of understanding: Virtue is a mean lying between two vices, a vice of excess on the one side and a vice of deficiency on the other. The temperate man keeps a middle position with regard to pleasure. In moderate spirit, he wants those things that make for health and a sound bodily condition, and whatever pleasures are not prejudicial to these ends, or costly beyond his means. He limits himself by the guidance of reason.[7]

SOME DEEPLY EMBEDDED ASSUMPTIONS UNDERLYING TECHNOLOGY

Let us assume for the moment that we might like to examine the alternatives of being temperate men of reason in our relations with nature. Then we would ask whether our reasoning methodology is consonant with

[7]Aristotle, "On Man and the Universe," Louise Ropes Loomis (ed.), Walter J. Black Inc., Roselyn, N.Y., 1943, p. 110 and 131–132.

ecological balance, or whether perhaps we make assumptions which are partly at the root of our environmental difficulties. The President's message referred to such attitudinal origins of the environmental crisis as "our failure to perceive the environment as a totality and to understand and to recognize the fundamental interdependence of all its parts, including man himself."

What is there about our attitude toward the environment which causes this omission, this failure to see ourselves as part of the interdependencies of nature? Some of it must stem from the assumptions behind the technology process.

One such assumption may be found in the work of R. J. Forbes, member of the Royal Netherlands Academy of Sciences, *The Conquest of Nature*, written following a conference of twenty scientists sponsored by the *Encyclopaedia Britannica*. Forbes said that the aim of technology has always been to harness the forces of nature and put them to man's service.[8]

The paradox of the argument is that, while the purpose of technology is to harness the forces of nature and put them to man's service in the process, nature suffers such degradation that the prospect is one of ecological disaster. How can we, at the same time, expect to harness nature to man's service while destroying it? This logical inconsistency is at the heart of the environmental crisis; and, if we understood how this inconsistency came to be, we would be at a better starting point to understand what to do to avert ecological disaster. To see the unfolding of this inconsistency, we need to have some perspective of the history of natural science.

SOME ORIGINS OF THOUGHT ON NATURAL SCIENCE AND THE ENVIRONMENT

The dominant body of thought in the Western world on natural science from the fourth century B.C. to the fifteenth century was found in the works of Aristotle. The science of biology had its origins in four of Aristotle's major works of which the *History of Animals* and the *Parts of Animals* are the most significant.

Aristotle compiled a detailed description of the habits, characteristics, and anatomy of more than 500 animals, divided into genera and species. His goal was to show the presence of purpose in nature, by relating the function of each anatomical part to the next higher function of the organism and, by this logic, to demonstrate the intricate interrelation of all of nature.[9] Aristotle's views on natural science, man, and purpose

[8]R. J. Forbes, *The Conquest of Nature*, Mentor/Encyclopaedia Britannica, 1968, p. 19.
[9]Aristotle, op. cit., p. 41.

are based on the idea that there is a final cause and a moving cause.

The modes of reasoning in natural sciences are different from those in theoretical sciences. Theoretical science starts with that which is the moving cause; natural science starts with that which is to be the final cause.

Natural science begins with the phenomena presented by animals, and proceeds afterward to state the causes of those phenomena, and to deal with their evolution.

Thus we say, "man is an animal" with specific characteristics, and these characteristics serve special functions which govern his development, and therefore evolution is accomplished in a succession related to the parts and functions of the body.[10]

Aristotle's natural science was, then, an a priori perception of final ends, with an interacting set of organisms, parts, and moving causes. From this concept came into being a hierarchical classification of nature which persisted for nearly 2,000 years.[11]

THE SCIENTIFIC VIEWS OF FRANCIS BACON

While Aristotle himself derived his ideas of nature from observation of phenomena and causes, natural science became very static under the classification approach, especially as it became associated with logicians and schoolmen of the church who associated this magnificent hierarchy with divine authorization. It was this static deduction from divine authority which Renaissance men attacked in their intellectual revolution. Francis Bacon (1561–1626), as one of the precursors of the philosophy of science, repudiated deductive reasoning in trying to establish instead the inductive process. His principal target was Aristotle, because of the long dominance of Aristotelian reasoning. In 1620, Bacon laid down his own approach in the book *The New Organon, or True Directions Concerning the Interpretation of Nature (Novum Organum).* In the process of developing his argument, he presents this view of the two intervening millennia since Aristotle:

> The sciences which we possess come for the most part from the Greeks. For that which has been added by Roman, Arabic, or later writers is not much nor of much importance; and whatever it is, it is built on the foundations of Greek discoveries. Now the wisdom of the Greeks was professorial and much given to disputations; and a kind of wisdom most adverse to the inquisition of truth.

[10]Ibid., "Parts of Animals," pp. 43–45.
[11]See Arthur O. Lovejoy, *The Great Chain of Being,* Harvard University Press, Cambridge, Mass., 1936.

Bacon then attacked Aristotle as corrupting natural philosophy by his logic, fashioning the world out of categories, imposing countless restrictions on the nature of things, and being more solicitous to provide an answer than about the actual reality of things. Aristotle came to his conclusion beforehand, a priori, and he did not consult experience, as he should have done, in order to frame his decisions and axioms.

Bacon's argument for the resort to experience and the senses to validate hypothesis was the essential feature of the scientific revolution which separates the modern from the medieval age. Copernicus (1473–1543), in *De revolutionibus orbium coelestium* of 1543, and Andreas Vesalius (1514–1564), in *De humani corpus fabrica,* were among the first to apply the scientific method.

GIORDANO BRUNO—PRECURSOR OF THE CONQUEST OF NATURE

Among those familiar with and influenced by Copernicus was Giordano Bruno (1562–1600), an Italian philosopher and monk, who was perhaps the earliest thinker to perceive the significance of the new world view provided by the scientific method and Copernican cosmology.[12]

Bruno's philosophy led him into constant disputations with both churchmen and Aristotelians; but worse, in the eyes of colleagues, he became the spokesman of the rising intellectual and commercial classes against the nobles and the church. In the *Expulsion of the Triumphant Beast* [*Lo Spaccio de la Bestia Trionfante* (1584)] he expresses a very modern view of materialism and the conquest of nature. *Lo Spaccio* is an allegory about Jove, a libidinous god, through whom Bruno satirizes the corruption, despotism, and violence of his times. On man's relation to nature, Bruno said:

> The gods had given intellect and hands to man and made him similar to them, giving him power over the other animals. This consists in his being able not only to operate according to his nature and to what is usual, but also to operate outside the laws of nature, in order that . . . he would succeed in preserving himself as god of the earth.

THE CONQUEST OF NATURE

Four hundred years ago with the rise of the intellect and science, modern man began to assume that he could operate outside the laws of nature. There is surprisingly little difference, except for the allegorical style,

[12]D. W. Singer, *Giordano Bruno, His Life and Thought,* Henry Schuman Inc., Publishers, New York, 1950, p. 88.

between the meaning of Bruno's words and those of Forbes in *The Conquest of Nature.*

While the idea of the conquest of nature is today commonplace, the same idea caused Bruno's death, which provides some evidence of change in cultural views in the interim. Shortly after writing *Lo Spaccio,* Bruno was lured back to Italy by Giovanni Mocenigo, who pretended to be his patron, but denounced him as a heretic to the Inquisition. The Inquisition drew up charges against Giordano Bruno, based upon *Lo Spaccio;* and finally, by direct papal order, he was burned at the stake.

Within a few years after Bruno's martyrdom, Galileo, Kepler, Descartes, William Harvey, J. B. Van Helmont, and Joachim Jung began to develop scientific thought in the vein of the Bruno prophecy. From then through the industrial revolution, to the surge of scientific discovery in the twentieth century, technology has been the driving force of progress.

What is not so well recognized is the inconsistency of present assumptions. Most of us would probably not argue with Aristotle, even today, that "man is an animal" and thus among the organisms of nature. But how can an animal, as Bruno says, "operate outside the laws of nature"? To do so would be to estrange ourselves from the earth, to act for our own ends, without knowledge of or regard for the interdependencies in nature. Logically, without prior knowledge of actual consequences, it would appear to be a calamitous resolve. Empirically, 400 years after the beginning of the scientific revolution, the actual consequences are that we are confronted with ecological disaster.

CONCEPT OF ENVIRONMENTAL ADMINISTRATION

What has all this to do with environmental administration?

Environmental administration is concerned with the management of human affairs so that we can live in more reasonable consonance with nature.

Environmental administration is not, as some might construe, concerned with the conquest, or reconquest, of nature. It is concerned rather with the conquest of ourselves.

Environmental administration seeks ecological balance; equilibrium between man, other species, and the food and energy cycles; minimization of our intrusions on the various ecosystems; maximization of the survival of all forms of life, however small and insignificant from our point of view, not out of magnanimity for "lesser creatures," but out of intellectual humility that we do not know what the loss of any species might do to the ecological balance.

Environmental administration is concerned with remedial measures, because we have already gone far enough in depredations of nature so that we and it are threatened. The remedial measures involve understanding what we have done, considering what we are doing, and trying to moderate or reverse our effects.

Because we have become a technical society, some of environmental administration is technology—biology, toxicity, deficiency, ecological quality standards, materials balance, transport phenomena, and scientific methodology.

Because we have become a very economic society, some of environmental administration is economics—marginal analysis of internal and external costs, market simulations of total costs, cost-effectiveness analysis, tradeoff analysis of costs and benefits, and examination of the concepts of economic growth.

Because we have become a managerial society, some of environmental administration is management—decision structures by which we arrive at present decisions, legal and institutional means we use to implement these decisions, planning methods as tools of degradation or improvement of environmental quality, financing of environmental programs, and what new decision structures might appear as alternatives to enable man to live more harmoniously in nature.

Because we have become a highly political society in which wants, needs, and value systems are compromised in the public arena, some of environmental administration is political—the representativeness of various interests which put demands on the environment; the comparative strength of various interest groups versus the public need for health and survival; and the arts of negotiation, compromise, and coalition to try to preserve the environment.

Because we have become a highly directed society moving toward goals of technological and economic progress, environmental administration is philosophy—the adequacy of our scientific methods, the nature of human values, what indeed is progress, and how can we try to decide what is better or worse in an environmental sense.

In the end, environmental administration concerns man himself and how he might continue to live and survive as a creature of the earth. As such, the field deals with the interaction of human activity with ecology. Man's social and economic wants alter the functions and structure of nature as decisions are made about resource use and waste disposal. With high and rising population densities, with high living standards in industrialized societies, human demands upon resources become so pressing as to be portentous in their effects upon life cycles in the environment. Environmental administration, therefore, concerns human decisions which affect and alter ecological systems; and most of those decisions are about man himself, his behavior, and his management of his affairs.

If such a field of study is ambitious, which it is, at least a start can be made to compile a first general catalog of ecological difficulties and their ramifications. From such a catalog of problems, scholars with greater depth in special fields can assess what may be done toward a solution. By making these assessments, we will have started biologically to accommodate nature, rather than having tried to conquer it. The conquest of nature, as Bruno foresaw, is in effect an expulsion from nature by our own choosing. Most of these expulsive assumptions lie in our decision structure, in the premises of economics, technology, law, and administration—both governmental and private. Environmental administration concerns itself with the decision structure by which we deal with nature and try to adjust our decison criteria to live more consonantly with our ecology for the sake of biological health and preservation.

SUMMARY

Environmental administration starts with the assumption that man is part of nature and has his being in the energy-nutrient cycles of the ecosystem. Since the ecosystem provides the very essence of his existence as an organism, he cannot live apart from it nor outside natural laws or biological processes.

Yet, ironically, a framework of thought and decision structure has come into being, from the scientific and industrial revolutions, that man can "conquer" nature and operate outside of its biological processes. This failure to include himself as part of the biological process is the crux of the environmental crisis, because the residuals from productive activity are overwhelming the ecosystem's ability to absorb the wasteload. The result is a potential ecological disaster.

Ecological disaster is latent in pollution and toxic hazards which are depleting other species and are detrimental to human health.

Environmental administration is a concept of managing human affairs in such a way that biological health, diversity, and ecological balance will be preserved. The approach to be made in this book is to examine past and present decision structures, to see how we came to place priorities on the satisfaction of short-run wants to the detriment of environmental quality. Then, alternative strategies and methods will be examined to see how environmental quality may be improved.

DISCUSSION QUESTIONS

1 What evidences of environmental deterioration, if any, have you observed in your own community? What seem to be their causes?
2 Try to recall all the goods you have consumed in the past week, and then enumerate the wastes associated with them from factory to your use. Do you think the volume of residuals is nearly equal to the usable product in these cases?
3 What are all the "free goods" which you have used in the past few days, for example, driving your automobile, breathing, drinking, washing, walking, playing? What price would you put on "free goods" if you did not have them?
4 Trace the history of your own learning process about biology, the categories and phyla. Do you think of species as being different from you? Part of a process? Are you part of their process? Was Bacon right about Aristotle?

PROBLEM

Make a field study in your vicinity for the purpose of inventorying some aspect of the environment, for example, a species count of flora or fauna, or some urban characteristic such as density or architectural features. Then try to reconstruct the data you have observed for a prior period, say twenty or forty years ago. You may be able to do this by a search of records, newspapers, or talking to older people. Then compare the two periods and describe the decisions which were the cause of the change. What new decisions would it take now to reverse the trend which you observed?

Chapter 2

Human Interaction
with the Environment

The decision structure under which we operate as a society has a strong bias toward short-term optimization of material results, with very little cognizance of ecological effects. This bias derives from the exclusion of biological data from the land-use, market, corporation, or personal decision criteria. In short, the decision mechanism seeks to operate outside of, or without regard to, nature.

In reality, nature can be ignored or excluded from decision criteria only so long as the waste burden of society can be disposed of in water, air, or sometimes land in a costless manner. Costless disposition assumes that air and water are "free goods," that is, that they are in such ample supply as to make them freely available, without cost. Upon this assumption corporations or individuals may put exhaust fumes or effluents into the air or water without reckoning their cost in accounts or profit and loss statements.

However, as high-quality air and water do become scarce in relation to a dense urban population, a kind of cost does become felt, not a cash, or accounting, cost to put in the income statement, but as a health, or biological, cost which presents a disease, or life, hazard to humans and other species. As these health costs or sacrifices become apparent, society must try to clean up the toxic elements in the environment, and a social cost is incurred in the form of taxation and public expenditure. So what started out to be a costless operation to the private entrepreneur becomes a health cost to some individual, or a social cost to the public.

If these are some of the ramifications of the present decision structure, we might then be curious as to: (1) who are the environmental administrators who make such decisions as we have been discussing, and (2) what have been some of their specific effects? The balance of this chapter will deal with these two questions under the following topics:

1 Who are environmental administrators?
2 Reasons for the environmental crisis
3 Chemicalization of the environment
4 Quality and beauty of the environment
5 Rectifying the ugliness of cities
6 Man's structural interface with the environment
7 The metabolism of cities
8 Sensors in the sea
9 The condition of estuaries
10 The spread of devastation
11 Impetus to change

WHO ARE ENVIRONMENTAL ADMINISTRATORS?

An environmental administrator is a decision maker whose resource allocation or product design affects ecological life cycles. The design may be of a physical product or service; and the design decision may be conscious or unconscious as to the materials' recycle effects upon ecology.

The most obvious environmental administrators are government decision makers who control resource use, for example, the Bureau of Land Management, the Bureau of Reclamation, the Bureau of Mines, the Corps of Engineers, the Department of Agriculture, the Forest Service, and many more who allocate or release resources to private users. In addition, there are the resource control agencies, such as the Office of Air Programs and Office of Water Programs, in the Environmental Protection Agency which take actions to protect air and water quality. In state and local governments, there are decision makers who determine water use, air pollution control, land use or zoning, and energy or transportation franchises. All these governmental officials are environmental administrators in the sense that they decide upon material standards and uses which, upon disposal or recycling, may change the ecological balance. Such government officials directly make decisions which characterize them as environmental administrators.

Other, and much more pervasive, environmental administrators are those executives in private business who indirectly create wastes, which become a burden on the environment, as a by-product of their design and production of marketable products. Such private industrial executives do not normally think of themselves as environmental administrators; but, in the future, they may be expected by public policy to become more concerned about their product design and waste disposal in direct relation to the degradation of the environment. For example, when the Governor of California called a hearing on the removal of lead from gasoline, on the grounds that the lead was not only toxic to biological species but was also a main obstacle to designing a "clean" car, the top executives of General Motors, Du Pont, and the oil companies appeared. They knew that their product designs and performance were viewed as the cause of atmospheric pollution; they knew that large investment decisions would have to be made to reduce automobile emissions; and they came in the role of men who would take actions as environmental administrators.

Now, there is, of course, no title today that says an executive in a business is an environmental administrator; but most research, development, and engineering executives will increasingly be called upon to play that role, either in cleaning up product designs which now are fouling the environment or in thinking in advance about the environmental consequences of industrial decisions.

The oil companies are being asked to consider such questions as the ecological damage caused by breaking the tundra and disturbing the permafrost in Alaska to build the pipeline from the North Slope, of controlling oil spills, of devising new safety devices to prevent fires on ocean oil-drilling platforms. They are also expected to calculate the cost of producing lead-free gas and of refining gas with high octane ratings without additives. These are all decisions in the area of environmental administration, whether they are called by that name yet or not.

The same types of decisions are being required in other industries: the auto companies to design a new emission-free engine, the chemical companies to meet stricter stream quality standards, the paper companies to restrict odors and get rid of black sulfur liquor without disposal in waterways, the airlines to reduce their emissions of particulates at takeoff and at high altitudes, the steel companies to reduce the sulfur dioxide and fluorine from the smelting processes, the pesticide manufacturers to get rid of mercury as a germicide on seeds, the power companies to select new sites away from airsheds already saturated with pollutants, the nuclear power industry to study effects of radiation or thermal pollution, and on and on. All these decisions are those of an environmental administrator.

The issue is not who presently identifies himself as an environmental administrator but where decisions are made which affect the environment. They are made in a wide range of industrial and governmental organizations. What these administrators need is not a new name for an old activity, rather they need a body of knowledge on how to deal with ecological problems. They need an approach and methodology to judge the impact of their actions on the environment.

Why, one might ask, when they got along without such an approach before? The simple answer is that an environmental crisis has emerged which requires a new perspective and a revised decision structure if the crisis is to be solved.

REASONS FOR THE ENVIRONMENTAL CRISIS

The environmental crisis appeared suddenly on the American scene, at least in the perception of most of its citizens. A rash of oil spills with petroleum-soaked birds, the worsening of visibility and air quality over most cities, water shortages, malodorous lakes, and the difficulty of finding unlittered or uncrowded recreational sites brought the realization that the quality of life and of the environment was wanting. Moreover, the youth of the country took up the environment as a cause and symbol of their discontent, with demonstrations and writings, which adults find hard to refute.

Perhaps more basically, the population has become more and more urbanized, and as the gross national product moved up to the trillion dollar level per year, the accumulated wastes in the cities became more than the natural environment could assimilate. While nature has considerable absorptive and self-cleansing capability, through wind and rainfall, bacteria in the soil, and dilution in the sea, the concentrated wastes have overwhelmed these regenerative forces. Rough estimates indicate that about 6 to 7 pounds of waste are produced per dollar of gross national product. That amounts to 6 trillion pounds per year, or 15 tons per person. Most of the population is now located in the major metropolitan areas; when 15 tons per person of waste and toxic materials are crowded into these few small areas, environmental degradation is bound to become obvious. To be more specific as to the causes for the rapid emergence of an environmental crisis in the last decade:

Population has increased between 1960 and 1970 from 181 million to 205 million, or by 24 million people, with another 23 million increase in prospect by 1980.

More than half the population is crowded into 1 percent of the land space, and two-thirds occupy 9 percent of the nation's land. The gross national product in real terms increased about 50 percent in the past decade and may be expected to increase another 50 percent in the next decade.

These data suggest that the active residual wastes concentrated in that 1 percent of the land area increased by about two-thirds in the decade. Such large increases in wastes, whether in tonnage or in percentage, become visibly a worsening of the environment.

CHEMICALIZATION OF THE ENVIRONMENT

In addition to the vast quantities of waste which have been thrust into the environment with a trillion dollar economy, there are special characteristics of the wastes which cause grave new difficulties. That is, the composition of waste is not as disposable as formerly, in a more simple society, where food, fiber, or human wastes could basically be digested in the soils. With rising technology, wastes of heavy metal, inorganic, or synthetic origin are increasing at a disproportionately high rate, and these chemicals are not easily decomposable in the soil. However, many of the chemicals are water soluble; but, once dissolved, the process is all but irreversible. Then the water cycle distributes the chemicals widely throughout the world.

No change has been more momentous to man during the past century than the chemicalization of his environment, with the consequence of unprecedented contamination in air, food, and water. As the rate of chemicalization increases, the human habitat becomes more menacing for a larger portion of the population. Prolonged exposure to low-level chemical pollutants has observable biological effects ranging from minor irritations to chronic diseases. Localized effects include inflammations of the eyes, intestines, nasal passages, skin, or frequent colds. Specific responses of a more advanced nature include asthma, hives, exzema, emphysema, and gastrointestinal disorders. More generalized symptoms are chronic fatigue, headaches, forgetfulness, and lowered levels of comprehension, initiative, or concentration. Ecological mental illnesses, including confusion, depression, and psychotic behavior, have been observed.[1]

These health consequences of environmental chemical exposure corroborate the conclusion of the medical task force on environmental health sciences (Chapter 1) that product safety has not been sufficiently

[1]Dr. Theron G. Randolph, in B. Jennings and J. Murphy (eds.), *Interactions of Man and His Environment,* Proceedings of the Northwestern University Conference, Plenum Publishing Corporation, New York, 1966, pp. 131–135.

assured, otherwise the number of persons susceptible to illness from chemical exposures would not be increasing.

If we are to improve future decisions regarding health hazards from chemical exposures, a means for monitoring the human population is necessary to detect disease or mutagenic change (i.e., a mutation is relatively permanent change in hereditary material in chromosomes or genes). A conference on the mutagenicity of chemicals, sponsored by the National Academy of Sciences and the U.S. Food and Drug Administration, found that many scientists now rank chemical damage, causing chromosome breaks, to be among the most serious of current biological hazards. Recent advances in the understanding of genetics brings a realization that mutations may be occurring from the uncontrolled release of new chemicals which persist in the environment. The genetic complexity of man and the enormous number of new chemicals in the environment create a high potential for mutation. Genes control protein synthesis, and many of the 1,500 diseases of genetic origin exhibit abnormalities or absence of proteins. The insidious effects of mutations appear in the form of a general physiological weakness, a lack of resistance to disease, a shorter life-span, and a decrease in fertility. Mutations, once introduced, remain in genetic material for as long as forty generations, with each generation exposed to increasing mutational hazard as it adds its own new mutations to those received from the past.[2]

QUALITY AND BEAUTY OF THE ENVIRONMENT

In addition to producing the chemical and physical changes in the environment which affect the life and health of all species, including man, the past decision structure has also produced environmental effects upon our aesthetic or emotional senses. We have feelings about our surroundings, whether they seem pleasant or unpleasant, whether we feel happy or unhappy in them. These feelings may be regarded as our assessment of the quality or beauty of the environment; and these features too, quality and beauty, have suffered from past decisions.

Joseph L. Fischer in an annual report of Resources for the Future, a research institute founded to advance knowledge of resource conservation, regards these quality changes as among our most significant problems. Population pressures, growing industries, and attitudes of indifference have caused serious environmental deterioration; water and air pollution are close to pandemic. The aesthetic effect of cities is all but ignored as urban areas sprawl over more and more countryside. The

[2]*Science*, vol. 171, no. 3966, Jan. 8, 1971, pp. 51–52.

gravest resource problems of the next generation are the threats to the quality of the environment.[3]

On the aesthetic side, an architect, Peter Blake, laments the uglification of America. The American people were endowed with a beautiful land, as varied and magnificent as anywhere on earth; yet this country is fast becoming the earth's greatest slum, a disgrace of vast proportions. The British have called it the mess that is man-made America. Cities do have isolated buildings which are handsome and a few rich neighborhoods done in taste. Beyond that, there are few handsome streets, plazas, or civic centers; and suburbs are an interminable monotony of little houses on little lots cut up by little streets, all interspersed with billboarded highways, garish diners, beflagged used car lots, and signs—everywhere the omnipresent, glaring signs filled with trivial messages. The junkiness of the human occupation presents hideousness to the eye without respite.[4]

President Lyndon B. Johnson expressed much the same point of view in his message to Congress in 1965.

Modern technology, which has added much to our lives, can also have a darker side. Its uncontrolled waste products are menacing the world we live in, our enjoyment and our health. The air we breathe, our water, soil, and wildlife, are being blighted by the poisons and chemicals which are the by-products of technology and industry. The skeletons of discarded cars litter the countryside. The same society which receives the rewards of technology, must, as a cooperating whole, take responsibility for control.

Every major river system is now polluted. Waterways that were once the source of pleasure and beauty and recreation are forbidden to human contact and objectionable to sight and smell. Furthermore this pollution is costly, requiring expensive treatment for drinking water and inhibiting the operation and growth of industry.

RECTIFYING THE UGLINESS OF CITIES

The ugliness of cities is mostly man-made. We know that cities can be beautiful; we go as tourists to older cities in Europe and Asia to see what a city can be, with broad plazas, open streets, handsome buildings, large parks which people use and enjoy, and artistic touches which we find quaint. Even the underdeveloped countries of the world have beautiful squares, plazas, parks, churches, and public buildings, although the populace generally is poor.

[3]Roderick Nash, *The American Environment*, Addison-Wesley Publishing Co., Reading, Mass., 1968, pp. 161–162.
[4]Ibid., pp. 165–170.

Cities basically have many admirable advantages, which get lost in their monotony, congestion, and monumental problems. Their advantages are diversity of activities; opportunities for education, culture, work, entertainment; and the chance to meet people of various views. In these aspects, the city is more richly rewarding than the countryside, however lovely the open landscapes may be. Indeed, the advantages of cities are undoubtedly why people prefer them, as seen in the long historic trend toward urbanization. The miserable and ugly aspects of cities are largely of human doing, a kind of thoughtlessness which can, with effort, be rectified. There are perhaps four faults of cities which stand out most sharply.[5]

First, the perceptual clutter, redolent closeness, and omnipresent noise make the city a place of emotional stress. The city is a malevolent embrace, instead of a spacious opening of arms. It is too close, too noisy, too confusing, too hot, too smelly, too dirty, too polluted in atmosphere and environment. The city does not need to be that way, and the great cities of the world give one a sense of invitation rather than a sense of incarceration.

The lack of visible identity is a second common fault of cities. An enjoyable environment is richly diverse, with distinct parts and a varied and identifiable character. We like to identify with the parts of the city, with places that feel like home or give us a sense of gaiety. The physical settings should be designed to express human diversity, rather than leaving us trapped in the cold monotone of uniform houses on uniform streets.

A third source of distress in our cities is their lack of coherence, the fitting together of its parts, a kind of legibility that lets us read its character. If we are to relate ourselves to the city and its many parts, we need a sense of recognition of the opportunities which we may share in a particular urban area. The language of cityscapes is now ambiguous, confusing, filled with discontinuities, which obscure the city's advantages and the rich experiences available within it.

The rigidity of American cities is a fourth disability. American cities look like what they are, a grid laid on the surveyor's section lines, with every lot crammed with as much cheap construction as would make the fastest dollar for its owner. Such mean objectives do not produce the open-ended accessibility which great cities have. A sense of individual freedom requires a certain availability to the physical setting, a sense of choice, a largeness of scale, a whimsy of waste, an unexpectedness, a new discovery to explore.

[5]Kevin Lynch, "The City as Environment," *Scientific American*, vol. 213, no. 3, September 1965, p. 209.

The drab, urban colossus looks permanent but is in fact changing rapidly, and in this change we have the means to create an enjoyable environment for all. The potentialities arising from the quality of the intimate setting, the house and its locale, but even more from the form of the city on a large scale are ours to create.[6]

MAN'S STRUCTURAL INTERFACE WITH THE ENVIRONMENT

If we are to consider restoring the beauty and purity of the environment in which we live, we need to understand both the general effects of our past decisions, which have already been briefly noted, and more importantly, the structural relationships of man's activity to ecological systems. That is, what is it that we do which affects other organisms? How do we do it? How do the results of our activities get into various ecosystems? We have seen that the effects of our activity have been the chemicalization of the environment, with its resultant pollution and biological hazards, and the uglification of the environment, which may be viewed as creating structures or installing materials inconsonant with the functioning of natural ecosystems. Let us look next at the structural nature of the environment to see the interactions which occur.

The structural characteristics of ecosystems are determined by two basic cycles: One is the energy and materials cycle which provides the metabolism for producing the user organisms, and the second is the biogeochemical cycle which is the nutrient rate or food chain. In a sense, the first of these is an input cycle by which energy is fixed into usable form, and the second is an output cycle by which usage is distributed and consumed.

Although we may speak of the energy and nutrient cycles as two broad processes in the ecosystem, each in fact is made up of many subcycles (for illustrations, see Figures 1 through 5 in Chapter 7). The process begins as the solar system radiates energy to the earth's surface. Plants use sunlight to fix nutrients from geological material and water. The atmospheric cycle distributes this material in the form of particulates or water vapor over large areas of the globe. The hydrologic water cycle is the principal transport function for distributing heat energy and cooling; distributing rainfall; moving materials as dissolved solids; becoming fluid agent in plants and animals; providing water power, underground water storage, and disposition and decomposition of wastes in streams and oceans.

Biomes are the subclimate ecologies created by the shape and structure of the earth's surface (parent geological material) in relation to

6Ibid., p. 219.

the available solar energy, meteorologic conditions, and hydrologic conditions at that site. These subclimatic pockets of the earth form the living conditions in which certain autotrophs, or producing organisms like plants or phytoplankton in the sea, utilize sunlight to manufacture nutrients and thus begin the nutrient chain. Within these same biomes, heterotrophs, or user organisms like plankton, bacteria, or animals, use the nutrients made by the autotrophic organisms to rearrange or synthesize the nutrients into a more complex form. These user organisms are plant or meat eaters (herbivores or carnivores) which grow and die; their remains are returned to the materials cycle by reducer organisms (generally bacteria).

These many cycles and subcycles provide ample opportunity for man's intervention into ecology, for the balances among the subcycles, and within the biomes in particular, are delicate and involve millions of organisms interacting with each other. Man, by his intervention at the interfaces in nature, has been able to create salinity in the soils, to desolate the Tigris and Euphrates Basins as well as portions of California, to create the dust storms of the 1930s, to produce an overpopulation of rodents in the West by destroying reptiles, to kill fish and pollute every major stream in the United States, and to turn many miles of coastline into underwater deserts by damming up silt behind 2,000 flood control dams. Having learned all this, we have culminated our knowledge by grander projects such as building the high Aswan Dam which is now reducing the fertility of the Nile and the fisheries of the Mediterranean, and at home we decimate the seabird populations off the Gulf and West Coasts of the United States by chemicalization of the oceans.

How do we manage to do it, without even trying? One would not suspect man of either the intent or the capacity for devastating and deranging all of nature.

The principal means of our cleverness is to load the transport systems of nature, the air and water cycles, with all our refuse and unwanted materials. The atmospheric and hydrologic cycles assure that these contaminant materials will have worldwide distribution, and thus they enter the biomes and the nutrient chain.

THE METABOLISM OF CITIES

We have even created structures in society similar to those in nature so that we affect nature intimately. The principal man-made structure which intervenes in nature is the industrial city. We may consider the city as having a metabolism, or energy-material cycle, in the same sense that nature does. That is, energy and materials are inputs into the city, are

Figure 2-1   Metabolism of a City

(Tons per Day)

Inputs		Outputs	
Water	625,000	Sewage	500,000
		Suspended solids	120
Food	2,000	Refuse	2,000
Fuel		Air pollutants	
Coal	3,000	Particles	150
Oil	2,800	Sulfur dioxide	150
Natural gas	2,700	Nitrogen oxides	100
Motor fuels	1,000	Hydrocarbons	100
		Carbon monoxide	450

processed, and then become outputs. The metabolism for a city of one million people may be illustrated by three inputs, water, food, and fuel, in Figure 2-1.[6]

These are by no means all the material and energy inputs and outputs for a city of one million people, because nothing is shown of industry or the industrial chemical wastes. Nor is all the natural input shown, for example, something of the order of 5 billion tons of atmospheric cover or air movement would be an input and output to such a city as well.

Nevertheless, the magnitude of the figures in the metabolism of a city of one million people is seen to be very large; and when one considers that there are over three billion people on earth, or perhaps 3,000 times as much materials and wastes as this, it becomes clear that the water and air transport systems of nature are heavily burdened with human residues.

The point is that human society has its own producer and user organic structures, like the autotrophic and heterotrophic systems of nature. Our producer structures take materials and energy from the earth, and our human heterotrophic components use the materials and return them to the earth. But the receiving system, the earth, is not an inert receptacle capable of utilizing sulfuric acid or whatever corrosive materials we wish to place in it. The receiving system is a biome, a territorial subclimate of nature filled with adaptive organisms, food makers, and food users, which need a particular chemical and materials balance to survive. When the output of our human user system is highly toxic, deficient, or mutagenic, the result in the receiving biome is often death. That particular death may

[6]Adapted from an article by Abel Wolman, "The Metabolism of Cities," *Scientific American*, vol. 213, no. 3, September 1965, p. 180.

not trouble us on sentimental grounds, but the problem is that the organism or species which died were part of the nutrient chain. In turn, the output of the heterotrophs in the biomes becomes the input (food) to the metabolism of the city. Sentiment aside, we have then reduced our food supply or introduced toxic agents into our own consumption. And this is exactly what we have done.

SENSORS IN THE SEA

One place where one may obtain some measure of our pollution and contamination of the environment is in sea life. Here in the rivers and seas, one can observe the environmental effects of man's activity most promptly, because water is such a marvelous hydraulic transportation system for moving materials from one ecosystem to another, including from the human ecology into marine cultures. It does not take very long for the metabolism of cities to be felt in the estuaries far downstream.

The estuaries, then, are efficient laboratories for environmental observation, and the marine life within them is the instruments and sensors through which one may see the interaction of urban metabolism upon the estuarian biomass. Estuaries are the place where stream flows of inland rivers meet the tidewaters of the sea, and because of the runoff of minerals and organic materials from the land, they are rich in nutrients and abundant in minerals. This basic richness is aided and distributed by wind and tidal mixing, particulate detention, marsh flushing, and circulation which deliver nutrients to the reaches of estuarine habitats in shallow, sun-bathed waters, where many organisms, fish, and shellfish thrive. While estuaries are more stressful than the sea in temperature and salinity, they are also far richer and more productive than either the ocean or fresh waters. The National Estuary Study of the Department of Interior notes that thousands of species of bacteria, plants, and animals thrive in estuaries. Estuarine waters are known for their shrimp, crabs, oysters, clams, scallops, striped bass, spotted seatrout, and flounder; their waterfowl and shorebirds; their marshbirds and seabirds; and for their aquatic mammals.

Fish enter estuaries for foraging, shelter, or migration. Estuarine waters serve migrating fish for acclimatization, nursery, and rearing areas.[7] Waterfowl, shorebirds, marshbirds, and seabirds use the estuary for nesting, feeding, resting, and shelter during migration and wintering. Aquatic mammals also use estuaries for foraging, shelter, rearing young, and year-round residence.

[7] *National Estuary Study*, U.S. Department of Interior, Washington, vol. 2, January 1970, pp. 20–21.

THE CONDITION OF ESTUARIES

The estuary, then, is the cradle of the sea today and for eons past. Long ago the reptilian progenitors of man crept from the estuary's marshy banks to become land creatures, hence our cradle was there too in estuarine waters. In what condition do we find the estuaries now?

Every one of the nation's estuaries in continental United States has been modified by man, 23 percent severely modified, 50 percent moderately modified, and 27 percent slightly modified.[8] The principal modifications have been dredging or landfill. Dredging, which is primarily for ocean-going or small boat harbors, may greatly change the productivity of an estuary by disturbing the rich nutrients and detritus on the bottom, deepening channels so less sunlight is available, increasing current strength and erosion, changing tidal flow and mixing patterns, and increasing turbidity. Filling of estuaries and marshes for landfill to create new sites for human occupation permanently removes the rearing beds of marine life from the nurture of the sea. From 1950 to 1969, 665,000 acres of estuarine zone were removed from their natural use by dredging and filling, or 4 percent of all the estuarine area in the United States.

Of all the uses of estuaries, waste disposal, intentional and vagrant, probably has the greatest potential for damaging fish and wildlife and esthetic values. Certainly estuaries trap waterborne wastes just as they do nutrients carried into them from bordering marshes and by the tides and from upland areas by river flow.

Biocides, especially long-lived insecticides, such as DDT, and heavy metals probably are the greatest threat to estuarine fish and wildlife. Petroleum wastes and spills as well as organic chemical wastes also can cause damage and impart disagreeable tastes to fish. Sewage released into estuaries may result in hazard to human health and may reduce dissolved oxygen to harmful or lethal levels for estuarine life.[9]

The Public Health Service began an annual census of fish kills in fresh and marine waters in 1960. In the 1964 census, 485 official reports of fish kills were reported, totaling 18,387,000 fish.[10] Two-thirds of the kills were caused by industrial chemicals, one-fourth by municipal waste, and most of the rest by agricultural toxic material. From some of the field reports on specific instances which occurred are the following:

A cement company regularly flushed tanks with wet cement grindings into the stream. The high alkaline content caused burning caustic

[8]Ibid., vol. 1, p. 2.
[9]Ibid., vol. 2, p. 108.
[10]"Pollution Caused Fish Kills in 1964," Public Health Service, U.S. Department of Health, Education, and Welfare, no. 847, Washington.

action, killing 1,500 fish and other marine life. The fish bore burned and bloody patches. Fish were reported trying to jump out of the water with odd gyrations and swimming ashore.

A slug of zero oxygen water, released from a dam, moved downstream killing about 2,000 fish.

An Army depot sprayed dieldrin on a house to remove termites. A sudden rain washed the dieldrin into a stream and killed the stocked trout.

A backhoe tractor struck a high-pressure pipeline. Despite rapid repair, 50 to 60 gallons of gasoline entered Warrior Run killing 3,252 fish.

A company, which had been warned to keep all substances out of a stream, allowed oil and sludge to enter the water. All aquatic life was destroyed for a 1-mile stretch and damage occurred for the entire 6 miles of the stream.

A potato farm worker washed 1 gallon of settlings from an endrin spray can into a farm pond which drained into a creek, which killed 14,850 fish.

Poorly treated sewage from a municipal plant caused low dissolved oxygen and high ammonia concentrations in the Salt Fork, with 2,000 fish killed over a 3-mile stretch.

A stream, stocked with trout, received 2,500 gallons per hour of strip-mine pumpings, and turned milky with fine clay deposits on the bottom. Trout died over the two-week period.

Five years later in 1969, the kill more than doubled to 41 million fish. One kill alone destroyed 26 million fish at Lake Thonotosassa, Florida, when faulty treatment plants reduced oxygen in water below the survival point.

THE SPREAD OF DEVASTATION

If the reported fish kills were the end of pollution, we might not have further concern. But the earth's hydrologic circulation is a wonder to contemplate, and all too soon these toxic agents appear everywhere. Of 400 mating pairs of pelicans off Southern California shores in 1970, only two eggshells were hard enough to incubate the baby pelicans. For the rest, chemicals in the marine life, eaten by the pelicans, inhibited the formation of shells, and the baby pelicans were crushed by their nesting parents. On the Gulf Coast the survival rate among pelican eggs was only slightly higher. In the Pacific Northwest the embryo of an eagle was found in a membrane with no shell formation at all.

In ocean waters far out to sea, tuna have been caught containing more than the 0.5 parts per million (ppm) of mercury which is considered a safe standard by the Food and Drug Administration. A tuna scare was precipitated in 1970 when a chemistry class in New York tested a can of tuna and found it contained twice as much mercury as safety standards allow. The Food and Drug Administration then tested 140 lots of tuna and found that nearly one-fourth contained mercury beyond the standard. These lots were ordered off store shelves.

Mercury pollution has been discovered in thirty-three states and in Canada, causing many fishing areas to be closed. Concentrations as high as 5 ppm have been found in the Great Lakes.[11] Mercury contamination found in freshwater fish in Sweden and Finland are similar to the levels in the United States.[12] However, fish consumption is much higher in Scandinavia, with the result that the human body burdens of mercury are near the levels reported for persons suffering from methylmercury poisoning in Japan. Japan had 111 cases of mercury poisoning, with 53 fatalities, between 1953 and 1960, from high dosages, which were traced to a chemical plant polluting Minamata Bay. Dr. Jun Ui of Japan, by research, discovered the presence of mercury in seafood at that time. Since then it has been found that heavy metals and pesticides can be concentrated from water by bacteria, shellfish, and other marine life; and, when subsequently eaten by some predatory species in the food chain, accumulates in the tissue of fish, birds, animals, and man.

The dose rate for mercury poisoning is not clearly known. European countries generally permit 1 ppm of mercury in food, twice the American standard. Evidence indicates that methylmercury causes brain damage, convulsions, and loss of bodily control. Safe dosages of mercury to adults may pose a threat to an unborn fetus, because of a tendency for mercury to concentrate in the fetus.

The source of mercury is partly natural, from weathering rocks, partly from agricultural fungicides and chemical waste. Perhaps the largest source is from the burning of fossil fuels. The mercury content of fuels is small. A sample of thirty-three American coals averaged 3.3 ppm of mercury. But fuels are consumed at such an enormous rate for industrial and electric power that they are a significant source of mercury contamination. Coal burning alone releases an estimated 3,000 tons of mercury into the environment, an amount much larger than that released by natural weathering.[13]

Mercury is not alone among metals as a toxic agent to man. Serious adverse environmental and health effects have been observed for roughly one-fourth of the metals in common economic usage today. The consumption of metals, and of synthetic chemicals which are alien to the natural environment, are increasing rapidly. Examples of the toxic effects

[11]*Ocean Dumping,* Council on Environmental Quality, Washington, October 1970, p. 16.
[12]"Hazards of Mercury," *Environmental Research, An International Journal of Environmental Medicine and Environmental Science,* vol. 4, no. 1, March 1971, Academic Press, Inc., New York, p. 6.
[12]Oiva J. Joensuu, "Fossil Fuels as a Source of Mercury Pollution," *Science,* Washington, vol. 172, no. 3987, June 4, 1971, p. 1027.

of metals are readily available. Compounds of nickel and berylium accumulate in the lungs and may cause fatal diseases. Inhalation of barium in sufficient quantities causes heart, intestinal, and neural disorders. Cadmium, lead, or selenium produced abnormal offspring among laboratory mice, and long exposures of arsenic and molybdenum altered sex ratios. Low doses of antimony shortened the life-span of laboratory mice, and a controlled experiment in a metal-free environment increased the life-span by one-fourth.[14]

The exact consequences of environmental contamination on human health are not clearly known, but surely one indicator is the decline in numbers of sensitive species such as birds and fish. The total fish catch in the oceans is declining. A biologist who had completed an analysis of a dead eagle's body found not only DDT, but dieldrin, mercury, lead, PCB, etc., a veritable chemical soup.[15]

Helpful as indicator species are in diagnosing environmental problems, the alarming possibility is that there are many forms of pollution in the environment which may not have a more sensitive indicator organism than man himself.[16]

The effects of human interaction with the environment go beyond its toxification and the poisoning of the nutrient cycle. Human activity has the potential for changing the solar energy cycle as well. In the last several decades, the aerosol (dust and particles) content of the atmosphere has approximately doubled, and at present rates the particulate content of the atmosphere could increase 6 to 8 times in the next fifty years, largely from fossil fuel combustion. An increase in the dust concentration and global opacity by a factor of 4 is calculated to decrease global temperature by as much as 3.5 degrees Kelvin. Such a temperature decrease over the surface of the earth for several years would be sufficient to trigger an ice age.[17]

IMPETUS TO CHANGE

These illustrations are perhaps sufficient to show that man's activities are dealing with enormous natural forces which are little understood by science or the human mind. We are literally playing a lethal game without knowing the rules. The consequence already has been destruction of indicator species. The President of the United States has warned of

[14] *Toxic Substances*, Council on Environmental Quality, Washington, April 1971, pp. 2–10.
[15] Don Moser, "A Lament for Some Companions of My Youth," *Life*, Jan. 22, 1971, p. 51.
[16] C. R. Goldman, "Is the Canary Dying?," *California Medicine*, November 1970, 113:21–26.
[17] Rasiik and Schneider, "Atmospheric Carbon Dioxide and Aerosols," *Science*, Washington, vol. 173, no. 3992, July 9, 1971, pp. 138–141.

ecological disaster. Need disaster occur before we are able to read the signs about us and in our past as in England a century ago?

With the rise of industrialization a century ago, England had an enormous increase in death rates in the large cities as country folk migrated to urban areas to work in the textile mills. The crowding out stripped the poor sanitation facilities, and the cities were filthy and pestilent. An alarming increase in number of deaths jolted the populace into crisis measures in public health to clean up their environment. The suddenness with which the people of England acquired a sense of sight and smell and realized for the first time that they were living on a dung heap, arose from both the promise and the adversity of industrial change.[18]

If now, more than a century later, industrial technology presents us again with new promise and adversities, then we must think through the mechanism for change now. Human and institutional change comes slowly, while the spread of contamination on the winds and streams moves swiftly. Ecological problems have been approached, so far, mainly by setting standards of environmental quality and expecting technological inventions to solve the problem, while we go on consuming in the same way and rate as in the past. But simple controls over emissions and effluents will not repair ecological damage. Technology alone cannot solve the problem; technology is the problem.

Our decision-making process in technological affairs is what has brought us to the environmental crisis. The solution is something else—a behavioral solution, a management approach, and a new decision methodology. Unfortunately, we ourselves are the problem in our conflicting objectives in the use of technology. Somehow we must learn to manage ourselves and industrial techniques to take cognizance of their long-run ecological effects, and not simply the short-term maximization of production. The balance of the book is concerned with how we make decisions and how we might manage ourselves more consonantly with the environment.

DISCUSSION QUESTIONS

1 Who are some of the environmental administrators whose decisons affect your life?
2 Make a list of all the chemicals and drugs which you use, directly or indirectly, in your ordinary activity. How do you dispose of them? Where do they ultimately go? How much do you know about their effects?
3 What do you observe about the aesthetic quality of cities and what might be done to improve them?

[18]S. E. Finer, *The Life and Times of Sir Edwin Chadwick*, London, 1952, p. 212.

4 How many and what type of environmental disasters do you recall from news accounts? What would be necessary to have avoided them?

PROBLEM

Visit your local public health department and obtain their assessment of the kinds of environmental health hazards which exist in your community in terms of noise, contamination, diseases, and chronic ailments. Ask how sewage is processed, how industrial wastes are disposed, how the quality of the water and air is maintained, and what is the ultimate end of residuals discharged into the environment. Then make your assessment of the degree of biological hazard in the area; and, if you see threat of biological damage, what do you think might be done about it?

Chapter 3

The Structure of Present Decision Making Relative to the Environment

The decision structure regarding the environment is exhibited most clearly in the allocation and use of resources. Economists speak of the elements of production for all types of goods or services as being land, labor, capital, and management. Land, in this case, refers to the territorial earth itself plus its primary products such as minerals, water, timber, or materials. Labor is, of course, the human means for processing the materials of the earth, and capital is the technological means for such processing. Management is the organizational and risk-bearing function which arranges the process by which land, labor, and capital are combined to produce goods and services to meet human wants.

If these are the principal means by which we supply human wants, then the decision structure can be seen in the way we apportion land, labor, capital, and management. The present decision structure, which has evolved in industrialized society, is reflected in four sets of policies or instrumentalities. These are (1) the public land and resource allocation policies, (2) market and price structure delegations of resource allocation,

(3) industrial organization preferences of management and the polity, and (4) private decision preferences and criteria.

Generally speaking land allocation is determined by public legislation governing land appropriation and tenure. Labor and capital are allocated principally by the market and price mechanisms authorized by law, although labor allocations are determined also partly by negotiation as well. Management effort is shaped by the market-profit mechanism and by public law on permissible industrial organization. Therefore, the primary allocations are determined principally by legal or institutional instruments, which are the expression of the body politic on the way it wishes to operate as a society, or more commonly, the way it does business. A secondary determinate is the private decision preference structure of individuals which becomes felt, as an input into the institutional system, through the market mechanism in the form of consumer demand for specific products or services.

If we are to understand, then, the workings of the decision structure as it affects the environment, we need to see how the institutional arrangements came into being and how they operate. Then we can observe how the individual preferences, within the institutional constraints in which they are allowed to function, exercise the decision system to produce usable services, or disutilities in the form of pollution or environmental degradation. The structure of decision making may be seen in the following topics:

1 Land-use appropriation policies
2 Land ownership practices of the United States
3 Ecological effects of United States land appropriation and tenure
4 Land parameters of the decision structure
5 The market-price mechanism
6 Efficiency of price mechanism
7 Industrial organization preferences
8 Ecological implications of industrial organization
9 Private decision preferences

LAND-USE APPROPRIATION POLICIES

The appropriation of land to specific human uses is the most fundamental of all decisions relating to the environment, because this decision determines what a man may do with, on, and to the earth of which he is a part. Land appropriation and tenure practices go deep into history and are perhaps the most complex and deeply embedded notions we have. They are so deeply embedded that we seldom think profoundly about them; they are obvious, taken for granted, rights, immutable. Few today question the right of an individual to use his own land as he chooses, subject perhaps to a few flexible zoning regulations. Yet the idea of land ownership as private property *in fee simple absolute* is a relatively recent invention, peculiarly American in its extremity, and a source of many of our problems, particularly exclusive and preemptive land use, and urban and farm tenancy.[1]

Primitive hunting and pastoral societies had varying customs regarding land use, but the more prevalent views were that tribe members might have certain rights *(usufructs)* although ownership rights, if such were recognized at all, were attributable to the village or tribe as a whole, to God, to earth itself, or occasionally to a lord who ruled for the group.[2] Generally then, land ownership was in common for the society; and rights were attached to usage for a term and a specific end, such as tillage, wood-gathering, or pasturage.

Under Roman rule, small farms or village common usages were converted into large slave-run estates owned by an aristocracy, and subsequently into estates with free tenants which later became a feature of the European manorial system. The breakdown of Roman law and order led to the sacrifice of free tenancy and small ownership by individuals, who gave up many personal rights in exchange for the physical and economic protection afforded by a feudal manor. The self-sufficing activities of the manor formed a type of security not otherwise obtainable in a period of chaotic change.

During its long history, feudalism has had two major features: (1) a system of personal relationships and (2) a form of land use.[3] The value of the personal relationships lay in the mutual system of loyalties and services—the tenant contributed labor and produce to the support of the manor, and the lord contributed protection, management, and care to the people of his estate. The mutual care of men, for each other and for the land, is one of the features lost with the end of the feudal system. This is not to express nostalgia for feudalism because its disadvantages weighed heavily against its advantages, and the disadvantages stemmed from land tenure. The tenant or serf became bound to the land with an ultimate loss of freedom of choice or equality of opportunity.

The abuses, or disadvantages, of feudalism did not lead to its demise so much as the Black Plague in the fourteenth century. In England the Black Death killed between 30 and 50 percent of the population. Feudal lords found themselves without the manpower to run the estates, with the

[1]Ronald R. Renne, *Land Economics,* Harper and Brothers, New York, 1958, pp. 266–373.

[2]Clawson, Held, and Stoddard, *Land for the Future,* Resources for the Future, Washington, 1960, pp. 470–474.

[3]Marion Clawson, *Man and Land in the United States,* University of Nebraska Press, Lincoln, Neb., 1964, p. 8.

result that prices and wages rose, farm labor demanded better tenure terms, and the manor lords sold portions of their land to free men or rented them to the more capable villagers and farmers. The Statute of Tenures in England in 1660 severely altered the legal structure authorizing feudalism.[4] Feudalism and serfdom gradually changed into the manorial system, with gentry, tenant farmers, and laborers under a wage system.

Another major development affecting land appropriation also occurred in England from the sixteenth to the eighteenth century—the *enclosure movement.* The village commons, or open-field farming, and the manorial commons were well suited to a local self-sufficient economy; but the industrial revolution brought increasing demands for food and fiber to be shipped to larger towns, to which labor had migrated to work in the textile industries. Rising food and wool prices made it profitable to farm individual fields with better methods. The enclosure movement converted and prorated ownership of common lands into private fields, thus reestablishing private individual ownership rights in land.

LAND OWNERSHIP PRACTICES OF THE UNITED STATES

This was the frame of reference in land appropriation that the American colonists were familiar with at the time of their immigration to the United States in the seventeenth century, and early American land appropriation reflected these practices. The initial settlers in New England obtained permission from the king or colony government to form a new town. The village was laid out, as in earlier days in England, with a small common grazing and meeting ground in the center, surrounded by houses with large yards for gardens. Men worked together to clear fields, and then divided them among all settlers, recording the titles as they went with each settler getting some good and poor land. There was little land speculation, and the cooperative effort fostered democracy and town hall government.

In the South, which was settled later, the idea of *headrights* was established. Like later homesteading, headrights conferred a tract of land, usually 50 acres, on each indentured servant who settled in the colony, as well as on the ship's captain, and the planter who paid the servant's fare. Subsequently, headrights were sold or obtained fraudulently. Survey and recording practices were poor. Land speculation was prevalant, and the speculation in headrights led to formation of large plantations.[5]

When the public domain of the United States came into being, first by the cessation of Western lands by the first colonies to pay debts and

[4]Ibid., p. 11.
[5]Ibid., pp. 28–30.

equalize size, and later by acquisition, the federal government encouraged rapid land sales and disposal in order to attract settlers and obtain revenue. The American immigrant had often been persecuted and dispossessed in his native land and came to the United States for quick riches. Immigrants frequently settled on the land before it was surveyed. The issues of preemption, or the right of a settler to buy land on which he had squatted at a fixed price without competitive bidding, became a heated political issue. Most early land sales were by auction, but in 1841, the Preemption Act allowed settlers the right to buy, with prior rights to ownership over others, at $1.25 per acre up to 160 acres. The Homestead Act of 1862 succeeded the Preemption Act but continued much of the same intent and practices. The Land Grant Acts from 1785 forward set aside public lands for the support of school systems and other public purposes.

What were the results of these land appropriation practices in the United States?

The United States became a geographical checkerboard land of scattered absentee ownership, with a cultural tradition of land speculation and private abuses of natural surroundings. Public land sales in the nineteenth century were a brawling affair fraught with fraud, trespassing, "fast-buckery," and waste. Congress did little to restrain the rampant, grab-bag aura, since many Congressmen were land dealers and speculators as well. Fraud in acquiring title to land took many forms, including the private land claim, preemption, and superficial improvements.[6]

The land blitz continues today in city council meetings where land is continually divided into smaller parcels and marked higher in price by zoning decisions. Fraud too persists in the best tradition of the West. A developer planted gold on a coveted parcel of land, filed a mining claim to get title, dug up the gold, and built a housing subdivision on it. Another opened a house of salacious repute on a national forest land claim, which was closed down by the United States Attorney for violating the mining laws, after the local sheriff refused to prosecute.[7]

ECOLOGICAL EFFECTS OF UNITED STATES LAND APPROPRIATION AND TENURE

The curious consequence of federal land policies is that they have had the opposite effect from that which was intended. Federal land policy was intended to encourage operator ownership of land; instead it created high rates of tenancy. Why?

[6]Ibid., pp. 78–80.
[7]"The New Shape of America," *Life*, vol. 70, no. 1, January 8, 1971, pp. 41–42.

The growth of tenancy came from granting title to land as private property in fee simple absolute, which permits land accumulation and transfer with practically no restrictions on its use or disposition. Our ancestors, who struggled so long to free themselves from the restraints of feudal land tenure system, undoubtedly went too far in the opposite direction in trying to prevent the rise of a landed aristocracy like that in Europe. Instead they created tenancy and corporate land ownership. The American system of land ownership in fee simple absolute makes land easy to mortgage and freely salable, which treats land like any other commodity.[8]

The idea of trading land as a commodity would be almost inconceivable in other cultural settings, for instance, to the American Indian who looked at land as the root of his being to be used in common, to the Chinese who base their maternal system on familial land tenure, to the East Indians who have elaborate cross-cousin marriage customs to keep land intact in a family, to the British whose primogeniture and entail laws cut off land claims to all but the eldest offspring. Throughout Europe the restrictions on land use are much more severe than in the United States, particularly through the role of city planners who practically direct how an owner may use his land within the public interest. Whereas here in the United States, the land developer and speculator can usually cajole, or occasionally bribe, a city council into giving him the zoning variances pretty much as he wishes. Zoning cases are the overwhelming business of many city councils, and council members soon learn the importance of placating most land-use demands in order to get reelected. Land speculation in the United States is today almost as ubiquitous as it was a century ago, except now the harvest centers on zoning and land-use demands rather than upon public land sales.

From a biological view, the idea of trading land as a commodity is also astonishing. The land (and the oceans) are the heart of the energy-fixing cycle of the earth, one of two great ecosystems on which all life depends. The second great ecosystem is the biogeochemical cycle, or food chain, which is the rate and character of nutrients (once they are first fixed in the energy cycle) that are generated and used by organisms. In the first cycle, the earth is the parent geological host material in which producing organisms, plants, or autotrophs fix light energy and manufacture food or nutrients. Without this energy fixing cycle of light energy, earth, and autotrophs, there would be no living things in our world. Equally important, the soil is host to bacteria and microflora which are the most efficient digestors of residue and waste in the ecosystem. The

[8]Renne, op. cit., p. 373.

ubiquitous *Bdellovibrio*, for example, are parasites to pathogens in raw sewage and render them innocuous. Other soil microorganisms decompose the synthesized nutrients made by the autotrophs. In an industrial world where we are succumbing to our own enormous waste burden, the soil and the oceans are the only place we can truly dispose of these residues by decomposition. In this sense, that we are willing to buy, sell, trade, barter, speculate, and abuse the parent geological material which provides the life-giving functions of the earth, our treatment of land as commodity is a Faustian bargain—trading early gains for long-term losses.

The land-use patterns which have come from this bargain are ecologically deleterious, because the land has become too fragmented as a natural ecosystem to preserve its species or balance. The public land disposal methods resulted in numerous small tracts scattered in shotgun fashion among many owners. The thousands of separate land parcels, combined with absentee ownership, defeated the possibility of working out effective land utilization.[9]

The original land survey cut up the United States into rectangular, haphazard squares which ignored ecological boundaries. The east-west or north-south section lines lay out roads and field layouts so that drainage runs up and down rather than around the slopes. Much erosion has been caused by these types of land use. Hindsight indicates that the rolling prairie or forest areas might better have been divided along natural drainage lines.[10]

LAND PARAMETERS OF THE DECISION STRUCTURE

A decision structure may be looked upon as a series of postulates and constraints, that is, the framework within which the decision maker views what he may or may not do. These assumptions dictate the form of the decision. We have been talking about the assumptions regarding land and its use, how they came into being and what they are. The postulates in the decision structure regarding land are:

1 Land is a commodity, owned in fee simple absolute, to be bought, accumulated, subdivided, used, or sold for the advantage of the owner.

2 Dependence on the land or operation of it is not a condition of ownership, and the owner may be absentee, with no interest in the land in either a subsistant or an ecological sense, but only a speculative interest in its market value.

[9]Ibid., p. 374.
[10]Clawson, op. cit., pp. 61–62.

3 Land may be traded in any parcel size, regardless of ecological effects, which suits the advantage of the owner and complies with minimal, flexible zoning regulations.

4 Land will ordinarily be subdivided upon rectangular lines within the boundaries of existing surveys, without regard to drainage or ecological characteristics.

5 Land may be held in use or disuse throughout time, transferred to heirs or assigns, without reference to societal or ecological needs.

6 Land may be preempted by the owner to exclusive uses, without any usage rights by others, because usufructs are not recognized in United States law.

7 Land may be used exclusively for its locational value, that is, as a situs and host for human activity, without recognition of its role as a parent geological host material for autotrophic or heterotrophic organisms (i.e., species which make, use, or decompose nutrients).

In addition to these postulates and assumptions in the decision structure, there are a few constraints that the decision maker must observe which reflect societal needs.

1 The owner of land must recognize the right of society to tax land to help support public services.

2 Society has the right of eminent domain, to acquire land for its own use, by paying the current market value. The fact that a speculative market value may be due to societal development surrounding the condemned land is immaterial under the law, and speculative or surplus value accrues to the owner rather than to the society.

3 Land use is constrained by broad zoning regulations which recognize special uses and parcels sized for the public convenience, but these zoning rules are subject to change through the political process; and land owners may exercise their interests under the political process to change land-use regulations to their favor. That is, conflict of interest, as a legal constraint, seldom arises in land-use cases.

The freedom of land use as situs for human activity carries with it corollary postulates for the primary materials of the land, namely minerals, water, and timber. Water rights are particularly important for human use, for agricultural use, and for industrial processing and waste disposal. It takes about 1,000 pounds of water to make 1 pound of milling wheat, and about 10,000 pounds of water for 1 pound of sugar. The water equivalent of food for human consumption is about 2,500 gallons per day.[11] In industrial processing, it takes about 770 gallons of water to refine

---

[11]George A. Nikolaieff, *The Water Crisis*, H. W. Wilson Company, New York, 1967, p. 15.

a barrel of petroleum, 3,500 gallons to produce an automobile, 200,000 gallons to produce a ton of viscose rayon, and 600,000 gallons to make a ton of synthetic rubber. Taken together, the food and industrial products requirements of the American consumer require use of about 15,000 gallons of water per person today. The rainfall in the United States approximates 5,000 billion gallons per day, but is unevenly distributed in time and place. This total rainfall supply is capable of supporting about 230 million people in the United States at present usage rates.[12] In 1970 the population was 205 million.

Water may then be viewed as a scarce resource, soon to be pressed by population beyond its bearing capacity. The decision structure regarding water use does not allocate scarce water in recognition of pressing or highest human need; rather the rule of appropriation is, somewhat as in land law, "first in time, first in right." This rule has become known as the appropriative doctrine.

The appropriative doctrine of water use developed in the gold fields of California, where prospectors and miners required water for sluicing gold in placer operations. The miners, like their agricultural counterparts in Utah, disregarded riparian rights and diverted streams whose normal channels were often many miles from mining operations.

Miners applied the same principle to water use that they did to their mining operations; that is, the first discoverer had the prior rights. The legal maxim was: first in time, first in right.

The doctrine of prior appropriation is the dubious contribution Western America has made to water law. The doctrine gives advantage to the first beneficial use of a water source regardless of later—possibly higher—beneficial uses.[13]

Whether the first use of water is the highest human or ecological need is very problematical, especially with the passage of time. Indeed, it is questionable whether the first use is the best use even at the time. Let us take, for example, the early gold miners of California, under whose vision the water appropriative doctrine was established. Before the gold rush, California was a land with a few large cattle ranches, and still the home of Indians who, largely ignorant of agriculture, lived bountifully on fish and game in the varied land of mountains, valleys, forests, streams, and grasslands. The Uurok, Karok, and Hupa Indians of Northern California especially prized the king salmon which was a large part of their diet; they reflected their awe and veneration for the salmon in elaborate rituals and ceremonies.

[12]Ibid., pp. 16–24.
[13]*Land and Water Use*, Wynne Thorne, ed., American Association for the Advancement of Science, Symposium, 1961, pp. 62–63.

The Sacramento–San Joaquin river system carried enormous stocks of California salmon, and the upper reaches of these rivers were their spawning grounds. Sacramento and San Francisco were the centers of a fishing industry in the period from 1860 to 1882 which realized as much as 12 million pounds of salmon per year; and California salmon were epicurean dishes in Chicago, London, and Paris. Hydraulic gold mining, originating in the 1850s, played high-velocity water streams on ore bodies and washed the dirt and silt downstream to expose the ore. Hydraulic mining devasted long stretches of the Sacramento River, creating mounds of silt up to 600 feet high, which flowed over valley lands and filled stream beds when the rains came. Hydraulicking was outlawed by court order in 1883, but the damage was done. By 1890 practically all the California salmon had disappeared from the Sacramento River.[14]

Was the first use of Sacramento River water for hydraulicking the highest human and ecological use, even in its own time? The answer depends upon one's views and values. From a short-run utilitarian and profit viewpoint, the gold miners gained wealth and their product, the gold, was eventually put back into the ground in a hole at Fort Knox. Over a very long run the market value of a renewable resource, salmon, will always be greater than that of an extractive or exhaustive resource like gold. To an ecologist the desolation of species is not only regrettable but a new unknown imbalance in the ecostructure. To the everyday sportsmen or nature lovers among the 20 million residents in California a century later, a Sacramento River teaming with salmon is preferable to tons of gold in Fort Knox.

> Of all the principles of ethics that men have been able to devise, none is so fundamental as the ethical postulate that we are morally obliged to meet the demands that coming generations would have imposed upon us were they able to speak to us today.[15]

THE MARKET-PRICE MECHANISM

A second fundamental cornerstone of our present decision structure, after land appropriation laws and customs, is the market-price mechanism, by which materials, capital goods, labor, and, to some extent, management, are allocated to the end uses of human wants. The market-price system, like the land laws, is largely taken for granted; though again, there have been many societies which operated without, or with only

---

[14] *Westways,* August 1970, pp. 13–14.
[15] C. West Churchman, *Challenge to Reason,* McGraw-Hill Book Company, New York, 1968, p. 16.

partial, market systems, such as the Romans; the feudal systems; the Incas; the Russians; and three-fourths of the world population in Asia, Africa, and South America today.

The money-market-price system as we know it is peculiarly Western: it originated in the Mediterranean; developed under textile trade beginning in the thirteenth century among Italy, France, Flanders, England, and Germany; rose to heights of perfection first under the German Hanseatic League, and then under the British Empire; was adopted full-blown by the United States; and was scarcely questioned until the Depression of the 1930s, when public goods and services (amounting to one-fourth of the economy) were pulled out from under the market-price system and dealt with by public appropriation, through what has become known, rather slightingly, as the welfare economy.

The foundations of the market-price structure are deep in the common law of England and the United States, in contracts, in agency, in negotiable instruments, and in personal liability. The law of contracts makes an agreed-upon price for the exchange of goods and services enforceable in the courts. The law of agency enables people to act on another's behalf in contractual activity. Negotiable instruments make various forms of payments for contracts enforceable in the courts; and personal liability pledges all the goods, services, and wealth of an individual, proprietor, or partner to fulfill payment of contracts. Briefly stated, as simple as they sound, they represent, nonetheless, the formidable arsenal of actions and remedies on which commercialism is based. Without them, there would be no markets; with them, everything is exchangeable as a commodity, including one's own work and the good earth.

The nature and working of the market-price system are such common knowledge in everyday experience that no attempt will be made to explicate further, except to note the exceptions. Some things have always been outside the price system, and others we have deliberately reserved from it after unhappy experience with the effects of the price system.

Although economy comes from a Greek word meaning management of the household, the family household economy has always been outside the market-price system in our society and everyone else's. Some few exceptions may come to mind, like the Jewish marriage brokers, or the black market in baby adoptions. But generally it is true that love, marriage, children, and family relations live by a different decision structure than the market economy. Family life is based on word rather than contract, personal contact rather than agency, free exchange of services rather than negotiable instruments, and voluntary retribution rather than personal liability. Given these customs in the family decision structure, the household economy is a place with a cooperative exchange system. Most of us spend almost half of our waking lives in this family economy, reserved from the market system, because everything there is too near to our lives for exchange.

Another exception to the market-price system came with the Great Depression of the 1930s when certain people were protected who were poorly equipped by training, health, or age to look out for themselves in the competitive bargaining of the market place. So another reservation was made from the price system to preserve human resources from the effects of the market; and farmers, aged, dependent children, unemployed, dependent mothers, the infirm and the sick, students, government workers—all were put under subvention to support their activity regardless of price. The move to make these human exclusions from the market system was bitterly fought then, and is still today, and the welfare state is of various repute depending upon who benefits and who pays for it. But whatever the merits of welfare as a concept, the society seemingly found it necessary to recreate some features of the tribe, of the extended family, of feudal care, to provide forms of common support.

The reservations from the price system of ecological regimes have been few, but there are exceptions. The national parks set aside natural scenery of extraordinary beauty outside of the commodity market in land. The twenty-four whooping cranes and the twelve Asian ibis are protected against hunters, as are sea lions and otters, which are shot nonetheless. The American bald eagle is a protected species, though disappearing anyway. Hunting and fishing laws protect some game species for a season, or out of season. The control of the pesticides to protect wildlife may perhaps be viewed as a protective removal of species from the effects of the market-price system.

Taken all together, these reservations from the market system indicate that there is a fairly substantial nonmoney economy. The market-price system, then, governs that limited portion of human affairs in the industrial and trade sector.

EFFICIENCY OF PRICE MECHANISM

In the industrial-commercial sector, the decision structure under the market system is crisp and efficient. There are few imponderables or qualitative judgments, because, as the saying goes in business, the bottom line of the profit and loss statement is what counts. The income, or profit and loss, statement summarizes the exchange prices in the market of a business, along with its volume. The price and quantity of products sold become the income; the cost prices, or materials, labor, and services, become the expense items; and the difference, which counts, is the remaining profit. The efficiency of this decision structure comes from its clarity, quantification, and unequivocal result. With so efficacious a decision tool, men of limited ecological knowledge can make quick decisions, like the California gold miners and those who bring their products to market today faster than they can be safely tested.

What are the deeper implications of the market-price decision structure? One is that test of benefit lies in short-term optimization of profit. Growth companies in the acquisition movement of the late 1960s spoke of optimizing their quarter-by-quarter net earnings per share. Now a quarterly decision span is very short indeed, considering that it took the miners twenty years to kill the California salmon, and it took twenty-five years for the pesticide DDT to proceed through the food chain so that it could be recorded in the stored fat on the human body. Nevertheless, the implication of the market-price system is very short-term optimization of results, and, in a few cases like the commodity trading pits or in land speculation, the optimization decision is almost instantaneous. Hence, the interesting question arises, does instantaneous, or short-term, optimization, or profit, take adequate account of long-term ecological damage?

The answer to this question is probably no, because the decision structure of the market only optimizes those things included in the price system. We have already seen that a portion of man's activity is excluded from the price structure, including the household, government, welfare, and some ecological processes. So what is the decision maker optimizing? Only the net trade on materials over the short run. Is there anything wrong with that?

No, it probably is a good thing for a manufacturer-trader to try to optimize the short-run activities in his operation, because in this way he becomes efficient, provides goods to the consumer at lowest cost, and makes a living for himself as well. Except there is one problem. The decision structure did not include even all his materials costs. If he is a pulp mill operator, the price of pulp did not include the cost of cleansing the water supply of the black sulfur liquor which he dumped into the stream. Nor did the cost of chemicals or oil refining include the cost of pollution they put into the water. Nor does the cost of electricity include the sulfur dioxide with which the power company pollutes the air. Nor does the cost of the automobile include the cost of air pollution, accidents, patrols, deaths. Nor does the cost of pharmaceuticals, high as they are, include untested health effects. On and on—the industrial system does not include the cost of any of its social or health effects. These are sometimes referred to, among economists, as external costs, or externalities. The market system includes none of the social costs of getting rid of wastes, residues, or toxicity. Considering that the amount of waste produced by industry is almost equal in quantity to the valuable produce they manufacture, the external costs can be seen to be enormous, perhaps again as much as what the consumer pays for the product, in either government cost, health effects, or degradation of the environment.

The market-price system, as it is conceived and practiced today, is a somewhat deficient decision structure from an ecological standpoint, however efficient it may be to the business enterprise. That bottom line of the profit and loss statement does not really tell anything, except the short-run benefit of the decision maker, and says nothing about the cost to or sacrifice of society, individuals, or species survival. In an ecological sense, the present market-price decision structure is a mechanism by which the waste-toxicity burden gets transferred as cost or sacrifice to humankind and other species generally and indiscriminately.

The market-price system can, of course, be corrected to include ecological costs, if we should choose to do so. This possibility is explored at length in Section Three.

INDUSTRIAL ORGANIZATION PREFERENCES

The third basic determinant of our present decision structure is the nature of our industrial organization, for that dictates who does business within the framework of contract law.

Many forms of industrial organization are possible; our preference is for large industrial corporations. The prevalence of industrial corporations as the principal model of business is scarcely more than a century old. The idea of incorporation is founded in municipal law. Early Roman law established the *municipium*, which permitted Italian cities to make general application for citizenship. Originally, then incorporation was a form of citizenship in a body politic for conducting the public interest. The expansion of municipal corporations through time gave to them certain contracting power to conduct their business as well as agency and taxation power.

The prevalent form of commercial organization in England and the American colonies was the single proprietorship or partnership of individual persons. Larger enterprises (such as the East India Company), which were few in number and somewhat privileged in their inception, were founded under royal charters. With the industrial revolution and the need for larger capitalization of business firms, the limited liability partnership developed in England and this was the dominant business form until 1855 when the Companies Act and a series of related laws were enacted to enable business firms to form limited liability corporations. The reason for the change was that partnerships became large, changing bodies of persons, and it was difficult to know with whom one was contracting and who was liable.

In the United States, both federal and state constitutions authorize legislatures to create corporations. Congressional power to incorporate presumably relates to some of the enumerated functions of the federal government; and Congress, except in the field of banking, has made limited use of incorporation. Most corporations are created by state law. State-created corporations include (1) public corporations such as cities; (2) private nonprofit corporations such as churches, universities, and charities; and (3) business corporations. In the early nineteenth century, most general corporations were municipal, religious, or nonprofit organizations. At that time, business organizations were more commonly formed by a charter through special act of a state legislature. These, as in earlier England, were costly to obtain and conducive to privilege and abuse. About the same time as in England, in the midnineteenth century, the states began to establish general incorporation laws.

The first real rise in the large industrial corporation movement came with the railroads and, in the 1870s, with the "trusts" in sugar, oil, coal, and other commodities. The power of the big trusts and railroads over the lives of the other citizens, who were single proprietors or farmers, was sufficiently ominous to start the Populist revolution; big corporations could exercise power over prices, rail rates, or availability of supply. These fears were real enough so that public clamor brought Congress to enact the Interstate Commerce Act in 1887 and the Sherman Antitrust Act in 1890 to regulate the railroads.

The Standard Oil trust which was formed in 1882 was dissolved by court order under the Sherman Antitrust Act; and other monopolistic practices have since been proscribed, like discriminatory pricing, dividing up markets, agreements to restrict competition, or other "conspiracies in restraint of trade." The antitrust laws do not prohibit monopoly or oligopoly as such, but only the use of monopoly power which reduces competition. The difficulty of defining what is the exercise of monopoly power has caused the courts to vacillate and rendered the enforcement of antitrust laws of dubious effect. In 1911 the Supreme Court ruled in the Standard Oil and American Tobacco cases that only abuse, predatory practices, and unreasonable restraints of trade were prohibited by law. This view was confirmed in the United States Steel case of 1920, which also ruled that bigness as such was not to be prevented. The predatory power theory gained further ascendancy in the Aluminum Company case

(1945) in which 90 percent control of the market was viewed as illegal, 30 percent as legal, and 64 percent as doubtful. The Philadelphia bank and other cases of the 1960s further judged that it was not total market power which determined abuse, but rather the horizontal market share in any territorial market segment. By this rule a company might dominate national markets by sheer size, while only holding a minor market share under its direct sales control in any city or geographic area.

The market power rule has enabled corporations to grow to gigantic size, either through national marketing organizations or through acquisition and merger of unrelated types of products and companies. Every major business boom in the last century, in the 1890s, 1920s, and 1960s, has produced a major industrial consolidation movement through merger and acquisition. The acquisition movement of the 1960s merged unrelated product line companies into vast financial conglomerates.

There has been no pretense in this consolidation movement that economies of size or scale would increase efficiency and lower costs to the consumer. Rather the claim was that the financial strength and management skill of the larger company would improve the operating stability and effectiveness of the miscellaneous collection of subsidiaries. This business principle became known jovially as "taking lemons and turning them into lemonade." As long as the price-earnings multiple of the acquiring company was higher than that of those acquired, or there was sufficient debt leverage in the subsidiaries to raise the earnings per share of the parent company, lemonade could be made by the promoters of the conglomerate. By the end of the decade, the lemons began to turn sour for the stockholders of conglomerates because of the unbelievable price-earnings ratios and the debt-credit pinch.

Meantime, through this whole century of merger, the industrial organization structure has become larger and larger until now the 500 largest corporations conduct about 64 percent of the manufacturing business of the United States. There are a number of advantages to these large-sized units, although the claim of efficiency and low costs is probably the least important, if not indeed of doubtful validity. The advantages of large industrial corporations are their ability to amass the large amounts of capital needed by complex technology, to produce the resources and stability to develop that technology and its capital goods requirements over rather long lead times, and to have the staying power to develop products and markets where the risks of technological obsolescence are high. These are significant advantages, particularly to a populace which places a high value on economic progress and security beyond all else, including health and environment.

ECOLOGICAL IMPLICATIONS OF INDUSTRIAL ORGANIZATION

Industrial corporations, or their product designs, are also the principal source of pollution and environmental degradation. They are the largest emitters of wastes and effluents of all kinds, into the air, the water, and the soils. Under such circumstances, it is not surprising that most of the species which have become extinct in the past 2,000 years have disappeared in the past 100 years during the era of large-scale industrial technology where the objective, whether the industry is privately owned or nationalized, is to optimize the output of goods. Russia too has preferred large-scale technical organizations intent upon maximizing production and has suffered severe pollution as its industrial technology manufactures wastes at the same rate as usable products.

The United States industrial corporation is founded on some very curious concepts from an ecological view. In the first place, a business corporation is conceived in the eyes of the law as an "artificial person," as contrasted with a "natural person." This basic assumption reflects the extraordinary subtlety of the legal mind, because it is hard for a natural person to imagine what an artificial person might be like. An artificial person is not something one can touch, see, scold, hold, or love. It is a figmental creature with the power to contract; designate agents; negotiate instruments; make and receive payment; buy and sell commodities, including land; accumulate wealth; and employ people. Such an artificial creature has many of the characteristics of a natural person, but not all.

An artificial person has limited liability, while a natural person is fully responsible for his acts and has unlimited liability. The artificial person has tax advantages for capital accumulation, i.e., accelerated depreciation, depletion allowances, capital gains, business expense deductions, not available to the ordinary person. The artificial person has enormous financial resources to own and hold the resources of the earth, while the natural person has relatively limited ability to possess the earth. The artificial person has no digestive tract to assimilate its own residues, while the natural person succumbs to toxicity and waste. The artificial person has unlimited life, and the natural person, after his brief span, dies.

Given two persons, one artificial and one natural, but both with equal legal powers to use the market-price system and the land appropriation system to their own advantage, would you expect them to behave the same from an ecological viewpoint? Yes, some would say, because after all the corporation, or artificial person, really is manipulated by actors who are human. No, others might say, because the human decision makers come and go and, during their brief stay, have modest sway over the actions of the corporation.

The form and framework of the corporate decision structure are capable of giving it a distinct bias of its own, regardless of the human actors in the scene. That bias is to objectify everything into things to be bought and sold, whether it is land, life, or labor; and to quantify everything into volumes, prices, and costs because its raison d'être is to use the market-price structure for an optimum, short-term profit, and to accumulate the maximum long-term wealth. Since it is the favored creature of the state, with limited liability, limited taxes, and unlimited funds, the artificial person can deal with the ecosystems of the earth on a scale unprecedented for natural persons. Finally, since it is immune to its own residues and cannot die, the artificial person need have no fear of pollution, disease, or environmental despoliation.

If one were to set out to design the perfect instrument for the conquest of nature or, more diabolically, the perfect instrument to destroy it, the modern corporation would fit that design specification exactly. Man, when he set out to become god of the earth, endowed the corporation with everything that he desired for himself, wealth, power, technology, preferential taxation, ability to operate outside the laws of nature, and immortality.

PRIVATE DECISION PREFERENCES

In all this elaborate structure of institutions and law regarding land, price systems, and corporations, the individual stands not as a helpless person, but capable of making vital decisions of his own. Two institutionalized instruments are in his own hands for ultimate control: his expression of preference through the price system in the form of consumer demand (after all he does not have to buy the products of industrial corporations if he feels their effects are noxious); and his power to vote, which can change the value scheme and institutional game completely if he chooses. The fact that the individual citizen-consumer has these ultimate controls and has not chosen to exercise them, suggests one or both of two things: either citizens are in accord with the present institutional game with its goal of economic progress, or they do not really know the magnitude of the economic-ecological tradeoffs which they are making. That is, they may not know that economic and material progress is being bought at the price of ecological disaster and their own life-span.

Assume for the moment that most citizens are deeply committed to the idea of material progress, but, if they realized a demonstrable hazard to their lives or the ecology, they would opt for environmental preservation as a superior priority; then, under these fairly realistic assumptions, what decision structure can and do citizens exercise?

The most conspicuous evidence of citizen preferences and the decisions they make lies in consumer spending patterns. The largest consumer expenditures are for family purposes, housing, food, medical care, and children's education. Beyond this, transportation and mobility assume high priority, followed by recreation in various forms. The overall allocation of consumer spending to functional purposes is not really as significant as the burgeoning mechanization of all these functions—more elaborate housing, temperature control equipment, kitchen and household equipment, garden equipment, snowblowers, lawn mowers, chain saws, automobiles, snowmobiles, dune buggies, campers, motor boats, etc., ad infinitum. All these energy-using mechanisms are polluters of the environment, and, since consumers outnumber corporations, their contribution to environmental degradation is more than negligible. Although the primary and most difficult forms of pollution may originate with the factory, particularly water pollutants and solid wastes, the consumers, with their many automobiles, are the biggest contributors to air pollution.

The decision structure to change environmental quality is, at least partially, in consumer hands. Business corporations are tremendously sensitive to the marginal changes in their volume of sales, because of the large fixed costs they build up in capital goods to carry on their business. In other words a small change in sales will have a large impact on most business decisions. Merely by stretching out purchases, making old products last longer, saving more money, consumers can exercise a strong influence on the course of business decisions. There are, of course, constraints on consumer choices, to the extent that they have no alternatives to the things they basically need. Most consumers can delay durable goods purchases for some time, but often not foods or pharmaceutical products. Even for transportation, the old car may be used longer; but, if there is no public transport system, the consumer in time has a limited freedom of choice in his options for getting to work.

Where limited freedom of choice exists, citizens can resort to their franchise and the political system for changes. They can vote for public transit systems, environmental controls, air quality standards, controls on emissions, land-use and zoning changes. The citizens have the ultimate power of control, if they choose to use it. But to exercise such control to improve the environment is difficult, because of other constraints. A citizen-consumer movement is generally not able to influence legislation against a corporate interest group, because the consumer interest is diffuse. It is harder to reach the mass of people. They have many cross-motivations and divergent views. A great deal of money, or a desperate crisis, is needed to organize a grass roots campaign. The corporations by contrast have large resources, special rather than general interests, and functioning organizational structures to run a campaign. A consumer movement will usually lose to the special interest campaign of corporation groups, unless the issues evoke powerful citizen motivates. In California for example, where the public ranked air pollution second in importance to concern over crime and violence, in a public survey, a public referendum (Proposition 18), to divert the local portion of gas tax funds to public transit, lost by a narrow vote. The highway lobby of automobile and oil companies reputedly spent $600,000 to defeat the proposition, more than 10 times what the citizen group was able to finance.

SUMMARY

On the whole, the framework of decision making has become highly institutionalized to favor corporation-oriented decisions, and, except in crisis, the consumer preference structure operates within a limited range of alternatives. Hence the prevalent decision structure under which we operate today tends to maximize material outputs, regardless of whether those outputs be useful goods or toxic wastes. In very real terms, the decision structure is insensitive to the distinction between useful products and wastes. If the two are concomitants, which they are in industrial processing of materials of the earth, then the wastes and residues get produced along with the useful goods. The wastes are then dumped upon the ecosystems on the presumption that waste disposal is costless and the ecostructure has unlimited capacities for absorption or dilution.

The fact that the ecosystems do not have this unlimited cleansing capacity has only recently been realized, and realized late in the despoliation of the environment. Whether the degradation of the environment can be turned toward ecological improvement depends to a large extent, not on wishes or patchwork controls, but upon a rethinking and overhauling of the decision structure. For the decision structure, as we have seen, has a bias toward environmental disaster, because it ignores biological effects.

The land appropriation system converts the earth, which is the principal biological host to all life, into a commodity or situs for human activity. The market-price system converts all material exchanges into short-term utility or profit, with no inclusion of social health or biological sacrifices. The modern corporation uses the tools of land ownership and the market system to produce economic growth, with no regard for the volume, toxicity, or disposal of its wastes. The corporation, as an artificial person, operates outside the laws of nature.

If we want to operate within the laws of nature, to prevent ecological disaster, we have to have a decision structure which enables us to function as human beings as part of, and within the ecosystems of the earth. The challenge, changing the decision structure, is no mean task; for it means reversing 400 years of complex technological, economic, and philosophical development; and we do not have nearly as long in the remaking as we had in the making.

DISCUSSION QUESTIONS

1 What observations of past land appropriation practices do you see around you, such as city, road, or field layout; tenancy; corporate land holdings; erosion? Select a terrain with which you are familiar and try to describe a land use consistent with native growth, drainage, and ecology.
2 What portion of your time and activity would you estimate is determined by factors of a market versus a nonmarket economy? That is, trace the origin of your activities to inputs from your surroundings and determine how the decision to allocate that input to you was made.
3 What does an "artificial" person mean to you, and how might its decisions differ from your own? Can you give an example?
4 What are the main instruments by which the individual citizen may make his wants known and effectuated? How extensively do individuals use their decision instruments with respect to environmental affairs?

PROBLEM

Go to a city council meeting when zoning cases are being heard and listen to the arguments for and against zoning changes, particularly on subdivision lot-splits and commercial or industrial zoning requests. Make a case analysis of the arguments on both sides including: what decision structure is the claimant using in requesting the zoning change? The city council? Is there a city planning department report presuming to reflect the public interest? How does its recommendations or decision assumptions differ from the claimant? What is the outcome of the decision in economic, community, and ecological effects? How often does the city council overrule the planning department? Go to a real estate broker, the register of deeds, or the assessor's office and determine the value of a zoning change by noting the price of land before and after rezoning, even without improvements. What contribution did the owner make to the change in value of the land? Why did the land value change and what does the change in value measure?

Chapter 4

Government as Environmental Guardian

The serious extent of environmental degradation, with some possibility of ecological disaster, requires strenuous efforts to restore and rehabilitate our natural surroundings, at least to a point of biological safety, and hopefully to ecological balance and a sense of beauty as well. One naturally thinks of the government as the agent best equipped with both the resources and the public purpose to undertake measures of such magnitude and social import. The government historically has done much to better the environment and has practiced a form of stewardship through its conservation programs, and undoubtedly the government can and will do a great deal more. But having recognized that, we must also be aware that the government is many things to many people, and in practicing its multiple roles, it has diverse priorities which make it the agency for compromise of social tensions. These diverse priorities and compromises, in the past, have made the government part of the problem as well as part of the solution.

The government has, historically, been the principal developer of the land through its land sales, appropriation policies, and tax structure. The government, through legislative policy, taxation, and expenditure, is also the principal developer stimulating research, technology, agricultural productivity, industrialization, and economic expansion; and these are the policies and acts which, in the end, result in intrusions into the environment. So when the government acts as steward and conservator of the land and natural environment, it is holding in check with one hand the depredations which it has set in motion with the other. At best the government has been an ameliorating agent in the environment, not neutral, but checking the worst of the excesses. That compromise, that ameliorating advocacy of expansionism, is not sufficient to correct the already grave disabilities in the environment.

The effects of chemicalization of the environment are not a subject of legislative will. The tolerance of species to toxicity and deficiency determines ecological consequences, and these are subject to natural laws of the energy or nutrient cycles. In ecological matters, then, men do not have the same latitude for compromise as they do in their own affairs. Legislation may be passed relative to the environment, but its effects will be determined, not by the law, but by natural processes.

Compromise is an art of settling men's differences with each other, and a very important art. But we are not legislating differences among ourselves in the environment, we are dealing with natural laws which are outside of our legislative jurisdiction. We do not operate outside these laws of nature, as we commonly suppose, and it is time to recognize that there are some forces superior to our own. When the government confines legislation to those things which are differences among men, and recognizes that natural laws regulate things ecological, perhaps we will have learned how to make the government function as an environmental guardian.

The purpose of this chapter is to show the role which the government has played in the past with respect to the environment, to see how it has played that role, to note what it is doing now, and finally to evaluate the effectiveness of its guardianship. The discussion will cover:

1 The concept of the commons
2 Tragedy of the commons
3 The exogenous factors in the decision process
4 The remorseless working of population
5 The natural balance as exogenous variable
6 The government as conservationist
7 The decline of conservationism

THE CONCEPT OF THE COMMONS

The commons consists of all those attributes of the earth which humans and other species use jointly, which is to say that there is no exclusive ownership right but rather some form of common usage rights. Perhaps the clearest form of such common usage is the oceans which encompass most of the globe. The oceans are used jointly by all nations for shipping and commerce, fishing, recreation, missile ranges, and research; and these uses are joint along with those of fishes, birds, sea plants, and the hydrologic cycle of evaporation and rainfall. Some claims to offshore territorial rights are in dispute, such as the 200-mile limit claimed by Ecuador, Chile, and Peru to preclude other nations from fishing in the richly inhabited Humboldt Current. But aside from these minor disputes, admiralty law is well recognized among the nations as providing "freedom of the seas." Freedom of the seas has not always been accepted as a right of individuals or nations. The Spanish Armada fought the British over the issue, and the United States fought the British over it in 1812. By now, however, freedom of the seas is a widely accepted precept.

Similar principles to those of maritime and admiralty law are now being worked out in the United Nations, and other diplomatic consultative groups, about the freedom of outer space. Internally, within the United States, we have principles about inner air, or the atmosphere, which place it in common usage. Except for a few aberrations, like "air rights" for building over railroad tracts, freeways, or real estate height limitations, the atmosphere is a property of common usage. Human beings and other species breathe it, plants use it and restore its oxygen content, and all forms of combustion engines have rights to it. The combustion process requires an oxygen input from the atmosphere to burn fossil fuels in power sources like internal combustion engines for automobiles, jet engines, or thermoelectric power plants. The use of the atmosphere for power sources presents some peculiarly difficult problems with respect to use rights of the commons.

Power sources are the principal polluters of the atmosphere, because incomplete combustion causes them to emit hydrocarbons, oxides of nitrogen, carbon monoxide, aldehydes, lead, pyrobenzines, sulfur dioxide, fluorine, and other chemicals. Some of these are harmful at high levels of concentration by themselves, such as carbon monoxide, lead, fluorine. Others like hydrocarbons, nitrogen oxides, and aldehydes are very reactive under heat and sunlight, forming the chain reaction called *photochemical smog* which results in high levels of oxidants. Oxidants cause aging of biological cells and impair their functioning.

As noted earlier (Chapter 1), the energy requirements for a technological society increase at a geometric rate many times greater than the natural increase in human or species population. This means that the consumption of air in the atmospheric commons by mechanical combustion engines is increasing at many times the rate of biological species, and thus contaminating the air to toxic levels at a geometric rate approaching or surpassing the life-limiting tolerances of species. Thus pine forests are dying on mountain slopes near contaminated airsheds, fruit yields are declining 50 to 60 percent, asthmatic and emphysema patients have shortened life-spans. In a sense, the rights of machines to the air commons is greater than, and prejudicial to, the rights of biological species to the commons.

The users of the machines, of course, and not the machines themselves, are the ones exercising their rights to the common. These users are the power companies, factories, airlines, and automobile drivers—in other words, all of us. Unfortunately, we tend to overuse the commons, because it is in our immediate self-interest to do so. That is, the oxygen for our automobiles costs us nothing, nor do the emissions which pollute the atmosphere. From the viewpoint of cost and convenience we find it advantageous to use private cars, instead of public transit. The consequence is multiple car ownership in most families, and individual trips rather than carpooling. In the end, we overuse the atmosphere and pollute it to our own health detriment.

TRAGEDY OF THE COMMONS

The heavy overuse of free goods is what biologist Garrett Hardin has called the "tragedy of the commons."[1] The commons has been abused from time immemorial, and we have not gained the wisdom to avoid repeating the experience. Primordial hunting societies overkilled their hunting ranges with the result of extinction of species and of their own food supply. The mastodon is gone, and so is much of the large game in North America and Africa, except on preserves. The overuse of common fields and the underproduction of food, during the industrialization in England, brought the enclosure acts which ended common, open-field farming. Again, Hardin gives the example of a rational herdsman using a common pasture, where his self-interest dictates that he add ever another animal to his herd.

Every herdsman is locked into a rationale dictating that he too

[1]G. Hardin, "The Tragedy of the Commons," *Science*, vol. 162, Dec. 13, 1968, pp. 1243–1248.

expand his herd; and there, in overuse of the commons, is the tragedy. Each pursues his own self-interest, in the name of freedom, while bringing ruin to all. Ruin is the end toward which we rush.[2]

The concept of the commons (i.e., common ownership and use) is idealistic in situations where resources are vastly greater than populations; but when population densities outstrip the resource, whether air, land, water, then freedom of the commons brings ruin and the attempt must be made to close the commons. Hunting and fishing are now partially closed, except as allowed by government license; the agricultural commons are closed; water resources and sewage disposal are subject to restrictions which have nearly closed the stream and ocean shoreline commons. We are still struggling to close the atmospheric commons to pollution by factories, automobiles, agricultural chemicals, and electric power installations.

The tragedy of the commons is an example of the workings of the law of supply and demand. As long as the supply of the resource, like air or land, appears unlimited with respect to the demands of a small population, the resource may be treated as a "free good," that is, without cost for its use. Once the resource supply becomes limited in relation to the demands of a large population, then the resource must acquire a price or cost which equates the worth of an increment of the supply with the marginal utility for it. If this pricing system does not come into being, and if society persists in the delusion that the commons represents a free good for all, even in the face of overwhelming demand and dwindling supply, then the consequence is overuse of the commons and its ruin by despoliation.

The environmental case is a special application of the law of supply and demand, for what happens is that the quality of the environment is affected rather than the quantity. In ordinary economic affairs, the supply diminishes in quantity if the price is too low. In environmental affairs, the quantity of air, land, or water does not diminish; but its quality diminishes as it becomes more toxic or deficient. Thus, we have air to breathe, but the quality of air is not sufficient for the long-term survival of people with respiratory ailments. Or again, the oceans do not diminish in size, but the fish in them become inedible due to mercury, DDT, or PCBs. One kind of solution to the tragedy of the commons, then, is to restructure pricing or incentives to preserve the quality of resources; such restructuring is one task which the government might undertake as an environmental guardian.

[2]Ibid., p. 1244.

THE EXOGENOUS FACTORS IN THE DECISION PROCESS

So far we have been talking mainly about a man-to-environment relationship, that is, how we behave relative to the environment and what the government may try to do to reprice our use of the commons in order to act as an environmental conservator. In a sense, this approach presumes that government can regulate human behavior, within limits, by various incentives.

We must recognize that there are some kinds of human behavior that do not respond readily to persuasions or incentives, and there are also natural catastrophes, large and small, beyond the influence of government. These events may be called *exogenous* (external) to the normal decision process. That is, they are factors to be recognized as external forces, either because they are beyond regulation or because we think they are.

Some of these exogenous variables are pestilence, climatic changes, changes in natural balance, and population growth. The first three are more clearly external forces than is the last. But population growth in our society has been an exogenous decision variable, because we prefer to leave procreation solely up to individual proclivities, and religious beliefs sanction this dogma. From the point of view of government in its decision process as environmental conservator, population has been almost as external a force as, say, pestilence or climatic change. That is, the government has had just about as much influence on the baby-making potential of society as it has had upon the weather. Perhaps this situation will change, hopefully so, and population growth will become an *endogenous* (internal) variable in the decision process, subject to influence and change by social policy.

Until this change is more apparent than it is now, we shall treat human population growth as an intractable biological force over which no one has much control, and this is part of the tragedy of the commons. The tragedy, of course, has two aspects: one is the rationale to overuse anything that is free and held in common, and the other is the inexorable increase in demand for resources caused by a rising population, by sheer numbers. In a sense, the inexorable increase in sheer numbers is the greatest tragedy of all, for it is what links supposedly intelligent human beings to the humblest, instinct-driven organism, like the dinoflagellates.

Dinoflagellates are tiny whirling organisms with whiplike appendages; they cause the red tides in the oceans. One variety of this species, *Gymnodinium breve*, is the source of red tides in Florida, and *Gonyaulax polyhedra* is its counterpart in California. Studies of *G. breve* in Florida indicate that heavy rains bring large runoffs of trace iron, tannic acid, and vitamin B_{12} from the streams into the oceans.[3] These nutrients stimulate the growth of *G. breve* to such sheer numbers that the ocean turns red with their color. *G. breve* blooms excrete a waste, or nerve toxin, which immobilizes the nervous system of fish, and the fish die in massive numbers. The enormous decomposition of fish provides more nutrient for the *G. breve* blooms, until the decomposition process exhausts the dissolved oxygen in the water, which in turn suffocates more fish and eventually extinguishes the bloom.

G. breve and *homo sapiens* differ in size and possibly intelligence, but neither difference matters much in view of their common inexorable urge to sheer numbers, which is their tragedy. "The essence of dramatic tragedy is not unhappiness," wrote philosopher Alfred North Whitehead. "It resides in the solemnity of the remorseless working of things."[4]

THE REMORSELESS WORKING OF POPULATION

The "remorseless working of things" has already brought the human population on earth to over $3^1/_2$ billion people, and a medium population projection for the year 2,000 is over 6 billion people. Today, as we have seen, there are already problems of waste disposal, toxicity, and deficiency not unlike those of our fellow organisms *G. breve.* By the year 2,000, the human population bloom will have nearly doubled, energy requirements will have increased perhaps 8 times over, and waste and toxicity will have increased at least fourfold. Rather than ask what the world will be like then, when the canary is already dying today, let us ask the obverse of the question: What would be an optimum population of the world, given its finite resources and present American living standards? One estimate places the answer at 1 billion people, or one-third of the present population.

H. R. Hulett, biochemist at the Stanford University Medical Center, has estimated that 1 billion people is the maximum world population supportable, at United States living standards, by present agricultural and industrial technology; the world population already has 3 billion more people than can live at our standards.

The idea that all countries should be able to grow food and support populations at the densities and living conditions of Europe is unrealistic on two counts. The first is that most countries have less favorable soil and climate than Europe; and the second is that Europe is not able to support its own food demands. Besides importing food, Europe also imports

[3]Wesley Marx, *The Frail Ocean,* Ballantine Books, Inc., New York, 1967, p. 17ff.
[4]A. N. Whitehead, *Science and the Modern World,* Mentor New American Library, New York, 1948, p. 17.

minerals, timber, and other resources from the rest of the world. Many of the underdeveloped countries with high population densities are in tropical, arid, or other regions of the world deficient in resources, climate, or agricultural soils. The soils of the tropics, for example, are not able to support intensive agriculture. Measured by nutrient availability, the earth as a whole is overpopulated, and individual regions must be regarded as overpopulated if they are using up their nonrenewable resources or causing their environment to deteriorate.[5] By this definition most of the world, including the advanced nations, is overpopulated.

Population increase is by far the greatest catastrophe with which governments must deal as environmental guardians, but the other exogenous variables are formidable as well. Famine and pestilence have been cataclysmic throughout history. The Black Death killed from one-third to one-half the populations of various regions in Europe in the fifteenth century. About 10 percent of the population of North China, over 9 million people, were destitute or dying from the famine in 1877. A century earlier, 3 million people died from famine in India. Every century or two, history records a major number of deaths from famine and pestilence; this occured in Russia, England, Ireland, France, Antioch, and also in Rome in 436 B.C.—all relatively developed countries for their time. Are we immune to these events? We like to think so, but only about one-sixth of the world's population today is well fed, and five-sixths (or 3 billion people) are undernourished. Of the 60 million deaths per year, from 10 to 20 million are from starvation or malnutrition.[6] Mass deaths from high toxicity levels are an increasing probability with each passing year as environmental quality deteriorates.

THE NATURAL BALANCE AS EXOGENOUS VARIABLE

Besides population, another exogenous, creeping form of catastrophe is the loss of natural balance which has laid waste many prosperous civilizations in the past, particularly those in the Middle East desert irrigated regions, but also in Ankor Vat and Chitzen Itza. Deserts have highly alkaline soils, and, as irrigation is used for crops, the water acquires a high burden of soluble salts.

Basin salt balance is one of the objectives of modern irrigation and water management, which means that the balance of salt leaving a basin should equal the amount of salt entering or dissolved by water within the basin. Salt balance can be achieved in part by tiling of irrigated fields, or

---

[5]Paul R. Ehrlich and Anne H. Ehrlich, *Population, Resources, Environment,* W. H. Freeman and Company, San Francisco, 1970, pp. 201–202.
[6]Ibid., p. 72.

evaporation reservoirs for highly salt-concentrated waters. But basin salt balance over the long distances of a stream bed is not easily achieved. The Colorado River which is derived from relatively salt-free, pure mountain snow in the Rockies has a dissolved solids (salt) content of about 700 ppm at Parker dam. After use in the Los Angeles Basin or the Imperial Valley, the dissolved solids are close to 1,000 ppm, making the water unusable for further human or agricultural purposes. This deterioration in water quality has been a major diplomatic dispute between Mexico and the United States for several decades, because the returned water in the Colorado is unusable for agriculture in Mexico. California is the largest single agricultural state supplying food and fiber to the nation, and the continuance of this supply is dependent upon the ability to maintain basin salt balances. These balances are manageable today; but heavier water usage under pressure of rising population could make basin salt balance more precarious, unless there are significant technological advances in desalination techniques.

Much the same might be said about climatic change. Climate changes slowly over long cycles. Currently much of the United States is in a long warming and drying cycle. Over several decades, areas once productive are no longer as suitable for agriculture. The result is that some arable lands go out of production, despite mounting populations, and may continue to do so unless new technology makes possible a modicum of weather control.

The ultimate consequence of exogenous variables, whether pestilence, population, natural balance, or climatic change, is to force ever-increasing expenditures for technological advances to offset these variables, just to maintain the status quo. In economic terms, this is an application of the law of diminishing returns; a heavier and heavier commitment of resources is needed to obtain a diminishing marginal return in terms of environmental quality. The meaning of this principle to society is that an increasing price or tax burden is necessary to just keep even. With population, energy, industrial growth, and wastes increasing at geometric rates, ranging from 1 to 8 percent per year, and the allocation of resources to environmental quality is subject to diminishing marginal returns, clearly one is playing a losing game. A government, acting as environmental guardian, which plays the role of stimulating growth on one hand while allocating resources to ecological clean-up with the other is employing a losing strategy.

THE GOVERNMENT AS CONSERVATIONIST

One must recognize in all honesty that, until very recently at least, the government has never really presumed to be the guardian of the environment. The government's historical role has been, at the most, ambitious as conservationist; and even the conservation movement came late in the nineteenth century after much of the exploitations had already occurred and only the most flagrant cases had outraged the public. One of the first expressions of outrage was from George Catlin, the artist who traveled frequently in the West to study paintings of the American Indians. Traveling along the Missouri River, Catlin arrived at Fort Pierre. Only a few days before he arrived in May 1832, an immense herd of buffalos had arrived on the opposite side of the river, almost blackening the plains for a great distance. Catlin wrote in his journal:

> A party of five or six hundred Sioux Indians on horseback, forded the river about mid-day, and spending a few hours amongst them, recrossed the river at sun-down and came into the Fort with *fourteen hundred fresh buffalo tongues,* which were thrown down in a mass, and for which they required but a few gallons of whiskey, which was soon demolished, indulging in a little, and harmless carouse.
>
> This profligate waste of the lives of these noble and useful animals, when, from all that I could learn, not a skin or a pound of the meat (except the tongues), was brought in, fully supports me in the seemingly extravagant predictions which I have made as to their extinction, which I am certain is near at hand.

Catlin then went on to propose that the Western plains be left open as a magnificent national park in which buffalo and Indians might preserve their lives "in all the wild and freshness of their nature's beauty." The idea of national parks remained dormant for nearly half a century after Catlin proposed it, and was not implemented soon enough to save the 75 million bison which once roamed Western plains.

By 1877 federal concern over the fate of public land and resources began to appear. Carl Shurz, Secretary of Interior, wrote in an annual report that the quantity of timber taken from the public lands without authority had been of enormous extent, probably far exceeding any estimates made on then existing data. The depredations had been carried on by organized and systematic enterprise, not only to furnish timber, lumber, and firewood for the domestic market, but, on a large scale, for commercial exportation to foreign countries. "The rapidity with which this country is being stripped of its forests must alarm every thinking man."[7]

The protection of forestlands did not occur for another twenty years, until a National Forest Commission was instrumental in the creation of 21 million acres of forest reserve. Gifford Pinchot, who was

[7]Annual Report of the Secretary of Interior 1877, Washington, pp. xv–xvi.

also a member of the National Forest Commission, became chief of the federal Forest Division a year later and brought into being the modern concepts of forestry management. He also strongly urged President Theodore Roosevelt to make conservation a political issue of national significance. President Roosevelt publicized his conservation program before a conference of governors in 1908. Roosevelt said that the enormous consumption of natural resources, and the threat of imminent exhaustion of some of them due to reckless and wasteful use, called for common action.

> We are coming to recognize as never before the right of the Nation to guard its own future in the essential matter of natural resources. In the past we have admitted the right of the individual to injure the future of the Republic for his own present profit. In fact there has been a good deal of demand for unrestricted individualism, for the right of the individual to injure the future of all of us for his own temporary and immediate profit. The time has come for a change. As a people we have the right and the duty, second to none other but the right and duty of obeying the moral law, of requiring and doing justice, to protect ourselves and our children against the wasteful development of our natural resources.[8]

Perhaps the principles of the conservation movement are best described by Gifford Pinchot himself:

> The first principle of conservation is development, the use of the natural resources now existing on this continent for the benefit of the people who live here and now.
> In the second place conservation stands for the prevention of waste.
> In addition to the principles of development and preservation of our resources there is a third principle. It is this: The natural resources must be developed for the benefit of the many, and not merely for the profit of a few.[9]

THE DECLINE OF CONSERVATIONISM

The spirit of the conservation movement helped preserve some forest lands, created the National Park system, and developed irrigation and reclamation of lands. But the heavy use of resources for high rates of economic growth continued to exact its toll in other ways, particularly the

---

[8]Theodore Roosevelt, "Opening Address of the President," Proceedings of the Conference of Governors in the White House, 1909, pp. 3–12.
[9]Gifford Pinchot, *The Fight for Conservation,* Harcourt, Brace, and Company, New York, 1910, pp. 42–50.

overuse of the remaining commons and the chemicalization of the environment. The quality of the environment succumbed to what President Theodore Roosevelt called "the right of the individual to injure the future of all of us for his own temporary and immediate profit." In the sense of the deterioration of environmental quality, the conservation movement all but died for half a century. The Department of Interior recognized this in its 1968 Fourth Conservation Yearbook:

> In the past, as the idea of conservation grew, we tended to separate our environment into its many components—forests, wildlife, minerals, soil, water—and to deal with each separately. This piecemeal approach has proved inadequate. As we deal with the various parts of the periphera, the core of the problem—which is mindless tampering with the environment—was creating new problems all over the surface.
>
> So profound and all-pervasive are the effects of exploding population and expanding technology that efforts to deal with environmental problems are unlikely to be effective in a long-term sense unless we turn our attention to these two root factors.[10]

The conservation movement was inundated by the huge waves of population and technology which overcame it. The prospects for its recovery are rather poor. Former Secretary of Interior Stewart Udall points out that true conservation is ultimately a state of mind, a belief in the future. Belief in the future is manifest in both a love for the land and a sense of responsibility toward future generations. A land ethic for tomorrow is difficult to conceive, because too many of us lack roots in the soil and respect for the environment which goes with such roots. Too many of us perhaps are not prepared to pay the price for reasonable abundance in keeping with an unspoiled environment.[11]

What that price may be is not specified, but it is a high price, at least in terms of change. We have seen enough of the causes and consequences of the deterioration in environmental quality to perceive that the price may include limiting economic growth and population, changing our life styles and management decision structures, plus raising taxes and product prices to pay for the cleansing of our surroundings. Such a price, however dimly perceived by the public, has apparently not seemed worthwhile so far. For that reason, the conservation movement subsided from its zenith in 1910, to make way for renewal of the government's main role, as the driving power behind development.

[10]U.S. Department of Interior Conservation Yearbook, *Man—An Endangered Species?* Washington, 1968, p. 14.
[11]Stewart L. Udall, *The Quiet Crisis*, Holt, Rinehart and Winston, Inc., New York, 1963, pp. 189–191.

SUMMARY

The federal government has historically been faced with conflicting roles in its management of the huge Western public domain. During the century-long, public land disposal, the government was presumably acting as both steward and developer. For the most part development dominated the day, partly because the immigrants were poor, land-hungry people, and partly because the country needed capital for its development. In any case, the concept of conservation and guardianship became obsolete before it was felt. Now the environmental crisis, stemming from that very development process, is requiring that stewardship be rediscovered to protect the public interest by preserving, not only resources, but also the environment and its quality.[12]

The government has been torn by divided objectives whether its environmental role is that of guardian, developer, both, or each in turn. The lack of a consistent view and policy has made environmental administration in the past a now-and-again intervention when environmental exploitation has become too blatant. The most persistent, and least controlled, type of exploitation is the "tragedy of the commons," in which the self-interest of everyone is locked into a system which brings ruin to all. This ruin is seen in overuse of air, water, and land resources. The remorseless tragedy lies in the inexorable increase in population, in a world already overpopulated threefold in terms of present Western standards.

As against the forces of population, resource depletion, or the change in natural balance, the government has not presumed to be guardian of the environment, except for a brief interim of conservationism brought on by excesses of fraud and waste. Then the government approach to conservation was piecemeal, dealing separately with minerals, soil, water, wildlife, and forests, never looking at the core problem, which is mindless tampering with ecological balance through population and technology. In the end, conservationism was overcome by that which it ignored, by a population which expanded its numbers, wants, and securities, and by a technology which set in motion new resource requirements and residuals. In the end, government returned to its primary role of developer, setting conservation aside as an avocation, and leaving guardianship for a later time when calamity might call for its return.

[12]Wynne Thorne (ed.), *Land and Water Use*, American Association for the Advancement of Science, Washington, 1963, pp. 349–350.

DISCUSSION QUESTIONS

1   What commons are now in general use? Who makes the largest or priority uses of these commons? What and whose priorities would you put on use of the commons? Do you think there is a tragedy of the commons? Discuss.
2   How would you attempt to measure or evaluate the issue of whether the world is overpopulated? Do you think using the Western living standard is a correct criterion? If not, what criteria of living conditions, use of nonrenewable resources, and biological health would you use? What population policy and means would be consistent with your criteria?
3   What vestiges of conservationism remain in the United States? What accounts for the opposition of conservationists to the "new environmentalism?"

PROBLEM

Suppose you were called upon to set up a policy and program for the "guardianship" of local land use. What would such a policy and program contain?

Chapter 5

The Government as Developer and Monitor

The government's role as developer may be viewed in relation to three of its policies for the handling of resources: (1) the transferring of resources from the public to private domain, (2) the extensive utilization of those resources, and (3) the intensive utilization of resources. The first phase corresponds roughly to the period of public land sales and the frontier stage of American life from 1820 to 1890. The second phase relates to heavy resource exploitation and industrial development, from 1890 to 1940, when labor was applied extensively to use the resources.

The third phase brought into being present technology, with its high wasteloads which have adversely affected the environment. This ecological damage has caused the federal government to pass legislation for the protection of environmental quality, and the agencies charged with this mission have assumed a new regulatory and monitoring role over productive activity. This evolution will be described in terms of:

1 First phase of development—frontier period
2 Land subsidies and their payment

FIRST PHASE OF DEVELOPMENT—FRONTIER PERIOD

With respect to the first phase of government's role as developer, in transferring of resources from the public to private domain between 1820 and 1890, we have already seen (in Chapter 3) how the early settlements in New England followed the British village or town common system; but this evolved quickly into the disposal by headrights in the South, and then into the Pre-emption and Homestead Acts which opened the West. That is, the integrating concept of a group of people with common ties to their terrestrial surroundings rapidly gave way to a concept of fragmentation, breaking up the land into small pieces and putting them into the hands of individuals as trading goods. The fragmentation of land was an impetus to development because it put free land into the hands of people whose labor was cheap. Under these circumstances, almost any improvement or development of the land has a marginal value beyond the marginal cost of the labor and land inputs.

The policy was an efficient means of converting surplus (hence low-value) labor into capital investment. The process was simple. The pioneers were land-hungry people with no capital and a great deal of time to apply to clearing fields, digging wells, building farm buildings, in addition to some subsistence cultivation. But that use of time for land development was, in fact, a form of savings and capital investment. Hence the development policy of the government was really to subsidize the land acquisition (by cheap disposal) for the purpose of creating developmental capital through the conversion of surplus labor into savings. That the policy was successful is attested to by the high state of industrialization and wealth that the United States has since achieved.

This development route to wealth does not really confirm either that the policy was efficacious in the long run or that the people were endowed with extraordinary virtues. Similar policies have been tried in most of the underdeveloped (cheap labor) regions of the world where there is unoccupied land, such as in South America, Africa, Australia, the Philippines, etc. The results have ranged from indifferent success down to outright failure. The obvious difference, one might say, must lie in the quality of the people. However, psychological measures do not support the idea of great variations in native ability among peoples on the basis of nationality or race. Then, perhaps the answer lies in determination and hard work. One could scarcely find any person, anywhere in time or place, who works harder than the laboring mestizo of Latin America, and he still labors in abject poverty.

A much more obvious explanation for the difference in success of these land development policies lies in the potential marginal value of the land. The land in the United States was and is enormously fertile in agricultural, mineral, and timber yields. This meant a small amount of labor would produce a large and early return, or as the vernacular goes, a fast buck. The United States was, and is, a fast-buck economy, which is only possible when the potential marginal value of the resources are enormously high.

Under these conditions of potentially high-value lands given away, a small amount of savings, in the form of work or surplus labor, yields a quick, short-term capital gain.

All of which is to say that the United States government policy of land development worked mainly because of the enormous size of the subsidy being granted in the form of underpriced resources. Since we would prefer to attribute success to our own sterling character or ideology, the attribution of success to the magnitude of government land subsidy may not seem acceptable. Yet there is an important principle involved here that bears examination and recognitition if true. That is, a subsidy is never free, except to the receiver. A subsidy comes from diversion, or transfer, of resources from a larger society. Hence, the farm subsidy today is paid by the consumer, and the old-age subsidy (social security) is paid by the producing workers.

LAND SUBSIDIES AND THEIR PAYMENT

Who paid for the subsidization of land development in the United States? Surely not the frontiersman, because he was the receiver of the subsidy with get-rich-quick incentives. The larger society that paid for these quick riches was the ecology of the time and future generations. The ecology of the time paid by species extinction—the bison, the California salmon—the denuded timber lands, the devastation of 2 million acres of strip-mining land turned into rubble with death to all its former inhabitants. The human generations of today are paying for the land development of the past by pollution and land use which makes no ecological sense. The land still lies in tiny parcels of trading goods, with no relation to stream basin characteristics and air basin ecology, with no preservation of ecological integrity in the form of meadowlands, marshlands, lake regions, or forestlands with their native flora and fauna. There is no integrating human principle, like the British town commons or the Indian village. The human ecology was fractured as the land was fragmented; surely a factor in our becoming alienated today from the land and each other. Beyond that, we still have residues and acid waters of old mines to cleanse, denuded hills and desolated mining lands to reclaim, abandoned marginal lands to restore, and poorly conceived cities to redesign. All these consequences of quick, short-term development will cost hundreds of billions of dollars to rectify, probably more than the original quick profits that were made. Who paid the cost of subsidizing land development? Succeeding generations of *homo sapiens* and other species bear the sacrifice or burden of the government's policies of transferring land from the public to the private domain, and transferring their costs to the future.

EXTENSIVE DEVELOPMENT OF THE UNITED STATES

By 1890 much of the public domain that had any significant potential value was turned over to individual ownership as private property. The lands remaining in the public domain were generally arid and mountainous, without minerals, timber, or sufficient water to be productive. The extensive development of the United States might be described as the period during which existing technology was applied by capital investment to available resources. Obviously such time periods overlap. The extensive development of Western land resources accelerated about 1850, and that of industry after 1870. By the 1890s large corporations began to dominate the resource-processing industries, such as sugar, grain milling, coal, textiles, iron and steel, oil, shipping. Subsequently the machinery industries expanded greatly through capital investment. By the 1920s the extensive development of electric power, electric machinery, radio, and automobiles stimulated the industrial growth of the nation. By the 1930s most of the major industries of a fully industrialized society were in place.

At the same time, the collapse of banking and capital markets in 1929 made further investment hazardous and difficult. The Great Depression was a period when economists described the condition of society as a "mature economy," almost as though that were a terminal affliction. Professor Alvin Hansen of Harvard, however, pointed out the need for intensive capital development for economic growth, as contrasted with the extensive capital investment of the past. Instead of building more of the same products out of existing technology, he saw the need for a more rapid acceleration of new product development based upon new technologies. He spoke of this as "channel deepening" rather than "channel widening." At the same time John Maynard Keynes noted the tendency of world economies to stabilize at equilibrium levels of underemployment, particularly during periods of anxiety and low confidence in the future, because of the liquidity preference of consumers. Savings and liquidity did not easily find their way into capital investment during a period of depressed expectations. The cure for this inadequate linkage between liquidity and investment was, according to Keynes, for the government to manage the economic aggregates, namely fiscal and monetary aggregates, so as to create social investment, such as public works, as a stimulus to private capital investment. Or more simply, the government policy he recommended was that it spend heavily, in excess of revenue, preferably on capital intensive goods such as construction. This would create a budgetary deficit which would be financed by the expansion of bank credit. The increased money supply and the increased government spending would then, according to Keynes, stimulate the economy, consumer spending, and private capital investment.

The first great test of this theory, following the "pump priming" of the Depression, was the massive government expenditures and credit expansion of World War II. The total federal deficits from 1940 through 1945 were $172 billion. Bank loans and investments tripled, from $40 billion to $124 billion; and at the end of the war, the banks held $90 billion in government bonds, which is the measure of the printing press money created by the war. That $90 billion was the liquidity which helped fuel the postwar boom.

The other fuel of the postwar boom was the development of technology—first the acceleration of intensive capital investment in farm equipment, secondly the development of aviation and rocketry, and thirdly the invention of the electronic computer. Much of the postwar boom for the next twenty-five years was built on the proliferation of these technologies.

INTENSIVE DEVELOPMENT IN AGRICULTURE

The most mundane, but the most remarkable, of these intensive capital developments was in farming. Tractor power and automated planting and harvesting equipment have raised farm productivity fivefold in thirty years. No other sector of the economy has raised output per man-hour so dramatically. Manufacturing productivity, which we usually think of as the epitome of America's economic achievement, only doubled, while farming productivity quintupled. As a result farm population has declined drastically. In 1940, farm population totaled 30 million people; in 1950, it was 23 million; and in 1970, less than 10 million. Nowhere else in the world does agriculture support, in abundance, twenty urban people for every one on the farm. This is the magnitude of the intensive land development which took place in three decades.

Perhaps the social significance of intensive agricultural development is even more profound than its economic importance. The success of intensive agriculture development released people from farms and supporting towns for the migration to the city. Hence the three postwar decades have also been a period of intense urbanization. Minority groups have moved out of agricultural occupations to inhabit the urban ghettos. The more fortunate and more skilled workers have become mobile, transient, rootless people—divorced from the land—with one-fourth of them moving every year to new residences. The United States is a society in movement and flux, in which neighborhoods are constantly changing, and the individual seldom has a permanent home.

In this intense urban flux, as we noted earlier, half of the total population live on 1 percent of the land, and this is the heart of the environmental problem. If the population were distributed more evenly over the land, the urban environmental crisis would be less acute. There would be less waste concentration and more ample opportunity to use the soil, which is a highly efficient digestor of waste, rather than concentrating wastes in streams and oceans which are not efficient at decomposing materials. More than that, the rootless, alienated urbanite has very little environmental pride or responsibility. It is not his land in the first place, and on average he will not live there more than three or four years anyway. So why should he care for his environment? Let the landlord, the next homeowner, the government clean it up.

GOVERNMENT AS INTENSIVE ECONOMIC DEVELOPER

The intensive economic development from aviation and the computer are more obvious to everyone. The mobile population crowds airports for vacation, business, or family visiting. Jets add noise and pollution to the atmosphere. Travel is worldwide, and so are communicable diseases. With faster travel, the pace of life can be speeded up. Computers speed it up even faster. With television, microwave relays, communications satellites, and computers, voices and numbers can be projected across space in astronomical quantities. All these developments make it possible for executives to manage more products, more materials, and generate more industrial waste at faster rates than ever before. The higher the rate of industrial output, the better the material life for the consumer, and the more waste to dispose of in the environment.

The enormous success of intensive capital development in the past three decades has produced constantly rising living standards and a steady economic growth rate. It has also increased wastes, and caused environmental quality to decline, at a geometric rate.

What has the government's role been in this intensive use of United States resources? That of developer. The government has faithfully produced deficits and more money when investment needed stimulating, and sometimes when it did not. When consumer spending has lagged, the government has produced tax cuts to provide more purchasing power. And in between, steadily, steadily, the government has spent enormous sums on research and development. Most of our modern passenger aircraft are descendants of military planes. Most of the electronic and computer technology, both hardware and software, had its origin in some guidance, navigation, or command and control system. On top of this, rapid amortization of new investments, high corporate depreciation allowances, large corporate cash flows, a tendency to shift taxation toward individuals and excises rather than toward corporations, and the subsidization of farming as well as corporations have all made the intensive use of technology possible. One could hardly expect more; the government has been an intensive developer of extraordinary virtuosity!

With such a record, how can one really believe that the depredations of the environment set in motion by such a powerful economic mechanism can now be held in check by the same mechanism?

THE GOVERNMENT AS MONITOR

The government has been a lightsome monitor for many years, first with the somewhat abortive conservation movement (described earlier) and more recently through the Food and Drug Administration, the Federal Trade Commission, and the Public Health Service. These agencies have kept the level of toxicity in foods and environment at tolerable levels, and the Federal Trade Commission has prosecuted flagrant deceptions in the form of false and misleading advertising or labeling.

While the beneficial effects of these agencies acting as government monitors have been considerable, it is an interesting commentary on their efficacy that it took a private individual like Ralph Nader to give spirit and fire to consumerism as a movement. What governmental agencies failed to do in automobile safety regulations was accomplished by an individual who single-handedly caused General Motors to discontinue its most hazardous car and then instigated and won a law suit against the corporate giant for invading his privacy. This sardonic contrast in performance of governmental agencies as monitors as compared to individual action is also seen in their lightsome tugging at the reins in the cases of air pollution, oil spills, stream quality, ocean dumping, health effects, and hazardous consumer products. The fact that oil spills persist year after year, as does air pollution, stream pollution, ocean dumping, and health hazards, is another indication of the ambiguous role which the government has played. It is not an easy role to whip the economy and technology into a gallop and then try to check the runaway damages which ensue. One day soon the government may have to make up its mind which is more important, being a developer, or safeguarding the people.

THE COUNCIL ON ENVIRONMENTAL QUALITY

Recognition that the day of choice is close at hand may be implied in a passage of the National Environmental Policy Act of 1969, Public Law 91–190, January 1, 1970. The act says in part:

> The Congress recognizing the profound impact of man's activity on the interrelations of all components of the natural environment, particularly the profound influences of population growth, high-density urbanization, industrial expansion, resource exploitation, and new and expanding technological advances and recognizing further the critical importance of restoring and maintaining environmental quality to the overall welfare and development of man, declares that it is the continuing policy of the Federal Government, in cooperation with State and local governments, and other concerned public and private organizations, to use all practical means and measures, including financial and technical assistance, in a manner calculated to foster and promote the general welfare, to create and maintain conditions under which man and nature can exist in productive harmony, and fulfill the social, economic, and other requirements of present and future generations of Americans.[1]

The act created the Council on Environmental Quality, which is charged with a policy role to examine all proposed legislation, new requests for funding by federal agencies, and executive orders for the purpose of ascertaining the following:

1   The environmental impact of the proposed action
2   Any adverse environmental effects which cannot be avoided if the proposal is implemented

---

[1]First Annual Report of Council on Environmental Quality, Appendix A, p. 244.

3 Alternatives to the proposed action
4 The relationship between local short-term uses of man's environment and the maintenance and enhancement of long-term productivity
5 Any irreversible and irretrievable commitments of resources which would ensue from the proposed action

The newly created Council on Environmental Quality issued interim guidelines on April 30, 1970, which required federal agencies to submit environmental impact statements for new legislative proposals. For the most part, the guidelines restated the five requirements listed above, with some amplification as to the meaning of the first point to be covered in terms of:

> The probable impact of the proposed action on the environment, including impact on ecological systems such as wildlife, fish and marine life. Both primary and secondary significant consequences for the environment should be included in the analysis. For example, the implications, if any, of the action for population distribution or concentration should be estimated and an assessment made of the effect of any possible change in population patterns upon the resource base, including land use, water, and public service, of the area in question.[2]

THE ENVIRONMENTAL PROTECTION AGENCY

These actions were followed by a message from the President to the Congress, on July 9, 1970, relative to Reorganization Plans No. 3 and 4, which created the Environmental Protection Agency. The Council on Environmental Quality is concerned with policy on new legislation and new programs relative to the environment. The Environmental Protection Agency is charged with responsibility for regulation or implementation of programs to improve environmental quality. The Reorganization Plans transferred the following activities to the Environmental Protection Agency:

> Functions of the Federal Water Quality Administration (from the Department of Interior).
> Functions regarding pesticides (from Departments of Interior, Agriculture, and Food and Drug Administration in Health, Education and Welfare).
> Functions of the National Air Pollution Control Agency (from Department of Health, Education and Welfare).
> Functions of the Bureau of Solid Waste Management, Bureau of

[2]Ibid., Appendix G, p. 289.

Water Hygiene, and portions of the Bureau of Radiological Health (from the Department of Health, Education and Welfare).

Functions respecting radiation criteria (from Atomic Energy Commission).

Authority to perform studies of ecological systems (from Council on Environmental Quality)[3]

The first administrator appointed to head the Environmental Protection Agency was William D. Ruckelshaus, formerly Assistant Attorney General in the Justice Department in charge of the Civil Division, once a practicing attorney, and former majority leader in the Indiana House of Representatives. A week after taking office he startled the mayors of Atlanta, Cleveland, and Detroit by giving them 180 days to stop polluting waterways or face federal court action. Then he was instrumental in persuading the Justice Department to file suit against Armco Steel Corporation on charges of polluting the Houston Ship Channel, against Jones & Laughton Steel Corporation for dumping cyanamides into the Cuyahoga River near Cleveland, and against the Burton Oxygen Company for polluting the Cuyahoga. The Cuyahoga River, running through central industrial Ohio, is one of the few streams in the United States regarded as a fire hazard.

Meantime in December 1970, the President initiated a major enforcement program to prevent water pollution by an Executive order directing that a federal permit program be established under an old statute, the Refuse Act of 1899. Under the rarely enforced act, applicants must submit information on wastes they plan to dump in navigable waters to the Corps of Engineers to obtain a permit. Industrial plants in operation were given until July 1, 1971, to obtain permits, and new plants must obtain permits before beginning operation. Some environmental groups expressed apprehension about the effect of the permit plant, fearing that the permits would provide a license to pollute and protect despoilers of water quality against legal action by citizens or the government. Despite such apprehensions, sixty-five citizens in Birmingham, Alabama, filed a 50-million-dollar suit under the 1899 Federal Refuse Act against nineteen large corporations, including U.S. Steel, Republic Steel, Du Pont, Allied Chemical, and Hercules Powder, for polluting the Warrior River and its tributaries.

Additional measures to strengthen environmental protection were submitted by the President to Congress in February 1971 in the form of fourteen pieces of legislation designed to give the newly organized Environmental Protection Agency additional powers to deal with pollu-

[3]Ibid., Appendix H, pp. 295–296.

tion control problems. The President's environmental plan permits the Environmental Protection Agency to set standards or require permits and licensing to control noise pollution, ocean dumping, sales of pesticides, mining practices, power plant location, water pollution, hazardous chemicals, air pollution, and land use.

About the same time, the President signed amendments to the 1967 Clean Air Act which required manufacturers to produce cars by 1975 which reduced emissions of common pollutants by 90 percent from 1970 standards. In an additional action, the Environmental Protection Agency also set standards on emissions of sulfur oxides, particles, carbon monoxide, nitrogen oxides, hydrocarbons, and photochemical oxidants. The enforcement of these standards is to be through state pollution control plans, to be formulated by mid-1972 and to be enforced by mid-1973.

The automobile manufacturers, to meet the new standards, continue to try to modify existing engines, by means of a modified carburetor, exhaust gas recirculation, a catalytic converter and an air pump, rather than seek new power plants. The effect of this equipment would be to act as an afterburner to complete the combustion process of unleaded gasolines and thus hopefully to reduce emissions to the 1975 standards. The equipment changes are estimated to add about $200 to the price of 1975 model cars.

In another action, the U.S. Court of Appeals augmented the responsibilities of the Environmental Protection Agency by directing it to review an administrative ruling of the Department of Agriculture regarding the use of DDT. In November 1969 the Department of Agriculture had ordered that all but essential uses of DDT be terminated by the end of 1969. However, the ruling was nullified by the Department of Agriculture on administrative appeal of six pesticide companies. The Environmental Defense Fund and the Sierra Club then requested the Department of Agriculture to reconsider and to reinstate its ban on the use of DDT. The Department refused, and the two environmental plaintiffs brought suit in federal court. The Department of Agriculture contended, before the U.S. Court of Appeals, that the court had no jurisdiction to review administrative determinations because it lacked legislative mandate or scientific expertise to do so. The Court overruled the Department of Agriculture, setting a new precedent with respect to administrative law. Chief Judge David L. Bazelon announced a "new era in the history of the long and fruitful collaboration of administrative agencies and reviewing courts," in which he said that in the future federal courts would no longer "bow to the mysteries of administrative expertise" in such matters as whether to ban substances alleged to be dangerous to the environment.

FORMS OF GOVERNMENT REGULATION
OF ENVIRONMENTAL QUALITY

Clearly the role of government with respect to the environment is now in transition and flux. The new legislation, reorganization plans, regulations, and court orders on the environment may set the stage for a new and more vigorous role of the government as environmental guardian; or the movement may prove somewhat abortive as have previous efforts such as conservation, pure food, and fair trade regulations. The outcome depends in part on the degree to which public support and interest reinforce the Environmental Protection Agency as it takes actions which are costly or to the disadvantage of existing business practice. In other words, will an environmental constituency develop to offset the special interests of those who have the funds and will to perpetuate their product practices regardless of environmental effects? The outcome probably depends upon the degree of health risk perceived by the public in environmental matters, and on the skill with which environmental regulations are administered.

The principal forms of environmental administration are standard setting, incentives, permissions regulation, and punitive controls. Environmental standards have been, or are being, set for air, water, and noise quality. Incentives are being offered to municipalities in the form of financial assistance to establish secondary sewage treatment plants. Permissions regulation is illustrated by the permits to industrial plants on the kind and amount of effluent they may discharge into streams under the Refuse Act of 1899. Punitive control is exemplified by litigation in the courts to force compliance with quality standards.

The forms of regulation available to the Environmental Protection Agency have been partly described by the recent legislation and regulatory actions, and they are partly discernible through past regulatory practices. A review of past regulatory acts provides some insight into the problems and feasibility of environmental protection.

We have already observed (in Chapter 1) that a medical task force for the Public Health Service concluded that new products are being introduced into the environment more rapidly than their safety can be determined. The new Environmental Protection Agency will have to deal with such a problem; hence we may fruitfully speculate on how this problem might be handled. Let us ask the question: If new products are being introduced into our society faster than their safety can be ascertained, whose responsibility is it to determine their hazard?

Historically, the responsibility has been that of the buyer or consumer, under the maxim of "caveat emptor" (let the buyer beware). Caveat emptor is of ancient usage and at least partially recognized in common law. In a highly technical society, caveat emptor places a heavy burden of information and knowledge upon the consumer. Each person would need to have almost the entire range of scientific knowledge of the society if he is to evaluate the safety of all products which he uses. That degree of scientific knowledge is more than he can reasonably be expected to assimilate, or acquire. In this sense, caveat emptor is an antiquated concept which today implies a willingness to expose people to health hazards of unknown gravity.

Another alternative is to assume that the government, through an agency such as the Environmental Protection Agency, should be responsible for determining the safety of all products from new technologies. On the face of it, this would seem to be quite a reasonable alternative. After all, government represents the total society, and its purpose is the protection of the public interest. Moreover, government has the resources to conduct technical assessments in every field of knowledge, plus the organizational means to define such inquiry into manageable tasks which specialists can then perform. In addition, ample precedent exists for such activity, under both the police powers of the states and the regulatory powers of the federal government, in such instances as the Food and Drug Administration and the Federal Trade Commission. With such precedent and resources, what counterarguments could there be to letting government assure the safety of products sold to consumers?

The government has played its regulatory role on product safety, so far, by acting as evaluator after the fact, that is, after the product is developed and on the market. Then, if the safety of the product comes to its attention, usually through accident or untoward circumstances suggesting hazard to citizens, the government conducts an inquiry ex post facto. It is precisely this ex post facto evaluation which is in question, because the public is exposed to serious hazards unknowingly, and these hazards threaten the public health and well-being, according to the Medical Task Force cited earlier. The implication is that the safety of the product should be evaluated before it comes to the market, which means even as it is being developed. This would indeed be a new and difficult regulatory role.

One problem of such prior, or ex ante, governmental regulation is that product development is highly decentralized in our economy. Each of the several million enterprises in the United States makes up its own mind what business it wants to be in, and that business is defined as a product to be made and sold. If the government is to evaluate all products for the purpose of ascertaining their safety, then the government would have entered into a new, pervasive relationship with every business, on a scale vastly more complex than attempted before. The second difficulty is that this pervasive overseeing of private product development would greatly alter the decision structure of the economy and put government into the very essence of private enterprises' decision role. The third consequence would be that private risk taking would be greatly altered; and the government, as party to risk-taking product decisions, would tend to become very cautious or culpable. In many cases of technological innovations, the risks of sheer scientific feasibility are very high, without regard, for the moment, for safety hazards. Scientific investigators take those risks mainly on their intuition, an act of faith in themselves and their ability to find a solution. The government, as regulator, cannot easily play the role of innovator at the same time. There are, then, some serious limitations on government's role in technological evaluation prior to the marketing of new products.

For these reasons, let us assume that government continues to act after the fact to regulate product safety rather than to become an ex ante partner in private product development. What other alternative is there to protect the environment and the public health? The present alternative in law, which might be considerably expanded, is to make a private enterprise liable for damages caused by pollution or unsafe products. This form of legal recourse by the consumer against manufacturers has been rather less used than, say, the filing of malpractice suits against physicians. Yet the development and sale of unsafe products, particularly those with adverse health effects, has many similarities to medical malpractice.

LIABILITY AND RESPONSIBILITY FOR HEALTH HAZARDS

Among the early significant cases against a business for failure to assure the safety of its products was the criminal proceedings in Germany against Chemie Gruenenthal for its sale of the drug thalidomide. The firm was charged with, and explicitly acknowledged, responsibility for the deformation of about 2,000 West German children whose mothers used thalidomide during pregnancy, as well as for about 300 cases of nerve damage to adults. The trial lasted $2^{1}/_{2}$ years, the longest criminal trial in German history, with 283 court sessions, 120 witnesses, 60 experts, and 72,000 pages of testimony. Chemie Gruenenthal set up a fund of $27.3 million to care for the deformed children and $1.1 million for the affected adults. The court found the firm careless in that it had failed to take necessary precautions when introducing the new product. The company was also said by the court to be lax in informing the public after alarming reports began to be heard about thalidomide. The firm allegedly covered up the reports and continued to promote the product as safe. Nevertheless, the criminal charges were dropped on the grounds that it was difficult to pin the responsibility in these cases to any individuals among the accused. The court regarded the financial damages, and the publicity on the danger of the product, as a reasonable settlement.

Another type of case in the United States was the federal government's prosecution of the automobile manufacturers under the antitrust laws for conspiring to restrain trade by delaying the utilization of antipollution devices to produce relatively smog-free cars. In this case companies were required to desist from such restraining practices. The court also ruled that individuals or communities who could show damages by the failure of the automobile companies to proceed with the development of low-emission cars might have bases for a civil liability suit. So far there has been no filing of such a claim, because of the difficulty of showing damages. The health effects of air pollution, while real, are difficult to trace from afflicted person back to the manufacturer, because of the many interactions of pollutants in the atmosphere and with human cells.

An even more difficult problem in tracing responsibility for pollution is found in the instance of mercury contamination of tuna. Scientists do not know for sure whether mercury in seafood could result from natural incidence in the oceans or whether it is caused by man-made pollution. The presumption of man-made pollution as the cause of mercury contamination of tuna is based upon the fact that the incidence of mercury in fish is higher in coastal waters and rivers, which are more subject to pollution. If the pollution is man-made, then the source might be any number of chemical or industrial processes, as well as mercury germicides washing off agricultural seed; but the ultimate responsibility and liability for the mercury found in tuna or swordfish are diffuse and indeterminate.

These cases are convincing illustrations that pollution, its sources, and health effects are deeply embedded in the technological processes of the entire society and concern everyone's behavior. Responsibility is difficult to determine, and hence regulation would be ambiguous to administer.

EFFECTS OF MONITORING ON INDUSTRY

Therefore, the interaction between government and private industry in regulation or product development decisions is likely to present increasing complexities and added risks to business in the years ahead. An example is the federal government's regulatory action banning the use of NTA, nitrailotriacetic acid, in detergents. The detergent and chemical companies had been under criticism for some time over their use of phosphates in washday detergents, because phosphates add nutrients to waste water supplies and stimulate the growth of algae. The nutrients and algae cause aging, or *eutrophication,* of lakes and ponds, which eventually threatens other marine life.

In response to criticism of polluting water supplies, the detergent companies spent millions of dollars in research funds to find a substitute for phosphates, and they came up with NTA as the solution. At least a dozen detergents containing NTA were put on the market, accounting for about 5 percent of the total usage. Subsequently, university and government research on NTA indicated significant birth defect hazards. In laboratory tests on rodents, NTA showed a tenfold increase in fetal abnormalities and fatalities. The Surgeon General of the United States and the administrator of the Environmental Protection Agency banned the use of NTA and said major manufacturers had agreed to stop using it. The Surgeon General added that there had been no indication that anyone had been harmed. In any event, the NTA case illustrates the large risks which private business may encounter in trying to clean up the environment, because in many cases it is difficult, costly, and time consuming to ascertain whether the new solution is really any better than the old. In the NTA case, the proposed solution was worse than the former product.

Much the same thing happened in the attempt to control air pollution. The automobile manufacturers were given a lower standard of hydrocarbon emissions to meet, which they did by an engine change that caused the oxides of nitrogen to increase threefold while the hydrocarbon emissions were brought down to standard. However, the oxides of nitrogen proved to be an even more active source of oxidants (the principal irritant and toxic agent in smog). Instead of making matters better, they became worse. Indeed, this is perhaps the most critical of all problems in environmental administration, that is, the difficulty of knowing in advance what is better and what is worse.

Still another example is found in the field of noise pollution, which the Public Health Service medical task force noted was reaching sound intensities in urban areas comparable to those associated with hearing loss in occupational groups. The noise level from the engine and gears of a diesel truck, or bus, can reach 100 decibels (almost the same sound level generated by a jet aircraft takeoff). The noise of a diesel bus is so intense that the driver can barely hear emergency vehicle sirens, which are only a few decibels higher. The combined noise from bus, truck, and siren sounds in urban areas is several times greater than the normal sound levels experienced by the human ear. Excessive noise can trigger cardiovascular, endocrine, respiratory, and neurologic changes; and long-term exposures may produce endocrine-metabolic deficits within the body which reduce the capacity to deal with other additional stress.[4]

The ironic aspect of the noise problem is that the electric street car and electric bus trolleys, which were replaced by diesel buses, were relatively quiet vehicles with low-frequency sounds. (Moreover, they did not emit hydrocarbons and oxides of nitrogen to pollute the air.) So a quiet vehicle was replaced by a noisy one. Noise consultant Paul S. Veneklasen, appearing before a California Senate hearing, summarized the situation in this way: With the improved electric trolleys there was a useful trend downward in the noise level of public street transportation. But with the replacement with diesel buses all of a sudden it (the noise level) reverted back up and now we're worse off than when we started.

WHAT IS QUALITY AND IMPROVEMENT?

These illustrations show the difficulty of defining quality and improvement in an environmental sense. The many interactions among materials, human behavior environments, and ecological systems often surpass our understanding of how to improve one aspect of an ecosystem without harming another. In the NTA case, the attempt to improve water quality substituted for phosphates a material which was damaging to human fetal development. The attempt to reduce hydrocarbons in the atmosphere ended up with an increase in the oxides of nitrogen, which were an even more reactive source of oxidants. These two examples illustrate the many unknown reactions which can take place in nature from sheer lack of knowledge or sufficient research.

The third example, of diesel buses as sources of urban noise pollution, is quite a different type of problem. Here one could conceivably argue that the ultimate volume of urban noise was predictable by those decision makers who were responsible for replacing trolleys with buses. But in all likelihood this decision alternate did not enter their considerations. At the time, trolleys were suffering losses in passengers, declining revenues, and rising costs. Track and overhead trolley wire restricted the flexibility of routing. Mass transit administrators thought that they could compete more effectively with passenger cars by more flexible schedules and routing. They also felt that buses would be cheaper than trolleys in capital outlay and operating expense. Hence, their decision criteria were to minimize cost and maximize performance through the use of buses in

[4]Task Force on Research Planning in Environment and Health Science, pp. 113–114.

lieu of trolleys, and noise probably never entered the decision at all, or at best very little. Gaseous emissions and atmospheric pollution also probably received negligible consideration.

If noise and air pollution are now significant factors in an environmental decision regarding mass transit, what has changed? What was wrong with the decision then, if anything?

The thing that has changed is the definition of quality or improvement. The bus was an improvement over the trolley only in terms of economics and flexibility, neither of which proved to be sufficiently persuasive to the public to save mass transit; but the bus degraded the environment, compared to the trolley, in terms of both air and noise pollution. Had quality in mass transit been defined in terms of air and noise pollution, as well as economics and flexibility, the decision criteria would have been different; and the outcome may have been different. Even at that time, say three decades ago, there was sufficient information about the noise and emission characteristics of buses to have made their pollution effects predictable. The problem in this case was not so much the myriad of unpredictable interactions in nature as it was use of a poor criteria of quality. At least the criteria can be said to be poor in retrospect, and that in itself is an instructive reminder. Poor quality criteria in retrospect implies poor use of foresight, or insight, as to human needs in the future. Perhaps we are guilty today of making equally faulty decisions with respect to the environment for the same reason, through lack of interest or insight into future human needs compared to our own immediate wants.

IMPLICATIONS FOR ENVIRONMENTAL ADMINISTRATION

The implications for environmental administration are that we need an expanded view as to the total effects and total costs of our decisions with respect to the environment. Fortunately most of us live long enough from birth into our own future to feel the impact of environmental decisions of our times. Those of us who lived through the demise of the trolley and the rise of the freeway have come to realize that we traded convenience for noise, traffic congestion, and air pollution. Was it a worthwhile tradeoff? That is, if we had predicted then some of the present facts we have now, would we have made the same decision? Possibly not, in that we might well have sought and found some alternative by which to achieve a greater measure of convenience in meeting our transportation needs at a less onerous cost in health, congestion, and noise.

This then is the essential point in environmental administration: costs cannot be reckoned merely as economic costs but must also include the external costs and sacrifices to the society, to the environment, or to other species in the ecology. The costs are not merely present cost but future total costs. The human wants to be satisfied are not merely immediate wants, but future human and environmental needs as well.

Environmental administration differs from traditional decision making in being more future-oriented in anticipating human need, more comprehensive in assessing total social costs as well as internal cost, more ecologically oriented in seeking to meet the survival needs of other species and not just human beings. The concern for the wants and needs of other species in the ecology is not so much altruism or magnanimity as a humble recognition that our own human health and survival depend upon maintaining ecological balance, and we do not have the omniscience to know when our disturbance of the environment is for better or worse, or at least not until the fatalities of some species (including man) have been counted. Then, of course, it is too late.

Hence the prudent environmental decision is one that imposes the least demands or change upon ecology at the same time as it tries to satisfy present and future human wants. The traditional decision was a simple one-dimensional model that signaled go or no-go based upon immediate utility and profit. The environmental decision is a multidimensional model which concerns itself with present and future, utility and disutility, energy and material transformations, total species sacrifice instead of immediate cost, ecological balance, and life cycle preservation. The answer to an environmental administrative decision is seldom go or no-go, profit or loss; the answer is generally a tradeoff, that some species gain and some lose, that better or worse are a matter of perspective as to who is making the decision, and that few decisions can represent betterment or the common good of all the species involved. Such decision making is highly value-oriented and complex, and those are the kinds of decisions which the government will face as environmental guardian.

SUMMARY

The frontier phase of United States development distributed undervalued resources to individuals as a means of converting surplus labor into savings and investment. This subsidization of the frontiersman is still being paid for by later generations in the form of ecological damage and social costs to rectify the environment.

The extensive development of United States resource, from roughly 1890 to 1930, saw the installation of large resource processing plants, and an increase in iron and steel, coal, oil, milling, textiles, and transportation.

This phase came to an end when the completion of such extensive investment coincided with a banking collapse, which then brought government intervention in the form of compensatory monetary and fiscal policy to try to smooth out business cycles.

The intensive development of the United States occurred as technology was applied in depth to agriculture, electronics, information handling, chemicals, and aviation. The success of this intensive investment created economic growth and increasing industrial wastes, which degraded the environment so that government had to assume the role of environmental monitor as well as developer.

With the passage of the National Environmental Policy Act of 1969, and the creation of the Environmental Protection Agency, the government has taken steps toward a more active role as monitor of the environment. The success of the government in this role will depend essentially on resolving two problems: First, the clarity with which the conflicting priorities of being monitor versus developer are resolved; and secondly, the skill with which anticipatory regulation can be applied. Government attempts to deal with product or environmental hazards in the past have essentially been after-the-fact, or ex post facto, regulation and control. By then, of course, the damage has been done; and some environmental threats, particularly those that are irreversible, demand prior action. The consequence is that public regulation will have to become anticipatory. Increasingly, public intercession into private product decisions and civil liabilities will impose new risks on business. These risks, to both business and the public, are of serious magnitude and require a rethinking of the decision process and criteria as to what constitutes environmental improvement, that is, defining what is better or worse. Attempts at such environmental improvement in the past have, knowingly or unknowingly, often produced worse results rather than better, either through lack of knowledge about natural interactions or through lack of attention to the range of future human needs.

Environmental administration to be successful must attempt to augment decision-making criteria to arrive at an expanded view of man's place in his ecological setting, including: establishing quality standards, monitoring and control measures, evaluation of external (social) as well as internal costs, measuring future human needs as well as present ones, prior evaluation of actions in terms of ecological balance and species survival, and broad public participation in environmental policy so that decisions represent, as much as possible, a consensus of the subjective tradeoff analysis involved. Subsequent chapters will deal with the purpose and means by which such environmental decisions might be made.

DISCUSSION QUESTIONS

1   What development efforts by government have you observed in your community which are intended to promote economic growth? Is there observable evidence still of the past phases of development, such as large land grants, railroads, large materials processing plants, or high technology rates? What benefits, security, pollution, and disadvantages have these industries brought to the community?

2   How effective do you think the National Environmental Policy Act of 1969 will be in improving the environment, judging from its authorized powers, organization structure, and initial actions? Do you see any problems with seeking environmental improvement through standards and controls? How would you suggest dealing with the problem of retroactive versus anticipatory regulation?

3   What are some of the forms of anticipatory regulation which have been attempted in environmental affairs? How effective have they been?

4   What are some of the liabilities, risks, and costs which industry may face under various forms of environmental regulation? How would you judge whether these burdens on industry are fair or worthwhile from the public viewpoint?

PROBLEM

Think of yourself, when you drive your car, as a polluter manufacturing about 1 pound of hydrocarbons, $1/4$ pound of nitrogen oxides, and 5 pounds of carbon monoxide per day. Suppose the total of all automobile air pollutants is causing 100,000 excess deaths per year in the United States in respiratory diseases, and plant and property damage of $16 billion per year. You, as the rational herdsman in Chapter 4, have been driven by the remorseless working of things to overuse the commons (the atmosphere) to the ruin of all. How would you propose to regulate yourself (and all others) through incentives or controls to reduce the death rates and biological damage?

Chapter 6

An Expanded View of Environmental Decision Making

Many of our environmental difficulties, as seen in previous chapters, stem from the narrow confines of our decision criteria which basically cover immediate production costs, without regard to biological effects or ultimate social costs. That is, Western philosophy is essentially utilitarian in the short term—we seek to maximize output, maximize satisfaction of immediate wants, and maximize profits. Short-term utility maximization implies a cost structure in the decision process which covers only the identifiable costs for the factors of production to the point of sale or, in case of government, to the point of delivery of an immediately consumed service.

Short-term utilitarianism, which has an honorable history in Western thought from Hobbes and Hume to Bentham, Smith, Mill, Freud, and Moore, is based on the maximization of pleasure and minimization of pain. This philosophy is coincidental in time with the rise of science and the industrial revolution. Essentially, it is a world view conditioned by poverty and underdevelopment. The assumption is that goods are scarce and poverty endemic to society. If this is true, then the way to maximize welfare, pleasure, or good is to increase material output; and the way to stimulate output is to provide a powerful incentive (profit) to produce goods which are priced to cover their immediate minimal costs. Minimal costs are the least increment of expenditures for land, labor, capital, and management needed to deliver a service to the point of immediate consumption. As long as the environment (air, water, land, flora, fauna) is ample, relative to population, the minimal costing approach delivers a maximum early output to satisfy human wants. But when the environment becomes scarce, relative to population and production, then the commons is overused, wastes cannot be absorbed by the environment, and the quality of the environment deteriorates—environmental quality gets priced out of the market. Like Gresham's monetary law, where good money is driven out of circulation by cheap money, good environment is driven out of circulation by cheap goods.

The consequence of deteriorating environment leads us to inquire into present and prospective decision-making criteria, in the following terms:

1   Present philosophy of poverty
2   Steps toward the future
3   Example of cost effectiveness applied to air pollution
4   Behavioral approach to satisfying human wants
5   Information problems of large-scale models
6   Systems approach to an environmental decision model
7   Environmental perception model
8   Ecological standards matrix
9   Materials-balance model
10 Environmental indicators
11 Environmental monitoring systems
12 Disutility added by manufacture
13 Gross national waste model
14 Cost-satisfaction assessment model
15 Behavioral adaptation
16 Air quality illustration of use of the model

PRESENT PHILOSOPHY OF POVERTY

In short, we are living with an economic philosophy based upon poverty, but, meantime, we have grown into an age of plenty, without having modified our economic or social concepts to adjust to the consequences of material affluence. The result is that while most of us live in private affluence everyone suffers public squalor.[1] This paradox is to be found in

[1]Kurt Baier and Nicholas Rescher, *Values and the Future*, The Free Press, New York, 1969, p. 369.

our lack of intellectual preparation for directing allocations between public and private goods. The commercial excitation of wants stimulates an insatiable desire for private goods. Meanwhile, lack of knowledge on how to produce a livable environment, or determine its cost, or value its worth, or advertise its satisfactions, coupled with an ideological bias against public expenditure, causes our social environment to deteriorate with neglect.

The opportunity to choose among public goods, relative to private goods, amounts to choosing among social environments. A choice among environments provides the occasion for individuals to consider what they will do with their lives, given the time and opportunities opened up by technology, and by affluence founded upon technology.[2]

In very broad terms, the nature of the choices of social environments might be among (1) economic growth, (2) more equitable distribution of income, and (3) improved allocation of natural resources to increase the amenities of living. The last alternative implies the establishment in law of amenity rights which would stand as protection of the individual to prevent one from being forced against his will to absorb the noxious by-products of the activity of others.[3] In a way, the environmental quality regulations of the new Environmental Protection Agency might be viewed as the beginnings of amenity rights. Such amenity rights become superior to property rights, as in the case of a water quality standard where the amenity right of the downstream individual to pure water is superior to the property right of an upstream plant to dump chemicals into the stream.

STEPS TOWARD THE FUTURE

The alternative choices among environments can be opened up by technology on the basis of new knowledge, particularly in the biological sciences and in resource economics.

In economic theory two useful concepts applicable to environmental problems are available, cost-benefit and cost-effectiveness analysis. The older, cost-benefit analysis, has been used frequently by the Bureau of Reclamation and by the President's Water Resources Policy Commission.[4] The calculation is intended to determine whether the net gain in benefits of irrigation or drinking water from river basin development is large as compared to the direct costs of dams or canals to develop water

[2]Ibid., pp. 386–387.
[3]Edward K. Mishan, *Technology and Growth*, Frederick A. Praeger, Inc., New York, 1970, p. 10 and p. 39.
[4]The President's Water Resources Policy Commission, *A Water Policy for the American People*, Washington, 1950.

sources. If so, the ratio of benefit to cost is favorable and presumably justifies the decision to develop the river basin.

The cost-benefit approach is also fraught with some conceptual difficulties.[5] For example, one analysis claims that the Commission's preference to relate private values based upon scarcity to public values based upon plenty is either meaningless or wrong.[6] That is, the benefit in terms of farm income from irrigated land, or the speculative capital gains which accrue to dry land when it is irrigated, or accrue to industrial and residential land supplied with water—all these enhance values in the private sector where productive resources are normally scarce. The cost-benefit approach also assumes that the costs, which are met from taxes, are allocated from a pool of funds or resources in plentiful supply. If public funds are plentiful, then their cost and value are low.

Thus, cost-benefit compares private values which are high by reason of scarcity with public funds which are presumed to be of low value and plentiful. Cost-benefit analysis offers no comparison of the alternative marginal revenue which might be created by the same amount of public funds spent elsewhere.

Cost-effectiveness analysis attempts to remedy this deficiency by comparing the relative utility of alternative choices, that is, by comparing marginal or incremental costs and gains. McKean argues that marginal costs and marginal revenues alone should be compared for alternative projects,[7] because this avoids the improper comparison of scarcity versus plenty. It assumes that both resources and benefits exist in an economy of scarcity, and that each project should pay its own way, so to speak, in terms of the net added value (utility or benefit) which it provides per unit of added cost. In a sense, cost effectiveness tries to apply to public goods the same test as a competitive market price applies to privately traded commodities.

Cost benefit and cost effectiveness are treated more fully as methodologies in Chapter 12. For the present we merely wish to see what usefulness the techniques may have in an expanded decision process.

EXAMPLE OF COST EFFECTIVENESS APPLIED TO AIR POLLUTION

A cost-effectiveness model could be applied to an environmental problem like air pollution. Assume that citizens are willing to pay a fixed sum of $1 billion to improve air quality; what is the most effective method of doing so? Let us say the measure of effectiveness is air quality, as measured by

[5]Wynne Thorne (ed.) American Association for the Advancement of Science, Symposium, 1961 *Land and Water Use,* p. 32.

[6]R. N. McKean, *Efficiency in Government through Systems Analysis,* Rand Corporation research study, Wiley, New York, 1958.

[7]Ibid.

oxidant levels. For example, the peak oxidant level in Los Angeles for one hour is 0.75 ppm compared with a state standard of 0.10 ppm, which was set on the basis of health effects. That is, beyond 0.10 ppm of oxidants, some deleterious health effects would be observed. Suppose, also, that three alternative choices are being considered to reduce air pollution: new car controls only, used car controls only, and car pooling of commuter transportation. New car controls may reduce emission by 90 percent by 1975, at a cost of $300 per car, but this improvement would apply only to about 500,000 new cars sold per year. Used car controls will, let us assume, reduce emission by 50 percent at a cost of $100 per car, and this improvement will apply to all five million cars on the road in the airshed. Car pooling would reduce emission by 75 percent by requiring commuters to ride four to a car, instead of alone, with an enforcement cost of $10 per year per car to regulate or fine people who violate car pooling ordinances. Which would be most cost effective? The answer is quite obvious, even without calculating it: car-pooling would be, by far, the most cost effective; second most effective would be used car controls; poorest would be new car controls. New car control is basically the public policy in air pollution control.

The reason that new car control is the policy is partially perhaps because cost-effectiveness findings have never been calculated nor explained to the public. The other is that neither legislators nor administrators are willing to take the political risk of either public enforcement or passing the cost of air pollution control on to the taxpayer. The cautious political compromise is to place the controls on the new car manufacturer, and let the manufacturer pass the cost on to the consumer through a large price increase for a new car. That way, the auto manufacturers bear the onus of the decision, rather than the politicians.

The consequence of the decision is that air quality will remain hazardous to health for another fifteen years. Even if all new car equipment controls work as hoped, everything for the best, air quality by 1985 will still see peak one-hour concentrations of between 0.2 and 0.3 ppm of oxidants, or roughly four times greater than the new federal air quality standard (of 0.08 ppm, beyond which there are hazards to health). But then, the public does not know these relative costs, effectiveness, or health effects, and may not know until morbidity or mortality make the facts more obvious.

BEHAVIORAL APPROACH TO SATISFYING HUMAN WANTS

One explanation for making the poorest decision might be that people do not act rationally. Classical economic theory is deductive, that is, not inductive or based on experience. Economics assumes that people make rational choices and act in a setting of pure competition where prices are definitive and, hence, choices are clear and determinant. As the complexity and instability of the environment increase, as the degree of competition becomes more ambiguous, as unpriced public goods increase relative to goods with market prices, economic theory becomes less adequate, because decision making occurs under conditions of uncertainty. The buyer (citizen) does not know, nor have the information for knowing, what the alternative choices are, or how to optimize them. In these circumstances, he makes the best choice he can, which means that he adjusts his aspirations to what seems attainable.

The decision to adjust aspirations to the attainable is enlightened more by game theory, or the psychology of human behavior, than by rational economic theory. The *binary choice experiment,* which psychologists call the *partial reinforcement experiment,* presents an individual with two choices and rewards each choice randomly, which simulates the uncertainty in future expectations. Assume that the choice is plus or minus, and minus is rewarded randomly two-thirds of the time. The best strategy would then be to choose minus every time, because no other decision would produce as many right decisions (in terms of optimizing rewards). But this is not how people customarily behave. Most people, in such experiments, choose plus or minus roughly in proportion to the frequency with which they receive rewards for each event. That is, their observed behavior is *event matching;* what they apparently seek to do is to minimize their regret, at the same time that they try to maximize their rewards. This behavior is called *minimaxing.* Regret means the difference between actual rewards and rewards which might have been received with perfect foresight. In short, they behave much as they would in a gambling game. The minimaxing of regret leads to event matching, and event matching, when there is a variety of goals, amounts to satisfying human wants rather than attempting to maximize them. That is, people get satisfied by reducing their aspirations to attainable goals.

Empirical studies of businessmen's expectations and decisions indicate that they, too, engage in something similar to simple extrapolation of events, or event matching to recent rewards. That is, they do not appear to have the information to relate marginal revenue with marginal cost, because to do so would imply an ability to estimate a smooth distribution curve of the joint probability of future events. Common sense tells us that businessmen do not make such estimates, nor do we find evidence that they do, by examining business forecasting methods.[8] To approximate the decision process of the real world, then, requires a large-scale adaptive

---

[8]H. A. Simon, "Theories of Decision Making in Economics and Behavioral Science," *American Economic Review,* 1959, vol. 49, pp. 253–283.

model which takes into account the consequences which will follow on each alternative, recognizing, of course, that alternatives are probabilities rather than fixed or known results.

INFORMATION PROBLEMS OF LARGE-SCALE MODELS

Suppose we pursue the idea that decisions with respect to the environment are essentially behavioral, and the problem is to estimate the probable consequences of alternative actions upon environmental quality. Then we face an arduous task of identifying the many alternatives and trying to estimate what consequences would follow upon the choice of each alternative. The prospect of constructing such a model of alternative choices is formidable because many of the biological and physical interactions in nature are unknown, to say nothing of the costs or health effects to man. As a result, the information obtainable for the model is only a fraction of what would be necessary to represent the real environment. At best, we could draw some inferences from such a model and submit the inferences to the test of controversy from intuition, experience, and common belief. That is to say, a large-scale decision model should enlarge our range of alternatives.

As soon as we begin thinking about a large-scale model of environmental decisions, we are caught up in what C. West Churchman calls the "ethics of the whole system," which, at its simplest, is stated in the following chicken-and-egg proposition:

The problem is that models do not mean anything unless they contain correct information. But we cannot determine what information is correct unless we understand how all the parts (models) interrelate to the whole system. The dilemma is: we need realistic information initially to build our models, but we need the models first to get the information.[9]

Obviously, we are now caught in a philosophical dilemma of how to break into a vicious circle. From experience one guide to this dilemma is to note that our environmental problems appear to stem from our failure to take as comprehensive a view of the environment as we possibly can. This pragmatic guideline tells us to design as large a conceptual framework of man's relation to nature as we know how, and then submit it to the test of data, experience, and controversy. This approach is exactly what the Council on Environmental Quality recommends in its first annual report to Congress.

The pressing need for tomorrow is to know much more than we do today. We lack scientific data about how natural forces work on our environment

[9]C. West Churchman, *Challenge to Reason,* McGraw-Hill Book Company, New York, 1968, p. 161.

and how pollutants alter our natural world. We lack experience in innovating solutions. We lack tools to tell us whether our environment is improving or deteriorating. And, most of all, we lack an agreed-upon basic concept from which to look at environmental problems and then to solve them.

Our ignorance of the interrelationship of separate pollution problems is a handicap in devising control strategies. . . . A systems approach is needed, but what kind of system? In this report the Council has suggested tentative answers to some of these questions. But much more thought is necessary before we can be confident that we have the intellectual tools necessary to delineate accurately the problems and long-range strategies for action.

Experience will help resolve some of the conceptual problems. We already know what problems are most pressing. Clearly, we need stronger institutions and financing. We need to examine alternative approaches to pollution control. We need better monitoring and research. And we need to establish priorities and comprehensive policies.[10]

SYSTEMS APPROACH TO AN ENVIRONMENTAL DECISION MODEL

The Council on Environmental Quality points out the need for a policy planning model for evaluating decisions with respect to the environment. The mechanism, which is in place by legislation and Executive order, is for the federal agencies to submit environmental impact statements to the Council on Environmental Quality on all new programs. Environmental impact statements should presumably contain the information needed to decide an issue in the conceptual framework of some environmental decision model. The use of such a decision model by federal agencies would, in time, imply that business decisions also would need to incorporate the elements of such a policy model, if the business enterprise planned to use resources monitored by the government. This means that an environmental decision model would become quite pervasive in use and should be, therefore, reflective of or able to satisfy as many alternatives and human needs as possible, in both the short and the long run.

It would also make human action as consonant with ecological balance as possible. We start with the constraint that ecological balance is a basic aspect of environmental quality, and, when this balance is perturbed, it becomes a peril to the survival of some species population. Whether man's survival is affected depends upon the place of the imperiled species in the energy-fixing food cycle or upon the toxicity of pollutants that directly affect humans.

An early evidence of degradation in environmental quality, then, is the appearance in ecological systems of toxicities or deficiencies which

[10]First Annual Report of the Council on Environmental Quality, op. cit., pp. 231–232.

stem from man's use of resources. The inquiry into environmental quality might, then, start from a series of questions along the following lines:

1   What boundary conditions or limits of toxicity or deficiency should be set as standards to preserve balance in various ecological regimes?

2   What chemical or physical conditions cause the toxicity or deficiency; and what are their quantities, origin, flow, and projected volume?

3   What other environmental problems (or standards) are perceived by people for physical, economic, social, or aesthetic reasons?

4   What indicators will measure the physical and perceived deficiencies?

5   How can the indicators be sensed in a monitoring net?

6   Based upon the indicators, what is the magnitude of disutility which society creates as a result of its total activity?

7   How can the aggregate of disutilities, or waste, be measured and compared with the sum of valuable products?

8   What technical alternatives are available to reduce the aggregate wastes?

9   What trade-off analysis can be made to determine the cost effectiveness of alternatives to reduce wastes and improve environmental quality?

10   How can human behavior adapt to maximize useful services while minimizing disutilities to oneself and the environment?

Answers to questions such as these should provide the basis for decision making to improve environmental quality. A plan to answer these questions and to develop a decision structure is described below as a set of interacting models, as shown in Figure 6-1. The schematic block diagram shows how various sets of information about the environment can be integrated into a decision structure. Perhaps the scheme will become clear by describing each block in the diagram, starting in the upper left corner with the environmental perception model.

ENVIRONMENTAL PERCEPTION MODEL

The environmental perception model is an attempt to see how individuals perceive their environment, and their satisfactions with it, through survey research methods and secondary source data. Samplings of public attitudes would reveal preferences regarding environmental quality, which may ultimately be interpreted into a set of environmental goals. Since we now have no sets of environmental goals, which are commonly recognized by the citizenry, to test as a starting point, we have to begin by a

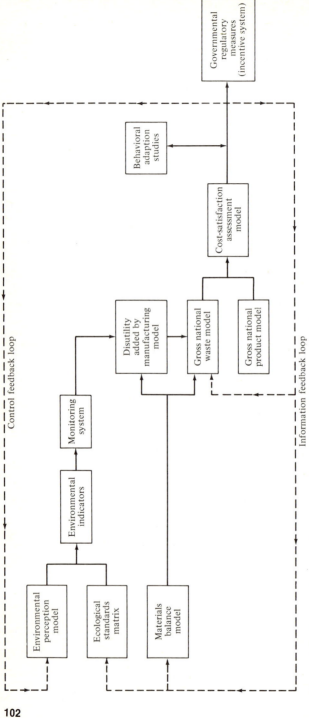

Figure 6-1 Schematic block diagram of an environmental decision model.

priori assumptions as to various indices of environmental quality. Then these indices may be tested to see whether they are perceived to be valued qualitatively by the public. If so, they will be indicative of preferred environmental qualities. If not, negative response will provide the basis for testing new hypotheses of quality in the perception of the public.

The a priori environmental quality features which might be tested against perception, could well be similar to the six suggested by Asch-mann as potential scaling values: (1) pollution levels, (2) diversity in physical appearance, (3) privacy versus opportunity, (4) energy versus amenities, (5) exclusive versus multiple land use, and (6) social blight.[11]

The hypothetical values, such as those suggested above, need some means of summarization into measures of significance once they are identified. Two forms of summarization seem likely: one in the form of preference scales or indifference curves; the other in a physical form such as ratios of density to open area, diversity, delinquency, or economic factors.

The overall purpose of the environmental perception model is to ascertain how people feel qualitatively about their surroundings, because these qualitative preferences are what we are trying to satisfy in subsequent subsystems in the model. If we can identify the qualitative judgments about the environment, then some external feature (or identity) can be measured quantitatively for periodic monitoring.

ECOLOGICAL STANDARDS MATRIX

Environmental protection agencies and the Council on Environmental Quality are faced with immediate decision making in the review of the environmental impact of new federal programs. Environmental impact statements are now required in the federal government for every new budgetary request which contains proposed actions that would affect the environment. The environmental impact statement (which is discussed in more detail in Chapters 12 and 17) generally contains data on how government actions will alter the physical or biological characteristics of the environment. To evaluate environmental impact, federal agencies need a decision structure, or screening method, to sort out the proposed programs which are critical and deserve analysis in depth.

One way to screen environmental impact statements is to set up boundary conditions or limits which are critical to species survival in

---

[11]Homer Aschmann, "Prolegomena to the Remote Sensing of Environmental Quality," *The Professional Geographer*, vol. XXIII, no. 5, January 1971, pp. 59–63.

various ecosystems. These life-limiting constraints would then be viewed as ecological standards.

Many ecological standards already exist in the form of water or air quality standards. These standards are very detailed and known mainly to specialists in these fields. There is a need for a workable comprehensive inventory of ecological standards, because:

1 Present standards may not be known to the nonspecialist, who may be making environmental decisions.
2 Standards for pollutants may have been determined by their effect on man, without a study of the effects in all ecological regimes.
3 Standards need changing as new knowledge on toxicity and deficiency in ecosystems is acquired.
4 There are many areas in which there are no standards for the effects of man or materials on ecosystems. This gap in knowledge needs to be filled, and the way to find out what one does not know is to categorize what one does know.

For these reasons, an ecological standards matrix is needed which categorizes the effects of materials recycling on ecosystems. In those cases where wastes are toxic or cause deficiencies to limit species populations, a boundary is set as a signal that environmental impact is critical.

An ecological matrix, to be useful at the decision-making level, should incorporate existing information into a form which will show interaction between suggested resource use and reuse, how levels of pollutants will be affected by the suggested use or reuse, and how these levels relate to existing standards. The initial level of screening should delineate the kind of ecosystem in which the resource under consideration is to be used, and the place where it originates. Probably the simplest means to develop these matrices, then, would be on a regional or project basis. Assuming matrices are to be developed for projects, initially broad-scale interactions should be considered. An example of the kind of matrix which would be developed for a mining project is shown in Chapter 17, Figures 17-1 and 17-2.

MATERIALS-BALANCE MODEL

The establishment of efficient, consistent, and comprehensive environmental control policies requires the integration of the three mediums of disposal, namely water, land, and air resources. Relatively restrictive air and water pollution control legislation may be beneficial to air and water, but simultaneously may induce an expanding solid waste disposal problem. The principle of conservation of matter-energy guarantees that unless recycling is undertaken, or material flow per capita reduced, the gross wasteload to air, water, and land resources will not be ameliorated. Thus, for comprehensive waste management planning, accounts need to be drawn up which identify the source, location, movement, and interaction of waste flows within an urban environment.

The proposed approach has two specific objectives. The first is to develop a consistent and practical accounting framework for classifying different types of waste flows in an urban environment. Clearly, a set of accounts containing *all* types of waste flows would be extremely cumbersome and unwieldy, and would be of limited usefulness for policy analyses. Therefore, a consistent aggregation approach needs to be developed where different types of wastes can be aggregated into a reasonably small number of categories. The aggregation procedure would be somewhat analogous to the gross national product accounts developed by economists, where meaningful distinctions are drawn between subcategories of the account, yet all categories are expressed in one unit of measure, the dollar. In developing waste flow and materials-balance accounts, it is not expected that a single unit of measure, beyond mass or weight, can be found which would yield complete consistency between subaccounts.

The second objective is a set of experiments conducted with several measures of waste intensity, such as biochemical oxygen demand, chemical oxygen demand, and minimum energy requirements (to centralize certain wastes), to ascertain whether such measures would yield meaningful aggregation weights. The resulting aggregation weights selected will then be applied to the subaccounts in an attempt to devise approximate ecoproduct accounts.

Once the accounting framework and aggregation weights have been developed, these may be applied to empirical data for an urban area in order to test the application of the accounts. Then the methodology and accounts could be expanded to approximations for the nation. These approximations and methodology would be utilized as part of a foundation for a set of national waste emission accounts, which then provide information into other subsystems of Figure 6-1.

ENVIRONMENTAL INDICATORS

The environmental indicators would be derived from the previous three models. That is, an environmental indicator would be the measure of some material which had a high degree of toxicity or contributed deficiency to an ecological system, which was generated in high volume in the materials energy balance model, and which the public perceives to be adverse from either its physical, social, or aesthetic effects. While these indicators are not predictable at this stage, we may speculate that they would include oxidant levels; PAN; hydrocarbons; aldehydes; dissolved solids and salts in water; pathogens in water; high-density land development without diversity or aesthetic appeal; high rates of intrusion into privacy as seen in crime or delinquency statistics; lack of opportunity as seen in economic or cultural deprivation; and in high risks, as perceived by the public, in hazards to which they are exposed.

The purpose of the environmental indicators would be to develop an information system which would alert policy makers, or the public, when signals of environmental hazard exceeded perceived level of acceptable risks.

The form of these indicators would probably be both tabular and graphic by sectors of the public or of biological systems affected. One might conceive of a gross measure of toxicity experienced in ecosystems, developed much by the same system as the weighted average of price indices. The weighting of toxicity would be related to the impact on species population. Similar indices might be developed upon deficiencies in ecosystems, perceived levels of risk, and human perceptions of privacy versus opportunity. The use of these indices would be to inform the public and policy makers of changes in environmental quality in terms of concrete environmental conditions.

ENVIRONMENTAL MONITORING SYSTEMS

Environmental monitoring systems would be the design of the instrumentation and data links which would be required to maintain the environmental indicators. Many of these sensors already exist in terms of air quality analyzers, water quality instruments, and social statistics from secondary sources. New sensors and measures may need to be developed, particularly remote sensing and pattern recognition of environmental conditions. The purpose of the monitoring system would be to accumulate sensory data into a communication network that would supply a continuous measurement of environmental quality as seen through the indicators.

DISUTILITY ADDED BY MANUFACTURE

Materials-balance models would identify the quantity of materials generated in the production process which are not put to use and are, therefore, disutilities or wastes. Sample materials-balance models would provide the basis for estimating the relationship of the value added by manufacture to the disutility added in the same process. Such calculations would provide a first approximation of the relationship of utility to disutility in the production process. More importantly, they provide the methodology by which a large aggregate national model could be constructed by federal agencies to show the disutility, or waste, by quantity and by industrial origin. This is a first building block to arrive at a national model of waste in the same sense that the value added by manufacture, and the income by industrial origin, is the principal building block on which the gross national product model was conceived.

GROSS NATIONAL WASTE MODEL

The gross national waste model would start with the disutilities added by manufacture and then extend the estimates to the other private service sectors, such as wholesale trade, retail trade, service industries, and governmental services, in order to account for the total productive activity in the nation. Rough estimates indicate that about 6 or 7 pounds of waste are generated per dollar of gross national product. The purpose of this model would be to show where that waste is generated and in what quantities. In other words, the gross national waste model would make possible a sector analysis of the waste-emission system in the nation, and this could then be compared with the gross national product model to compare and trade off the comparative value of productive product to waste. Such a measure would give an indication of the critical area in which environmental solutions or regulations would be needed to maintain environmental quality.

COST-SATISFACTION ASSESSMENT MODEL

The cost-satisfaction assessment models would compare tradeoffs between performance and cost in trying to improve the environment. The trade-off analysis could be derived from data in the gross national waste model, from the materials-balance model, and specific technical studies on processes for improving environmental quality.

An example of such technical study might be a comparison of the energy balance and environmental impact of alternative power sources. The study would look at the energy requirements for the future. Based upon these projections, an evaluation could be made of various alternatives of mobile, decentralized, and centralized power sources, including fossil fuels, natural gas, and nuclear reactors. The inputs, outputs, and emissions would be studied for prospective generalized sites with an estimate of environmental effect. The object of the study would be to minimize environmental impact while maximizing power availability.

In addition, a group of economists and social scientists could undertake a cost analysis of power generation alternatives, materials-disposal costs, and costs of waste avoidance and pollution control. This economic analysis would be used to generate the cost side of the cost/performance model. The degree of preference for amenities of living based on power consumption (see environmental perception model) would then suggest the marginal satisfaction which people would derive from a given cost/performance level of electric power generation.

BEHAVIORAL ADAPTATION

Behavioral adaptation examines the means by which human activity and behavior might be altered to be more consonant with environmental improvement. Behavioral adaptation may be approached in at least three ways: first, through preferences and value schemes (together with latent value systems) to provide incentives for change; second, through psychological means of changing behavior as a step toward inducing subsequent attitude change; and third, through institutional regulations as a method of change.

Behavioral adaptation in the end probably comes down to some minimal form of regulation of emissions into air, water, or land, plus a substantial change in incentives to reprice goods and services more in line with their total cost to pay for or eliminate their waste burden. The total cost, in this sense, is the sum of the direct product costs, plus the social costs of getting rid of wastes.

AIR QUALITY ILLUSTRATION OF THE USE OF THE MODEL

Perhaps the environmental decision model (Figure 6-1) which we have been describing seems abstract, because it presents no real data or alternatives. The generation of the data would, in itself, be a research project of large cost and magnitude; in the absence of actual data, the model remains somewhat intangible. However, the environmental decision model can become more understandable by a word description of how the model would be applied in the case of an air pollution decision. For illustrative purpose, then, let us go briefly through each block in Figure 6-1 with some tentative or suggested data regarding air quality.

1 *Environmental perception* The perception of air quality as a significant problem is widely recognized, in California at least, as noted in public attitude surveys; most citizens feel that very little is being done to correct the situation. The University of California undertook an integrated research program, "Project Clean Air," on air pollution; one of the program's objectives was a survey of attitudes regarding air quality.

> Among these 57% who report that something bothers them, one in three *spontaneously* mention air pollution or smog in this respect.
>
> When confronted with a listing of ten specific domestic social problems (e.g. taxes, unemployment, crime and violence in the streets, etc.), the proportion who select air pollution as among the three "most serious" problems these days rises to a definite majority of the state (59%). Only "crime and violence in the streets" was selected somewhat more frequently (63%).
>
> The point to be emphasized in these findings is that, despite the perhaps popular image throughout the country of the happy life in California, there does exist a considerable amount of dissatisfaction among the state's residents; and a substantial portion of this dissatisfaction has become focalized on air pollution or smog.[12]

2   *Ecological standards matrix*   The current operational measure of air toxicity is mainly the oxidant concentration. Oxidants cause aging in biological cells and, thus, are deleterious to health. California air quality standards have been that no more than 0.10 ppm of oxidants should be in the atmosphere, and a proposed federal standard lowers it to 0.08 ppm for the nation as a whole. Air pollution frequently exceeds the state standard by three or four times in California; peak concentrations for one hour have reached 0.75 ppm. Inland areas may have air pollution in excess of the state standards more than 200 days per year. Alerts are called in many areas to avoid playground activity among school children when oxidants exceed from 0.20 to 0.27 ppm.

Air quality standards on oxidants were derived partly from the attempts to control hydrocarbons in exhaust emissions. Hydrocarbons in the atmosphere, under sunlight, start a photochemical reaction which produces ozone and oxidants. The 1967 new car control standards reduced the hydrocarbon emissions, but, in meeting them, the automobile manufacturers produced an engine modification which emitted three times as many oxides of nitrogen. The oxides of nitrogen have proven to be an even more reactive source of oxidants than hydrocarbons.

There are at least eighteen intermediate reactants fixed in the internal combustion process which become emissions into the atmosphere. The resulting pollutants include hydrocarbons, oxides of nitrogen, aldehydes, PAN (peroxyacl nitrates), benzopyrenes, carbon monoxide, and lead particulates. In the atmosphere, the photochemical process can

---

[12]David Gold, *Public Concern about Air Pollution*, Project Clean Air, University of California, Riverside, Calif., 1970, Research Reports, vol. 3, Project S-11, pp. 2–3.

generate scores of other chemical reactions, many of whose atmospheric behavior and toxicity are unknown.

An ecological standards matrix for air pollution should identify all the atmospheric chemistry, final products, and their toxicity. The new 1975 car standards set controls on many of the known chemical emissions, such as hydrocarbons and oxides of nitrogen, but they say nothing about aldehydes. Aldehydes, of which formaldehyde is one type, are compounds which are very reactive and tend to combine with proteins. Failure to understand and control aldehydes could, conceivably, produce higher levels of toxicity than yet experienced. This possibility shows how important it is to have a comprehensive set of standards in an ecological standards matrix.

3 *Environmental indicators*   Environmental indicators of air quality would include all the elements of the ecological standards matrix, that is, the total chemical emissions of vehicles and stationary sources. In addition, other environmental measures such as obscurity or color of the air have important aesthetic effects in human perception. Lead emissions are estimated to contribute about 8 to 25 percent of the loss of visibility in the atmosphere. The other main contributors to obscurity are the oxides of nitrogen which, in atmospheric photochemical reaction, form a yellowish obscurity. Measures of the chemical pollutants and obscurity would constitute the environmental indicators.

4 *Monitoring system*   An air quality monitoring system would need sensors in every air basin capable of measuring each of the chemical outputs from photochemical smog. Some of these measuring instruments are available; some new ones would need to be designed. Multiple sensors of each type are needed at strategic locations in the airshed, the location being determined by patterns of wind drift and meteorological dispersion.

The dispersion and mixing of air is one of the fundamental pieces of knowledge needed to estimate the surrounding air quality at any point where a human being senses or perceives it. This means that the meteorology of the airshed must be determined sufficiently to create an atmospheric model, enabling one to calculate the spread and dispersion of the pollutants measured by the sensing instruments. In this way, estimates of air quality can be made for key locations on a periodic basis.

5 *Materials-balance model*   The atmospheric model provides one set of information for determining materials balance; that is, it shows the input of emissions from auto exhausts into the atmosphere, and the output from atmospheric chemical reactions of toxic agents delivered at nostril level to the individual. There are other materials transformations in the whole system as well. For example, there is the input of petroleum into the internal combustion engine and the output of exhaust emissions. There is also the input of crude petroleum into the refinery process and the output of gasoline. There is the input of metal parts and labor into an automobile assembly line and the output of a motor vehicle. There is the input of concrete, asphalt, labor, and equipment into the road-building process and the output of highways. The entire personal vehicle transportation system consists of the automobile manufacture, auto service, petroleum refining and distribution, casualty insurance, highway patrol, accident incidents, hospital care for the injured, mortuary facilities for the dead, highway construction, street construction, street maintenance, snow removal, etc.—truly a large and costly system. The outputs from the personal vehicle transportation system consist of such things as: convenience in human time utilization, passenger miles driven, air pollution, injuries, deaths, and a sense of power and liberty provided by individual control of a speeding vehicle.

The materials-balance model attempts to measure the inputs and physical outputs of the entire personal transportation process. The outputs in air pollution, for example, would be about 1.3 pounds per day of hydrocarbons for the average uncontrolled car, 5 pounds per day of carbon monoxide, and $1/4$ pound per day of oxides of nitrogen. This converts to about 20 g/m (grams per mile), 82 g/m, and 4 g/m respectively.[13]

The purpose of measuring the physical materials flows, of course, is to try to ascertain which methods or alternatives best accomplish a human purpose, such as personal transportation, with the least amount and toxicity of inputs and outputs. These inputs and outputs become crucial later on in the decision structure for calculating a cost-satisfaction assessment. No one has yet generated enough data to make possible such an assessment for a personal transportation system. One might surmise the outcome from the comparative costs of capital investment alone. An eight-lane freeway has a person-trip capacity of 9,000 at a capital cost of $1,600 per person. A mass transit system has a person-trip capacity of 50,000 at a capital cost of $440 per person, or five times the traffic at one-fourth the cost.[14] Of course, this calculation does not include the satisfactions of power and liberty which have so dominated the motivations for personal car ownership.

Materials-balance data allow us to estimate the disutility added by manufacture. Consider only the manufacture of an automobile, which is but a small part of the personal transportation system. Assume the automobile weighs 3,000 pounds and sells for $4,000 with a value added of 40 percent. That is the auto companies buy minerals, metals, parts, and fabrics for about $2,400 and add about $1,600 in labor and management cost. The value added becomes a contribution to the gross national product. If the waste production of automobiles is about the same as other manufacturers, then the manufacture of an auto produces about 10,000 pounds of waste. The 10,000 pounds consist of waste water,

[13]Paul Downing, *Benefit/Cost Analysis of Air Pollution Control Devices,* Project Clean Air, op cit., pp. 10–11.
[14]Leland Hazard, *Challenges for Urban Policy,* in *Values and the Future,* op cit., p. 326.

chemicals, scrap iron, scrap fabric, other unusable materials, and air pollutants emitted from stationary power sources. This 10,000 pounds of material is the disutility added by manufacture, which contrasts with the 3,000 pounds of valuable product in the form of a finished car.

In addition, the finished car, which will last perhaps fourteen years, will produce during its lifetime another 30,000 pounds of air pollution. The net effect is that 3,000 pounds of value added by manufacture, in the auto case, also result in 40,000 pounds of disutility added by manufacture. This 20 tons of waste must be disposed in the air, water, or land. The disposition adds 20 tons of material which, in part, at least adds to the toxicity of the environment.

The gross national waste model then aggregates all the disutilities and wastes by sector of the economy, to compare with the valuable product, to ascertain where the most adverse ratios of utility to disutility occur. In the personal transportation system, for example, the gross national waste model would aggregate all the disutility from the car manufacturing (shown above), from auto service, petroleum refining, highway building, street maintenance, casualty insurance, highway patrol, accidents, deaths, etc., compared to the utility of personal transport. These aggregations would provide some measure of the true social costs of the services which we demand as consumers.

Even the preliminary facts generated in our materials-balance and disutility-added models suggest that both the cost and the waste burden of a personal transportation system are exceedingly high, compared to alternative forms of transportation. The question then becomes, is that extraordinary cost worth it? Consumers and citizens have never had the alternatives put before them to choose. Presumably, if they knew the alternative costs and satisfactions of various transportation possibilities, survey research methods and market demand studies could ascertain their true preferences.

The preferences would have to be obtained with some perception of biological consequences, as well as costs and performance. The biological consequences are not clearly definable at the moment because of insufficient medical research to identify all the complex interactions between pollutants and human health. Medical research does indicate that: oxidants cause aging in cells, ozone adversely affects pulmonary mechanics and resistance to respiratory infections, vigilance is impaired upon prolonged exposure to carbon monoxide in freeway driving, motor vehicle accidents are higher with elevated pollution levels, a clear-cut relationship exists between carbon monoxide levels and myocardial infarction, and benzopyrene is a potent carciogenic hydrocarbon which shows some tendency to bind to new and unreplicated genetic cells.[15] The answers about the medical effects of air pollutants are not in, but enough inferential data are available to suggest caution and possible adverse health effects.

How the public would view the cost/satisfaction–health-effects consequences of air pollution cannot be known until the choices and preferences are clearly presented. However, they should be available so that the people know what the real costs of air pollution alternatives are. If they knew, they might then choose to change their behavioral patterns.

Behavioral change occurs when individuals realize intellectually or emotionally that the costs (health, social, economic, and sacrifices) are not worth the relative satisfactions received. Behavioral change occurs also when public policy legislates that a particular behavior is no longer in keeping with public interests; and then imposes regulations, incentives, and penalties to cause the change. An example of a change in incentives would be to charge the polluters of air the cost of keeping the air clean. This might mean imposing taxes on the manufacturers and drivers of automobiles. What this implies, of course, is that personal vehicular transportation is at present a heavily subsidized system. It is subsidized in terms of providing free, pure air which is returned polluted. It is also subsidized in terms of highway construction, highway patrol, medical attention, and shortened life-spans for biological species. If these subsidies were removed, then personal vehicular transport would be less attractive to the user. The subsidy could be removed by making users pay for the cost of clean air, and also by transferring the public subsidy to an alternative and less deleterious form of transportation.

What all the ramifications of these behavioral changes might be cannot be identified without detailed studies by the method of the environmental planning model (Figure 6-1). However, some authorities in their fields have speculated qualitatively what some behavioral changes should be. Professor Renne, for example, lists several attitudes which he believes must change based upon his study of land use. The attitudes which must change are basically the freedom to use the commons individually without constraint as to the general and environmental welfare of all. The conquest of nature needs to be replaced with public action programs to preserve our habitat.[16]

Other suggestions to change incentives and behavior, with special reference to land, have been to revise the real estate tax to prevent slum

---

[15]Project Clean Air, op cit., Research Reports, vol. 2.
[16]R. Renne, *Land Economics*, Harper and Brothers, New York, 1958, pp. 542–546.

formation, and to remove the tax advantages for speculative capital gains on land.[17]

With respect to the air pollution illustration, tax schedules could be imposed as incentives and disincentives to favor cars with low-emission characteristics. Some popular notions regard large cars as having higher emissions than small cars, and thus a tax on horsepower would be fair. In fact, smaller cars frequently have the higher emissions, particularly if they have high compression ratios and also high weight-to-power ratios. A plausible tax schedule that tries to relate the tax burden proportionately to emissions calculates the tax on compression ratio, cylinders, model year, transmission, odometer reading, and carburetor type.[18]

SUMMARY

Environmental degradation stems from inadequate decision criteria which relate immediate costs of production only to the point of sale. This short-term utilitarianism is a poverty-conditioned perspective, which takes no account of large social and biological costs.

A step toward the future is to develop an advanced level of economic theory jointly with the biological sciences, in effect to create an ecological technology. The Council on Environmental Quality also sees the need for a new conceptual framework for making decisions to protect our ecological well-being. One example of such a framework is an environmental decision model which includes key sets of data on environmental perception, ecological standards, materials balance, environmental indicators, environmental monitoring, disutility added by manufacture, gross national waste, cost/satisfaction assessment, and behavioral change. A description of this model, and its air pollution example, suggests that there are enormous bodies of information wholly omitted from our decision making at present. Most important to include in the future would be all the social and biological costs which are now suffered without alternative choices being presented. The presentation of these alternatives is the main mission of environmental administration with its expanded view of decision elements important to ecological balance.

This chapter has attempted to present an overview of a new environmental decision structure. Subsequent chapters will develop further its individual parts. Chapters 7 through 9 describe the biological interactions of man with the environment. Chapters 10 through 18 elaborate on

---

[17]M. Clawson, "The Land Use System in the U.S.," *Man and Land in the United States*, University of Nebraska Press, Lincoln, Neb., 1964, pp. 144–145.

[18]Ralph d'Arge, *Auto Exhaust Emission Taxes*, Project Clean Air, op. cit., vol. 3, S-12.

methodological approaches to develop an environmental decision model. Chapters 19 through 24 cover management methods which would implement an environmental improvement program, and the political implications of environmental decision making. The whole is intended to provide an integrated conceptual framework with which to explore the improvement of environmental quality.

DISCUSSION QUESTIONS

1   What arguments or examples can you think of to challenge or support Braybrooke's contention that most of us enjoy private affluence but even the richest suffer public squalor? Do you feel there are adequate choices open to you among "social environments" in which you have the options that you desire as to what to do with your life?

2   What applications or economic theory are useful in measuring environmental change? What are their advantages and limitations? What applications from game theory to environmental problems are plausible? Take an example of some recent decision of your own, would you say you decided it rationally more upon cost effectiveness, or upon event-matching grounds?

3   What is the dilemma, or vicious circle of thinking, in model building? Why might models be applied to environmental decision making anyway? What limitations must one watch out for in developing environmental decision models? Critique the statement of the Council on Environmental Quality regarding the need for a basic concept from which to look at environmental problems.

4   Consider the several models which are suggested in the chapter as part of a basic concept from which to look at environmental problems, and consider also the dilemma that you need information to define the models at the same time that you need the models to identify the data. What data do you think might be most feasible to obtain for inputs to the suggested models? What models or data would you start with to try to arrive at environmental decisions?

PROBLEM

Try to calculate a rough materials-balance model for your community, perhaps along the line of the metabolism of cities discussed in Chapter 2. That is, call the city utilities or waste disposal departments to get some idea of the volume of discharges into the environment from the city. Then work backward to calculate what the input into the city must be in terms of tonnage of fuel, food, and other materials. Check your rough estimates (guesses) with a few industrial companies or food distributors to see if your input tonnages are reasonably correct. You have now constructed a crude materials-balance model. What do you conclude from it?

Section Two

The Ecological System

The emerging problems in environmental administration described in Section One stem basically from inattention to biological processes and failure to include ecological effects in our decision structure. Population density and high wasteloads are impinging on the ecological system, causing deterioration of life support capabilities, and it is this deterioration which makes it necessary for us to become attentive to biological processes in decision making.

Attention to biological processes means that we must first understand them, secondly, know their limits and tolerances, and thirdly, know when our actions cause irreversible ecological changes. Chapter 7 deals with the basic biological processes of energy conversion; the food cycle; species distribution; and the role of water, air, and nitrogen in living organisms. The limits and tolerances of organisms to changes in temperature, or chemical composition in soil and water, are discussed in Chapter 8, which gives some idea of the boundary conditions of human decisions. Human acts which go beyond those bounds and cause irreversible ecological consequences are described in Chapter 9. Together, the three chapters are intended to show the framework of natural forces within which human beings exist, and which are the constraints on human decision making.

Some ideas and concepts regarding the workings of the ecological system may appear at several points in this book. For example, the biological damages caused by contaminants in the food chain were discussed briefly in Chapter 2. The nature of the nutrient cycle as an energy conversion process, and as one of the fundamental characteristics of the biology of the environment is explained in more detail in Chapter 7. Later, in Chapter 11, we will examine the dispersion and circulation of materials in the ecosystem, particularly in the food chain and hydrologic cycles. This concern for the energy conversion and circulatory processes of the ecosystem is not a duplication, but, rather, an emphasis on different facets of the most basic principle in environmental administration—everything interacts with everything else.

The environment is an open system, with incoming energy and materials, which can change nutrients and species populations. In this respect, environmental administration is unlike other management problems, which are generally closed systems of select materials converted to specific final products. There are no final products in environmental administration, only various stages of growth, development, and change. Environmental administration is concerned with the management of change in its ultimate and most complex set of interrelationships. To understand and deal with these intricate patterns of interaction, as best we can, require examination of biological processes from many aspects: the effects of human actions, the basic energy conversion cycles, and the dispersion of materials which alter these conversion cycles, and thus alter the ecosystem itself.

Chapter 7

The Biology
of the Environment

The externalities of environmental decisions can only be understood by recognizing the biological implications of administrative decisions. An understanding of biological systems is therefore important if all pertinent information is to be considered in making a decision. Even though biological systems are very complex, with many interacting reactions, there are approaches to getting a simplified overview. There are basic energy and material flow cycles on which nature's metabolism depends. These will be referred to as "life support" cycles for convenience. The basic food, oxygen, carbon dioxide, hydrologic, and nitrogen cycles are important. Disruption of, or input to, the cycles by man would obviously have implications for the system. These cycles will be briefly described and the influence of man's activities on them will be discussed. The following is an outline of the main topics.

1 Life support cycles
   a Basic food cycle
   b Oxygen and carbon dioxide cycles
   c Hydrologic cycle

LIFE SUPPORT CYCLES

Basic Food Cycle

The basic food chain is illustrated in Figure 7-1. Producers (plants and phytoplankton), by the process of photosynthesis, use energy provided by the sun to combine CO_2, water, and various minerals into carbohydrates, fats, proteins, and vitamins. A plant, or part of a plant, is used as a food source by a herbivore which transforms some of the material into body tissue, utilizes some as an energy source, and passes the remainder through the digestive tract where it is eliminated as waste. Carnivores feed on herbivores (or other carnivores), transforming their body tissues into usable food materials. Eventually all individuals die, and reducer organisms comprised of fungi and bacteria transform dead organic materials to minerals which may be used to begin the cycle again. The basic food elements are conserved and thus allow continuous cycling as long as the energy source from the sun is available.

Oxygen and Carbon Dioxide Cycles

Water, O_2, and CO_2 are vital components of the biological system which undergo cyclic processes. The O_2 and CO_2 cycles are illustrated in Figure 7-2. Carbon dioxide is removed and O_2 is added to the aerial environment by photosynthesis, and the reverse gas exchange results from respiration. Photosynthesis is the process where energy from the sun is "captured" to keep the food cycle in motion and is also the process which resupplies the atmosphere with oxygen. Whereas, both plants and animals respire, photosynthesis occurs only in plants; thus all animals are dependent upon plants for survival.

The pathway between the aerial environment and the respiration site is an important factor in gas exchange. High resistance or blockage of the pathway can have serious effect on the cycle and organisms involved. The

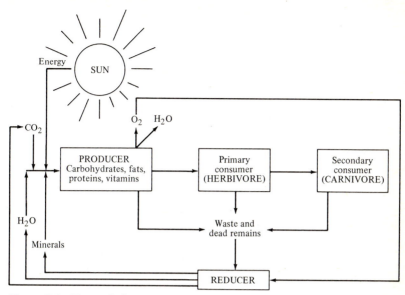

Figure 7-1 The basic food cycle.

soil imposes a resistance between the aerial environment and plant roots and reducers growing underground. The extent of resistance is dependent upon soil factors such as compaction and water content. Fish extract O_2 from the water in which they live rather than taking it directly from the atmosphere so the oxygen must dissolve in water before it is useful for the fish. If oxygen consumption by aquatic life is more rapid than the rate at which the oxygen can dissolve in water, the supply will become depleted and the aquatic life will suffer. Terrestrial animals, on the other hand, breathe the air directly into the lungs, and the CO_2 and O_2 exchange occurs there. As long as the passage to the lungs is clear and the atmospheric concentration is adequate, terrestrial animals will not suffer oxygen deficiency.

Hydrologic Cycle

An illustration of the hydrologic cycle is presented as Figure 7-3. Water reaches the earth's surface through rain or snowfall, infiltrates into the soil, or flows over the land surface as runoff. The water entering the soil will be stored in the soil profile. If precipitation is great, water will flow through the soil, following the more permeable strata to underground water storage or to the surface again at lower elevations to become

122

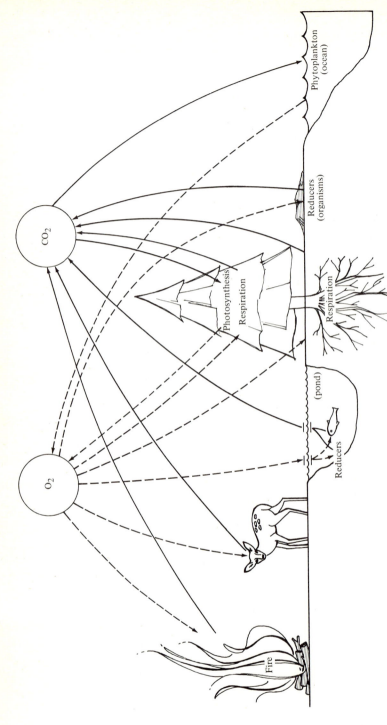

Figure 7-2 The oxygen and carbon dioxide cycles.

springs. The water from springs combines with runoff water to form streams which flow to lower elevations and eventually reach oceans or "landlocked" lakes.

Part of the energy received from the sun converts water from a liquid to a vapor allowing its return to the aerial atmosphere by evaporation. The water vapor forms clouds which lead to precipitation, thus completing the cycle. Evaporation may take place from the soil, plant, stream, lake, ocean, or animal surfaces. As evaporation occurs, the dissolved and suspended materials are left behind. Evaporation is the link in the hydrologic cycle which allows complete repurification of the water. However, partial repurification of water may occur without evaporation. For example, reducer organisms can attack and break down organic compounds which may be dissolved in water.

Water is one of nature's most important transportation vehicles. Fast flowing water carries suspended particles, causing erosion of one area and sediment deposits in another area, causing continual alteration of the earth's surface. Mountains and hills are gradually eroded and deltas are developed at the mouth of streams. Water is also an excellent solvent, dissolving minerals and organic compounds as it moves through the soil. Soluble minerals released from rocks through weathering are transported and concentrated in oceans and lakes which have no outlets. Obviously, the earth's surface has undergone several changes through time; it is not static. Man's activities can, however, accelerate or in other ways modify natural earth surface changes.

Nitrogen Cycle

Nitrogen is the most abundant gas in our atmosphere and is important in biological systems. Nitrogen gas is not used directly by higher forms of plants and animals, but must be converted to other forms before it can be used. Figure 7-4 illustrates the nitrogen cycle. Some N_2 is converted to nitrate (NO_3^-) by lightning, but the quantity is not great. Most of the nitrogen fixation is by *Rhizobia* and other microorganisms which live symbiotically on the roots of legumes and certain other nonleguminous plants. Some fixation is by free-living soil microorganisms, and perhaps by organisms on the leaves of tropical plants.

Nitrogen fixed by *Rhizobia* is available directly to the host legume plant and indirectly to other plants. Dead legume parts, or wastes from animals having eaten legumes, are decomposed by reducer organisms which "free" nitrogen into the soil, making it available for other plants. Ammonia is released first; it may be lost to the atmosphere or converted to nitrate. Ammonium ion (NH^+) or nitrate can be taken up and utilized by

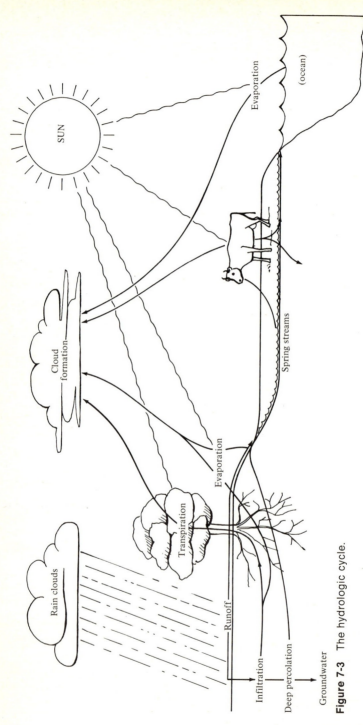

Figure 7-3 The hydrologic cycle.

SUN

Evaporation

(ocean)

Cloud formation

Spring streams

Evaporation

Rain clouds

Transpiration

Runoff

Infiltration

Deep percolation

Groundwater

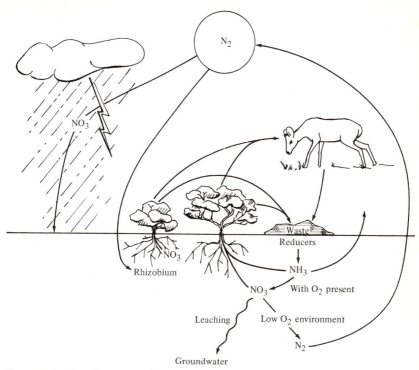

Figure 7-4 The nitrogen cycle.

plants. Nitrate is soluble in water and may be carried from the root zone if sufficient water is applied to cause leaching. The nitrate concentration in ground waters is generally low under native vegetation because the release of nitrate by reducer organisms is gradual and the plants remove the nitrate from the soil quite rapidly. Nitrate will be reduced to N_2 in a soil zone deficient in oxygen (excessively wet). The N_2 escapes to the atmosphere.

Water, minerals, CO_2, O_2, and N_2 undergo complete cyclic processes. Thus the environment is a self-perpetuating system which uses the sun as its source of energy. An organism finds itself linked to the environment through these cycles. The organism is dependent upon the regenerating processes for a continued supply of water, nutrients, and gases required for metabolic processes. On the other hand, organisms play a vital role in perpetuating the cycles. For example, if reducer organisms were eliminated from the systems, wastes would accumulate; the mineral cycles would be shunted; and minerals would accumulate in the waste and dead remains.

SPECIES DISTRIBUTION AND ENVIRONMENT

The types and quantities of plant and animal species living in a given ecosystem are dependent upon abiotic (nonliving) factors such as water, light, temperature, soil, and on biotic (living) factors such as complementary or competitive plants and animals. Usually a few species comprise the majority of the total population, but there are a large number of other species present with very few individuals. The diversity of species seems to be greatest under moderate physical environment conditions and decreases under more harsh environmental conditions. Tropical rainforests and tundra serve as examples of extreme differences in physical environment with concurrent differences in species diversity.

Stability of the ecosystem is believed to increase as diversity of species increases. The more species present, the greater the possibility for adaptation to changing conditions. Greater diversity also provides for better "checks and balances" through regulatory interactions of the functions of individual species in the ecosystem. Introduction to, or elimination of, a species in the ecosystem can create an imbalance which has pronounced effects on the ecosystem. Since individual species have tolerance limits, their elimination from a given ecosystem can be brought about by changes in the environment.

The environmental conditions in which an organism exists are not independent of the organism. For example a large tree has several effects on the environment. Transpiration from its leaves has a cooling effect. The soil beneath its outstretched limbs is cooler during the day because of shading. Soil properties are influenced by the roots of the tree and leaf drop. Each organism has its pronounced effect on the environment. The environment would in some form or other be modified if a given organism was removed from the system.

MAN'S IMPACT ON ENVIRONMENT

Man's activities have a pronounced effect on the environment. It is impossible for the environment to be the same with man in the system as without man in the system. Then what effect is man having on the environment and what impact does this have on other species?

Man is considered to differ from other species because of his ability to make rational choices. Thus man's impact on the environment depends upon the decisions he makes. Man's activities have changed through the years. A review of his activities and concurrent effect on the environment could provide insight to those actions which have the greatest impact on the environment.

Early Agricultural Practices

Man's first agricultural endeavors involved propagation and protection of desirable plant and animal species. Seeds of the intended crop were planted and competing plants were eradicated. A diverse system was reduced to a simple monocrop system in a given area. Continual planting of the same crop proved unsuccessful as yields gradually declined. Although the "undesired" plant species provided competition, they also provided a function in the ecosystem which helped support the "desired" species. For example, legumes served as hosts for *Rhizobia* which fixed nitrogen and their removal shunted the nitrogen cycle. Similarly, grasses had an extensive fibrous root system which maintained good soil physical conditions. Furthermore, plant material was removed from the field which shunted the mineral cycle on that field. Insects and pathogens which thrived on the crop found a haven of ample food and little competition.

Some of these problems were overcome by crop rotation practices. Legumes were periodically grown to regenerate the nitrogen cycle. Grasses were introduced into the rotation to provide soil physical conditions. Barnyard manure was spread on the land to return some of the minerals removed with the crop. The rotation also caused a disruption in the life cycle of insects and pathogens and decreased their disruptive capacity.

Man exercised considerable control over plant species in his environment, but he could only maintain control by allowing the basic life support cycles to flow and by maintaining some species diversity. Man's impact on the environment under this system was in selectively altering the distribution of plant species. His influences did not range far from the territory of his control.

Man was not always successful in exercising his dominion. He was usually successful in establishing agriculture in areas which originally had a "simple" system lacking great diversity. He was generally unsuccessful in sustaining agriculture in stable diverse systems such as forests. The natural system had as one of its mechanisms a wide range of species for quick reforestation of cleared areas. The diversity of the forest caused defeat of the competing simple system.

Domestication of animals occasionally caused an imbalance in the ecosystem. Animals were protected from their predators by providing shelter and killing the predators. A classic example of the effect of the killing of predators by man is the case of the deer in the Kaibab plateau of Arizona. About 4,000 deer lived on the Kaibab plateau at the beginning of this century. Many mountain lions, coyotes, and wolves were taken in the period from 1907 to 1939. The removal of the predators allowed a spectacular increase in the deer population; it reached about 100,000 in 1924. At this time, starvation and disease lowered the deer population to about 10,000.

Fluctuations in the animal kingdom population also have an effect on the plant kingdom. The Kaibab deer example serves to illustrate how plants can be affected by the animal population. When the deer population got large, normal yearly vegetative production was insufficient to provide food. As a result, the desperate deer ate parts of the plant which they would not ordinarily eat. Branches and bark were chewed off. This caused severe plant damage and decreased the vegetative productivity of the area, which further compounded the problem. The carrying capacity of the area was decreasing at a period when additional food resources were necessary.

Man's activities have also led to decreased productivity of an area. Cases of overgrazing of the range by sheep and cattle are documented. Overgrazing often leads to increased erosion, decrease in productivity, and change in species distribution (overgrazing of edible plants allows nonedible plants to take over). Wildlife and range management programs were developed to overcome the above-mentioned problems. Man tried to maintain a balance on a system which was thrown out of balance by his actions. Some animal species were protected from man's direct killing by law. Hunting seasons were declared on other species to maintain a given population. Grazing on public lands was restricted.

The above description of man's activities as related to the environment applies during the period of time when he was primarily agriculturally oriented. It applies to a time when energy sources were limited to animal energy (man and his beast of burden). This source of energy actually emanates from the sun and passes on to the animals through plants. Man was therefore restricted in what he could do by the amount of energy available. He had to maintain some sort of balance in the environment so that the flow of energy for his activities could be maintained. Activities which shunted the life support cycles had to be changed. Man was forced to modify his decision to accommodate the biological system. Greatest destruction occurred when man avoided the consequences of his detrimental activities by moving to new, unexploited areas.

Use of Supplementary Energy and Technology

Man's influence on the environment became more pronounced when he started to use supplemental energy sources (fossil fuel and nuclear energy) and technology. Energy and technology placed man in a different

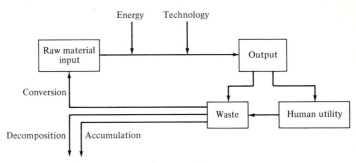

Figure 7-5 The materials-balance cycle.

sphere as compared to other animal species. He was placed in the position of having more alternative decisions. Seemingly, less concern for the life support cycles was necessary. Living in harmony with other species appeared less important. Increase in technology and energy supply has been associated with increased production and environmental degradation. What factors have led to this situation, and what courses of action must be followed to alter the direction in which we are headed? The remainder of this chapter will be devoted to analyzing some of man's activities as they relate to the basic biological life support cycles and interactions between species.

Materials-balance Cycle Man, through energy and technology, has created a cycle which may be referred to as the technological, or materials-balance, cycle which is linked with the life support cycles. (Linkage of the technological cycle, which is illustrated in Figure 7-5, with biological cycles has not always been recognized.) Raw materials are processed into desired output goods which are for human utility. Some wastes are produced in the process of manufacturing. Eventually the utility of the good diminishes, and it also becomes a waste. The waste can then accumulate, decompose, or be converted into raw materials to regenerate the cycle. Most raw materials have been rather plentiful so a minimum of conversion (recycling) has been done. Thus the waste either decomposes or accumulates. Since the cycle is not complete, a drain on natural resources occurs.

Whether the waste accumulates or decomposes has been left primarily to "nature." The common link between the materials-balance cycle illustrated in Figure 7-5 and the biological-food cycle illustrated in Figure 7-1 is waste. Man has dumped his waste into the water or onto the land, expecting the reducer organisms to do the decomposing. Failure to achieve decomposition of waste has been a key factor in many of our environmental problems.

Let us consider some of the cases and reasons why natural decomposition of wastes has not occurred. Man has synthesized many chemicals which do not occur naturally. In some cases, there are no reducer organisms which are effectively capable of breaking down the chemical, so breakdown is slow or occurs only under very specific conditions. Detergent molecules which are nonbiodegradable, plastics, and DDT are examples of man-made chemicals which resist decomposition by natural reducers. The same problem occurs, for opposite reasons, when man overloads the system with naturally degradable compounds, particularly in water. Reducers, being supplied with an ample food source, multiply rapidly and busily attack and decompose the waste. Oxygen is generally required in the decomposition process, and it may be used faster than it is dissolving in the water and become depleted. This leads to the death of oxygen-requiring organisms in the water, including the reducers themselves. Thus, failure to get decomposition may result from overloading the system. Still another reason for waste accumulation is the introduction of materials harmful to the reducer and other organisms.

Until recently, most attention and benefit-cost analyses were given to processing raw materials and getting them to the consumer. Cost of handling the waste was not considered. Preferably this waste can be converted into useful raw materials. Second choice could be decomposition into innocuous forms. The last choice would be accumulation. There are situations when accumulation cannot be avoided. In such cases, planning must be done to accumulate and store wastes in a manner least harmful to the environment.

Quite obviously technology and energy must be expended to handle wastes if environmental quality is to be maintained. We can no longer afford to ignore the step beyond human utility.

Nitrogen Cycle   The nitrogen cycle has been affected by some of man's activities. Crops were frequently found to respond positively to nitrogen fertilizer, and commercial nitrogen fertilization removed the need for a legume in the crop rotation. Soil fertility programs have had the positive effect of great increase in food production to feed the peoples of the world. On the other hand, it must be noted that nitrate can be leached with water. There are two negative aspects to nitrate leaching. First, nitrate is harmful to animals, particularly to infants, if it is too concentrated in the water. The level of 0.45 ppm has been set as dangerous. Second, nitrogen in water will stimulate unwanted plant growth in certain areas. Growth of algae in waterways and lakes is usually undesirable. Judicious application of nitrogen and other fertilizers may be considered as a positive enhancing of the life support cycle by increasing nutrients available for productivity. It is only overloading of the system with nitrate which leads to negative effects.

Another factor affecting the nitrogen cycle is the concentration of a large number of cattle into a small area such as feedlots or dairies. Decomposition of animal wastes by reducers is part of the nitrogen cycle, as well as part of the natural food chain. The problem is one of overloading the system. Too much nitrate results and leaching can occur with the negative feedbacks previously mentioned. The economic values of concentrating animals in small areas must be balanced by economic considerations of distributing wastes, or, in some other manner, assuring freedom from undesirable nitrate concentrations in water.

Oxygen and Carbon Dioxide Cycles   Oxygen and carbon dioxide are vital gases in biologic systems. They are recycled through the processes of photosynthesis and respiration. Man's influence on these cycles is indirect and results primarily from using the air as a "dumping site" for wastes. Gases which were not present, or present in extremely low concentrations, are being introduced into the atmosphere. Some of these gases are harmful to biologic systems. Air pollutants affect the respiratory system of animals and cause damage to leaf tissues of plants. Air pollutants therefore act as inhibitors to the O_2 and CO_2 cycles as well as causing outright biological damage.

The oxygen cycle involving aquatic life may be affected by dumping of wastes into water as previously mentioned. Organisms attack organic wastes causing their decomposition and consume much oxygen in the process. Water offers a resistance to oxygen flow from the atmosphere to aquatic life, and if the demand exceeds the supply rate, oxygen becomes depleted and the oxygen-dependent organisms suffer. Oxygen and carbon dioxide exchange is vital to life on this planet. Severe disruption of this exchange could be disastrous. Man's activities must be carefully analyzed with regard to their effect on CO_2 and O_2 cycles.

Hydrologic Cycle   Man has introduced significant changes along the water pathway in the hydrologic cycle. Much water has been diverted and used to irrigate lands, resulting in increased productivity of arid regions. Productivity can be maintained in irrigated regions only by periodically adding sufficient water to cause leaching of accumulated salts from the root zone. Often artificial drainage systems are required to remove the excess water. The drainage water either returns in some manner to a surface stream or becomes part of the ground water supply. In either case, salinity of the water increases, and the water becomes less useful for most land and freshwater plant and animal species. Benefits from increasing productivity of a given area by irrigation must be balanced by the possible decreased productivity in adjacent areas because of the increased water salinity or the cost of removing salt from the water. The latter is an extremely expensive operation. Decomposition is not one of the alternatives in the disposal of salt wastes. Thus far the benefits derived from increased productivity resulting from irrigation have exceeded negative aspects. Salt concentrations in some of our waterways, however, are rapidly increasing, so that careful analysis must be made of activities which will further increase the salt concentration.

Irrigation is not the sole contributor to increased salinity of water. It is estimated that passage of water through a municipality results in about a 300-ppm increase in salt concentration in the water.

Man has altered the temperature of much water with resulting implications on the species which flourish in that water. Great amounts of heat are produced by industries which need water for cooling. The electric power industry uses more water for cooling than any other industry, and the demand for electricity is great and has been doubling every six to ten years. Tremendous amounts of water for cooling purposes will therefore be required.

We may soon face a dilemma. Obviously wastes cannot continue to be discarded into the environment with the expectation that "natural" processes will cause their decomposition. Production of much waste has been brought about by technology and energy, so it is reasonable that disposition of the wastes will also require technology and energy. Energy used to handle wastes may contribute to another environmental hazard in the form of heat. (In fact, a two-page advertisement by a power company pointed out that all devices designed to reduce pollution which have been patented require electricity for operation.) Thus steps taken to improve the environment for one condition may create a negative environment for a different condition.

Construction of buildings in flood plains is another example of man not giving adequate consideration to the hydrologic cycle and its implications. Expensive flood and erosion control programs have been required to protect buildings. These are external costs which usually were not considered in initial investments in construction on flood plains.

Continued Need for Supplementary Energy   The advent of supplementary energy and technology has allowed man to exercise greater control over other plant and animal species. "Undesirable" plant species were mechanically destroyed or sprayed with chemicals. Insect numbers have been controlled by applying chemicals. In one sense, a stable ecosystem has been made unstable to favor man by the input of energy. Emphasis has been on maximum production rather than maximum protection. Continuous input of energy is required to maintain the instability. Fields left unattended will become infested with weeds. Insect populations would rapidly increase until a new steady state with the environment was reached, if no control was exercised. Thus man is faced with a continual struggle to maintain the position he has reached, and the position becomes more precarious with time. Some insecticides are persistent in the environment and are being accumulated in the food chain with adverse effects to nontarget organisms. DDT residues are sufficiently high in some soils that certain crops grown on these soils cannot be marketed. Furthermore, resistant strains of insects have developed requiring either higher application rates of present insecticides or development of new ones.

Present agricultural practices are productive, particularly in developed countries. Modern agriculture has large areas of essentially one crop. Attack of the crop by disease or insects over which man cannot maintain control could destroy a large amount of food because there are no natural barriers. Food requirements increase as human population increases, so pressure exists for continued productivity. Whether agricultural practices which are more in harmony with a balanced ecosystem, considering food requirement for present and predicted human population sizes, are possible will be discussed in another chapter.

SPECIES SURVIVAL

Survival of some species is questionable in the present environment. Need we be concerned about these species? Certainly, from a moral point of view, we must be concerned. Others would argue for the species on the basis of their aesthetic value to man. Both of these viewpoints would result in "value judgments" based upon individual desires. But is the situation more basic? Is man's survival dependent upon other species? Elimination of a species decreases diversity and possibly decreases the ecosystem stability. Each species has a function in the ecosystem which provides "checks and balances." Removal of sufficient checks and balances results in great fluctuations in other species populations. Species populations which remain relatively constant from year to year tend to be associated with moderate environmental conditions and great species diversity. Species populations which fluctuate considerably from year to year tend to be associated with harsher environmental climates and less species diversity. Man's activities have set a trend toward making the environment less suitable for life and eliminating some species. These activities could lead to population fluctuations which would mean sooner or later a population crash for man.

It may be foolish to suggest maintaining reasonably stable population sizes of the various species when that of one, *Homo sapiens*, has grown and continues to grow at a tremendous rate. Can one species population grow at a much greater rate than others without causing a serious imbalance? It seems reasonable that increased productivity resulting from input which enhances the life support cycles could be used to the benefit of one species without seriously jeopardizing others. Activities which overload or interrupt the life support cycles or those actions which result in extermination of other species could lead to ultimate disaster and should be avoided.

SUMMARY

The basic energy and material flow cycles on which nature's metabolism depends were referred to as "life support" cycles. The more important cycles are the basic food, oxygen, carbon dioxide, hydrologic, and nitrogen cycles.

Man's activities which have bearing on the life support cycles were examined. The activities which either shunted or overloaded a cycle have contributed to environmental degradation. The activities which enhance the life support cycles have had a net positive effect by increasing productivity. Therefore it is important to analyze the effect of any decision on the life support cycles as to the balance between positive and negative results.

DISCUSSION QUESTIONS

1   Are there any reasons why the use of Colorado River water by the United States for various projects should have any bearing on Mexico as long as a predetermined quantity of water is allowed to flow into Mexico?
2   Some of man's activities have reduced the number of predators for a given animal species. How has man tried to make adjustments for maintaining balance without the predators?
3   In what ways would waste disposal in a water body by a chemical plant affect water life differently from waste disposal from a food processing company?
4   Why is photosynthesis so vital to the well-being of animals when photosynthesis occurs only in plants?
5   Do you consider it more advisable to use aluminum containers which can be recycled but resist corrosion rather than "tin" cans which are not so easily recycled but will rust and eventually become an integral part of the soil?

Chapter 8

Limits and Tolerances within the Ecostructure

Plant and animal species have a range of tolerance to various abiotic factors and chemicals. A modification of one or more environmental factors could cause a disruption in the ecostructure. This chapter discusses some of these limits and tolerances. It also reviews man's modification of some environmental factors and to what extent these modifications alter the biological system. The following is an outline of the chapter.

1 Abiotic factors
2 Commercial chemicals
   a Toxicity
   b Interference with communication
   c Tolerance development
3 Man's effect on physical environment
   a Temperature of water
   b Temperature of soil
   c Temperature of air
   d Gaseous composition of water

    e Gaseous composition of the atmosphere
        1 Effects on humans
        2 Effects on plants
    f Inorganic chemicals
    g Commercial products

ABIOTIC FACTORS

Each plant and animal species has tolerance to a range of values of abiotic factors such as temperature, light, oxygen, pH, and salinity. The range of tolerance is sometimes expressed as maximum, minimum, and optimum values for each species. These values are, however, dependent on other variables and cannot be precisely established for a given species. For example, a fresh-water fish transferred immediately from a water low in dissolved salts to a considerably higher-salinity water may die. If the fish is conditioned by successively being transferred to higher-salinity waters, it can eventually adapt to waters quite high in salinity. Age and type of metabolic activity also influence tolerance. An organism may be able to tolerate a given condition but lose its ability to reproduce.

Although the exact range of tolerance is difficult to establish, differences between species and an appropriate range of tolerance are clearly recognized. Knowledge of species tolerance to environmental factors has been used extensively in planning food production where crops and animals have been selected for various areas based upon their productivity in the specific environment. The extensive plantings of citrus in California, Florida, and Arizona; planting of cotton in the Southern states; and production of corn in the Midwest were not by accident. They resulted from understanding the relationship between crop production and environmental conditions and the selective propagation of the species best adapted to the given area. This example also serves to demonstrate that the range of tolerance differs between species. Citrus and cotton cannot be grown productively in the north, whereas corn can be grown in all the states. Man has clearly demonstrated awareness of species tolerance to environmental conditions in choosing crops and animals for a given locale. This same awareness should be demonstrated in making decisions on programs which will alter the environment and consequently affect organisms growing in the area. Man knows that he cannot "grow" all species in a given environment. He should also recognize that changing the environment could alter the species able to "grow" in the area.

A schematic representation of relative productivity of a given species as relating to an environmental index (in this case water tempera-

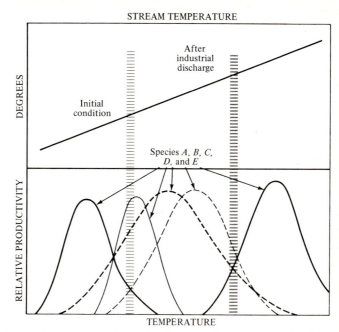

Figure 8-1 Typical relationship between the relative productivity of five species and temperature. The effect of modifying water temperature by industrial outcharge on species survival is also indicated.

ture) is presented in Figure 8-1. It can be noted that the initial stream temperature allows some productivity of species *A*, *B*, *C*, and *D*. Assuming that industrial discharge results in a temperature change as indicated in the diagram, species *A* and *B* would fail to survive and species *C* and *D* could remain. The temperature now falls within the range of productivity of species *E*, but this does not necessarily mean that species *E* will then appear in the locale. First, species *E* was not initially present and must either migrate or be transferred to the locale. Secondly, although species *E* is able to tolerate this particular temperature, there are other environmental indices of that locale that species *E* might not tolerate. Furthermore, all physical requirements of species *E* may well be within the limits of tolerance and yet species *E* may fail as a result of biological interrelations. Most organisms are dependent on other organisms to complete the "food web." It is even possible that species *C* or *D* would fail to survive if either species *A* or *B* was vital in the food chain of species *C* or *D*.

COMMERCIAL CHEMICALS

Toxicity

Besides the physical environment, we must consider the many new chemicals man has introduced into the environment. Some of these have been called toxic; however, toxicity is not a very specific term. Indeed, all chemicals may be considered to be toxic if taken in sufficient quantities. Much confusion has arisen by referring to a chemical as being toxic, or nontoxic, without being specific as to the quantity considered. An individual suffering from headache gets quite different results whether he takes one aspirin tablet or whether he takes a bottlefull.

Chemicals have both positive and negative inputs into the environment. They are designed and produced for their positive effect, often without due consideration or recognition of the negative effects. On the other hand, overreaction to the environmental degradation can lead to overemphasis on negative aspects without proper consideration of the positive factors. Arguments too often center on whether a chemical is "bad and should be banned" or "good and should be produced" without recognition that the answer depends to a large extent upon the methods and level of chemical use and the knowledge of people using them.

Again, using aspirin as an example, several deaths, mostly of children, have resulted from accidental overdoses, yet no great outcry for banning aspirin has arisen. Why? Possibly because most individuals have personally found beneficial uses for aspirin and readily recognize its "usefulness." Society has a balanced understanding of the usefulness and hazards associated with aspirin. The safety approach has not been one of "banning," but one of developing containers difficult for children to open and educating adults on the harmful effects of overdoses and the necessity to keep the supply from children.

Evaluation of positive and negative effects of a given chemical depends upon knowledge of the degree of toxicity and side effects which one can expect. Unfortunately, the quantitative establishment of the degree of toxicity of any substance may be quite difficult. Acute toxicity (rapid death resulting from taking one dose) is easier to observe and establish than chronic toxicity (slow death or gradual disablement by long-term small doses). However, even the determination of lethal limits is not simple since both intrinsic (body size and sex) and extrinsic factors and interactions of multiple factors can influence response. Whether a chemical induces chronic toxicity is very difficult to determine and is often established only after many years of society being subjected to the given condition. For example, the detrimental effects of cigarette smoking have only been recently established (some still do not accept the conclusions), after many people have had their health impaired by smoking to establish significant trends. Establishment of the detrimental effects of cigarette smoking was only possible because some individuals did not smoke, so that statistical comparisons between smoking and nonsmoking populations could be made. Many are concerned by the possibility of all society being subjected to a factor which is causing chronic toxicity without detection. Thus we find those who are opposed to introduction of any "foreign" chemical into the environment. On the other hand, we can readily recognize examples of individuals who are perfectly willing to subject themselves to the possibility of chronic toxicity for other benefits which might be achieved from a given chemical. Again, we may use cigarette smoking as an example. Despite the overwhelming evidence of the harmful effects of cigarette smoking, a large percentage of our society is willing to accept this danger rather than to forego the "satisfaction" that they achieve from smoking. Those who have an economic stake in the tobacco industry are also not willing to forego this personal profit for the sake of society health.

Decisions on environmental issues related to health are difficult. Concrete evidence of harmful effects is often difficult and time-consuming to obtain. On the other hand, a most frustrating fact is that it is impossible to prove a chemical completely safe. One can only conclude that from the "materials tested and the results observed" no detrimental effects appeared.

Abatement programs have generally occurred but only after much concrete evidence has been achieved. In an open hearing on air pollution in Riverside, California, it was stated that it was necessary in developing abatement procedures to get specific medical information on just how much harm certain pollutants do and at what levels and "not go off half cocked." Counsel stated, "When you're getting into enforcement, you have to have something to back it up." Unfortunately, something to back it up may be the impaired health of many people, animals, and plants.

Interference with Communication

Research is indicating that small amounts of pollutants can turn a thriving marine community into a dying one by disrupting the chemical communication systems on which fish and other marine species depend rather than causing direct damage which is usually investigated. Attraction to food, attraction of male to female, recognition of predators by prey, recognition of home stream territory by migrating fish are some of the actions triggered by natural chemicals, either released from other organisms or produced in the aquatic environment. Lobsters have been observed to be attracted to the extremely low concentrations of kerosene which cause changes in normal lobster behavior resulting in a decrease of local population density. Great concern is expressed on the effect of pollutants on some far-ranging fish such as salmon which spawn only in streams where they were born. Slight modification of the home streams or sea, which fouls up the communication systems of salmon, would be very detrimental.

Tolerance Development

Limits of tolerance to a given chemical may change with time. DDT serves as an example of this phenomenon. Levels which killed certain insects in early years of application later became ineffective and higher and more frequent applications were made, contributing to world contamination. The observation that insects were developing tolerance led one individual to state that we need not be concerned with DDT contamination because "if the insects develop tolerance to DDT, so will the pelicans." Actually, the term "tolerance" is not an accurate description of what has occurred. Application of DDT caused the death of all treated insects but a very small percentage that had a genetic characteristic for DDT resistance. This very small percentage survived and reproduced. Successive applications of DDT killed off the more susceptible individuals leaving the more resistant individuals to live and reproduce. Repetition led toward successively selecting and developing a resistant population of insects. (This also serves as an example of how genetic variability serves as a safeguard against species extinction.) The pelicans probably will not fare so well. Insects develop resistance in a relatively short time because of (1) extremely large number of offspring produced, (2) relatively short life cycle, and (3) elimination of susceptible species by treatment. None of these apply to pelicans—or to humans.

MAN'S EFFECT ON PHYSICAL ENVIRONMENT

To what extent are man's activities changing the physical environment and which segments of the environment seem to be most affected? Are these changes significant enough to alter species numbers and distribution? These questions need to be posed and answered if possible. Unfortunately, this chapter will not completely answer the questions. However, some changes in the environment brought about by man's activities and the relationship between the changes and certain species tolerance will be discussed. The environmental factors to be discussed are water, soil, and air temperature; gaseous composition of water and the atmosphere; inorganic chemicals and commercial products. Extensive detailed and quantitative relationships between environmental indices and various species productivity will not be presented. Books such as *Water Quality Criteria*[1] and *Environmental Biology*[2] can be consulted for such information.

Temperature of Water

Man's activities have had tremendous effects in changing water temperature, particularly on inland waters. The main effect has been a raise in water temperature caused by industries which produce great amounts of heat and require water for cooling. An estimated 70 percent of the waste heat discharged into the waterways in the United States results from generating electricity. With the demand for electricity doubling every six to ten years, the annual production of electricity is expected to reach 2,000-billion kilowatt hours by 1980. Production of this electricity will require about 250 billion gallons of water per day for cooling of which about 200 billion gallons will be from freshwater sources. This constitutes one-fifth of all the fresh water available in the country. Usually the warmed-up water is returned to the nearest waterway, causing a pronounced effect on aquatic life.

The species in the waterway are adapted to the water temperature as it was before being used for cooling. Exposing the fish, for example, to a higher water temperature can have noted negative effects. An increase in water temperature causes a decrease in oxygen solubility but an increase in fish requirement for oxygen. Fish such as trout, which require relatively high concentrations of oxygen, find it difficult to survive.

The life cycle of many aquatic organisms is closely regulated by water temperature. Migrations, time of spawning, days required for eggs to hatch are all influenced by temperature. For example, trout eggs require 165 days to hatch at 37°F, 32 days at 54°F, and won't hatch at temperatures greater than 59°F. "Food chain" organisms are also affected by temperature. Some eggs may hatch so early in the spring in warm water that the fishes' natural food organisms are unavailable. Trout and salmon waters appear to be the most critically affected by temperature increases; they should be protected, and no heated effluent should be discharged in the vicinity of spawning areas.

Production of electrical power provides a good example of the direct confrontation between man and the environment and how man has tended

[1] *Water Quality Criteria*, Report of the National Technical Advisory Committee to the Secretary of the Interior, Federal Water Pollution Control Administration, Washington, Apr. 1, 1968.

[2] Philip L. Altman, and Dorothy S. Dittmer (eds.), *Environmental Biology*, Federation of American Societies for Experimental Biology, Bethesda, Md., 1966.

to use the environment as free goods in the past. As population increases and our standard of living continues to require more energy per individual, the demand for electric power will increase. Additional energy will be required to dispose of material waste. Society is concerned and unhappy about temporary blackouts such as occurred in New York City when the peak power requirements exceeded supply. Nevertheless, society has recently become quite critical of plans for construction of electric power plants. As an example, it was announced in 1968 that an 830-megawatt, nuclear-fueled, electric power plant was to be constructed on the shores of Cayuga Lake in New York. Waters from the lake were to be used for cooling purposes. After much public protest, the utility agreed to provide cooling towers to dissipate the excess heat. Use of cooling towers rather than the waters of Cayuga Lake results in an increased cost which the public will pay for with higher rates. An administrator may very well find himself in the unenviable position of being criticized for any decision which significantly alters the environment on one hand and protests from unhappy customers who must pay the higher price for protecting the environment on the other hand.

Although most of man's activities have involved increasing the temperature of water, there are examples of the reverse case. For example, cold bottom water from the Fontana Dam Reservoir on the Little Tennessee River in North Carolina is released downstream into the river, eliminating for many miles the warm-water fish usually characteristic of Southern rivers. Thus the important factor is not whether the temperature will be raised or lowered by the action, but merely that the temperature is changed.

Possibly of greater consequence than a "permanent" change in water temperature are fluctuations in water temperature. In other words, the plant may be disposing water to a river which raises the temperature. With time, and possibly with introduction of new species, adaptation to the new temperature might be possible. However, if the plant was to shut down only for one or two days and the river temperature returned to its original temperature, the biologic system will again be disrupted. Periodic pulses of water temperature make adjustment of the flora and fauna to either warm or cold water impossible.

Temperature of Soil

Soil temperatures tend to be nonuniform and everchanging because they are related to the aerial temperature of the locale. Soil surface temperatures tend to follow diurnal variations of the aerial temperature, heating up in the daytime and cooling off at night. The average temperature of the profile will follow seasonal changes, becoming cold in the winter and warmer in the spring. Plants and animals associated with the soil therefore are not subjected to a constant uniform temperature to which they adapt. Nevertheless the plants have ranges of tolerance for soil temperatures. Some plant species seeds will germinate only at relatively high temperatures, whereas other species will germinate only at the lower temperatures.

Man's activities have not had a tremendous influence on soil temperatures except in small areas of intensive activity. There have been deliberate attempts to manipulate soil temperatures to increase production. A black mulch has been laid over the seedbed in the spring to increase soil temperatures, causing more rapid and complete germination of seeds. Quite often protective covers are placed on vegetable crops early in the spring to raise the temperature for protection against frost and to increase the rate of growth. These efforts are primarily for extending the period of time that the soil temperature is in a range allowing good plant growth.

Consideration has been given to using the heat produced by power plants to raise soil temperature and increase crop productivity in some of the colder regions of the world. In Oregon experiments have been conducted where pipes were installed underground and hot water passed through them. Increase of soil temperature by this means allowed for an increase in production of several crops growing on the site. This is an example of using heat produced by the power plants for a positive purpose. However, the cost of installing and maintaining the system may exceed the beneficial results.

The proposed pipeline across Alaska to transport heated oil is a recent controversy which centers upon the effect of such action on soil temperature. However, the prime concern is the possibility of melting the tundra, which might set off landslides or landbuckling causing a rupture in the pipeline and spewing of oil over the landscape. The primary concern, therefore, is not related to the effect of changing soil temperature on biological activity directly; it is the indirect effects which are of concern.

Temperature of Air

Man's activities have had local effects on air temperatures. For example, cities on an average have a temperature of approximately 1°F higher than the surrounding countryside. Smudge pots or large propellers which circulate the air have been used for frost protection of citrus and other susceptible crops when the temperature drops to a few degrees below freezing. This is an example of man modifying the environment to protect certain species and increase productivity. Widespread irrigation in arid regions has caused a slight lowering of the temperature. In terms of biologic response, an average change of 1 or 2 degrees would not generally be considered too significant. However, the main concern is about possible changes of the average world temperature which could bring about tremendous climatic changes.

Several of man's activities can lead to change in average world temperature. The carbon dioxide content of the atmosphere, which has a tendency to cause increase in temperature, has been increased by burning of fossil fuels. Carbon dioxide in the atmosphere has a very small effect on the incoming radiation from the sun but traps much of the long-wave radiation being emitted by the earth's surface. Thus the heat loss through radiation from the surface is reduced by carbon dioxide and is known as the *greenhouse* effect. Other activities of man tend to have a temperature-depressant effect. He can decrease atmospheric transparency thus reducing the amount of energy reaching the earth's surface by introducing dust, aerosols (tiny solids or liquid particles floating in the air), or cloud condensation nuclei (small particles around which raindrops can form). At this time, enough is known about the physical environment to establish the fact that inadvertent modification is occurring, but not enough is yet known to confidently predict the consequences of atmospheric changes.

Gaseous Composition of Water

The concentration of oxygen and carbon dioxide dissolved in water is of prime concern. Oxygen is required for all forms of aerobic organisms whereas carbon dioxide at high concentrations tends to be detrimental to the organisms. There are many bodies of water which have been drastically affected by man's activity with regard to oxygen concentration. As pointed out in the last chapter, dumping of organic waste into water supplies caused rapid depletion of oxygen from the water by the organisms which decompose the organic matter. Furthermore, increasing the temperature of the waterways enhances this problem by increasing the biological activity which depletes the oxygen and decreasing the solubility of oxygen in water. Fish species differ in their tolerance to low oxygen supply in water. Trout and other fish which chiefly inhabit cold streams require relatively large concentrations (7 to 11 cc/1) of the dissolved oxygen. On the other end of the scale are fish such as carp and goldfish which can live on as low as 0.5 cc/1. (It is not strictly because of size and appearance that children have goldfish swimming in a bowl on their dresser rather than trout.) Alteration of the water environment to the extent that it will not support one fish species but be adequate for other fish species does not necessarily mean that the first will disappear and the second take over. Very likely the second species is not even present in the environment to start with. For example, one does not find carp in our mountain streams. Thus depletion of oxygen in mountain streams will eliminate the trout but not increase carp population. Generally, species diversity and numbers decrease.

A study conducted in Ohio serves to illustrate the effect of modifying environment on a number of individuals and species present. Immediately below an industrial outfall, no fish were observed or collected in the stream. Eight species were present 2 miles downstream, and at a distance 2 or 3 miles further downstream, a larger number of fish and twelve species were represented. Thirty-two species were observed at a distance of about 8 miles below the outfall. Apparently the effects of the outfall were being dissipated as distance increased. The number of species which could survive decreased as the environment became more harsh.

Gaseous Composition of the Atmosphere

Man has altered the gaseous composition of the air so that in some areas the biological activity has been significantly affected. The main gases emitted are carbon monoxide, sulfur oxide, hydrocarbons, and nitrogen oxides. In addition, under the influence of sunlight, nitrogen oxides combine with the gaseous hydrocarbons to form a complex variety of secondary pollutants called *photochemical oxidants.* Ozone, peroxyacetyl nitrates (PAN), aldehydes, and acrolein are some of the photochemical oxidants which have developed.

Effects on Humans Air pollutants have become sufficiently concentrated at times to have caused obvious damage to plants and animals. Two major disasters have been recorded as being attributed to air pollution. Twenty individuals died and several thousand inhabitants of Donora, Pennsylvania, fell ill in 1948 when weather conditions were such to keep the air pollutants entrapped over the city for several days. In 1952, the number of deaths in London was about 1,600 more than would have normally occurred without the infamous "killer smog." Although these two incidents are dramatic evidence of the acute effect of air pollution, as great a concern should be related to the more subtle long-range chronic effects on human health resulting from exposure to low-level, longer-lasting pollution. It is very difficult to separate pollution from other biological and physical stresses to which people are subjected as the cause of chronic diseases which constitute a major public health problem of our day. Nevertheless, there is mounting evidence of the adverse effect of air pollution on human health. For example, in comparing areas which have high and low pollution, there is clear evidence that increased respiratory disease, bronchitis (both acute and chronic), and lung cancer are associated with the high-pollution areas. There is an apparent difference in susceptibility of individuals to air pollutants. Concentrations of SO_2, between 0.3 and 0.5 ppm cause physiological effects in some individuals but not in others. As individuals are exposed to concentrations between 1 and 3 ppm, the physiological effects become more uniform. All individuals exposed to concentrations between 5 and 10 ppm are affected. The fact that humans apparently differ in their tolerance to air pollutants is an interesting biological factor but should be of little consequence in decision making. Certainly our concern for our fellow man should be such that we would not be willing to "write off" that percentage most susceptible to the pollutants.

It will probably be virtually impossible to completely eliminate air pollutants in some areas. Then the question is, What levels are safe? Unfortunately, the nature of chronic disease makes it almost impossible to provide precise information on this question. The matter is further complicated by concentration-time relationships which must be established. We know that some areas very definitely have air pollutants at adverse levels much of the time, and effort should be made to alleviate the obvious problem.

Effects on Plants   Plants are also adversely affected by some components of air pollution. Indeed, it was the observation of silvering on the lower surface of leaves of leafy vegetables and petunias in the early 1940s that let man know that "something was in the air" in the Los Angeles Basin. Sensitive plants were used as indicators for the presence of air pollutants before instrumentation was developed to make the measurements. Not all plants are affected by air pollutants to the same extent. In fact, varieties within a given species show great variation in resistance to air pollutant damage. For example, of several varieties of corn grown at Riverside, California, in 1970, some of the varieties showed no visual symptoms of damage whereas others showed extreme damage to the plant. The great variability in plant and animal resistance to air pollutants and the complication of time-concentration relations preclude quoting concentration values which can be considered harmful.

Variability of varieties to air pollution damage may serve to illustrate the importance of maintaining species diversity on this planet. Species diversity provides stability. If all the varieties of corn were susceptible to air pollution, that crop would be eliminated from areas suffering from high levels of air pollution. However, by having a resistant variety, corn can be maintained in the locale. It is not difficult to conceive how this same principle might apply to other diseases which might attack a given plant or animal species and essentially eliminate it.

Inorganic Chemicals

Inorganic chemicals are neither created nor destroyed, except by extremely complex procedures. They have always existed and will continue to exist in the environment. Some of these chemicals are extremely toxic at relatively low concentrations, and man's activities have created situations where they are in a position to be dangerous. Inorganic mercury compounds are used by many industries, and water discharged from these plants contains mercury. The classic example of mercury poisoning occurred in the vicinity of Minamata Bay, Japan, in 1953 when over 100 people became ill with a strange series of disorders, many cases ended in either death or permanent disability. Cause of poisoning was traced to the eating of fish containing a high concentration (38 to 102 ppm) of mercury which originated at an industrial plant which discharged a large amount of mercury into the Bay. (Discharged mercury was inorganic and insoluble and was considered nonhazardous. However, when it settled to the bottom, it was converted into the water-soluble methylmercury which accumulates in organisms and is passed along the food chain.) Currently, in the United States, levels of mercury above Food and Drug Administration standards have been discovered in more than twenty states, resulting in cases of sport and commercial fishing being curtailed and recall of some canned fish products on the market. Organic mercury compounds are used extensively as fungicides in industry and agriculture. Seeds are treated to inhibit growth and molding during storage and after planting of the seed. Birds can become exposed to mercury by eating sown grain.

Concern is increasing about lead poisoning because several children have died and many others been affected after ingesting paint containing lead pigments. Lead is also being widely disseminated in the atmosphere by emission from vehicles using lead-containing fuel additives. The average body tissue concentration of lead in United States inhabitants is increasing, indicating that efforts must be made to curb exposure to lead.

Several other heavy metals or compounds derived from heavy metals are harmful at relatively low concentration. They include silver, arsenic, cadmium, chromium, copper, nickel, zinc, and beryllium. The degree of harm is associated with concentration-time relationships. Indeed, a small amount of copper is actually required for plants and animals to grow and develop properly.

Commercial Products

Several commercial products are harmful to life. Pesticides have been designed and used for the specific intent of destroying, or limiting, population of some species. Insecticides have been effectively used to control insects and thus reduce some diseases and increase food and fiber production. Concern has arisen about the damage to nontarget organisms and the widespread distribution and persistence of some of the pesticides. DDT has been the no. 1 target of attack, leading to restricted use or a complete ban in some states. There is fairly conclusive evidence that DDT (or one of its decomposition products) is causing soft eggshells, thus restricting reproduction of some bird species. Relatively high DDT levels have been measured in body tissues of animals, but it is not known whether any harmful effects are associated with the DDT accumulation. Furthermore, many of the analyses are suspect because it is difficult to distinguish between DDT and polychlorinated biphenyls (PCB). Many of the reported levels of DDT prior to 1968 may have included PCB. The balance sheet on positive versus negative effects of certain pesticides is difficult to draw because of the complexity of the matter and inadequate factual information on some facets. The tendency has been to substitute one product for another with the hope of maintaining the positive effect of control and minimizing the negative aspects. In some cases, the substitutes have not been investigated, and they lead to more negative effects than the original. Unfortunately, quick decisions are often demanded on matters which require much more time to gain adequate information upon which sound decisions would be made.

Detergents serve as another example of commercial products which have had significant effects on biological systems. Alkylbenzene sulfonate (ABS) was the basic component of many detergents which resisted biological degradation and remained in waters causing foaming of streams. Pressure was placed on industry to market biodegradable detergents, and so industry responded by replacing ABS products with products containing phosphate. Phosphorus is a plant nutrient which causes increase in vegetative growth (particularly algae) in waters which originally were low in phosphate. Abundant algae growth depleted oxygen from water at night when respiration occurs but photosynthesis does not, because of darkness. Fish kills resulted from oxygen depletion. This problem is most serious in deep, slow-moving waters which are not readily replenished with oxygen from the atmosphere. Phosphorus-containing detergents were attacked and even banned in some communities. Legislation was introduced in some states to forbid the sale of phosphorus-containing detergents. Industry responded by proposing other substitutes including nitrotriacetic acid (NTA) as a substitute. NTA was found to have possible links to cancer and birth defects which led the government to urge state and local governments to reconsider any laws they had passed banning the use of detergents containing phosphates. The Surgeon General stated, "My advice to the housewife at this time is to use a phosphate detergent. The safest thing in terms of human health is the use of phosphate." Pesticides and detergents represent a few of a vast array of commercial products which are being produced for various reasons. Information on the total impact of these products on the biological system is often lacking and difficult to obtain. Decision makers face the dilemma of making a decision without complete information or delaying decision awaiting information while possible damage occurs during the interval of data collection.

SUMMARY

Plant and animal species have a tolerance to a range of values of abiotic factors and chemical additives to the environment. The precise range is often difficult to define because factors such as body size, type of body function, age, and time influence the tolerance. Chemicals added to the environment may cause harm depending upon the concentrations involved. It is impossible to prove that a chemical is perfectly safe, and whether it will cause chronic toxicity (slow death or gradual disablement by long-term small doses) is difficult to establish. Many decisions are therefore required with the incomplete quantitative information available. Man's activities have definitely altered such factors as water temperature and gaseous composition of water and air with significant effects on biological activity.

DISCUSSION QUESTIONS

1 Discuss alternate ways of managing heated waters which have been used for cooling purposes and estimate the effect on biologic activity for each alternative.
2 Why is it impossible to prove that use of a chemical in the environment is safe?
3 Can value judgment be eliminated in deciding whether a given action has a net positive or negative impact on the environment?
4 Assume 5 percent of the population is adversely affected by oxidant levels in the air of 0.12 ppm and no one is affected at a 0.06 ppm level. The cost, in terms of dollars, inconvenience, and sacrifice, for the public in lowering the ambient oxidant level from 0.12 ppm to 0.06 ppm is tremendous. How much consideration should be given to the 5 percent affected?

Chapter 9

Reversible and Irreversible Ecological Processes

Man's activities have indeed had significant effects on the environment of planet Earth. Many of these activities have resulted in degradation of the environment for many forms of life. The question naturally arises whether the degradation is reversible. Can the environment be improved from its present condition, and if so, will the improvement occur spontaneously by terminating practices leading to degradation or will other action by man be required to bring about the desired change? Equally important as the question of reversible or irreversible environmental modifications is the rate at which reversible processes can be expected to occur by either spontaneous or induced action. An outline of this chapter is as follows:

1 Reversibility as a factor in decision making
2 Reversibility of various types of degradation
  a Water pollution
    1 Oxygen-demanding wastes
    2 Disease-causing organisms
    3 Synthetic organic chemicals

        4   Inorganic chemicals and metals
        5   Plant nutrients
        6   Types of water bodies
  b   Air pollution
        1   Plant recovery
        2   Human recovery
  c   Landscapes
  d   Populations
        1   Animal species
        2   Plant species
  e   Agricultural practices
        1   Increased diversity
        2   Application of insecticides

REVERSIBILITY AS A FACTOR IN DECISION MAKING

Reversibility of environmental conditions is a vital factor to be considered by decision makers dealing with the environment. Activities which are leading to irreversible or very slowly reversible environmental degradation should receive top priority for curtailment as compared to equally destructive activities which lead to reversible damage. Furthermore, man is endeavoring to undertake new activities having effects on the environment which cannot be accurately predicted. For example, considerable controversy exists on the feasibility of developing supersonic transports (SSTs), and qualified scientists cannot agree on the ultimate effect of a large fleet of supersonic transports on the environment. In this and other similar projects of which the ultimate effect on the environment cannot be accurately predicted, the seriousness and reversibility of the predicted damage should be vital factors in the ultimate decision. If the potential damage is reversible, one might be willing to authorize the project with the option to terminate should the activity prove to be harmful. Since the damage can be corrected, relatively little is lost in the "experiment." On the other hand, if the potential damage is irreversible, one would be considerably more reluctant to proceed with the project. In the SST case, the potential damage is both serious and irreversible. At the time of this writing, Congress had not been willing to authorize the project.

    To summarize, information on the reversibility of environmental degradation is important in developing program priorities for environmental enhancement and in future decisions on programs which may or may not have negative aspects on the environment. The remainder of the chapter will be devoted to various types of environmental degradation and their degree of reversibility.

REVERSIBILITY OF VARIOUS TYPES OF DEGRADATION

Water Pollution

There are several types of water pollutants which, for convenience, might be classified as oxygen-demanding wastes, disease-causing agents, synthetic organic chemicals, inorganic chemicals and metals, and plant nutrients.

Oxygen-demanding Wastes These are microbiologically decomposed compounds which, when placed in water, stimulate microbial activity resulting in oxygen depletion. If oxygen consumption exceeds supply, the oxygen concentration of the water becomes very low and aerobic forms of life in water suffer. This type of pollution is reversible. If oxygen-demanding wastes are not dumped into our waterways, the original wastes are gradually decomposed by the microorganisms until they are essentially all consumed. The rate of reversibility is dependent upon the rate at which oxygen can be supplied to the water. Deep, slow-flowing streams (particularly those which may have considerable amounts of organic matter settle to the bottom) may require considerable time for repurification because the rate of oxygen supply within the water is extremely slow. On the other hand, fast-moving streams with shallow waters receive rather rapid enhancement from oxygen, increasing the rate of waste decomposition. The rate of decomposition can be increased by any means of supplying oxygen to the water.

Disease-causing Organisms Water is not a very suitable growth medium for most disease-causing organisms. Thus, if the source of contamination is curtailed, waters will become relatively free from disease-causing organisms in a short time. This is especially true for groundwater. Movement of water through the soil is an extremely effective way of purifying the water from a disease point of view. Sunlight is also effective in destroying the organisms, so shallow-flowing streams are quite rapidly purified. Waters which would take longer for purification are the deep, slow-moving water bodies.

Synthetic Organic Chemicals Numerous types of synthetic organic chemicals have been introduced into the environment. Several of these have accumulated to the extent that they are a definite source of pollution. The principal factor involved in the rate of organic chemical disappearance from the environment is the degree to which they are decomposed by microorganisms. Some molecular structures are readily attacked and broken down into the innocuous forms of CO_2 and water, but other organic structures are broken down very slowly and sometimes only under very specific conditions. Some of the first detergents marketed were composed primarily of alkyl benzene sulfonate (ABS) which was very slowly decomposed by microorganisms, so that only a small fraction of the detergent was removed during an ordinary secondary sewage treatment process. Many of the surface waters became polluted with ABS. The soil serves as a relatively effective adsorber for ABS so most ground waters were relatively free of ABS. Detergent companies substituted linear alkylsulfonate (LAS), which is decomposed by organisms in a relatively short time, for ABS.

Pesticides represent another group of organic chemicals which have been synthesized and introduced into the environment. Again, some chemicals are more readily decomposed than others. The organochlorines which consist of such insecticides as DDT, dieldrin, and lindane tend to be slowly decomposed; so they have persisted and accumulated in the environment with repeated application. If application of these chemicals was terminated, the chemicals would gradually disappear from the environment. However, it would take several years for complete degradation of some of these chemicals. Generally, if the log of the concentration is plotted against a linear scale of time, a straight line results. The term *half-life* has been applied to the duration of radioactivity, and the same concept can be applied to organic chemicals. Half-life is the time required for half of the original material to be decomposed. For example, if the half-life of a chemical is ten years, the concentration would be decreased one-half in ten years. During the second ten-year period, half of what was left would be decomposed (one-fourth of the original material). Thus one-eighth of the chemical would be in the environment after thirty years and one-sixteenth after forty years. Complete elimination requires many years. Thus, synthetic organic chemicals introduced into the environment may be decreased in concentration if application is stopped, but they will persist for several years depending upon their resistance to degradation. DDT, for example, has a half-life varying from two to fifteen or more years, depending upon the soil in which it resides.

Inorganic Chemicals and Metals   These are persistent in the environment and may be one of our most troublesome types of water pollutants. The concentration of dissolved salts in the water increases each time the water is used. In some cases the increase in salt content results from salt addition to the water, in other cases it results from water evaporation concentrating the salt already in the water. Water originating from a mountain snowfall can be used several times as it flows toward the ocean. Each time it is used, salt concentration increases so that eventually the concentration might be sufficiently high to be of little value for practical use. There are methods of removing salt from water but they are very complex, expensive systems which have been used on a very limited scale thus far. In some respects, pollution of water by salts may be considered to be an irreversible process. That is, the water will not become free from salt by natural processes. Evaporation is a water-purifying process, however it is only the evaporated water which is purified, and the water which is left behind becomes higher in salt concentration. In nature, the salts have been accumulated in oceans, seas, and landlocked lakes. Similarly, man will eventually have to develop programs and processes for the concentration of salts in some waters and storage of these waters in desirable places.

The Salton Sea in Southern California represents an example of man's use of a body of water to accumulate salts. The Imperial and Coachella Valleys which are adjacent to the Salton Sea are very produc-tive agricultural areas. Irrigation is required for agricultural production in these valleys. Climatic conditions are such to cause large evapotranspira-tion from the irrigated lands. Salts accumulate in the soil profile and soon would reach levels that would reduce or eliminate plant growth. Irrigation water is applied in greater quantities than required to meet the evapora-tion demand so that salts can be flushed from the soil profile into the drainage systems which are installed. The drainage lines lead to the Salton Sea. Over the years, evaporation has occurred from the Salton Sea, and the salt concentration will soon be sufficiently high to eliminate most forms of water life. Presently, the Salton Sea is used as recreation area, and present water quality sustains certain forms of fish life. The benefits of using the Salton Sea as a "dump" for the salts of the Coachella and Imperial Valleys, thus maintaining their high productivity, are being balanced by the decreasing value of the lake for recreational purposes. Decisions will be required to determine the relative values and/or alternative steps that can be taken.

"Seawater intrusion" is another problem associated with water pollution by salts. As groundwaters are pumped from lands adjacent to oceans, the water table can be lowered sufficiently for ocean water to flow in and resupply that which is removed by pumping. Once the salt water from the ocean has flowed into the area, it is virtually impossible to reverse the effect. Seawater intrusion is a possibility anywhere along the coastline and should be closely investigated. Recent reports indicate that saltwater intrusion may become a problem on Long Island in New York. The household water comes from groundwater, in many cases from backyard underground wells. After household use the water is collected in sewer systems, treated, and then discharged into the ocean. Thus there is continual removal of water from the ground without replenishment. As the water table falls in the area, salt water from the ocean may move in. If this occurs, the well water would be unfit for human use.

Thus far, the discussion on the effects of inorganic chemicals on water quality has centered on the high concentrations which may occur. Other problems associated with inorganic chemicals center around those elements which may be toxic at relatively low concentrations. These would include some of the heavy metals. The source of this problem is usually industrial dumpage into the waterways. This form of water pollution represents an extremely slow reversible process. Heavy metals are adsorbed by various forms of organic and clay particles. Material containing adsorbed heavy metals hopefully would settle or in some other manner protect biologic systems from excessive concentrations of heavy metals. Mercury represents a unique problem in that it is converted into a water-soluble form while it resides in the sediment of the water. The water-soluble form may be accumulated in organisms and passed along the food chain. As the organisms die, the mercury is redeposited into the aquatic environment and cycled so water contamination by mercury is not reversible.

Plant Nutrients These, notably nitrates and phosphates, have recently been considered as water pollutants. The chief problem is associated with profuse growth of algae or other higher forms of plants in waterways where plant growth is not desirable. The natural aging process of lakes can be accelerated by addition of plant nutrients which increase biological activity. The enhanced aging of lakes resulting from additional plant nutrients is probably irreversible. The nutrients tend to be recycled through the biologic process. In other words, they are taken up by the plant, used by the plant, and then redeposited in the lake after biological breakdown of dead plant tissue. The same cycling system could occur in streams; the nutrients are moved when they are in a water-soluble form and thus the effect in one location would be gradually reversed if the supply of nutrients was stopped.

Most soils have relatively high adsorptive capacity for phosphates. Water percolating through soil is "stripped" of phosphate, and so most groundwater is relatively low in phosphate. On the other hand, nitrates are readily mobile in the soil system, moving along with the water. Denitrification of nitrate in the soil can occur in a zone of deficient oxygen if denitrifying organisms are present with sufficient energy source to accomplish the breakdown. Nitrates reaching the groundwater which is to be pumped may create a serious problem. Nitrates in addition to being plant nutrients can be harmful to animals, particularly children and pregnant animals, if the concentration gets too high. Special treatment must be applied to the water to lower the nitrate concentration.

Types of Water Bodies   In general the degree of reversibility of water pollution is greater for surface waters as compared to groundwater. Reversibility is also greater for streams as compared to lakes or reservoirs. Streams would tend to revert back to the original state if addition of pollutants was terminated. If plant or animal species are destroyed by the addition of pollutants, reintroduction of the species into the locale may be required for complete reversal. On the other hand, polluted groundwaters would tend to remain polluted and create a serious problem which requires close attention. Polluted water which enters land surfaces may require years before it arrives at a well. Thus, groundwater pollution may not be detected until several years after the pollution has been introduced. It would take at least equally long to have the polluted water removed and replenished with unpolluted water.

Air Pollution

Most aspects of air pollution are reversible. Indeed, places like New York City or the Los Angeles Basin may have a day of relatively high pollution followed by a day of very low pollution or vice versa. If the source of air pollution was terminated, air pollution would cease to be a problem almost immediately. Exceptions to this might be the gradual buildup of CO_2 concentration, which has the effect of increasing the average temperature of the planet, or the buildup of particulates in the atmosphere which has the opposite effect of causing a lowering of the average planet temperature. Rather drastic climatic changes which could not be reversed are likely if significant changes in the planet temperatures were to occur. Introduction of pollutants into the stratosphere where very little mixing occurs could also have more long-range detrimental effects.

Although the presence of oxidants, nitrous oxides, sulfur dioxide, etc., in the atmosphere could be very rapidly eliminated by eliminating the source, there is still the question of reversibility of damage which has been caused by the presence of air pollution. In other words, will plants suffering from air pollution damage recover and flourish, or will they be permanently damaged? Likewise, is human health permanently impaired?

Plant Recovery   Most experiments indicate that plants recover very rapidly after being exposed to pollutant-free air. The toxicant is not part of the plant. Visible damage to the plant such as necrotic parts of the leaves, is not reversible. However, the plant puts out new growth and rapidly recovers. Eastern white pine suffer a disease known as *chlorotic* *dwarf* caused by the ozone and SO_2 in the air. Pine trees suffering from chlorotic dwarf recovered very rapidly when exposed to filtered air to remove the pollutants. Approximately 80 percent of the pine trees in the San Bernardino Forest in Southern California have only about one year of needles retained because of air pollution. Trees receiving filtered air start retaining their needles and progressively recover from air pollution damage. A major problem in the San Bernardino area is insects attacking weakened trees and killing them. Once a tree is severely infected by insects, it will not recover even if subjected to clean air.

Human Recovery   Much less quantitative information is available on the effect of air pollutants on human health. The reason is rather obvious. Experiments can be set up to expose plants to various concentrations of pollutants and observe the effects. Application of a treatment which results in plant death is acceptable. On the other hand, it is not reasonable to subject humans to treatments which will permanently impair their health. Much of the information on human health is obtained by comparing health of populations exposed to different ambient air pollution conditions.

Carbon monoxide (CO) affects health because it has a greater affinity for hemoglobin than oxygen. Metabolic processes are dependent upon the pick up of O_2 in the lungs by hemoglobin and its distribution throughout the body. When CO is in the lungs, it becomes attached to hemoglobin rather than O_2, and the body may suffer from insufficient oxygen. It takes about eighteen to thirty-six hours for the hemoglobin and CO to separate after the lungs are freed from CO. Little is known on the permanent damage done to the body by rather frequent exposure to CO. There has been a statistically significant increase in the number of deaths from cardiovascular disease on days of increased CO as compared to very low, or no, CO days. Apparently CO causes an additional strain on the body which might be sufficient to cause death of susceptible individuals. There is also evidence of cellular damage in bronchial tubes as a result of CO. Cellular damage would tend to be irreversible.

Ozone causes irritation of cells lining the nasal passageway from the atmosphere to the lungs and causes them to swell. Increased airway resistance results and, in severe cases, causes chest pain. Cilia are hairlike bodies capable of lashing movement which line the sinus, nose, throat, and bronchial tubes to move mucous and other foreign material out. Ozone interferes with the action of these bodies, causing the retention of mucous which may contain harmful material and cause infection. Direct cellular damage can be caused by high ozone levels. Increased airway resistance and inhibited cilia action are reversible when ozone is removed from the atmosphere. Cellular damage may be irreversible, and infections might or might not be reversible depending upon the seriousness of the infection.

Sulfur dioxide (SO_2) causes increased airway resistance, affects cilia, and causes a thickening of mucous. Long-term exposure to SO_2 by some industrial workers has led to chronic bronchitis. The length of exposure required and degree of reversibility of intermediate stages of damage are not clearly known.

Landscapes

Man has been actively engaged in earth moving and construction projects. Huge buildings, an extensive network of railroads and highways, dams of a variety of sizes along streams have all significantly altered the landscape of the planet in a rather irreversible fashion. The effects of old roads, even though unsurfaced and not used for several years, on vegetation is obvious. Indeed, a section of the Mormon Battalion Trail through New Mexico can still be detected from the air by a thin line of foliage which marks the trail. This is an interesting observation because the battalion moved through the area over 125 years ago, and that section of the trail has not been used since. Rainwater collected in the slight depressions made by the wagon wheels in the sand thus promoting growth in the hollows. Slight modifications by earth movement or vegetation removal would be expected to have more long-lasting effects in the harsher environment found in deserts or in the tundra as compared to the moderate environmental conditions which are more conducive to rapid vegetation growth.

Mining operations have contributed to significant alterations of the landscape. Strip-mining operations are noticeably destructive. Soil and rock along with the growing vegetation is stripped off to reach a desirable coal strata. Until recently, strip-mined land was abandoned after the coal was gone, leaving desolate, steep piles of discarded earth to scar the land. The more fertile surface soil was often buried, and the exposed material was acidic and unfertile, preventing extensive vegetative development. In certain parts of Kentucky, the seams occur in strata near ridge tops. Road building and mine operations dump material down the sides of mountains to bury some vegetation and collect in the valleys. Severe erosion occurred during rainfall. Presently, there are stricter laws requiring backfilling of trenches and efforts to revegetate the area.

Populations

History, as recorded by fossils, indicates that extinction is a natural process. Organisms are replaced sooner or later by better-adapted or newly evolved forms. Man has directly or indirectly caused the extinction of some species and greatly reduced a number of other species to the point of endangered survival. Obviously, the extinct species can never be returned to the environment. Can the endangered species be saved and population numbers be increased?

Animal Species   Rate of population increase is related to a number of factors but the reproduction rate is probably the most important. For example, some female insects may lay hundreds of eggs. The offspring soon reach the reproductive age and each female lays hundreds more of eggs. Thus in a very short time a relatively small insect population can grow to enormous numbers. The extremely rapid recovery of insect populations has allowed several of these species to survive the all-out attack by man to eliminate them from the face of the earth. On the other hand, a pair of California Condor birds produce only one egg every two years. With such a low reproduction rate, population growth is extremely slow and the birds are susceptible to complete elimination.

Fortunately, for some species, man has undertaken positive steps to protect their existence. Wildlife management programs not only protect some species from overkill by man, but also limit their population to the carrying capacity of their habitat. Hunting permits are designed to maintain a "balanced" population level.

Overexploitation of fishes in the sea may have serious consequences. Modern fishing practices use extremely effective equipment for both locating and capturing the fish. Furthermore, several countries are involved in fishing activities, and no one country can assume the responsibility of protecting the fish. Populations can be reduced to very low numbers in a relatively short time by consistently capturing more fish than are produced each year. A decline in population is illustrated in Figure 9-1 for the case when 6.5 percent more fish are killed than are produced each year. Although 6.5 percent overkill may not appear to be excessive, the population can be reduced by 92 percent over a forty-year period. Obviously a higher percentage overkill would cause a more rapid population decline. Incidentally, the curve presented as Figure 9-1 closely follows the shape of the number of blue whales harvested over the years and may indicate that they have been removed at a rate of about 6.5 percent more than they are produced.

Plant Species   These have been affected by man's activities related to lumbering and grazing. The land can be stripped almost completely of more palatable species when exposed to overgrazing practices. Overgrazing often sets into motion an irreversible process. The land, stripped of its

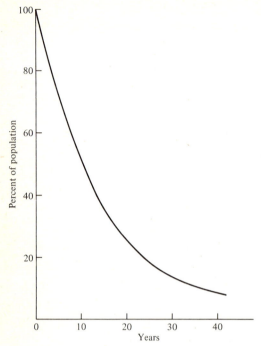

Figure 9-1 The change in population with time resulting from practices which cause 6.5 percent higher death rate than birthrate.

protective vegetation, is exposed to severe erosion hazard. Much of the more fertile topsoil is eroded away leaving the less fertile subsoil exposed at the surface. With increased erosion, the productivity of the land decreases. With less vegetation, the grazing animals are forced to eat the less palatable species thus intensifying the problem. Erosion is an irreversible process. The soil which is removed will never return to its original site unless manually transported back. Soil formation does occur; however, the development is an extremely slow process. Thus overgrazing, which contributes to erosion, creates a situation where the original vegetation will not occur. Nevertheless, studies have indicated that vegetative production is enhanced after an area is protected from overgrazing. The degree of recovery is dependent primarily upon the extent of erosion.

Man has made extensive use of wood products, leading to the cutting of many acres of forested land. Initial "cut out and get out" practices followed by the lumber industry contributed to considerable damage to our forestlands. Heavy equipment used in lumbering practices caused severe disruption of the land surface leading to tremendous erosion during rainfall. Irrepairable damage was done by such practices. Man has, however, recognized that his timber resources are not infinite but that timber is a renewable resource which can be regenerated by good management practices. Replanting and other management practices allow for regeneration of the cut-over land with minimum amount of damage.

Agricultural Practices

Agriculture is the art, or science, of crop and/or livestock production. Basically, man has chosen "desirable" plant and animal species and encouraged their production by providing suitable growing conditions and protecting them from competition. Breeding programs have been used to develop highly productive strains, or varieties. Many acres of land supporting a diversity of plant species have been converted into a less stable monoculture. Stability has been maintained by energy input in the form of mechanical cultivation, fertilization, and use of pesticides. Modern agricultural practices have led to increased food and fiber production. Some fear, however, that modern systems are susceptible to disaster. An uncontrolled pest could severely damage vast areas of a crop.

Increased Diversity   Are modern agricultural practices reversible in the sense of reverting to a more diversified cropping system and decreased usage of pesticide? Obviously it would be impossible to return to the "natural" state of complete plant species diversity and still feed the populations on the earth. There could be a shift toward a more diversified cropping sequence and pattern, if man decided to follow this route. It is not likely, however, that such decisions will be made unless something quite drastic happens. Each grower is interested in making the maximum return from his property. This is accomplished by planting his entire acreage with the highest-value crop that he is able to grow in his particular locale. Providing greater diversity in crop pattern by growing lesser-value crops would not be in his best economic interest. Furthermore, agricultural practices have become highly mechanized. Huge, elaborate machines are used for tilling, planting, cultivating, and harvesting crops. These machines are cumbersome and difficult to use on relatively small fields. They are most useful in expansive fields. Each crop has its unique set of production machinery. A grower could afford to "tool up" for one or two crops, but could not afford the entire line of machinery for a number of different crops. These are pressures which lead growers toward a monocrop rather than a diversified crop system.

Application of Insecticides   In a very diverse plant community, there is usually no large outbreak and devastation of vegetation by a given insect species. This is because of the large number of plant and insect species which interact and serve as checks and balances on each other. However, by eliminating the plant diversity, insect diversity is also decreased. This allows, in some cases, extensive damage of the crop by a given insect species. To overcome this difficulty, man has applied commercial insecticides which were found to be very effective in killing insects. When insecticides were first used, rather dramatic increases in yield were observed along with the reduced insect damage. However, with time it was found that, although the first application of an insecticide greatly reduced the insect population, the resurgence was often greater than the initial population. This was brought about partly because the insecticide did not differentiate between insect species. All types of insects, including the natural predators, were killed off. Although large percentages of the insect population were killed, there were a few who would survive. Because of the rapid reproductivity of insects, there could be a resurgence in population. However, at this time the predator population was so reduced that they would not provide "natural" control. As resurgence of populations developed, further applications of insecticide were necessary. Indeed, in some cases insecticide was applied on a regular basis without determining whether there was an insect infestation. In general, insecticide application was relatively cheap, and it was felt that it was better to apply rather than risk the possibility of insect damage. Eventually the insect species developed a resistance to the insecticide. In an attempt to overcome this problem, more frequent, higher application rates were applied. When this failed to achieve control, new chemicals were used. Usually the insect developed a resistance to the new insecticide in even less time. This sequence of events has occurred in a number of cases.

The more persistent insecticides such as the organochlorines have become widely distributed on the planet. They have become concentrated in some animals. The prime question is whether the system is reversible. Can we revert to less extensive insecticide use and still maintain food and fiber production? If we can decrease or eliminate the use of insecticides, will the planet ever become free from the contamination which has already occurred?

A classic example of a modified insect control program is the one in the Canete Valley of Peru. The Canete Valley is an essentially self-contained agroecosystem. It is a coastal valley, isolated by intervening ridges. In 1920, the major crop was shifted from sugar cane to cotton. Currently about two-thirds of the valley is planted in cotton. When synthetic organic insecticides were brought into use, they were essentially applied as a blanket over the entire ecosystem, and the entire biota of the valley was repeatedly exposed to these insecticides. The parasite and predator fauna were decimated which in turn relieved the key pest species as well as potential pests from biotic repression. Later resistance to insecticide rapidly developed in the pest species. These events led to marked cotton yield decreases to the point that the 1956 yield was the lowest in more than a decade. Clearly, an alternative approach to insect control was required. The agricultural experiment station located in the valley was requested to formulate a plan to bring about relief from this problem. A plan which called for changes in pest control practices as well as adoption of certain cultural practices was formulated by the experiment station and approved by the Peruvian Ministry of Agriculture. Deadline dates for planting, plowing under or burning crop residues, pruning ratton cotton, and applying irrigation were established. The valley was repopulated with beneficial insects introduced from other Peruvian valleys or from foreign areas. Use of synthetic organic insecticides was prohibited, and a return to the older materials (calcium and lead arsenates and nicotine sulfates) was recommended, except for exceptional cases approved by a special commission. These procedures, along with a number of other cultural practices that were recommended, resulted in a rapid and striking reduction in severity of cotton pest problems in the Canete Valley. Most important, there was an impressive increase in cotton yield as compared to the organic insecticide era.

Although the crop insects and geographic features of the Canete Valley are not representative of every condition which exists, the example does serve to demonstrate the feasibility of cutting back on the use of synthetic insecticides and development of cultural practices to maintain insect control. The present trend among entomologists is to develop "integrated control" procedures. The general philosophy appears to be changing from complete elimination of insects to controlling insect populations at a level which will not be economically detrimental. This does create a problem with vegetable crop production. The FDA has rather rigid requirements on the number of insect remains which will be allowed on produce which is processed. Furthermore, the consumer severely discriminates against the purchase of fresh fruits or vegetables which have any sign of insect damage. These basic conflicts in the approach to insect control in vegetable products must be resolved.

The prospects are that the use of synthetic insecticides can be greatly reduced. However, even the most ardent, knowledgeable supporter of "biological control" recognizes that the use of some synthetic insecticides will be required to maintain crop productivity. *Integrated control,* therefore, is the combination of cultural practices and insecticide use to maintain control.

Assuming that the use of synthetic pesticides will be greatly reduced or eliminated, how long will the present environmental contamination persist? All pesticide chemicals are subject to decomposition. The rate of decomposition, however, is dependent on both the chemical and the conditions to which it is exposed. In general, the organochlorine pesticides (chemicals such as DDT, chlordane, dieldrin, and lindane) persist longer than the other chemical types. Phosphate insecticides and carbomate and aliphatic acid herbicides are relatively short-lived. They will disappear from the soil environment in a matter of weeks. Most of the other herbicides tend to persist in the soil for a matter of months. Actually, disappearance of chemicals from the environment follows a logarithmic relationship to time. In other words, they behave much as radioactive decay. The concentration decreases quite rapidly initially, and then the rate decreases with time and final disappearance may require a considerable length of time.

The average concentration of DDT in fatty tissue of humans in the United States in 1970 was 5.14 ppm. It is estimated that if the use of DDT was completely curtailed, DDT concentration would decrease to 2.23 ppm in 1986 and to 0.36 ppm in 2022. These figures indicate that DDT would persist in the fatty tissue of humans for many years. For comparison, it is estimated that the average concentration would be 2.60 ppm in 1986 and 1.03 ppm in 2022 if the present rate of DDT use was continued. Thus, there would be a significant decrease in DDT in human bodies even if present use of DDT was continued. The reason for the decrease is that much of the DDT in our body now is the result of much higher uses of DDT in earlier years. The 1970 use of DDT was approximately one-seventh of the amount used in the United States in 1966 (peak year of DDT use). DDT represents one of the most persistent pesticides, and so the above figures represent estimates of the worst condition for insecticide persistence.

Some of the methods for food production have resulted in detrimental effects on the environment. Some of these practices can be altered with resultant beneficial effects to the environment. Increase in human population, however, may preclude reversal of many of these practices. As the population increases, there will be an increased demand for food production. The demand for increased food production may pressure individuals to develop practices which are based on increased productivity without regard to environmental effects. As population demand and maximum food production approach each other, the following chain of events often occurs. Population increase → overexploitation → less productivity → disaster. The degree to which we can reverse the negative input that man has made into the environment is to an extent dependent upon the pressures resulting from population size and mode of life.

SUMMARY

Some alterations on the earth by man's activities are reversible while others are either irreversible or very slowly reversible, sometimes requiring special efforts to bring about the change. Oxygen-demanding wastes and disease-causing organisms tend to disappear from water bodies if their input is terminated. This is especially true in shallow, running waters. Synthetic organic chemicals will become decomposed at a rate dependent upon the nature of the chemical and conditions under which it occurs. Inorganic chemicals and heavy metals added to the water are only removed with considerable effort. Air becomes relatively free from pollutants in a relatively short time; however, some of the damage to plants and animals by air pollution may not be reversible depending upon the extent of injury. Increased population and "high standards" of living cause pressure for increased energy consumption and productivity which make reversing of many of our present practices difficult to achieve.

DISCUSSION QUESTIONS

1 What types of water pollutants are generally removed from the city water by treatment prior to delivery and which types of pollutants are not?
2 Assume a stream flows through a city serving as both the water supply to the city and the water body into which sewage water receiving secondary treatment is discharged. What differences would you expect if you examined the water before it entered the city and after it left the city? What steps would be required to make the sewage effluent the same as the intake quality?
3 Do you ever expect the bison to roam the prairies as they did centuries ago? Why?

Section Three

Observing and Measuring Ecological Processes

The previous section has shown the intricate dependence of biological processes and species upon each other, from which it follows that human intervention in the environment can seriously alter delicate balances of the ecology. This being so, a decision maker who takes actions affecting the ecosystem needs some measures of the consequence of his decisions if environmental quality is to be preserved.

Federal policy now requires private industry to meet quality standards and environmental controls. In meeting these standards, private executives become engaged in a new form of decision process which seeks to anticipate future ecological impacts. Private executives are involved in environmental administration because they must attempt to foresee and justify whether their product designs will meet rigorous quality standards, at what cost, and whether side effects may entail more damaging consequences than those they were trying to remedy, as in the case of NTA detergents, or in auto emissions with the substitution of oxides of nitrogen for hydrocarbons.

Environmental decisions are, then, pervasive in their consequences,

167

from which substantial costs or liabilities can ensue. Hence the decisions deserve to be made with as much information, skill, and understanding as can be brought to bear upon them. The purpose of Section Three is to describe the skills and methodologies for improving predictability and understanding in environmental decision making.

The flow of materials in the industrial process, and how it relates to the ecosystem, is described in Chapter 10. The following chapter then traces the dispersion of these materials through the natural cycles in the environment. These two chapters together, then, give some basis for estimating the possible biological consequences of a decision.

We next wish to relate these biological consequences to human activity, and this is done in Chapter 12 by developing a simulated market to reflect environmental costs. Chapter 13 continues the environmental cost analysis by showing various methods of treating costs in theory and practice. Once costs are known, they need to be related to human decisions, and this is the topic of Chapter 14, where the methods for dealing with uncertainty are discussed. Since costs and benefits accrue in varying degree to different groups, some tradeoff of costs versus benefits among various beneficiaries becomes the crux of decision; and this is treated in Chapter 15.

All these several techniques are integrated in an environmental impact analysis, Chapter 16, to arrive at a net assessment of the quantitative and qualitative judgments in a decision. One perceives in this chapter that quantitative measures of environmental impact do assist in the predictability of final effects, but some of the effects themselves can only be judged qualitatively, for example, what is the value of a species? This leads to a discussion, in Chapter 17, of issues which arise in setting criteria for decision making, and at what point quantitative decision criteria shift to social choice making, which is more value-oriented.

The entire section is intended, in the end, to show the range of techniques available to enlighten environmental decision making, together with an indication of the possibilities and limitations of the techniques to the executive in measuring environmental impact and quality.

Chapter 10

Materials Balance

Materials balance accounts for the flow of materials through a process in a format that makes the inputs, transforms, and outputs identifiable and traceable. The process may be any of a wide variety of technical or natural processes. For example, engineers customarily use the concept to examine the flow of materials in a steel mill or oil refinery. The analysis identifies the inputs of iron ore, scrap iron, limestone, coal, oxygen, electric power, etc., in relation to the yield of pig iron, ingot steel, blooms, billets, finished shapes, slag, fly-ash, or air pollutants.[1] Materials balance is also a way of studying the productivity of a dairy feedlot in agriculture in terms of the input of forage and grains, water, salt; and the output in milk, or dairy, products and animal wastes. The metabolism of cities, discussed in Chapter 2, was a materials-balance approach. The nitrogen cycle, or the hydrological cycle, in ecosystems is likewise a form of materials balance.

Material flow may be a relatively simple, closed system—for

[1]C. S. Tsao and R. H. Day, "Process Analysis Model of Steel Industry," *Management Science,* vol. 17, no. 10, June 1971, pp. B588ff.

example, the circulation of freon in an air conditioner. Or they may be highly complex, open systems such as the solar energy system, in which case they become descriptive of the total environment because their flows and transformations are so ramified. The simpler the materials flow, as in the industrial case, the more understandably and completely it can be described and modeled quantitatively. The more complex and open the system, the more care must be taken in identifying variable inputs and modeling the system. The materials balances we are concerned with in the environment are of the complex and open order; and therefore, we shall have to proceed descriptively from the simpler to the more complex, in the hope that we can begin to account for the main elements of material flows in human ecologies as they interact with natural ecosystems. This interaction is ultimately the crux of the entire environmental problem, for we are trying to assess the degree to which humanly originated material processes alter the life cycles in the natural systems.

The purpose of materials balance then, in the environmental sense, is to trace the interaction of human processes upon the natural systems. A second noteworthy aspect of materials balance is that it is an accounting concept, which tries to account for the origin, flow, use, and final resting place of all the materials in a process. Materials balance is, therefore, a technical accounting system, in the same sense that a business has a financial accounting system. As with any form of accounting, the accounts in some sense are expected to balance. Financial accounts balance because the money spent by the business should equal the money received, if only for fiduciary reasons. In technical or natural processes, the materials outputs are equal to the materials inputs because of the law of the conservation of matter; that is, matter cannot be destroyed, but may only be transformed into energy or other molecular structures. Materials-balance studies attempt to trace the significant energy or molecular transformations.

The organization of this chapter will develop the concept of materials balance by covering the following topics:

1   Materials balance and accountability
2   Illustrations of materials balance
        a   Food consumption
        b   Food processing
        c   Agriculture
        d   Solid waste
        e   Energy conversion
3   General flow of services and materials

MATERIALS BALANCE AND ACCOUNTABILITY

The fact that materials balance is a form of accounting makes it more than a technical methodology; it is also an administrative means for establishing environmental accountability. We are interested, as environmental administrators, in improving the quality of our surroundings. A fundamental principle of administration is to establish accountability for the acts of all of those who affect the process you are trying to manage. Materials balance is such a device, but to use it we must understand the processes in detail, which is a monumental task in dealing with the ecosystem. To simplify the task, we will deal at first mainly with the summary or broad accounts, because the essence of accountability does not necessarily lie in the detail of the data but in the explanations or reasons for changes in the environment.

What does it mean to be accountable? For public bodies or environmental administrators, public or private, to be accountable means to give explanations for actions taken, and to be responsible for the consequences of those actions. It is not enough to submit a report of materials or financial accounts. The public has a right to know why the accounts reveal, for example, that there are more pathogens in the water supply to the detriment of the public health. Then the citizens are entitled to know what was the process or flow of materials to cause the bacteria to increase.

Still, it is not enough that the materials accounts record the quality of the environment, or that the administrator explain them; they should also be capable of independent evaluation, whether in the form of scientific inquiry or public audit. The public or private administrator, who is an actor in the piece, has difficulty being an evaluator of himself. Therefore, accounts and reasons should be capable of independent review. This is particularly true in dealing with goods or services provided to the public by government, when there is no independent market data to coroborate value.[2] For such public goods, the biggest problem is finding an acceptable measure of performance and benefit. We shall see that there are enough difficulties with benefit-cost analysis to make independent evaluation highly desirable.

An independent evaluation of environmental decisions is possible by the method of materials-balance accounting. Kneese, Ayres, and d'Arge have developed an input-output model of materials flows based upon the

---

[2]L. R. Smith and D. C. Hague, *The Dilemma of Accountability in Modern Government*, Carnegie Corporation and Macmillan, New York, 1971, proceedings of the Ditchely Park conference, pp. 317, 357, and 376.

theoretical model of Leon Walras, which was more recently implemented by Wassily Leontieff. The materials-balance model relates resource services to product output and final demand. Sets of equations relate prices of intermediate goods to the prices of basic resources, which also include prices for utilizing the natural environment's scarce waste assimilative capacity.

The interdependency of the materials prices describes, quantitatively, an exchange system, which is connected to physical materials flows by regarding the environment as the source of material inputs into the production process and final consumption as emitting output into the environment. The flows to and from the environment are equal, since mass is conserved, and the system is in physical balance.

Since the amount of materials returned to the environment must approximately equal the amount taken from it, in a closed economic exchange, the tonnage of residual disposals exceeds that of basic materials process in the production system. These tonnages of residuals disposed into the environment result in external costs in the form of air, water, or land pollution. Traditionally these external costs have been treated as minor anomalies in an otherwise smooth exchange system, but their magnitude is such that they cannot continue to be dismissed so easily. The residuals and external costs are so inherent in the economic process of highly developed nations that it becomes a function of government to integrate these external costs into the exchange system in order to have an efficient resource allocation.[3]

ILLUSTRATIONS OF MATERIALS BALANCE

Human Food Consumption

The nature of one of these sectoral accounts, in a materials-balance calculation, may be illustrated by the estimated annual food consumption, with its attendant inputs and outputs. In the following table, we see that the human population is estimated to have consumed 50 million tons of food in 1963, made up mainly of carbohydrates with lesser amounts of fat and protein, or carbon, oxygen, hydrogen, and nitrogen. The nitrogen element, while small, is essential to protein formation, and thus the nitrogen cycle is one of the crucial characteristics of the environment for human beings.

Note next the enormous outputs from the human biological combus-

---

[3]See Allen V. Kneese and Ralph C. d'Arge, *Pervasive External Costs and the Response of Society*, Joint Economic Committee, U.S. Congress, *An Analysis and Evaluation of Public Expenditures: The PPB System*, 91st Cong., 1st Sess., Washington, 1969, pp. 87–91.

Figure 10-1 Hypothetical Materials Balance for Humans, 1963
(Dry Weight $\times$ 10^6 Tons)

	Carbon	Oxygen	Hydrogen	Nitrogen	Total
Food inputs:					
Carbohydrate	14.74	16.30	1.99		33.12
Fat	7.36	1.11	1.11		9.63
Protein	3.92	1.67	0.51	1.16	7.25
Total	26.01	19.17	3.65	1.16	50.00
Outputs:					
Garbage	5.99*	3.12*	0.80*	0.09*	10.03
Respiration†	12.84*	9.79*	1.84*		24.46
Sewage‡	6.44*	6.06*	0.91*	0.98 + 0.06	14.39
Losses due to death§	0.46	0.12	0.06	0.06	0.70
Added biomass (population growth)	0.28	0.07	0.03	0.03	0.43

*Estimates based on plausible allocations of protein, carbohydrate, and fat.
†Not including oxygen from the air; proportions based on combustion of sugar ($C_6H_{10}O_5$) yielding CO_2 and H_2O.
‡Sewage solids estimated at 0.55 lb per capita per day.
§Assuming the population increase is 1.2% (of the biomass) per year, and the death rate is 2% (of the biomass).
(Source: Allen V. Kneese, Robert U. Ayers, Ralph C. d'Arge, *Economics and the Environment*, Resources for the Future, Johns Hopkins, Baltimore, 1970, p. 57.)

tion process, especially the 24 million tons of respiration, 10 million tons of garbage, and 14 million tons of sewage. There are also losses in biomass due to deaths, and additions due to births. The portion of the human output which goes into sewage interacts, in the environment, with the water supply. The materials input into the water supply from domestic sewage consists of about 40 percent minerals and 60 percent organic material, most of which is dissolved rather than suspended in water.[4]

The organic portion of waste in water is normally converted by bacterial action back into its basic elements of carbon, oxygen, hydrogen, and nitrogen by decomposition. The decomposition process normally is by microbial action using dissolved oxygen in the water. Thus the degradable organic materials in household waste impose a demand on the dissolved oxygen in the waters by which they have been received. This dissolved oxygen requirement is usually measured in terms of the five-day biochemical oxygen demand (BOD_5) at a temperature standard of 20 degrees centigrade. BOD_5 may be thought of as a characteristic of water, the amount of dissolved oxygen which is required in decomposing one gram of organic material. In this sense, BOD_5 is a measure of the degree to which organic residuals can be removed from the water.

[4]G. M. Fair and J. C. Geyer, *Water Supply and Waste Disposal*, John Wiley and Sons Inc., New York, 1956, p. 563.

When too much organic material is deposited in the water source so as to exceed the available dissolved oxygen, the process becomes *anaerobic*, that is, active in the absence of free oxygen. Microorganisms then cause chemical decomposition in the absence of oxygen (anaerobic), which results in the characteristic stench associated with polluted water. The absence of oxygen causes fish kills which produce additional nutrients for algal growth, and the body of water ages, or eutrophication takes place. To prevent degradation of a water source, then, the organic effluents discharged into it by human society cannot exceed the available dissolved oxygen measured by the equivalent biochemical oxygen demand, if biologic equilibrium is to be maintained.

One form of materials balance at the interface between human and natural processes, then, is the flow of organic substances from human society into ecosystems. If the human organic wastes are discharged at a rate which exceeds the decomposition rate in the ecosystem, the consequence is death to marine life. The materials-balance accounts for the human food consumption sector, then, are the metabolism requirements and waste discharge rates of the human ecology balanced against the decomposition rates of the receiving ecosystems.

Food Processing

The wastes disposed into the environment as a result of human food consumption are but a small part of the wasteload accounted for by all sectors of the economy. In addition to food consumption, other final products used by consumers are soft goods, like textiles and household supplies, and durable goods such as automobiles and appliances. In addition, the materials-balance accounts would need to cover sectors such as construction, mining, transportation, utilities, wholesale and retail trade, finance, services, government, and more than twenty major categories of manufacturing. One of these categories of manufacturing, accountable for less than 10 percent of all industry, is food processing, and one of the smaller elements of the food-processing sectors is beet sugar manufacturing. The materials-balance accounts for beet sugar processing would show a large input of water relative to the sugar beet input, and a small output of refined sugar compared to a large output of waste.

Sugar processing is a heavy user of water. Gross water usage varies considerably based upon design and operation of the plant, but the range of water use is from 2,000 to 8,600 gallons of water per ton of beets, with an average of 4,100 gallons per ton. The largest factor responsible for this variation in usage is in the means for transporting and washing beets, particularly in flume and washer design. These huge water withdrawals

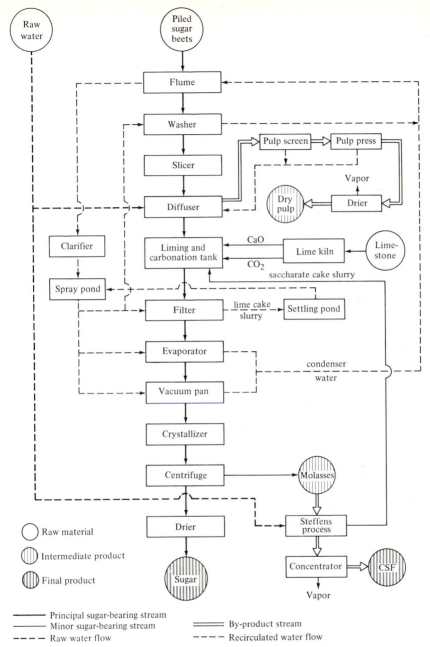

Figure 10-2 Residuals from production and consumption. *(Source: Allen V. Kneese, Robert U. Ayres, Ralph C. d'Arge, Economics and the Environment, Resources for the Future, Johns Hopkins Press, Baltimore, 1970, p. 47.)*

also mean that there is a large water disposal after processing; and the wasteload from sugar beets, being largely organic carbohydrates, represents a very high biochemical oxygen demand (BOD). The BOD load coming from this small part of the food industry is almost two-thirds as large as the residuals from all municipalities in the entire United States.[5]

The materials flow process in a beet sugar plant is illustrated in Figure 10-2, which shows the main processes to be intake through the flume, washing, slicing, diffusing, liming, filtrating, condensing, and crystalizing the sugar. The water consumption and contribution to the BOD wasteload for these processes is shown in Figure 10-3.[6]

Considerable reductions in the wasteload in beet sugar processing are possible by water recirculation, substituting drier for wetter processes, and other technical changes. While technical changes have been made in the industry, there has been no strong need nor concerted effort to reduce the water intake or effluents. The result is that the gross water usage has not been greatly altered, and the BOD wasteload is still high. The reason is, of course, that water is a cheap resource. An external stimulus, such as an effluent charge or effluent standard, may induce the further installation of techniques by the industry itself to eliminate some 70 percent of the BOD now contained in waste water from factories which use no recirculation, or treatment, processes. The Federal Water Quality Agency, in cooperation with local governments, is now carrying out a $4 billion program to reduce municipal wastes (including industrial wastes handled by municipal systems) by installing new treatment plants, which amounts to a public subsidy for industrial waste treatment. This approach should be coupled with economical opportunities in industry to

[5]George O. G. Lof and Allen V. Kneese, *The Economics of Water Utilization in the Sugar Beet Industry RFF,* Johns Hopkins, Baltimore, 1968, pp. 3, 4, and 45.
[6]Ibid, p. 22.

Figure 10-3
(Per Ton of Beets Sliced)

	Gallons of waste water flow	Pounds of BOD
Flume water	2,600	4.5
Screen water	640	3.0
Press water	180	2.6
Silo drainage	210	12.3
Lime cake slurry	90	6.5
Condenser water	2,000	0.7
Steffens waste	120	10.4
Total	5,840	40.0

reduce waste discharge by in-process changes and recirculation.[7] The industrial processor has considerable capability to reduce wastes cheaply through proper incentives.

Another industry which is a heavy user of water is pulp and paper processing. The water intake per ton of pulp was estimated at 57,000 gallons by the National Council for Stream Improvement, New York (1959). Of this the consumptive use in pulp and papermaking was 3,300 gallons per ton, with the residual 53,700 gallons disposed of in stream beds. This effluent contained a wasteload of 68 pounds of BOD per ton of paper.[8]

Here are examples of two industries, then, whose wasteloads range from 40 to 68 pounds of BOD per ton of usable product produced. Obviously the BOD effects on water quality are enormous when the tonnage of all outputs in all industries is taken into account. We shall not attempt so exhaustive a review at this point, because the implications are clear. Industrial output places very heavy demands upon water sources for pure water intake and discharges large tonnages of effluents which pollute the streams. The costs of such effluents have generally been subsidized by public treatment facilities, but industry itself is able to economize on water usage by putting in the appropriate technical improvements which maximize its return on investment. These costs to industry, ranging from perhaps 0.1 to 3 percent of production costs, depend upon type of treatment.[9]

Agriculture

Agricultural residuals are derived from pesticides, fertilizers, animal wastes, plant fibers, or mechanical outputs, which, as residuals, may take the form of air pollution, water pollution, or soil wastes. The pesticides, which are relatively smaller in tonnage of wasteload, are nevertheless of great significance because of their potential toxicity to other species, and because they tend to become concentrated during successive ingestions in the food chain. For example, soil containing 1 unit of insecticide per gram will result in earthworms, living in the soil, containing 10 to 40 units of insecticide per gram; and in woodcocks feeding on earthworms, the insecticide level will rise to around 200 units per gram.[10] This tendency of pesticides to concentrate in the tissue of animals higher in the food chain, of course, is what causes carnivores to be most subject to biological hazard, for example, the eagle being affected by DDT.

[7]Ibid., pp. 86 and 106.
[8]Allen V. Kneese and Stephen C. Smith, *Water Research, RFF,* Johns Hopkins Press, Baltimore, 1966, p. 146.
[9]Ibid., pp. 150, 168–170.
[10]Barry Commoner, *Science and Survival,* The Viking Press, Inc., New York, 1966, p. 26.

Another important waste disposal problem in agriculture is that of animal wastes. The wastes from a cow, measured in BOD, for example, are 6 times greater than that of a human being. In terms of nitrogen residues, a cow accounts for 16 times as much as a human.[11] Nitrogen is also deposited in the soil by fertilizers. The consequence is that, in an area with high animal populations plus heavy fertilizer applications for crop production, the nitrates in the water table may become quite concentrated. Moreover, the nitrates may accumulate in the water table over many years, as has happened in the Santa Ana River watershed on the eastern edge of the Los Angeles coastal plain.

Until recently, the Santa Ana River basin was mainly devoted to agricultural production, namely citrus fruits and livestock. More recently the area has become urbanized with fairly high densities of population in Orange County and in Riverside County. The Santa Ana River riverbed itself is usually dry, except during a few months of the winter rainy season; but the underground water table provides a substantial reservoir supplied by melting snow from the mountains or by water recycling, particularly from irrigation. The underground rock strata forming the reservoir comes to the surface at several points, where there are both natural and artificial dams. One such dam is the Prado Dam which has become a convenient point for measuring water quality, as well as a legal line of defense since it separates one urban area from another. One of the issues, besides the normal one of water rights, is the rising nitrate concentrations in the water table. The consequence has been a certain amount of research as to the origin and causes of the nitrate concentrations; and this has proved to be an interesting case because, being in an arid region with rather small quantities of water recharge or flushing of the aquifers (strata), the water usage cycle is a relatively closed system. Thus one can observe it in a laboratory sense more easily than many streams with high water flows.

The safe level of nitrates in drinking water has been set at 45 ppm. Consumption of water or food containing more than 45 ppm of nitrates can lead to a disease called methemoglobinemia which causes a depletion of oxygen in the blood stream of infants. Dr. Parker Pratt, professor of soil science at the University of California, Riverside, analyzed the question of the contribution to nitrates in the underground water of the Upper Santa Ana from fertilizers, dairy wastes, municipal and industrial sources. A partial report of findings indicates that some groundwater contains high levels of nitrates often exceeding what is normally considered safe for human consumption. In the dairy area, the top layer of

---

[11] *Water Research*, op. cit., p. 483.

underground water had from 63 to 945 ppm of nitrate, while waters from deep wells had from 6 to 44 ppm of nitrate. The situation of shallow wells with undesirable levels of nitrate, and deep wells of excellent quality, may exist in the basin for an indefinite period. Mixing of the top layer with the deeper water in the *aquifer* (underground reservoir) is a slow process.

Dr. Pratt also studied the process by which nitrates leach through the soil and arrive at the water table. Nitrates in the upper basin of the Santa Ana River take about twenty to fifty years to reach the water table depending on the depth to the water table and other factors. Some wells have nitrates from citrus fertilizer used twenty to forty years ago.

The total nitrogen in the basin is about 25,000 tons every year. Municipal wastes account for 3,900 tons; industrial wastes, 81 tons; animal wastes, 4,500 tons; fertilizers, 8,500 tons; water supplies, 5,100 tons; and rainfall, 4,600 tons.

Fertilizers are distributed over a large amount of land, so that their effects are less immediate. Animal wastes tend to be highly concentrated in local areas and have a direct, measurable impact on the water supplies. This highly concentrated source of waste creates a hazard to water supplies and ultimately human, plant, and animal health.

> There are several ways to reduce the nitrates that find their way into water supplies. We must increase, for example, the efficiency by which crops recycle nitrogen that is added to the soil. This leaves less nitrates to be removed from the soil to the groundwater.
>
> "We must also find ways to increase the efficiency of the fertilizer, so that we use less. We might find that slow-release fertilizers are the answer. In any event, an answer must be found."
>
> The alternative is pollution of a vital natural resource—underground water supplies—that can take hundreds, if not thousands of years to cleanse themselves.[12]

This example suggests that, with growing demand for meat, dairy, and poultry products by our society, animal production units have been increased quantitatively to the point where waste management and disposal are critical environmental problems in many areas. The escape of animal waste materials, and products of decomposition of waste materials, create serious pollution of air and water. Whether the wastes are decomposed in soils, in various digestion processes, or by burning, the mineral elements remain as potential pollutants.

Thus, to quantify the impacts of both animal and crop production units on environmental quality, we need to trace the input materials

[12]University of California, *On Campus*, June 1971, pp. 2–3.

through the systems to their ultimate fate into air, water, and land. Materials balances need to be made to identify the pathways and end products so that methods of recycling and reducing adverse effects can be determined.

Crop or animal production units, where input records and crop removal records have been kept during the past ten to twenty years, can be sampled to determine (1) accumulation in the soil, (2) the soluble materials being transmitted to the groundwater, and (3) the transit time of such materials. Transit times are measurable from water retention characteristics of soils and water balance and leaching fraction data. Sampling of soils to the 30-meter depth or to the water table, if it encountered above this depth, can be done using a power-driven bucket auger.

A materials balance on an elemental basis with emphasis on nitrogen and soluble materials could, for example, be made on a dairy production unit where the waste is put on irrigated land. Elemental inputs would be determined by analysis of feeds, water, and salts consumed. Removal in milk and meat could be determined and the amount and composition of waste measured. The loss of nitrogen to the atmosphere by ammonia volatilization from manures is measurable, and some estimate of its distribution in the atmosphere and reabsorption on land and water surfaces can be made. The nitrogen, other nutrient elements, and soluble salts that go onto land surfaces can also be measured; and the quantities that move to the water table are recycled into feed crops and accumulate in soils can be determined.

Techniques developed by the materials balance on a dairy unit are applicable to other animal production units. The techniques could also be applied to animal production units where aerobic digestion of liquid and/or solid waste is used as an alternate disposal procedure or as a pretreatment before land disposal.

Although part of animal wastes are disposed in water, the largest portion of all agricultural residuals are solid wastes. Solid wastes represent the largest bulk and a major share of the tonnage of all forms of residuals. Fortunately their disposal represents less of an ecological problem than air or water pollutants, mainly because there is less dispersion into the environment. The difficulties with solid waste disposal are largely quantity, sanitation, and cost.

Materials Balance—Solid Waste Example

A materials-balance model for solid waste would have to start with all the products of industrial production in the entire economy as the inputs into the solid waste system. Because all products become junk eventually, the

Figure 10-4   Quantitative Estimates of Solid Waste Production

Types of waste	Annual quantity in million tons		
	1967	1985	2000
Municipal wastes			
Residential	8.9	16.1	25.9
Commercial	9.7	15.7	22.7
Demolition	3.0	4.4	5.9
Special	1.3	2.0	2.7
Subtotal	22.9	38.2	57.2
Agricultural wastes			
Animal manure	21.8	28.5	32.7
Fruit and nut crop	2.4	3.6	3.9
Field and row crop	10.7	13.8	15.7
Subtotal	34.9	45.9	52.3
Industrial Wastes			
Food processing	2.1	3.7	6.3
Lumber industry	8.0	2.7	1.0
Chemical and petroleum refining	0.5	0.5	0.8
Manufacturing	3.1	4.8	7.0
Subtotal	13.7	11.7	15.1
Total	71.5	95.8	124.6

question is one of aging the stock of durables until their salvage time. In a sense then, the national product by industrial origin represents the input portion to a set of accounts on solid materials. The output is the solid waste disposal volume. Obviously these inputs and outputs represent enormous quantities and to detail them would entail a reconstruction of the national product accounts. We can visualize a portion of the output side of the accounts, as an example, by looking at the estimates of the Department of Public Health on the solid wastes for the State of California, which represents roughly one-tenth of the national economy.[13]

Residential waste consists of refuse, garbage, rubbish, cans, bottles, paper, and packaging. Commercial waste includes tires, cans, cardboard boxes, wastes of restaurants and wholesale and retail stores. By weight, nearly half of all municipal wastes are paper, about 20 percent garden trimmings, 7 percent metals (mostly ferrous), and the balance is plastics, textiles, leather, and rubber.

The common form of disposal for solid waste is sanitary landfill,

[13]Report of Panel on Solid Waste Management, Assembly Science and Technology Advisory Committee, Sacramento, Calif. 1971, p. 23.

which means compaction into unused land area, like a ravine or lowland, and covering the refuse with soil to prevent exposure to flies or rodents. Such landfills not only accommodate wastes, but they also form reclaimed level sites for parks or recreational areas. From the composition of the waste, noted above, it is clear that recycling of all residuals is not practical, especially garden trimmings and used remnants of textiles or plastic. However, the separation and recovery of paper and metals for recycling could be quite feasible with appropriate incentives. The concentration of metals in municipal refuse, for example, is higher than in many commercial ores. The handling, separation, and recycling of solid wastes is largely a cost problem. There have not been many significant technical innovations in solid waste handling nor do there appear to be major cost-saving methods on the horizon.

One way to encourage solid waste recycling is to alter the cost structure to favor the use of recycled materials rather than continue the current disincentives in legislation which discourage recycling. For example, producers of virgin materials such as minerals and timber have favorable depletion and depreciation allowances, while the producer of recycled material has none. Moreover transportation rates favor virgin material and discourage reclaimed materials. Product specifications in law and in practice often require new materials rather than recycled material. In short, disincentives now discourage recycling.

There is good reason for us to reconsider these disincentives to recycling for a number of reasons. The solid waste problem centers on three major concerns: (1) the depletion of resources now discarded in wastes, such as metals and paper; (2) the increasing costs of disposal to local governments; and (3) the increasing scarcity of landfill sites and the degradation of the environment which could ensue from the lack of adequate solid waste disposal means. The burning of solid waste is not a practical alternative to landfill, because of the air pollution which burning would bring. Pyrolysis, which is the heating and breakdown of material in an inert atmosphere, avoids the air pollution problem, but is high in cost. The comparative costs per ton of processing solid wastes are shown in Figure 10-5.[14]

These data show that there is no method competitive in cost with land disposal at present, and of course disposal itself is only part of the total cost. The general collection of municipal solid wastes, for example, with a rear-loading compactor truck, costs about $10 to $20 per ton, plus another $6 for transport to a disposal site, plus another $8 to $15 per ton if any manual separation is required.

Again one solution is the same as that suggested in the beet sugar

[14]Ibid.

Figure 10-5   (Cost in Dollars per Ton)

Landfill	$1 to 4
Incineration	4 to 10
Pyrolysis	15 to 23
Composting	5 to 7
Landspreading	1 to 3

industries, to put the effluent charges upon the polluter, in this case the householder, to pay for the disposal costs. The householder can exercise some control of the nature and volume of residential solid wastes, according to the incentives available. Would housewives be as receptive as they are to present packaging practices, for example, if they had to pay a throw-away charge to get rid of packaging materials? Residential solid waste is a case where the householder is creating an external, or social, cost, not accounted for in the normal pricing system. When the absorption of these costs is not contained in the market price or that of public goods, the consequence is an environmental cost, that of degradation.

While considerable reference has been made to examples of business failing to absorb its external, or social, costs, the same can be said of all of us as householders. One might argue, of course, that all householders taken together are the taxpaying public, and therefore there is no grave inequity in the incidence of taxation for failing to place a price on waste disposal. This is true, but aside from the question of tax equity is the issue of incentive or disincentive. The present system of making solid waste disposal a low-cost public good tends to encourage excesses in convenience and high waste burdens. A direct assessment of the social and environmental costs on the solid waste disposal would, contrary to present practice, discourage the householder from high solid waste burdens. In the end, it is the discouragement of excessive solid wastes, and the conservation of resources now disposed in waste, that would bring better balance with the ecosystem by placing less demands upon it, for either new resources or the absorption of such high volumes of residuals.

Energy Conversion

Most materials usage in the economy is dependent upon energy conversion to provide power for the process. Thus power conversion is a universal requirement in an industrial economy. Primary energy consumption in 1965 by type of usage is estimated to be about 32 percent industrial, 24 percent transportation, 21 percent household and commercial, and 20 percent utilities.[15]

[15]Allen V. Kneese, Robert U. Ayers, and Ralph C. d'Arge, *Economics and the Environment, RFF,* Johns Hopkins, Baltimore, 1970, p. 17.

In terms of quantities, the fuel sources or inputs into the energy conversion system consisted of 1.3 billion tons, with fuel being petroleum, coal, and natural gas, in that order of importance.

On the output side, the thermal power residuals consist of gaseous emissions in the form of stack gas consisting of carbon dioxide, sulfur dioxide, oxides of nitrogen, water vapor, hydrocarbons, fly-ash, and fine particulates. In addition there are the solid wastes in the form of bottom ash, dust, clinkers—some of which are disposed of in land and some in water. The gaseous emissions are of most significance in terms of health effects, because sulfur dioxide with particulates forms the London-type smog which is prevalent in the cities of the Eastern U.S., and the oxides of nitrogen plus hydrocarbons from stationary power sources add to similar vehicular emissions to create the Los Angeles-type of photochemical smog. The thermal power combustions residuals quantitatively in millions of tons are shown in Figure 10-6.[16]

If we now take these emissions from stationary power sources and add to them all the vehicular emissions for a particular area we may account for the total output of energy conversion into the atmosphere. As an example, the gaseous emissions in New York City for 1965 are seen in the following table (Figure 10-7) in terms of tons per day:

Another way to view the total materials processing output for industry would be to add the energy conversion residuals to the materials residuals by type of industry. While this would be a substantial statistical task, some idea of the composition of gaseous emissions, in addition to energy residuals, is suggested by the data which show gaseous emission to range from 0.25 to 3 percent of the material processed.[17]

The typical industrial process can be expected to emit aerosols in the form of dust, mist, fumes, gases, and vapors of the order of a fraction of 1 to 3 percent of the weight of the material input; and the nature of the

[16]Ibid., p. 21.
[17]Ibid., p. 39.

Figure 10-6

	Tons (millions)
Carbon dioxide	807
Water vapor	231
Sulfur dioxide	13.6
Ash	25
Oxides of nitrogen	3.7
Particulates	2.4

Figure 10-7   Gaseous Emissions in New York City, 1964

Source	Gaseous residual (in tons per day)				
	Carbon monoxide (CO)	Hydro- carbons (HC)	Sulfur dioxide (SO_2)	Oxides of nitrogen (NO_x)	Particu- lates
Stationary sources:					
Electric power	1	4	754	254	35
Industrial	2	2	140	54	26
Commercial, institutions and					
large apartments	76	21	678	212	37
Small residential	4	4	67	78	24
Refuse combustion	291	120	6	7	75
Miscellaneous*	750	31	n.a.	705	7
Motor vehicles	3,784	695	14	162	22
Total	4,908	877	1,659	1,472	226

Source: Tri-State Transportation Commission, "Electric Power and Fuel Consumption. 1965–1985," New York. July 1967.
    *Mainly gasoline marketing, commercial dry-cleaning, etc.

emissions are, of course, derived from the chemical composition of the inputs.

GENERAL FLOW OF SERVICES AND MATERIALS

We have now reviewed illustrations of specific materials flow examples in human food consumption—food processing, agriculture, industry, and energy conversion—which provide some conception of the methodology by which it would be possible to trace the flow of materials through the entire economy. Economics sometimes refers to the production process as creating time, place, and form utility. The inputs to the economic system are fuels, foods, and raw materials. These materials are processed into different form utilities for a time, but they are never really "consumed" in the sense of being used up. The law of conservation of matter prevents such obliteration. Instead, the materials are held in a temporary form utility by which they render a service, and then they are transformed into a higher state of fabrication or are discharged into the environment as waste.

From an abstract, ideal point of view, we can conceive of the economy as not consisting of materials at all but merely consisting of a flow of services rendered by temporary states of form utility. Thus consumption consists of the service of a ride to work, rather than a car, of recharging the human combustion process, rather than a lump of sugar. What satisfies our wants are the ride and the energy recharge, not the car

Figure 10-8   Weight of Basic Materials Production in the United States plus Net Imports, 1965

(In Millions of Tons)

Material	1965
Agricultural fishery, wildlife forest) products:	
Food and fiber:	
Crops	364
Livestock and dairy	23.5
Fishery:	2
Forestry products (85% dry wt. basis):	
Sawlogs	120
Pulpwood	56
Other	42
Total	607.5
Mineral fuels:	1,448
Other minerals:	
Iron ore	245
Other metal ores	191
Other nonmetals	149
Total	585
Grand total	2,641

Source: R. U. Ayres and A. V. Kneese, "Environmental Pollution," in *Federal Programs for the Development of Human Resources,* a compendium of papers submitted to the Subcommittee on Economic Progress of the Joint Economic Committee, Congress of the United States, vol. 2, 1968.

or the sugar. Then the important consideration is that the want of a ride and a recharge be satisfied and yet remain consistent with the balance of the whole system, which means the materials balance of the economy and of ecosystems. If we wished to look at the economy in this way, we would trace first the service and then the basic materials through the various states of fabrication and usage. The initial input would be that of basic materials, which is illustrated in Figure 10-8.[18]

Kneese and d'Arge have suggested a schematic diagram,[19] as well as a mathematical model, for tracing the materials flow through the economy (see Figure 10-9). The schematic which is attached depicts the interrelations of many of the processes previously illustrated. Among the principal residual emissions in the diagram are elements of the gaseous emissions,

[18]Ibid., p. 10.
[19]Ibid., p. 9.

sewage effluents, and solid wastes. About three-quarters of the active inputs, by weight, are eventually discharged into the atmosphere as carbon monoxide, carbon dioxide, and hydrogen combined with atmospheric oxygen as H_2O. The discharge of carbon dioxide may be considered harmless in the short run, because vegetation and oceans have a large capacity to reabsorb this gas. But a few scientists estimate that the continued combustion of fossil fuels at high rates could increase carbon dioxide in the atmosphere by as much as 25 to 50 percent by the year 2000, which could give rise to significant and adverse weather changes for the entire world.[20]

The remaining residuals in the form of gases or dry or suspended solids are potentially harmful in the short run by reason of their impact on ecological systems. We can avoid some, perhaps a large part, of these deleterious residuals by recycling and reuse. Material residuals do not necessarily have to be discharged into the environment at their present rates. The reasons that they are discharged at present rates is that the cost structure and incentives in society make it profitable, or least costly, to get rid of them in this way.

One solution to the waste problem is to reprice the residuals. The large volume of material residuals discharged into the environment represents a market failure. The market does not include the pricing of human utility (demand) for quality in the environment nor does it cover the external social costs of wastes. If a governmental agency developed the necessary information on materials-balance accounts and economic interdependencies, a coherent and consistent set of prices for environmental services could be determined.[21] The application of these environmental materials prices, to industry and householders, would change the cost structure of present services, and thus serve as an incentive to recycling and as a means of covering the social cost of residual disposal. An important element of research for such a government agency, in addition to developing and costing the materials-balance accounts, would be to estimate the demand function of individuals for various attributes of environmental quality. That is, how much social damage is perceived in the various forms of pollution, either as health effects or as environmental stress? One measure of these costs of environmental stress might be the avoidance costs which people assume in order to move away from undesirable environments. The relocation decisions which people make to move to cleaner air, out of traffic congestion, to more healthful locations are measures of the alternative costs which people are willing to assume to pay for a different environmental quality. The notable migration and

[20]Ibid., p. 11.
[21]Ibid., pp. 103 and 116.

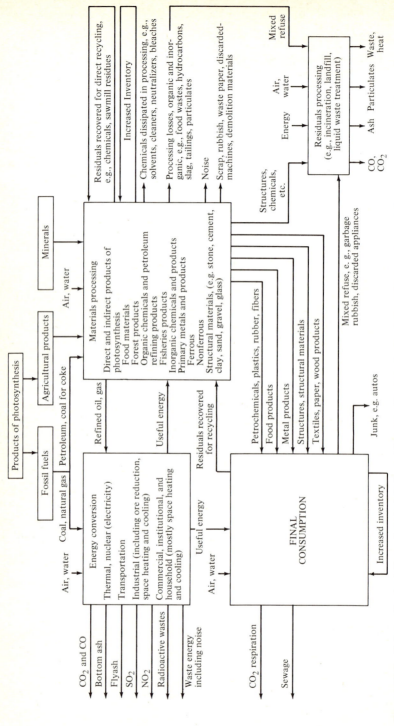

Figure 10-9 Schematic depiction of materials flow. (*Source: Kneese, Ayres, d'Arge, Economics and the Environment, p. 9.*)

188

relocation in recent years of families to Canada, Australia, Idaho, Guadaljara, or just "away from it all" are cost measures of the demand for environmental quality, as perhaps are the social drop-outs among youth. The evidences of environmental degradation and social stress are sufficient to raise the possibility of new Malthusian prophecies if we fail to understand and correct ecological problems. One of the ways to understand ecological problems is through materials-balance accounts and the repricing of residuals.

SUMMARY

Materials balance is a technical accounting model for tracing the inputs and the outputs of a production process. The residuals constitute an external cost to society, either a monetary cost for their disposal or a biological damage cost to the environment. Among the disposal or damage costs from human consumption or food processing is the biochemical oxygen demand needed for decomposition of organic materials in waterways. The depletion of oxygen in streams is a major cause of death to marine species.

Materials-balance models in agriculture show the buildup of nitrate levels in underground water from commercial fertilizers and from animal wastes. In areas of concentrated disposal, nitrate levels in water are known to exceed levels considered safe for human consumption.

Solid waste disposal accounts for the largest tonnage of residuals, and the lowest-cost disposal method has been sanitary landfill. With rising populations and wasteloads, disposal sites are becoming scarce; thought might well be given to incentives which reduce household wastes.

Energy conversion discharges large quantities of carbon monoxide, hydrocarbons, oxides of nitrogen, sulfur dioxide, and particulates into the atmosphere. These emissions in high levels of concentration are hazardous, particularly in the form of respiratory diseases.

In general the total flow of materials and residuals in the economy are of such volume and impact on the environment that their damage and cost effects need to be carefully assessed in making environmental decisions. Subsequent chapters will be concerned with the means for analyzing external costs which have been identified by materials-balance studies.

DISCUSSION QUESTIONS

1   How does materials balance differ from normal accounting? In what way are they related? What are the essential characteristics of accountability?

2 How does one identify and estimate external costs from materials-balance studies? Give examples.
3 What are the principal wastes in sewage and what environmental impact may these wastes have?
4 What are some of the problems and possibilities for recycling solid wastes?

PROBLEM

Take a city of the size and type in which you live and construct a materials-balance model for energy conversion, using data in the chapter for scaling and estimating the approximate residuals.

Chapter 11

Dispersion and Circulation of Materials in the Ecosystem

Materials balance represents the rate of transformation of resources and food from the natural ecosystem through the human production-consumption cycle, and the subsequent return of residual wastes from the human cycle to the environment. The interaction between the human and the natural ecologies, then, is one of transfer and exchange of materials. We have examined some of the human and industrial wastes, such as high BOD outputs from municipal sewage and food processing, nitrates from agriculture, and toxic residuals from industry. These outputs from the human production-consumption cycle become the inputs into the natural ecosystem.

The natural ecosystem has circulation cycles of its own, particularly the solar energy flow and the circulation of materials. When the residuals from human waste enter the natural materials cycles, a dispersion of human wastes circulates throughout the ecosystem. This dispersion of residuals, such as BOD, nitrates, and toxic wastes, results in a distribution of human wastes throughout the biosphere. Some of the consequences of this dispersion have been noted in earlier chapters, particularly the biological hazards to health, for both humans and species generally.

191

What we wish to examine at this stage is not so much the consequences of human waste in ecosystems, but rather the mechanics of dispersion and circulation of materials; for if we understand better the dispersion and circulation of materials, we may, as environmental administrators, have a better perception of the control points at which to exercise restraint upon the flow of deleterious residuals from the human to the natural ecosystem.

The basic ecological cycles were described in Chapter 7 with the objective of showing how they function and interrelate. In this chapter we will consider some of the same cycles again with a different objective of showing how they disperse residuals and materials throughout the ecosystem.

This chapter then builds on the previous discussion of biological processes and human effects from residuals to show more clearly how the dispersion of wastes takes place. Most importantly, it shows how the residuals enter the nutrient cycle, and eventually into human consumption. An outline of the main topics is shown below:

1 Energy and material flow
2 Solar energy conversion
3 The nutrient cycle—carbon
4 The sulfur cycle in aquatic ecosystems
5 The nitrogen cycle
6 Nutrient budgets in ecosystems
7 The hydrologic cycle and materials transport
8 Atmospheric dispersion of pollutants
9 Pollution as a worldwide problem

ENERGY AND MATERIALS FLOW

Ecologists historically have been concerned about the flow of energy and materials within the natural ecosystem itself. Indeed, the one-way flow of energy and the circulation of materials are two great principles of general ecology.[1] The one-way flow of energy is a universal phenomenon of nature evident in physics and biological systems. The first law of thermodynamics in physics, which is equally applicable in biology, states that energy may be transformed (for example, from light energy to food) but is neither created nor destroyed. The second law of thermodynamics, which is especially fundamental to biological processes, is that any energy transformation will always be associated with a degradation of energy from a more concentrated to a more dispersed form. Some energy is

[1]Eugene P. Odum, *Ecology*, Holt, Rinehart and Winston Inc., New York, 1963, p. 38.

always dispersed into unavailable heat energy, with the result that no transformation can be 100 percent efficient. Indeed, most biological processes range in efficiency of energy conversion from a fraction of 1 percent to an upper range of around 30 percent. The human organism, along with all its creations (like the internal combustion engine), also operates in these low energy conversion ranges.

The low efficiency with which species convert energy has important ecological implications, for it means that there must be a very high energy and nutrient input at the bottom of the food pyramid for each higher order to subsist. At the high end of the food pyramid are the carnivores who, for every 1 calorie in equivalent food they consume, require that perhaps 10,000 calories of energy be absorbed by phytoplankton or green plants *(autotrophs)*. Through every stage of the long food chain from green plants to carnivores, a dispersion of energy and a concentration of nutrient occur. As the nutrient concentrates, the trace pollutant elements from human residuals concentrate as well. A few parts per million of DDT in the oceans become absorbed by phytoplankton; concentrate successively through microscopic plankton, mollusks, and fish; and finally reach high concentrations in the flesh of predators. The second law of thermodynamics explains why an eagle's body has become a chemical soup. The chemical dispersion of pesticides and other residuals from human activity into the ecosystem is the concern of this chapter, to see how it happens and what the circulation processes are which bring it about.

Let us start with materials balance, or the flow of materials in the human production cycle discussed in the last chapter, to establish its relationship or interactions with the ecosystem. Figure 11-1 shows the interactions of natural and human ecologies. On the right half of the diagram is the materials-balance model represented by the withdrawal of food and resources from the ecosystem, their processing through industrial production, their delivery to human consumption, and the return of the human residuals to the biogeochemical materials base of the earth, in some cases in the form of pollution.

The natural energy-materials circulation is shown on the left half of the schematic, beginning with the one-way flow of energy from the sun. A small part of the solar energy is absorbed by the autotrophs which, with parent geochemical materials in the form of minerals, soil, air, and water, convert the energy into biological cellular structures. A portion of these plant structures return to the earth as organic, detritic materials which are, in fact, forms of stored solar energy. They become the organic base and compost from which trees and flora eventually form. Another part of the green plant cells of the autotrophs are ingested by the herbivores and become transformed from botanical to zoological species. The her-

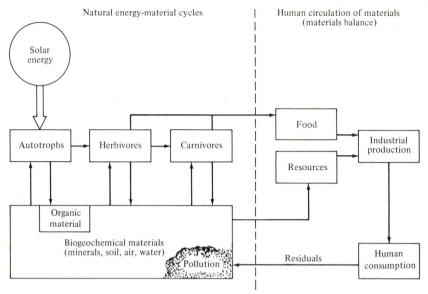

Figure 11-1   Interaction of natural and human ecologies.

bivores, in turn, form the food supply for carnivores. All these species return organic and inorganic residuals to the soil. Soil microorganisms decompose the organic materials, and thus the cycle can continue.

In addition to the so-called natural residuals coming back into the ecological base are the manufactured residuals from human productive activity. Many of these are inorganic materials, and some of the organic chemicals are not biodegradable in the soil (i.e., detergents, DDT, PCB/s, etc.). The consequence is that these persistent man-made chemicals become pollutants in the biogeochemical base and begin dispersing and recirculating with all the other materials in the food conversion processes. These persistent pollutants become part of the cellular structure of the autotrophs and heterotrophs and, if toxic, can cause organic malfunctions. For example, the effect of DDT in the diet of birds is to cause structural damage to the cellular structure of eggshells. Professors McFarland and Garrett, using an electronic microscope to examine eggshells of quail fed trace amounts of chlorinated hydrocarbons, have shown that DDT inhibits the formation of calcium in the middle shell layer, which normally provides the structural strength. Instead of a solid granular structure, the "weak shell" has open spaces in the middle layer, leaving it with a lacework, corrugated structure (see Figure 11-2). Pesticide dosages as low as 5 ppm, in the birds' diet for twenty-one days, caused measurable eggshell defects. Human body fat normally contains about 10 to 20 ppm of DDT, although DDT is not considered to be harmful to humans. Fish and birds may build up concentrations in the visceral fat reaching several thousand parts per million of pesticides.[2] These phenomena of concentration of chemical elements in the food chain are part of the energy conversion process in the ecosystem, and thus we will find it useful to trace how solar energy becomes converted into nutrients.

SOLAR ENERGY CONVERSION

If we are to trace the effects of human activity on ecosystems, we need to perceive the interactions in three grand cycles: (1) solar energy conversion, (2) the natural materials circulation, and (3) human materials balance and dispersion. The flow of solar energy is sometimes referred to as

[2]First Annual Report, Council on Environmental Quality. Op cit., p. 133.

 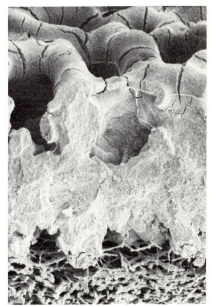

Figure 11-2   *(left)* Without DDT in its diet a laboratory-bred Japanese quail produces eggshells like this. Cross-section of shell has been vastly magnified by a scanning electron microscope. *(right)* With DDT added to the quail's diet, the middle layer of the shell deteriorates and the outer layer acquires corrugated look. Peregrines and brown pelicans in the wild are now laying eggshells with similar structural defects. (*Source:* UC News, *University of California, Berkley, Calif., Vol. 46, No 49 May 25, 1971.)*

energy dynamics, or the trophodynamics, of ecosystems. Raymond Lindeman was among the significant pioneers in developing the concept of trophodynamics from basic measurements on the conversion of solar energy in Cedar Bog Lake, Minnesota. His measurements show the gram calories per square centimeter per year (gcal/cm²/yr) of gross production in the standing crop of species in the lake. Lindeman traces the conversion of solar energy into the gross production of autotrophs, herbivores, and carnivores, together with their respiration and decomposition rates. The flow of solar energy is depicted in Figure 11-3.

Among the notable characteristics of solar energy flow is the very small portion (one-tenth of 1 percent in this case) of incoming radiation which is utilized by green plants. The largest portion of incoming radiation is reflected, and a small amount is dissipated as heat from the leaf surface temperature. The minute amount of light absorbed becomes incorporated with geochemical materials from soil or water in the cellular structure of the plant. The gross production of the autotrophs, in this case 111 gcal/cm²/yr, is used partly to maintain its own respiration (23 gcal/cm³/yr). The remaining net production is the standing crop of green plants, of which 80 percent is not utilized, a small portion is decomposed, and 15 gcal/cm²/yr becomes the nutrient for herbivores. Again, in the herbivore production, much of the energy is not utilized, a portion is used for respiratory functions, a fraction decomposes, and a small portion (3 gcal/cm²/yr) becomes the nutrient for carnivores. The carnivores make relatively heavy use of energy respiration. At the end of the cycle, the net production among carnivores is less than one/one-thousandth of the incoming solar radiation.

Other studies have shown that the production efficiency of organisms is higher in more southerly latitudes where more solar energy and moisture are available in the conversion process. A study of energy conversion at Silver Springs, Florida, showed that the conversion efficiency of autotrophs was an order of magnitude (10 times) higher at that latitude than at Cedar Bog Lake, Minnesota, and the conversion efficiency of herbivores was about twice as high.[3] The efficiency of carnivores was unchanged.

The latitude, or incident solar radiation, is the most significant variable in accounting for differences in primary production among ecosystems around the world. The pattern of world distribution of primary production varies, also, according to the available water and nutrients. The deserts are low in primary production due to the lack of water. The oceans which cover much of the earth are low in production due to lack of available mineral nutrients, which are at such submerged

[3]H. Odum, Ecological Monographs 27:55–112, 1957; also Edward J. Kormondy, *Concepts of Ecology,* Prentice-Hall, Englewood Cliffs, N.J., 1969, p. 26.

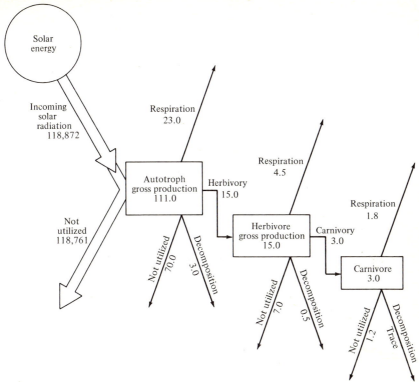

Figure 11-3   Conversion of solar energy in autotroph-based ecosystems in gramcolories per square centimeter per year (gcal/cm²/yr) *(Source: Edward J. Kormandy,* Concepts of Ecology, *Prentice-Hall, Englewood Cliffs, N.J., 1969, pp. 22–23. Data of R. Lindeman,* Ecology, *1942, 23.399–418. Energy Flow in Cedar Bog Lake, Minnesota.)*

depths that light energy is absorbed by the water before reaching them. These deficiencies of minerals, energy, or water are illustrations of Liebig's law of limiting factors in community populations. The "law of the minimum" of Justus Liebig (1840) states that the rate of growth of organisms is dependent upon the availability of the minimum materials or energy for their metabolism. The law may also be extended by recognizing that there are certain maximum levels of tolerance to species growth, particularly of toxic elements. E. P. Odum restates Liebig's law to convey that the growth of community populations depends upon a complex of conditions (energy, minerals, nutrients, water), and any one of these conditions which exceeds the range of tolerance, minimum or maximum, of an organism becomes a limiting factor.[4]

[4]E. P. Odum, op cit., p. 66.

The limiting factor in many ecosystems is becoming, increasingly, the residuals of human activity which exceed the tolerance limits of species in the ecosystem. Thus, the high BOD imposed by human wastes upon lakes, rivers, and estuaries becomes the limiting factor, by depleting the dissolved oxygen in water, which accounts for fish kills. The fact that we regularly kill twenty to forty million fish per year in United States waters is only one indication of the enormous scale of limiting factors which human activity imposes upon ecosystems.

An indication of the extraordinary range of productivity within ecosystems which exist because of limiting natural factors (deficiencies in energy, water, minerals, or other materials) can be illustrated by the tropical reedswamps. Tropical reedswamps and tropical perennial plants have among the highest productivity rates of any organisms on the planet; they are able to convert about 30,000 kilocalories of energy per square meter per year (kcal/m²/yr). By comparison, temperate zone perennials, conifers, and submerged sea plants have a productivity of about 12,000 kcal/m²/yr. Ocean phytoplankton have a productivity of 800 kcal/m²/yr and desert plants 400 kcal/m²/yr. Therefore, we can see there is as much as a 100-fold difference in primary productivity among plant species, depending upon the availability or deficiency of energy, minerals, or water.[5]

These differences in productivity are, of course, what account for the pattern of distribution of food resources. Since much of the earth's surface is arid, oceans, or lacking in solar energy, the fertile areas are proportionately small, mainly at the interfaces of the estuaries, coastal plains, or temperate savannas. These small fertile areas are where the human populations congregate in high-density communities, which means, also, that high-density waste materials are being dumped into the environment. So the human population perpetrates its pollution on the very areas which it is most dependent upon for primary production of nutrients. Here, the human chemicalization of the environment is most intense; and, when one considers the further concentration capacities of many species (an oyster, for example, being able to concentrate materials, including toxic ones like pesticides, up to 70,000 times the parts per million in the surrounding ocean), we can see that man, at the apex of the food chain, is destined to ingest the quintessence of his own residues.

THE NUTRIENT CYCLE—CARBON

The degree to which human residuals enter the ecosystems, and return for ingestion through the food chain, depends upon the circulation of materi-

[5]Kormondy, op. cit, pp. 19–20.

als in the nutrient cycles. Among the most basic of the nutrient cycles is that of carbon, since carbon is an essential building block in combustion processes, whether plant, animal, or mechanical. Carbon is found in the ecosystem in two large reservoirs, the atmosphere and the oceans (see Figures 7-1 and 7-2). The concentration of carbon dioxide is only about 0.03 to 0.04 percent of the total atmosphere. The ocean is estimated to contain 50 times as much carbon as the air, mostly in the form of dissolved carbon dioxide (CO_2) which forms carbonic acid (H_2CO_3). The CO_2 enters the oceans from the atmosphere through precipitation, or, since all the reactions are reversible, it may be released to the air if there is a depletion in the concentration of atmospheric CO_2. The regulatory mechanism which controls the balance of atmospheric CO_2 to aquatic CO_2 is the alkalinity of the water or the CO_2 concentrations in the air.

The basic cycle of carbon, as a nutrient to living organisms, originates in the atmospheric reservoir and moves to producer and then to consumer organisms. The autotrophic organisms fix carbon in the photosynthesis in immense amounts, as much as 4×10^{13} to 9×10^{13} kgram annually, which means, of course, that very large transfers take place among air, ocean, and organisms.[6] The carbon is returned to the atmosphere by the respiration (CO_2) of producer and consumer organisms and by decomposers while processing the remains of other trophic levels. The deposition of plant material also results in the storage of carbon in peat, coal, oil, and carbonate rocks. Carbon is released from these forms, either through combustion or through weathering and dissolution. Added to these natural sources of carbon are the large organic wasteloads from municipal sewage and agricultural wastes, which are also high in carbon compounds.

THE SULFUR CYCLE IN AQUATIC ECOSYSTEMS

A second important nutrient, especially in aquatic environments, is sulfur, which is reduced by autotrophic plants and incorporated into amino acids for protein synthesis. The sulfur cycle also is an interesting example of the exchange of materials among geological, aquatic, and atmospheric regimes. The available form of sulfur in water is generally an ion SO_4^{--}, sulfate. Upon decomposition of plants and animals by heterotrophic microorganisms, hydrogen sulfide (H_2S) is released, and this becomes part of the deposition in sediments.[7] There, in the slow flux of deep sediments, specialized sulfur bacteria reconvert some of the hydrogen sulfide back to sulfate again, and the process continues.

In addition to the sulfur circulation in sedimentary types of ecosys-

[6]Ibid., p. 41.
[7]E. P. Odum, op. cit., p. 56.

tems, industrial emissions contribute to the circulation of hydrogen sulfide in the atmosphere. The hydrogen sulfide is oxidized in the air and eventually is converted into sulfur, sulfur dioxide, sulfuric acid, and sulfate salts. The sulfur dioxide is absorbed directly by plant life into the ocean.

In spite of the natural sinks to absorb sulfur, a rising concentration of sulfur compounds in the air over Europe began to be observed in the early 1960s, which has been attributed to the increased use of sulfur-containing fuels (oil and coal). Rain and snow absorbed the sulfur, causing precipitation to become more acid. By 1966, the area in which acidity had reached pH 4.5 (a value of 7.0 is considered neutral) had extended over Holland to Central Europe and Sweden. The precipitation into surface waters dropped the pH in the Morrumsan River from 6.8 to 6.2. Acidity is a threat to aquatic life, since most organisms cannot live at less than pH 4.0, and some fish, such as salmon, are wiped out at pH 5.5.

The global importance of sulfur emissions from man-made sources into the atmosphere is not known, although estimates indicate that such emissions account for about one-third of all the sulfur going into the air annually. Whether sulfur is accumulating in the atmosphere is not known, but a layer of sulfate particulates has been observed in the stratosphere worldwide, and there are indications of a net increase globally in these particles. Concentrations of particles in the air can affect mean global temperature, and particulates have been found to be important agents in both photochemical and London-type smog. Thus, the man-made emissions of sulfur compounds cannot be ignored in the long run in the biogeochemical cycles.[8]

The abatement of sulfur emissions into the atmosphere from man-made sources can be attempted by changing the industrial chemical processes or power sources which cause the emissions. In most cases, of course, these are solutions which increase costs. The city of St. Louis had a controversy over air pollution control which centered about the best way to minimize emissions. Coal burning at stationary power sources accounts for about one-third of total emissions into the atmosphere of the city in the form of sulfur dioxide, nitrogen oxides, and particulates. A linear programming model was construed to determine how best to minimize pollutants, given the location of stationary sources and the capability to modify their combustion equipment. One conclusion was a need to shift to low-sulfur coal and natural gas, both of which are relatively scarcer and higher-cost fuels than those which had been used. A second conclusion was that, since the cost structure of the power sources

[8]*Cleaning Our Environment,* American Chemical Society, Washington, 1969, pp. 30–32.

was altered by the fuel conversion, the air pollution authorities should have decided the order and priority of conversion because it would affect the profitability and return on investment of the power generation units.[9]

THE NITROGEN CYCLE

In the biosphere as a whole, the circulation of materials is of two types: the sedimentary type such as the sulfur cycle, and the atmospheric type such as the carbon cycle. The carbon cycle is among the simpler circulations because carbon can be used by organisms directly in its atmospheric form (CO_2), and because carbon dioxide is returned to the atmosphere at nearly the same rate that it is removed. Nitrogen ranks along with carbon, hydrogen, and oxygen as one of the major nutritional elements in the ecosystem. Nitrogen is essential to the formation of amino acids, nucleic acid, and proteins and is prevalent in autotrophic and heterotrophic organisms. Nitrogen is among the most plentiful of elements, since 79 percent of the atmosphere is composed of nitrogen.

In spite of the nitrogen-rich atmosphere in which all organisms live, none of the higher plants or animals have the ability to fix nitrogen or use it directly in its atmospheric form. Specialized microorganisms in the environment convert atmospheric nitrogen into nitrate (NO_3^-), and the autotrophs assimilate it in this form (see Figure 7-4). The nitrogen fixing organisms are blue-green algae and a relatively few species of bacteria, which fortunately are quite abundant, especially in the soil. Yet, such is the dependency of the entire life stream on these few species of nitrogen fixers that their preservation should be a matter of universal concern.

Fortunately, none of man's activities or pollutants are known, so far, to be limiting factors in the survival of nitrogen-fixing organisms. Indeed, the nitrogen cycle appears to operate in a steady state with self-regulating biological mechanisms. The flow of atmospheric nitrogen to nitrates, nitrite, ammonia, amino acids, and protoplasm has sufficient pathways and organisms, so that any change in flow along one path is compensated for on other paths.[10] Although nitrogen circulation remains in balance over normal seasonal cycles, local shortages of nitrogen do occur due to net losses or slow adjustment in a particular biome, and then nitrogen does become a limiting factor to organic growth. The large injections of nitrogen oxides into the atmosphere by motor vehicles and stationary combustion engines are not known to perturb the general stability of the nitrogen cycle. Nitrogen oxides generally appear in the form of NO or

[9]Robert Kohn, "Application of Linear Programming to a Controversy on Air Pollution Control," *Management Science,* Vol. 17. No. 10, June, 1971, p. B609.
[10]E. P. Odum, op. cit., p. 57; Kormondy, op. cit., pp. 43–48.

NO_2 from engine emissions. The solar energy in the atmosphere causes photochemical changes which disassociate the oxygen, returning nitrogen to the atmosphere and releasing active oxidants which are the source of irritation and cell damage.

NUTRIENT BUDGETS IN ECOSYSTEMS

Sufficient illustrations of individual nutrients have now been given to convey the general character of materials circulation. However, we should recognize that any particular ecosystem, like a forest, an estuary, or a grassland plain, uses many minerals and nutrients for growth. The sum of all these biochemical requirements for an ecosystem may be looked upon as its nutrient budget. The nutrient budget includes not only the individual biogeochemical cycles but, also, the stored nutrients which are bound up in the biomass of the ecosystem over long time periods, such as the nutrients in the trunks of standing trees in a forest. Eventually, these stored, or bound, nutrients are released by decomposition to other organisms. Among the few examples of composite nutrient budgets, which include several minerals, are the data of Professor J. D. Ovington on a Scots Pine plantation in England, showing the utilization of nitrogen, calcium, potassium, magnesium, phosphorus, and sodium by trees and ground flora.[11] The portion of the nutrient which becomes bound up in trees may range from about one-fourth to one-half of the total uptake; and the remainder, of course, becomes litter in the falling of leaves, cones, and branches.

Plants take more nutrients from the soil than are released to the soil by decomposition. Hence the forest is not a closed ecological regime in the sense of having a balance of nutrients required for growth into plant structure being supplied from available decomposition. Obviously, then, the net uptake represents an importation of materials from some other ecological cycles or biogeochemical sources. The exchange of materials from other ecosystems is part of the nutrient circulation, and man-made injection of residuals into these nutrient cycles becomes part of the food chain elsewhere in the biosphere.

THE HYDROLOGIC CYCLE AND MATERIALS TRANSPORT

The net exchange of nutrients and materials from one ecosystem to another takes place largely through air and water circulation, although there is some transport within the soil. The transport mechanisms are of

[11]Kormondy, op. cit., p. 56; also, J. D. Ovington, *Advances in Ecological Research,* vol. 1, New York., Academic Press, 1962.

Figure 11-4   Distribution of Fresh Water

	Percentage
Polar ice and glaciers	75
Groundwater (at less than 2,500 feet)	11
Groundwater (at more than 2,500 feet)	14
Lakes	0.3
Rivers	0.03
Soil moisture	0.06
Atmosphere	0.035

interest to us because they are the principal means of dispersion of pollutants from man-made sources into the nutrient cycles of the biomes and escosystems. The most ubiquitous of these transport mechanisms is the hydrologic cycle, which may carry minerals as particles, as dissolved solids, or gases in the form of dissolved oxygen or carbon dioxide (carbonic acid). The meteorological circulation of the atmosphere plays the same transport role for gaseous materials and very fine particulates. The two fluid states, that of water and air, are the main transportation arteries for dispersion and circulation of materials (see Figure 7-3).

About 90 percent of the water content of the earth is bound up in the *lithosphere,* or solid parts of the earth, and unavailable for organic use. Of the available water 97 percent is contained in the oceans, leaving 3 percent or 33 trillion acre-feet of fresh water. The distribution of the fresh water is approximately as shown in Figure 11-4.[12]

Although the amount of atmospheric moisture is very small at any one time, compared to the total reservoir, the circulation rate of moisture through the atmosphere is relatively high. The annual precipitation over land surfaces, for example, is about 30 times as great as the moisture in the air over the land.

In the hydrologic cycle, most of the rain (nearly 80 percent) falls on the ocean, the balance on the land. The distribution of the rains depends mainly on the wind movements and, secondarily, on the land structure. The main trade wind movements are from cooler to warmer latitudes, taking up moisture by evaporation as they go and depositing it in the equatorial region. This wind movement within the horse latitudes (30°N and 30°S) leaves the coasts of California, Mexico, Chile, North Africa, South Africa, and Australia relatively arid. The westerly winds which move from warm to cool latitudes, outside of the horse latitudes, provide fairly heavy precipitation to the Pacific Northwest and Europe. The air masses from the Gulf of Mexico moving inland provide rainfall within the

---

[12]Abel Wolman, *Water, Health and Society,* Report to the National Academy of Sciences, Indiana University Press, Bloomington, 1969, p. 6.

United States. In continental United States, the East receives two-thirds of the rainfall.

The hydrologic cycle may be thought of as beginning with evaporation of fresh waters, largely from the oceans, using solar energy. The air movements and land structures cause cooling and precipitation. Moisture enters the plant through the root system and is returned by transpiration from leaves. The annual precipitation in the continental United States is estimated at 4,750 million acre-feet (1 acre-foot equals 326,700 gallons),[13] and the uses of this water flow are depicted in Figure 11-5.

The diagram shows the flow of water as it precipitates out of the atmosphere and falls into land uses (70 percent) and into stream flow (30 percent). A large portion (30 percent) of the rain which falls on nonirri-

[13]Ibid, p. 7.

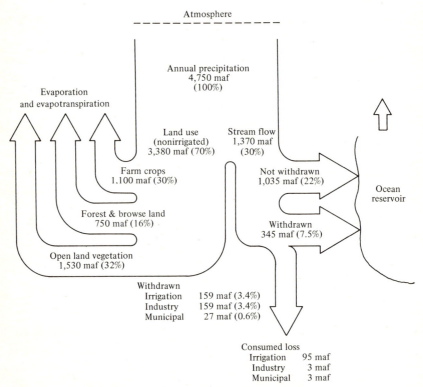

Figure 11-5 Hydrologic cycle for continental United States, in millions of acre feet (maf). *(Drawn from data of Abel Wolman,* Water, Health, and Environment, *1969, p. 7.)*

gated land becomes utilized for farm crops, and the balance falls on forest and browse vegetations (16 percent) or upon wild, noneconomic vegetations (32 percent) on open land. All this water, after some storage in plant tissue, eventually returns to the atmosphere through evaporation from the soil or through evapotranspiration of the plants. That portion of the rain which becomes stream flow (30 percent) in large part goes through the river systems to the sea, with about 7.5 percent withdrawn for some form of human use for irrigation, industry, or municipal water. Although these withdrawal rates are relatively small, compared to the total annual precipitation of the ocean reservoir, these human uses, along with those on nonirrigated farm croplands, are the principal sources of contaminants to the water system, in the form of pathogens, pesticides, fertilizers, and industrial chemicals. That such a small portion of usage could degrade the entire hydrologic system, so that every major stream in the United States is polluted, fish kills exceed twenty million a year, and seabirds are unable to reproduce, is telling evidence of the effectiveness of water as a dispersion and transport mechanism.

This transport and dispersion function of the water cycle is not well understood. Materials and chemicals move through a water system by flow or convection and disperse by dissolution, diffusion, or mixing. The transport process determines the impact of waterborne substances upon the quality of water throughout the hydrologic cycle, and, thus, transport and dispersion processes are fundamental to ecology. The American Chemical Society, in a technical assessment of the water environment, came to the conclusion that adequate balances have not been worked out for most water pollutants. Hence there are major uncertainties in the degree and details of water degradation. Even in domestic wastes the major organics are only partially known. Only 75 percent of the total organic carbon could be accounted for in one analysis of domestic sewage, and only 35 percent of the total chemically oxidizable organic materials could be accounted for in the effluent from secondary treatment.

Lack of data on waste composition extends to municipal storm water runoff, which at times contains more suspended solids, coliform bacteria, and chemically oxidizable organics, than domestic sewage.[14]

Among the other unknowns, in both air and water transport processes, is the role of particles. Particles are ubiquitous in air and water; they vary widely in chemical and biological properties; and they can absorb and otherwise bind other chemicals, can serve as site for bacterial growth or chemical reaction, and can strongly affect the transport and degradation processes. The role of waterborne particles in the transport

[14]American Chemical Society, op. cit., pp. 98–99.

of pollutants has been studied only in limited degree, most of which was stimulated by the fact that some pesticides, such as DDT, are present in low concentrations (a few parts per billion) in almost all surface waters in the United States. Pesticides and other organic compounds absorbed by particles are deposited in bottom muds, and these residues then can accumulate in lakes through absorption by sediments. We have already seen, in the sulfur cycle, how the slow flux of bottom sediments becomes part of the nutrient chain through action of bacteria, and this is one means by which the initially diluted pesticides may begin to concentrate in higher species.

The acute episodes of fatal poisoning by pesticides are fairly well defined and have remained reasonably constant over the past twenty-five years at a rate of about one per one million people per year.[15] Most major pesticides have contributed to fatal poisoning, most frequently by accidental ingestion, and most often among children. The long-term effects of low-level exposures of pesticides or toxic wastes are virtually unknown. The most intensive studies have been on the accumulation of chlorinated hydrocarbon insecticides (such as DDT and DDE) in fatty tissues of human beings, and it is generally agreed that humans carry a body burden of 10 to 20 ppm of these residuals in their tissue, although measurements as high as 30 ppm have been found in some samples in India. Within the United States, the daily human ingestion of chlorinated hydrocarbon insecticides in complete meals is estimated to range from 0.04 to 0.5 milligrams. Volunteers have tolerated 35 milligrams of DDT per day for periods up to twenty-one months without a detection of adverse health effects.[16]

Some explorations have been made of suspected relations between pesticides and leukemia, anemia and other blood diseases, hepatitis, and cancer. So far, there is no evidence that low-level exposure to pesticides has caused deleterious effects on humans, nor is there any clear evidence that they do not. Meantime, the benefits of pesticides to higher food production and to the reduction of serious diseases like malaria are obvious.

In a situation where long-term health effects are poorly known, the ultimate decision about pesticide use by each individual is likely to rest upon his own perception of risk, that is, his attitude toward early benefits as a tradeoff against unknown long-term effects. Perhaps many people, conditioned by the utilitarian tradition, would choose in favor of early benefits such as higher food production. Others, with a different value

[15]Ibid., p. 230.
[16]Ibid., p. 233.

scheme oriented toward long-term ecological balance of species, might prefer greater proof and validation of biological effects, on the part of human producers and users of pesticides, before their widespread application.

ATMOSPHERIC DISPERSION OF POLLUTANTS

The other fluid process (besides water) in the ecosystem, with broad transport and circulation implications, is the atmosphere. Air circulation in the atmosphere is capable of carrying immense quantities of pollutants, estimated in the United States at 214 million tons per year of carbon monoxide, particulates, hydrocarbons, and nitrogen oxides.[17] In addition, a recent study suggests that coal burning may be a principal source of mercury, amounting to 3,000 metric tons per year, or 10 times the quantity released by the natural weathering of rock, and this toxic agent is widely distributed by winds and water. Excessively high levels of mercury have been found in the tissues of wildlife studied in Sweden, as well as in fish in most oceans. The increasing accumulation of mercury in the biomass is a recent phenomenon and a dangerous one since mercury is toxic to humans and animals.[18]

Meteorological stations are widely distributed for weather forecasting, yielding excellent historical data on air pressure, wind velocity, temperature gradients, precipitation; but the measurement of the composition or quality of air is limited to very few stations in a few selected air basins. The result is that a good deal is known about high- and low-pressure areas, weather fronts, and wind movements; but not much is known about the complete composition of air content in the winds. Until recently, the measurements which were made at the few air pollution monitoring stations were mainly for hydrocarbons and oxidants. More recently, carbon monoxide and oxides of nitrogen were added to the inventory. Many petrochemical derivatives, emitted from stationary or vehicular sources, still are not monitored at all, for example, aldehydes which are a particularly reactive and potentially deleterious substance.

The monitoring of air quality requires that an atmospheric model be created to identify the composition, flow, and concentrations of pollutants in the moving air mass. This monitoring requires a large number of observation points for measuring air quality, plus meteorological data, and a computerized mathematical model to integrate the data points and show the convections and air flows. Such an atmospheric model and

[17] *Environmental Quality,* op. cit., p. 63.
[18] Oiva I. Joensuu, "Fossil Fuels as a Source of Mercury Pollution," *Science,* vol. 172, June 4, 1971, p. 1027.

contour mapping of the Los Angeles Basin was developed on a pilot basis at the University of California.[19] The report observes that the effects of air pollution have been well-documented in terms of eye irritation, plant damage, visibility reduction, material degradation, and respiratory and other potential health effects. In order to decide how best to control air pollution, a technique is needed which would allow us to relate possible courses of action with the effects. Such a technique requires a model of atmospheric dispersion showing the concentration, time, temperature, solar intensities, and spectral distribution to determine the rates of reactions leading to photochemical air pollution.

The research carried out under this project was aimed at simulating the history of oxidant formation, dynamic irradiation, and dispersion of diluted automobile exhaust. One output of the research was a series of computer-produced contour maps of the Los Angeles Basin over a time cycle of a normal summer day.

The contouring procedure is programmed to reflect air convection currents from mathematical models of meteorological data. The maps represent the concentration variations of total oxidant for August 21, and August 22, 1969. A legend shows the oxidant concentration of the contours. The time of day for the particular map is in the lower left-hand corner of the picture. The sequence selected for illustration on August 21 starts at 8 A.M. and continues to noon, 3 P.M., and 6 P.M. The maps clearly

[19]Joseph V. Behar, *Simulation Model of Air Pollution Photochemistry*, Project Clean Air, 1970, Research Reports, vol. 4, Project S-14. University of California, Riverside, Calif.

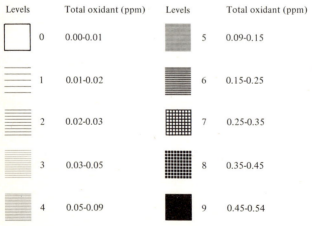

Levels		Total oxidant (ppm)	Levels		Total oxidant (ppm)
	0	0.00-0.01		5	0.09-0.15
	1	0.01-0.02		6	0.15-0.25
	2	0.02-0.03		7	0.25-0.35
	3	0.03-0.05		8	0.35-0.45
	4	0.05-0.09		9	0.45-0.54

Figure 11-6 Oxidant contours in the South Coast Basin—computer generated, in parts per million.

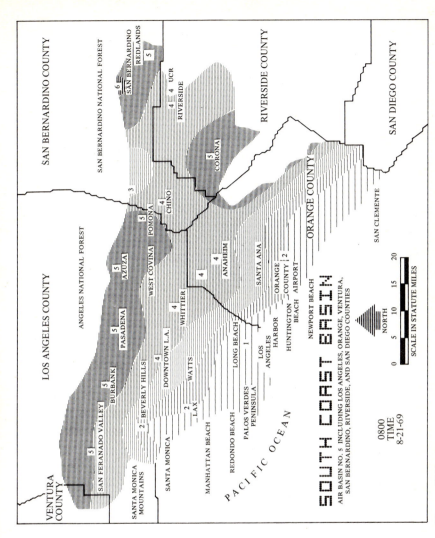

SOUTH COAST BASIN

AIR BASIN NO. 5 INCLUDING LOS ANGELES, ORANGE, VENTURA,
SAN BERNARDINO, RIVERSIDE, AND SAN DIEGO COUNTIES

0800
TIME
8-21-69

NORTH

SCALE IN STATUTE MILES

0   5   10   15   20

Figure 11-7

209

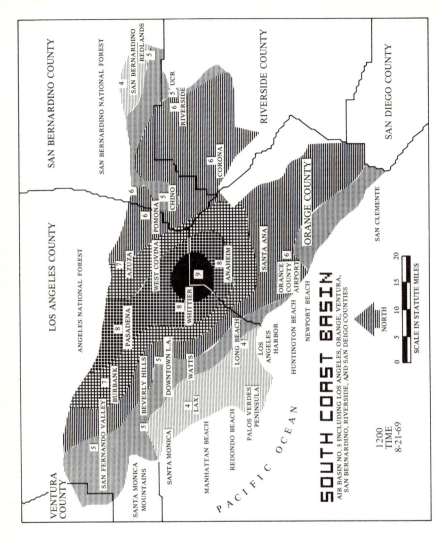

SOUTH COAST BASIN

AIR BASIN NO. 5 INCLUDING LOS ANGELES, ORANGE, VENTURA,
SAN BERNARDINO, RIVERSIDE, AND SAN DEIGO COUNTIES

1200
TIME
8-21-69

NORTH

SCALE IN STATUTE MILES

0   5   10   15   20

Figure 11-8

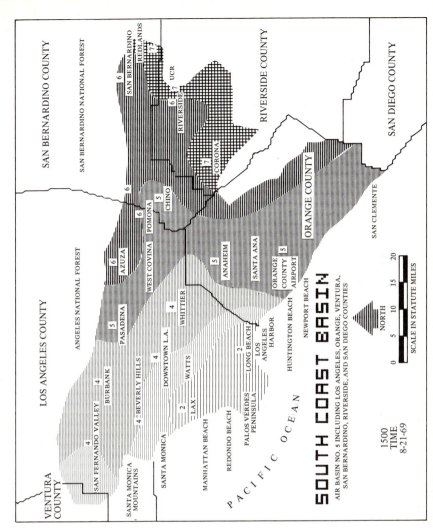

SOUTH COAST BASIN

AIR BASIN NO. 5 INCLUDING LOS ANGELES, ORANGE, VENTURA,
SAN BERNARDINO, RIVERSIDE, AND SAN DIEGO COUNTIES

1500
TIME
8-21-69

SCALE IN STATUTE MILES

0   5   10   15   20

NORTH

Figure 11-9

211

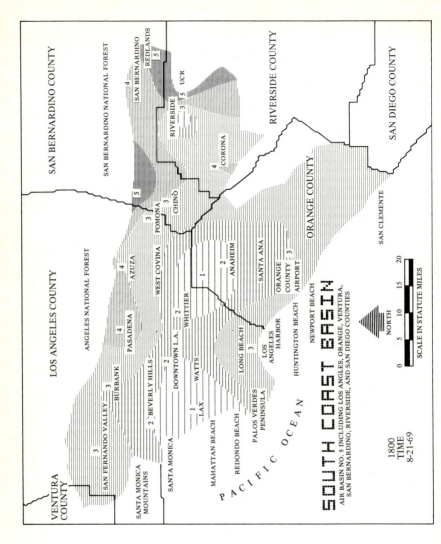

SOUTH COAST BASIN

AIR BASIN NO. 5 INCLUDING LOS ANGELES, ORANGE, VENTURA,
SAN BERNARDINO, RIVERSIDE, AND SAN DIEGO COUNTIES

1800
TIME
8-21-69

NORTH

SCALE IN STATUTE MILES

0   5   10   15   20

Figure 11-10

illustrate the location and movement of the oxidant-containing air masses. Their advection from west to east becomes evident as we look at the maps for later hours of the day. The movement of the polluted air mass corresponds with the general direction in which the wind is moving.

The first map, 8 A.M., shows the coastal area fairly clear of oxidants, and the smog (represented by the darker areas) rising over the principal freeways along the mountain base, downtown Los Angeles, and Anaheim. By noon, shown on the second map, the entire South Coast Basin is heavily covered with high-smog concentrations. At 3 P.M., the ocean breezes from the west have begun to clear the smog from the westerly coast and compact the oxidant concentrations inland. By 6 P.M., as the sun wanes and the photochemical reactions subside, the entire basin becomes fairly clear of smog, except for a few traces inland against the mountains. The contour maps of nighttime and early morning hours, from around 8 P.M. to 6 A.M., are essentially clear of oxidant concentrations.

While the oxidant concentrations are regularly monitored in Los Angeles and in many cities, many other air pollutants are not; for example, lead, a toxic heavy metal, is not regularly measured. A special study by the University of Cincinnati for the U.S. Air Pollution Control Office found that between 1961 and 1969, in some areas of Los Angeles, lead concentrations in the air had increased as much as 64 percent; in Cincinnati 33 percent; and in Philadelphia, 36 percent. Dr. Ronald Engle, of the Environmental Protection Agency's Air Pollution Control Office, concluded from these findings that the problem hardly justifies a wait-and-see attitude. Clearly there is need to prevent environmental lead exposure.

Engle theorized that lead is absorbed into the body from the air, adding substantially to the lead content in the blood and body tissue. The absorption of airborne lead might push some people, already exposed to high-lead concentrations, into the toxic range of lead absorption. Children who have swallowed paint chips, for example, are particularly susceptible, according to Engle.[20]

The Environmental Protection Agency, out of concern for these high concentrations of air pollutants, has adopted very strict new car emission standards for the 1975 model cars, which reduce oxides of nitrogen by 90 percent. Other measures require low-lead gasolines. Most rigorous of all is a requirement that cities and states come up with a plan to regulate the level of air polluting activity, such as limiting traffic and industrial production, if concentration of pollutants exceeds federal standards.

[20] *Los Angeles Times*, June 4, 1971.

POLLUTION AS A WORLDWIDE PROBLEM

Pollution problems often appear to have a local or regional character which one can shrug off, like smog in Los Angeles, mercury in tuna in the Pacific, killer smog in London, or DDT in Gulf Coast pelicans. But the fact is that pollution is a worldwide problem, and the global circulations of air and water guarantee that it will remain so. Pesticides have been measured in the tissue of Eskimos, and mercury concentrations are worldwide.

Because pollution is a worldwide problem, the United Nations has initiated a number of conferences on environmental problems, the first in Rome in 1954 on world population; in 1961 on water pollution; 1963 in Geneva on the application of technology to underdeveloped countries. The General Assembly adopted a resolution in 1968, at the suggestion of Sweden, for a global conference on environmental problems to be held in Stockholm in 1972. Preparatory meetings for the Stockholm conference have been held in Prague. The Scandinavian countries, Britain, Finland, and Russia generally agreed at Prague that no one country acting alone can do the job of improving environment, and the global polluters must be controlled through international agreements.

In the Baltic Sea, overconcentrations of mercury have been found with increasing frequency in fish, which is a prime food source for many of the surrounding nations. Other incidents impelling the Baltic nations to take remedial action are the closing of swimming beaches in Sweden because of pollution from raw sewage originating in Denmark near Hamlet's castle; the dying out of kestrels, once a prolific bird species in Britain, due to DDT in mice they eat; lead contamination found in water samples for forty English boroughs; the appearance of "brown snow" in Sweden caused by industrial stack emissions from the Ruhr Valley. As a result of such problems, Sweden has a strong incentive-subsidy program to encourage pollution control equipment on all industrial facilities. Switzerland claims to be the first nation to have made environmental protection a constitutional mandate, and Britain the first nation to establish environmental affairs as a department of cabinet rank. Peter Walker, first Secretary of State for the Environment, has identified five major problems: Better land utilization on a crowded island, reconciling urbanization and waste dispersal, eradicating derelict buildings, preserving historic heritages, and trying to incorporate a good life in greener spaces as part of rising living standards. Among the early acts of the department has been the consolidation of 1,200 local borough control agencies into 400 environmental control units. The machinery of local government in Britain has not been changed since 1888, before the days of the automobile or such intensive industrialization. The overhaul of local government came as a recognition by boroughs that air and water pollution do not recognize artificial boundaries.

The circulation of materials, including pollutants, is a global phenomenon due to the worldwide distribution of nutrients and water through the natural cycles. The low efficiency with which organisms convert energy has, as its consequence, the dispersal of energy (in accord with the second law of thermodynamics), and, as its concomitant, the concentration of pollutants for higher species. The nature of the biogeochemical cycle, the hydrologic and atmospheric cycles, and the concentration of materials which takes place make inevitable the degradation of the biologic quality of the environment at geometric rates with every increase in human population and human residuals, unless we offset the contamination effects of the wastes; but that offset requires increasing technological inputs and costs.

Consider the geometric ratios involved to achieve the offset where the effect of human activity is neutral upon the ecosystem, even at today's degraded quality level. Human populations are increasing at rates from 1 to 3 percent per year, and their increased usage of industrial output and energy ranges from 3 to 8 percent per year. The combined population-energy-materials demand upon the ecosystem is of the order of a 5 to 10 percent increase per year, which also means that the waste residuals are increasing at a rate as high as 10 percent per year.

This increasing wasteload is disposed into the ecosystem, and there it tends to become assimilated and concentrated in the nutrient cycle. The conversion efficiencies of species range from 1 to 30 percent; let us take 10 percent as a simple average. If conversion efficiency is 10 percent then nutrients and pollutants become concentrated tenfold for every trophic level through which they pass. We have already seen that, from the microautotroph through the carnivore, this concentration in nutrient-pollutant can reach 10,000 times its dilute state in the ambient surroundings, and we have already recorded such concentration with some pollutants in organic tissue structures. Next, we must recognize the consequence of compounding a 10,000-fold concentration by 10 percent per year (the population-energy-materials demand upon ecosystems). This means that every year, concentrations of toxic materials in higher species could increase at rates as high as 10,000 times 10 percent of the ambient state of that pollutant annually. One does not have to be a mathematician to perceive that, with a geometric increase by orders of magnitude annually, wasteloads can pile up at astronomic rates unless preventive action is taken.

SUMMARY

The dispersion and circulation of materials in the ecosystem are significant to administrative decisions because human transformation of materials ultimately affects the nutrient cycle upon which man and all species subsist. The conversion of solar energy is at low rates of efficiency, which means that materials are fixed through each trophic layer at increasing levels of concentration. Moreover, the various cycles in the nutrient chain, carbon, sulfur, nitrogen, and others, are interactive. Also, the water and atmospheric cycles assure dispersion and circulation of materials worldwide throughout the ecosystem. In the end, pollutants become concentrated and dispersed throughout the world. The combined population-energy-materials demand is increasing at nonsustainable geometric rates, because residuals, accumulating at these same geometric rates, adversely affect the nutrient cycle. The consequence is pervasive biological damage.

Since the laws of nature are inexhorable, and at odds with our present waste practices, a tragic outcome is a clear possibility, tragic in either its cost or its health effects. We can still choose something other than a tragic course. We can alter our decision processes, incentives, institutions, and individual behavior to act more in consonance with ecological constraints. By recognizing the dispersion and circulation of materials in decision making, we can intercept the withdrawal or disposal of materials when harmful to the ecosystem. Through regulation or incentives at these points, the reduction of wastes, waste recycling, or biodegradable products can be encouraged. Then the recirculation and dispersion of residuals in the ecosystem would have less dire consequences than they do now.

DISCUSSION QUESTIONS

1 Discuss why contaminants concentrate in the nutrient chain and what effects you are aware of from your reading or experience.
2 How does the carbon-nutrient cycle interact with, and depend upon, the hydrologic and atmospheric cycles?
3 Suppose your public health department detected a high coliform (intestinal) bacteria count in the city water supply. How would you go about trying to trace it to its source? A high nitrate level? Lead? Mercury?
4 Suppose you were a delegate to the Stockholm conference on worldwide pollution, what agenda items and proposals would you submit for discussion?

PROBLEM

Make a chart, such as Lindeman's on the conversion of solar energy in autotroph-based ecosystems, for a tropical reedswamp. Use the information from Odum's analysis of energy conversion at Silver Springs, Florida, along with the information on the productivity of various ecosystems. Assume that Cedar Bog had the same energy conversion characteristics, in kcal/cm²/yr, as ocean phytoplankton.

Chapter 12

Impact Statements and Benefit-Cost Analysis

A traditional approach of government, in dealing with resource or environmental problems, has been to look at the benefits of public programs in comparison with their costs, an approach which has come to be called benefit-cost analysis. The benefit has usually been regarded as human economic gains, and relatively little consideration has been given, until recently, to the environmental or biological consequences of government programs.

Benefit-cost analysis has frequently been applied during this century to public works, especially to dams and reclamation, irrigation, flood control, and navigation projects. The benefit is estimated in terms of economic gains to beneficiaries, such as the added value of crops by providing irrigation water to farmers, or the prevention of dollar loss by a flood control project to homes built on a flood plain. The cost is estimated as the dollar investment of public funds, at some assumed interest rate over the future period during which benefits or income accrue, to accomplish the construction of the project. The two are then compared, the benefit in relation to the cost, to arrive at some judgment as to the value or worth of the undertaking.

Such calculations normally have not covered the damage effects to the environment caused by human actions, and, as these damage effects have become more serious, government policy has recently tried to take such effects into account by requiring environmental impact statements to be submitted prior to approval of all public works. The environmental impact statement seeks to identify the changes in materials balance and the dispersion of residuals into the environment, which concerned us in the past two chapters. That is, a governmental agency, in planning a new program, must submit an impact statement which shows the changes in environment which could be expected from a new highway, dam, flood control, or other public project. This impact statement shows first the physical changes caused by the project, and then the interaction upon the environment in terms of effects on biota, chemical or natural processes, or aesthetics. The means for evaluating these environmental impact statements is not yet well developed, because the requirement for impact statements is relatively new, beginning in 1970. Indeed, the purpose of Section Three is to describe the various methodologies which might apply to environmental impact analysis. This chapter will consider present and traditional governmental methods, which include the following topics:

1 Environmental impact statements
2 Council on Environmental Quality as a clearing house
3 Benefit-cost analysis
4 Example of interest rate effects
5 Example of indirect benefits
6 Example of income redistribution effects
7 Care in the analysis of cost-benefit relationships
8 Experiments with productivity measures in civilian agencies

ENVIRONMENTAL IMPACT STATEMENTS

The creation of the Council on Environmental Quality by the National Environmental Policy Act of 1969 (see Chapter 5) established in the federal government an overall policy-making and review function with respect to environmental problems. The principal mechanism for bringing these problems and issues to the attention of the Council is through the submission of environmental impact statements. Section 102 (2)(C) of the act requires all federal agencies to submit an environmental impact statement to the Council for all new budgetary programs which may alter the ecology by construction, disposal, resource use, or other activity. These environmental impact statements are abstracted in a publication of the Council called the *102 Monitor*. The *102 Monitor* reports a large number of impact statements and construction items from the highway program of the Department of Transportation; the flood control, harbor, and navigation projects of the Corps of Engineers; the reclamation projects of the Department of Interior; as well as lesser numbers from the Forest Service, National Park Service, Atomic Energy Commission, Geological Survey, Department of Agriculture, and other agencies that deal with land, air, and water resources.

The Corps of Engineers has implemented the requirements of the Council of Environmental Quality for the submission of impact statements by a carefully prepared procedural manual which contains the following directions:

1   Environmental statements will contain a project proposal with the name, specific location, purposes, authorizing document, current status, benefit-cost ratio, and environmental setting.

2   The statement will "identify environmental impacts, viewed as changes or conversions of environmental elements which result from the direct and indirect consequences of the proposed action. A thoughtful assessment of the environmental elements under both a 'with' and 'without the project' condition should aid in determining impacts. For example, the filling of a portion of the wetlands of an estuary would involve: the obvious conversion of aquatic/marsh areas to terrestrial environments, the loss of wetland habitats and associated organisms, a gain in area for terrestrial organisms, a change in the nutrient regime of the runoff water entering a portion of the estuary, alteration of the hydrology of some given area, perhaps the introduction of buildings or roads, curtailment of certain commercial uses, conversion of wildland aesthetics to less-pristine attributes, perhaps the removal of some portion of popular duck hunting grounds or unique bird nesting area, etc. Such impacts shall be detailed in a dispassionate manner to provide a basis for a meaningful treatment of the trade-offs involved. Quantitative estimates of loss or gains (e.g. acres of marshland, number of ducks nesting or harvested) will be set forth whenever practical."

3   A discussion of the beneficial and detrimental aspects of the environmental changes and conversions should be included, with an identification of remedial, protective, and mitigation measures which would be taken in response to adverse effects of environmental impacts.

4   The various alternatives, their differences in environmental impact, and the reasons considered in arriving at a judgment of each should be described. These alternatives shall consider both natural and man-induced changes which may ensue, and the economic justification of each choice.

5   The cumulative and long-term impacts of the proposed action shall be assessed with the view that each generation is a trustee of the environment for succeeding generations. Special attention should be given to considerations which would narrow the range of beneficial uses

of the environment or pose long-term risks to health or safety. "The propriety of any action should be weighed against the potential for damage to man's life support system—the biosphere—thereby guarding against the short-sighted foreclosure of future options or needs. It is appropriate to make such evaluations on land-use patterns and development, alterations in the organic productivity of biological communities and ecosystems and modifications in the proportions of environmental components (water, uplands, wetland, vegetation, fauna) for a region or ecosystem."

6 Irreversible and irretrievable commitments of resources should be carefully weighed including changes in land use, destruction of archaeological or historical sites, unalterable disruptions in the ecosystem, and other effects that would curtail the diversity and range of beneficial uses of the environment.[1]

After environmental impact statements are prepared by federal agencies, along lines more or less similar to the directive of the Corps of Engineers, they are submitted to the Council on Environmental Quality for review. A staff member analyzes the adequacy of the data, may prepare a statement of environmental issues, suggests some tentative problems or recommendations, and then circulates the statement for evaluation by interested agencies, both public and private, which may be affected.

An example of a rather extensive coordination and review procedure is seen in a project submitted by the Federal Highway Administration of the U.S. Department of Transportation. The report is titled "Environmental Report and Advanced Planning Study, Final Environmental Statement, Project I-90-1, U.S. Interstate 90, West Snoqualmie to Tanner, State of Washington." The statement concerns a section of highway about 40 miles long between West Snoqualmie and Tanner, in which five alternative highway routings have been studied. The terrain of the area is that of a river basin surrounded by hills and mountains. The grade differentials are the least, and therefore construction costs less along the river basin, which are generally the northern alternative routings. However, this river basin flatland is also the most populated, so land acquisition costs are higher than the more southern routings which hug the foothills and mountain range. The southern routes, being in more primitive area, disturb the natural woodlands and wildlife, and, of most concern, these highway routings would cut a major game migration trail from the mountains to the water and feeding grounds below.

The recommended routing of the federal and state highway agencies

---

[1]Council on Environmental Quality, *102 Monitor*, Washington, vol. 1, no. 2, March 1971, pp. 11–15.

was a southerly route, E-3, for two major reasons: one was that the net cost per mile would be lower considering the lower land acquisition cost in relation to somewhat higher construction costs; and secondly, the route would most effectively serve the through traffic in saving both time and distance. The northerly routes would tend to have more local traffic and be somewhat slower and longer. The major remaining concern, then, was what would happen to the wildlife if their main migration crossing were cut.

To evaluate the significance of this issue, the Council on Environmental Quality circulated the environmental impact statement on Project I-90-1 (which consisted of three volumes in folio format approximately 15 by 24 inches with highway design drawings and descriptive text) to the following agencies for their review:

>Environmental Protection Agency, Seattle, Washington
>Department of Interior, Bureau of Outdoor Recreation
>Department of Interior, Fish and Wildlife Service
>Corps of Engineers, Seattle, Washington
>Department of Housing and Urban Development, Seattle, Washington
>U.S. Department of Agriculture, Soil Conservation, Spokane, Washington
>State of Washington: Office of Program Planning
>Planning and Community Affairs
>Department of Ecology
>Department of Game
>Department of Fisheries
>Parks and Recreation Commission
>Natural Resources Commission
>Puget Sound Governmental Conference
>Town of North Bend
>Town of Snoqualmie
>King County
>King County, Air Pollution Control Office

The several agencies reviewed the impact statement and wrote their findings and recommendations to the Council on Environmental Quality. Most of the agencies concurred with the routing E-3 recommended by the Highway Department. The Washington State Department of Game expressed concern about the current of the wildlife migration trails but had no specific estimate as to how adverse an effect this might have on wildlife habits or population. Game crossings had been monitored and most of the wildlife made the crossing between 2 A.M. and 5 A.M. The Department of Game believed that the effects of the highway could be mitigated by installing a 10- by 30-foot lighted game tunnel to permit the wildlife migrations. The recommendation was incorporated into the highway design and the project was adopted.

THE COUNCIL ON ENVIRONMENTAL QUALITY AS A CLEARING HOUSE

A first reaction to this decision procedure, which at the time was less than a year old, is that it represents a great improvement and a substantial concern for environmental factors in decisions. Indeed, one is a little amazed at the large number of agencies to whom the environmental impact statement was sent.

A second and more thoughtful reaction may be that the principal issue in the environmental impact statement was not really adequately addressed. No one seemed to know what the effect on wildlife population and habits would be by cutting the migration trail, and that was the principal environmental issue. In the end, the effect of migration on wildlife populations and habitat is a research question, which the responding agencies might not be expected to know. The Department of Game did have an ameliorative proposal which undoubtedly helps somewhat, but in the end, one finds it a little hard to picture these now urbanized wildlife creatures commuting through a 10- by 30-foot lighted game tunnel from 2 A.M. to 5 A.M. It sounds like an anthropomorphic solution, what we would do for the after-theater crowd crossing 42d and Broadway in New York. Maybe the sly, wild fox does not care to become so urbane; perhaps he would rather slink across the highway at the risk of being hit by a car, or go back to British Columbia from whence his forefathers came. Somewhere, someone must know the answers to such questions as the ecological effects of cutting a migration trail, or be prepared to find them out. Research biologists and naturalists in universities and research institutions undoubtedly have deep interest, and perhaps have done considerable research, on the impact of migration upon species populations. Before making a decision, we really ought to find out. However, the implication of such a procedure would be to make the Council on Environmental Quality a clearing house of very wide dimensions. Either the Council would have to have an inventory of the competence of scientific personnel in all environmental specialties, which would be a huge data bank indeed, or else it would have to make a very widespread referral or referendum to elicit both factual and value judgments.

In the end, of course, there is a value judgment of considerable significance in the project. Suppose that informed scientific opinion determined that, even with a 10- by 30-foot lighted game tunnel, migration would be so inhibited that wildlife population in the region would decline by 10 or 30 percent? At what point would the depletion of wildlife population become a significant enough factor to offset the human convenience and cost preference for route E-3? More important, who could make that tradeoff, who could decide such a question? Could the Department of Game or the Department of Ecology for the State of Washington decide; if so, how representative would be their judgment? These are the kinds of value questions which are raised in even the seemingly routine environmental impact statements.

BENEFIT-COST ANALYSIS

In many cases, of course, the environmental impact statements deal with an issue which is primarily economic, such as the value of an irrigation project to cropland productivity. In such cases, the traditional benefit-cost approach can be usefully employed.

Benefit-cost analysis is an attempt to make a rather straightforward transposition of the market-price mechanism into the field of public goods. As such, the benefit-cost approach is an economic rationale, and not a biological one. Otto Eckstein has made the transposition clearly by citing the marginal-cost versus marginal-price theory of economics and then relating them to public benefits.[2] He observes that marginal-cost analysis can be carried directly over into the public sector because production costs are merely the exchange price of intermediate goods which are finally determined in the market place by consumer willingness to pay for the output. Hence, the cost analysis of public goods may be treated by the same methodology as private goods.

Benefit also fits readily into the private marginal utility model, in that benefit is the value of the public good or service to the user. We can then assume that, in equilibrium, benefit is a measure of value which reflects the consumer's willingness to allocate his marginal income toward that benefit by comparison of its worth to other alternative purchases.

This equilibrium between marginal costs and benefits also leads to profit maximization. That is, public goods are produced to the point where the cost of producing the last unit is just equal to its incremental benefit to the user. Then we may say that economic welfare is maximized when the last added unit of benefit equals the marginal cost.

Having posed the public goods equivalent of private marginal utility theory, Eckstein then proceeds to enumerate some conceptual problems and difficulties.

[2]Otto Eckstein, *Water Resource Development*, Harvard University Press, Cambridge, Mass., 1958, pp. 24–25.

1   Many public projects, particularly large dams or water systems, have large fixed investments with a total capacity beyond current use, which is one reason why the government has to engage in their development rather than leave it to private utilities. Such large fixed investment projects are characterized by decreasing average unit costs as the facility is more fully utilized, and this leads to increasing marginal returns.[3] Discriminatory pricing, common in utility rates, could be used to induce marginal users of different categories to make as full use of the project as will cover marginal costs and make some contributions to capital charges. But on large public works projects, it may still take many years before demand develops sufficiently to cover the annual capital charges.

2   Many environmental projects are characterized by multiple use, particularly land and water developments. A watershed may be used for recreation, water storage, flood control, irrigation, potable water, and electric power. Moreover, the river basin may have a series of dams. The entire series of dams and the multiple water uses must be operated to recognize their physical interdependence; otherwise, the water use cannot be maximized.[4] That is, if one dam is operated to maximize its electric power output regardless of its effect on irrigation, flood control, or potable water uses, the river basin will be suboptimized on all water uses. That is, the last added unit of cost of power output on the dam may just equal the marginal benefit for power from that dam, but it will not equal the marginal benefit for all power or all uses for all dams.

3   Public projects frequently change the income distribution of those who use them; indeed, that is usually the purpose of the undertaking. For example, an irrigation project supplies more water, usually at lower prices, to farmers, thus increasing their crop yields and their incomes. Changes in income distribution and crop yields may then cause changes in demand. This redistribution of income may in turn alter prices, which could then modify the original calculation as to the worth of the project.[5]

4   Some public goods are nonmarketable and have no price equivalents; rather they are based purely upon a subjective social choice. Defense and education are such examples. When the benefit is not measurable in terms of some marginal gain (converted to dollars), there is no way of constructing a cost-benefit ratio.[6]

5   Public projects frequently have large investments and long service lives of 50 to 100 years. This raises a serious question of people's time preference for present consumption over the value of future benefits. That is, what rate of future flow of goods or benefits is sufficient to compensate consumers for sacrificing their present consumption? The present value of a future flow of benefits may be adjusted by an ap-

[3]Ibid., p. 30.
[4]Ibid., p. 31.
[5]Ibid., pp. 35–37.
[6]Ibid., p. 41.

propriate interest rate to equal the present marginal satisfaction of current consumption. The interest rate which equates future income or benefit flows with present values is thought of as the social rate of time preference. However, this may be something different from current market interest rates, which carry within them risk factors, as well as current supply-demand prices for money caused by the monetary policy of a central bank. Hence, the appropriate rate of interest to express social time preference is a thorny problem.[7] Moreover, the interest rate is a crucial one in benefit-cost calculations when the life of the project is long. Cost-benefit ratios for most government projects are calculated on the assumption of a 3 percent interest rate as an expression of time preference. Eckstein estimates that the social rate of time preference is probably more like 6 percent. An interest rate of 6 percent in cost-benefit analysis would preclude the justification of most public works projects.[8]

6   Benefit-cost ratios cannot readily be compared with the average rate of return on investment, which is a common criterion for private capital allocation. The rate of return on investment tends to favor capital extensive projects with large volume and high margins, while benefit-cost ratios tend to favor capital intensive projects with low annual operating costs.

The consequence of these several differences and conceptual problems is that benefit-cost ratios do not effectively enlighten the question of how to allocate resources between private and public goods. Since the social rate of time preference is not comparable to market interest rates, and benefit-cost ratios pose different investment criteria than return on investment, the cross-sectoral allocation problem is not solved. Cost-benefit analysis may be of some use, nonetheless, as a means of ranking governmental projects against each other, but not as a justification for using social capital for public goods in preference to private goods.[9]

EXAMPLE OF INTEREST RATE EFFECTS

In developing the water resources of the nation, the United States is faced with decisions to make multiple uses of government land or river developments. These uses include recreation, preservation of wilderness, parks, grazing, timber production, flood control, irrigation, land reclamation, navigation, as well as direct private uses such as electric power generation or potable water for municipal utilities. The allocation of resources to

[7]Ibid., pp. 42–45.
[8]Ibid., p. 99.
[9]Ibid., pp. 55–59.

these several ends requires a careful analysis of the several benefits in relation to costs.

An example of such a decision was the licensing of the Idaho Power Company in 1955 by the Federal Power Commission to build a three-dam development on the Snake River, along the Hell's Canyon Reach in the Idaho-Oregon-Washington border region. The principal benefits of the river development were electric power production, some flood control benefits, and a small amount of navigation services. The Idaho Electric Power Company preferred the three-dam development system to other alternatives, because the three dams were best adapted to the small electric system which it operates.

The federal government retains rights to the hydroelectric potential of navigable streams, and part of the alternative installations were to be on government land. One of the approaches was for the federal government to build a high dam which would provide more power production and, also, form more flood control and navigation. The high dam would have developed the full 602 feet of fall of Hell's Canyon Reach and generated 961,000 kilowatts of power. The three dams of the Idaho Power proposal would have had water heads ranging from 117 to 277 feet and generating about 700,000 kilowatts of power.

The annual cost of the high dam was first calculated on the basis of a 2.5 percent interest rate, which was in keeping with the cost of federal

Figure 12-1   Hell's Canyon High Dam Cost-Benefit Calculation
(In Thousands of Dollars)

	Benefit	Annual Cost	
		at 2.5%	at 5.5%
Benefits			
Value of prime power	$39,958		
Value of flood control			
benefits	2,600		
Value of navigation benefits	250		
Total annual value of			
benefits	$42,808		
Costs:			
Interest and amortization		$10,898	$23,721
Interim replacements		1,545	1,545
Payment in lieu of state and			
local taxes		1,999	2,145
Operation and maintenance		1,495	1,495
Total annual costs		$15,937	$28,906
Excess of benefits over costs		$26,871	$13,900

capital assumed at that time. However, a private power company would have to pay at least 5 percent interest for capital. Therefore, annual cost of the high dam, which required an investment at the time of about $400 million, was also calculated at a 5.5 percent interest cost. The difference in the two calculations is shown in Figure 12-1.[10]

While the gains in benefits over cost are large at the 2.5 percent interest rate, they are approximately cut in half by the 5.5 percent rate. Moreover, compared to the three-dam alternative development of the river, the High Dam does not show a clear economic advantage, even though it is, in some respects, the most efficient multiple river use over the long term. In part, excess capacity makes the full utilization problematical at an early date. Thus, the high dam would show decreasing returns over a longer period of time, but it would not show as early a return on investment to a private power company as three smaller dams.

A study was made of a third alternative in an attempt to combine some of the efficiencies of the high dam with the lower costs of three small dams. That is, a medium dam with a 325-foot head was contemplated at the Brownlee site in lieu of the high dam. The resulting two-dam system, with a medium-height dam at Brownlee, would have cost about a $200 million investment, slightly less than the three dams. The two dams would develop about $30 million in annual value of prime electric power, and $1,800,000 in flood control benefits, compared to $28 million in power and $1,400,000 in flood control for the three dams. The calculation of cost versus benefit, at a 5 percent interest rate, for the two proposals would then appear as in Figure 12-2.

Table 12-2 shows that the three-dam development of Idaho Power had about the same net economic gain as the high dam approach, but significantly less than the two-dam alternative. In view of the gains and efficiencies of the two-dam proposal, why did Idaho Power prefer, and the FPC license, the three-dam approach? One reason was that the increased power generation and flood control was at the downstream site, which

[10]John V. Krutilla and Otto Eckstein, *Multiple Purpose River Development*, Resources for the Future, Johns Hopkins, Baltimore, 1958, pp. 142–159.

Figure 12-2   Cost Benefit of Two Versus Three Dams on Hell's Canyon Reach

(In Thousands of Dollars)

	Two dams	Three dams	Gains of two over three
Annual average value of benefits	$31,513	$29,317	$2,196
Average annual costs	15,397	15,869	472
Average annual economic gain	$16,116	$13,448	$2,668

would be at a federal installation used partly for navigation services, for which the power company would receive no compensation. Federal law construes additional benefits by private development as a quid pro quo for the granting of a license. The result was a decision toward a suboptimum solution.

EXAMPLE OF INDIRECT BENEFITS

The Hell's Canyon project illustrates direct economic benefits, but some developments entail secondary and tertiary benefits as well, which become more difficult to measure. The President's Advisory Committee on Water Resources has recommended that benefit-cost evaluations should be computed on the primary or direct benefits alone, such as the net economic gain to the farmers themselves, as illustrated above. However, an agency may also submit estimates of secondary or supplemental benefits as well. These indirect benefits are the estimated impact or gain to the rest of the economy generally. A somewhat abbreviated example of the Department of Interior's Reclamation Manual's illustration of indirect benefits (2.2.6) (Figure 12-3) is shown on page 230.

The indirect benefits are calculated from profits accruing to those who handle the additional farm produce as a result of irrigation purchases in the local and national economy. Under Benefit A, local wholesalers and retailers buy an additional $340,000 of farm produce and sell it at an average profit rate of 5 percent; thereby, they have a profit from their trade of $17,000 more than they would have earned otherwise. Similarly, national manufacturers and distributors, with higher profit rates, earned an additional $178,750 annually as a result of the irrigation. Those merchants who sell goods to farm families, for living or production, earn an additional $158,800 under Benefit C.

In this type of analysis, then, two types of benefits are accounted for: those that accrue directly to the farmer as added income, and those that are imputed as indirect economic benefits to the economy as a whole. Notice that so far we have been concerned solely with benefits measurable in terms of dollar values, that is, monetary benefits to society. Presumably, in environmental issues, we might also be concerned with nonmonetary benefits. Our earlier query, as to the value of better health, or the value of pelicans as a species, is not addressed by these historical cost-benefit studies. The reason, in part, is that the measurement of such intangible and subjective values would be even more imprecise than in the illustrations which we have already reviewed. Morever, public policy has not, until recently, regarded these intangible benefits as being an admissible concern in the decision process. The President's Advisory Commit-

Figure 12-3 Indirect Irrigation Benefits
(Annual Values under Full Development)

	With irrigation (dollars)	Without irrigation (dollars)	Difference (dollars)	Average profit rate (percentage)	Indirect benefit (dollars)
Benefit A: Sales to local wholesale and retail business (includes fruit, vegetables, hay, and forage)	350,000	10,000	340,000	5	17,000
Benefit B: Sales for national processing and marketing (includes grains, fruits, vegetables, dairy, livestock, poultry, wool, and seed crops)	1,000,000	90,000	910,000	20	178,750
Benefit C: Purchases for family living and production expenses			882,500	18	158,800
Total indirect benefits A, B, and C					$354,600

tee on Water Resources, for example, recommended that only the direct monetary benefits be considered, ruling out the indirect benefits. If cognizance is not taken of indirect benefits, then intangible and subjective values would likely be of even more remote interest.

One reason for omitting indirect effects is that sufficient conceptual problems have already been encountered in trying to measure the economic aspects of cost-benefit relationships, without adding still more subjective ones. We have so far considered two of these conceptual problems, namely, (1) what social rate of interest should be assumed? and (2) what shall be the measure of direct and indirect economic benefits included in the analysis? A third, and still more thorny problem, is related to: (3) what are the income redistribution effects?

EXAMPLE OF INCOME REDISTRIBUTION EFFECTS

Income redistribution effects of a public project will be illustrated by a potential development of the Willamette River in central Oregon. The Willamette River runs from the Middle Fork River near Eugene, north through Salem, and into the Columbia River at Portland. In progress the Willamette is confluent with the McKenzie, Middle Santiam, North Santiam, and Callapooya Rivers. A series of dams on the several rivers would provide about $27 million in estimated annual benefits, of which $12 million would be from flood control; $6 million from drainage, $5 million from power, and the balance from lesser services such as navigation, irrigation, recreation, pollution abatement, and domestic water supply. A variety of different annual costs might be estimated depending upon whether the development is by federal agency, local government, or private utilities.

The total project cost was estimated (House Document 531, *Columbia River and Tributaries Northwest*, 1950) at about $22 million. The annual changes would vary from $1,500,000 to $3 million depending upon public or private development. The main difference in cost is due to bond interest or stock dividends to recompense the invested capital required by the project.

A study of the distribution of gains from the project indicates that the first-round effects accrue to the customers of the electric power, who receive the additional energy at rates less in cost than they would from the next attractive alternative. Second-round income effects are benefits to those who gain from the flood control and drainage services of the project, as well as from navigation, recreation, and other minor services. Of the total annual costs, about $1,500,000 is covered by power charges to electricity users in the Pacific Northwest. Another $850,000 represents unmet opportunity costs shifted to other regions of the United States in accordance with the incidence of general taxes. The Middle Atlantic and the East North Central states, which have the largest tax base and bear the preponderant tax incidence, would absorb about half of the redistributed cost of the project which is not sustained by the electric power consumers in the Pacific Northwest.

However, still other successive rounds of income distribution effects are also encountered stemming from gains through stock or bonds ownership incurred in financing the project. Assuming that the Willamette River development is carried out by a private utility company, which takes advantage of the rapid amortization of investment then available, the final distribution of gains would appear as in Figure 12-4.[11]

The table shows some rather surprising results. If you had been asked for example, what you thought the effects would be of a private utility project to develop the drainage flood control and power potential of the Willamette Valley in Oregon, what would you answer? The obvious, simple answer would seem to be that the principal benefits and cost would rest upon those who live in the area. But the table below indicates such an answer is not correct.

After all the income redistribution effects are calculated, the principal benefits, aside from those to electric power consumers in the Pacific Northwest, accrue to citizens in the New England and Middle Atlantic regions, which are rich in surplus capital for investment. The main costs

[11]Ibid., pp. 199–261.

Figure 12-4   Distribution of Gains and Costs by Region, Including Accelerated Amortization and Net Annual Income Transfers

Regions	Distribution of gains by regions (percent)	Distribution of increased general tax liabilities (percent)	Net annual income transfers among regions* (thousand of dollars)
New England	32.92	7.05	+64,520
Middle Atlantic	29.97	24.35	+14,016
South Atlantic	3.87	9.96	−15,189
East South Central	1.70	3.42	− 4,290
East North Central	10.47	25.55	−37,560
West North Central	4.32	7.86	− 8,829
West South Central	0.45	6.40	−14,839
Mountain	2.55	2.89	− 848
Pacific Coast	13.08	12.49	+ 1,471

*Discrepancy in net of transfers caused by rounding.

of the project, after income redistribution, are borne by the East North Central states, which are high in current taxable income but relatively low in capital. This illustration makes it quite clear that the income redistribution effects, which are often the most important criteria for a project, may have widespread and surprising ramifications which need careful analysis and exploration.

CARE IN THE ANALYSIS OF COST-BENEFIT RELATIONSHIPS

Perhaps these examples, however brief, have been sufficient to suggest that the measurement and allocation of both cost and benefits are fraught with a number of knotty problems. Roland McKean has concerned himself with these issues and arrived at a number of rules for guidance to avoid the pitfalls of cost-benefit measurements. These rules are not simple axioms, easily applied, but rather broad directions on how to approach the analysis of value in the case of public goods. He believes that if these pitfalls are not avoided, quantitative analysis in governmental decisions may do more harm than good.[12] However, better quantitative analysis, well done, holds promise of greater responsiveness and economy in government. The real problem is to determine the right criterion. In government operations the overall objective is so complex, and the size of the "firm" so large as compared to private enterprises, that it is more difficult to select appropriate criteria for measurement or judgment. Among McKean's suggestions are the following:

    1   Care should be taken, in breaking down a problem to make it more manageable, that one does not end up with a piecemeal analysis which results in suboptimization.
    2   Closely related to the suboptimization tendency is the danger of inconsistency of a piecemeal solution with higher-level criteria.[13] The Hell's Canyon illustration, for instance, suboptimized the river development upon local electric power distribution, without regard to the higher-level criteria of maximizing flood control, navigation, or national power output.
    3   The spillover effects of a project should be carefully studied to be sure that secondary interactions do not result in unknown costs or biological effects.[14] In economics these interactions of one firm's gains upon another's costs are called external economies and diseconomies. For example, forcing brine into an oil well to increase its yield of crude oil may create salinity in the underground water table, reducing the fertility

---

[12]Roland N. McKean, *Efficiency in Government through Systems Analysis,* John Wiley and Sons, New York, 1958, Rand Corporation, p. 14.
   [13]Ibid., p. 32.
   [14]Ibid., p. 39.

of neighboring farmlands. Then the gain of the oil well operator has created a spillover, or diseconomy, which adversely affects the farmer. Similarly, in water resource projects, a multiple-purpose development involving damming a river may alter the stream flows and change the chemical content of the water which ultimately is used in domestic or industrial water supplies.

4 Neglect of spillover effects, higher-level gains, or valuable inputs may lead to wrong definitions of cost and gain.[15] The gain in personal automobile transportation convenience at the manufactured cost for a new car, for example, ignores the spillover effect of air pollution. A higher-level gain may be possible by optimizing urban planning and transportation systems together, along with the social cost inputs of highway construction and air pollution control costs. In other words, present transportation decision criteria ignore most of the social and biological costs.

5 The most appropriate criteria are the measurement of maximum gains minus all costs, with either gain or cost fixed.[16] The practice of treating benefits as a ratio of cost can be erroneous because it may ignore the absolute dollar value of the benefit. The real concern is the amount of net benefit over cost. The reason for keeping either benefit or cost fixed is that there will be some common basis for comparison, control, or standard of one project to another. If both cost and benefit are varying from project to project, comparison becomes unreliable. The common tendency of maximizing benefit while minimizing cost should be avoided, as a logical impossibility.

6 Alternative courses of action should be compared with costs calculated by at least two discount rates so that a realistic measure of present worth is reckoned under differing social preferences as to the value of a future time stream of benefits.[17]

These basic principles are supplemented in a later work by Hitch and McKean, where attention is paid to the treatment of uncertainty in the future, and the discounting rates used to recognize the time factor.[18] When unknowns and uncertainties exist in a problem—for example, the amount and duration of oxidants which may be expected to cause damage to lung tissue—the procedure should be to calculate the contingency at both a high value and a low value, in order to construct a range of probability.

The application of the several principles above has been tried experimentally over the past decade in a number of agencies, the most

[15]Ibid., pp. 40–41.
[16]Ibid., pp. 46ff.
[17]Ibid., pp. 99 and 124.
[18]Charles J. Hitch and Roland N. McKean, *The Economics of Defense in a Nuclear Age*, Harvard University Press, Cambridge, Mass., 1960 (Antheum edition, 1965), pp. 193–200 and 209–211.

notable attempt being in the Department of Defense. The intercontinental ballistic missile threat was subject to considerable useful analysis by cost-effectiveness methodology, because the final output was definable and measurable as target destruction capability. With a finite and known number of targets and a measurable output, the problem was quite tractable, and the results helped resolve the question of the size of a missile force and its relative advantage compared to bombers. The applications of systems analysis to other defense problems were not so useful, because the outputs were difficult to define and measure. For example, what is the most effective mix of armament for limited warfare purposes? In limited war tactics, the contingencies are so numerous that the outputs become imponderable. The first contingency is that of search, and if one does not have the technology to find the enemy and know where they are, there is no way to optimize superiority of one's own forces. About all one can conclude quantitatively is that rifles are relatively useless in suppressing an enemy, compared to mortars for example, but, psychologically, what soldier would care to go into battle without any sidearms?

However, we are not particularly interested in the defense examples of cost-effectiveness studies in this book but, rather, in the experience of civilian agencies which might have some bearing on environmental problems. Unfortunately, outside of the water resource studies of the type already cited, there are few civilian agency examples. One set of experiments conducted by the Bureau of the Budget on productivity measurements, based upon input and output studies, has similar enough resemblance to our interest to warrant examination.

EXPERIMENTS WITH PRODUCTIVITY MEASURES IN CIVILIAN AGENCIES

In 1962, the Bureau of the Budget asked five agencies to join in an experiment to develop input-output measures of their operations, which might ultimately yield some productivity indicators. The Budget Bureau stated its purpose in these terms:

> In private enterprise, the guidance of what to produce and the incentive to produce it with maximum obtainable efficiency are provided by the workings of the profit motive in a market system. Moreover, business enterprises can gauge their success from the financial statements. But, in Government, the system of goals and incentives is different and, with very few exceptions, the managers of Government agencies have no general indicator of the effectiveness of their choices or the efficiency of their performance compared to the profit and loss statement. Measures of productivity for

individual agencies do reflect the efficiency with which the agencies produce their service. By providing objective measures of service output and unit cost, development of productivity data can contribute, also, to better evaluation of choices of outputs to be produced.[19]

The statement of purpose indicates that no real attempt is being made to measure benefit to the user: rather, the purpose is to ascertain the costs of an existing service or output which is assumed, for the time being, to be socially desirable. The implication is that, if one knew the cost, it might be easier to find out whether society had any preference for the service.

In any case, one has to start somewhere, and the Bureau of the Budget chose to start on the costs of present operations. As a matter of fact, most operations research tends to start with cost analysis, rather than with demand estimation, simply because it is easier.

The five agencies and functions which participated with the Bureau of the Budget in the study were: (1) the Division of Disbursements in the Treasury, producing checks and savings bonds; (2) the Department of Insurance in the Veterans Administration, life insurance accounting; (3) the Post Office Department, mail handling operations; (4) the Federal Aviation Agency's Systems Maintenance Division, maintaining the air navigation and air traffic control facilities for civilian aviation; and (5) the Bureau of Land Management in the Department of the Interior, handling land and mineral claim cases, cadastral surveys, and range and forestry programs.

The study was extensive, involving analysis of a large amount of data about individual transactions in the several agencies. Very briefly, the findings were that, over various years ending in 1962, the productivity of measured operations of the Veterans Administration increased at an annual rate of 9.8 percent, the Treasury by 9.4 percent, the Post Office by 0.3 percent, the Federal Aviation Agency decreased by 4.0 percent, and the activities of the Bureau of Land Management proved to be un-measurable with the time and effort allotted.

The Bureau of the Budget concludes that the productivity findings are determined by three major factors: (1) a uniform, definable, and not diversified output; (2) a comparatively small number of locations; and (3) a radical change in production technology.[20]

What happened in the study is clear. The activities which proved measurable were simple accounting operations that had increased in

---

[19] *Measuring Productivity of Federal Government Organization,* Bureau of the Budget, 1964, Washington, p. 3.
[20] Ibid., pp. 14–15.

productivity by installation of data processing equipment. The two agencies with a high labor input, the Post Office and the FAA, made a poor productivity showing. The agency with the subjectively valued outputs—that is, the Bureau of Land Management—was not readily measurable.

The conclusion one might correctly draw from this experiment is that the measurement of inputs and costs for government services in many cases is difficult, and the measurement of outputs is even more so. But it is not a correct inference to go on to assume that, because of its difficulty, the approach should be abandoned. There are two kinds of answers, propounded by Kneese, to such a surmise.

First, any attempt at benefit-cost analysis requires a rigorous statement of objectives, which in itself requires some rethinking as to whether an activity is worth doing.

The second is that an attempt to specify the cost of an activity, its quantities, or causative relationships has the effect of revealing nonessentials as well as establishing some approximate values.

Even if the inherent complexity of determining the value of public goods makes optimum solutions unattainable, due to lack of information or conceptual difficulties, the examination of these issues at least helps define better what government is doing, why, and at what cost.[21]

In the end, however, we need to recognize that there are limitations to the use of benefit-cost measures, which is, after all, the attempt to transfer marginal analysis from the private market to public goods. Some public goods are, in fact, distinctly different in character from private goods and, thus, not susceptible to the same logic. Public goods are distinct in being highly interdependent, that is, characterized by joint supply. Public health protection is an example of joint supply; if it is provided to one person, it is provided to all. Moreover, individuals cannot elect how much public health protection they wish to consume individually, as they can for discrete products in the private market. In air pollution, for instance, one individual cannot choose to consume an air quality of 0.10 ppm of oxidants, while another may be satisfied with an air quality of 0.25 ppm oxidants at lesser cost. If public health policy achieves an air quality standard of 0.10 ppm, then the atmosphere has that quality for all. True public goods are characterized by interdependence in consumption and joint costs in their supply. One may wish to measure a benefit to individuals, since the value of a particular standard of air quality, for example, will vary from person to person. That is, each has his own demand curve and marginal value for a particular level of air quality. But

[21]Allen V. Kneese, *Water Pollution*, Resources for the Future, Washington, 1962, pp. 40–41.

what one needs to ascertain for public policy is where the average (or majority) value lies for all beneficiaries, because this average represents democratic consensus in political reality.

Public goods, in the end, are valued by the political process, because of their joint and interdependent characteristics. Environmental quality standards, public health, and protection against force are all public goods of this nature. Market values do not exist, nor can they be readily imputed, because there cannot be individual choice about the amount of discrete consumption or supply.[22] The environment has one quality for all within it. If environment is to be improved, it is by group choice, and this form of social valuation is political.

If environmental issues are political valuations in the end, of what purpose is the attempt at quantitative measurement, i.e., comparing costs to benefits? Would quantitative measures have any impact upon decisions, given the cross-currents of political motivations and compromises?[23] Lobby influences, pressure groups, pork barrel politics, logrolling, empire building, spoils, party loyalty, and just plain getting elected next time—these are all powerful political forces associated with a representative form of government, and are often decisive in shaping legislative actions.

One reason political forces are so powerful is that legislators are rarely presented with analytical choices; if they were, there is reason to expect legislators to pay some heed—if only because the voters back home, who are the only ones who can keep the politician in office, would tend to favor lower cost or higher benefit choices. This does not mean that cogent analysis would promptly prevail, but neither is the pessimistic view warranted that better quantitative analysis is without influence. Many legislators are frequently in search of objective information upon which to make informed judgments responsive to the public interest. The availability of objective data on environmental impact or benefit-cost relations would improve their decision process.

SUMMARY

The increasing concern for biological damage has brought into being a government policy to require environmental impact statements on all new public programs. These statements are intended to identify the extent of environmental change caused by public actions and to assess their beneficial or detrimental aspects. Long-term, irreversible actions are to be

[22]Ibid., p. 97.
[23]McKean, *Efficiency in Government*, op. cit., p. 15.

scrutinized particularly to see whether other alternatives mitigate disruptions to the ecosystem.

In practice the environmental impact statements have been subject to review through distribution to other concerned agencies or community groups. The Council on Environmental Quality has served as a clearing house to identify issues and adverse effects. However, there does not yet appear to be a methodology or expertise clearly related to environmental impact analysis.

Historically, the government has weighed benefit versus cost as a means of deciding whether projects should be approved. Typical of such projects have been dams, irrigation, reclamation, navigation, and flood control works. The benefits and costs have been related largely to human economic activity, and indirect effects or biological costs have, until recently, been neglected in the decision process.

Benefit-cost analysis, even when applied to economic projects excluding subjective consequences, has encountered three difficult conceptual problems. The first has been to determine what interest rate would fairly allocate resources among public and private capital markets. The government has generally used low rates of social time preference (2 to 3 percent), but at higher interest rates more similar to private markets (5 to 6 percent) many public projects are not justifiable.

The second conceptual problem has been how to relate indirect effects to the direct economic benefits to users. Secondary and tertiary effects have been estimated to show how increased sales, trade, or employment may be derived from public projects, but generally these have been illustrative only and not included as part of the decision criteria.

A third problem has been to estimate the income redistribution effects of a project. Indeed, this may be the most important of all consequences, because in most cases the government undertakes projects specifically for the purpose of redistributing income. Yet the redistribution effects, when calculated, often show that the major income changes go to those supplying the capital rather than to those who are beneficial users of the project's output.

These problems demonstrate that considerable care needs to be exercised in benefit-cost analysis, particularly to avoid suboptimization and spillover effects. The most appropriate approach is to compare alternatives at several interest rates on the basis of gains minus costs, with either gain or cost held fixed in the comparison among alternatives.

The difficulties with benefit-cost studies have raised some question as to whether they are worth the effort, especially when the judgment in the end is dominated by political influences. One answer to such a query is, perhaps, that an attempt might be made to make even political decisions more objective in terms of choices among alternatives.

DISCUSSION QUESTIONS

1 What social rate of interest do you think is equitable as a means of allocating resources among public and private uses? Why? How would you make such an interest rate effective?
2 If you were asked to judge the environmental impact statement for the West Snoqualmie to Tanner highway, what would be your criteria and judgment?
3 Explain the reasons why the three-dam approach was chosen for Hell's Canyon Reach, instead of the high dam or two-dam approach? What were its economic and environmental consequences?
4 What are spillover effects and how do they occur in benefit-cost studies?

PROBLEM

Make a benefit-cost analysis of your own college education, showing the effects of various interest rates, indirect benefits, and income redistribution effects. What are the benefits? Who are the beneficiaries? What are the costs? How are the costs and income effects distributed? From the results, what would you conclude about the value of a college education?

Chapter 13

Market Simulation of Environmental Costs

The study of economics concerns itself with the efficient allocation of resources to optimize the satisfaction of human wants. The principal means for accomplishing this optimization is through the market mechanism, by which individuals express preferences for the kind and quantities of goods and services that satisfy their wants. The efficient allocation of resources is achieved, also through the market, by supplying factors of production to a point where the marginal costs to producers are in equilibrium with their marginal revenue.

The criterion of efficiency in this allocation process is sometimes referred to by economists as *Pareto optimality,* after the economist by that name. An economic state is said to be Pareto optimal if it is impossible to make anyone better off without making someone else worse off at the same time. A situation is inefficient when it is possible to make at least one member of society better off without worsening the condition of someone else.[1]

---

[1]Otto A. Davis and Morton I. Kamien, *Externalities, Information and Collective Action,* Joint Committee on Economic Report, Analysis and Evaluation of Public Expenditures, vol. 1, Washington, 1969, p. 69.

The condition of the environment, with its high wasteloads, toxic concentrations, biological damage, and social costs, is clearly something less than Pareto optimal. Some members of society could obviously be better off in terms of environmental quality, clean air, pure water, and improved health effects. That is, the removal of pollutants from the environment would make a great many members of society better off. Would removal of pollutants make anyone worse off? Temporarily, perhaps, the reduction of pollutants would cause producers of emissions some administrative travail and increased costs to eliminate or recycle residuals now dumped into the ecosystem, but in the longer run, the producers would adjust to a new cost structure and equilibrium where the (presumably) higher marginal costs would again just equal the marginal revenue. Perhaps at higher costs and higher prices, the volume of goods sold by an individual producer might be less than it was formerly without pollution controls, but this does not make him worse off, in economic theory, because the quantity of goods is determined by the amount which satisfies consumer wants and not producers. In other words, the producer is no worse off as long as he can adjust the allocation of his resources and factors of production to a new cost structure, and this he can do. In consequence, we must conclude that the environmental situation is not Pareto optimal because we can make a great many consumers or receptors of ecological effects better off without making producers worse off.

The idea of a more optimal, simulated market to improve the environment will be discussed in terms of the following topics:

1 What is optimal?
2 Market failure in the environment
3 Market simulation of ecological effects
4 Forms of ecological usage charges
5 The use of shadow prices
6 The estimation of shadow prices
7 Present suboptimal structure and rules
8 Rule making as a form of shadow pricing
9 Social indicators as measures of worth

WHAT IS OPTIMAL?

The previous study of materials balance and dispersion of residuals into the environment provides us with some information on the locus, incidence, and impact of human actions on ecology. We now want to examine that impact in relation to some standard or criteria to assess whether the effect is for better or worse. Concepts like better or worse, good or bad, progress or degradation are value judgments, which we subjectively apply as normative standards compared to an event. If the event falls short of the norm, the judgment is that one is worse off; if the event exceeds the expectation in the norm, one is better off. The normative standard itself is usually culturally derived from historical events, and we have seen that many of the norms regarding material progress and the conquest of nature were derived from the industrial revolution and the attempt to overcome general poverty.

The cultural indoctrination from this historical era provides us with norms which condition us to say that free enterprise and free market prices are "good," because they can be logically linked to the maximization of output which satisfies human wants. Other norms regarding the value of human life, from theology and ethical philosophies, condition us to say that health damage effects from toxic residuals in the environment are "bad," because they increase morbidity and mortality rates among human and other species. Now we are in the logical dilemma, however, that one of our "goods" is contributing to a "bad." That is, the "good" market price structure is associated somehow with "bad" health damage effects. What can we do to reconcile this paradox?

One approach is to back off from the ideal expectation regarding market prices or health effects and say that we would like to achieve as much of benefit from each as is internally consistent between the two. That is, we would like to maximize the material output through free market exchange to the extent that it is consistent with a satisfactory level of health. This is a concept, not of the ideal, but of the optimal—optimum means to achieve sufficiently those qualities conducive to an end, such as the most favorable conditions for the growth of an organism. Optimal, then, is a most favorable or satisfactory state, considering the conflicts and interactions among means. It implies a tradeoff, or exchange, of satisfactions, one against another, in increments until some balance or equilibrium is reached which is minimally agreeable to all.

This principle was stated by Pareto: society should try to achieve an optimum in which each individual realizes maximum satisfaction (or utility) without subtracting from anyone else's satisfactions. That is, if society could add one increment of utility to one individual's satisfaction, without detracting an increment of utility from someone else, it should do so. This is the basic criterion of welfare economics. A condition where such an equilibrium among incremental satisfactions has been reached is known as Pareto optimality.[2]

Pareto optimality would probably not be a useful concept were it not also for the development of concepts in modern welfare economics which

[2]David W. Miller and Martin K. Starr, *Executive Decisions and Operations Research*, Prentice-Hall, Inc., Englewood Cliffs, N.J., 1960, p. 46.

implement the idea. The most important of these developments can be viewed as one of the central theorems of economics. Given the following: (1) the divisibility of capital equipment to prevent increasing returns with scale (size), (2) the availability of information, (3) the absence of monopoly power, and (4) private goods without side effects, or externalities, then there exists a set of market prices, by which profit-maximizing firms and utility-maximizing customers will automatically cause the economic system to attain a Pareto optimal position.[3]

All these boundary conditions to the economic theorem are essential to achieve an optimum, and their failure to be realized in the real world precludes optimality. All these conditions need to be examined for their reality, and certainly there is grave question whether technology is infinitely divisible, or whether perfect competition and perfect information exist in the marketplace. These questions are amply explored in economic literature. For our purpose, we need only examine whether all goods in the market are "private" goods, without side effects, or "public" goods. That is, a private good is one which has a discrete unit in utility; has no side effects; is privately produced, privately and discretely consumed, and privately exchanged in the market place. If all goods are of this type, then there would be no "public" goods, which are commonly used, jointly produced, and jointly consumed. But we know as ecologists, (Chapters 7 through 11) that all the goods and services derived from the environment are commonly used and jointly consumed. There is no discrete unit of air quality, privately produced and available to one but not all. Air quality, water quality, solar energy conversion and availability, and the quality of nutrient in the food chain are common to all species. Moreover, private production does produce side effects such as toxicity, quality deterioration, social costs—all external to the private market mechanism. Therefore, the existence of side effects and externalities from private goods, if nothing else, negates the achievement optimality.

MARKET FAILURE IN THE ENVIRONMENT

The fact that the market mechanism has not created optimal environmental satisfactions is sometimes referred to in economic literature as a "market failure." A market failure exists in ecological conditions because the market is unable to make an efficient allocation of resources to optimize human wants. That is, resources are not allocated efficiently because an overabundance of waste and toxic materials are produced. Human wants are not satisfied because too little clean air and environ-

[3]Davis and Kamien, op. cit., p. 69.

mental quality are produced relative to material consumer goods. The reason for the market failure in the ecological case is that many of the resources going into the human production process are not priced. They enter the market presumably as "free goods," like air, or if not free, at least underpriced, like water.

Pollution presents a somewhat embarrassing problem to economic theory, which has refined the logic that the market works reasonably well in allocating resources. The apogee of theoretical achievement has been to show that, under certain conditions, the market comes to a competitive equilibrium which is also Pareto efficient. Pollution, externalities, and other spillover effects have been treated as isolated and minor welfare deviations in the economic system, but their prevalence now demonstrates that they are neither minor nor isolated. The air resource allocation problem, with its widening disparity between actual and desired levels of air quality, is but one example of many of the welfare failures caused by the market's present structure.[4]

The preoccupation of economists with the exchange of goods in private markets has caused environmental social costs to be viewed historically as aberrations of an otherwise stable and comprehensive equilibrium. The erroneous perspective of viewing economic exchange as composed of *goods* was discussed by Irving Fisher in 1906 and F. H. Knight in 1921.

> The only true method, in our view, is to regard uniformly as income the *service* of a dwelling to its owner (shelter or money rental), the *service* of a piano (music), the *service* of food (nourishment).[5]

Pollution and adverse environmental effects of rising wasteloads may be said to create a disservice or disutility to the consumer.

The emergence of human environmental dissatisfactions from the flow of economic services has been aggravated by rising population, urbanization, and industrialization in recent years. These dissatisfactions or disutilities to the consumer are also referred to as external diseconomies, social costs, spillovers, or damage effects. Kneese, Ayres, and d'Arge argue that these disutilities can no longer be set outside of economic theory as insignificant. They say:

> 1 External diseconomies are not freakish anomalies but inherent parts of the production-consumption processes.

[4]Robert J. Anderson, Jr., and Thomas D. Crocker, *The Economics of Air Pollution*, Project Clean Air, University of California, Riverside, Calif., Assessment, vol. 3, pp. 6–2.
[5]Irving Fisher, *Nature of Capital and Income*, A. M. Kelley, New York, 1906.

2 While external diseconomies may be negligible in a low-population, underdeveloped economic settling, they become progressively more important as population rises and technological output increases.

3 The diseconomies cannot properly be dealt with by considering land, air, and water separately because the ecosystem is in common use by man and all species and its natural reservoirs of dilution or assimilation become exhausted.[6]

If we accept the notion that environmental diseconomies reflect a market failure, because they are an integral rather than a freakish part of an urban industrial society, then economic theory should encompass these external costs in its calculus. Failure to incorporate these externalities and damage effects into the cost structure has two related consequences: (1) it perpetuates and augments the biological damages, and (2) it causes a misallocation of resources. The misallocation of resources takes place because some resources are underpriced and that results in the overproduction of goods which have adverse damage effects.[7]

MARKET SIMULATION OF ECOLOGICAL EFFECTS

The "market failure" to allocate resources efficiently in the environmental case, then, results in overproduction of underpriced goods which have adverse biological effects. We can correct this misallocation by repricing the resources to reflect more accurately human needs and satisfactions, including biological effects. The difficulty is that biological effects and environmental quality are services not traded in the commodity markets, which is, of course, the reason why their valuation was left out of allocation decisions in the first place. This means that we must find a way to introduce ecological effects into the market by some means, which may be an actual or surrogate cost. That is, we must treat the ecological inputs and outputs in the human production cycle as though they were reflected in the market with some real or artificial price. Thus, we will simulate a market to incorporate ecological effects in order to correct our allocation decision process.

Market simulation of the environment becomes feasible at those points, which we discovered in the last chapter, where administrative control can be exercised at the human interface with the ecosystem. Let us recreate, from the last chapter, a simplified diagram (Figure 13-1) of the relation of the ecosystem to human productive activity, and introduce

[6]Allen V. Kreese, Robert U. Ayers, and Ralph C. d'Arge, *Economics and the Environment, Resources for the Future,* Johns Hopkins Press, Baltimore, 1970, p. 14.
[7]Orris C. Herfindahl and Allen V. Kneese, *Quality of the Environment, Resources for the Future,* Johns Hopkins Press, Baltimore, 1965, pp. 7–8.

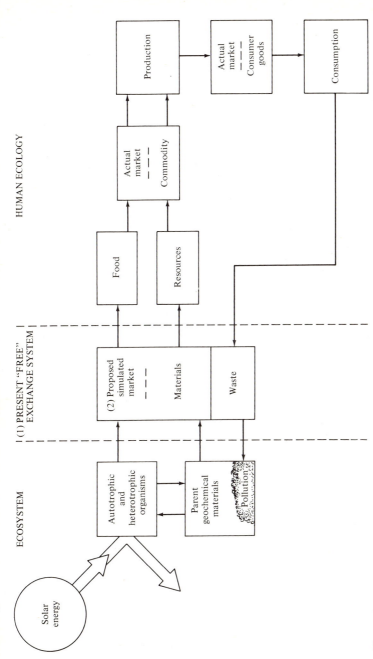

Figure 13-1 Market exchange systems in human activity and ecosystems.

into the diagram the points at which price mechanisms can be made to work. The diagram shows two related but separate circulatory systems, the energy-nutrient cycle of the natural ecosystems, and the human production-consumption cycle. The human activity cycle has actual markets interposed at the exchange between food and resources with the production process, and this is a commodity or materials market. Again, the exchange between human producers and consumers has an intervening market, the actual market for consumer goods. (In this much simplified form, the interchanges of labor and capital equipment are not shown, but they would merely proliferate the market sectors in which prices and exchanges occur.)

The natural ecosystem has no intervening "markets" as such in its circulatory processes, mainly because they are self-regulating. That is, the first and second laws of thermodynamics create an equilibrium in energy conversion, nutrient cycles, and species populations. (Human wants and appetites have no such natural constraints, rather they are near-infinite, and thus we interpose markets in the human production-consumption cycle to substitute for the regulatory functions of natural law.) The natural ecosystem is essentially a closed system, except for incoming solar energy; that is, the nutrient-species processes are self-contained and circulatory within themselves. The human ecology is an open system, with newly imagined wants entering the demand side of the markets, with increasing demands upon the resource base, and with increasing wastes disposed on the ecosystem.

The open human demand system has no regulatory function in its relation to the environment, either in the form of a market or natural laws (other than mankind ultimately poisoning itself into extinction). Since we do not want to rely on the natural laws of toxicity (poisoning ourselves) as the regulator, some other form of regulation is needed.

Presently a "free" exchange system exists between the natural ecosystem and the human ecology. That is, we withdraw food and resources from the ecosystem without any costs or charges to ourselves or compensation to the ecosystem, and we dispose toxic wastes upon the ecosystem without cost and charges to ourselves. This "free" exchange coupled with the infinity of human desires is what has created the ecological crisis. (There is seemingly no limit to the amount of resources we withdraw from, nor the amount of wasteload we dispose upon, the environment.) The result of this "free" exchange system has been a failure in our own human markets, a misallocation of resources, and an overproduction of wastes to our own biological detriment. How can we correct this misallocation?

One solution is to interpose a simulated market between the ecosystem and ourselves, so that the withdrawal of resources and the disposition of wastes have a price. What should that price be? One alternative form of pricing would be to interpose a sufficient charge to avoid adverse biological effects. The definition of adverse might be Liebig's law of the minimum, that is, any effect outside of the tolerance range of species. The *Genossenschaften* in the Rhine use such a definition when they base their effluent charges upon pollution concentrations which are lethal to fish. The charge is then sufficient to clean up the water to prevent fish kills. The BOD level at which fish kills occur may be only one standard of biological damage; for example, another common criterion is to reduce the coliform bacteria in sewage to prevent the incidence of human disease. The sufficient charges in either case would be an amount necessary to cover the costs of removing pollutants to prevent such biological damage.

FORMS OF ECOLOGICAL USAGE CHARGES

Charges in the simulated market exchange between the natural system and the human ecology might be at either the input or output phase. Effluent charges for sewage are on the output side of the human processes, that is, upon the return of waste from human activity to the ecosystem. In some cases, it would be administratively more feasible to place the charge on inputs, that is, upon the movement of materials from the natural ecosystem into human processes.

For example, surface mining, in present practice, underprices the minerals by including only the fixed and operating costs of extraction, but not the reclamation of the land afterward. About 3,200,000 acres of land have been devastated by surface mining, and about 2 million acres are still in need of reclamation. New surface mining operations are adding about 150,000 to 200,000 acres of overturned land per year to this total. In strip-mining of coal alone, there are some 25,000 miles of spoil banks of upturned land. Spoil banks and mine tailing frequently have high-acidity characteristics, some below pH 4 in which plants cannot survive. The reclamation of these lands costs from perhaps $100 to $700 per acre, not to put them back into natural contours, but to grade them sufficiently for planting and to prevent mine-acid runoff into streams.[8] Such reclaimed lands may still lie in huge furrows or long hillocks, but they would have some limited use for recreation and wildlife.

One reason devasted mining lands lie unreclaimed is that there is no practical way to impose a charge for the social costs of reclamation after extraction is completed. The mining company then has moved on to other

[8] *Surface Mining*, a special report of the U.S. Department of Interior, Washington, 1967, pp. 42, 52, 54, 82, and 90.

operations and has no incentive to reclaim the land. The consumer cannot identify the portion of his car which represents underpriced coal and iron that came from surface mining, and hence there is no fair charge to the consumer after the fact. The result has been that government, with tax dollars, has undertaken what limited, pilot reclamations have been attempted.

The time at which an environmental charge could administratively be placed upon the surface mining to cover the cost of land reclamation is at the time of extraction as a cost per acre or per ton of ore mined. The cost per ton would depend upon the yields of ore and the reclamation costs in each case, but as an average the cost might be as much as $1 per ton, considering that something like 30 billion net tons of crude ore are mined annually. An additional user charge of $1 per ton of ore could result in a 10 to 20 percent increase in price for some ores, and this may be viewed by some as upsetting the market, meaning changing the demand and quantity relationships in the private price market. That is probably true. But again, the object of economic activity is not to maximize the volume of materials flow, including waste, spoil banks, and mine-acid in streams. The objective is to optimize human satisfactions. The market should accurately reflect that preference. In this case, our simulated market would most accurately reflect that preference by placing a user charge on the input of the resource into the human production process, because there is no practical way to impose a unit usage charge after the fact of extraction.

We have noted two types of ecological usage charges, the effluent charge imposed upon waste disposal as an output from the human processes to the environment, and a mineral usage charge imposed as an input from the environmental to the human production process. We might observe, of these ecological usage charges, that they added costs sufficient to avoid or repair biological damage to the ecosystem. In a sense, we are compensating the ecosystem for a loss. Surface mineral extraction or effluent wasteloads represent a biological loss in the ecosystem to some species. The ecological usage charge is a compensation to avoid degradation in the first instance, or to restore the nutrient-species balance to its condition prior to human intervention. The essence of the ecological usage charge is then basically simple; it is a compensation sufficient to maintain a nutrient-species equilibrium.

There are at least two other means of achieving the same effect of maintaining ecological balance, besides the direct user charge, that is, (1) by incentives and disincentives, and (2) by shadow prices.

An example of an incentive is the policy of the Swedish government to grant tax concessions or subsidies for the installation by industry of pollution control equipment. Rapid depreciation allowances for new equipment which is low in emissions would be another form of incentive. The obverse would be to discourage human behavior which causes pollution by disincentives or penalties. For example, a tax on automobiles proportionate to their air pollution emission characteristics would be such a disincentive. Then autombile owners would have to take into account the added costs of using and polluting air, and this cost element would be a factor in their decision as to what kind of car or transportation they preferred.

D'Arge calculated an illustrative disincentive to air pollution in the form of tax schedules and found that a series of automobile characteristics could be related to emission levels. The characteristics included were compression ratio, model year, number of cylinders, transmission type, make, odometer reading, and type of carburetor. The emission levels were then related to health damage effects of the emissions. The assignment of damage per ton of gaseous emissions from automobiles requires more research on the health hazards caused by air pollution. However, if the health damages of air pollution were valued at $10 per ton of emissions, for example, the tax disincentive on a 1968 Chrysler with 22,600 miles on the odometer, for example, would be $3.60. If the damage effects were determined to be $200 per ton of emissions, the tax would be $72.[9] This type of disincentive is very like an effluent charge for the use of the environment (in this case, the use of oxygen from the air for combustion and the discharge of residuals into the atmosphere), with the exception that the charge is based on a calculation of damage rather than upon a direct usage measurement.

A third general type of ecological usage charge is shadow prices. Shadow prices are applicable particularly to public projects where the government finds it necessary to undertake a public investment program with broad common usage such as in river basin development, multiple land usage, sewage disposal, or public transportation system. These are cases in which the production of the service is indivisible and, if provided to one, the service is available to all. That is, shadow prices are applicable to public goods in common usage.

THE USE OF SHADOW PRICES

The need for public investment programs in the environment is based upon the assumption that isolated user charges and incentives are not sufficient, in themselves, to achieve a coherent program of environmental

---

[9]D'Arge, Clark, and Bubik, *Automotive Exhaust Emission Taxes*, Project Clean Air, University of California, Riverside, Calif. 1970, Research Report, vol. 3, S-12, p. 18.

quality.[10] For example, suppose that disincentives to automobile driving were legislated in the form of taxes based upon emissions, and assume also that a large number of drivers then preferred a public transit system. They would have no alternative choice to use a public transit system unless there had been, concurrently, a public investment program to create such a transportation system.

Benefit-cost analysis is one means of trying to evaluate the costs of public investment projects, but benefit cost is, like the industrial accounting system, concerned mainly with allocating fixed and operating costs to beneficiaries. Shadow prices represent an attempt to extend benefit-cost techniques to impute additional intangible values which people treat as satisfactions.

In the automobile–public transit case, for example, land values and proximity are social values of some significance. Are they reflected accurately in present decision making? The gasoline tax in California, as in most states, is dedicated to highway construction, and high interests have successfully defeated public referenda to repeal it. The consequence is that about one-sixth of the land in the Los Angeles area is paved in highways and streets; the withdrawal rate of land from other uses to highways continues each year because there is nothing else the gas tax can be spent upon. Is the continuous withdrawal of land, to pave it over, an optimal ecological use?

To examine such a question, the application of shadow prices would be useful. Presumably there is some value to the land withdrawn measurable in (1) market price, (2) alternative human use, (3) proximity or time effects on work-home locations, and (4) alternative ecological uses of the soil. The present calculus for deciding upon highway locations, presuming that a given number of acres must inexhorably be paved out of ecological existence each year by reason of a constitutional provision, is to consider mainly the element of market price of land in relation to traffic densities and convenience. The alternative uses, particularly alternative ecological uses, do not normally enter the decision. The function of shadow prices would be to introduce the social value into the decision, such as the benefit to ecology, wildlife, or other human needs.

In the Los Angeles Basin, or any metropolitan area, where a large portion of the land is already paved over, thus removing its ecological usage, shadow prices might attach values to future alternative uses such as residential use, recreational use, commercial use, agricultural use, and species preservation uses. These last two alternatives, of plant and species usages in an ecosystem, are no inconsequential values, especially

---

[10]Kneese, Ayres, and d'Arge, *Economics and the Environment*, op. cit., p. 14.

since man has chosen to place cities in the fertile fringes which represent a small portion of the world's land and a large portion of its ecological productivity. Shadow prices could reflect nutrient-species losses, as well as alternative human use values. For the freeway construction decision, shadow prices should also be attached to the health damage effects of air pollution, associated with highway construction and usage.

Similarly for public transit, as an alternative to automobile-highway transportation, shadow prices could be assigned to its land usage, and alternative forms of remaining land usage, also to the air pollution caused by the power generation needed to operate a public transit system. Public transit would presumably occupy less land than a highway system, because of the higher densities of traffic it can carry. Air pollution emissions would apparently be less for the same reason, although the composition of the emissions might change to heavier concentrations of sulfur dioxide and less toward the ingredients of photochemical smog. For Los Angeles, this shift might not have adverse health effects, since the basin generally has low sulfur dioxide concentrations. For Eastern cities, already high in sulfur dioxide, the tradeoff might be deleterious. In addition to these factors, some attention must be paid to the convenience factor to humans.

Convenience is undoubtedly one of the critical social values which favor private transportation, and hence a shadow value for convenience needs to be included. What the outcome would be of such a calculation of actual and shadow prices for public versus private transportation systems is difficult to foresee, but at least it would clarify the social choice involved. Intuitively one can see from the problem formulation that the decision is likely to depend finally on a tradeoff between environmental quality (including better land use and air quality) as opposed to travel convenience. Such a social choice has never really been put before the public because the environmental quality option has never been offered, either quantitatively (cost) or descriptively.

THE ESTIMATION OF SHADOW PRICES

The use of shadow prices in public investment decision would require the valuation of intangibles which are now unpriced. Professor Margolis has suggested some estimating procedures for arriving at shadow prices.[11] He notes that shadow prices are computed to reflect social values. The correction of market prices, by these imputed values, is applied to both inputs and outputs. In principle, inputs tend to be valued at their oppor-

---

[11]Julius Margolis, "Shadow Prices for Incorrect and Nonexistent Market Values," Joint Committee on Economic Report, *Evaluating Public Expenditures*, vol. 1, op. cit., pp. 538–546.

tunity cost, or what they would have produced elsewhere. The result is that most of the controversy in correcting market prices centers on the valuation of outputs. Three forms of estimating procedures have been used:

1   The most common technique is to value the public output, say an acre-foot of water, as an intermediate product and then estimate its marginal value in further production for increasing the producers' income. A farmer, for instance, using an acre-foot of water as an intermediate product in further crop production, would then have a marginal increase in his crop output, which presumably reflects the value of the acre-foot of water. The "shadow price" of the water, then, is reflected by its incremental income to the farmer, and presumably the farmer should be willing to pay something near this cost (less some entrepreneurial margin) for the water. In practice the farmer is seldom charged that much for agricultural water from public projects, due mainly to risk and alternative water costs in farming.

2   The cost savings to users represents a second technique for estimating shadow prices. This approach is commonly used in transportation and power projects. The comparison is made by estimating, say, power costs from a proposed dam site with some alternative, like existing power rates or a new fossil fuel generating plant. The cost-savings approach faces two difficulties: identifying realistic alternatives and apportioning the cost savings to users. Unfortunately, public agencies are notoriously poor in developing alternatives.[12]

3   Estimation of user prices by market information is the third technique, which in many cases is both the most fruitful and the most difficult. In some cases there are near substitutes for collective consumption, as in the private educational, health, or recreational markets. Then the problem is to identify the differences in services with the differences in cost to arrive at a comparative value. The differences in services between a public and private health clinic may be sufficiently definable to compare services and costs. In other cases, for example, the differences in nuclear research between an Atomic Energy Commission laboratory and that of a private nuclear equipment company may be so different in terms of output and cost as to make them incomparable. Nevertheless, to the extent such market comparisons are possible, they are among the more reliable means of estimating shadow prices.

The main difficulty with shadow prices is that decision makers may not care to use them once they are calculated. Shadow prices assume that efficiency in productivity is the basis of decision. Payoffs to decision

[12]Ibid., p. 544.

makers may not be based upon maximizing national welfare but rather on getting elected again. Gains to a locality rather than to the nation, averting risk and responsibility, and party loyalty are among many personal motivations. Shadow prices are useful pieces of information if they fit the decision structure of the public official, but he may have a different decision model in mind as to what constitutes the public interest. For a market simulation to function properly, based upon shadow prices or ecological charges, there must be some agreement on whose interest is being optimized and how. For instance, is the Pareto optimality of economists the criterion of public decision making, or are the collective self-interest groups the focus of policy, or a little of both? If so, how much of each?

> The thrust of the above remarks is that the problem of shadow price determination is not simply one of calculation. If shadow prices are to guide behavior, then those who must make and implement the decisions require incentives to provide the "correct" information needed for calculation and to use the prices. Therefore the study of shadow-pricing rules opens up the even more difficult study of the optimal structure of government.[13]

PRESENT SUBOPTIMAL STRUCTURE AND RULES

The optimal structure of government is a study beyond the scope of this undertaking, but we might improve our knowledge of market simulation of the environment if we examined the decision rules and structure which are suboptimal at present. The evidence that present decision making is a suboptimal structure is seen in the ecological and biological damages which occur. One problem with the present structure is that the payoffs to present public decision makers are in local interests, special interests, and personal interests rather than in the national interest, which more closely approximates ecological welfare. This bias toward special interests is inherent in a representative form of government because an elected representative is charged by the constituency and special interests which keep him in office to advocate their peculiar desires. These special desires cover both public and private interests, and hence representative government creates incentives for the benefit of private markets in the process of creating public goods, often with counterproductive results. Some of the problems encountered by government in mixing and confusing its rule making over public and private actions are pointed out by Charles Schultze in testimony to the Joint Economic Committee of Congress.

[13]Ibid., p. 546.

Many of the Federal Government's most important expenditure programs involve a mixture of public and private actions. The majority of public programs are an attempt to take account of external costs and benefits in the production of private goods. Public programs seek to modify, in quality or quantity, the outcome of private production and investment decisions. Urban development programs, air and water pollution controls, and flood protection are examples.

Since the Flood Protection Act of 1936, the Federal Government has spent some $7 billion on flood protection projects. National policy has been to build flood protection at public expense and assist states, localities, and individuals to recoup against large flood losses.

However, public policy ought not to be expressed primarily in terms of criteria for flood prevention. Rather, it should encourage rational use of flood plain lands. A policy should induce investment in flood plains only if the advantages are greater than alternative sites by an amount which exceeds expected flood damages.

Present public policy, which concerns itself almost solely with public projects, sets up a series of monetary and political incentives which induce distinctly uneconomic private investment decisions in flood plains.

Once the flood plain is developed, the standard cost-benefit calculation will often show that the construction of flood prevention or protection works is worthwhile in terms of expected damage avoided. However, in all too many cases the preferred alternative would have been a much less intensive development of the flood plain or no development at all.[14]

The suboptimal structure of government decisions, in this case, is that representative government responds first to the special interests of land speculators who seek to develop low-investment-cost lands in the flood plains, and then responds to the plight of unsuspecting buyer-victims to minimize real or potential flood damage. Both voting blocks represent local interests which keep the representative in office, but neither represents the national or ecological welfare which would favor low-density development or nondevelopment of flood plains. Much of the misdirection of private investment into nonproductive and nonecological uses comes from the misincentives of tax laws. Schultze illustrates this further by the effect of tax incentives on zoning decisions:

Urban development plans establish zoning for differential uses, which may be esthetic, to control development along lines of efficient urban transportation, or for other purposes. The principal effect of zoning is to reduce the potential rent on specific parcels of land below the rent which could be

[14]Charles L. Schultze, "The Role of Incentives, Penalties, and Rewards in Attaining Effective Policy," Joint Committee on Economic Report, *Evaluating Public Expenditures*, vol. 1, op. cit., pp. 203–204.

earned without zoning restrictions. Even under favorable conditions, this characteristic would make zoning hard to enforce. But this problem is substantially increased by the present tax system, because the potential rewards from securing a change in zoning can be realized as capital gains, and will be taxed at much more favorable rates. As a consequence, the energies and capital of real estate developers are channeled into land speculation and into massive efforts to secure favorable changes in zoning codes. This kind of activity yields returns which pay less than half the tax securable by investment in physical improvements. Small wonder that urban development plans in most metropolitan areas quickly succumb to the relentless pressure of land developers.

More generally, the availability of highly favorable tax treatment for those who speculate in land, tends to work counter to most of the objectives contained in urban plans. A change in the tax system would not itself automatically channel urban investment into socially desirable directions—there are a host of other factors which influence such investment. But the system could be made more neutral with respect to planning objectives, rather than being highly counter-productive as it now is.[15]

The process of decision making in land-use cases, then, throws some light on why the structure is suboptimal from the viewpoint of national or ecological welfare. The payoffs to the elected representative largely favor his acceding to the interests of the land speculator, and the tax incentives to the land speculator impel him toward the earliest gain on the land regardless of the social or ecological effects. To reverse these counter-productive effects, one would have to change the incentives, which might be attempted by such alternatives as (1) reducing the dependence of elected representatives upon special interests for getting reelected, (2) involving a broader spectrum of citizenry in land-use and ecological decisions, and (3) removing the capital gains tax incentive on land speculation.

RULE MAKING AS A FORM OF SHADOW PRICING

The land-use cases illustrate that social choices in the form of rule making are a form of shadow pricing. A piece of land has a relatively constant ecological potential determined by its biogeochemical material and its location in reference to solar energy and hydrologic, atmospheric, and nutrient cycles. Given these ecological phenomena, a piece of land has a variety of biological (including human) alternatives. These biological alternatives do not vary with the zoning decision about the land, they vary only with the natural cycles.

[15]Ibid., p. 212.

The natural cycles are the real determinants of land-use potential, not the city council. The city council, or county board, can make a ruling on density of human use in zoning. Whether that rule making vacates the use of the land or determines its interim human use to be residential or commercial, it creates a temporal market value. The market value will vary greatly, depending upon the density of use permitted whether agricultural, single residence, multiple dwelling, industrial, or commercial. In any event, that market value is a figment of the political rule making.

This fictitious land value then becomes reflected in the costs of agricultural produce, in mineral outputs, in the fixed costs of industrial products; and now we say that we have a "market price" which is objectively determined because it represents competitive bidding for products and factors of production. But the initial price of the land was a fictitious or shadow price in the first place, created by fiat of elected representatives who, in the suboptimal structure of government, coveyed a price to the land in accession to special interests. How, then, can the subsequent market values be any more objective or real than the fictitious price on which the whole cost structure was created? One might argue quite similarly with respect to the initial values assigned to all other factors of production. The implication is that all prices, market or nonmarket, are shadow prices in their origin, created by a rule-making process which is supposed to reflect social choice. The question is then moot whether the rule-making process indeed reflects present social choices, or whether the entire market-price structure is an historical accident of past rule making.

The thrust of this argument is that all prices, market or nonmarket, shadow or money prices, need to be validated periodically by reexamining the critieria upon which they are based. The lack of periodic validation causes price and decision structures to get out of line with current needs and wants, results in misallocation of resources, large external and social costs, or alternatively causes a decline in quality. All these characteristics are symptoms of suboptimal decisions. That is, the combination of market prices and rule making have not achieved Pareto optimality. The solution to suboptimal market structures are to correct the rule making and shadow prices, and to simulate a total market which corresponds with human wants, including environmental quality.

The question may be raised as to where these corrections in shadow prices or rule making need to be made. At least two indicators are useful in helping identify areas for remedial examination. One is where environmental quality has declined, and many illustrations of such degradation have already been given in prior discussion. A second is where social indicators show that qualitative wants are not being realized by present markets or public programs. The role of social indicators as measures of worth or optimality is, then, of some interest to explore further.

SOCIAL INDICATORS AS MEASURES OF WORTH

The difficulty of valuing intangible qualities like health, personal security, and education has led to research on social indicators as a means of identifying progress over time. The social indicator approach attempts to eastablish priorities or preferences and to show progress which may be the result of action taken. The Department of Health, Education and Welfare has undertaken such research, and Isabel Sawhill has reported on some of their findings.

The higher the level of decision making, the more difficult it is to develop satisfactory indicators of performance. This is particularly true in the case of social goals and programs. At the higher levels of decision making, it is not now possible to construct quantitative measures of progress. Only the judgment of the voters and their political representatives can determine whether an extra dollar spent on schools and parks increases the well-being of the nation more than an extra dollar spent on guns or butter. However, when the choice is narrowed, social indicators can play an important role and serve to reorder our fundamental national priorities, by drawing greater attention to social problems.

Social indicators are quantitative measures of social conditions designed to guide decision making and to allocate expenditures among various social programs, such as health, education, or the control of pollution.

> Table 1 (Figure 13-2) presents a list of some of the statistics which were used to measure social conditions in Toward a Social Report. They are not in every case the best social indicators which could be used. New data and/or different definitions of social goals could lead to the use of a different set of indicators. However, they will serve to illustrate some of the possibilities and problems involved in social measurement.[16]
>
> Program analysts like to work, whenever possible, with output measures which are expressed in dollar terms. However, measuring benefits in this way often puts a serious constraint on the kinds of problems which can be analyzed. Social indicators will help to fill this gap. Most of the indicators in Table 1 (Figure 13-2), for example, are expressed in nonmonetary units. . . . If program analysts don't insist on using dollar values, they will

---

[16]*Toward a Social Report.* U.S. Department of Health, Education and Welfare, January 1969, p. 188.

Figure 13-2   Some Social Indicators Used in *Toward A Social Report* to Measure Major Social Conditions

Aspect of life to be measured	Some social indicators
Social mobility	Correlation coefficient between father's occupational status and son's occupational status
Health	Expectancy of healthy life (free of bed disability and institutionalization)
The physical environment	Ratio of a city's actual level of pollution to an acceptable standard Proportion of housing that is substandard or overcrowded
Income and poverty	Personal income per capita Number in poverty
Public order and security	FBI Uniform Crime Reports Index of crimes Value of property involved in theft per $1,000 or appropriable property
Learning, science, and art	Performance on selected achievement tests Technological balance of payments Attendance at theaters, operas, ballets

have more flexible yardsticks with which to measure social conditions, but there will be disadvantages as well.[17]

That is, the benefits in different social areas are not commensurable; the benefits cannot be aggregated; and a benefit-cost relation cannot be calculated. Nevertheless, some indication of relative priority or improvement is often possible, which is frequently more than can be determined without such indicators.

SUMMARY

The ecological condition is something less than optimal, in the Pareto definition of national welfare, with high wasteloads and consequent biological damage. This suboptimal condition is a result of a market failure to take into account all the costs and biological effects of the human productive process. We can correct for market failure to some extent by simulating a market, including the ecosystem, in which prices are assignable to both the resource withdrawals and the wasteload

[17]Isabel V. Sawhill, "The Role of Social Indicators," Joint Committee on the Economic Report, *Evaluating Public Expenditures*, vol. 1, op. cit., pp. 473–482.

disposals from the human production cycle upon the environment. These price assignments may take the form of a variety of ecological usage charges, such as effluent charges, incentives and disincentives, and shadow prices for public investment decisions. Regardless of form, the ecological usage charges are designed to compensate the environment for its losses, that is to say, for its damage or degradation. A variety of techniques are available for calculating shadow prices (or ecological charges) such as contribution to marginal revenue, cost savings, or comparative market pricing.

However the simulated prices are estimated, the real test lies in whether the present public decision structure will use the information, because the payoffs to public decision makers are not based upon productivity (national welfare) as much as on response to local or special interests. The result is that a workable market simulation of ecological effects requires more optimal decision rules and structure than now are available. Particularly, the rule- and choice-making functions should allow individuals to express preferences on specific issues involving biological damage. In short, the affected citizen should have some participative role in assigning values and shadow prices to outputs. This quasi-public–quasi-private form of choice may seem, superficially, to change the character of the private market, but deeper examination indicates that all money prices in the private market are shadow prices in the sense that they are derived from a value determined by public choice making. Therefore, the private market values and social choices may usefully be combined into alternative benefit-cost calculations which incorporate subjective valuation of ecological damage.

The valuation of biological damage and environmental quality becomes difficult, even by social choice-making procedure, in the treatment of uncertainty. The relation of cause to health effects is probabilistic and the risk factors with respect to mortality or morbidity differ for each individual. Moreover, the sufficiency of biological quality or the value of life may vary among individuals. Ultimately, biological quality and life values are the "service outputs" of the ecological system. Some quantitative social indicators have been attempted which provide insight into relative rates of improvement in social or environmental conditions. But on the final decisions regarding the value of output, in terms of degree of biological quality or damage which is sufficient to warrant a given level of expenditure or change in life style, the priorities can probably only be set by a public consensus. One may conclude that the mechanisms of a market simulation for the environment are feasible in terms of cost inputs, but the ultimate value of the output (degree of biological quality) depends upon a more optimal structure of public choice making.

DISCUSSION QUESTIONS

1 What examples from your own experience can you cite to achieve a higher degree of Pareto optimality in the environment? In other words, in what ways could you be made better off in your perception of environmental quality without making someone else worse off?
2 What is the "market failure" in the environment? How might it be corrected?
3 What are the various forms of usage charges which you might consider applying to improve water quality or land use in your community?
4 Give an example of present pricing and of shadow pricing in land development or flood control, and show the difference in decision outcomes which might follow from each.

PROBLEM

Select a group of social indicators which measure a social problem of your choosing, and then make an analysis to determine: (1) whether progress is being made in the solution of the problem, and (2) whether a reordering of priorities is indicated to arrive at a solution.

Chapter 14

Marginal and Opportunity Costs in Environmental Analysis

The concept of a market simulation model for the environment provides us with the opportunity of interjecting a shadow price between the ecosystem and the human production cycle for the purpose of compensating the ecosystem for biological damage done to it by human residuals. The "compensation" is a charge sufficient to avoid the biological damage, or to repair it. The reason we wish to compensate the ecosystem is that the ecosystem encompasses all of us, as human beings or biological species, and by this compensation we maintain environmental quality for our own lives as well as for others.

In other words, the ecosystem is the largest "commons" of all; to prevent a "tragedy of the commons" in the form of quality degradation, we attach costs to the commons (e.g., materials of the ecosystem) the same as we do to our own productive process. In this way, we intend to prevent biological damage to ourselves and to other organisms. More plainly, we are trying to expand the recognition of our biological interdependency so that we do not slowly poison ourselves. The method for regulating our relations with the ecosystem is to place a "market" between ourselves and the ecosystem, the same as we do among our human institutions in the exchange of land, materials, labor, and capital.

The creation of a simulated market to regulate the exchange between ourselves and the ecosystem may seem an awkward contrivance to deal with our own biological processes in relation to the larger processes of nature, and, indeed, this is so. But public officials, bureaucrats, businessmen, and scholars are all given to limited imaginations, and one finds it hard to conceive of mechanisms greatly different from what we have, even though they lack the elegant simplicity of nature's self-regulating mechanisms. But more than that, practical decision makers do not have the option of creating the environmental resources base and cost structure anew. The industrial system is a going, functioning entity with whatever good and bad environmental implications and decisions there may be in it. The ecostructure is given by creation. We may change ourselves and our industrial institutions, but we are not about to change the ecostructure.

The question then is, what can we change in our industrial institutions which will improve biological quality? The suggestion is that we introduce costs via a simulated market between ourselves and the ecosystem. This simulated market would then provide total environmental cost data which are basic to decisions, in the same sense that financial statements are basic to business decisions. Moreover, we are unlikely to be able to change everything at once, which would result in chaos, so environmental decisions—like business decisions—will tend to be incremental, or one thing at a time.

Incremental decision making is found in economic literature as marginal-utility and marginal-cost theory. We will do well, then, to explore the extent to which marginal-cost analysis may assist in making environmental decisions, what its limitations are for this purpose, and what other alternative concepts might be helpful. Thus, this chapter will cover marginal theory and opportunity costs in the following topical headings:

1 Marginal-cost analysis
2 Marginal-utility theory applied to environmental quality
3 The influence of uncertainty upon marginal theory
4 What is cost?
5 Opportunity costs

MARGINAL-COST ANALYSIS

Decisions tend to be made incrementally through time, and economists have concerned themselves with the conditions upon which such decisions turn. The conditions or criteria of the decision process are not the unique province of economists, because political scientists, psychologists, practical executives, and statesmen, too, have their own mental model as to what constitutes a decision. The economist's model is defined by his own sense of mission, which is to seek the optimum allocation of resources in response to human wants. The achievement of this mission would constitute Pareto optimality, in which no one could be made better off without someone else being made worse off. But what does "better" mean in this sense? Better generally means the satisfaction of identifiable or tangible wants, and tangible wants tend to be measurable, which disposes economic analysis more toward things than toward feelings.

To make the problem tractable, economists make two explicit assumptions, in which every beginning student of economics is assiduously drilled, but whose limitations become obscured in practice. The two assumptions are that the model describes (1) the behavior of *homo economicus* in an exchange, where (2) part of the situation is qualified as *ceteris parabus*. That is, the model describes a rational man making an economic choice in an exchange of goods or services with another buyer or seller where other things (other than the exchange) are equal. "Other things being equal" means that other things are fixed, given, certain, or immaterial to the exchange. These are two extremely simplifying assumptions which greatly limit the applicability of the theory. There are fairly few instances when a person acts wholly rationally in an economic exchange where all other things are equal or excluded from consideration. Nevertheless, attempts are made to apply marginal theory (e.g., as in benefit-cost analysis), and, hence, the understanding of its uses and limitations merits attention.

Perhaps the easiest way to understand the idea of marginal costs is through an example. Let us consider an extension of a case in air pollution which has already been discussed. The improvement of air quality is critically dependent upon reducing emissions of used cars because there are so many of them in use, and they are high emitters of pollutants. One technical proposal is to retrofit a used car with an afterburner and a catalytic muffler. The afterburner's function is the further combustion of unburned fuel elements, and that of the catalytic muffler is to pass the spent gases over a bed of some catalyst (gold being one example) which would hasten a chemical reaction to remove the residuals from the gaseous emissions. These two pieces of equipment, added to the exhaust system of the used car, would reduce pollution emissions into the atmosphere.

Assume that we are entrepreneurs who wish to manufacture and sell exhaust emission control equipment consisting of an afterburner and a catalytic reactor. The fixed investment in tools and machinery to make the emission control devices is $500,000 to start on a small scale, and with this fixed investment we can build from 1,000 to 12,000 control devices per year. We estimate our labor and materials costs (variable costs) at $350,000 for the first 1,000 units, which would give us a total cost of $850,000 (with the fixed costs), or an average cost of $850. Common sense indicates very little market at such a price, because perhaps one-fourth of all used cars on the road are not worth more than that. Intuition and heresay suggest the desirability of getting the price down to a lower figure if we are to sell any, even if there is control legislation requiring drivers to install emission control devices. Hence, we make some additional estimates, which indicate that the same tools and machinery will produce 2,000 units with no additional fixed investment, so that makes it attractive to add more labor and materials. We find that for $500,000 in labor and materials we can produce 2,000 units, which lowers our average cost of $850 per unit to $500 per unit. In fact, the added (marginal) output costs us only $150 per unit. This is so attractive that we continue our marginal analysis to see what every added increment of output will cost us, and these calculations are shown in the following table.

We find our plant in a condition of decreasing costs (average unit cost column) as production is expanded out to 8,000 units of output; then increasing average costs are encountered. The explanation for the decreasing costs, of course, is that the fixed investment in tools and equipment contributes to declining unit costs as the investment is spread over a larger volume of output. However, as output rises we have to add proportionately more and more labor and materials to push production

Figure 14-1   Example of Total and Marginal Costs and Revenues
(All Figures in Thousands of Dollars, Except per Unit Costs and Revenue)

Units	Fixed cost	Variable cost	Total cost	Per unit Average cost	Per unit Marginal cost	Total revenue	Per Unit Average revenue	Per Unit Marginal revenue
1	500	350	850	850	350	800	800	800
2	500	500	1,000	500	150	1,300	650	500
3	500	625	1,125	375	125	1,700	567	400
4	500	775	1,275	319	150	2,050	512	350
5	500	950	1,450	290	175	2,350	470	300
6	500	1,150	1,650	275	200	2,600	433	250
7	500	1,375	1,875	268	225	2,825	403	225
8	500	1,625	2,125	266	250	3,025	378	200
9	500	1,925	2,425	269	300	3,200	355	175
10	500	2,275	2,775	278	350	3,350	335	150
11	500	2,700	3,200	290	425	3,475	316	125
12	500	3,200	3,700	308	500	3,575	298	100

upward until a point of diminishing returns is reached (at 8,000 units), where the factors of production begin to be used less efficiently, and average costs go up.

The marginal costs of added production units are low in the early stages, on the order of $125 to $150 per unit, but they rise rapidly as production is increased. How shall we decide at what point to stop adding new increments of outputs? In other words, how do we decide when marginal costs are getting too high?

We may make this decision by comparing the marginal costs with marginal revenue, the last column in the table. The demand curve is represented by the average price which buyers are willing to pay for our emission control device. The total revenue is the income of the enterprise, or the average price multiplied by the number of units sold. The marginal revenue is the addition to total revenue for each increment of new output sold. That is, we find we can sell 6,000 units at $433 each for a total income of $2 million. If we produce 7,000 units, each sells for $403 for a total revenue of $2,825,000 units. The 1,000 additional units produced $225,000 in additional revenues, or a marginal revenue of $225 per unit.

We can also observe that at $225 of marginal revenue we just cover our marginal cost of $225 per unit. So we stop expanding production at 7,000 units, because from this point on any added units yield less marginal revenue than our marginal costs. If we produce 8,000 units, for example, the added production costs $250 per unit, but the added revenue amounts to only $200 per unit. Hence, our point of optimum profit is 7,000 units, which is the point of equilibrium at which marginal revenue just covers marginal costs.

The same marginal analysis can be portrayed graphically, the form in which it is most commonly presented in economic literature. The following graph (Figure 14-2) shows the demand curve with a negative slope to the right, as added customers can only be found by attracting them with lower prices, and this lower price becomes the average price for all consumers, including those who would have been willing to pay more. The marginal revenue lies below the demand curve because each added unit is brought on to the market at a lower-than-average price. The average unit cost generally presents a U-shaped curve, reflecting first decreasing unit costs as the fixed investment is spread over a larger volume, and then rising costs as diminishing efficiency sets in. The marginal costs rise more sharply than average costs, because each added unit is being produced with diminishing efficiency.

The point in the graph at which marginal revenues intersect the marginal-cost curve is the point of equilibrium and maximum profit. Hence, marginal theory in economics tells us that the rational economic

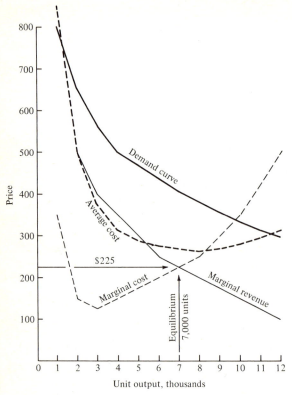

Figure 14-2 Example of marginal costs and marginal revenue.

producer will add output until his marginal revenue just covers his marginal costs.

What about the consumer who is buying the emission control equipment? After all, the crux of the decision for the producer depends upon the position of the demand curve, because it is the marginal revenue which tells him when to stop producing. Then where does the demand curve come from? According to economic theory, the demand curve originates in the subjective evaluation of consumers. That is, each consumer has in mind (since he is a rational economic being) a utility function which looks much like a demand curve; that is, negative sloping to the right, which is to say that added units of the same product have diminishing satisfaction to him. The consumer is also aware of supply-cost curves, in effect the sum of the marginal-cost curves of the producers. The consumer goes through a mental calculus such as we have just illustrated for the producer. That is, the consumer purchases a quantity of a good to that point where the added utility (satisfaction) to him just covers the marginal cost to him. By this hypothesis, then, economics can offer a theory of economic equilibrium and of economic welfare. That is, resources are optimally allocated when the marginal utilities of all consumers are just equal to the marginal costs of producing those services, because at this point no one could be made any better off.

MARGINAL-UTILITY THEORY APPLIED TO ENVIRONMENTAL QUALITY

While this brief sketch of marginal theory can hardly convey an adequate impression of the scope and subtlety of economic literature in the field, still one can see some basic assumptions at work. First, something crucial happened in perspective as we shifted from the producers to the consumer's perception of marginal theory. To the producer, all the data inputs were objective, that is, factual costs and market prices. From this objective data the producer could calculate an optimum profit and equilibrium. However, as we shifted to the consumer perspective, all the data became subjective, that is, concerning his feelings about the degree of utility or satisfaction of the goods or service.

This shift in perspective from the objective to the subjective marks one of the great changes in thinking which took place in economics around 1870. Prior to that time the early economists had been concerned about the theory of the firm and how a firm might arrive at an optimization of profit. The view of early economists, like Smith and Ricardo, was somewhat Newtonian. That is, they sought to explain the mechanism by which the economy arrived at a position of equilibrium which best satisfied consumer wants. While they formulated much of the basic theory about supply and demand, diminishing returns, optimum allocation of resources, and equilibrium at a price which equated supply with demand, they never really satisfactorily explained prices in terms of how they were determined. In other words, they never explained value or where the demand curve came from.

This omission in classical economic thinking led to a revolution in economic theory in the late nineteenth century as a result of the work of William Jevons, Karl Menger, and Leon Walras. They conceived of the consumer as having a marginal-utility function in his mind which subjectively determined his willingness to pay a particular price. That price would reflect the point where the marginal utility or satisfaction of a purchased good just equaled the marginal cost to obtain it. If there is such a point in the individual's mind where marginal utility equates with marginal cost, two characteristics of the decision are apparent: (1) it is not expressed in dollars, but the utility is some subjective sense of satisfaction; and (2) because it is not measurable in dollars or some overt satisfaction unit, the decision process becomes wholly subjective, knowable only to the decider, and not observable by any outsider. For this reason, marginal-utility economics became known as "subjective-value economics" and the doctrinal revolution carries the name of subjective economics, to contrast it with the classical cost-of-production theory which was based upon objectively observable market costs and prices.

Marginal-utility economics may be used to illustrate the decision process invoked by a consumer purchasing an air pollution control device, or any other choice involving environmental quality. Crocker and Rogers give several such examples,[1] and graphically they appear to resemble the marginal analysis of the producer. An illustration would appear as follows in Figure 14-3.

The vertical axis, as in the former case, is price, but the horizontal axis, shown in the illustration, represents the level of cleanliness or quality of the environment desired by the buyer, rather than the quantity of output. The individual is presumed to have some scale of values in mind, relative to environmental quality, which expresses his preference as to the degree of cleanliness desired. Suppose an individual is concerned about the level of lead in the atmosphere because of the health damage resulting from lead poisoning. To prevent a lethal level of lead, he would pay a very high price. As the lead concentrations in the atmosphere

[1]Thomas D. Crocker and A. J. Rogers, III, *Environmental Economics*, Dryden Press, Hinsdale, Ill., 1971, p. 63.

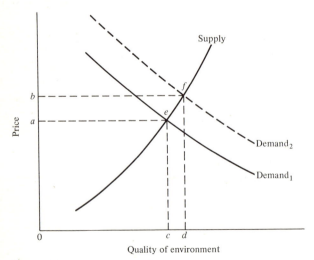

Figure 14-3

became less and less, below the lethal level, he would be willing to pay a declining price to improve air quality. That is, he would become more indifferent to the utility of removing lead from the atmosphere as its biological damage declined. Hence, we observe the negative sloping utility function, labeled as Demand$_1$.

The supply of lead-free fuels with high-octane ratings comes at increasing prices, which yields the supply curve rising to the right on the graph. The oil companies have said that the cost of unleaded gasolines, with octane ratings sufficient for high-compression engines, might cost from one to three cents per gallon more than present fuels, due to increased investment costs to refine unleaded gasolines. As the demand for level of cleanliness becomes more stringent, then the supply cost of clean-burning fuels rises. In this hypothetical example, the consumer would be willing to pay price *a* for an air quality designated as *c*. The utility function (demand) intersects the supply curve at point *e* which represents the equilibrium point in this set of circumstances.

Suppose now this same individual reads *Science* (vol. 173, July 9, 1971, p. 130) and finds that animals at the Staten Island Zoo are dying from lead poisoning. In the first case, an eleven-month-old leopard became weak, started losing its hair, and refused to eat. The animal was taken to the New York Medical College for testing; the pathology department found no evidence of disease, but the leopard died twenty-four hours later.

Three weeks later, the leopard's fraternal twin was found lying paralyzed in his cage. Again, there was no evidence of disease, but a toxicologist made a test for heavy metals and found extremely high levels of lead in the animal's hair, blood, and feces. After six weeks of intensive treatment, the leopard was well enough to return to the zoo, but shortly the lead level in his body began to rise again and he went into convulsions. The leopard was taken back to the hospital for recuperation, and the NYMC decided to check other animals.

They found high concentrations of lead in other species, from reptiles to primates, especially among those caged out of doors. For some time, snakes at the zoo had been dying after having lost the muscular coordination to slither. Chemical analysis of the preserved carcasses of the snakes and the first leopard revealed high-lead contamination. A test of the grass, leaves, and soil on the zoo grounds showed lead concentrations as high as 3,900 micrograms per milligram dry weight, an amount equal to that found along the sides of major highways where automobiles emit 180,000 tons of lead annually. The pathologist directing the study suggests that zoo animals serve as potential barometers of the biological effects of pollutants in the city's air. The effects on indicator species have ominous implications for the people who live in that area.

The Council on Environmental Quality, in a report on toxic substances, make it clear, however, that this is not a local problem:

> The increase in air pollution is now global in scope. For example, between 1904 and 1964, lead concentrations in Greenland snow increased 16-fold.
>
> Lead is one of the oldest known pollutants. In the 2nd century, the wealthy class of Rome was decimated by sterility, child mortality, and permanent mental impairment. According to one theory, this decline can be traced to lead poisoning from wine and food vessels. The lower classes survived because they could not afford lead utensils.
>
> Today, lead is absorbed by humans in a more democratic way, because all social classes are exposed to lead in the atmosphere. Lead particles in the air eventually settle to land and water, mixing with other sources of the metal and following complex pathways in the environment.
>
> Although the acute toxicity of lead has been a health problem for 2,000 years, the effects of ambient levels are not known. . . . The data are not conclusive, but in the opinion of at least one recognized expert, "There is little doubt that at the present rate of pollution, diseases due to lead toxicity will emerge within a few years."[2]

Suppose now, returning to the diagram, our consumer becomes more highly concerned about the level of environmental cleanliness, particularly atmospheric quality with respect to lead. He feels subjectively an increasing want for clean air, which means lesser concentrations of lead particulates in the atmosphere. Then his utility function or demand curve shifts to the right, as illustrated by Demand$_2$. That is, he is willing to pay a higher price for any specific degree of air quality. He now is willing to pay price b for a higher degree of air quality d, and equilibrium with supply is at point f.

In summary, then, marginal-utility theory illustrates the subjective process by which an individual equates his feelings about a human want with price. His want is expressed as a utility function, or a negatively sloping demand curve, and economic theory can then demonstrate the relation of this subjective utility function to the marginal costs (supply curve) of producers.

THE INFLUENCE OF UNCERTAINTY UPON MARGINAL THEORY

The intersection of a marginal-utility curve and a marginal-cost curve at a precise equilibrium point implies that the buyer and the seller have a very clear idea of the exact cost and the expected benefit. That is, they operate

[2]U.S. Council on Environmental Quality, *Toxic Substances*, Supt. of Documents, Washington, April 1971, pp. 10–11.

with a high degree of certainty and knowledge about costs and benefits. Indeed, in any general market with many buyers and sellers, each would require perfect knowledge of all utility functions and all cost curves in order to arrive at a precise equilibrium between supply and demand at a specific price. That is, marginal theory presumes something close to omniscience on the part of the participants in the market.

In the air pollution case, however, we found that the buyer especially was far from a state of certain knowledge about the benefit or utility of his demand for clean air or pollution control equipment. A high degree of uncertainty exists about the relationship of lead emissions to biological damage. We surmise that the Roman nobility succumbed to lead poisoning, and we have known for 2,000 years that lead is highly toxic. We know that zoo animals have died from lead concentrations similar to those found along highways and freeways. But it is not entirely clear to us, as buyers, exactly what the relationship is between the level of lead emissions and the biological damage of lead poisoning in our own lives.

Moreover, the suppliers operate under a similar veil of uncertainty, because it is not clear exactly what amount of investment or cost will be incurred to produce low-lead gasolines, and, if they reduce the lead content, it is not known how much improvement in air quality will occur. Therefore, the suppliers do not know what it will cost them to arrive at varying levels of air quality. The consequence is that both buyers and sellers operate within a broad range of uncertainty, which means that their supply and demand function are represented by wide ranges rather than lines. Hence, the diagram might be redrawn as shown in Figure 14-4.

Actual demand may lie somewhat between demand curve D_1 and D_2, depending upon what biological damage is believed to be involved. Similarly, the supply curve may lie somewhere between S_1 and S_2, depending upon what the costs are to achieve specified levels of air quality. The result is that both buyer's and sellers, operating under uncertainty, find no exact price at which supply equates with demand. The area *abcd* in the diagram is the range within which supply and demand come together, but the exact price, quality, or quantity is indeterminate.

The higher the level of decision which a person must make, higher being the more vital and crucial to his well-being, the more uncertainty which surrounds the choice. It is more uncertain to choose a spouse than a loaf of bread, more uncertain to choose a career than an auto. Bread and autos have relatively ascertainable performance characteristics. Spouses and careers are full of imponderables. Environmental problems and biological damage are, like spouses and careers, fraught with interactions

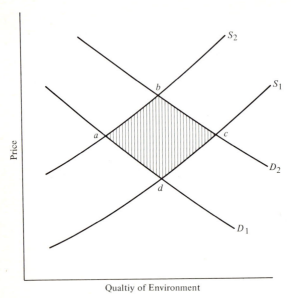

Figure 14-4

involving many unknowns. Decision making under uncertainty is not easily described by the marginal-utility theory, because the degree of utility or satisfaction is doubtful and probabilistic.

WHAT IS COST?

Marginal theory presumes to maximize human welfare by allocating resources in such a way that marginal cost is equated with marginal utility. This optimizes welfare because the last added unit of cost is just equal to the last added satisfaction or gain, and so no one could be made better off without making someone worse off.

But we have already seen that the utility or benefit is uncertain, probabilistic. Therefore, the degree of benefit or gain is a matter of doubt to its recipient. If the consumer does not know what his degree of satisfaction is, how can satisfaction be optimized? Similarly, if the seller does not know what his costs are, costs cannot be minimized. So we need to ask the question, what are costs? Can they be known and minimized at the margin?

The first reaction may be that the nature of cost is obvious. Cost is what we pay for something. This definition of cost is the sense in which classical economists used the term in their cost-of-production theory, and in this sense, costs are indeed observable and measurable. One can observe the costs in the market and check the actual invoice in the accounts to see what was paid for an item. But, if we are speaking of accountant's costs, they are something which occurred in the past, and past events have very little to do with making decisions.

Decisions are prospective. They look to the future and not to the past. Decisions are concerned with present and future needs, wants, and satisfactions. A decision occurs when an individual finds his present state unsatisfactory in some respect, and he wishes to change to a more satisfying state in the future. A cost in the past has nothing to do with achieving a more satisfying future state, except perhaps in an intellectual and historical perspective. Rather, the subjective assessment in the mind of the decision maker is to determine what future sacrifice he must make for a future gain.

Suppose an individual of limited means lives near the Staten Island Zoo and feels that his present health risks are unsatisfactory. He does not wish to go the way of the reptiles and leopards—to become weak, lose hair, lose muscular coordination, and then expire in convulsions from lead poisoning. Rather, he would like to have a more satisfying future state, that is, to be healthy and vigorous. He considers that he has three choices to reach the more satisfactory state: (1) To go into politics and place severe controls on the lead emissions, which means fighting the lobby of auto and oil companies, (2) staying in Staten Island and at his present house but air conditioning his home with charcoal filters to remove as much lead pollution as possible, and (3) moving to Maine. The probability of his cutting lead pollution in his lifetime by the political route is perhaps rather low, and he does not have the wealth for political campaigning. Filtering the air in his present home enables him to stay at his present job, but it is uncertain how effectively he will improve his home air quality or reduce the biological risks. The move to Maine has the highest probability of solving the lead poisoning problem but the lowest possibility of his earning a living.

In other words, this is not a decision *ceteris parabus*. Other things are not equal at all, nor can they be excluded from the decision without vitiating his choices. No, he must decide among his sacrifices. If he goes to Maine, he sacrifices his occupation. If he installs air filtration, he sacrifices time and effort (paying for the installation) and, possibly, a portion of his lifespan. If he is a man of limited means and goes into politics, he sacrifices, for a time at least, his occupation and the improvement of ambient air quality in his home. Or more simply, every gain involves giving up other things which one might have had. We sacrifice other things for every gain we make.

OPPORTUNITY COSTS

These sacrifices, or foregone gains, are called "opportunity costs" in economics. Opportunity costs always deal with the future; they are what one is willing to give up in order to gain a satisfaction. Opportunity costs are exactly descriptive of the ecological sacrifices involved in environmental problems. The gain in transportation by automobile travel is obtained by the sacrifice of smog, ill health, and lead poisoning of some species. The gain in food production, by using DDT as an insecticide, is obtained at a sacrifice of bird populations. We then decide to ban DDT and substitute an organic phosphate pesticide like parathion instead; then the gain in food production is obtained by the sacrifice of the health of farm workers. Some deaths of farm workers from parathion poisoning have been documented, and the California Department of Health estimates that as many as 150 out of every 1,000 farm workers suffer symptoms of pesticide poisoning.[3]

The opportunity costs of a decision are the foregone gains. The opportunity costs of automobile driving are bronchial asthma, plant damage from ozone, traffic accidents from carbon monoxide entering the blood, lower levels of physical activity, earlier death to people with respiratory diseases, and lead poisoning to at least some creatures. The opportunity costs of an enlarged food supply have been the sacrifice of bird populations from DDT and parathion poisoning for farm workers.

The opportunity cost is expressed, in these cases, in biological data rather than in dollars. The sacrifice is in terms of biological damage, or the foregone gain is in terms of health. The foregone gain, in the case of the auto or pesticide, is biological well-being.

Biological health as a lost opportunity is, like accounting costs, retrospective. Biological health as in choosing to move from Staten Island to Maine is prospective, looking to the future. Thus, we have at least two meanings for opportunity cost as a theory of choice, besides the accounting cost of classical economics. Buchanan has called these several kinds of costs: (1) "objective cost," meaning accounting costs of classical economics; (2) "choice influenced costs," meaning opportunities lost, as in the case of lead poisoning of zoo animals; and (3) "choice-influencing costs," meaning prospective sacrifices, as in the case of deciding to move from Staten Island to Maine.[4] The last of these, choice-influencing costs, are the only significant form of costs which enter into making choices. Hence, one might conclude that the choice-influencing opportunity costs are the requisites for making economics a predictive science. Curiously enough, in the history of economic thought, however, economists have

---

[3] *Wall Street Journal*, July 16, 1971, p. 1.
[4] James M. Buchanan, *Cost and Choice*, Markham Publishing Co., Chicago, 1969, pp. 44–45.

attempted to base their predictive science on objective, or accounting costs, applied to marginal cost and marginal revenue models.

The notion of opportunity costs (in the choice-influencing sense) goes back to Adam Smith who observed that: If among a nation of hunters, *it usually* costs twice the labor to kill a beaver as it costs to kill a deer, one beaver should naturally exchange for two deer. In this case, relative labor costs determine the exchange ratio, and the hunter will be indifferent to what he hunts as long as the labor ratios and the exchange rates are in accord. If the exchange rate should become three deer to one beaver, he will no longer kill deer but only beaver, because he will end up with three deer by exchange rather than one deer by hunting.

This concept of subjective opportunity cost, while always present in economic thought, becomes subordinate to the idea of objective accounting costs during the nineteenth century's preoccupation with the problems of production. Thus, the cost-of-production theory of the firm, based on accounting costs, was intended to describe the level to which output should be expanded to satisfy human wants.

Beginning with the twentieth century, a renewed interest in opportunity costs emerged and a number of economists, mostly British, attempted to reincorporate it into the main body of economic theory. Philip Wicksteed noted that the cost of production is a historical and irrevocable fact that has no influence on the value of things produced.[5] Wicksteed was a major influence on the cost theory that emerged at the London School of Economics under Robbins, Mises, Hayek, Coase, Thirlby, Wiseman, and Lerner.[6] In the United States, Davenport and Knight also concerned themselves with opportunity cost theory.

Thirlby particularly emphasized the ephemeral nature of cost. Cost, in the sense of sacrifice or foregone gain, exists only in the mind of the decision maker at the time he is deciding. Because it is subjective and ephemeral, cost cannot be discovered by another person at another time. Opportunity cost is not observable and not measurable by a third party; the weighing of the sacrifice is knowable only subjectively to the decider.[7] This direction of thought leads Buchanan to note that opportunity cost is subjective, ephemeral, anticipatory, and exists only in the mind of the decision maker. Thus, cost is borne only by the decision maker and cannot be discovered or measured by an observer.[8]

This highly subjective view of cost was not easily incorporated into economic theory, perhaps because economists viewed their discipline as Newtonian in character, observable like science, and deterministic in an

[5]Philip H. Wicksteed, *The Common Sense of Political Economy*, Macmillian & Co., Ltd., London, 1910, p. 380.
[6]Buchanan, op. cit., pp. 16–37.
[7]G. F. Thirlby, "The Ruler," *South African Journal of Economics*, December 1946, pp. 253–276.
[8]Buchanan, op. cit., p. 43.

equilibrium outcome. In such a model, subjective costs, which are nonobservable and nonmeasurable, have no place. They are excluded by definition. Whatever the reasons, opportunity costs seem to have lost their place among the paradigms of modern economics.[9]

The inacceptance of opportunity costs as a cogent force in contemporary economic thinking is regrettable because the concept is a principal contribution which economics could make to environmental decision making. Environmental decisions revolve upon "choice-influencing costs," that is, the prospective biological sacrifices inherent in the situation. The choice to buy an automobile, at the moment of decision, is a subjective preference for future personal convenience in transit time at the expense of the biological health of organisms to be damaged by air pollutants. Biological processes are based upon energy exchange in which there is no net gains but only transformation and entropy, which eventually become a diffusion of heat and death.

The biological exchange is, therefore, unlike the market exchange; in biological terms there is always a loss to some species in the ecosystem from every human choice. Opportunity costs conceptually recognize that every human choice (satisfaction) is made at the expense of biological damage elsewhere in the ecosystem, whenever the supply of energy or materials limits the life support capability of natural cycles (which is most of the time).

The resurrection of opportunity costs as a tool of analysis in environmental economics depends upon a willingness to deal with prospective opportunity costs rather than with retrospective accounting costs. This change alone would constitute a major reorientation in economic thinking. Retrospective costs have about them a rigor likened to the physical sciences; they can be measured, quantified, and submitted to extensive mathematical manipulation, however real or unreal their meaning.

Prospective opportunity costs are, at best, probabilistic estimates of subjective judgments. As such they have a high degree of uncertainty about them, because they represent two kinds of imponderables. The first is the lack of complete information about any situation. The second is that choices (opportunity costs) are made on a collection of behavioral, subjective, or psychological data.

Economics avoids these imponderables by assuming that the decision maker (1) possesses perfect or complete information, and (2) acts rationally. The constraints, or perhaps unreality, of the economic model of man have recently led to the emergence of new disciplines which attempt to take into account the uncertainties derived from imperfect

---

[9]Ibid., pp. 35 and 49.

information and subjective behavior. These disciplines are called variously management science, operations research, systems theory, information theory, or simply behavioral sciences. They have in common a different set of assumptions than economics, in that they presume that a decision maker (1) has incomplete information and therefore faces uncertainty as to the outcome of his decision, which tends to make him minimize risks by acting on the probabilities of the outcome; and (2) acts frequently on the basis of preconditioned learning, subjective, emotional, or psychological factors, as well as—at times—rationale. These differences in assumptions, or view of reality, generate a different paradigm of the decision process, which is the subject of the next chapter.

SUMMARY

The thesis of this and preceding chapters in Section Three has been that the human decision process must reflect biological data within the decision parameters, if the resulting choices are to encompass and approximate the external condition of the ecosystem. Thus, if we wish environmental quality, then there must be biological, qualitative parameters in the decision logic. The argument has been advanced that neither the market price structure nor economic theory presently encompasses such qualitative or biological data, because they are both based upon historical accounting costs in which costs or prices have been attached to the exchange value of the factors of production. It is the lack of recognition, indeed exclusion, of biological damage data in the decision process which causes environmental quality to deteriorate.

This exclusion of biological data can be remedied in two ways: first, by introducing probabilistic data into the decision model which reflect the condition or quality of the ecosystem (that is, the estimated degree and loci of biological damage); and secondly, by creating a simulated market in which the condition of the environment is specifically incorporated into the cost tradeoffs which constitute the decision. By this means, biological damage would become a specific and internal function in the decision, rather than being an "externality" as it is now.

The inclusion of a biological damage function in the decision would foster ecological diversity, balance, and well-being, because the minimization of damage would enable the natural processes of the ecosystem to function normally without aberration caused by human residuals. If this inclusion of biological data were accomplished, then many of the concepts of economic theory could be adapted to environmental decisions. That is, environmental decision, like economic decision, can be related to marginal-utility theory, in which the last added increment of human satisfaction is just equal to the marginal increment of opportunity cost. By opportunity cost is meant those choice-influencing costs which reflect the prospective sacrifices to the individual or the ecosystem. Such opportunity costs will have the characteristic of uncertainty; the exact location of supply and demand functions will not be known because of the incompleteness of qualitative information. Even more important, they will be uncertain because of the futuristic, ephemeral, and subjective quality of the decision. This means that decision sciences will become, at best, an aggregation of future probabilistic estimates reflecting qualities which people subjectively desired in themselves and their environment. Such a decision art will be less precise than the Newtonian paradigm of equilibrium economics, but it may also be more real in taking into some account the qualities of the ecosystem upon which our own organic sustenance depends.

DISCUSSION QUESTIONS

1   Some business executives have a tendency to make a decision to produce to that point where average cost equals average revenue, instead of equilibrating marginal costs and revenues. By examining the table and charts on pages 266 and 268, calculate the difference in gross profit by producing 7,000 units compared to 11,000 units.
2   If you were to convert the marginal-utility concept to an environmental decision, what qualities of the environment might you try to measure on the horizontal scale labeled quality of environment in Figure 14-3 on page 270? Give examples.
3   Suppose you are the individual living near the Staten Island Zoo at the time of the deaths of zoo animals from lead poisoning. What alternatives would you consider in a decision, and what costs would be associated with each decision? What are the bases of cost in your several alternatives?
4   Give examples from your own experience of decisions which you have made which involve (a) objective costs, (b) choice-influenced costs, and (c) choice-influencing costs? Which of these decision examples seem the most germane to you?

PROBLEM

Suppose that the probability rate of human death from respiratory disease is 1 per 1,000 at an average oxidant level of 0.15 ppm. Assume also that morbidity rates are estimated to rise directly with the increase in oxidant levels. That is, if oxidants double to 0.30 ppm, then morbidity rates double to 2 per 1,000. Now create a demand curve with this data using level of cleanliness on one scale and mortality rates as cost on the other. Next invent a supply curve of your own design, and explain your decision. What kinds of costs are involved? How did you equate the mortality cost with other costs?

Chapter 15

Systems and Information Theory Applied to Ecology

Even though choice-influencing costs found little place in economic theory, opportunity costs moved over, under the pen of mathematicians and behavioral economists like von Neumann, Morgenstern, and Simon, to become game theory, or the gains and losses in a payoff matrix. The fields of probability theory, operations research, management science, and systems theory are found upon choice making under conditions of more-or-less uncertainty. What was *ceteris parabus* to economics became the sine qua non of the new decision-making disciplines. That is, what economics chose to exclude, viz., uncertainty and subjective values, became the substance of the new decision theories. There is scarcely yet a developed systems theory. Still, we will find it useful to contrast what systems theory there is with economic theory, because the differences will tell us something about the nature of environmental problems and how costs or sacrifices may be regarded in ecological decisions.

   The crux of choice making, as seen in management science, is the handling of uncertainty, and uncertainty is derived from the lack of

information. To reduce uncertainty in a decision requires that one increase the amount of information.

The amount of information contained in the ecosystem, to describe
all its processes and interactions, is myriad, and human cognition has
limited informational capacity. Hence the question becomes, how much
information is enough to reduce uncertainty to an acceptable risk level,
given the limited capability of the human mind? To understand this
question, one needs to explore the nature of whole systems (viz., the
ecosystem), the informational content of systems, and what requisite
variety of information about the whole system is needed to reduce
uncertainty. These points will be discussed in the following sequence:

1 Open and closed systems
2 Steady state versus entropy
3 Biological exchange systems and equifinality
4 Examples of state-maintaining and purposive organisms
5 Information systems
6 Energy and information requirements of a steady state
7 Information as selection to reduce uncertainty
8 Uncertainty, gain, and loss
9 The requisite variety of information regarding environment
10 Foregone gains and opportunity costs in the environment

The purpose of this chapter is to describe more adequately what is
the measure and meaning of opportunity costs in the sense of biological
damage in the environment. Those who find the content of the chapter too
technical for their interest may obtain the general sense of the chapter by
reading the materials under headings 1 through 4 plus 9 and 10 (omitting 5
through 8). These sections will convey the general concept that choice-
influencing opportunity costs are the biological losses suffered by reason
of uncertainty and inadequate information.

OPEN AND CLOSED SYSTEMS

A closed system is one which has no environment; an open system is one
that does.[1] Marginal theory in economics describes a closed system,
because *ceteris parabus*, all other things are equal, which is to say, the
environment is excluded. Hence, if economic theory chooses to exclude
the environment and to deal only with past costs or observable market
prices (past demand), the economic model or system becomes deterministic. That is, the economic model is a static or one-state system in which no
events occur and the equilibrium is posited in the data.

[1]Russell L. Ackoff, "Towards a System of System Concepts," *Management Science,* vol. 17,
no. 11, July 1971, p. 663.

People do not live in such a closed or static system. They live as organisms in an environment of interacting biological processes and changes. The characteristic of biological species, including humans, in such an environment is to be adaptive to change. Biological phenomena exist in an open and dynamic system. Moreover, the purpose of biological events is not to achieve equilibrium, but to maintain disequilibria.

Equilibrium is found in the physical world in closed systems which are governed by the one-way flow of energy. The second law of thermodynamics demonstrates that the higher forms of energy, such as light, chemical, or mechanical energy, are irreversibly degraded to heat; and the heat gradients diffuse into a random distribution among physical elements. This process is called entropy and is a tendency toward maximum disorder, randomness, and a leveling of differences. The universe moves toward entropy death as all energy is converted into heat of low temperature, and the physical processes come to equilibrium.[2] At equilibrium all energy is uniformly distributed, and with no energy conversion no work can be done.

The attainment of equilibrium means death.[3] The process of life, biologically, is to move counter to the tendency in the physical world of dissipation into entropic disorder, and instead to move toward a higher state of order and organization within the organism. This counterflow, moving from disorder toward order, has been called *negative entropy*. In open biological systems, the living organism imports complex molecules high in free energy from the environment. The imported energy is used biochemically for cellular production, which is a form of storing potential energy; for maintenance as in respiration; and for work such as the production of movement. The production of work, or the conversion of energy to activity, is associated with positive entropy as in the physical world, that is, with a dissipation or distribution of heat energy. The importation of energy from the environment for energy storage or maintenance, however, constitutes negative entropy. By this importation and storage of energy, living systems can maintain themselves in a steady state, avoid the increase in entropy, and may develop toward higher states of order and organization.

A STEADY STATE VERSUS ENTROPY

Entropy may be looked at statistically as a probability distribution. A closed system in equilibrium is a state of complete disorder, disorder being a uniform distribution or dissipation of heat energy throughout the

[2]L. von Bertalanffy, "The Theory of Open Systems in Physics and Biology," *Science*, vol. 111, 1950, pp. 23–29.
[3]L. von Bertalanffy, *General System Theory*, George Braziller, Inc., New York 1968, p. 191.

system. The most probable distribution of a mixture of red and blue glass beads, or molecules of different velocities, for example, is that of randomness or disorder. Suppose all high-temperature fast molecules are contained in one space with all slow molecules in a second, then the distribution represents a highly improbable statistical state. Such an improbable distribution, in living organisms, is the disequilibria (or steady state) they maintain vis-a-vis the environment.[4]

The tendency for living organisms to be in a steady state of disequilibria was noted, among early systems thinkers, by Koehler and Cannon. They observed that living organisms absorb and emit energy, exchanging it with the environment, but at times they absorb much more than they emit, which makes them reservoirs of potential energy. Organisms are by no means in equilibrium with respect to their environment. Mammals, for example, frequently stand when at rest; and many fish, when at rest, are positioned with the heavier parts of their body turned away from the direction of gravitational force. In a state of physical equilibrium, the center of gravity of both mammals and fish should be lowered as much as possible; in other words, they would be top-side down as they are in a condition of death. In their living condition, no outer physical forces keep mammals standing or fish swimming against the pull of gravity. Hence, this unstable position must exist by internal processes and vectors within the organism which prevent the attainment of equilibrium. These factors represent a certain amount of reserve energy in living organisms, which is unlike physical systems that are unable to preserve an energy potential to avoid reaching equilibrium. The conclusion is that living organisms are able to reserve enough energy to depart from equilibrium sufficiently to maintain their internal organizational structure, and frequently perform work functions as well.[5]

BIOLOGICAL EXCHANGE SYSTEMS AND EQUIFINALITY

Thus, a biological organism is an open system which may be defined as a system of exchange of matter between the organism and its environment, and this exchange results in the importing and exporting of energy by building up and breaking down its material components. The rate at which energy is converted by the organism is subject to the organism's own regulation, that is, its own metabolic rate or genetic code. The steady state at which an organism arrives is determined by the metabolic rate at which it imports and stores energy, and this steady state is called *equifinality*. Equifinality is the optimum energy potential of the organism; and it may be approached at different rates depending upon nutrition (energy im-

[4]Ibid., pp. 39–41.
[5]F. E. Emery, *Systems Thinking*, Penguin Books, Baltimore, Md., 1969, pp. 61–62.

ports) and environmental conditions such as temperature, water, or limiting factors such as pollutants. Equifinality is the growth characteristic of an organism.[6] An experimental demonstration of the equifinality of growth was conducted feeding a control group of rats a normal diet, but interrupting the diet of the experimental group from the 50th to the 200th day with a vitamin deficiency. With a regular diet the control group gained weight along a normal growth curve for 300 days. Those with vitamin deficiency stayed at a constant, subnormal weight from the 50th to the 200th day, but regained all the weight (stored energy) from the 200th to the 300th day to recover to normal weight.[7] In other words, both groups arrived at the same equifinality, or steady state, determined by their species organizational characteristics despite early growth at different rates stemming from environmental conditions.

The profound difference between most physical and living systems can be expressed in the contrast between equilibrium and equifinality. Physical systems are closed, separate from an environment, without the ability to reserve energy, and, hence, energy dissipates to an equilibrium state. Living systems are open to the environment, import energy from it, store the energy in a reserve determined by their self-regulated growth rate, and by this negative entropy maintain a disequilibria which becomes a steady state, or equifinality.

Perhaps some illustrations of different kinds of systems would make their characteristics more clear. Koehler gives the flame as an example of system. Enclosed in a bell jar with a given amount of air, the flame represents a closed system whose chemical energy conversion will dissipate at a calculable rate depending upon the amount of fuel and oxygen, and, as heat dissipates, the system will arrive at an equilibrium with the flame extinguished and the heat randomly distributed at a less-concentrated level. This illustrates that in closed systems the equilibrium is predetermined by the starting state of the system.

A flame in the atmosphere is a part of an open system in that the flame can draw from its environment almost an unlimited store of chemical energy (for example, in the flaring of a natural gas well). The system will then operate at the maximum rate which the energy can be spent by the flame. The flame contains the maximum potential energy, and thus there is no reserve unspent.

EXAMPLES OF STATE-MAINTAINING AND PURPOSIVE ORGANISMS

An organism, like the flame, operates in an open system, drawing energy from the environment; but unlike the flame, the organism converts and

---

[6]Ibid., p. 76.
[7]von Bertalanffy, op. cit., p. 142.

contains within itself large stores of food or energy. The potential energy is not spontaneously spent outside the organism at its maximum rate.[8]

Systems may be looked upon as increasing in complexity as they derive energy and information from the environment to achieve a higher state of organization. Closed systems do not import energy or information. A clock would be an example of a closed mechanical system whose state is described by the theories of conventional physics. A flame or organic cells are simple examples of open systems whose theoretical model is found in principles of heat conversion, metabolism, genetics, and information. Man himself represents an example of an open system with a higher organizational state, whose behavioral model is found in theories of nervous systems, learning, and communication. At a higher systems level still, in terms of organizational complexity, are sociocultural systems among populations and communities, whose theoretical models are found in population ecology, economics, sociology, and statistics.[9]

Ackoff has generalized these organic systems further by describing them as state maintaining, goal seeking, purposive, and purposeful.[10] State-maintaining organisms (for example, simple forms of sea life) may react to their environment in various ways, but the outcome in terms of bodily state is fixed.

Purposive systems are multigoal seeking; they may choose the means to pursue their goals, but the goals are determined by initiating events. Animals may be purposive in seeking food, reproduction, relaxation; but, as in the example of the rat experiment, their final goals of growth and potential energy (equifinality) are determined by their initiating event, that is by their birth and genetic code.

Humans and human organizations are the most familiar examples of purposeful systems. A purposeful system is one which can select its ends as well as its means under constant conditions. Organizations are the most adaptable of the open systems, capable of importing and exporting energy and materials at varying rates from their environment for a variety of ends.

INFORMATION SYSTEMS

The selection of ends, as well as means for importing and exporting energy, are basically informational processes. The metabolism of organisms, that is, their importing energy by eating, drinking, and breathing, is the means by which they avoid the decay into an inert state of equilib-

[8]Emery, op. cit., pp. 64–67.
[9]von Bertalanffy, op. cit., pp. 28–29.
[10]Ackoff, op. cit., p. 665.

rium. Schrodinger has called this process the *feeding on negative entropy*. He notes further the formulation of entropy in heat mechanics by Boltzmann to be expressed as

$$\text{Entropy} = k \log_n \Omega$$

in which k is the Boltzmann constant of gases (3.293×10^{-24} cal/°C), Ω is a quantitative measure of the atomistic disorder of the system, and $\log_n$ may be to the natural log base e (2.71828—). Or, another way of expressing the idea is: Entropy is the probability of a given heat distribution and is a logarithmic function of the number of microscopic ways (probabilities) that the macroscopic state (entropy) can be realized. The formulation says that the heat distribution will increase logarithmically as it dissipates until it reaches complete disorder, which means that all energy velocities are equally distributed in the system rather than being concentrated.

But living organisms by their metabolism feed on negative entropy, that is, acquire energy to maintain a steady state of order within the organism, and this can be expressed by rewriting Boltzmann's equation

$$\text{Negative entropy} = k \log (1/\Omega)$$

From this formulation comes the awkward expression "negative entropy," which is semantically a double negative meaning to decrease the rate of disorder. Hence, negative entropy is really a measure of order. Or more understandably, perhaps, living organisms have the ability to extract order from the environment.[11]

The expression for negative entropy is also the same as the measure of information in information theory. The measure of information I may be defined as:

$$I = K \log_n P$$

where I is the information of one outcome which has P possible states, all equally probable; K is a proportioning constant; and $\log_n$ is a logarithm frequently to the binary base 2. This concept, first applied by Shannon to electronic communication and channel capacity, has since been used more broadly for psychological and biological measurement of information. The expression says that information always decreases, and never increases, as a result of being communicated. Entropy and information

[11]Walter Buckley (ed.). *Modern Systems Research for Behavioral Scientists*. Aldine Publishing Company. Chicago, 1968, pp. 144–146; from Erwin Schrodinger, *What is Life?*. Cambridge University Press, Cambridge, Mass., 1945, chap. VI.

then are isomorphic but differing in sign, entropy increasing and information decreasing when randomness occurs. That is, information, in sign, is a measure of negative entropy.

ENERGY AND INFORMATION REQUIREMENTS OF A STEADY STATE

The maintenance of a steady state in an organism may be viewed as being accomplished in part by the importing of molecules high in free energy and in part through stimuli communicating information to avoid the degenerative process of entropy. In simple, single-cell organisms, the molecular information for the arrangement and replication of the cell may be sufficient for it to assimilate food and energy for a considerable period of time without any added information. Any stimulus applied to the cell, if only a change in the food supply, communicates new information to the cell which, along with the stored information in the structure of the cell, is used to determine its new state or adaptation.

In more complex organisms, communication takes several forms: electrochemicals in nervous systems, pressure in vascular systems, or the generation of hormones and enzymes. The control of body growth through a chemical agent secreted by the pituitary gland is an example. Another example might be the regulatory relation of insulin to sugar metabolism, which requires individuals to inject this information into themselves; otherwise they would die from its lack.

Complex organisms which store a large amount of information neurologically connected or programmed to elicit rapid response to a wide variety of stimuli, or informational inputs, from the environment have historically been the most adaptable and successful in biological evolution.[12] The most complex organisms capable of storing information for adaptable response are higher animals (biological systems) and sociological systems in the form of communities. At any level of informational content, however, information may be looked upon as the agent of negative entropy, or the means of selecting orderliness out of the environment.

Another way to look at the information process is to regard biological organisms as a catalyst capable of carrying information to direct the rate of specific chemical or physical reactions. The information serves to order and hasten a thermodynamic process which may otherwise be slow or complicated by competing reactions. The catalytic information creates negative entropy in molecules formed in the desired reaction. That is, catalysts are rate information. The second law of thermodynamics makes

[12]Ibid., p. 160; from Richard C. Raymond, "Communications, Entropy, and Life," *American Scientist*, April 1950, 38 pp. 273–278.

no reference to time; it merely postulates that entropy will tend to increase over some unspecified time period. Information then is the rate function of energy conversion in open systems, which enables living organisms to create the energy reserve which constitutes negative entropy. Without this rate information capability, closed physical processes degrade toward entropy death, or equilibrium.

Viewing organisms as catalysts carrying rate information, however, presents a new problem, and that is, catalysts tend to become poisoned. This is true in physical processes as well as biological. The lead in gasoline "poisons" noble metals (platinum or gold) used as catalysts in a catalytic muffler to hasten the rate of reaction in burning residual hydrocarbons or oxides of nitrogen. Similarly, lead is a "poison" to human life. A poisoned catalyst, in biological systems, is one which has become disorganized in its own structure and thus low in information content, or high in entropy.[13] Ozone, another air pollutant, causes aging in cells, which might be viewed as a disorganization of cellular structure, making it lower in information content, and less able to match or select orderliness (rate of energy reactions needed by its cellular structure) from the environment.

INFORMATION AS SELECTION TO REDUCE UNCERTAINTY

The cardinal feature of information theory is that it is a theory of selection,[14] the selection of reaction rates needed to respond to stimuli. In simpler systems, which are state maintaining or goal seeking, the amount of stored information is less than in complex systems and the response may be directly reactive. In purposeful systems, with large and complex information storage, there are technical, semantic, and value problems. These levels of problems cause the information transmission to become iterative, going through various translations, and these translations are what constitute the pattern of communication. Communication is a somewhat enlarged informational set. In large purposeful systems, such as human beings and societies, Ackoff views communications as consisting of the transmissions of (1) information, (2) instruction, and (3) motivation.[15]

Information is a measure of one's freedom of choice when selecting a message. A message is a man-made sign or symbol which signifies a change in state or response. The amount of information in a message

---

[13]Ibid., p. 160.

[14]Ibid., p. 139; from Anatol Rapoport, "The Promise and Pitfalls of Information Theory," *Behavioral Science*, 1956, vol. I, pp. 303–309.

[15]Ibid., pp. 209–217; from Russell L. Ackoff, "Toward a Behavioral Theory of Communication," *Management Science*, 1957–1958, vol. 4, pp. 218–234.

usually relates to two aspects of response: (1) information which describes potential choices, and (2) information which shows the efficiency of the choice. Suppose you enter a theater and are told that there are two exits, to your right and to your left; and left is nearer. The message informing you of two exits describes your potential choices. The message that the left exit is nearer informs you of the efficiency of an action based upon the choice.

Instruction modifies the probabilities of success in such a way as to give the individual greater control of the outcome. That is, suppose an individual had the objective of going from one point to another by two alternative choices: say, one by climbing on foot over a high mountain, and the second, by driving around the mountain on a road in a car. The second choice may have a higher probability of success, if the individual has been put in control of a sufficient vector of energy. The information, then, of the amount and vector of energy under one's control among various choices, is instruction.

Motivation is the transmission of the basis for preferences among various purposeful states or outcomes. If an individual has no preference among a variety of outcomes, he has no motivation within his present state. If an individual is in a theater when a fire alarm sounds but has no preference for which exit he seeks, or whether he seeks an exit, he may be viewed as having no motivation to change states.

In summary, information is obtained by reducing uncertainty, and uncertainty is potential information. Thus, the measure of the amount of information is the same as the measure of the amount of uncertainty.

The amount of uncertainty is a function of the number of outcomes which may occur. We arrive, therefore, at this important conclusion: The amount of information in a communication is not a function of what happened but, rather, a function of what could have happened but did not.[16]

UNCERTAINTY, GAIN, AND LOSS

Decision theory is concerned with the selection of information which will reduce uncertainty and thus modify the probability of success by changing the outcome. Suppose, for example, that an organism possessed information, I_1, in its cellular structure which enables it to convert food or energy, E_1, from the environment. Let us say, also, that in a particular state, S_1, the environment contains only the one form of energy, hence, any encounter between the organism and its environment will make E_1 available. Under these conditions the organism is able to maintain a

[16]Wendell R. Garner, *Uncertainty and Structure as Psychological Concepts*, John Wiley and Sons, New York, 1962, p. 7.

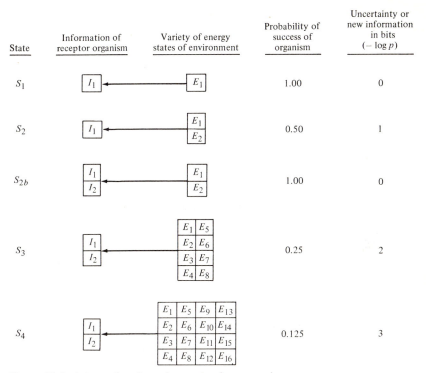

State	Information of receptor organism	Variety of energy states of environment	Probability of success of organism	Uncertainty or new information in bits $(-\log p)$
S_1			1.00	0
S_2			0.50	1
S_{2b}			1.00	0
S_3			0.25	2
S_4			0.125	3

Figure 15-1 Informational requirements of an organism.

steady state, because it has all the energy it needs and the necessary information to convert it in its own cellular process. As long as the environment remains in state S_1 the probability of success (i.e., maintaining a steady state) of the organism is 1.00, or certainty. Also, the amount of uncertainty or new information received by the organism upon each encounter with nature is zero. There are no surprises; every encounter delivers a recognizable energy source which is usable.

Now, suppose the environment changes and is in state S_2 in which there are not one, but two, forms of energy, E_1 and E_2, equally distributed and equally available. Information, I_1, relates specifically to energy condition, E_1. That is, I_1 is used to convert E_1, I_2 for E_2, etc., distributed and equally available. Now the organism may encounter either E_1 or E_2 with equal probability. When it encounters E_1, it can assimilate it and convert the energy because it has information I_1, which informs it how to do so. But when it encounters E_2 half of the time, it cannot use the energy because it does not have the requisite information I_2. The result is that the organism now receives only one-half the energy that it formerly did.

Next we will assume that the organism has sensory feelings, and, because it is now undernourished, the organism feels pain when it encounters E_2 and continues to do so until it adapts and acquires the information on how to convert this form of energy. Thus, the organism is adaptive and has acquired a new bit of knowledge, I_2. This returns it to a steady state with the environment (see third level of Figure 15-1, S_{2b}) where the probability of success is again 1.00 and the uncertainty has returned to zero.

The environment now changes again to state S_3 which contains eight types of energy, but the organism still has only two forms of information. The probability of success has dropped to 0.25 and the new information or uncertainty has become 2 bits (binary digits). A fourth environmental state, S_4, brings sixteen forms of energy, the probability of success drops to .125 and the uncertainty to 3 bits.

The only way that the organism can reduce uncertainty and improve the probability of success is to acquire as much information as there are stimuli in the environment. This is Ashby's law of requisite variety, that the variety of outcomes can only be decreased by a corresponding increase in the information of the receptor.[17]

THE REQUISITE VARIETY OF INFORMATION
REGARDING ENVIRONMENT

Unfortunately, the environment presents such myriads of stimuli that organisms can seldom acquire the requisite variety to remain in a steady state or to respond with certainty. The result is uncertainty, frequently a high degree of uncertainty, and the problem to a receptor organism in the environment is to reduce the average uncertainty with a minimum number of tries, or responses. The measurement of average uncertainty is similar in formulation to negative entropy, that is

$$\text{Average uncertainty} = -\Sigma p \log_2 P$$

where p represents the probabilities of a series of events or stimuli. For example, if a bent coin is thrown in the air and it turns up heads 9 times out of 10, then the surprisal of the event, or new information appears with the tails. The information contribution of heads is $\log 1/.90 = \log 1.11 = 0.15$ bits. The information contribution of tails is larger: $\log 1/.10 = \log 10 = 3.32$ bits. The weighted sum of these two values is their average contribution to uncertainty (also, their information content). Hence, $.90 \times .15 + .10 \times 3.32 = 0.47$ bits. That is, in the case of the bent coin, an

[17]Ibid., from W. Ross Ashby, *An Introduction to Cybernetics*, Chapman and Hall, London, 1956, chaps. 7 and 11.

average of only 47 bits is necessary to describe completely a series of 100 throws.[18]

An organism faced with a series of 100 stimuli with a biased probability of .90 for one event and .10 for the second, would only need forty-seven attempts (correctly received and coded) to "know" all 100 events and fifty-three of the stimuli would be "redundant." The reduction of uncertainty could then be accomplished with 47 bits of new information.

The function of information is to enable organisms to select a response to stimuli. The communication in a series of messages informs the organism as to courses of action, efficiency of response, and value; or, as previously pointed out (by Ackoff), a message informs, instructs, and motivates. If a person has acquired the requisite variety of information (i.e., reduced his average uncertainty), then he is equipped to implement his goals. That is, he is sufficiently informed to achieve the *gains* and satisfactions he seeks. If he is inadequately informed or misinformed with respect to courses of action, their efficiency, or value, then his efforts to satisfaction may be abortive, in which case he *loses*.

The quality of information available to an individual, then, determines his gains or losses. This brings us back to our starting point about costs, especially opportunity costs.

Opportunity costs may be viewed as the losses, or the gains which an individual gives up. In informational terms, these losses may be viewed as the inability to reduce his average uncertainty. The insufficiency of information is also an inability to reserve energy and acquire negative entropy. Hence, the losses, in biological terms, are the entropy incurred.

That is, opportunity costs are deviations from the steady state, the drift to entropy death rather than feeding on negative entropy, the tendency toward disorder (equilibrium) rather than toward improbable disequilibria (steady state). The measure of opportunity cost, then, can be expressed as the deviation from the requisite information content, which is expressed as the probability of failure by reason of insufficient information. For instance, in Figure 15-1, in the last example of state S_4, the organism has a .125 probability of success in matching its available information to respond appropriately to sixteen stimuli from the environment, or a .875 probability of failure. Suppose there is a population of 1,000 organisms of the same species, with the same information characteristics, and the consequence of an unsuccessful response is death. That is, the mortality rate is 1 per unsuccessful response. Then we can see that 875 out of the 1000 organisms would die (1,000 × 1 × .875). The

[18]Garner, op. cit., pp. 20–23; and also Fred Attneave, *Applications of Information Theory to Psychology*, Holt, Rinehart and Winston, Inc., New York, 1959, pp. 5–10.

opportunity cost, in this example, is 875 lives of the species. We can generalize the expression of opportunity costs in the following manner

$$O_c = nrp$$

where O_c is the opportunity cost, n is the number of population or units exposed to uncertainty, r is the rate of loss or damage at risk, and p is the probability of failure by reason of an inadequate response or uncertainty. (If the probabilities are unequally distributed among the environmental stimuli, then the probability of failure would be derived from the average uncertainty $-\Sigma p \log_2 P$.)

Suppose, in another illustrative calculation, there are 30 million people in major cities, such as New York, Chicago, and Los Angeles, exposed to concentrations of air pollutants which are capable of causing a respiratory morbidity rate of .003, or 3 cases of illness per 1,000 exposures. Suppose also, (in case S_4, Figure 15-1), that I_1 and I_2 are knowledge of successful control and response to oxidants and sulfur dioxide, which are environmental stimuli E_1 and E_2. But there are also fourteen other air pollutants in the atmosphere, E_3 through E_{16} which also present risks. (*Note:* There are about eighteen organic reactant emissions from automobiles. Three of these alone, the alkanes, olefins, and aldehydes result in four or five types of reactions involving scores of different reaction partners.[19]) Then, the opportunity cost of the automobile emissions for inadequate knowledge and response to these reactions, would be 30,000,000 × .003 × .875 = 78,750 cases of respiratory illness. Or more simply, opportunity cost is the prospective losses suffered by inability to reduce the uncertainty (information) and risk (biological damage).

FOREGONE GAINS AND OPPORTUNITY COSTS IN THE ENVIRONMENT

The opportunity costs in the environment are the lost gains (entropy) which cause the ecological system or the individual to deviate from a steady state (disequilibria). The lead poisoning of leopards in the Staten Island Zoo is a loss of metabolism, a loss of ability to reserve energy, with the consequence of entropy death. The cause was lack of information or uncertainty with respect to the probabilities of the distribution of lead particulates in the environment; that uncertainty in turn was caused by the lack of information on the relation of lead emissions to atmospheric chemistry and meteorological distribution; and that uncertainty was

[19]Harold Johnston, *Reactions in the Atmosphere*, Project Clean Air, University of California, Riverside, Calif., 1970 Task Force Assessments, vol. 4, no. 7, pp. 3–11.

caused by the lack of information about thermodynamic reactions of leaded gasolines in combustion chambers.

The general public assumed that the use of automobiles had a relatively low probability of biological damage with a high probability of satisfying personal transportation wants. That assumption represented lack of information, or we may say the public acted on misinformation.

That is, the public did not have the requisite variety of information to reduce the uncertainties caused by the greater varieties of events in the ecosystem. The opportunity cost of the decision, then, was the loss of the mammals and reptiles in the zoo, due to a shortfall of information. That is, the public assumed a lower probability of biological damage, due to uncertainty and lack of information, than were the actual varieties of interaction and damage in the environment.

Moreover, the uncertainty continues. The probabilities of human biological damage from low-level lead poisoning remain unknown, and individuals do not have the requisite variety of information to know the degree of their exposure to entropy. The result is that we can say that opportunity cost, or loss of negative entropy, is measured by the deviance of the actual information upon which the public is acting from the actual distribution of uncertainty in the environment. Or in the vernacular, the opportunity cost of automobiles is that we do not know the extent to which we are dying.

SUMMARY

We are so accustomed to thinking about what we know as a certainty, that we seldom relate it to what we do not know, which constitutes uncertainty. This tendency to act on the knowns and ignore the unknowns exposes us to extraordinary biological risks. The number of interactions (energy states and information) in the ecosystem are myriad, while the human mind is comparatively limited in its informational capacity, which means that in ecological matters we act with a great deal less information than we need to reduce the average uncertainty or risk. As an example, we act on the information that an automobile provides personal transit convenience and that lead in gasoline prevents knocking in automobile engines. These are the knowns. The unknowns are what atmospheric reactions take place as a result of lead emissions, where the lead finally reposes in the ecosystem, and what toxic effects lead has on the energy conversion of all the organisms in the ecosystem. The amount of information upon which we act is small compared to the amount of ecological information needed to reduce average uncertainty and risk to acceptable levels.

To reduce biological risks to acceptable levels, we need to understand something about systems and information theory. Most of our logical paradigms from science, that is in the physical sciences and economics, apply only to closed systems. A closed system is one which has no environment, a one-state system, in which no events occur, and the equilibrium outcome is posited in the situational data. Such scientific methodology has little application to biological organisms.

Biological organisms exist in open systems, importing energy from their environment. Organisms avoid entropy death by maintaining disequilibria, or a store of energy, with which to sustain vital internal functions or perform external work functions. The higher the degree of energy reserve or informational selection which living beings possess, the higher their state of organization or purposiveness.

Humans and human organizations are purposeful because they can select ends as well as means. The selection of ends and means is basically an information selection process. Organisms adapt to environmental change by selecting information upon which to act, thus reducing the average uncertainty or risk. Indeed, one can say that prospective losses (opportunity costs) are the extent to which the information upon which one acts falls short of the information required to reduce average uncertainty. This brings us back to the hypothesis that the interactions and states of nature are myriad compared to the requisite variety of information available to human minds. If this is so, then we are exposed to high risks of biological damage by the emission of alien residuals into the environment, especially for those materials demonstrably toxic to organisms.

DISCUSSION QUESTIONS

1 What do entropy and negative entropy mean to you after reading this chapter? To what extent have you encountered the incorporation of the concept of entropy and negative entropy into theories of disciplines outside the physical or natural sciences? Does the incorporation of the concept of negative entropy into decision processes make any difference?

2 What is the distinction between equilibrium and equifinality? Can you illustrate the idea of equifinality in a sociocultural system?

3 How would you explain or calculate the requisite variety or information in a given situation? Illustrate a situation with a low-requisite variety of information, with a high-requisite variety.

4 What are the informational requirements of measuring opportunity costs? Why do you think cost-influencing opportunity costs did not find a significant place in economic theory?

PROBLEM

Consider a normal day in which you emerge from the door of your home to go to work, school, or shopping; and make a list of three or four alternative risks which you encounter as you enter into the open-system environment. Describe verbally how you would estimate the informational requirement and the average uncertainty of these several alternatives. In which of the alternatives are you exposed to the greatest opportunity costs?

Chapter 16

Trade-off Analysis: Cost Burdens and Beneficiaries

Biological processes reserve energy or dissipate it; that is, they are subject to relative gains or relative losses. Human beings, as biological organisms, also obey the laws of positive or negative entropy. Whether the entropy of a human biological system is positive or negative depends upon the state of information of the human system, that is, whether the human organism has the requisite variety of information to reduce the average uncertainty of environmental events sufficiently to maintain a steady state. Since the environment always has more variety than the human organism has information, the tendency is toward entropy or death. The most an organism can accomplish is to stay awhile the inevitable entropic end, and this staying power is accomplished by storing energy sufficiently to gain a little more time.

The process of decision making, or of life itself, may be looked upon as a balancing of relative probable gains against losses. The human organism is a stochastic system governed by relative probabilities, never with the requisite variety of information to act with certainty, always forced to make choices among probable gains versus probable losses. Choice theory concerns the means by which human decision making can obtain a relative gain minus the least relative loss, and this decision function may be called the trade-off analysis.

Trade-off analysis is the subjective calculation by which the probable gains minus the probable losses yield a preference. In arriving at a trade-off analysis, the decision maker always suffers opportunity costs, which are the relative losses. If inadequate information or misinformation causes the decision to yield larger relative losses than gains, the human organism moves from its present state toward one of greater entropy. That is, the decision was a poor one in accumulating more biological damage to the organism than energy. Or more simply, the decision lost time, in a life-span sense, instead of gaining it.

The application of trade-off analysis to environmental decisions will be approached through the following topics:

1 Time as a measure for trade-off analysis
2 Trade-off analysis compared to cost effectiveness and cost sensitivity
3 Air pollution example of cost-effectiveness analysis
4 Air pollution example of trade-off analysis
5 Air pollution example of cost-sensitivity analysis
6 Biological tradeoff—the fluoride case

TIME AS A MEASURE FOR TRADE-OFF ANALYSIS

To gain or lose time is the essence of a trade-off decision for human organisms, for time is life itself. Pollution in the environment causes biological damage which shortens life-span, and this is a loss of time, of lifetime. Moreover, time is interchangeable with energy, because it is the storage of potential energy by the organism which gives it lifetime potential.

The economist Irving Fisher noted that we should not view exchange as a means of obtaining products, but rather view its service as an object of exchange (Chapter 13). Thus the buyer does not purchase food, but the services of food; not a piano, but the services of a piano; not a dwelling, but the services of a dwelling. What are these services? They are a form of energy. The services of food are its caloric yield to maintain a steady state in the human organism. The service of a dwelling is heat protection to conserve the potential energy of the body by preventing its dissipation through convection or conductance. The services of a piano are in its ability to convert kinetic energy into sound waves.

The energy placed at the disposal of its user is the service of all material objects, and it is this acquisition of energy utilization which is the object of economic activity and exchange. The utility of an object is in energy potential, and it is this energy service which provides satisfaction. Energy services are a source of satisfaction because the organism then avoids expending its own energy (entropy); and by the avoiding of expenditure of its own energy, the organism has preserved its own energy potential for a future time. That is, the energy reserve is the means by which the organism extends its time, extends its life, and delays its death.

The common denominator in ecological trade-off analysis is, then, time. In normal trade-off calculations in economics, the net gain is expressed in monetary terms. But the ecosystem does not deal in coin; its media is energy, matter, and time, where time is the rate variable of the conversions between energy and matter. If biological health may be assumed to be the mission of ecological studies, then, the criteria for trade-off analysis are the species population affected and their life-spans, or time dimensions.

The time dimension of species populations is a function of the incoming solar energy of the sun, which is a major rate variable determining the conversion of energy to nutrient and thus the total biomass which can be sustained. We have seen, in Chapters 11 and 14, that the ecology is an open system with a one-way conversion of energy, in which the energy is always transformed from higher to a lower state of order (entropy). The efficiency of this conversion is generally low, which means that much of the energy is dissipated as heat.

This broad physical tendency toward entrophic disorder, and death, is counteracted by biological organisms which store energy from the nutrient chain sufficiently to achieve, for a time, a more highly organized state of activity, or equifinality. This temporal equifinality is the species' life-span. The total species populations, their time-spans, and the rate of reaching equifinality are all alternative variables dependent upon comparative advantage or access to the nutrient chain. That is, those species most favored by climate, circumstance, adaptibility, or cunning to feed upon the common flow of nutrients (energy reserve) increase in numbers, life-span, or rate of reaching equifinality; and these favored species acquire, then, their time and rate dimension at the expense of the disadvantaged species. That is to say, one species' gain in nutrient, or access to the common energy reserve, is another species' loss. The consequence is that every volitional action affecting the nutrient cycle is a tradeoff, favoring one species at the expense of another.

The human decision process is not presently constructed to recognize these tradeoffs, because there is no biological parameter in the decision mechanism. The decision mechanism presently recognizes only material and energy inputs being converted into services to satisfy human wants with a net monetary profit for the conversion service. The mechanism does not recognize that the useful goods are produced with an equivalent volume of residual wastes which changes the nutrient cycle and causes biological damage. By these omissions, the decision calculus always favors providing nutrient and energy reserves to the human species at the expense of other species. But the paradox is that the other disadvantaged species, denied nutrient or energy reserves, as they succumb, diminish the remaining available food supply for humans.

Logically, then, it can be argued that every human decision is a choice as to which species will survive and expand by its access to an energy reserve. In this light, the concept of profit from human activity becomes a fictitious gain, which is contrived only by failing to account for all the costs. If all costs and biological damage are accounted for, net profit is a logical impossibility because it is contrary to the second law of thermodynamics, since energy may be transformed but always at a loss, that is, from a higher- to a lower-energy state. We may surmise, then, that the concept of net profit really has the effect, by not accounting for all costs, of shifting the biological damage to other organisms who then pay the compensatory loss by a deficiency in energy and time. Thus an emphysema patient pays, in time lost and by a shortened life, for air pollution; and the eagle pays, in loss of time and life, for pesticides.

The objective of ecological trade-off analysis is to determine which species pay in energy, time, and life losses for the gains sought in human satisfactions. Human satisfaction is goal seeking for a gain (in energy use and time). Trade-off analysis looks to determine the time and life losses caused by the choice, for the purpose of asking which gains will entail the least undesirable losses.

The absence of this question of gains versus losses is what has brought us close to environmental disaster, because without knowing the losses, we assume our satisfactions to be a sheer net gain, in a kind of Santa Claus fantasy that something is to be had for nothing. Our preferences for gains should be made only in light of all the losses, because then we will know what it costs us. We need to know our opportunity costs, where the loss of time, life, and energy is occurring, if we wish to live in the real biological world, rather than in a material fantasy land of our own creation. Trade-off analysis is a means of trying to bring ourselves back to earth.

TRADE-OFF ANALYSIS COMPARED TO COST EFFECTIVENESS AND COST SENSITIVITY

The elements of a trade-off analysis are implicit in the semantics of the phrase. To trade off means a willingness to make an exchange for gains which are valued more than some acceptable level of losses. A tradeoff is, thus, a preference and choice of means. The choice of ends was discussed previously in terms of cost effectiveness or benefit-cost analysis. Indeed, there are several levels of analysis in choice making, which may be distinguished as follows:

1   A cost-effectiveness study examines whether a goal is worth its cost. The goal satisfactions are judged in relation to monetary, biological, or other costs.
2   A trade-off study determines whether one alternative is better than another for the same goal.
3   A cost-sensitivity analysis determines how much it costs to change the performance specifications of an alternative.[1]

Or more summarily, cost effectiveness is a measure of worth (value), trade-off analysis is a measure of alternative means, and cost-sensitivity analysis is a measure of performance requirements. All three methods involve costs, sometimes much the same cost elements. All of them also are concerned with benefits or satisfaction—but with different levels of degrees of satisfaction. Cost effectiveness relates to the overall satisfaction or benefit of the system. Trade-off analysis is concerned with the best alternative means to achieve the benefit. Cost-sensitivity analysis, by varying performance specifications (the output), tries to determine what is a sufficient degree of satisfaction.

AIR POLLUTION EXAMPLE OF COST-EFFECTIVENESS ANALYSIS

Perhaps the import of these different methods of looking at costs would be more obvious if we considered an example. Suppose we are asked to recommend a solution to the air pollution problems of major cities, by choosing among several alternatives shown below:

1   New car emission controls only
2   Used car emission control by retrofit equipment
3   All car inspection
4   A rapid urban transit system

The first of these alternatives has been the main thrust of state and federal regulations. The second alternative has had study, but little implementation. The other alternatives have yet to be seriously developed on a broad scale for all urban areas throughout the nation.

First, we will examine the economic costs of several alternatives in

[1]E. S. Quade and W. I. Boucher, *Systems Analysis and Policy Planning*, Elsevier Publishing, New York, 1968, pp. 20 and 138.

terms of cost effectiveness. To make the example brief, a few simplifying assumptions will be made. Assume there are 80 million cars on the road used, with 8 million being replaced each year at an average cost of $3,000 per car. Assume also that the cars are used mainly for urban transportation to work and carry 100 million people per day on round trips. Also, we will assume that used car inspection and control costs $50 per year, used car control equipment costs $150 per unit to install, and an urban express transit system has a person-trip capacity of 50,000 at a capital cost of $440 per person compared to an eight-lane freeway with a person-trip capacity of 9,000 at a capital cost of $1,600 per person.[2] These figures become our cost inputs.

Now we need to determine some effectiveness measures. For simplicity we will use the air quality standards adopted by the state and federal governments. The ambient air quality standards for photochemical oxidants are 0.08 ppm for one hour; for carbon monoxide, 35 ppm for one hour; for nitrogen oxides, 0.24 ppm for three hours; for sulfur dioxide, 0.14 ppm for twenty-four hours; for hydrocarbons, 0.24 ppm for three hours; and for particulates, 260 micrograms per cubic meter for twenty-four hours. Let us assume that they all increase proportionately, so that if we double the oxidant reading, all other pollutants also double. We shall assume also that when the ambient air quality has pollutants four times the standard (i.e., oxidants at 0.32 ppm and all other pollutants increase fourfold) that observable deterioration in physiological functions occurs, that is, lower respiration and metabolism rate such that athletes and workmen slow down in their activity. When pollution reaches eight times the standard (0.64 ppm), morbidity and mortality rates rise for those with respiratory and heart diseases.

Next in the hypothetical case we need to assign some relationships between the various alternatives and the reduction of air pollutants. We assume that the 1975 cars can meet the air quality standards at operating temperatures, but one-third of the emissions occur during the first forty seconds of start up with a cold engine. Car inspections and proper tuning are believed to reduce emissions by 50 percent, and emission-control equipment on used cars will reduce emissions by 40 percent. Also the energy required for a transit system from an electric generating plant is assumed to supply the power with only 20 percent of the emissions of automobiles moving a similar volume of traffic.

If the urban areas under study presently have ambient air quality of 0.26 ppm of oxidants for extended periods, then we can calculate some rough cost-effectiveness numbers for each alternative.

[2]Kurt Baier and Nicholas Rescher, *Values and the Future*, Free Press, New York, 1969, p. 326.

Figure 16-1

	New car controls	Used car retrofit	All car inspection	Urban transit
Air quality, ppm	0.14	0.19	0.17	0.05
Initial cost, in $ billions	240	12	4	44

The application of new car emission-control equipment would reduce emissions by two-thirds of the difference (0.18 ppm) between present ambient air quality of 0.26 ppm and the standard of 0.08 ppm. The cost would be $3,000 per car to replace all 80 million cars on the road, because, until they are all replaced, the used cars would continue their present emission rates. The total cost of the first alternative is $240 billion with the resulting air still containing almost twice the pollution it should to meet the federal standards.

The initial cost of the second and third alternatives are only a small fraction (one-twentieth and one-sixtieth respectively) of the new car control alternative and only slightly less effective. As a result, one would say they are much more cost effective, since they cost relatively little and do almost as good a job.

The only alternative that meets the air quality standards is urban transit at a cost of about one-sixth of new car controls.

Despite the fact that it is the poorest choice (least cost effective) of the four alternatives, new car emission controls have been the principal thrust of federal and state regulations up to the present. However, the purpose of this example is mainly to present the methodology of cost effectiveness, which would normally be portrayed graphically, as shown in Figure 16-2.

Cost is shown on the horizontal axis in billions of dollars, and effectiveness in shown on the vertical axis in air quality. The purpose of cost-effectivenss analysis is to determine the worth of the system. The new car control system is not worth the cost because it is vastly more expensive than any alternative and does not meet the air quality standard. The cost-effectiveness chart shows that only urban transit reaches the air quality goal. The other two alternatives, being relatively low in cost, may merit some further attention in arriving at a mix of systems to meet air quality standards. However, the all-car inspection costs $4 billion per year, compared to a one-time capital cost of $12 billion for used car retrofit equipment. After three years the annual inspection costs would exceed the used car retrofit costs. Hence, in choosing a system system over a long period of time, we would probably rule out the inspection alternative.

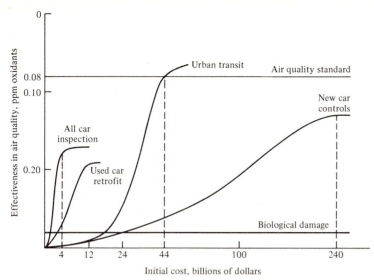

Figure 16-2   Cost effectiveness of air pollution alternatives.

Two alternatives have now been eliminated from our decision process: (1) new car controls because of their exceedingly high cost for effectiveness, and (2) all-car inspection because its annual costs soon outrun used car retrofit costs.

AIR POLLUTION EXAMPLE OF TRADE-OFF ANALYSIS

So far we have been mainly concerned with cost-effectiveness analysis, whether a system is worth the cost, in itself or compared to another alternative. Two alternatives have not been worth the cost and are eliminated. Now let us look at trade-off analysis directly, which is whether one system is better than another in terms of either cost or performance. That is, shall we choose urban transit or used car retrofit, or a mix of both? We cannot choose used car retrofit by itself, because it will not attain the desired air quality standard. However, the urban transit system exceeds the air quality standard, perhaps providing cleaner air than we need. Perhaps, then, we can reduce the cost of reaching the air quality standard by some mixture of the two alternatives. Simple arithmetic shows that the used car retrofit reduces ambient air pollution by 0.01 ppm for every $1.7 billion of expenditure, while urban transit requires $2.3 billion for an equal reduction. Graphically the comparisons of the two alternatives in reducing pollution would look like Figure 16-3.

The slope of the line shows that air pollution can be reduced faster

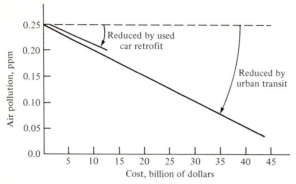

Figure 16-3   Cost of reduction in air pollution.

per dollar by used car retrofit than by urban transit, but only by the limited amount of 0.07 ppm. Therefore, we would choose to carry the reduction in air pollution as far as we could by the used car retrofit alternative. That is, we would trade off the used car retrofit system against the urban transit system to get more air pollution reduction per dollar. The mix of alternatives which we would need in the end, assuming we can apply systems proportionately in parts, to achieve a 0.18 ppm reduction in air pollution and reach the federal standard for air quality of 0.08 ppm, is shown below in Figure 16.4

By making the tradeoff between systems, we arrive at a mix of the two alternatives which achieves our air quality standard for $37 billion, rather than spending $44 billion for the urban transit alternative alone, and we also end up with a mixed transportation with greater flexibility than any one alternative.

The tradeoff of performance or dollars of one system against another, as in the above example, has been the most prevalent form of trade-off analysis for hardware systems in the past. One might conceive of a more biologically oriented tradeoff by introducing time as the exchange media. Suppose we continue the same example in air pollution

Figure 16-4

	Reduction in air pollution, ppm	Cost in $ billion per 0.01 ppm	Total cost, $ billions
Alternative			
Used car retrofit	0.07	1.7	12
Urban transit	0.11	2.3	25
			37

from the subjective point of view of the individual, rather than from the technical, dollar view of society as a whole. What is the crux of the individual's decision about air pollution? He may be quite interested as a citizen and voter, to be sure, in whether a safe air quality of 0.08 ppm of oxidants can be reached, and, if so, how, and for how much. He may even be pleased to know that the standard could be reached for $37 billion rather than $44 billion, and as a voter he might cast his ballot for the $37 billion mixture of alternatives. But it really is not all his $37 billion —perhaps only $500 is his tax share which becomes lost in the noise, He may then feel that his influence upon dollar cost is small or insignificant. There is, however, a kind of cost that is very pertinent to his own decisions, and that is the opportunity cost of the several alternatives. So let us now try to turn the tradeoff into subjective opportunity costs expressed in time.

The first form of time with which we will concern ourself is the comparative convenience time in travel among the several alternative systems. Let us assume that the average driving time for an automobile commuter is forty minutes per trip, and this would be applicable in the case of new or used cars, or the type of auto control equipment upon emissions. The inspection of cars, however, takes a small amount of time for the check up, repairs, and tuning required to keep the car in good operating condition; and we shall presume that this would require several hours every six months which, when pro rated, adds an average of three minutes to every trip. An urban express transit system will, say cover the same trip mileage as the auto trip in thirty-five minutes, but an added fifteen minutes is consumed by the waiting and walking at both ends of the line, making a fifty-minute trip. These various times may then be plotted against the air quality with which they are associated to produce a supply curve expressed in terms of time and effectiveness (Figure 16-5).

This chart indicates that air quality can be improved by the sacrifice of time. If a person is willing to add ten minutes per trip to his travel time, air quality can be improved to the federal health standard level. Even this portrayal is rather remote from the individual's subjective sensitivity, because it is not obvious that he would be willing to trade off travel convenience for air quality. What is there about air quality which he might value, or regard as a benefit and satisfaction? If he knew the relation of air quality to biological damage, he would then be in a position to make a subjective tradeoff of travel time versus lifetime.

Hence, we will take the same chart above and convert the air quality scale to life expectancy and the convenience scale to life-time travel. The supply curve (of clean air) has also been extended to make a smooth curve, on the assumption that more energy applied to travel could cut

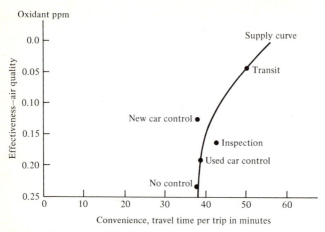

Figure 16-5 Time-effectiveness supply curve in air pollution.

travel time and increase emissions. Care should be taken to observe that this is a hypothetical illustration. Medical authorities do not know the precise relation of air quality to morbidity or motality; hence more research would be needed to determine the actual relation of air quality to life expectancy (Figure 16-6).

The hypothetical chart below is drawn on the assumption that a person thirty-years-old has a life expectancy of about forty years. At air quality levels of 0.08 ppm of oxidants, no health effects upon longevity are probable, and life expectancy remains at forty years. At sustained air pollution levels of 0.20 ppm oxidants, a three-year loss in life expectancy is assumed; at 0.30 ppm, a four-year loss is presumed. At sustained levels over 0.50 ppm the presumption is that persons with respiratory diseases may experience an average mortality which reduces life expectancy by twelve years.

This hypothetical diagram (Figure 16-6) says that a forty-year life expectancy can be supplied to a thirty-year-old at an opportunity cost of $2^{1}/_{2}$ years in lost travel time, or inconvenience in commuting. In the present assumed state, with no car emission controls and an average air quality of 0.24 ppm of pollutants, the individual is trading off a three-year loss in his life-time for a half-year gain in travel time over that same period. If he wished to save even more travel or convenience time, he could, hypothetically from the supply curve, gain one additional year of travel time by sacrificing twelve years of his life-time.

Somewhere at the lower end of the curve, the individual would subjectively feel the tradeoff to be a bad one, because he loses too much lifetime to gain too little convenience time. At the higher end of this curve, which is a measure of biological damage as well as a supply curve, individuals might have somewhat different preferences.

The rational man, *homo economicus*, would clearly prefer the urban transit system because a half-year gain in travel time would cost three years of lifetime. From a long-term perspective, that is a costly tradeoff. However, many people have a short-term time perspectives and may prefer time now to more time in the future, even at the high trade-off ratio of 6 to 1. If one is in love and in the heat of passion, perhaps one can do a great deal in one hour now that cannot be done with six more hours at age seventy. As one gets older and closer to the anxiety of death, a six-hour (or six-year) gain in life versus a one-hour loss of convenience seems like a better tradeoff. Even among more objective or elderly people, however, there undoubtedly is some discounted time preference for time now compared to time in the future. Then, let us take the time supply curve from the above diagram and transpose it to Figure 16-7, adding two hypothetical demand curves, one for the young, hedonistic person, and a second for the more mature, objective individual.

The rational time preference demand curve shows something near unity, a willingness to trade one year of convenience time for one plus years of lifetime. The more hedonistic curve trades perhaps one year of

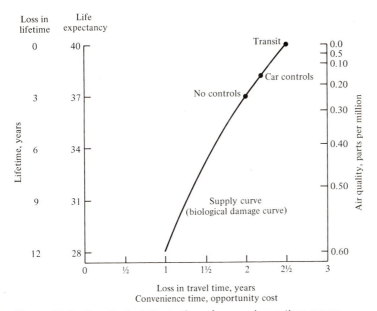

Figure 16-6 Hypothetical illustration of convenience time versus life expectancy in varying states of air quality.

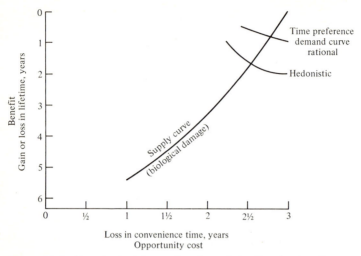

Figure 16-7 Hypothetical demand and supply for time in air pollution case.

convenience time for two years of lifetime. Thus the subjective trade-off curves would indicate that the rational individual would tend to prefer an urban express transit system, while the more hedonistic one would tend to prefer a private automobile with emission controls. In this trade-off context based upon time preferences, the rational man would say that the urban express transit is a better system than private automobiles, while the more hedonistic person would say that private automobiles with emission controls are a better system than urban transit.

AIR POLLUTION EXAMPLE OF COST-SENSITIVITY ANALYSIS

Suppose that even a hedonistic and power-loving individual looks at these time tradeoffs and says; "The alternatives you picked are all a bad deal. I am willing to trade off convenience for dollars, but not for much of my lifetime. No one ever showed me before that I was paying for my car with my life, and I don't want to do that. It does not fit my satisfactions or utility functions. I want to roar down the highways and chase pleasures, but not at the expense of my lifetime. There must be some other alternative."

At this point you pause and explain patiently that there is no Santa Claus or getting something for nothing—to which he replies that he does not believe that kind of bunk and some red-blooded American enterpriser has to have a better alternative, like an antigravity machine or a steam engine. Then he demands an alternative. You reply that, well, one possiblity is to create a Manhattan project out of the small gas turbine engine and put all the best technical manpower available to solve the materials problem of how to build the rotor to stand up against high heat at low cost. At the present pace of technological improvement, gas turbine engines do not seem likely until the year 2000, but a crash development program might bring it down to five or ten years. To this, he says that, if we can engineer our way to the moon, we ought to be able to lick a little rotor problem; and he then roars off in his 450-cubic-inch displacement sports car and shouts back, "Do a cost-sensitivity analysis, or something like that, and let me know how it comes out."

Cost-sensitivity analysis is a means of determining how variations in the design or operational specifications of a particular system affect the resource costs of developing it.[3] The operational specifications of the gas turbine engine are believed to meet low-emission criteria because of the higher uniform burning temperature which combusts almost all the fuel residuals. The crucial specification to be met is the design of a turbine rotor which will withstand high heat and be reasonably competitive in price with the internal combustion engine. Thus, this Manhattan project contemplates a large corps of engineers and scientists who work toward the design specifications of developing the materials to form a gas turbine rotor at competitive costs for a nearly emission-free engine. What this will cost is no better than a guess; but the best guess of the engineering staff, after they have studied the problem a bit, is that the research and development will cost $1 billion per year for five years and the cars will cost 10 percent more than present automobiles. Further, they conclude, the first cars will be available in the fifth year, and all 80 million cars can be replaced by the tenth year. That is, if everything goes as hoped, in ten years an automobile engine which would bring air quality down to the federal standards which presumably avoid biological damage would be in general use. Then, in the tenth year, what would the gas turbine alternative have cost? That is, what is the cost sensitivity of the performance specification? The change in performance specification is vis-à-vis the internal combustion engine, which cannot meet the required air quality standards. How much more does it take in cost to make the engine change to meet the standard? That is the cost-sensitivity question, which we can approach by comparing the cost of the two systems.

We already have seen in the earlier analysis that redesign of internal combustion engines to reduce emissions costs about $240 billion for new car replacement over ten years and air quality would improve to 0.14 ppm

---

[3]Quade, op. cit., pp. 138ff.

of oxidants but still be 75 percent over federal standards. The gas turbine car, under the assumptions given above, would cost about $275 billion over the same period, and would at the end of the decade (1975–1985) bring ambient air quality within the federal standard. The cost-senstitivity analysis would look something like Figure 16-8.

The diagram indicates that the present internal combustion engine is highly sensitive to increasing costs as attempts are made to reduce its emission characteristics by equipment changes. A redesigned internal combustion engine to respond to the 1975 air quality standards represents a higher annual cost than present internal combustion engine production. Presumably the redesigned engine has lower compression ratios, electronic timing, fuel injection or improved carburation, and a catalytic afterburner to reduce emissions to a low level at operating temperatures. This redesign entails a higher development investment by the company and increased car prices to the consumer. At these higher investment levels of about $24 billion per year, the redesigned internal combustion engine is relatively insensitive to cost until an air quality requirement of 0.14 ppm of oxidants is reached, and thereafter costs increase rapidly even though the engine is unable to achieve the federal standards.

Even after redesign and improvement, however, the internal combustion engine always has the problem of the cold engine wall during the first forty seconds after starting, when one-third of the emissions occur, which is inherent in its design. This cold wall causes incomplete combustion at the edges of the cylinder chamber as the flame front burns across the chamber, due to the lower temperature of the gasoline vapors. This

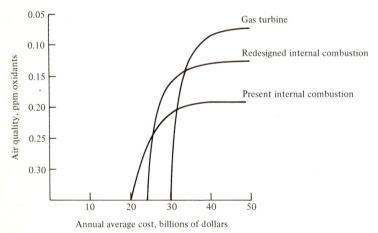

Figure 16-8 Hypothetical cost-sensitivity analysis in air pollution case.

thermodynamic differential between the flame temperature and the cold wall temperature presents a physical limitation which means there will always be some irreducible minimum emissions from an internal combustion engine at start up. The gas turbine avoids this limitation by having a higher uniform burning temperature which causes more complete combustion of residuals, but, of course, the gas turbine also costs more. On the chart the annual average cost is estimated at $28 to $30 billion, but thereafter the cost is relatively insensitive to higher air quality requirement until it reaches 0.08 ppm of oxidants, then it increases. However, at 0.08 ppm the federal air quality standards have been reached, and the engine is in compliance with the emission control regulations.

Now let us assume that a decision is made immediately on the three systems to carry out the research on each of them now with production following in the 1975–1985 decade; then we would like to see the rate at which the air quality approaches the federal standard (Figure 16-9).

The chart is self-explanatory in showing that the improvement of air quality may be expected to take ten to fifteen years, and two of the alternatives are not likely to reach the required air quality at all. These are the two alternatives currently being most actively pursued by both industry and regulatory agencies.

BIOLOGICAL TRADEOFF—THE FLUORIDE CASE

Another type of trade-off example might be examined to illustrate the exchange of one set of biological gains for other biological losses. The Polk County area of Florida in the early 1960s had 120,000 head of cattle grazing on 500,000 acres of grassland and also produced about 15 percent

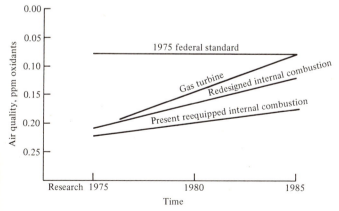

Figure 16-9 Hypothetical rate of air quality improvement.

of the nation's citrus.[4] The growing conditions seemed favorable to both crops until they began to be damaged by fluorine emissions from local phosphate fertilizer plants.

The Polk County fertilizer industry produces about 75 percent of the phosphate rock used for triple superphosphate (TSP) which is a very important ingredient of fertilizers used throughout the nation. The processing of phosphate rock releases large amounts of fluorine in both gaseous and particulate form.

The gaseous fluorides in volumes of 5 to 16 parts per billion interfere with the photosynthesis process of citrus leaves and adversely affect growth and production. The particulate fluorine settles on grasslands, is absorbed by the plants, ingested by cattle, and then causes fluorosis in the animals. Fluorosis is accompanied by loss of appetite and body weight, vomiting, bloody diarrhea, and painful joints, forcing the animal to lie down. The affinity of fluoride for calcium causes lumps and bony spurs on the skeleton and joints until the cattle are finally immobilized and die of starvation.

Several years elapsed while ascertaining the cause of the biological damage, trying to get regulatory agencies to impose emission controls on the fertilizer industry, and in court actions. The final outcome was that the fertilizer companies were given two options: (1) to bring their fluorine emission control in a range of 99 percent efficiency and reduce fluorine concentrations in grasslands below 40 ppm, or (2) buy up the grasslands affected which amounted to about 250,000 acres. The cost of achieving high efficiency in emission control was very costly in the 1950s and the companies found it an advantageous tradeoff to buy up land at $100 to $150 per acre instead of going very far in emission control. The companies bought 200,000 acres of land over a period of years. As emission control technology improved, they then also invested $6.7 million to achieve a 95 percent control efficiency and then another $16 million to reach 99 percent control. A trade-off diagram of this situation might appear as shown in Figure 16-10.

The diagram indicates that land acquisition was the most attractive tradeoff for achieving environmental protection in the early stages, because it was cheaper to buy land than reach 99 percent control over emissions. The regulator agencies then required the fertilizer companies to do both, and as higher efficiencies of emission control were achieved by added investments, the costs became very close and parallel. By that time the fertilizer companies were such big landholders, they had gone into the cattle business, too, by leasing out their land, and it became their own

---

[4]Thomas D. Crocker, and A. J. Rogers, III, *Environmental Economics*, The Dryden Press Inc., Hinsdale, Ill. 1971, pp. 93ff.

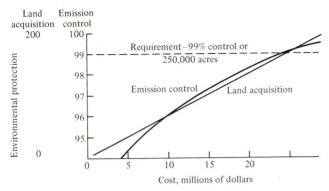

Figure 16-10 Land acquisition vs. emission control—fluorine pollution.

self-interest to protect the cattle on their own land by additional emission control. Hence as emission control reached the 99 percent efficiency levels, there was no more trade-off advantage to buying land; but there was the continued incentive, as long as they had the land, to keep fluoride emissions to a minimum level to maintain high productivity among the herds on their land.

There is another question, which did not become part of the actual dispute in the Polk County deliberations, but which represents an interesting public policy question. From the point of view of the national interest in maintaining ecological balance, should the fertilizer plants have been closed down or was the regulatory solution an equitable one? The argument for closing the plants would be that they did extreme biological damage within Polk County to cattle, citrus, and perhaps other biological life. The argument for continuing production of superphosphate fertilizer, aside from the employment benefit, would be that the fertilizers increased the general yield of farm production throughout the nation. Posed in this way, we see a biological tradeoff between the losses in Polk County and the gains in biological growth nationally. Suppose we try to measure this tradeoff hypothetically by assuming that Polk County produces 10 percent of the biomass (i.e., the total standing crop of biological life) in the United States, including citrus, cattle, and all other organisms. Let us assume also that TSP increases farm yields by an average by 20 percent. Then the loss of Polk County fertilizers would reduce production of the national biomass by 15 percent (75 percent of all TSP is produced in Polk County times the 20 percent increased productivity in yields). Then we can compare the loss in biological life in Polk County due to fluorine with the gain in biomass elsewhere from TSP fertilizer (Figure 16-11).

The United States gain in biological production (biomass) from

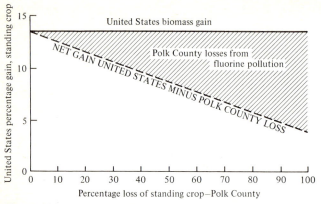

Figure 16-11   U.S. biomass gain compared to Polk County loss.

fertilizers is 13.5 percent (90 percent of the production times 15 percent gain). The Polk County biological losses are the percentage of crop lost due to fluorine multiplied by its 10 percent share of United States production. Suppose the cattle, citrus, and biological losses were of the order of 40 percent, the decline in Polk County farm activity and income would be severe. The net loss in all United States production, caused by the Polk County crop declines, would be 4 percent (40 percent loss times 10 percent of United States production). However, this is more than offset by the gains to national agriculture from the fertilizer, which is 13.5 percent. We may then say that the net gains are 9.5 percent, that is, the 13.5 percent minus the 4 percent loss. Even if 100 percent of the Polk County standing crop were lost, there would still be a net gain of 3.5 percent to the United States generally from the fertilizer production. This kind of analysis ignores any special species losses, which might be critical or of great value in themselves. But simply on the basis of total biological production, it would have been undesirable to close the fertilizer plants, and the protective policy of land acquisition and emission control seems an equitable solution.

SUMMARY

Trade-off analysis is a means by which an administrator may determine whether one system is better than another in terms of its relative gains over losses, in either a biological or a monetary sense. The method also shows who gains and who loses, so that there can be some relative judgment of its effects. The trade-off technique is closely associated, and often used in conjunction, with cost-effectiveness analysis and cost-sensitivity studies. The cost-effectiveness analysis attempts to determine the worth of a project, in itself, or in relation to others. The cost-sensitivity study is concerned with the relative cost of changes in performance specifications. Together these several techniques aid the environmental administrator in making decisions among several alternatives. The value of the studies is to take specific congnizance of losses in advance of a decision, to try to avoid unpleasant surprises later in the form of unrecognized biological damage.

Our failure to include biological losses in our decision calculus is one of the principal causes of our environmental difficulties. These difficulties arise because we proceed under the false assumption that a net gain or net profit is obtainable, free of constraints; but this assumption violates the law of conservation of matter, and we need to come to grips specifically with the biological damage and losses caused by human decisions. This chapter has attempted to show how cost-effectiveness, trade-off, and cost-sensitivity analyses can be used to incorporate a specific recognition of biological losses, and thus minimize them to some acceptable level. If we can do this, we will have taken the first major step to preserving the environment. Generally, such a recognition and calculation will require that we reckon costs in biological losses and damage, as well as in dollars.

DISCUSSION QUESTIONS

1 What instance can you give from your own experience of a tradeoff in which you have chosen to devote time to one activity rather than another? How did you come to your choice?
2 Suppose you were assigned the task of making a trade-off analysis, a cost-effectiveness analysis, and a cost-sensitivity analysis of reducing fluoride emissions in Polk County, Florida, how would you describe what you would do?
3 How would you decide the tradeoff of your own life expectancy against convenience time among alternative transportation choices (see Figures 16-6 and 16-7)?
4 What would your decision be on the issue of whether or not to begin a crash program to produce a feasible gas turbine auto engine? Why (see Figure 16-8)?

PROBLEMS

1 Develop your own assumptions as to costs and air quality effects of various technical solutions to the air pollution problem and recalculate a cost-effectiveness analysis as in Figures 16-1 and 16-2.
2 Assume that you live close to your work in an area with a high asbestos

content in the air, which originates from brake-band wear of automobiles on nearby freeways. Asbestos inhalation increases the probability of *mesothelioma,* a form of lung cancer for which there is presently no cure, twenty or thirty years after exposure. Suppose that each year of exposure, by remaining where you are, costs you two years of life expectancy twenty years hence. Draw a trade-off chart of life expectancy versus loss in convenience (travel time) by moving further away from your job, as in Figure 16-6. How long would you wait before moving?

Chapter 17

Environmental Impact Analysis

Environmental impact analysis is the integrating process for synthesizing all the elements of an environmental decision into some form of action. It may be considered in two parts: (1) the evaluation and screening of projects which affect the environment to determine any adverse ecological reactions, and (2) special studies of ecological impacts to ascertain the degree of biological damage and how it may be mitigated.

The first of these, evaluation and screening, can be approached by a technical assessment of the environmental impact statement currently required by the Council on Environmental Quality, and by a number of state environmental agencies as well. The general content of an environmental impact statement was discussed in Chapter 5 and will be covered more explicitly here.

The second part of an environmental impact analysis, that is special studies of biological damage, may be approached by applications of the techniques previously covered in Chapters 10 through 16. That is, the specific impact may be examined by determining materials balance, dispersion of materials in the ecosystem, benefit-cost analysis, a market simulation of environmental costs, marginal-cost studies, and trade-off analysis.

The purpose of an environmental impact analysis, then, is to apply systematic techniques to measure the gains and losses in the environment and see who or what species are affected adversely or beneficially. As such, the environmental impact analysis is a summing up, an integrative device. The purpose of this chapter is to describe and illustrate how such a summing up may be approached. In the process, techniques previously covered will be used, and hence the only new conceptual material needed will be an understanding of how an environmental impact statement may be evaluated and screened for ecological significance. The following will be covered:

1 Evaluation and screening of environmental impact statements
2 Evaluating impact by an environmental matrix
3 Phosphate mining lease—example of use of matrix
4 Applying environmental analytical techniques to the matrix
   a Step 1—materials balance
   b Step 2—dispersion models
   c Step 3—market simulation
   d Step 4—marginal-cost studies
   e Step 5—trade-off analysis
5 Test of the decision criteria
6 Reexamining the measures of worth
7 What really happened in the phosphate case

EVALUATION AND SCREENING OF ENVIRONMENTAL IMPACT STATEMENTS

The Council on Environmental Quality, under section 102 of the National Environmental Policy Act of 1969 (Public Law 91–190, January 1, 1970), requires that all federal agencies shall "utilize a systematic, interdisciplinary approach which will insure the integrated use of the natural and social sciences and the environmental design arts in planning and in decision making which may have an impact on man's environment." The law then says that every new proposal for legislation or major federal action shall identify (1) environmental impact, (2) adverse environmental effects, (3) alternative actions, (4) short-term uses versus long-term environmental productivity, and (5) any irreversible commitments.

Lower court decisions have interpreted the National Environmental Policy Act to be a broad delegation of powers to the Council to assure reasonable compliance in a process which envisions:

. . . that program formulation will be directed by research results rather than that research programs will be designed to substantiate programs already decided upon. . . . The (environmental) statement must be sufficiently detailed to arrive at a reasonably accurate decision regarding the environmental benefits and detriments to be expected from program implementation. The statement should contain adequate discussion of alternative proposals to allow for program modification during agency review so that results to be achieved will be in accordance with national environmental goals.[1]

The required content of environmental impact statements has been specified by the Council on Environmental Quality in revised and detailed guidelines to federal agencies. The following points are to be covered.[2]

1 A description of the proposed action including information and technical data adequate to permit a careful assessment of environmental impact by commenting agencies. Where relevant, maps should be provided.

2 The probable impact of the proposed action on the environment, including impact on ecological systems such as wildlife, fish, and marine life. Both primary and secondary significant consequences for the environment should be included in the analysis. For example, the implications, if any, of the action for population distribution or concentration should be estimated and an assessment made of the effect of any possible change in population patterns upon the resource base, including land use, water, and public services, of the area in question.

3 Any probable adverse environmental effects which cannot be avoided [such as water or air pollution, undesirable land use patterns, damage to life systems, urban congestion, threats to health or other consequences adverse to the environmental goals set out in section 101 (b) of the Act].

4 Alternatives to the proposed action [section 102 (2) (D) of the Act requires the responsible agency to "study, develop, and describe appropriate alternatives to recommended courses of action in any proposal which involves unresolved conflicts concerning alternative uses of available resources"]. A rigorous exploration and objective evaluation of alternative actions that might avoid some or all of the adverse environmental effects is essential. Sufficient analysis of such alternatives and their costs and impact on the environment should accompany the proposed action through the agency review process in order not to foreclose prematurely options which might have less detrimental effects.

5 The relationship between local short-term uses of man's environment and the maintenance and enhancement of long-term productivity. This

---

[1]EDF vs. Corps of Engineers, D. Ark., LR-70-C-203, 1971; EDG vs. Hardin, D., D.C., CA 2319-70, 1971.

[2]*Federal Register,* Apr. 23, 1971, vol. 36, no. 79, pp. 7ff.

in essence requires the agency to assess the action for cumulative and long-term effects from the perspective that each generation is trustee of the environment for succeeding generations.

6 Any irreversible and irretrievable commitments of resources which would be involved in the proposed action should it be implemented. This requires the agency to identify the extent to which the action curtails the range of beneficial uses of the environment.

7 Where appropriate, a discussion of problems and objections raised by other Federal, State, and local agencies and by private organizations and individuals in the review process and the disposition of the issues involved. (This section may be added at the end of the review process in the final text of the environmental statement.)

A number of states have passed legislation requiring environmental impact statements similar in concept to that of the federal government, and several of the states, too, have organized environmental protection agencies or councils to carry out the evaluation and review of such statements. In addition, the operating departments of federal and state governments have found it desirable to provide more specific instructions, as to required information, to persons within the agency preparing impact statements. An example of some of the specific requirements defined by the Corps of Engineers is shown below:

> Statements should not be limited to ultimate conclusions, but should demonstrate that the Corps has adequately considered the potential impact of the proposal upon the environment. The statement should summarize information and cite source of overall appraisals which are based upon judgments of complex matters (e.g., water quality by Federal Water Quality Agency).
>
> Statements should include and comment on the view of those opposing the proposals for environmental reasons, if any. The summarized view of agencies having environmental responsibilities, and with which the proposals have been coordinated, should also be included.
>
> The statement should include a full and objective appraisal of the environmental effects, good and bad, and of available alternatives. In no case will adverse effects, either real or potential, be ignored or slighted in an attempt to justify an action previously recommended. Similarly, care must be taken to avoid overstating favorable effects.[3]

Beyond this policy directive as to approach, the Corps of Engineers circular described specific elements to be included in the impact statement (see Chapter 9) and then listed numerous environmental elements

---

[3]Council on Environmental Quality, *102 Monitor*, vol. 1, no. 2, March 1971, pp. 4ff.

which should be particularly identified, including geological, hydrological, botanical, zoological, and archaeological elements.

The number of environmental elements potentially affected by human or governmental action is, of course, very large; and as the quantity of environmental impact statements submitted by federal agencies to the Council on Environmental Quality has swelled, a technique for identifying and measuring the many impacts has become essential to any systematic evaluation process. An attempt has been made to accomplish this identification and screening by the use of an environmental evaluation matrix.

EVALUATING IMPACT BY AN ENVIRONMENTAL MATRIX

The U.S. Geological Survey has proposed a procedure of evaluating environmental impact intended to provide both the uniformity and the specificity necessary for critical judgment among alternatives for a wide variety of projects. The heart of the evaluation is a matrix or reference checklist to serve as a reminder, and identification, of the many environmental interactions associated with man-made projects. The number of human actions, which federal agencies might potentially propose, consists of 100 types of projects listed horizontally across the top of the matrix. The environmental elements or characteristics are listed vertically on the table and total eighty-eight ecological situations. The matrix contemplates the possibility of 8,800 possible interactions; but in use, the matrix may be telescoped to a smaller number of related items, or expanded to a larger number. While the combinations are too numerous to record here, a few examples will be given to illustrate the content of the matrix, and those with deeper interest might wish to examine the course document.[4] From the horizontal axis of the matrix, the first set of proposed actions (13 items out of the 100) which may affect the environment are identified as follows:

A. Modification of Regime
    a Exotic flora or fauna introduction
    b Biological control
    c Modification of habitat
    d Alteration of ground cover
    e Alteration of groundwater hydrology
    f Alteration of drainage
    g River control and flow modification
    h Canalization

[4]Luna B. Leopold, Frank E. Clarke, Bruce B. Hanshaw, and James R. Balsley, *A Procedure for Evaluating Environmental Impact*, U.S. Geological Survey Circular 645, U.S. Geological Survey, Washington.

    i Irrigation
    j Weather modification
    k Burning
    l Surface paving
   m Noise and vibration

The first two sections of the existing environmental conditions, characteristics, which might be affected by proposed action, shown on the vertical axis of the table are these:

1 Earth
    a Mineral resources
    b Construction material
    c Soils
    d Land form
    e Force fields and background radiation
    f Unique physical features
2 Water
    a Surface
    b Ocean
    c Underground
    d Quality
    e Temperature
    f Recharge
    g Snow, ice, and permafrost

The most efficient way to use the matrix is to check each action (top horizontal list) which is likely to be involved significantly in the proposed project. Generally, only about a dozen actions will be important. Each of the actions thus checked is evaluated in terms of "magnitude" of effect on environmental characteristics on the vertical axis, and a slash is placed diagonally from upper right to lower left across each block which represents significant interaction. . . .

    After all the boxes which represent possible impact have been marked with a diagonal line, the most important ones are evaluated individually. Within each box representing a significant interaction between an action and an environmental factor, place a number from 1 to 10 in the upper left-hand corner to indicate the relative "magnitude" of impact; 10 represents the greatest magnitude and 1, the least. In the lower right-hand corner of the box, place a number from 1 to 10 to indicate the relative "importance" of the impact against 10 is the greatest.

    Assignment of numerical weights to the "magnitude" and "importance" of impacts should be, to the extent possible, based on factual data rather than preference. Thus, the use of a rating scheme such as the one suggested here discourages purely subjective opinion and requires the author of an environmental impact statement to attempt to quantify his judgment of probable impacts. The overall rating allows the reviewer to follow the originator's line of reasoning and will aid in identifying points of agreement and disagreement. The matrix, is in fact, the abstract for the text of the environmental assessment.

The text that accompanies the completed matrix should be primarily a discussion of the reasoning behind the assignment of numerical values for the "magnitude" of impact effects and their relative "importance." The text should include a discussion of those actions which have significant impact and should not be diluted by discussions of obviously trivial side issues.[5]

PHOSPHATE MINING LEASE—EXAMPLE OF USE OF MATRIX

The use of matrix analysis may be illustrated by applying it to the application for a phosphate mining lease. A mineable deposit of phosphate, located in Los Padres National Forest, Ventura County, California, is estimated to include about 80-million tons of crude ore, in sand-sized pellets, of an average content of 8.7 percent P_2O_5. The beds crop out on hillslopes over a 5-mile length and are about 90-feet thick with an overburden ranging from 0 to 200 feet.

A prospecting permit was granted in 1964, extended in 1966, and currently the U.S. Gypsum Company has applied to the U.S. Department of Interior for a lease to mine the property.

The environmental impact statement indicates that the deposit occurs in a semiarid region receiving an average rainfall of 23 inches per year, with principal drainage by Sespe Creek which is 2 miles south of the mine site. The region is sparsely populated.

The planned mining operation would be open-pit, with V-shaped cuts to strip the overburden running parallel to the ore beds. An ore processing plant, constructed at the mine site, would crush the ore and leach the phosphate out with acid. The resulting pregnant liquor would be neutralized with quicklime to precipitate dicalcium phosphate in granular form. The quartz sand tailings from the leach process would be washed, dewatered, and stored in the open-pit areas where mining had been completed. The major raw materials required are quicklime and sulfur, imported by a 2-mile paved road to be constructed; and the finished phosphate would be shipped by truck out on the same road to market. The water demand for the processing is small and to be supplied by a 1,000-foot well.

The principal environmental impacts of the mining operation would

[5]Ibid., pp. 5–7.

be: Possible adverse effects on the habitat of the California condor, a rare and endangered species; the impairment of wilderness quality by imposing man-made constructions in a recreation area; and some level of air pollution, water pollution, and soil erosion.

The adverse environmental impacts are shown by notation in the reduced matrix for those characteristics affected by the phosphate mining lease. In the illustration below, note that the highest number 10 has been assigned to indicate the *importance* of the impact on the California condor, while the rating 5 has been assigned to the *magnitude* of the threat to this rare and endangered species. The other high ratings (meaning adverse potential impacts) are attributed to the mine's effect on wilderness quality; atmospheric quality; and the effects of spills and leaks on water quality, plants, and fish.

The matrix (Figure 17-1) as illustrated, is an abstract of the environmental effects. The text of the impact statement should explain the impacts in more detail. An abbreviated version of the text includes the following information:

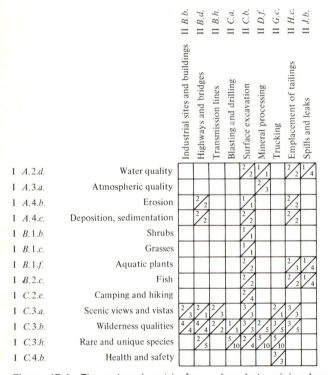

Figure 17-1   The reduced matrix for a phosphate mining lease.

1   The Sespe Condor Sanctuary in the National Forest lies 15 miles to the east of the mining area. The ordinary flight and soaring patterns of the condor would pass over the general area of the mine, range along the crestline to the northwest and across the center of the National Forest. One abandoned condor nest has been noted a few miles west of the mining site but the other known nests are within the condor sanc-. tuary.

2   The lease site involves 2,434 acres of land, which is small compared to the total forest. The site is 15 miles east-southeast along the mountain ridge from the San Rafael Wilderness, an undeveloped public land usable for recreational purposes potentially needed to relieve California's population pressure. Wind dispersion of atmospheric pollution would be toward the east, that is toward the San Rafael Wilderness.

3   Some level of air pollution is possible from noxious gases, in the form of fluorine, SO_2, and fuel residuals, as emission from the ore processing plant. The *importance* of these emissions was rated 3 because of the sulfur and fluorine content; but their *magnitude* was rated 2 due to the small size of the plant.

4   Wilderness qualities and scenic views were given moderate- to high-impact ratings due to the industrial building, highway construction, transmission lines, open-pit mining cuts, trucking, and emplacement of tailings which would be visible from considerable distances and impair, to some extent, the effectiveness of the San Rafael Wilderness Area.

5   Some increase in soil erosion and sediment load in stream channels is to be expected, but the extent of the impact depends upon how effectively the stream channels crossing the ore body are protected from the open-pit mines. The possibility of water pollution from phosphate ore is low because the phosphates in ore form are quite insoluble. The effectiveness of erosion control measure will determine the quantity of sediments, including particulate phosphate minerals, added to Sespe Creek.

6   The liquid chemicals handled at the plant are to be confined within dikes, and the main hazard to water quality would occur from accidental spills and leaks. An expanded matrix with detail of the impact on water quality (Figure 17-2) indicates that the greatest dangers of adverse affects to water quality downstream from the mine come from industrial waste water, sewage, acidity of yard runoff from the mine, erosion of fill at tailings emplacements, and spills or leaks from dikes or trucks.

As an outcome of this matrix analysis, the critical environmental effects are apparent; and the reviewers of the project could ask the petitioners for the phosphate lease to identify those actions which can be taken to reduce the adverse impacts.

Industrial sites and buildings			Highways and bridges			Transmission lines		Surface excavation			Mineral processing		Trucking	Emplacement of tailings			Spills and leaks			
Waste water	Sewage	Washing	Runoff from paving	Runoff during construction	Runoff from finished road	Sediment from cleared zone	Construction sediment	Sediment from fill	Effects of ore exposures	Effects of deep seepage	Sulfuric acid use	Acidity of yard runoff	Spilled sulfur compounds	Erosion of fill	Deep seepage	Acidity of seepage	Highway truck spills	Tailings pond leak	Tailings dams washout	Plant spills of acid
Water quality 3/3	3/3	1/1	1/2	1/1	1/2	1/1	1/1	2/2	1/1	1/1	1/1	1/1	1/1	3/4	1/3	1/2	1/2	1/3	1/3	1/1

Figure 17-2 Expanded matrix showing actions which would impact water quality.

APPLYING ENVIRONMENTAL ANALYTICAL TECHNIQUES TO THE MATRIX

Answers to the questions raised by the matrix would require additional analytical studies of the special impacts on the environment, centering upon those that appear most adverse, namely the endangered species, wilderness-recreational effects, air pollution, soil erosion, and water pollution. These effects could be measured by applying the analytical techniques covered in Chapters 10 through 16.

Step 1—Materials Balance

The first and most basic analysis would be to construct a materials-balance model of the phosphate mining operation, by a measurement through samples and calculations of all the materials inputs and outputs. The most basic input, of course, is the phosphate ore; and the other principal inputs are sulfur, quicklime, fuel, and water. The exact chemical composition of all these materials would be analyzed first, and then a model would be constructed by calculation or pilot demonstration to see what residuals remained after conversions in the processing of the ore.

The exact amount of fluorine in the ore would, for example, be important to calculate the degree of concentrations which would impinge on surrounding environment either as fluorine gas or as particulates settling on vegetation. The soil and rock in the region is known to contain significant parts of salts and boron, the latter being high enough in concentration to inhibit plant growth over large areas of the nearby west slope of the San Joaquin Valley. The exact quantity of boron, minerals, and salts should be determined to estimate the residual quantities which would enter the atmosphere, water supply, and soils of the surrounding area. Beyond this, the sulfuric acid and quicklime content of tailings and leaching waters needs to be measured to determine the concentrations of these chemicals which may be expected to reside in tailings stored in open-pits, in the liquors placed within dikes, in stack-gas emissions into the atmosphere, in the industrial effluents discharged into the stream bed, or in the seepage or leaks which might enter the soil or underground water table.

Step 2—Dispersion Models

The second major analytical study would be the dispersion of these residuals into the ecosystem. A measurement of the wind patterns and meteorological conditions would show how far the fluorine, sulfur dioxide, and hydrocarbons might be expected to disperse in the atmosphere, and whether the concentrations upon dispersal might be sufficient to cause biological damage, such as fluorosis in animal life. Similarly a measurement of the dispersion of the toxic residuals in the waste water and sewage would seek to determine if there would be biological damage to the aquatic plants or fish downstream. Since this is an arid area in which stream beds are often dry, the discharges might possibly be transported by sporadic flooding in high concentrations to standing ponds with plant and fish life downstream. Similarly the study of deep waste seepage or leaks into subsoils of the water table would be needed to estimate the potential dispersion underground. Since water table recharge and movement is irregular and slow in arid regions, the transport effects would have to be considered over a period of many years. We observed in a previous chapter that the nitrates now measurable in the Santa Ana River basin had their origins in fertilizers applied thirty or forty years ago. Similarly in the Sespe Creek region, the underground movement of industrial wastes would depend upon the soil and rock structures in which water basins are contained.

Step 3—Market Simulation

The third step, if the materials concentrations and dispersions were known, would be to construct a market simulation of the ecosystem by attaching shadow prices to the unpriced values in the ecosystem. The market priced components include the costs associated with development of the industrial site and buildings, the road construction, the fuel, sulfur and lime materials, the equipment and labor for the strip-mining operations, the ore-processing costs, the transportation to market, and the market price of the phosphates.

The unpriced components of the ecosystem in which this mine will be located are the values attached to water quality, air quality, wilderness qualities, scenic views, biological health, species balance, and potential hazard to the condor. Because no market prices are attached to these values, the decision to mine phosphate is biased in favor of a net cash gain without regard to the ecological effects. The failure to value these environmental qualities, or to include the cost of removing residuals, is what has caused the "market failure" with respect to maintaining the quality of human life.

Some of the unpriced components can be valued at the cost of rectification or avoidance. For instance, the cost of air and water quality can be arrived at by estimating the cost of removing the emissions and effluents. For example, if 40 ppm of fluorine is the dosage which causes fluorosis in biological species, while 3 ppm is a safe dosage, then the cost of air quality would be the investment in air pollution control equipment required to keep the dispersed fluorine concentrations down to 3 ppm. Similar calculations may be made with respect to other air pollutants, sewage effluents, spillage and seepage, or erosion. In short, most of the causes of biological damage can be valued at the cost of control measures which avoids the damage.

The valuation of aesthetic qualities presents more difficulties. For example, the loss of scenic views or wilderness qualities is rated as having a high environmental impact in the matrix. To some extent, avoidance costs can be used here, too, to prevent aesthetic damage. For example, underground transmission lines would help maintain scenic views and wilderness quality. The design and site of the ore processing plant could be developed so the structure would blend into the environment, or be visible only for a short distance. An extreme measure, in cost and effectiveness, would be to put the entire plant underground in order to preserve wilderness quality. The large scars and benches from open-pit mining would present more severe problems, if one wished to preserve scenic views and wilderness qualities; but one could estimate costs of backfilling the pits and replanting with native dryland foliage. Despite these difficulties, careful planning, perhaps on a scale never contemplated by mining operations, could minimize the aesthetic damage, probably at very considerable cost.

The purpose of the market simulation model is precisely the measurement and exposure of these costs, so they can become part of the decision. A mining operator will naturally contend that any of these costs are unnecessary and unbearable, because he has never had to pay them before, and he does not know the competitive effects of incorporating them into his market price. He will fear that the added costs will make him noncompetitive in the market. This fear can be minimized, of course, if all like mining must bear similar environmental costs. In that case, with an industry bearing comparable costs, the effect will be a shift in prices, demand functions, and the preferences of consumers among products. Such shifts in consumer preferences among products can, of course, cause a certain anguish of adjustment within an industry; but presumably that is what a free market is all about, to adjust the volume of production to the preferences of consumers in keeping with their real costs and utilities. The fact that many products now are sold for less than their real costs, including the social and environmental costs of their unpriced components, is not an argument for deleting the external costs (as we have in the past) in order to avoid industrial adjustments. Rather, the argument is that a freely functioning market must include all costs or encounter a market failure, the failure to deliver the quality of human life which corresponds to consumer preferences and utility functions.

While the industrialist will argue that all external environmental costs cannot be included in the market simulation model without bankrupting him, the genuine conservationist will argue to the contrary, that the mine or plant should not be allowed to operate at all if it disturbs the pristine quality of the wilderness. In other words, the conservationist would insist that all costs be included in the market simulation to maintain a pristine state of nature, or else the economic enterprise should be denied the right to operate. The maintenance of the environment in a pristine state, in the case of the phosphate mine, would probably require that the entire installation, including the mining of ore, be done underground with a smokeless fuel and no emissions to the atmosphere or water. Such an alternative is probably not technically feasible, and if it were, would be extraordinarily expensive. Such a conservationist view would be as extreme as the industrial view. While the conservationist wants to include all the costs of a pristine state, the industrialist wants to include nothing but his direct production costs. This contrast in views, in their extremes, brings forth crucial questions in environmental decisions. How clean is clean? How aesthetic is aesthetic enough?

Step 4—Marginal-cost Studies

As the questions imply, there are degrees of environmental quality just as there are increments of costs applicable to each degree of quality. The fourth step in our analytical process is to estimate the marginal costs against their marginal returns in terms of environmental quality. For example, assume that the phosphate ore is high in fluorine; and without air pollution control equipment, the fluorine content would reach 40 ppm in a surrounding area of 250,000 acres, roughly the same as in the Florida case. This would be an area about 20-miles square and would come perilously close to the condor preserve, as well as affecting all the rabbits, rodents, and reptiles common to a desert biome. Therefore, we may estimate that the danger of death from fluorosis would be, say, a 98 percent probability for most zoological species within the area.

The amount of investment is small to achieve a large reduction in fluorine emissions, and thereafter the incremental investment becomes greater as to make smaller marginal gains in air quality, until the last 1 percent of fluorine removal is very costly indeed. Suppose, for example, the cost of phosphate is $20 per ton, and it cost $1 per ton to remove 80 percent of the fluorine emissions. This would reduce the fluorine in the ambient atmosphere from 40 ppm to 8 ppm. Suppose it cost another $9 per ton to get to 5 ppm and another $70 per ton to reach 3 ppm. Then, the incremental cost curve would appear as in Figure 17-3.

The cost of supplying relatively pure air (that is, free of fluorine) is low up to 8 ppm, and so the cost curve is very flat. But the cost curve rises very steeply as an attempt is made to press air quality beyond 5 ppm of fluorine.

Step 5—Trade-off Analysis

The demand for phosphate plus a fluorine-free environment can next be superimposed on the cost curve to arrive at some tradeoff between cost and biological damage. In this illustration we assume that consumers would pay a very high price, of $100 per ton, to hold the air quality down to 20 ppm of fluorine. To explain such behavior, of course, we need to establish some relationship with biological damage. We noted earlier an assumption that at 40 ppm of fluorine, the probable mortality rate among biological species was 98 percent within a 20-square-mile area surrounding the proposed plant.

Few people would like to see such high mortality rates, even among animals (we assume). Therefore, consumers would pay very high prices, up to $100 per ton in this hypothetical case, to bring the probable mortality rate down to 40 percent. Once the majority of species were preserved, the human demand curve for environmental quality might decline rather sharply. On our hypothetical demand curve, for example, consumers would pay $30 a ton to bring fluorine concentrations down to 5 ppm and the biological damage down to a probable mortality of 6 percent. The next increment of quality, to reduce fluorine to 3 ppm and to reduce

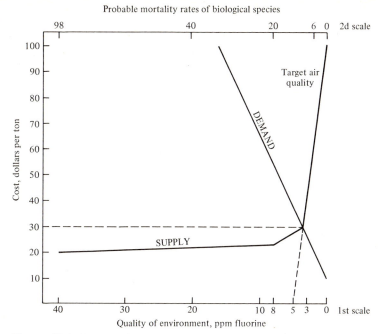

Figure 17-3 of biological species

Figure 17-3 Hypothetical cost-damage illustration of fluorine emissions.

the probability of biological damage, would cost $100 per ton. This next increment becomes too costly in relation to human utility; that is, the zero probability of mortality comes at too high a price.

The tradeoff between the demand for quality and the cost of quality is equated at $30 per ton, with the 6 percent probability of mortality. In other words, given the circumstances in the chart, people would allow a few (6 percent) of the weaker species to succumb to minor amounts of pollution (5 ppm of fluorine) rather than pay more than $30 per ton. They are willing to pay $10 per ton, over the $20 direct production cost, for a "nearly pure" environment. But they are not willing to pay $100 per ton for a truly "pure" and pristine state.

In summary, there is some subjective point at which human beings equate the degree of environmental quality against cost, and this point is ascertainable by a careful study of biological damage in relation to incremental avoidance costs. In all probability, human beings cannot afford as pure an environment as they might ideally like to have, and hence we need an analytical means for estimating how pure is good enough, and at what price. The market simulation of total environmental costs compared to biological damage provides such an analytical tool.

TEST OF THE DECISION CRITERIA

The five analytical steps so far have followed decision criteria which have been explicit in previous chapters of the book. That is, the decision process seeks to satisfy a gain in human utility with a minimum acceptable loss in the ecosystem. We recognize that a net gain or net profit is impossible in ecological decisions because of the law of the conservation of matter. Also, it is clear that all decisions are ultimately ecological just because we, as human beings, are a biological species which is part of the ecosystem. Moreover, the pervasiveness of ecological devastation wrought by human actions, unintended perhaps, but real nonetheless in biological damage and extinction of species, convinces us that environmental decisions should be approached with substantial humility about the limits of human knowledge with respect to ecological interactions.

The expression of that humility is to seek to maintain the existing balance of biological species as undisturbed as possible, which is the same as to say that we will try to restrict human impact on ecology to minimum acceptable losses. We have to accept some losses in the biosphere to achieve some gains in human utility. The tradeoff then is to restrict human wants to a modicum consistent with negligible losses to the ecosystem.

In the previous phosphate mining illustration, the gain in human consumption of foods and products derived from phsophate was "bought" at a price, not of $30 per ton, but with a probable 6 percent mortality rate among all the species in the Sespe Creek area. The $30 per ton merely represented the sum of the transaction prices at which human beings exchanged their services among each other, and thus was irrelevant as a "cost" in the sense of "sacrifice." There was no sacrifice involved in the exchange, because if the services had not been exchanged in this way for phosphate, they would have been exchanged for something else. Monetary prices do not represent sacrifice costs, they merely represent shifting utility preferences in the exchange of services. The sacrifice costs are borne elsewhere, by the death or biological damage of species. In the hypothetical phosphate case, the sacrifice cost of the decision is the probable death of 6 percent of the species in the Sespe Creek region. In the previous air pollution example in New York, the "cost" of automobile transport is not the price of the car and its gasoline, but death of 10,000 people from respiratory damage and leopards in the Staten Island Zoo from lead poisoning.

The methodology we have followed, then, allows us to tradeoff human utility gains against acceptable levels of biological damage. The analytical methods can be applied at either the biological level or the aesthetic level. That is, we can use the methodology of environmental matrix analysis, followed by materials balance, dispersion, market simulation, marginal-cost analysis, and trade-off studies, to examine species mortalities or to examine the preservation of "wilderness quality." In applying the methodology to wilderness quality, or scenic views, the avoidance costs of disturbing the wilderness can be calculated in comparison with the degree of scenic change which is tolerable to potential observers. For example, we may convert our previous damage illustration from fluorine damage to scenic damage by assuming it costs $100 per ton to put the plant completely underground and backfill all the spoils banks in order to maintain the pristine state, or to have zero aesthetic impact on the environment. Suppose that for $30 per ton of product, the processing plant could be blended into the background and be observable only from short distances, that power lines and highways could be depressed, and spoils banks could be contoured and replanted like hillocks. Then the demand curve, or environmental utility preference by observers, might indicate that this degree of wilderness scenery was "aesthetic enough." In other words, the aesthetic damage would be held to an acceptable minimum.

Since our methodology will allow us, conceptually at least, to arrive at trade-off evaluations for both biological and aesthetic damage, as well as monetary costs, we may conclude that the decision criteria are generally valid for ecological judgments. That is, we have tested the decision criteria against the environmental impact matrix and have found we can make trade-off analysis to resolve most of the issues raised in the matrix. However, there is one exception, and that is the most important judgment of all—what is the worth of a rare and exotic species like the California condor?

The methodology we have used is not very appropriate to the issue of the survival of the condor, because we have relied upon trading off avoidance costs against acceptable damage levels as our decision criterion. In the case of the condor, there may be no avoidance costs which are possible. The condor is a remote and shy species, not given to habitats in contact with man. Moreover, the condor is a bird of prey, feeding on small animals and carrion. Like man and the eagle, the condor is at the pyramid of the food chain, where small parts of toxic material in the ambient environment can concentrate into lethal dosages to the carnivore (see Chapter 11). Therefore, what may appear to be acceptable concentrations of pollution in terms of biological damage to most species may present unacceptable survival risks for the condor, in the same manner that chlorinated hydrocarbons (DDT and PCB) threaten the survival of the peregrine falcon and the eagle. That is to say, perhaps no amount of money spent on avoidance costs can bring the level of pollutants low enough to preserve the condor, given the concentration effects in the food chain where small parts of toxicity become lethal dosages through successive species ingestion. Such an issue is, of course, subject to research, to determine what the food chain effects, or habitat effects, might be upon the condor. In the meantime, present knowledge suggests the number of remaining condors are few and the interactions affecting their survival are in very delicate balance. With this delicate balance of interactions unknown, an unintended outcome of the environmental decision on the mining project might well be the extinction of the condor. In other words, the plight of the condor is not a probable mortality rate, as we applied in our methodology to other species, but rather extinction or survival. The decision, then, is an irretrievable, all-or-nothing, life or death decision regarding the species. Marginal analysis of gains versus incremental damage is not applicable to such all-or-nothing decisions. Hence, with respect to the condor, the decision criteria used so far do not meet the test. We cannot decide the issue of survival of rare and exotic species by some form of marginal trade-off analysis.

Although every other issue contained in the environmental impact matrix appeared susceptible to resolution by the methodology of marginal cost-damage, trade-off analysis, the issue of the impact upon the California condor requires some other measure of worth. In short, we are forced to reexamine our measures of worth.

REEXAMINING THE MEASURES OF WORTH

Our measure of worth so far has been to equate the marginal gain in human utility with the marginal loss in the ecosystem caused by biological or aesthetic damage. While these measures imply numerous surveys or tests of attitudes and subjective judgments, they are, after all, based upon some recognizable form of quid pro quo. The quid pro quo is a biological exchange based upon an extension of human identity and empathy to other biological species. While such an empathy requires a substantial stretch of imagination, as well as a broader dissemination of biological knowledge, still it is not impossible for most of us to feel that our own well-being depends upon low mortality rates among other species. Most people experience anguish and outcry against fish kills, epidemics among plants and animals, or other evidences of high mortality rates because we intuitively fear that such ecological disasters or imbalances imply higher mortality rates to ourselves. Thus, the mechanism of quid pro quo, biological gain in exchange for loss, has an organic psychological base in human cognition. Most individuals, on the basis of this quid pro quo, would be likely to recognize that some price, however large or small, must and should be paid to keep the species mortality rates at Sespe Creek down to some low, acceptable level, even though Sespe Creek is a tiny place and the individual does not know where it is.

The identification of the human condition to the condor is, however, an even greater abstraction, which must relate, not so much to subjective quid pro quo mechanisms, as to a scheme of values or philosophy. After all, if a price has been paid to preserve the overwhelming majority of species, say 94 percent of the biomass, at Sespe Creek, then one may hope that the condor survives but not feel very anxious for one's own biological health if the condor perishes. No, the valuation of the worth of the condor depends upon something else than the empathetic identification with biological health. The worth of the condor depends more upon some general feeling about the quality of life, some emotional feeling that Schweitzer called a reverence for life, or some intellectual perception that diversity, comprehensiveness, or elegance of design, in man or nature, is inextricably bound to the quality of life.

The media for expressing these human values and social choices is political, through votes, elections, legislation, courts, law enforcement, and, sometimes, lawlessness. Thus, the decision process governing life and death issues (such as wars, abortion, birth, marriage, homicide, rebellion, and treason) is not determined in market places, real or simulated, but socially and politically. Some of the problems in social choice making related to the environment are explored in Chapter 18 and Chapter 24.

WHAT REALLY HAPPENED IN THE PHOSPHATE CASE

The illustration of the Los Padres (or Pine Mountain) phosphate mine has been used in this chapter merely because it happened to be the example selected by the Geological Survey to demonstrate the use of an environmental impact matrix. Most of the cost-damage data, beyond the matrix, has been assumed for further illustration to make a hypothetical case showing the use of analytical methods leading to marginal trade-off studies. These assumptions were hypothesized because there are no detailed materials-balance data on inputs, outputs, and costs. If data were available, the methodology would permit some rational decisions, particularly if a referendum also sampled the measures of worth to apply to the survival of the California condor.

Meantime, in the real world, which is unencumbered by such concepts of social choice, referenda, or marginal cost-damage analysis, there was a dispute between the U.S. Gypsum Company, which sought a lease to the phosphate site under a century-old mining law, and conservationists who wished to preserve the wilderness and the condor. The dispute had all the classic adversary arguments of economic development versus pristine beauty which have characterized the battle over resource use for a century and a half (see Chapter 4).

The company argued that there is no evidence that the mining will be a major degradation of the environment, and that the phosphate is needed for the well-being of mankind, particularly in use as fertilizer, matches, fire retardant, and detergent.

The conservationists argued that the proposed project could have serious impact on the environment in terms of potential dangers to the biological community, plus the probable increase in fire hazards, water, noise, air, and visual pollution. In addition, there is potential damage to wildlife, the condor, the watershed, and recreational resources.

Rare unanimity was expressed among politicians and community groups in opposing the project at a two-day hearing. Joining the opposition were two United States senators, local politicians, the Sierra Club, the Environmental Coalition of Ventura County, civic organizations, private residents, and the Southern California Chapter of the American Institute of Architects.

Appearing in support of the project were the resident manager for U.S. Gypsum, the landlord of U.S. Gypsum's pilot plant nearby, a trucking operator, and a number of consultants. Aside from the name of the project, the words of the disputation were similar to those advanced by land developers versus conservationists for over a century since the mining acts and the Preemption Act of 1841.

The only factual evidence reported was by the County Air Pollution Control District which estimated that the emissions of sulfur dioxide from the plant might be as high as 2.5 tons per day, more than doubling the emissions in the entire county which had totaled 2.1 tons of sulfur dioxide from all stationary sources.

Aside from this evidence, there was no materials-balance study, no dispersion analysis, market simulation, marginal-cost analysis, trade-off studies, estimates of biological damage, decision criteria, or measure of worth. Also, there was no decision.

As in countless other environmental cases argued without analysis or criteria, the result of the verbal disputations was a stalemate. The Department of Interior, for the first time, considered not granting a lease, although in practice, under the Mineral Leasing Act of 1920 and earlier mining laws, a permit had been granted automatically. By not granting the permit, the Department of Interior faced legal action from the mining company; by granting it, it faced a suit from the conservation groups. In short, the administrative decision machinery broke down, and the decision process was headed for the courts. The best that can be said for the proceedings is that, at least, they will provide the first test cases of the century-old mining laws, and whether the Environmental Quality Act of 1969 modifies the old decision process.

SUMMARY

Much of the inability to arrive at decisions in environmental cases lies in the irreconcilable nature of two diametrically opposed national goals which are embedded in law, folklore, and emotion, that is, development versus conservation. Expressed in their verbal extremes, these are both shibboleths which defy reconciliation and frequently result in stalemate, and the resulting political inaction satisfies no one.

Some of the obstacles to the decision process could be avoided by shifting from exhortation to analysis. An analytic method is available to arrive at a tradeoff of costs versus biological damage. The first stage of the method is a general assessment of the critical areas of environmental impact by the use of a matrix. The second stage consists of a series of analytical studies to arrive at a marginal cost-damage tradeoff.

The seven analytical tools to arrive at a decision are studies of (1) materials balance, (2) environmental dispersion, (3) market simulation, (4) marginal cost-damage estimates, (5) trade-off analysis, (6) testing the criteria, and (7) referring critical sacrificial costs to social choice by referenda. Each of these analytical approaches has been considered in detail (see Chapters 10 through 16), and in this chapter their integration has been illustrated through an environmental impact analysis applied to a phosphate mining application.

In the end, the development of a usable technique, whether this one or a better alternative, for arriving at environmental decisions is crucial, not only to the prevention of biological damage, but also for the stability of the political structure. A political structure which has no objective decision function becomes unworkable and unstable in a densely populated nation, because inaction, belated action, or misaligned action frustrates both the public will and the public itself. The attempt to develop a feasible environmental decision process is, therefore, a test case on whether we can re-create, not only a viable ecology, but also a viable political process in our own time.

DISCUSSION QUESTIONS

1   After studing the Corps of Engineers' guidelines and the instructions to those preparing environmental impact statements, what is your opinion of the ability

of a person, who must also justify the initiation of a project, to make an "objective appraisal of the environmental effects, good and bad?" How would you deal with this problem?

2 What strengths and weaknesses do you see in the environmental impact matrix proposed by the U.S. Geological Survey?

3 How would you evaluate the phosphate lease at Sespe Creek?

4 What decision criteria would you suggest for dealing with the threat to the condor?

PROBLEM

Use the approach of the environmental impact matrix of the Geological survey to evaluate an environmental problem in your own vicinity.

Chapter 18

Social Choice Making on Environmental Issues

An adequate decision criterion in environmental problems contains some form of mission analysis or definition of purpose, so that the program decision can be organized to fulfill that mission or goal. Missions and goals are normative, value judgments of what is worth doing and thus a social choice. Without a sense of mission, the solution becomes fragmented into components or patchwork remedies which are nonsolutions, as in the air pollution case. Environmental impact statements are now being generated by federal agencies under the requirements of the Environmental Quality Act of 1969, and these statements raise fundamental questions about the impact of human decisions upon biological processes. Some of these environmental impacts could cause biological damage to other species or to ourselves.

When biological damage occurs, or may potentially occur, we are faced with a value judgment of whether the benefits of our normal productive activity are worth the cost or biological sacrifice borne by ourselves or some species. In the case of the phosphate lease at Sespe

Creek in the last chapter, after all the analyses had been made as to the costs of reducing air pollution, spoil banks, leaks of pregnant liquor, or aesthetic intrusion into the wilderness, the ultimate question still remained as to the relative value of the phosphate mineral as compared to the preservation of the California condor. That is, the final decision in biological issues, which are at the heart of environmental problems, is frequently a value judgment, as to the worth of one species or quality of the environment versus an economic gain. The private mechanism for settling such cross-sectoral issues, and so the value judgment, if it is to be made at all, require some form of social choice making, usually in a political forum.

In another example, pesticides diffuse into the world's water sources; and eventually the eggshells of some birds, including pelicans and eagles, are so fragile that the young are crushed. Hence, some species face depletion. Are the uses of pesticides and chemicals, which cause such destructions, worth the consequences? Against the loss to bird populations must be placed the gains to human food supplies. But, still, the question remains, are the gains in human food supplies sufficient to overcome all the losses and biological damage which ensue? Ultimately a subjective value judgment governs such issue. That is, we seek to measure the gains in relation to the losses in such a way that a social choice can be made about the relative worth or value of the outcome.

Society has, of course, been making choices for a long time, and there are precedents and parallels on how such value judgments can be resolved. The purpose of this chapter is to explore those choice mechanisms to try to apply them to environmental issues. The most obvious means of making choices or valuations traditionally has been through the market price mechanism, and the private marketplace has served over most of United States history as the principal means for determining values. Historically, the private sector has been large relative to the public sector; for example, federal government purchases of goods and services accounted for less than 1 percent of the gross national product prior to 1930. Now, the federal government itself absorbs 10 percent of GNP and, with state and local government, accounts for nearly one-fourth of all economic activity.

The large intrusion of government into decision processes over the past forty years has changed the role of the private market place to a somewhat more specialized function. Rather than allocating all the resources and factors of production, as they had done historically, the private market prices serve the more restrictive role of distributing private capital and consumption goods. In the public sector, government has historically allocated resources to serve the general welfare based upon priorities applied to program needs. That is, the public needs are decided politically by votes, and programs are developed, in keeping with the voting priorities, for the government to supply or satisfy the public needs and services. These governmental services are sometimes called public goods, to distinguish them from private goods supplied in the commercial and industrial market places. Public goods originate in the political, or social, choice-making process. The nature of social choice making as it applies to environmental issues will be discussed under these headings:

1   Market prices versus social choice
2   Environmental problems as cross-sectoral choices
3   Environmental decisions as biological and probabilistic
4   Environmental decisions as qualitative value judgments
5   Varieties of social choice
    a   Direct democracy
    b   Voting under representative government
    c   Lobbying
    d   Legislative compromise
    e   Bureaucratic programming
    f   Participative technology
    g   Administrative appeal
    h   Judicial recourse
    i   Initiative and referenda
    j   Survey research
    k   Nonparticipation

MARKET PRICES VERSUS SOCIAL CHOICE

The government decision-making process is of quite a different character from the price mechanism. The price mechanism deals with the time, place, and form utility of discrete products or services, and equates the wishes of individual buyers with individual sellers. As such, prices are identified with cardinal numbers, linear relationships, rational behavior, quid pro quo, and scalar satisfactions. In short, prices deal with the relation of one buyer to one seller, one product to one use, one unit of service to one recognizable want, one need in one place or at one time. A man in spot x is hungry at time y and buys one loaf of bread from one seller to satisfy a recognizable want. In satisfying wants of this character, prices tend to deal with the more elemental human needs which can be simply counted and simply met. True, one may argue, to the contrary, that prices also deal with very large systems in which buyers procure complex services. For example, a large company may buy a communications network to interconnect all its offices and plants at many locations with voice and data transmissions, and, so, it has procured a complex network of services. Even though the communication system was purchased in aggregate by a rational process of assessing company needs, this does not vitiate the fact that an individual message or call itself is a discrete unit of service, relating one talker to one listener at one time, and a cost can be assigned to the value of such a call separately from the system as a whole if one chooses. The scaling up and aggregation of products or services for purposes of buying and selling do not disprove the discrete and individual satisfactions involved; they only prove the ability to rationalize the wants in the price mechanism.

Government decision process is not so rational, because the product or service is not so recognizable or discrete to an individual's sense of need. A police car patrolling the streets to prevent crime is performing a community service, but the individual citizen sitting in his living room at night reading the newspaper does not necessarily know that the police car is on patrol and, if he does, probably would not feel an individual and personal sense of satisfying a want, in the same sense as a hungry man eating a piece of bread. That is to say, governmental services are more typically joint benefits to many citizens, more cultural and less elemental, more subjective and less rational, more ordinal, nonlinear, nondiscrete. Consider a standing army for instance. In peacetime, the army is of no direct benefit to an individual citizen, except, perhaps, those in it. The benefits of a peacetime army are all potential; they are cultural as a means of enforcing foreign policy to maintain a life style, subjective as to the value of the army or the life style, ordinal in being lower or last among individual priorities, nonlinear in not relating one service to one present want, and nondiscrete in having no recognizable bounds to the army's essential quantitative size. In wartime, the army continues to present the same ambiguous characteristics to the individual, but all the values are reversed. Instead of being last in priority, the necessity for the army now appears to be first; the benefits are emotionally viewed as being of crisis proportions; life and death are at stake; size and cost of the army are no object; preservation of territory, culture, property, and way of living are what seem to matter.

All social choices do not have the crisis proportions of war, but lesser issues have much of the same characteristics. For example, unemployment, depression, injustice, health, all have this same subjective, nondiscrete, joint benefit aspect. Hence, the government does not really provide services on a one-to-one basis, but it tends to respond all or none, or much more or much less. Instead of discrete prices then, the social choice is expressed first in votes, elections, representatives, legislative actions, and finally in block appropriations. The voting mechanism of the polling booth, or through representatives in the legislature, rank orders the blocks of appropriation in some rough social choice, which is at best an approximation; and since emotions are unstable, the issues, needs, and appropriations change frequently. Despite its ephemeral and imprecise nature, the voting mechanism does serve to express social choice, and thus provides a means for meeting human needs that cannot normally be satisfied by the private sector or the market-price system.

Thus, we see that two substantial sectors of our society have existed side by side for nearly half a century, each with its own separate decision system, its own method of arriving at worth. The interesting thing is that these two decision systems do not really intermingle very much. They are more like two institutional structures with a wall between them. The wall may move, or things on each side of the wall, but the two decision structures do not easily change nor mingle. Rather, the jurisdiction for the service is shifted. For example, most urban transit systems were once private, now they are generally public. Medical services have historically been private, but health care is now making the transition to the public sector. In the other direction, the army arsenal system once supplied most of the munitions, now private defense companies build most weapons. When such transitions occur, the service tends to conform to the acquired decision system. Thus, transit fares and medicare are now decided esentially by the political process rather than by individual fee or price. On the other hand, weapons system acquisition has tended to move from block appropriation (or cost plus a percentage fee) to a fixed price or fixed fee, after the manner of a market price, and in the process in wringing out the defense industry.

ENVIRONMENTAL PROBLEMS AS CROSS-SECTORAL CHOICES

The peculiarity of environmental problems is that they cannot easily be forced into the mold of either (1) the appropriation decision system of the government sector, or (2) the price mechanism of the private sector. Unlike urban transit, health care, or defense systems, environmental issues will not stay put in one sector or the other, nor conform to a single decision process. The reason is that the material-cost element of environmental problems is basically in the private sector, but the output or benefit element is felt in the public sector in the form of a generalized biological quality. Then it becomes difficult to equate the material values determined in the private sector with the biological consequences in the public sector.

The difficulty is that the costs are rational and the benefits are emotional, the inputs are linear and the outputs are discontinuitous. Worst of all, the decision makers differ, and there is no evaluation point at which to adjudicate the worth. The chemicals for a pesticide may cost a few cents, be sold for a profit at a few dollars, be well worth it to the agriculturist who increases his yield by a few hundred dollars, and end up in the water sources as toxic agents which accumulate in fatty tissues of man and animals.

Who can judge the question of worth with which we started: Is a pound of pesticide, at whatever its price, worth a pelican's egg or toxic accumulations of unknown gravity in human tissue? The chemical manufacturer does not consider that question—only his cost and selling price; nor does the agriculturalist, the food consumer, or the voter; nor does the politician. True, if all pelicans died, or if many human beings died, the voter and politican would react on a crisis basis by some regulatory control; but that really has very little to do with a solution, because the chemical manufacturer and agriculturalist would then have to decide upon a different pesticide, on a cost-price basis again, rather than a biological basis, which might turn out to be better or worse than the one that was banned. The point is that the public sector has neither the technology nor the cost-price knowledge to alter the pesticide business, and the chemical manufacturer has neither the ultimate biological knowledge nor the criteria to decide the relative value of food output versus species populations.

The consequence is that, in a very ramified and peculiar sense, environmental problems present us with cross-sectoral choices which require a new decision structure. That decision structure will have at least two important characteristics: One will be a feasible method for individuals to express detailed preferences on the allocation of resources among services across private-public sectoral lines, and the other will be a means for equating economic costs with biological gains. There is no good way to accomplish either of these goals at present, which certainly says something important about the deficiencies of current decision structures.

Suppose, for instance, that you live in a congested urban area and are one of those people with sensitive respiratory tracts who are adversely affected by air pollution. The city is industrial with a high concentration of oxidants, sulfur dioxide, and particulates which you feel cause you adverse health effects. Assume further that you are head of a household, earning $15,000 per year, and half your income goes into fixed expenses like taxes, house payments, insurance, pension contributions, and the like. You have one fairly new family car which is used to drive you to the commuter station in the morning where you take a train or subway to work. The commuter service is old, slow, and congested, with frequent breakdowns. Your total transportation costs are $1,500 per year, including depreciation, insurance, and operating expenses for your car plus your commuter train fares; and it suddenly occurs to you that you are spending one-fifth of all your disposable income for a transportation system which you find to be miserable. After further reflection and study, you conclude that the quality of your life would be vastly improved if the city upgraded its commuter service into a fast, comfortable transit system, reduced the central city auto traffic, and developed remote siting of power plants using sulfur-free or nuclear fuels. You conclude further that you could afford to pay 3 or 4 times as much for your commuter fare, use compact rental cars for your weekend driving, and still spend no more than the $1,500 you now allocate to transportation. Reliable research suggests that air pollution could be reduced by three-fourths in the city under such a transport utility plan, and you feel that your asthma and respiratory afflictions will largely disappear. What you have decided in your own mind is a question of worth; you have decided that you are willing to sacrifice some of your personal convenience in pleasure transportation for gains in commuting and biological effects. This is a subjective appraisal on your part, but it is very real and very strong, because you feel that the quality of your life will be greatly enhanced if you spend less time each day getting to work and if your health and vigor improve.

Now that you have arrived at this decision, you find, unfortunately, that there is no way to express the choice or implement it. You cannot express your choice in the private marketplace because automobile manufacturers sell only cars and air pollution, not transportation systems. You can express your preference to the transit administration; but they cannot do anything because, in this illustration, it requires a reallocation of resources from auto manufacturing to capital improvements in the commuter system. You can express your preference to elected representatives in your local government, who could, conceivably, through taxation or regulation, upgrade the transit system and the power plant siting. However, municipal finance being what it is, the poverty-ridden stepchild of government, the city officials hardly feel justified in such action unless it is of crisis proportions. Your biological condition is not of crisis proportions, even to you. You are not dying, you just spend most of your life not feeling very well; and that is too bad, but the decision system is just not geared to respond to you. The consequence is that you are frustrated, live out your debilitated life, and vote unenthusiastically in general elections for office seekers who claim that the quality of life will soon be better. But it does not seem to happen, and the basic reason is that there is no way that biological or environmental effects enter into the social decision structures short of catastrophe.

One is hard put to accept the idea that we must be satisfied with decision systems that let us choose mainly between catastrophes and half-living. That is why a new decision system is needed, a decision system profoundly cross-sectoral and capable of responding to people's assessment of environmental quality and anxiety over biological damage.

ENVIRONMENTAL DECISIONS AS BIOLOGICAL AND PROBABILISTIC

In addition to being cross-sectoral, environmental decisions are biological and probabilistic. That is, they are concerned with how well, biologically, people prefer to live. An environmental choice is one that concerns the quality of health one desires for oneself, and what biological quality is desired in the ecosystem. In a sense, the degree of biological quality is the "service" which the consumers choose or "buy" in the simulated market. To be sure, an individual cannot unilaterally buy a particular degree of air quality, because everyone else uses the common atmosphere as well, and the aggregate residuals of others affect the cleanliness of air available to any one person. This commonality is what makes the choice a social one, rather than a discrete one in the private market, and, because the service must be jointly and commonly provided to all, it is a public good which can only be supplied by government.

That is, a consumer, who chooses that air quality (and health quality) not to exceed 0.08 ppm of oxidants in any day, has basically posed several kinds of options and costs—i.e., (1) much less driving with more expensive lower-emission cars (which means walking or living nearer to work), (2) an elaborate public transit system, or (3) dispersal of factories and cities into rural areas. The choice or purchase of clean air, then, really involves a number of related choices about living style—to live closer to work and drive costly cars, to become a public transit commuter, or to move with one's employment to a rural area.

Certainly this kind of choice making of ecological services is much more complex than buying a television or a car. The television or car represents a piece of hardware with certain performance characteristics and service uses which are tangible, discrete, and separable with a price tag on them. Still they are services. It is the service of music which one buys, not the piano. It is the transportation service one buys, not the car. In the ecological choices regarding air pollution, it is the service of breathing clean air for one's own health sake that one buys, not a low-emission auto or a public transit system. As services become more removed and abstract in a complex society, less obvious as hardware, and more intangible as services contributing to biological health, the choices become more difficult to understand and more personal. Because choices are more complex and personal, only the individual can make them for himself—no representative or industrial executive can make them for him.

A personal decision upon biological quality is essentially a probabilistic decision. Health and biological qualities are not certain states; they are shifting and uncertain states. One feels a little better or a little worse from one day to the next, and it is not entirely clear whether a small amount of lead poisoning, pesticide, oxidant, or a common respiratory infection is the cause. Since the precise cause is not known, and perhaps not knowable in the short term, it is a matter of risk and judgment as to what "solution" will provide the desired service which the individual wishes to purchase, namely better air quality. There is also the uncertainty as to what degree of air quality will be sufficient for each individual. This means that each individual is making a judgment about a service (environmental quality) in a state of uncertainty, and the individual must then be aware what risks and probabilities he is willing to accept about his own health or biological condition. Some flavor of the kinds of judgments involved in ecological issues may be seen by the report of the medical task force on Human Health Effects for Project Clean Air (a University of California research document on the subject of air pollution).

> Air pollution must be safe for not only the healthy adult but also the ill, the infant, and the aged, who are recognized as being most susceptible to the threatening effects of air pollution. Even among healthy adults, we can recognize differences in the levels of pollution that may so interfere with oxygen utilization of an athlete as to prevent him from achieving a record-breaking performance, but may produce no presently measurable diminution in the performance of a sedentary clerical worker.
>
> The question is sometimes raised as to what percentage of the population (i.e., 99.9%, 99.99%, etc.) we should seek to protect by ambient air quality control; and what percentage (i.e., 0.1%, 0.01%) we should take care of by other means such as their relocation to areas or structures having a cleaner air supply, or medical treatment. Answers to this question require the best possible information as to how large the percentage at risk really is, and as to the nature of the disability (for example, respiratory vs. psychomotor) with respect to functions to be performed by persons exposed to polluted air.

In addition to these risk factors, other questions recur in the cause and effect relationships between disease and air pollution, and what is a sufficiency of quality.

> One (question) is what we mean by injury or damage. As experimental techniques improve, we are increasingly able to detect subtle physiological

and psychological deviations from the norm that can be attributed to pollution. The norm in this case is exposure to unpolluted air and the deviation may be reversible when exposure to the pollutant stops. Some will argue that only irreversible deviations should be considered and that any deviation, however reversible, should be considered benign until proved deleterious. However, the fact that a deviation is reversible on cessation of exposure is not, of itself, assurance that we are willing to allow such a deviation to occur. Prudence would argue for considering measurable deviation from the norm as deleterious until proved benign. If a temporary reduction in sensory perception or reaction time occurs, for example, during the operation of a motor vehicle or other machine with moving parts, fatal accidents may occur. This argument is invoked in regulations on smoking (and drinking) by airplane pilots and may be equally applicable to ordinary citizens driving on the freeway at times of high air pollution. Thus temporary, presumably reversible, physical effects of air pollution cannot be dismissed for lack of lethal potential.[1]

Even when the lethal potential is observable, the question of valuation of human life becomes a profoundly difficult and personal question. A report indicated that New York City has about 10,000 excess deaths—mainly those most susceptible, the ill, infants, and aged—per year that are attributable to air pollution. If New York with its population and air quality has 10,000 deaths per year because of air quality, one might hazard that among the dozen largest cities, there may be 80,000 to 100,000 deaths per year attributable to air pollution directly or indirectly. Assuming this to be so, what method of valuation is appropriate for 100,000 lives? To the afflicted individual, and to his family, his life is unique and of infinite value, because all other values disappear with its extinction. In an economic sense, the value of a life is at least its potential future earnings. Somewhere between these two extremes, which in any case range from several millions to billions of dollars, is some subjective valuation, peculiar to each individual, as to what level of sacrifice or expenditure would be worthwhile to achieve a more salubrious degree of air quality and health.

ENVIRONMENTAL DECISIONS AS QUALITATIVE VALUE JUDGMENTS

The fact that environmental decisions are cross-sectoral, biological, and probabilistic makes them qualitative in character. That is, they are not deterministic or quantitative; they do not have an obvious "right" answer.

---

[1]Project Clean Air, op. cit., Task Force Assessment vol. 2, p. 2.

A qualitative decision is one which suffers from a deficiency of information (see Chapter 15), and because information is deficient, the outcome has a considerable degree of uncertainty or risk. The reason environmental decisions are deficient in information is that the biological processes are highly interactive, and the ecosystem itself is made up of countless interdependent phenomena. There are several thousand chemical compounds, alone; and these, with a variety of energy states, give the potential of billions of combinations of molecular and biological interactions. Compared with these countless natural interactions, which constitute an information requirement for predictability, the human knowledge and information available to understand these phenomena are miniscule. The consequence is uncertainty, and this uncertainty makes the decision qualitative. For now, the individual must decide whether an uncertain outcome is worth its probable cost or effort.

By introducing the issue of worth of the outcome, as compared to its uncertain costs (damage), one is confronted with a value judgment. A value judgment is one in which the requisite variety of information as to ultimate effect is far greater than the information available to the decision maker. Such value judgments are made every day. The seeking of friendship, companionship, or marriage has an uncertain outcome, because the compatibility of two individuals' interactions is unknown. That is, individuals may interact with each other in countless ways, and the variety and compatibility of those interactions are unknown. The seeking of friendship is then a prediction that the interactions will be more compatible than incompatible, but this estimate is based on inadequate information, since human beings are too varied to be predictable. Therefore, the choice is probabilistic, uncertain, and risky. The risk is one of emotional costs and perhaps psychological damage to oneself. That is, if one makes an emotional commitment to another person, which leads to psychological dependence on the other's reactions, then incompatible reactions will cause anxiety and unhappiness.

Biological reactions are similar in principle, except they involve physical rather than emotional interactions. In the ecosystem, the variety of interactions is very large relative to the available information. For example, the number of photochemical reactions in the atmosphere is very large relative to human information about air pollution. Very little has been known, until recently, about the distribution of nitrogen oxide concentrations in the upper atmosphere. Very little is known still, about the role which particles play in photochemical smog, or about the concentrations and reactions of aldehydes in the upper atmosphere. Still less perhaps is known about how all these chemical interactions affect human health, except to conclude that the interdependent relations are difficult to measure. Yet we act every day on this minimal knowledge, assuming that the transportation convenience which results in air pollution is worth the uncertain health outcome.

This air pollution illustration demonstrates that culturally we are more conditioned to respond to measurable economic utility than we are to complex biological hazards. Yet even on economic grounds, there are serious value judgments and social choices to be made. Let us look at the magnitude of some of the environmental problems before us.

The present annual expenditure to dispose of solid wastes is about $3.5 billion per year,[2] and this can be expected to increase in the future at least proportionately to the growth in population and the economy.

The projected cost to improve water quality is about $5 billion per year at current prices, totaling something like $150 billion by the year 2000. Compared to this, the total appropriations for water resource development from 1824 to 1954 were only $14 billion.[3]

The damage effects of air pollution are about $16 billion annually in health, vegetation, materials, and property values; and the abatement costs to control air pollution are about $5 billion per year.[4]

On this basis, without attributing any large expenditures to pesticide or noise pollution abatement, the total cost of cleaning up the environment may be expected to range between 20 and 40 percent of the increase in gross national product,[5] depending upon the environmental quality with which we will be satisfied.

If something over one-fourth of the gains in our future income is likely to be allocated to keeping the environment clean, or failing that we suffer biological damage, all of us have a keen and personal interest in the social choices regarding pollution control. Pollution poses a problem in designing an efficient, interdependent system of waste disposal, in which which the social costs are held to a minimum.[6] Social costs, as we have observed earlier, are the external diseconomies or wastes which are by-products of the normal production process. These wastes are disposed of into the environment, without any charge in the private price system to cover their removal. Hence society bears the social cost through taxation to clean up the wastes, or else suffers the biological and health damages of their residual effects. Clearly these are social choices involving value judgments in which the worth and uncertainty of potential effects are weighed against costs and alternative benefits.

[2]Allen V. Kneese, *Economics of Environmental Pollution*, Resources for the Future, Washington, paper prepared for the Atlantic Council, December 1970.

[3]Allen V. Kneese, *Water Pollution*, Resources for the Future, Washington, 1962, p. 2.

[4]Second Annual Report, Council on Environmental Quality, op. cit., 1971, pp. 107 and 111.

[5]*Economics of Environmental Pollution,* Allen V. Kneese, op. cit.

[6]*Water Pollution,* Allen V. Kneese, op. cit., p. 97.

VARIETIES OF SOCIAL CHOICE

Social choices emerge when a common service is desired which involves cross-sectoral, uncertain, and qualitative criteria. The characteristic of cross-sectoral choice, in environmental issues, is that the costs and side effects are generated in the private sector, but the damage or benefit is felt in the public sector. That is, pollutants originate from private activity but are felt commonly by the public (or ecosystem) in the form of biological damage. Even if we understand the cost side of an environmental issue, by the methods discussed in Chapters 10 through 17, we have dealt with only half of the cross-sectoral choice. The other half, which we now address, is how to evaluate uncertain benefits, costs, and damages in a biological case.

The qualitative effects of a prospective environmental action by government may be either (1) aggregated from individual judgments of the citizens, or (2) attributed to the citizenry at large by a representative who presumes to reflect the public will. The aggregation of individual judgments is seen in voting on specific issues, in voting for representatives or political parties who seek identification with public opinion on broad issues, or in survey research and polling of attitudes and desires.

The voting mechanism is relatively infrequent (every two years or so) as compared to the number of individual social choices to be made. In the private market the individual makes many specific buying choices daily; in the public market he makes a few nonspecific choices very infrequently. Under these circumstances, the private market is more closely aligned to individual needs than the public market.

Information control theory shows that any system operating with a long delay-line in its feedback loop is bound to yaw off course and go into an oscillation. This oscillation is observable in the political system in the form of overreaction or underreaction, which has as its concommitant the overprovision or underprovision of public goods. Examples are the periodic overprovision or underprovision of welfare, medical care, employment, money supply, inflation, national defense, education, law enforcement, and environmental quality. The present political choice-making process is an oscillating system due to infrequent and nonspecific choices. This was not as serious a deficiency in the past, when government was 1 to 3 percent of the national economy, as it is now when government is 25 percent; and that 25 percent includes the major joint cost services which contribute to the qualitative conditions of life.

The deficiencies of social choice making in recent years have led to some attempts to fine tune the political system by such devices as public opinion polls, consumerism, and referenda. The polling of public opinion by survey research methods has the advantage of a more frequent aggregation of individual views, but such surveys have no institutional status in government and tend to be dismissed as nonrepresentative by those who disagree with the findings. Consumerism is a kind of grass roots opposition, by community or court action, against public or private institutions which appear nonresponsive to public wishes. Consumerism has forced numerous corrective actions, but it is a relatively costly and cumbersome way for individuals to deal with institutional change. A more flexible way to deal with insitutional change is via referenda, and referenda on important issues have become more common in state elections. However, elections are still infrequent and referenda do not offer continuity of choice similar to private markets. The fine tuning of social choice making, then, still has a way to go to prevent oscillation and to achieve a social steady state.

The difficulties of trying to make a highly institutionalized society responsive to individual choices are particularly severe when it is also a very interdependent, technological society with side effects that degrade environmental and life quality. To deal with these difficulties, we might do well to review the varieties of social choice mechanisms available from history and experience, to see if some means might be found to shorten the delay-line in the feedback loop. Some of the varieties of social choice are:

1 Direct democracy
2 Voting under representative government
3 Lobbying
4 Legislative compromise
5 Bureaucratic programming
6 Participative technology
7 Administrative appeal
8 Judicial recourse
9 Initiative and referenda
10 Survey research
11 Nonparticipation

Of these several historical attempts to deal with social choice, four of them are aggregative of individual judgments, i.e., direct democracy, referenda, survey research, and nonparticipation. All the rest are basically social choice by attribution, where the judgment of a public figure is attributed to the public generally. Let us look at each of these social choice mechanisms more carefully.

Direct Democracy

Direct democracy was born in the city states of Greece and Rome and has survived today only in the limited form of town hall meetings and the local party caucus. Direct democracy has the advantages of providing a forum, direct voting, and direct aggregation of individual wishes. It worked reasonably well in colonial America, but was discarded for a republican form of government on the presumption that democracy was size-limited, and would only be applicable in a small community.

Community size was not the only factor which was changing at that time; property rights were changing as well. The New England town, like the British village, held part of its property in common. The abandonment of the town hall meeting form of government occurred after the Southern headright system influenced other colonies to divide property into individual parcels owned in fee simple absolute, which converted the land into a commodity.

Was it then really community size, or was it the treatment of land as a commodity, which caused direct democracy to languish? Under the New England town system, everyone had some mutual interest in property owned in common, as well as their own individual property and interests. There was little mutual interest or need for direct democracy after the common property had been converted to a commodity in the private market.

Today we are beginning to realize that much of our environment is still held in common, particularly the air and water; moreover, these common environmental properties are deteriorating in quality due to private actions causing their overuse. The commonality of the environmental problem commends a reexamination of direct democracy, at least on some limited scale, as a plausible mechanism to deal with ecological issues.

Voting under Representative Government

The creators of the United States Constitution created a representative, republican form of government, rather than a democracy, on at least three conditions which were applicable to their time. The first was that there was little commonly used property, since land was owned in fee simple absolute, and air and water were in surplus supply relative to the small population. The second was that only property owners were permitted to vote under many state franchise laws, and there was no presumption that the whole populace generally was entitled to a voice in government. The third was that communication and transportation were very slow: therefore, if one presumed to aggregate the choices of the large property owners throughout the colonies, a representative form of government was a logical outcome.

In fact, none of these conditions prevail today. Common air, land, and water resources are scarce relative to their usage and to population size, with the result that air and water quality, especially, have been deteriorating steadily. Revision in voting laws have gradually enfranchised male nonproperty owners, females, minorities, and youth, in an attempt to make the voting base universal, except for the very young. Transportation has become rapid, communications instantaneous, and technology is in hand to make direct voting simple.

Although needs, conditions, and technology have drastically changed, we still retain the colonial voting system. The consequence is that the principal social choice mechanism available today is to vote for representatives every two or four years, in which the choice is basically on very generalized issues reflected by two parties.

The two parties once had distinctive platform positions, such as free trade versus tariff protection, easy versus stable money, deficit spending versus balanced budgets, preemptive versus selective land disposal, progressive versus nonprogressive taxation, broad versus narrow voting enfranchisement, social versus individual economic security, internationalist versus isolationist foreign policy, a minimal versus a strong military posture, and many more. These differences on issues between the parties have largely disappeared, and voting options today relate more to the personality of the candidates than choice among the issues. The consequence is that the election process and media have created a government of men more than of law, contrary to the intent of the founders who sought to create a government of laws and not men. The disappearance of social choice on specific issues defeats the intent to establish a government of laws, because only by choice on specific crucial issues can the individual citizen influence what the law shall be.

Lobbying

As differences among parties on issues progressively declined, lobbying and institutional size increased. Lobbies are a means for influencing specific issues by special interest parties through direct persuasion on representatives. Since the rise of large business at the turn of the century, and similarly large institutions in labor, government, foundations, education, and trade associations, lobbies have been a principal instrument for influencing legislation favorable to their advocates. Institutional lobbies have become well-financed and well-staffed for persistent persuasion in legislative halls.

The phenomenon of representation by interest groups is sometimes called "pluralism" by political scientists. A pluralist society is one in which individuals reflect their needs and choices via an institutional organization (lobby). Presumably, if every individual was a part of an institutional organization through which he could vote, and if all lobbies had equal influence in legislation, then a pluralistic society would also be democratic.

Unfortunately all individuals cannot reflect their choices equally through a lobby, and all lobbies are not equal in their influence. The general public interest is not reflected by lobby at all by definition, since lobbies are special interest groups; and broad interests like consumerism, civil rights, or environmental quality are poorly represented in the lobbying structure as compared to specific interests like a labor or manufacturer's association.

Indeed, the political scientists find themselves and their pluralist theory about where the economists were 100 years ago with their assumptions about pure competition. If the economy were truly competitive, with equal access to resources, equal ease of entry, and infinitely divisible capital, then the economy would reach an equilibrium reflecting the general welfare in which consumer satisfactions would be optimized (Pareto optimality). But individuals do not have equal access to resources, there are substantial barriers to market entry, and capital requirements of industrial technology are not divisible—they are massively indivisible. The consequence is oligopoly, or at least imperfect competition, rather than competitive markets. The large firms in the economy have become, on the political side, institutionalized lobbies with disproportionate influence on legislation and administrative rulings. That is, inequalities in competition due to large-scale economic organizations are reflected, via the lobby, in a pluralism characterized by political inequality.

The political inequalities have much the same characteristics as in the economy: (1) individuals do not have equal access to lobbying resources to effectuate their social choices; (2) there are barriers to entry into lobbying determined by scale and minimum sizes of influential voting blocs; and (3) individuals cannot readily exercise persistent persuasion on all the issues in which they wish to express social choices, simply because organized lobbies do not exist for all consumer and general welfare problems. There are, for example, no antitoxicity, anti-ocean-dumping, or clean air lobbies of the same national scope and force as their industrial counterparts.

Legislative Compromise

The process of legislation in representative government is one of compromise, in which the various advocates have a chance to express their preferences through their representatives by personal calls or letters to legislators, as well as by lobbing. Hence it may be argued that the individual voter still has a chance to express his preferences to legislators on a personal, ad hoc basis, even though he does not belong to a lobby. In this manner, through personal input to legislators, the individual may be said to affect legislation and legislative compromise.

Legislators do, in fact, pay attention to their mail and their constituencies, if for no other reason than to get reelected. As a general rule, perhaps, legislators may tend to vote for the interest of their general constituents, against the interest of a special lobby, whenever it is obvious to them that a preponderant public opinion exists. The difficulty is that legislators do not often get enough mail or personal calls to obtain a representative body of opinion. Letters tend to be written by citizens only under extreme anxiety or provocation, and thus the letters or calls to a representative tend to reflect the extremes of an issue, rather than the broad middle spectrum of opinion. The legislator frequently cannot tell from the anxious fringe what a representative opinion would be. In this case, the legislator may well come to believe that the collective opinion of lobbyists is an approximation of opinion generally, when in fact it may or may not be representative of the public interest.

Bureaucratic Programming

Policy is made, not only in legislatures, but by administrative rulings or executive decisions within the bureaucracies in government. Administrators in the government bureaus are, most frequently, intelligent, well-educated, dedicated people who, by training try to act in the general interest. Moreover, since they do not have to run for reelection, they are often able to carry out a more consistent program of what they regard as the public interest than are legislators. While bureaucracies are prone to the public interest and democratic representation, they have no means for measuring the public will or acting upon it. The elected official asserts that he alone represents the public, and the civil servant has no grounds on which to claim greater representativeness.

The bureaucrat has, moreover, a grave obstacle to overcome to be representative of the public will, even though by training and intent he tries to be so. That is, he gains an identity and emotional investment in the program to which he has been assigned. His experience, knowledge, and expertise in that assignment give him a commitment to solve the administrative problems as he understands them, and he probably understands them better than the legislator or voter. But his very sense of commitment militates against change, particularly change in priorities and goals. If his program has been to design new spaceships to go to the moon, he wants to continue to develop space exploration, even though the public may now think it is time to solve problems on earth. The bureaucrat is not experienced in or attuned to earth problems, and so the bureaucracy resists priority and personnel change. The result is that the main way to start new initiatives and new programs is to get new people and start a new agency, often without eleminating the old ones.

As far as social choice by individuals is concerned, bureaucracies are frequently very sensitive to citizen inputs and choices in their early stages of development when they are searching for a constituency and support for appropriations, but, as they become established in their procedures and appropriations, bureaus tend to be less open to citizens' voices or participation. Since most agencies are established ones, the citizen often has rather little influence or choice in bureaucratic programming.

Participative Technology

The one case where citizens may continue to have a high input into a bureaucracy is when the program is a highly technical one. Then the administrators need scientific and technical advice on the management of their programs. This advice takes the form of technical assessments to determine the practicality of alternative programs, for example, on the effectiveness of various weapons systems. Participative technology is an essential means for the transfer of knowledge and the assurance that government programs are feasible. However, it is not particularly suitable as a vehicle for obtaining representative opinion. First, the scientific community which does the advising is a very small and elite portion of the population, whose views are not necessarily typical of the public at large. Secondly, many of the advisors come from the very industries or disciplines affected by the program, and thus have the same self-fulfillment desires found in bureaucracies and lobbies.

Administrative Appeal

Even if direct input into the legislative or administrative process fails, and if the citizen feels that public decisions are opposite to his choice, the individual generally has the opportunity of administrative appeal. That is, he may appeal, formally or informally, to the bureau which made a ruling in order to protest it. Administrative appeal has been a principal instrument by which consumerism has been effective, in automobile safety, health care, or pesticide regulation. Administrative agencies do have due process procedures, which are available to individuals or groups to reflect persuasions and choices. However, these appeal procedures have some of the same problems associated with lobbies. To use the appeal procedures, the individual has to be very knowledgeable in his subject, devote a great deal of time to the proceedings, and amass a voting bloc to support his view. All of this adds up to substantial resources for persistent influence upon the administrative agency, a requirement which most individuals cannot realize.

Judicial Recourse

When both legislative and administrative means fail, the individual may also seek redress in the courts. While a court case takes time and effort also, it may often not take as much investment in money or energy as legislative or administrative appeals. The main limitation to an individual bringing suit against a public ruling has been the difficulty in showing direct damages to himself. The court has recently relieved this problem by permitting class action suits, or suits where the individual acts on behalf of the public interest on evidence of constructive damages caused by a defendant. Indeed, it is under such class actions that much of the consumerism and environmental issues have been effectuated. Again, however, this route for social choice presumes either that the individual is himself a skilled attorney, which many consumerism advocates are, or that he has access to the resources for legal proceedings. Judicial appeal has recently become a new instrument of social choice making, but it lacks ready accessibility to most individuals as a regular means of expression.

Initiative and Referenda

Initiative and referenda are means for individuals or groups to introduce critical issues on the ballot for a general election. Usually the initiative requires a large number of signatures on a petition, or a resolution by the legislature, to place the issue on a ballot. The referenda are then voted on in the next election, and this provides a vehicle for direct expression of social choice. The referenda are a form of direct democracy, which has recently come into more general use, often through legislative action rather than through the initiative. That is, legislators have tended to put controversial issues, which they did not themselves care to resolve, on the ballot. The main limitations of referenda are the difficulties for the public to introduce issues on the ballot and the infrequency of the elections.

Survey Research

Survey research refers to the sampling of opinion on specific issues, through either public opinion polls or market research techniques. Business uses market research surveys widely to determine consumer attitudes, product preferences, consumer acceptance of products, pricing strategies, channels of distribution, packaging, and advertising. Marketing research is, to business, an integral part of decision making. The same cannot be said for the use of survey research in public affairs. It is true that politicans use public opinion polls to shape their campaign style or to suggest general shifts in platform. But these are adjustments to broad, rather than specific, issues; and give individuals no way of aggregating their specific choices. It need not be so. The government could conduct surveys on specific choices, but there has been no attempt to use such surveys in the public decision process. Until survey research findings are institutionalized into the government decision process, they will remain what they are, newsworthy pieces of information, but not persuasive.

Nonparticipation

In the absence of direct input into social choice making, the citizen always has one recourse if he feels frustrated by nonresponsiveness of government. That is, he can ignore government, fail to participate, or get out. In Eastern Europe this phenomenon became known as "voting with one's feet." In the United States, this type of unobtrusive voting has taken diverse forms, such as dropping-out, drugs, deviant subcultures, protests against the establishment, disregard of the law, riots, and militant revolutionary movements. For the most part, these forms of nonparticipation or protest have been treated symptomatically, as behavior to be repressed, rather than for what they more properly are—votes of no confidence. A no confidence vote in a parliamentary system is an extreme mandate, which requires the government to stand for reelection, so that a new government may be brought in if desired by the public. The United States political system has no provision for handling a no confidence vote. The many forms of nonparticipation on the American scene can plausibly be read as extreme mandate that social choice-making mechanisms need to change, or they will be changed indirectly by nonparticipation.

How might social choice making be changed? We have reviewed eleven varieties of social choice mechanisms available to the public, seven of which require the individual to work through an institutional intermediary. Direct democracy, referenda, survey research, and nonparticipation are the only forms of social choice where the individual can express his own preferences directly, without going through some institutional structure which is usually costly, difficult, and dilutes his preferences. At least one way to try to deal with the widespread nonparticipation apparent today is to seek to develop more means for direct participation by which the individual can express his social choices regularly as a matter of course and of right, just as he does in the private market.

SUMMARY

While the varieties of social choice making are many, the prevailing ones in use require the individual to express his wants through an institutional intermediary, which makes difficult a direct choice on a specific issue. Direct choices on specific issues are vital to deal with value questions related to the environment. Environmental issues are peculiarly cross-sectoral, uncertain, interactive, probabilistic, and qualitative because a deficiency of information makes the value of the biological sacrifices and outcome unique to each individual. This is, the quality of each individual's life is affected differently and uniquely; only he can appraise his preference and life quality for himself.

The social choices as to environmental and biological quality are a different order of decisions from those established historically in the marketplace and the early American voting system. The marketplace and historic American electoral practice were designed to deal with the more tangible, subsistance requirements of a developing nation. Most of those needs were commodities, discrete products, and a few tangible services like land disposal and postal services. Government was scarcely a recognizable factor in the economy for 150 years, and only recently has it emerged to account for one-fourth of the nation's activity.

Yet the choice-making apparatus still functions as it did traditionally, providing discrete products in the private sector, and public goods on the basis of programs and priorities. In either case, the selection of the products or the programs is on a one-by-one basis, or more of this and less of that. Thus private and public choices alike are unilinear, proceeding in line from stage to stage as though they were independent transactions. But they are not independent transactions when biological issues are concerned, because the environment is highly interactive. The biosphere is so interactive that most environmental choices present a requisite variety of information for predictibility, well beyond available knowledge. This information gap makes the choice qualitative, rather than deterministic, and commends the value judgment to the individual, rather than an intermediary, because his biological well-being is affected.

The means for enlightening the cost aspects of an environmental decision are reasonably approachable, as we have seen from the methodologies described in Chapters 10 through 17. But when all the cost analysis is finished, the ultimate question is still a value judgment—is the phosphate worth the condor's extinction, or parathion worth the farm worker's health, or the automobile worth shortening an emphysema patient's life? Who can make such ultimate environmental choices? Surely the more frequently and directly these can be made, without obstacles or intermediaries, the more accurately will common public goods respond to public will. Also, the more infrequently and indirectly such social choices are made, the more oscillation and nonparticipation may be expected in the sociopolitical system. On the whole, even though institutional change is difficult, the advantages would seem to lie in making social choices more immediate and personal, not only for the sake of environmental quality, and personal biological health, but for achieving a more stable state in the society itself.

DISCUSSION QUESTIONS

1 What are the differences in choice making between the private and public markets? Consider the way various forms of communications have been provided historically and the differences which occurred according to whether they were supplied as private or public goods.
2 What are some of the problems encountered in cross-sectoral choice makings? Give examples from the environmental and other fields.
3 What is the cause of the uncertainty and qualitative nature of biological issues?
4 Which of the varieties of social choice making do you feel are available to you? Why?

PROBLEM

Take the example of the phosphate mine at Sespe Creek and describe how you think the value judgments involved would be exercised under each of the varieties of social choice.

Section Four

Implementation of Programs in Environmental Administration

The three previous parts of the book have described the emerging problems of the environment, the biological processes involved, and some methods for assessing and improving environmental quality. These concepts provide the essential background for what to do about the environment, which is the question addressed in Section Four. That is, we have defined the environmental problems and how they might be approached, but the real issue is doing something about it. The act of doing, of concerted action, of problem solving is the function of management; hence we are concerned in this part with managerial actions.

The first managerial actions normally taken to solve a problem are the establishing of objectives, framework, and organizational structure to deal with a situation. The objectives or policy of environmental administration were defined in the Environmental Policy Act of 1969. Some of the framework was also contained in that legislation and subsequent executive orders, which consist of evaluating environmental impact statements, setting quality standards, and seeking compliance with the standards. The

365

organizational structure created to carry out these goals is dealt with in Chapter 19, where federal, state, industrial, and community organizations participating in environmental issues are described. These various organizations have conflicting interests and goals among themselves, which both shape and constrain the public administrative structures. What we observe are the varieties of social choice making (from Chapter 18) coming into play as pressures on the environmental organizations, by raising real questions as to shifting roles in government; and the means by which these conflicting pressures can be reconciled.

At least one means for dealing with disparate goals is to create administratively a coordination and interface among the interest parties. The means for creating such an administrative interface, the subject of Chapter 20, strains the organizational art, but it is at least conceptually possible to envisage interlocking ecological organizations which may partially integrate disparate views. The problem, in the end, of course, is to see the ecology as a whole and to deal with it managerially. This is a large undertaking, but filled with challenge and fruitful possibilities.

The problem of seeing the environment as a whole, and managing the various institutions to some common purpose for ecological improvement, may be aided by systems management techniques, particularly by the development of an environmental mission analysis, which is the concern of Chapter 21. Mission analysis is a means of describing a set of purposes in storylike fashion, by a scenario, which lets individual actors pursue different activities or subgoals that are integrated by a common criterion, in this case, environmental quality. If such a criterion among organizations can be established, then individual organizational units may engage in their different pursuits but move concurrently toward a common objective of environmental improvement.

The program organization and control for such a systematic effort at environmental improvement (Chapter 22) require first the identification of a competent decision maker; second, the determination of the major functions of the system; and finally setting up the budgetary and task assignments to carry out the mission. As the program manager breaks jobs down into their specific tasks, he may expect to encounter communications problems, particularly the proclivity of technical organizations to redefine their tasks into what they know how to do rather than what they ought to do. There is no remedy for this other than a manager who gives attention to detailed, tight specifications, and then engages in patience and dialogue to see that they are met. Such skills, while seemingly simple, place an order of competence on administrators seldom realized by present training.

The entire network of interactive events, required in environmental administration to coordinate dispersed activity, requires above all a comprehensive flow of information (Chapter 22). Three information systems are needed, an operational network to control work tasks, a monitoring network to measure results, and a public environmental information system to convey factual data on the biological risks to which humans are exposed. The data on biological risks will be, as we have seen (Chapters 15 and 18), probabilistic and subject to various interpretations. The variety of interpretations will, of course, thrust many environmental issues back into the political arena.

The politics of environmental administration revolve about three questions: (1) what is adequate quality for biological safety? (2) how does one choose among technical alternatives to improve quality?, and (3) who shall bear the costs? In issues such as these, of course, there are no experts, because each individual is and chooses to be his own expert. Moreover, he must be because the deficiency of information makes the judgments qualitative and uncertain. The main policy means by which such questions become resolved is the subject of Chapter 24, the politics of environmental administration which examines the administrative and social choice-making means by which diversity, balance, and biological safety can be realized.

Chapter 19

Environmental Management Systems

The serious impacts upon the environment from industry, technology, and urban populations can be identified through a variety of analytical studies, including environmental impact matrices, materials balance, environmental dispersion, market simulation, marginal-cost analysis, trade-off studies, and social decision criteria (see Chapters 10 through 17). Such studies help define environmental problems and show what needs to be done, but then the real question becomes how to do it. This is a management question, that is, how to organize and carry out an implementation program to improve environmental quality. We turn our attention next, then, to the managerial means by which environmental administration may carry out its programs.

A useful starting point is to examine the existing management structures which have been created to deal with the environment. This chapter describes some typical environmental administrative organizations in federal, state, and industrial institutions, including the following:

1 Council on Environmental Quality
2 Environmental Protection Agency
3 Proposed Department of Natural Resources
4 Environmental administration in state and local governments
5 Interest groups and issues in state environment plans
6 Industrial environmental organization
7 Citizen organization and participation in environmental quality
8 The interfaces among the many organizations

COUNCIL ON ENVIRONMENTAL QUALITY

The Council on Environmental Quality is the principal policy-making body in the executive branch of the federal government on environmental matters. The Council was created by the National Environmental Policy Act of 1969 (Public Law 91–190, January 1, 1970) for these purposes:

1 To develop and recommend national policies to foster and promote the improvement of environmental quality to meet the conservation, social, economic, health, and other requirements and goals of the nation
2 To conduct investigations, studies, surveys, research, and analyses relating to ecological systems and environmental quality
3 To document and define charges in the environment, including plant and animal systems, and to interpret the underlying causes of changes in environment trends

The Council on Environmental Quality is made up of three members appointed by the President with the advice and consent of the Senate. The Council is located organizationally in the Executive Office of the President and derives its chief policy-making role from the requirement that it review all new legislation and programs of federal agencies prior to their submission to the Bureau of the Budget or to Congress. The Council's staff is small, about a score of professionals, organized mainly into an environmental program development staff and an impact evaluation staff, plus a general counsel and technical advisors in the areas of science, economics, and international affairs.

Legislative relations of the Council, initially amicable, have shown some stress as a result of an industry drive against pollution controls. The Iron and Steel Institute proposed to the Senate Public Works Committee that an "independent nine-member board" be set up to hold hearings on water standards in lieu of the Environmental Protection Agency. The chairman of the House subcommittee on appropriations for environmental agencies proposed a legislative requirement that the economic impacts also be included in the environmental impact statements submitted by federal agencies.

Russell E. Train, the first chairman of the Council on Environmental Quality has been sensitive to the possibility of an industrial backlash against environmental improvement and has said:

> I absolutely do not think that we are dealing with a confrontation between environment and the economy. That's ridiculous. Pollution in the ultimate sense is inefficient use of resources. When you put mercury into the water and sulphur into the air, its a waste of resources. It can't even be good business. I have a strong feeling that in dealing with pollution problems in the long run we will be developing more efficient ways of doing business to everyone's advantage.[1]

The initial investment by the nation in environmental improvement is, of course, large. It is estimated by the Council to be $105 billion for the five-year period 1970 to 1975. However, even this investment is less than the cost of biological damage. For example, the economic cost of damage by air pollution to human health, plants, crops, and equipment is about $16 billion annually, compared to an annual investment of about $5 billion to reduce atmospheric pollution to air quality standards. These facts led Train to conclude:

> The costs we see involved in meeting air and water pollution standards, for example, while very significant, are far less than the annual wage increase that the American people take as a matter of course. The American economy has adjusted to a high level of wages, high level of worker security, protection and safety. I see absolutely no reason whatever why the economy can't adjust just as successfully to the requirements of a decent environment.

The role of the Council on Environmental Quality, then, is to review all new federal programs, to determine their impact, to initiate policies to improve environmental quality, and to pace the rate of environmental improvement consistently with the financial temper of the economy.

THE ENVIRONMENTAL PROTECTION AGENCY

While the Council concerns itself with policy, the Environmental Protection Agency is concerned with implementing the regulations or controls needed for environmental improvement. The Environmental Protection Agency (EPA) was created by Executive order through consolidation of

[1] *Los Angeles Times*, Aug. 6, 1971.

the functions of the Federal Water Quality Administration, the National Air Pollution Control Administration, the Bureau of Solid Waste Management, and pesticide control and radiation criteria from several federal departments and agencies.

Although the Council has a small staff concerned with determining environmental quality goals, the EPA is an operating agency whose activities in pollution control required a staff of about 7,200 with a budget of $1.3 billion in 1971. For the fiscal year 1972 a budget request was made for $2.45 billion for EPA and a staff of 8,850. EPA has organized its activities under five Assistant Administrators; three are in functional areas of (1) planning and management, (2) enforcement, and (3) research and monitoring. A fourth Assistant Administrator is concerned with the substantive pollution programs in air and water quality; and a fifth supervises the pesticide, radiation, and solid waste programs. Figure 19-1 is an organization chart for the EPA.[2]

The Office of Air Programs administers air pollution control, which was notably strengthened by the Clean Air Amendments of 1970. The amendments require stringent national emission standards for new automobiles, amounting to a 90 percent reduction in most emissions from 1970 levels. The amendment also empowers the EPA to set emission standards by sources and to establish a framework for the states to realize the national air quality standards by 1972. If the state plans submitted to EPA are inadequate, the federal government may promulgate a plan of its own which takes precedence.

The Office of Water Quality sets standards for water quality and implements its programs in part, by assisting municipalities in financing construction of sewage treatment plants. Congress appropriated $1 billion for waste treatment plants for fiscal year 1971, and EPA estimated that another $12 billion is needed during the 1972–1974 period for municipal waste treatment plants. A second means for enforcement of water quality is by the approval of permits to discharge effluents into navigable waters under the Refuse Act of 1899. To obtain such a permit, an industrial discharger must disclose what kind, and how much, effluent he intends to discharge. The Office of Water Quality may require installation of waste treatment equipment to reduce pollution as a condition of receiving the permit. Failure to comply with the effluent standards specified by the permit subjects the discharger to enforcement proceedings.

The Office of Pesticide Programs administers legislation which requires that all pesticides shipped in interstate commerce be registered with the EPA. When the label of the product is inadequate to prevent

[2] *Environmental Quality*, Second Annual Report of the Council on Environmental Quality, August 1971, Washington, p. 5.

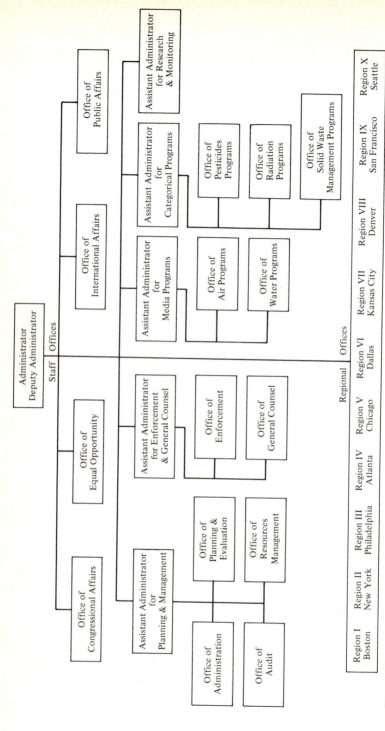

Figure 19-1 Environmental Protection Agency.

"imminent hazard" to man or other organisms, the registration of the pesticide can be suspended, which immediately stops interstate shipment. The EPA issued notices for cancellation of all registrations of pesticides containing DDT, and has initiated cancellation proceedings for aldrin, dieldrin, and mirex. A lengthy and complex appeals procedure may require a year or more before the cancellations are effective.

The Office of Radiation Programs sets radioactivity standards on nuclear reactor effluents. Standards have been established which would keep radioactivity from nuclear reactors to less than 5 percent of the ordinary human exposure from natural sources, such as cosmic rays and radioactive rocks.

The Office of Solid Waste Management Programs places emphasis on recycling materials, issues guidelines for the construction and operation of acceptable solid waste disposal systems, and authorizes funds for demonstration grants for recycling systems.

These several offices constitute the main substantitive program of the EPA. In addition several service and enforcement departments were established. The Assistant Administrator for Research and Monitoring is concerned with establishing an instrumentation and monitoring network which will provide an index of environmental quality. The research office also studies the effects of environmental insults, ecological relationships and processes, and pollution control technology.

The main enforcement activity by the General Counsel for the EPA has been under the Refuse Act of 1899. Over 300 criminal actions were brought in fiscal years 1970 and 1971 against violators of effluent standards, resulting generally in fines upon conviction. Fourteen civil actions in water quality cases were also successfully concluded in 1971. In addition, water enforcement conferences have been initiated with state government participation, public hearings; these are resulting in compliance guidelines for water usage. Three major cities, Atlanta, Cleveland, and Detroit, were issued violation notices for water pollution. A major industrial manufacturer was subject to enforcement proceedings for air pollution. On the whole, the enforcement program has been an active and essential part of the EPA's first year's efforts to improve environmental quality.

The balance of the EPA functions shown on the organizational chart are generally managerial or liaison in nature, and thus similar to the normal housekeeping requirements of a governmental agency. The entire organizational structure took place relatively rapidly, being effectively operational within about half a year after its creation December 2, 1970.

PROPOSED DEPARTMENT OF NATURAL RESOURCES

The Environmental Protection Agency is principally a control agency, which seeks to change materials usage and economic activity after the fact of environmental degradation. However, prior determination of how materials should be used in keeping with ecological balance is also essential for environmental improvement. This means that the disposition of resources and materials should be guided by policies consistent with environmental quality. The federal agencies concerned with resource usage and disposition are now scattered in the government and could be better coordinated. To deal with this problem, the President's Advisory Council on Executive Organization recommended that a Department of Natural Resources be created from the following units: the Department of Interior, the Forest Service and the Soil Conservation Service of the Department of Agriculture, the civil works planning of the Corps of Engineers, civilian power functions from the Atomic Energy Commission, and the National Oceanic and Atmospheric Administration from the Department of Commerce. The President sent legislation to create such a department to the Congress on March 25, 1971. The new Department of Natural Resources would consist of five main organizational entities: land and recreation; energy and mineral resources; oceanic, atmospheric and earth sciences; and Indian and territorial affairs. An organization chart for the proposed department is illustrated in Figure 19-2.[3]

ENVIRONMENTAL ADMINISTRATION IN
STATE AND LOCAL GOVERNMENTS

State and local governments have, traditionally, been the principal administrators of environmental affairs, through the residual police power reserved to them by the constitution. These powers have meant that most health, land use, transportation, and general welfare measures have been governed by state or local legislation. The federal government's intervention in environmental protection has been mainly in preserving parks and wildlife, and very recently in water and air quality standards. The local governments have historically governed land use through zoning ordinances and have provided for waste disposal. State governments have regulated transportation, water basin usage, and more recently air basin emissions.

Even with the new and more stringent environmental policy legislation at the federal level, and the control and enforcement functions of the Environmental Protection Agency, much of the daily implementation and

[3]Ibid., p. 7.

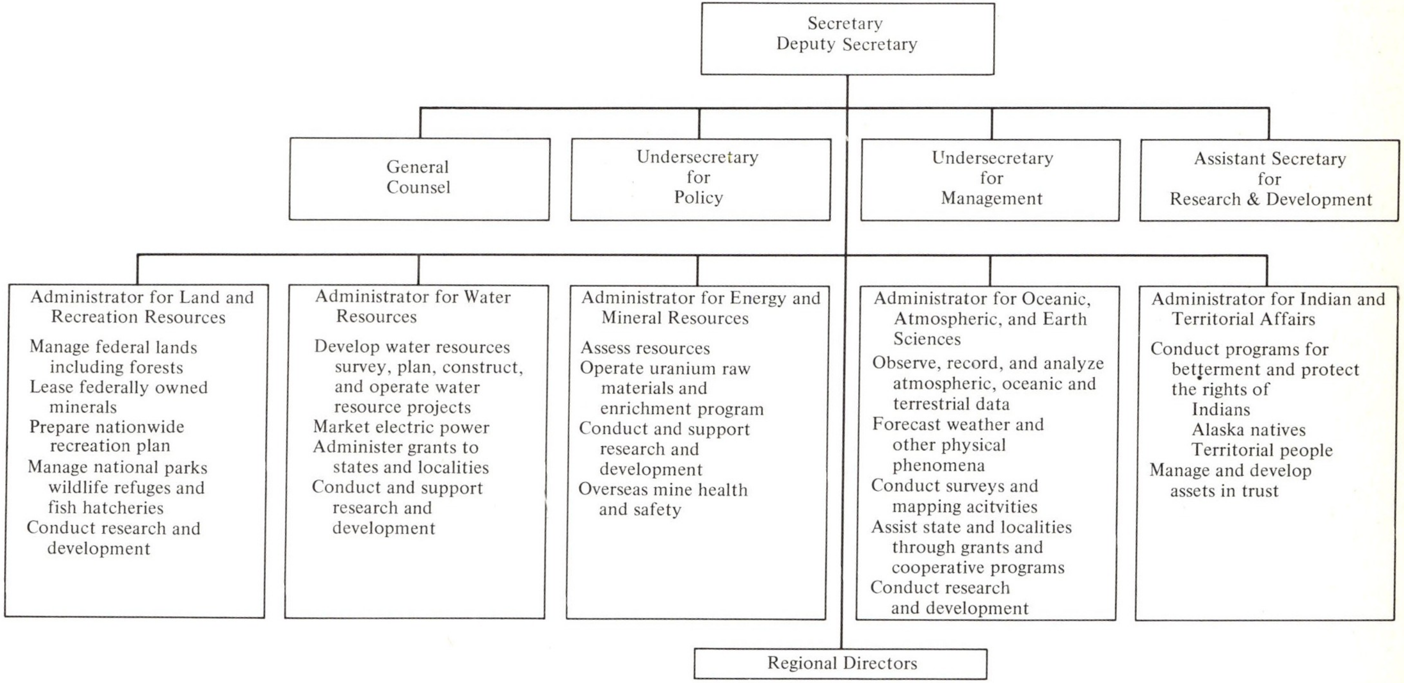

Secretary
Deputy Secretary
General Counsel
Undersecretary for Policy
Undersecretary for Management
Assistant Secretary for Research & Development
Administrator for Land and Recreation Resources
Manage federal lands including forests
Lease federally owned minerals
Prepare nationwide recreation plan
Manage national parks wildlife refuges and fish hatcheries
Conduct research and development
Administrator for Water Resources
Develop water resources survey, plan, construct, and operate water resource projects
Market electric power
Administer grants to states and localities
Conduct and support research and development
Administrator for Energy and Mineral Resources
Assess resources
Operate uranium raw materials and enrichment program
Conduct and support research and development
Overseas mine health and safety
Administrator for Oceanic, Atmospheric, and Earth Sciences
Observe, record, and analyze atmospheric, oceanic and terrestrial data
Forecast weather and other physical phenomena
Conduct surveys and mapping acitvities
Assist state and localities through grants and cooperative programs
Conduct research and development
Administrator for Indian and Territorial Affairs
Conduct programs for betterment and protect the rights of
Indians
Alaska natives
Territorial people
Manage and develop assets in trust
Regional Directors

Figure 19-2 Proposed Department of Natural Resources.

operation of environmental programs will rest with state and local governments. Local governments must develop plans and authorize bond issues for matching funds, for example, to develop municipal sewage treatment plants under the federal funding provided by the EPA. The degree of water purity achieved by a treatment plant is largely a matter of local determination. Primary treatment consists of the removal of solids and sediments from waste water; secondary treatment utilizes bacteriological processes to digest organic materials; and tertiary treatment utilizes chemicals, in addition to bacterial treatment, plus percolation through soils to achieve a high degree of water quality. While the long-run objectives of the EPA are to recycle waste water into potable usage, most of the early effort is being made to prevent raw sewage from going into the water basins and to see that sewage receives at least primary and secondary treatment. A few tertiary treatment plants have been installed, mainly on a pilot demonstration basis. One in the city of San Diego processes waste water and returns it first into a recreational reservoir for the city population and eventually to drinkable water. Such recycling of water is still a long way off for most metropolitan areas, although future population pressures will require cities eventually to develop such processes.

Similarly, local and state governments are crucial in the final implementation of air pollution control, solid waste disposal, new transportation systems, or revised land-use planning. The EPA can set national air quality standards, but air basin monitoring and vehicle inspection, which are the key to ultimate air quality, are matters for local government to implement. Solid waste disposal methods may be influenced by federal policy and finance, but local governments will carry the programs out. If there is to be any substantial change in urban transportation systems or land-use plans, state legislation will have to be enacted, because these problems cut across local government boundaries and jurisdiction.

Despite the importance of recent initiatives at the federal level to establish more compatible environmental policies, it is still largely up to state and local governments, at the operational level, to determine exactly what kind of environmental quality will be achieved. States have shown considerable innovative ability in environmental improvement. Wisconsin led the way, before federal action, in banning DDT. California has been the precursor of many of the air pollution control measures. Minnesota created a consolidated environmental Pollution Control Agency several years before the federal government followed suit.

Almost all states have taken steps to effectuate environmental improvement. For instance, all states have legislated authority to set air emission standards, and all but two (in 1971) had provided for inspection and punishment of violators. In solid waste management, ten states are in the inventory stage of determining their disposal requirements, and all the rest are in the planning stage or have completed solid waste disposal plans.

The organizational structures for dealing with environmental administration vary considerably among the states. New York has one of the most comprehensive environmental organizations, enacted on Earth Day 1970, to bring together in one agency all resource management functions as well as all pollution control activity. The new Department of Environmental Conservation is basically divided into an environmental quality section concerned with all forms of pollution control and an environmental management section responsible for resource management, including minerals, lands, forests, marine, and wildlife resources. The Department of Environmental Conservation, whose organization structure is shown in Figure 19-3,[4] is administered by a Commissioner, who reports in turn to a State Environmental Board made up of citizens and representatives of other state agencies. The Board is advisory to the Governor on broad environmental policy, including environmental quality, economic impact, and population growth. The Board also has veto power over environmental standards and rules and regulations proposed by the Commissioner.

The State of Washington created a new Department of Ecology, less comprehensive in coverage than the New York agency, in 1970. The Washington Department of Ecology consolidates the pollution control functions into one agency, including air and water quality, solid waste management, and water resource uses. However, the Department of Ecology does not incorporate the resource management functions in its administration. These remain in separate state agencies. The Department of Ecology is structured organizationally into functions, such as standard setting, planning, and enforcement without regard to the media, e.g., air, water, or solid waste; and in this sense Washington represents a departure from other environmental organizations. Another feature of the Washington structure is that it sets up a strong environmental administrator directly accountable to the Governor, eliminating the interagency or special interest boards which have been common in other states. The Ecological and Biological Commission are advisory to the administrator, rather than having legislative or veto powers over him. A quasi-judicial Pollution Control Hearings Board provides for appeals from the control

[4]Ibid., p. 50–51, from Elizabeth Haskell and Victoria Price, *Managing the Environment, Nine States Look for New Answers*, Smithsonian Institution, Washington, April 1971, p. 271.

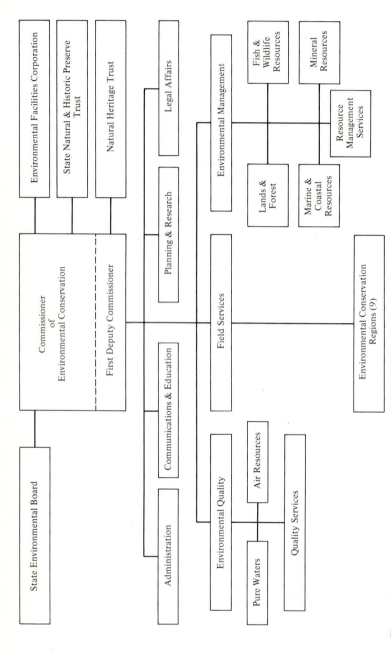

Figure 19-3 New York State Department of Environmental Administration Conservation. *(Source: E. H. Haskell, et al.)*

regulations of the administrative department. The organization structure (Figure 19-4)[5] should provide an interesting test whether a strong executive form of environmental administration will be more effective than the representative board forms used by a number of other states.

A third form of organization is found in Illinois where the framers acted upon different assumptions than in most other states in that they sought to separate planning, policy, and administration rather than to consolidate them. The result is an unusual and innovative organization, with a Pollution Control Board engaged in setting standards and making policy, an Environmental Protection Agency engaged in administration and enforcement, and an Institute for Environmental Quality engaged in long-range planning. The Illinois framers acted on three principles different from other states: First, they sought to strengthen the policy-making function by professionalizing it, making it full time, and giving it its own staff; secondly, they acted on the theory that some functions such as prosecution and adjudication conflict in a single agency and should be separated; and thirdly, they presumed that some duplication of functions heightened competition and maximized action against pollution. The organization chart which resulted from the Illinois Environmental Protection Act of 1970 is shown in Figure 19-5.[6]

Despite the differences between Illinois and New York, a study by the Smithsonian Institution of nine state environmental organization plans classified the two states as essentially of the type which seeks to combine environmental management activity into a more rational administrative grouping. The nine-state study describes four general types of organizations among the states:[7]

Type 1   Consolidation of environmental management activities, in Illinois, Minnesota, New York, Washington, and Wisconsin
Type 2   Land-use control commissions, in Vermont and Maine
Type 3   Statewide waste management service for solid and liquid wastes, in Maryland
Type 4   Citizen suits in state courts, in Michigan

INTEREST GROUPS AND ISSUES IN STATE ENVIRONMENT PLANS

The outcome of the state environmental reorganizations, whether of these four types or variations of them, depended partly on the prior conditions

[5]Ibid., p. 53; from Haskell and Price, op. cit., p. 185.
[6]Ibid., p. 55, from Haskell and Price, op. cit., p. 187.
[7]Elizabeth Haskell and Victoria Price, *Managing the Environment, Nine States Look for New Answers*, Smithsonian Institution, Washington, April 1971, Summary vol., p. 1.

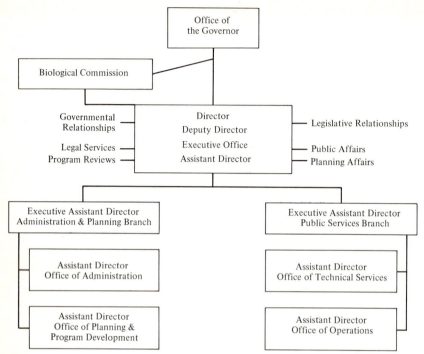

Figure 19-4 Washington Department of Ecology. *(Source: E. H. Haskell, et al.)*

or history of environmental protection in the state and partly on the character and strength of the constituencies seeking change.

In terms of history, for example, Illinois had experienced part-time standard setting boards that were ineffective; the boards met infrequently, attendance was poor, and some members on the board represented polluters seeking to avoid enforcement. The Illinois framers also felt the courts had been "soft" on polluters in terms of enforcement and fines. The role of the courts was thus minimized. Michigan, with a different experience and history, turned to the courts as the principal focus for enforcement. The Michigan Environmental Protection Act gives every citizen the right to sue any public or private entity under a class action on behalf of himself and others to forestall environmental damage. The Michigan legislation thus draws the state judiciary more actively into the field of environmental control.

The several constituencies which affected the outcome of the environmental reorganizations might be classed as (1) the traditional conservationists, (2) the public health group, (3) the new environmentalists,

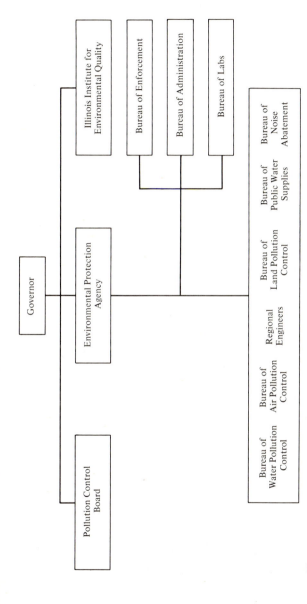

Figure 19-5 Illinois Interim Environmental Organization. *(Source: E. H. Haskell, et al.)*

and (4) the polluters. The traditional conservationist group, made up of sportsmen, outdoorsmen, and wilderness advocates, is basically rural-oriented; and it tends to fear that its conservation interests would be diluted if combined into pollution control agencies. The public health groups generally were faced with giving up jurisdiction over pollution control programs which they had previously administered, and they neither liked the loss of function nor the prospect of new administrators emphasizing environmental quality control rather than public health. The "new environmentalists" were basically urban activists concerned about the crowding, pollution, and blight in cities which had not been prevented by tough enforcement in the past.[8] The special interest groups of polluters were basically everyone who did not want to bear the costs of change. Of course, no one wants to be a polluter or likes pollution, but everyone from the car driver and his automobile club to the industrial polluter and his trade association looked with some apprehension on the cost of environmental improvement. The result was that many organized lobbies took stands against change or the enforcement of tighter environmental quality standards. The outcome in any state, of course, represented some kind of balancing and compromise among the constituencies, based on their relative strength, and upon the prior conditions or history in the state. It is not surprising that a diverse and fertile set of organizational changes occurred.

Out of all the diversity and flux, however, emerge certain key issues to watch, according to Haskell and Price.[9] These are:

1   What are the merits of environmental "superagencies" combining both pollution control and resource management? The implication here is that pollution control is essentially consumer oriented, and resource management is basically producer oriented. Can you indeed integrate the interests of two diverse constituencies in one agency, or will the result be stalemate and inaction?

2   What are the merits of structuring the organization around media or programs, such as air or water quality, or around functions, such as planning, standard setting, and enforcement? For example, one planning function might better deal with the whole ecosystem interactions, to prevent air pollutants from becoming water pollutants, or vice versa. But then, how can such a planning group make intelligent recommendations without understanding all the biochemistry of the media? That is, air pollution interactions are different from those in water or on land. Do we really have enough environmental knowledge to be able to integrate administrative actions in separate scientific disciplines?

[8]Ibid., pp. 24–27.
[9]Ibid., pp. 42ff.

3 Are there, indeed, conflicts of interest within environmental functions which should cause them to be separated? Should standard setting be separated from enforcement, as in Illinois, or combined as in New York? The separation of powers is applied in government generally—why not in environmental administration? But then, when the powers were separated previously in environmental affairs, inaction resulted. How does one reconcile these differences?

4 Does a competitive environmental system with some duplication, as in Illinois, produce more effective pollution control than the single agency or more confusion and cost?

5 Do policy formation boards result in "soft environmental administration" compared to policy determination by a single executive? And if so, are the policies more socially representative and thus more desirable, or merely more amenable to lobbying?

6 To what degree should private citizens participate in actual decisions regarding the environment? If at all, is the Michigan mechanism workable or does it only provide access to enforcement by those who can afford to initiate a lawsuit? If judicial recourse is elitist, what broader public participation is possible?

7 Where pollution control and resource management are separated, how will state policies for environmental protection be integrated with the big resource development agencies, such as highway departments, water resource, and electric power regulation?

8 What changing roles are implied in environmental administration for the three branches of government? Will the judicial branch become the objective recourse for individual citizens, in which case it becomes more administrative? Or will the individual citizens take more direct part in environmental decisions, in which case the body politic will reassume some of its sovereignty from the delegated powers to the legislatures?

9 Where will responsibility shift among federal, state, and local governments? Federal initiatives appear at the moment to be preempting the environmental decision process, but the federal government cannot really carry out a land-use or a solid waste disposal operation. Will the states emerge as stronger environmental administrators than in the past because they can make uniform regional plans? Or will local government finally recover from its supine place in the governmental hierarchy through the environmental issue because it is closest to the problem?

These and other issues suggest that the environmental problem could bring about a far greater change in governmental structure than the reorganizations to date have contemplated. But progress comes one step at a time, and a first step has been taken. Before we can speculate on where environmental administrative and organizational structures are headed in the future, we need to take cognizance of other actors in the piece, namely, the corporations and citizen groups.

INDUSTRIAL ENVIRONMENTAL ORGANIZATION

Industry has operated historically under an economic and pricing rational which excluded "external" environmental costs from its decision processes (see Sections One and Three). The change in public wants relative to environmental quality, and the legislative actions which express those desires, have caused industrial organizations to expand their concern to include the effect of their operations on the environment.

Industry produces the greatest share of the nation's goods and services, and since wastes are a by-product of production, they are also the greatest generators of wasteloads. About one-third of all the air pollution and solid wastes comes from industry, as well as 80 percent of the water pollution and most of the toxic wastes. Paper, chemicals, steel, petroleum, and utilities have been the heaviest polluters in the past, and now they are the hardest pressed to innovate a control technology to reduce wasteloads, which also means they must make the heavy investments needed to improve environmental quality. Generally, industry has been making considerable improvement and investment in pollution control equipment.

Industry investment for air and water pollution control increased by a dramatic 50 percent, from $1.7 billion in 1969 to $2.5 billion in 1970. The planned expenditure for 1971, at $3.6 billion, represented another 50 percent increase. Despite these large increases in outlay, they are small compared to the total requirement of $18 billion to meet the air and water quality standards of 1971.

The need to make these heavy investments, and to plan for more rigorous pollution control, has caused many companies to reorganize and create a special departmental function concerned with environmental impact. Historically, pollution control has been one of many quality control problems residing in engineering departments, and this is still true in many companies today. However, a survey by the National Industrial Conference Board found that 51 percent of 174 companies with heavy wasteloads, such as chemicals, utilities, food processors, pulp and paper, mining, and petroleum, had reorganized to give increased emphasis and focus to environmental effects and pollution control.[10] Some of these reorganizations created separate corporate units or special environmental departments. One example, shown in Figure 19-6, is the General Motors organization which created an Environmental Activities Staff, headed by a vice president, on the Operations Staff of the corporation. The functions of the Environmental Activities Staff include product assurance, automo-

[10]Second Annual Report, Council on Environmental Quality, op. cit., pp. 79–86.

tive emission control, automotive safety engineering, as well as plant and environmental engineering activities.[11]

In another survey of the 500 largest companies by *Fortune* magazine, 69 percent of the top management executives said that they now participate in industry and community pollution control activity. The private sector is the key to ultimate environmental quality improvement; and industry for its part, though it still has far to go to reduce its wasteloads, has shown a steady increase in involvement and commitment to pollution control.

CITIZEN ORGANIZATION AND PARTICIPATION IN ENVIRONMENTAL QUALITY

Perhaps even more important than industry activity is the role of individual citizens and consumer behavior in determining environmental quality. The individual's willingness to change his transportation habits, to sort and recycle materials, to give up some convenience in packaging or transit, to find satisfactions other than in noise and speed, to live in greater proximity to his life functions, to walk more, to know more about ecological balance, to have higher regard for continuing the lives of "lesser" organisms, in short, perhaps, to live closer to the Aristotelian mean are the final determinants of environmental quality.

If this is the final test, is there any reason for optimism, or even hope? Perhaps optimism would be too strong—but hope, yes. The limited rationality of *homo sapiens* is gradually being reinforced by the unpleasantness (pain) of crowding, toxicity, and biological degradation. Eventually the tradeoffs will favor individual health instead of noise, speed, and convenience.

While man's rationality alone may not be counted on to improve the environment, his innate and unvarying inclination to ease and comfort can. When it becomes more healthy and comfortable to amble through his own urban pathways rather than to go roaring through ecological disaster areas, the decision process will have changed. Since every major stream is polluted, the sea is chemicalized, the air is fouled, and the land is crowded, we are perhaps closer to the day of decision than might be supposed. While the future may find Aristotelian virtue still to be rare, a new sense of comfort is in the making. In short, there are sufficient biological pressures and damage affecting the human race to have some hope that the ecosystem will right itself.

The realization of these biological pressures and damages has led to

---

[11]The Organization of General Motors, Office of the Assistant Secretary, General Motors Corporation.

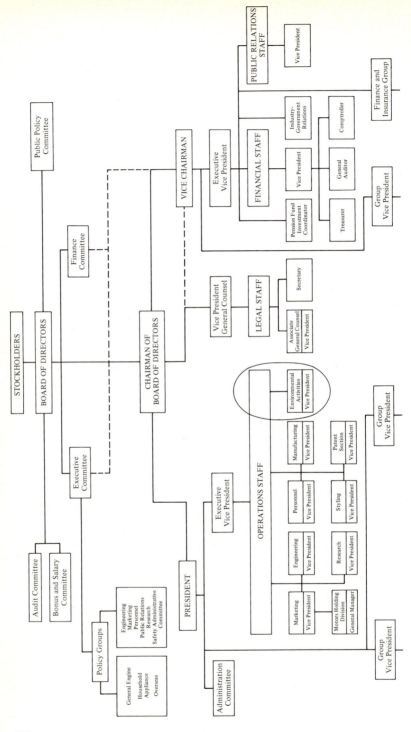

STOCKHOLDERS

BOARD OF DIRECTORS

Public Policy Committee

Audit Committee

Bonus and Salary Committee

Finance Committee

Executive Committee

CHAIRMAN OF BOARD OF DIRECTORS

VICE CHAIRMAN

Executive Vice President

PUBLIC RELATIONS STAFF

Vice President

FINANCIAL STAFF

Industry-Government Relations

Vice President

Comptroller

Pension Fund Investment Coordinator

General Auditor

Treasurer

Group Vice President

Finance and Insurance Group

Vice President General Counsel

LEGAL STAFF

Secretary

Associate General Counsel Vice President

Environmental Activities Vice President

Policy Groups

Engineering
Marketing
Personnel
Public Relations
Research
Safety Administrative Committee

General Engine
Household
Appliance
Overseas

PRESIDENT

Administration Committee

Executive Vice President

OPERATIONS STAFF

Manufacturing Vice President

Patent Section Vice President

Personnel Vice President

Styling Vice President

Engineering Vice President

Research Vice President

Marketing Vice President

Motors Holding Division General Manager

Group Vice President

Group Vice President

386

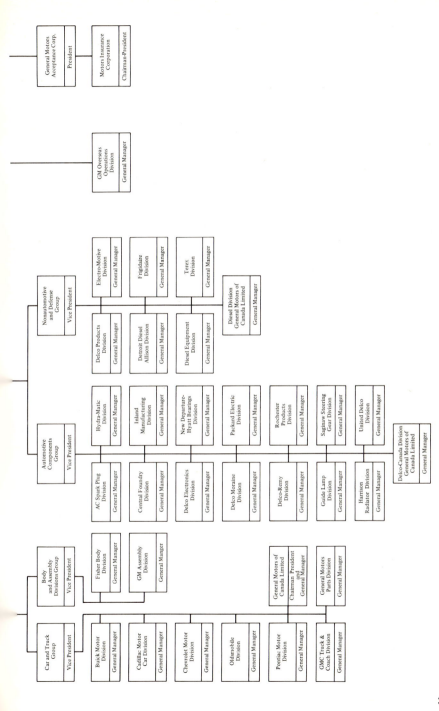

Figure 19-6 Organization chart for General Motors Corporation.

387

a significant increase in citizen action groups in recent years. There are estimated to be over 3,100 citizen environmental organizations active in the United States, not including civic, church, or school groups. They vary greatly in size and activity, but most appear to be concerned with antipollution action programs and public information, with legislative and law enforcement activities not far behind. Water pollution leads in citizen concern, followed by solid waste, air pollution, land use, and conservation of natural areas.

In addition, local ad hoc groups frequently form to combat some new development perceived as environmental deterioration; perhaps a new industrial plant site, smoke emissions, thermal pollution, noise, or rezoning for dense occupancy will trigger a community coalition to stop such projects. Formerly, such groups have had limited success in the face of money in the hands of developers and an expansive frame of mind by politicians and public policy. More recently, the ecological concerns of the general public have brought together coalitions of environmental groups who have had more muscle to influence administrative decisions. For example, the Michigan Steelhead and Salmon Fisherman's Association and the Lake Michigan Federation, were joined by the Thermal Environment Must be Protected and the Sierra Clubs to challenge the issuance of an operating permit by the Atomic Energy Commission for a nuclear plant to prevent thermal and radioactive discharges into Lake Michigan.

The five largest national environmental organizations, the National Wildlife Federation, The National Audubon Society, the Sierra Club, the Izaak Walton League, and the Wilderness Society, have increased almost one-third in membership during 1971. In addition to these traditional conservationist groups, new types of groups are coming into being, like the Environmental Defense Fund which institutes citizen suits on significant ecological issues.

Environmental issues have also made strong showings at the polls. Water and sewer bond issues succeeded in elections for 90 percent of the dollar volume proposed compared to 60 percent for other bond issues. Only two major referenda were defeated in 1970, one in California on the use of gasoline taxes for mass transit, the other in Washington to ban nonreturnable beverage containers. In each case the defeat is attributed to massive political campaigns financed by industry associations.

On the whole, the American citizen is becoming better informed on the major pollution issues, is organizing, lobbying, and beginning to influence elections. In the process of influencing others, he may even manage to change himself.

INTERFACES AMONG THE MANY ORGANIZATIONS

We have reviewed a number of organizational entities, enough to begin wondering whether they have sufficient common purpose, or can be coordinated, to produce environmental betterment. Or will they work at cross-purposes to each other? Certainly the industrial and the citizen groups have worked partially at cross-purposes in the past. In addition to the organizations we have examined, there are many more including several hundred local governments and control districts which influence environmental action. Where do they stand? Sometimes they are agents of change trying to implement state and federal programs. Sometimes they represent the status quo and are obstacles to change. For example, the Environmental Protection Agency has encountered considerable difficulty in encouraging state and local plans which will be effective enough to meet the air quality standards for 1972. At least in some cases, the reason is that air pollution districts, local government, or state agencies are sufficiently attuned to automobile users and suppliers so that they do not really want an effective air pollution plan which entails any cost or change in transportation patterns. Thus control plans are easily dismissed by saying they cannot be done in so short a time.

With these examples of polluters versus antipolluters, or other examples such as economic growth versus zero population growth advocates, the question arises whether these several organizations will produce some positive environmental improvement or cancel each other out? This is an administrative problem in social coordination involving the effective interfaces among diverse organizational groups.

Organizational interfaces are usually coordinated in society by a common philosophy, mission, or homogeneous set of goals. Whether this process is called "the social drill" as Toynbee termed it, acculturation, socialization, or nationalism, the result is similar—a kind of like-mindedness about personal and institutional endeavors. This like-mindedness makes possible legal, exchange, and social mechanisms which enable people to act in concert more by custom than by premeditation and enforcement. The like-mindedness of Americans for three centuries has been a common purpose in seeking individual self-determination, rising living standards, economic development, security, a market economy, and representative republican form of government. Since most accepted and few questioned these goals, until recently, the United States society could act in concert, with maximum reliance in custom, minimum enforcement, and still realize the expectations of most citizens.

But expectations change, and now the younger population especially shows more interest in peace, equality, individuation (nonconformity), and environmental quality than in the old value scheme. American society has had little experience in shifting its value schemes in its 300-year history, only perhaps over slavery during the Civil War, and over economic security during the Depression—both periods were marked by turmoil and violence.

A change in value schemes would be facilitated if there were a regular and responsive social choice merchanism. But we have seen, in Chapter 18, that our traditional social choice mechanisms are relatively inaccessible and infrequent. The result is that, if there is to be an accommodation to new goals, it is more likely to come about by administrative means rather than by social choice making. This raises the question whether administrative organizations can be devised which will enable diverse interest groups to interface with each other on at least a modicum of goals, like individuation, equality, and environmental quality. This question is a subject to be explored in the next chapter. Meantime, one can say that numerous new environmental organizations have come into being, and they need to interface with each other.

SUMMARY

The public policy to evaluate impact on the environment of both government and private actions has resulted in new administrative organizations to implement legislation. The Council on Environmental Quality reviews all new federal programs for their ecological effects and develops policy with respect to improving environmental quality. The Environmental Protection Agency performs the control functions of setting quality standards and regulating compliance by a variety of means, including monitoring, permits, requiring pollution control equipment, or legal action in the courts.

The state and local governments are, and will remain, crucial in the daily operational monitoring and control of environmental quality under federal standards. States have organized their environmental agencies variously to carry out this responsibility. The four most common forms of state environmental organization are: a consolidation of environmental management activity, land-use control commissions, establishment of a statewide solid and liquid waste management service, or use of the state courts for environmental rulings.

The form which state and local organizations take depends partly on the nature of various interest groups and political pressures and partly on pragmatic results of recent experience. The main environmental constituencies are the traditional conservationists, the public health group, the "new" environmentalists, and organizations representing polluters. In effect, the conflicting interests among these pressure groups become embodied in state environmental organization structure and raise questions about resolution of the public interest. These resulting pressures are sufficiently disparate so that questions emerge about the changing role of branches and levels of government.

The response to environmental quality standards has caused industry to reorganize somewhat to adapt to environmental impact analysis and to install pollution control equipment. Generally the engineering departments have assumed a major environmental role, but some special new departments have been formed; and, in any case, top executives report increasing involvement in environmental decisions.

Finally, a large number of both new and old citizens organizations are participating in environmental activity, generally by presenting their views at administrative hearings or in legal proceedings. Altogether the spectrum of participation and interaction among the many groups has now become large enough to raise questions about how the various views can be reconciled. The two most likely methods for such interface are through improvements in social choice making or in the administrative machinery for coordination.

DISCUSSION QUESTIONS

1 What is your assessment of the administrative effectiveness of the Council on Environmental Quality, the Environmental Protection Agency, and the proposed Department of Natural Resources? Or put another way, since environmental problems eventually affect everything, how do you think the federal government should be organized?
2 What is your judgment of the outcome of the issues described by Haskell and Price?
3 How does the environmental organization of your state fit into the four general types of state organizations?
4 How do you think the nation will arrive at a common mission or purpose in environmental quality, in view of the many organizations and pressures involved in the issues?

PROBLEM

In your own community or state, identify a specific environmental issue and try to categorize the parties involved as to their organizational structure, and secondly as to whether they are conservationist, public health, new environmentalist, or polluter groups. How would you assess the pressures and outcome of the issue, given the organizational relations you have described?

Chapter 20

The Interface of Environmental Organizations

New management organizations have come into being, as we saw in the last chapter, to deal with new goals in the environment. Changes in goals and values are attended by conflicting interest groups in and among organizations. The job of the administrator is to bring these conflicting organizations and goals into some resolution or interface.

The newly emerging social goals of peace, equality, individuation, and environmental quality go to the very core of everyone's life style. One need only review the wide-ranging implications of Section Three to realize that environmental quality alone will shift our whole decision structure, to say nothing of the ultimate purport of nonviolence, equal rights, and individuation which are beyond the province of this book. But just to raise the question for a moment, what kind of society will there be if individuation and nonconformity replace our past reliance on the social drill? Nonconformity and social drill are antithetical. We cannot have both. If individuation and nonconformity prevail, then what takes the place of social drill as the glue which enables society to function with accord?

The answer, if there is an answer that works at all, is likely to be some form of administrative mechanism which enables diverse interest organizations to interface with each other at least on a modicum of goals—like nonviolence, equal rights, or environmental quality. So the social glue, which has been the realm of custom and drill, now becomes an administrative procedure. We will need to know how to organize and administer better and more responsively than ever before.

Are administrative theory and mechanics ready for such an undertaking? The answer is likely no; administrators are probably not knowledgeable enough to use decision processes in lieu of custom, any more than the human body can do without habit or the involuntary nervous system.

But what administration can do, with great effort and determination, is to create flexible enough organizations, and linkages among them, so that the social glue holds broad groups together, while individual habits and desires have greater play in ordinary affairs.

That, in essence, is the interface problem, and it exists primarily because of the evolutionary change from simple authoritarian organizations in past history to the more complex, technical, and free-form organizations today. One need only think of early military organizations compared to modern technostructure to apprehend the difference. Indeed, the review of historical organization types may provide some insight as to future environmental structures.

The topics to be discussed are:

1 Historical organization types
   a Military
   b Military general staff organization
   c Mercantile organizations
   d Early industrial organization
   e The technostructure model
   f The sociotechnical model
2 Ecological organizations of the future
3 Problems of managing the whole system
4 A holistic decision structure
5 The errors of conventional design—Air pollution example

HISTORICAL ORGANIZATION TYPES

Military

The structure of military organizations has not changed in essential details, except size, from Alexander's phalanxes to the Franco-Prussian War. Military organizations are basically single-purposed, authoritarian, and direct in line of command. The purpose is strategic, to defeat an enemy, which includes only a few subsets of goals like defense, interdiction, and tactical maneuvers. The goals being few and the purpose of crisis proportions to the society, the internal organization has no choices, cannot dissent, and is authoritarian in the extreme. Being authoritarian, the organization has one decision maker whose orders proceed verbatim down the chain of command. The military organization type still persists in field armies and looks essentially like Figure 20-1.

The line of communication in military organizations is essentially one way by reason of its authoritarian premise; but, even if it were not, the troops would have difficulty setting up two-way communication under the weight of the administrative hierarchy.

Military General Staff Organization

With the disappearance of cavalry and the coming of armored firepower, the technology of war changed, making necessary specialists who knew

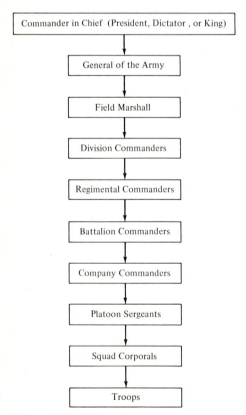

Figure 20-1 Military line organization.

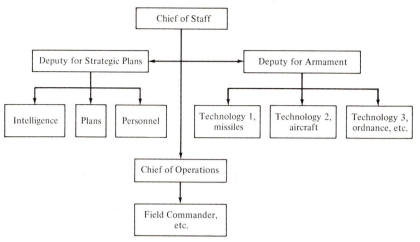

Figure 20-2 Military general staff organization.

the technologies of explosives, ordinance, tanks, and gunsights, also eventually of aircraft, electronics, computers, and missiles. Around the turn of the century the Germans recognized the need for incorporating technology and specialists into military organizations and created the German General Staff, which all nations have since followed and elaborated as technology advanced. A military line and staff organization may be portrayed schematically as in Figure 20-2.

Mercantile Organizations

Commercial organizations developed later than military organizations, but along somewhat similar lines because poor communications and transportation made local operators, like the field commander, the locus of risk responsibility and hence authority. Mercantile establishments were common in Italy (arising from trade in the Renaissance), in the German Hanseatic League, in the British textile trade, and among the American colonial merchant sea captains. The mercantile organization differed from the military mainly in specialized functions which represented its several purposes in moving goods in trade channels. A simplified schema might look like Figure 20-3.

Early Industrial Organization

In early industrial organization, production was the most demanding art and therefore became the chain of command. Early industry had single or few products, was high in production and market risks, and, for that reason, was authoritarian. As a result, early industrial organization bor-

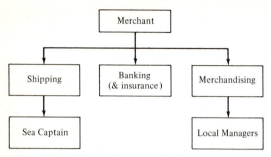

Figure 20-3   Mercantile organization.

rowed heavily from the military line and staff, as well as from mercantile organization. Figure 20-4 represents an early industrial organization chart.

In the 1920s, Du Pont and General Motors began to divisionalize their production operations as they became larger in size. This led to the decentralization movement throughout American industry, which became especially widespread in the 1950s. The General Motors Organization chart shown early in Chapter 19 may be viewed as the prototype of the large, modern production corporation.

The Technostructure Model

As science and technology began to change more and more rapidly following World War II, industry became less oriented toward mass production (à la General Motors) and more oriented toward developing a technology (viz., IBM). The technical companies became more multipurposed, pursuing whatever products and services in which they had a competitive advantage in the state of the art. This meant that pushing the

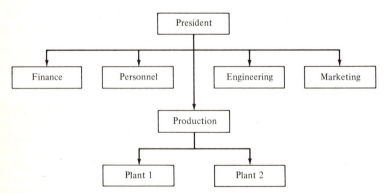

Figure 20-4   Early industrial organization.

frontiers of knowledge and the state of the art became a prime mission of the business. To organize for such technological progressions, companies had to strengthen their research and organize around their technologies. Products and services then became "programs" carved out of the technology by a matrix organization, on the assumption that the technology life would be longer than the life of its derivative products. The organization of a technical company might appear as in Figure 20-5.

The Sociotechnical Model

Increasingly in recent years attempts have been made to bring higher technologies to bear on social problems, particularly in areas like health care, welfare information systems, transportation networks, law enforcement, or solid waste management. Organizationally this means the enterprise must have an outward-looking focus on social issues as well as

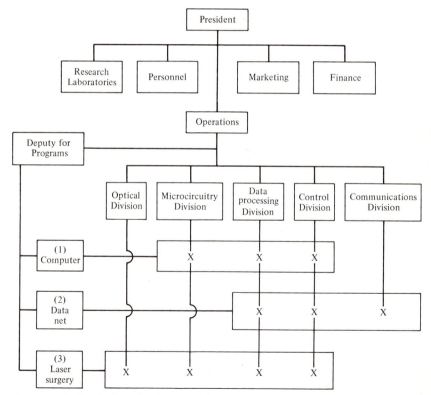

Figure 20-5 The technostructure model.

an inward-looking focus on technologies. Historically, organizations have been inward looking, concentrating on their few purposes or technologies and finding their niche in a limited variety of social applications.

As companies become outward looking and seek to apply interdisciplinary technologies to many broad social problems, the interactions and interfaces become more numerous. Greater flexibility is needed to accommodate differing social needs. Conventional organizational charts or ideas become less adequate. We might try to adapt the conventional organization chart to see which way the eyes are looking, inward or outward (see Figure 20-6).

In this portrayal of a sociotechnical organization, the marketing-application engineers are looking outward at social problems. The technology teams are looking intensively at specific scientific advancement. The rest of the organization is looking internally at the president (for decisions) and at everyone else for markets, technologies, products, and staff services.

Other authors, who apparently do not like the idea of everyone looking at everyone else in an organization, have portrayed the new sociotechnical structures differently. For example, Kast and Rosenzweig illustrate organization as a sociotechnical system in this way (Figure 20-7).[1]

Talcott Parsons advanced pioneering concepts on how technical requirements shape the character of organizations. He submits that there are three hierarchical levels in complex social structures: (1) the technical or production level, (2) the organizational or managerial level, and (3) the institutional or community level.[2]

The technical level performs the actual productive tasks in the organization. In business, it provides the scientific, technological, engineering, product, marketing, distribution, and financial knowledge which make the enterprise economically viable. Similarly, the doctor performs the production task in a hospital, the lawyers in a courtroom, the professors in a university, and the scientist in a laboratory. The technical core is the principal identity of the organization, its competitive or monopolizing power, and thus is protected and nurtured by the organization, in the same way that fighter ants protect their queen.

The managerial level serves and protects the technical core, assigns and coordinates its tasks, finds money and markets to keep it busy, and thus markets its productive effort. The organizational level is made up of

[1]Fremont E. Kast and James F. Rosenzweig, *Organization and Management, A Systems Approach,* McGraw-Hill Book Company, New York, 1970, p. 121.
[2]Talcott Parsons, *Structure and Process in Modern Societies,* The Free Press of Glencoe Inc., New York, 1960, pp. 60ff.

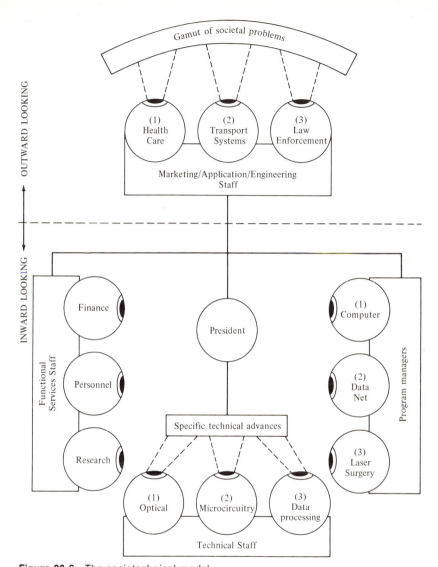

Figure 20-6 The sociotechnical model.

middle management and the information processes of top management.

The institutional level is concerned with relating the institution to its (social) environment. That is, it is concerned with legislation, public affairs, its own legal identity, lobbying, consumer wants and dissatisfactions, markets, money sources, community affairs, civic pride, and social

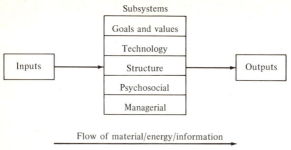

Subsystems

Figure 20-7

trends of the times. Usually the board of directors and chief executives are the principal participants at the institutional level.

Or perhaps more simply, the technical level is concerned with production, the organizational level with management, and the institutional level with politics. The technical core operates as a closed system with known inputs and identifiable outputs. Thus the technical level has an insulating boundary that enables it to function in a world of certainty, largely of its own illusion. The organizational level has some inkling of the real world, but is so busy translating it into the technical illusion that the boundary between fact and fiction is blurred. The institutional level lives in the real world of open systems and variable inputs, and thus is never really understood or trusted by the technical core, because institutional executives, while technically emphathetic, bring in real-world messages like—money is tight, customers do not like our products, or competition is killing us. These real-world messages disturb the illusion and tranquility of the technical core, making production difficult and creating perturbations in the process of technological extrapolation.

These boundary layers between the technical, organizational, and institutional levels have caused Petit to suggest an organizational chart of concentric circles (Figure 20-8).[3]

The term *environment* is used here in a social sense, rather than in an ecological context. Even so, the concept is clear that the more expansive the concentric circles become, the more outward looking the institution and the greater the outer-to-inner stress and adjustment.

ECOLOGICAL ORGANIZATIONS OF THE FUTURE

We have reviewed half-a-dozen evolutionary organizational types without any mention or recognition of ecology. The institutional level merely functions to adjust the organization to its societal context. Who adjusts

[3]Thomas A. Petit, "A Behavioral Theory of Management," *Academy of Management Journal,* December 1967, p. 346.

the organization to its ecological setting, that is, to environmental quality? Clearly some superdecision function needs to be added to atune the institution to environmental quality. We might expand the preceding organization structure in the manner shown in Figure 20-9.

Figure 20-9 attempts to portray the idea that every production unit, whether in government or business, has an ecological decision interface beyond the normal technical, organizational, and institutional levels. That is, if we are to live in the natural environment with some recognition of its constraints upon us to achieve environmental quality, then the decision process needs to include more than the technoeconomic, managerial, and sociopolitical issues. The decision process must encompass the interaction of human activity with the ecosystem as well.

Present organizational structures and executives are not well-adapted to make such ecological decisions, because they do not acquire enough information or possess enough knowledge about ecological interactions to make appropriate choices. Moreover, it is doubtful if they can acquire the necessary knowledge and information under present organizational concepts, unless the structures are expanded to include an ecological level with linkages to all organizations and to the ecosystem. This new form of organization would be very much more complex than any past administrative form, and would include most of the features contained in our six historical models. That is, an environmentally oriented organization becomes too complex to chart because it contains the following features:

1 An ecological level that possesses scientific insight into the natural process of the ecosystem, a quality monitoring information system, and linkages with all other organizations with environmental quality information. In other words, the ecological level comes close to being a global environmental monitoring and information system.

2 An institutional level capable of negotiating and adjusting its

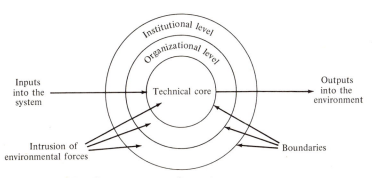

Figure 20-8 The firm as a composite system.

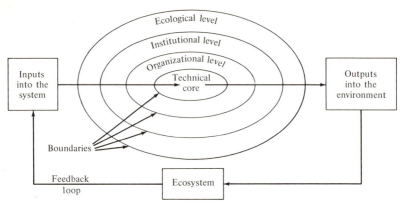

Figure 20-9 Interface of an organizational subsystem within the ecosystem.

production system to take into account the objectives of both the social and the natural environment.

3   An organizational level with sufficient flexibility and knowledge to make decisions based upon shadow prices and simulated markets to achieve ecological balance (see Section Three), as well as acting on profit motivation. Perhaps even more important, the managerial level must have the skill to translate the ecological interactions and costs to the technical core.

4   The technical core will have to be more interdisciplinary than ever before, to have social and natural scientists and environmentalists on its product development and production teams.

5   The organizational level will have to strengthen its marketing application engineering staffs appreciably to maintain an outward-looking adaptability to new societal problems and needs (Figure 20-6) as well as to discern the behavioral change potential of its customers. Since most environmental problems are basically behavioral at heart, the marketing staff will have to perceive what the behavioral response of users will be to changes in technical product and service which are necessary to meet ecological standards.

6   The managerial-technical levels will need much more complex matrix organizations (Figure 20-5) and interdisciplinary teams than ever before to solve the combined technological/shadow-pricing/consumer-behavioral changes which are essential for environmental quality.

7   The enterprise will need a functional line and staff organization to provide the essential services to the institution.

8   The enterprise will need a highly decentralized direct-line-of-command authority within small interdisciplinary production programs.

If one were to try to portray these relationships graphically in an organization chart, then the technical level would contain (1) an interdisciplinary matrix organization and (2) a line organization; the managerial level would contain (3) a functional organization and (4) a general staff; the institutional level would contain (5) a decentralized or divisional structure, (6) a marketing or applications planning structure to relate to new societal problems, and (7) a political liaison activity; and the ecological level would contain (8) an ecological research unit, and (9) an ecological information structure appropriately linked to other organizations. The latter information system linkage (item 9) might appear as a set of organizational interfaces (see Figure 20-10).

What this rather involved and planetary form of organization schematic is trying to convey is that all organizational units function within the content and constraint of the ecosystem. Because the ecosystem encompasses everything, any one organizational unit is in touch with only a part of it at any time. Moreover, all other organizations are in touch with part of the ecosystem all the time, drawing resources from it or discharging emissions into it along with their output. Therefore, the only way that any organization can develop the ecological information system needed to monitor the environment, or know what is happening to environmental quality, is to be in touch or linked with all other organizations. The information system linking one organization to another needs to transmit the following content: material withdrawals, energy use, process conversions, outputs, emissions, dispersions, and consequent effect on local environmental quality.

Each organizational unit will make use, moreover, of all the administrative analytical skills described in Section Three, that is, environmental impact matrices, materials balance, environmental dispersion, market simulation, marginal-cost analysis, benefit-cost analysis, and trade-off studies.

If all these organizational interfaces and analytical techniques make administration in the future more complicated than it is today, it is because management will, in fact, be more complex if we want to improve environmental quality. The problem is that the environment encompasses everything, and the result is that an administrator will need to know as much as he can about everything (all the processes) in the environment, if he is to make an intelligent decision about his own business or behavior.

PROBLEMS OF MANAGING THE WHOLE SYSTEM

The need to know the whole design before making a decision on any part of it has been called the "ethics of the whole system."[4] That is, we cannot judge improvement of any individual part unless we have some

---

[4]C. West Churchman, *Challenge to Reason*, McGraw-Hill Book Company, New York., 1969, pp. 4 and 171ff.

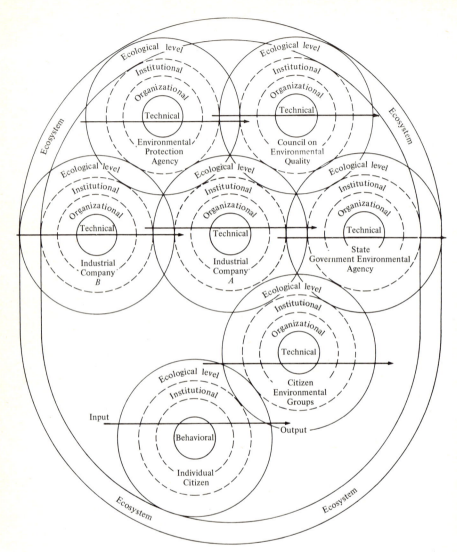

Figure 20-10 Schema of interface and linkage among environmental organizations.

understanding of the whole system in which the individual entity exists. To make judgments of quality, of what is better or worse, only on the basis of individual desires, results in suboptimization or segmentation; and it is precisely such suboptimization which constitutes ecological degradation. A firm wants to make a quick profit, or an individual wants speed and convenience, with the result that the firm suboptimizes on profit without regard for its effluents, or the individual suboptimizes on speed without regard for air pollution. The choice of how much profit and how much speed, or what product and what service, can only be made in the light of its effect on the ecosystem. To improve the quality of the ecosystem, then, we must refrain from making segmented and suboptimal decisions.

An environmental administrator, who seeks to avoid segmented decisions and tries instead to make decisions on individual parts consistent with the design of the whole system, will find himself in deep philosophical difficulties. The problem is essentially, how can one (the decision maker) know what is "right" or "better" in the context of the whole system (the ecosystem)? The decision maker would first need to know the purpose of the ecosystem; and secondly, he would need to be omniscient about all its parts and processes. In the absence of this, any decision he makes is suboptimal. His problem then is to make as systematic and holistic a decision as he can but, recognizing himself to be something less than omniscient, to find a "reference" against which to compare his decision. In other words, he has to inquire into the nature of the system with which he is dealing. Where can he find that reference in his inquiry?

Leibniz and other philosophical designers of the seventeenth century claimed that an inquiring system needed some guarantor—a God—in the management of its affairs, else control and stability of the system is impossible. The guarantee needs to be very basic—for example, that the laws of physics will continue to work in the future as they have in the past. The physicist does not guarantee the workings of physical laws; he only observes them. The "system" (universe) needs a guarantee that the observable will persist, whether in the physical, natural, or social sciences. In short, a decision process requires certainty somewhere in the system design, or else one cannot control (i.e., predict) the effects of a decision with respect to any part of the design.

While the Leibniz argument about the need for a guarantor in an inquiring system has never been successfully refuted by philosophical argument, the problem was disposed of by ignoring the issue. It is precisely because the whole system was ignored that we have the current environmental crisis. In contemporary philosophy, there is no guarantor, though we often act as though science were. Yet science is incapable of generating an adequate basis for management decisions, because science does not distinguish between good and bad, and thus has no measure of progress or quality.

Yet we must have some measure of progress and quality if we are to make decisions which affect the whole system, or judge environmental improvement. Where are we to find that measure?

A pragmatic way to perceive the whole system design is through public participation, by informing the public and ascertaining their social choices. Individual officials or executives cannot see the whole system because they are not the whole system. The whole system is all the people and how they behave relative to the ecosystem, and the only ultimate secular reference is how they perceive the quality of their environment in the light of their own behavior. This behavior and perception of the whole system would be facilitated by the ecological organization interfaces, discussed in the previous section, because the administrative relations and information system would organize knowledge of all the behavioral parts and processes.

The perception of the whole is then necessary to measure progress, which, applied to the ecosystem, means how to determine environmental quality. Philosophy answers that there are two basic approaches to determine the "ethics of the whole system," one is to re-create certainty, which we have been timorous about doing in recent years, and the other is to submit environmental quality issues to evaluation and critique through public discourse. If we want to improve the environment, if we want to see the system whole, if we want to create the reference which makes environmental decision making possible, if we want control and stability within an environmental administrative system, then there is no obvious alternative but to find some appropriate way for broad public evaluation and choice on issues of environmental quality.

A HOLISTIC DECISION STRUCTURE

Let us assume, for the moment, that we have solved the problems of (1) ecological organization interfaces, and (2) perception of the design of the whole system, along the lines of preceding sections. The next order of business, then, is to consider a holistic decision structure by which to link the organizations and goals and to consider what elements the decision structure must contain to relate it, in turn, to the environment. First, the decision process in environmental cases is vastly more complex than in normal business or governmental policy matters because environmental quality is multidimensional; it covers (1) ecological processes and standards, (2) human perceptions of an interaction with the environment, and (3) economic utility and disutility of materials drawn from the environment. Normal business decisions concern themselves with only one of these elements, economics. Governmental decisions also depend mainly on economic criteria plus, occasionally, human perceptions about vital issues. None of the traditional decision processes try to encompass all three dimensions. However, we need to define and extrapolate from present business and government decisions to build toward an environmental decision model.

A schematic outline of a holistic decision structure would include the following elements:

1   Human values to determine whether a problem exists, or whether there is need for a decision. That is, when external events deviate sufficiently from human expectation, a problem exists and a decision is required to improve the existing state.

2   Problems to be solved by missions, or a set of purposive acts, which are designed to adjust the existing state of events to a more desired state which considers the interactions of the whole system.

3   Mission analysis to explore what is the most ideal holistic state which can be conceived and then establishes some bounds or constraints on the problem to arrive at feasible alternatives in light of time, knowledge, and resources.

4   A feasible mission or design target to be performed by evaluation of work functions, which identifies the functional causes of the present state, and then alters the performance of these work functions to arrive at the feasible desired state.

5   The change in functional performance specifications to be approached by examining alternative sets of technical and cost possibilities.

6   A workable decision to be selected by choosing among the technical-cost alternatives, through a series of trade-off choices, that one which yields the largest gain in performance for an acceptable cost. This becomes the mission goal.

7   The chosen alternative to be developed into detailed design decisions (i.e., performance changes and implementation events) which are tested in progress for functional performance against the standards provided by the mission goal. Achieving the mission goal, by definition, means solving the problem satisfactorily.

8   The decision to be put into effect, with some control or informational feedback to see if it works, that is, solves the problem.

In business decisions, the value judgments are so routinized by cultural norms that the decision process is highly truncated and starts at step 5 with the examination of technical and cost alternatives. That is to say, the profit goal instilled in the executive has so many value judgments and missions subsumed into it that he really does not have to think of the full implications of what he is doing. If profit deviates from human expectation, the obvious decision is to change the technology or cost structure so as to make a gain in profit performance. He then implements this alternative and installs a control system to see that it works.

An engineering decision is somewhat more complicated than a

business decision because it must start at step 4 and analyze the work functions which cause the existing state to deviate from a standard—that is, to go off an existing target or what is normally expected of profit or product performance. Because engineers frequently begin their analysis by examining the existing system, they are attuned to improving existing designs. That is, they seek to make better cars, better televisions, better houses, or more profit; all are certainly laudable endeavors. The result, however, is a methodology which is highly analytical; that is, analytical in the sense of probing deeply into alternative technical solutions without too much attention to what the problem really is in the first place. This analytical method, while highly effective in extrapolating technical improvements in an existing system, can lead to what has been called "the errors of conventional design."[5] Errors of conventional design can lead to monumental mistakes which amount to solving the wrong problem. Much of our environmental difficulties are caused by these monumental mistakes in solving the wrong problem. We will shortly consider an air pollution example to illustrate an error of conventional design. In the meantime, however, let us complete our brief inventory of decision processes by examining governmental decisions.

Governmental decisions usually are political and value-oriented. Thus they start with step 1 in the decision process outlined above; but then they usually skip the mission analysis (steps 2 and 3) for lack of information, time, or understanding and go on, like engineers and businessmen, to steps 4 and 5, the examination of technical functions, costs, and alternatives. That is, government decisions are highly traditional, founded on voting blocks, which means on the existing state of art and society. The consequence is that political policy is the compromised adjustment of the existing system to try to make it a little better. The governmental decision process seldom asks the question, "What might be?" but only, "How can things be a little better?" That distinction in questions may seem trivial, but in terms of framing a problem definition, it makes an enormous difference.

The question, "How can things be made better?" translates into such issues as, how can water quality be improved; how can wildlife management improve the deer population; how can air pollution be abated; how can employment be increased; how can inflation be checked; how can we make multiple uses of present river basins or idle lands? These may seem like good questions but they subsume in them all the existing practices of industry, art, society, and present individual behavior. And when one has subsumed all that, there is very little room indeed for change, except for upgrading of minutiae.

[5]Gerald Nadler, *Work Design, A Systems Concept*, Richard D. Irwin, Inc., Homewood, Ill., 1970, pp. 488-500.

The other question of what might be translates into such issues as: What might be the use of water that achieves the greatest human and ecological balance; what might be the environment in which the deer population would achieve its natural climax in various ecosystems; what might be the way we meet our transportation needs in an atmosphere of clean air; what might be the incentives to productive institutions which would utilize all human skills of whatever proficiency; what might be the exchange system which would equate the level of production with the means of payment; what might be the most prolific ecosystem of a river basin from a species population view?

The first set of questions on how can things be made a little better leads to the errors of conventional design. The second set of questions on what might be leads to mission analysis and the full exercise of the eight steps in the decision process outlined above. Through value judgments and mission analysis the full range of new human needs and ecological impacts is capable of being explored. In contrast, traditional decision processes in business, technology, and government, usually result in amelioration, the "quick-fix" on the existing state. The reason is that many people see incremental change as a more practical approach than total system change.

THE ERRORS OF CONVENTIONAL DESIGN—AIR POLLUTION EXAMPLE

In air pollution we can say that a problem exists. The public has, let us assume, a value scheme which presumes that people want to be healthy. The expectation then is that the environment and air should be clean enough not to present damaging health effects. The actual condition of the air is that it regularly contains pollutants in excess of the air quality standards set by government based on the desirable level to avoid adverse health effects. In Eastern cities, the concentrations of particulates and sulfur dioxide exceed air quality standards, and in Western cities the oxidants exceed the standards manyfold. Therefore, we can say that air quality does not meet human expectation, and there is need for a decision because a problem exists.

What should the decision be? The government decision process applied to this issue has been to examine the functional causes of air pollution which are primarily from automobiles and secondarily from stationary power sources. The work functions which cause these air pollution emissions are the transforming of fossil fuel energy into personal motive power and into electricity. Next then, we examine the work functions of an automobile as the source of the personal motive power. These include the internal combustion engine, the power train, the wheels, the carriage body, the highway network, the gasoline fuels, and the automotive mechanical services to keep the cars going. Of these work functions, then, where is the source of polluting emissions? Largely in the internal combustion process, because all the fuel is not burned, and also in the composition of the fuel itself. Then the decision is to change the performance of the internal combustion engine and the composition of gasoline fuels to reduce the amount of emissions and thus improve the quality of the air.

Now that we know the major functional causes of air pollution, and have a design target to reduce the emissions from engine and fuel sources, we will next look at the technical and cost alternatives for redesign. Technical expertise suggests that removing the lead from gasoline, avoiding the volatile aromatic additives, and trying to keep the octane rating up by improving the cracking and distillation process is one alternative. The oil refiners estimate that this would cost at least $3 billion in capital investment in refineries and raise the price of gasoline one to three cents a gallon. The lowering of compression ratios in internal combustion engines and the use of catalytic afterburners to complete the combustion of unburned fuels before emission are other alternatives. Electronic timing and improved fuel injection are additional alternatives. The various costs of these alternatives range from perhaps $30 to $300 per car.

This set of information being at hand (in more detail of course), a government decision is now possible. In real life, the actual decision made by both federal and state governments has been to impose new car emission controls to cut the rate of emission of carbon monoxide, hydrocarbons, oxides of nitrogen, and particulates to one-tenth of their present levels. These decisions have become, in fact, the 1975 new car standards. Thus, the decision is made, and the problem is presumably solved.

But what problem was solved? The solution was to control emissions from new cars by 1975. Are new cars the whole problem? We started out saying that health effects and air quality were the problem. Engineering analysis led us to believe that engine design and fuel composition were the most identifiable functions contributing to the problem. Therefore, we solved the problem analytically and incrementally where we could most practically fix it and most easily influence it politically.

The analytical approach used in the air pollution case, which is a current real-life example, is an error in conventional design which amounts to solving the wrong problem. First, the automobile manufacturers say they cannot meet the 1975 car standards. Secondly, if they met the 1975 standards, the emissions would be reduced on less than 10 percent of the cars on the road, and all the old cars would continue to pollute the air at the same rate they always have. Thirdly, even if the best available equipment were put on used cars as well as new cars, and if everything worked as well as technically projected (an unlikely probability). then the amount of air pollution in 1985 would still be 3 to 4 times greater than the air quality standard. So our decision will result in air pollution fifteen years hence only slightly better than today, if at all. If that is our best decision, it was really no solution. What went wrong?

The environmental administrators making the air pollution decisions did not have a holistic decision structure. They used the conventional governmental, technical, business decision methodology without realizing that it had grave omissions from a social and environmental point of view. The environmental administrators skipped over the mission analysis (steps 2 and 3). They forgot to ask themselves about the whole system and what an ideal state might be?

Suppose we ask the question, what might be? Then we will see if we are led to the same design target as the government finally arrived upon.

What might be to bring air quality down to a level of 0.08 ppm of oxidants as one of the standards which the government says will avoid adverse health effects? We know that new car controls and redesign will not do it, nor will control equipment on used cars, because scientific study indicates that, even if every technical alternative worked out according to its best-estimated performance, air pollution would still exceed air quality standards threefold or fourfold.

Let us make the daring assumption, for the moment, that human beings do value their health more than their power-convenience preferences as expressed in driving an individual automobile for all their commuting and shopping needs. At least, let us assume this long enough to figure out another possible alternative and give the public a choice. Suppose we also admit that the exact health hazard and damage is unknown, so there is an uncertainty and risk factor whether as stringent an air quality standard as 0.08 ppm of oxidants is, in reality, the real borderline between potential health hazard and safety. Maybe the standards could be 0.15 ppm or maybe it should be 0.03 ppm. We only know that the best estimate of scientific-medical teams was that 0.08 ppm should be an appropriate standard. Our mission goal is therefore, to achieve no more than 0.08 ppm of oxidants at peak concentrations for one hour. Some plausible alternatives are:

1   New and used car emission-control equipment
2   Regular inspection of new and used car emissions for all cars on the road
3   Incentives or enforcement of car pooling for commuters
4   Closing of main freeways and thoroughfares to automobile pas-

senger traffic when pollution exceeds air quality standards, and implement and improvise rapid transit systems of buses using freeway lanes

5 Beginning the design and construction of mass transit systems to avoid individual car use

6 Beginning the redesign of cities to avoid urban sprawl and minimize urban transportation requirements by compact, vertical cities in which people live closer to work and shopping

7 Changing the incentives on land speculation and industrial concentration so the population becomes more thinly distributed across all the land in the United States, as it used to be under a more agricultural society, that is, re-create industry in small towns

Among these potential alternatives of what might be, only the first one has actually been examined carefully, and since it really will not work to solve the problem anyway, it is basically a nondecision.

The second alternative has the potential of reducing all emissions by 50 percent relatively quickly, but it would require all motorists to keep their cars tuned, to install emission control equipment, and to spend several dollars plus several hours twice a year having their car inspected and adjusted. Politicians are apprehensive about discommoding millions of drivers (millions of votes) that much, on the assumption that drivers love their cars better than their health, which may indeed by true. However, an argument can also be made that maybe the drivers (voters) ought to have the factual alternative and choice themselves.

The third alternative could potentially reduce air pollution immediately by 60 to 80 percent, by requiring all commuters to ride four or five to a car instead of alone. The actual reduction in emissions would also depend on how noncommuter traffic is regulated. Still there is no technical or cost-alternative as effective as this one. A reduction of 80 percent in emissions for *all cars* is *not* now a technical possibility, but reducing emissions by reducing trips 80 percent is quite feasible, if people will stand for that much regimentation for the sake of their own health and pocketbooks. Car pooling would also reduce transportation costs by close to 80 percent, require no new capital equipment, reduce the need for highway expansion, enable the gas tax to be converted to urban redesign or transit—the sort of things that the highway lobby would not want. But, is anyone willing to wait for ten or fifteen minutes a day for his car pool? The politicians think not, and again they may be right. But what if the voter knew the costs and health effects of his choice?

The third alternative would also reduce air pollution by 80 or 90 percent, at modest cost; and the fourth could make a still larger reduction in pollution at a somewhat greater cost.

The sixth solution is a long-range one which may not cost any more than the future investments which will be made anyway to meet the living needs of a growing population, and with appropriate planning there might be much less environmental pollution and greater convenience than we experience today.

The seventh alternative is also long term, but in some ways the simplest because much of the capital investment is already in place in the smaller town and cities which are now underpopulated and underutilized. In other words, a decentralization of industrial employment could go a long way to resolving many of our environmental problems, by redistributing the population across the land in low-density concentrations.

This review of the alternatives which might solve the air pollution problem (that is, actually improve air quality to the 0.08 ppm oxidant standard) obviously cannot arrive at a recommended decision at this stage. In the first place, the exact data for the technical-cost analysis of the alternatives are not available and would take a great deal of work. Secondly, the matter is one so entwined with the values and life style of the whole population that it could only be decided by a broad social choice of the preponderance of voters.

The first alternative is really the only one which can be made without affecting the general populace. The first alternative only affects three automobile manufacturers directly, and affects the general public indirectly when the price of new cars goes up to pay for the emission-control devices. The fact that the first alternative is a nonsolution is not nearly so important to a public official as the fact that it appears to be doing something, and it is politically feasible. All the other alternatives are politically unattractive because they imply altering the behavior of millions of voters. Meantime, real environmental choices have not been addressed in the absence of a holistic decision structure.

SUMMARY

We started out in this chapter to examine two things: (1) alternative ways to interface environmental organizations with differing goals and interests, and (2) methods of dealing with a managerial problem peculiar to environmental administration, namely, the design of the whole system.

As to the interface problem, the historical evolution of various organizational models includes: military line of command, line and general staff, functional mercantile organization, industrial line and staff, a technical matrix model, sociotechnical organization, and ecological interface organizations. These organizational structures become progressively more complex as they attempt to take a larger view of their place in the decision-making process, until at the ecological level they try to take a holistic view of the entire environment.

The peculiar managerial problem in environmental administration is seeing the whole system, that is, seeing how one's own decisions affect the many interactions of the ecosystem. A holistic decision structure would include: identifying problems and goals from human expectations and values, viewing the problems in terms of what might be a more ideal whole state, using a mission analysis to describe the ideal state in terms of constraints and alternatives, and identifying the work functions needed to realize the performance specifications. From this overview of what might be, the decision process proceeds traditionally to choose among technical alternatives and costs, detailed design, and control over implementation. The traditional decision process, which omits the holistic overview, is subject to errors of conventional design, that is, solving the wrong problem. As an example, the analytic and incremental approach to air pollution problems has led to reliance on a new car emission control program, which, though politically feasible, is likely to leave pollutant concentrations 3 to 4 times the government's air quality standard over the next fifteen years.

Generally, one may conclude that solution to environmental problems will require a considerably different form of organization as well as a new and holistic decision structure. The realization of these managerial changes will strain the administrative art, but the possibilities are there, and environmental quality depends upon it.

DISCUSSION QUESTIONS

1 How would you describe existing organizations with which you are familiar (give cases), and compare them to historical types? What determines the type and configuration of organization in each case?
2 Suppose you contemplated starting a new business to manufacture air monitoring instruments, how would you organize your company internally and how would you interface with all other ecological organizations?
3 How would you go about applying a holistic decision structure to the proposed air monitoring instrument business? That is, what is a holistic decision structure, in this case, and how does it differ from traditional business decisions?
4 Think of some decisions which you regarded as mistakes and ask the questions—Were there errors of conventional design? If so, where and how did the error occur?

PROBLEM

Select a business or government unit whose decisions affect the environment, (i.e. the air monitoring instrument business) and draw an organization chart reflecting all its internal and external interfaces which you can portray, using elements from Figures 20-5 through 20-10.

Chapter 21

Environmental
Mission Analysis

The critical determinant for the environmental administrator, in making a specific ecological decision, is his perception of the design of the whole system. To the extent that he correctly perceives the purpose and state of the ecosystem, he can make a decision which is consistent with the whole. Otherwise, he inadvertently makes a segmented or suboptimal decision, which has as its consequence environmental degradation. The ecological degradation which we experience today, its chemicalization, pollution, and hazard to biological health, is a consequence of segmented decision making without discerning the design or state of the whole ecosystem.

That is to say, the environmental administrator makes his decision in a context. That context is the purpose of the individual part, upon which the administrator proposes to act, within the design (purpose) of the whole system. It is this context which we shall call a "mission analysis." A mission analysis is a rationale and justification for the decision, showing its purport in contributing to the quality of the whole ecosystem. Therefore, the mission analysis must state some measure of quality or progress with respect to the ecosystem and a linkage which demonstrates how the individual decision contributes to that progress or quality.

A mission analysis is, then, a word model which describes the state of the system (ecosystem) today, the state in the future, the way a proposed decision will generate the future state, and why the future state is "better" than the present. In this sense, the mission analysis is the administrator's statement of what he believes to be the whole system. The mission analysis may be looked upon as the administrator's belief and justification of what constitutes better environmental quality. In another way, the mission analysis may be looked upon as a story, the story of how the administrator proposes to decide and act in the future. Or, in Jungian terms, it is the living of the administrator's legend, psychoanalyzing his own behavior with respect to the ecosystem and how he proposes to interact with it. Because a mission analysis has this character of a story or legend, it is often referred to as the "scenario," the setting of the scene and the script which tells what might be.

The nature of mission analysis and scenarios will be discussed according to the following outline:

1   Content of a mission analysis
2   The present scenario
3   An alternative mission analysis
4   A future environmental scenario.
5   A criterion for environmental quality
6   Operational principles
7   Measures of worth

CONTENT OF A MISSION ANALYSIS

In any new field, where social change is imminent, the rationale of decision making is perhaps more important than a specific decision, because the rationale is the mission analysis with which, by concurrence or controversy, a new life view is forged. A mission analysis is, then, a story of the future, or what might be, which people can critique, revise, or embrace as a means of behavioral adaptation and change. The content of a mission analysis usually contains:

1   A description of the present state of the system, which may also be called a definition of the problem. Since there are no problems without some normative judgments about what is better or worse, the mission analysis is also a preliminary statement of qualitative or ethical assumptions.
2   A description of the contingencies of the future, or alternatives of what may be.

3 A statement of criteria by which to evaluate the alternatives.

4 An evaluation of the alternatives against the criteria.

5 A selection of the "best" alternatives according to the criteria; that is, which approach provides the most ideal solution to the users or beneficiaries.

6 An assessment of the state of the art available to carry out the best alternatives, in other words, how feasible at what cost?

7. A definition of specific outputs and implementation plans to carry out the best alternatives.

8 A final summary statement of the worth of the proposed goals and decisions, which quantifies or epitomizes descriptively the criteria, the feasibility, the methodology, the benefits, costs, and overall worth of the proposal in the value scheme of the users.

While a mission analysis will usually include many or all of the eight elements above, the art of systems analysis and social change is new and developing, with the result that scenarios and mission analysis may vary considerably in format and content. Some scenarios may be expressed as mathematical models or in computer language, as contingency plans or potential technical requirements. The irreducible essence of scenarios is that they are concerned with (1) the criteria for evaluation of a decision, and (2) some objectives and alternatives.

THE PRESENT SCENARIO

The present scenario did not originate today but rather 100 or more years ago, with the takeoff of the industrial revolution in the Western world. In other words, we still operate under the preindustrial assumptions. Hence, the scenario reads of the past as well as of the present.

1 *State of the system as of 1870* The total population of the world is slightly over 1 billion people (circa 1870) and the doubling time of population is nearly 200 years. Over half the people in the United States and Europe live on farms, mostly subsistence farming with a small cash crop. The city population is largely unskilled labor, living in cold-water flats, several people to a room, with annual incomes a few hundred dollars per family. Public utilities consist of urban transit systems, horse-drawn or electric; street maintenance for those who walk or ride bicycles; urban water quality, generally satisfactory by low bacteria counts and pathogens; public baths for personal cleanliness; primary sewage treatment plants in large cities and latrines elsewhere; and some gas-lighting utilities in major urban centers. Public health is generally protected against epidemics and plague; average life expectancy is forty-five years; and major health problems are respiratory infections, industrial accidents, and malnutrition.

The need of the public is to improve its nutrition, to prevent crowding and exposure to respiratory infection, and to increase consumption goods, generally. The technology is available to increase production. Technology produces some problems, notably belching smoke, slag and refuse piles, and dangerous working conditions. Generally, however, there is still a large amount of open space away from the factories, and the working hazards are mainly mechanical against which the worker can protect himself by caution. On the whole, the public benefit of raising living standards to improve comfort, health, and individual development, by increasing production and technology, far outweighs the disadvantages (costs) of industrialization. Therefore, an appropriate social choice is to stimulate economic growth.

2   *State of the system as of 1970*   The contemporary version of the same scenario reads as follows: The total population of the world is 3.5 billion people, doubling every thirty-seven years. In the United States, two-thirds of the people live on less than 10 percent of the land; urbanization and urban densities continually increase. Farm population has dropped to less than 10 percent of the total. The urban population is largely skilled; live in suburban homes, several rooms per person; with an annual income of $12,000 per family. The exception is that about one-eight of the population is unskilled, unemployed, or elderly and lives on the poverty fringe.

Public utilities consist of aging mass transit systems almost useless; elaborate street and highway maintenance for the majority who drive their own cars; adequate palatable water quality; inadequate treatment plants for industrial and municipal sewage so that every major stream in the nation is polluted; and electric utilities which generate 8 percent more power each year for industrial production and home conveniences. Public health is generally free of major epidemics; average life expectancy is sixty-five years; and major health problems are environmental, resulting from exposure to toxic materials, noise, microwave radiation, and low-level pollutants, which contribute to elevated death rates from respiratory diseases.

The technology is available to increase production. Technology produces some problems, notably in environmental health. Open spaces near cities are disappearing, and it is difficult for most of the population to get away for long from the environment of industrial complexes, but the citizen can protect his health somewhat by limiting his environmental exposure. On the whole, however, the public has become accustomed to rising living standards, greater comfort, and easier working conditions. These economic advantages appear to outweigh the environmental disadvantages. Therefore, an appropriate social choice is to stimulate economic growth still more, so that the productivity gains may be used to ameliorate the environmental problems and the condition of those on the poverty fringe.

3   *Contingencies and alternatives of the future*   The future presents a variety of opportunities for choice—to increase technology and output,

to provide for greater individuation, to seek to improve environmental conditions. While there is some speculation in the scientific community that the golden age of science is past, there is still ample room for technological improvements, particularly in automated control systems, information handling, new materials development, medical care, weather modification, and communications. The result is that economic and technical growth can continue unabated, limited only by the availability of capital, energy, and environmental problems. The energy requirements can be met, at least for the interim, by nuclear power plants. This may create new environmental problems from radiation or thermal effects, and these may cause some degradation but are regarded as manageable.

The environmental problems can be dealt with generally by devoting a larger portion of the productivity gains to pollution controls. This raises some economic issues, particularly how to divide productivity gains among labor, pollution, and capital; control inflation; remain competitive with foreign labor; and make investment attractive enough to continue to create capital. However, these problems can be dealt with by greater governmental controls on prices and foreign exchange. The higher degree of internal and external regimentation, while regrettable, is preferable to foregoing the benefits of economic growth, with its rising consumption standards and pollution abatement potential. Most people are judged, by attribution of public leaders, to prefer economic growth even if individuation is sacrificed to some extent. The major alternatives of the future then are:

a Stimulate economic growth further by incentives for intensive technical and capital development, while holding inflation and side effects in check by increased government regulation over individuals and the economy.

b Maintain current encouragements to technical and capital development, using a larger portion of productivity gains for environmental improvement, and recognizing that the consequence may be inflation and loss of competitiveness vis-à-vis other nations, but there would be little change in personal freedoms or individuation.

c Encourage individuation and greater personal freedom of choice in work and self-development, by higher wages and government transfer payments to nonworkers and for cultural pursuits, within some reasonable constraint of a lowered economic growth rate and minimal environmental improvement.

4 *Statement of criteria* The criteria to evaluate the best alternatives will be: first, the measure of economic growth shall be the gains in production output per unit labor input in economic organizations measuring their effectiveness by profitability; secondly, the measure of regimentation versus individuation will be the relative votes received in elections by government representatives who espouse inflation-wage-price controls versus those who advocate larger transfer payments for welfare and environmental functions.

5 *Evaluation of alternatives against criteria* The criteria of economic growth as measured by productivity would favor alternative (*a*) over (*b*) and (*b*) over (*c*). The social choice on regimentation versus individuation is unknown and will become apparent only in future elections. A working hypothesis might be advanced, upon which most political candidates seem to be operating, that individuals will resist further regimentation but they will also resist lowering the economic growth rate.

6 *Selection of the best alternative* The "best" alternative, according to the two criteria, is 3*b*, because it attempts to maintain the current economic growth, while improving the environment and leaving personal freedom unchanged. The fact that this alternative may cause the United States to decline as a world power, relative to other nations, is regrettable and undoubtedly will stimulate resounding nationalistic oratory. But diminished international influence is a long-term effect, and as such is not part of the criteria, for the criteria show that the nation is interested in short-term benefits in the form of economic growth, individuation, and some environmental improvement. Future generations may worry about being a world power, or in the interim an election may inject that issue as a criterion, if the current generation becomes sufficiently concerned. The fact is that the United States is the leading world power; the loss of that status is speculative, to be worried about when it happens.

7 *Technical state of art and costs* The technical state of the art and future foreseeable technology are adequate to maintain productivity gains of 3 to 4 percent per year, with improvements likely in control automation, data handling, communications, and nuclear energy. With labor continuing to receive most of the productivity gains, and with environmental improvement costing something over 2 percent of gross national products per year, the ultimate costs of this scenario will be continued inflation and probably static profits. The resulting pressure on profit may impair the accumulation of capital and the willingness to invest domestically, in which case further economic growth becomes limited by the lack of capital. The slackening of economic growth would be accompanied by internal social difficulties, because productivity increases are largely in the manufacturing and construction areas, while most of the employment is in the services. The failure to improve the service efficiencies at the same rate as the rest of the economy will cause the burden of inflation to rest most heavily on the service employees, the aged, and the disadvantaged. Their failure to share in economic gains, plus the decline in the availability of services, would adversely affect the life quality of most of the population, causing social unrest. The real costs of this alternative, then, would be inflation, unequal distribution of productivity gains, and social unrest.

8 *Specific outputs and implementation plan* The specific outputs would be reflected in an extrapolation of the gross national product accounts into the future. The implementation plans are the present economic and budgetary plans of government and the business plans of industry.

9 *Worth of the proposed mission* The worth of this mission is found in its achievement of a reasonable economic growth rate, consistent with constraints caused by: (a) economic pressure groups, (b) the fact that technical innovations are mainly in hardware areas, and (c) minimal changes in individual attitudes. The benefits of the mission include gains to organized groups in the economy and some pollution abatement. The losses or costs in the system are largely due to: (a) inflation, (b) the uneven burden of costs upon service workers and disadvantaged, and (c) consequent social unrest. On the whole, however, growth in the economy continues to be the principal goal of most citizens, and, therefore, the social costs appear to be worth the economic gains obtainable.

AN ALTERNATIVE MISSION ANALYSIS

Perhaps the contemporary scenario is not altogether appealing, especially to those who do not share equally in the economic gains, who desire a higher order of environmental quality, or who prize individuation. The majority of service workers, aged, and disadvantaged do not share equally in economic gains during an inflationary period; and these represent a larger portion of the citizenry. The portion of citizenry that might desire a greater improvement in environmental quality is possibly a minority, mainly those with health problems, plus the new environmentalists. Those who seek individuation in preference to economic gains are mainly youth. By the process of elimination, then, we arrive at the estimate that the present scenario appeals mainly to the older, upper-middle-class population, who are perhaps stronger in their institutional influence than in sheer voting numbers. But, in any case, they are aging; and within ten to fifteen years new voting patterns, social preferences, and institutional chieftains will appear. They may pursue a different rationale. Let us examine an alternative mission analysis which may better fit those who seek relatively greater equality, environmental quality, and individuation.

This entire book is, in fact, an alternative mission analysis with respect to environmental quality. If we take the eight major elements which comprise the content of a mission analysis, discussed previously in this chapter, we may relate them to the content of this book. For example:

1 The description of the present state of the system is found in Chapters 1 through 5, in which the biological hazards from chemicalization and pollution of the environment are described, together with the historical origins of how the decision structure came to tolerate environmental degradation by suboptimizing on economic development.

2   A description of alternatives or contingencies of the future, or what might be, is given summarily in Chapter 6 and continued in Section Three. Chapters 7 through 9 also suggest an alternative based on return to the natural state. The general proposition is advanced that the quality of the environment can be affected for better or worse by the cost structure and incentives which pertain to common goods, which are now called "free" and therefore are unpriced in the market structure. It is the lack of pricing of these "external" or social costs which leads to overuse and environmental degradation. Some alternative means of perceiving, viewing, measuring, and pricing wastes are suggested, with the kind of behavior change which would have to accompany this social and environmental restructuring.

3   A statement of criteria on how to evaluate environmental decisions against a measure of worth is given in Chapters 16 through 18. Generally, the measure of worth suggested is the maintenance of ecological balance, which implies the optimization of diverse species populations, rather than the optimization of consumption goods for human beings. The optimization of diverse species populations is a biological objective, rather than an economic or technical one and, as such, has some corollary implications which are contrary to prevailing views. One corollary is that human population, and human demands on ecosystem resources, may need to be limited to provide living space for a balance of other species. A second is that human wastes cannot continue to be dumped indiscriminately into the ecosystem without biological damage to other species and ourselves. These are, in fact, drastic corollaries if one considers the social and behavior change which would ensue from their acceptance and realization. Since these are drastic changes in viewpoint, it is incumbent on their proposer to explicate their worth. The worth of diversity and balance in the ecosystem is based on the need to preserve our health and habitat. It is important to observe that this scenario has an evaluation criterion—viz; ecological balance—which is observable, measurable, quantifiable; and that this evaluation criterion has a view of its whole system (the ecosystem), which differs significantly from our contemporary perspective of the whole system as the technoeconomic system.

4   A methodology for evaluating the alternatives against the criteria is provided in Chapters 10 through 16. That is, the alternative decisions affecting environmental quality will be evaluated by materials balance, dispersion in the ecosystem, market simulation of environmental costs, marginal and opportunity costs, and trade-off analysis. In essence, the trade-off analysis inquires into the question of which organisms and species bear the sacrifice (cost) of a decision. Since the tradeoff seeks to achieve the largest biological gains with the least biological losses, the objective of ecological balance is maintained.

5 The selection of the best alternatives according to the criteria is described in Chapter 17. That is, the environmental impact analysis, which summarizes the evaluation methodology into the most feasible solution, is the means of selecting the best approach to satisfy the wants of users and beneficiaries.

6 The assessment of the state of the art to carry out the best alternative is the subject of the present section, Section Four, on implementation programs in environmental administration (along with Section Three which has provided the cost and technical assessments).

7 The definition of specific outputs and implementation plans to carry out the best alternative is dealt with in Chapters 22 and 23.

8 A final summary statement of the worth of the proposed goals and decisions is the concern of the present chapter. That is, here in this chapter we shall try to demonstrate that the final mission is to maintain ecological balance, and ecological balance is the best criterion for design of the whole system.

The entire book is arranged slightly differently than a mission analysis for purposes of presenting concepts and methodology. Also, the book is not a mission analysis in the sense of taking one specific problem and developing it consistently throughout each phase. For such a purpose, other books are available.[1] Rather, in this exposition, a variety of illustrations have been given in the several chapters to give some sense of the range of applications which are pertinent in ecological studies.

Nevertheless, the concept of a mission analysis, and what it is, should be apprehensible by a brief review of the book in the context of the eight elements of the mission analysis which have just been illustrated above. Indeed, one should be able to carry out a mission analysis, applying it to a specific envirommental problem, by following the methodologies set forth.

Let us assume, then, that enough has been said about mission analysis, what it is, and how one can go about applying it in real cases; and let us now try to make that application by writing a brief environmental scenario for the future. The scenario will be much abbreviated from the contents of the book, but it will serve to show how a word model becomes converted into an administrative program.

A FUTURE ENVIRONMENTAL SCENARIO

Let us play the role of "futurist" for the moment and assume the time is now the year 2000. A futurist, a professional from one of many interdisciplinary fields, thinks about the future and what its alternatives might be.

---

[1]See, for example, E. S. Quade and W. I. Boucher, *Systems Analysis and Policy Planning—Applications in Defense* (Rand McNally), Elsevier, N. Y., 1968.

In this speculation about the future a variety of scenarios have been developed, mainly dealing with economic or social alternatives. Many of these scenarios are quite elaborate and complete; and rather than repeat them here, we will merely make reference to them.[2] For the most part, the environmental scenario will subsume much of the economic and cultural projections found in the references. Our concern will be what is the state of the ecosystem. Any future scenario is speculative, and reflects merely one of many futures which are possible.

1   *The state of the system* In the year 2000, world population has now almost doubled since 1970, and there are 6 billion people. The population growth in the United States has been slower, from 205 million to 275 million; but the population is even more highly urbanized that it was with 75 percent of the people living on about 10 percent of the land. The city cores are badly decayed, old buildings and urban sprawl are general, except for high-rise new towns for the middle class on the urban outskirts. The poor are generally in the decayed buildings in the city core or at the far reaches of the urban area living in trailer-type units on otherwise unusable land. Municipalities have all built the best sewage disposal plants available, but the sprawl to the trailer parks and the aggravated industrial pollution have made all waterways unsafe for use, except with heavy chemical treatment. The trillion-dollar economy of 1970 has doubled to two trillion (at 1970 prices), and the doubling of production output has also doubled the wastes. Although industry spends $40 billion per year on waste treatment, the toxic, metalic, and material residuals create environmental health exposure problems, which limit the places to which one can venture, and the time of day for going out of doors. Public health studies show that morbidity and mortality rates are one-fourth higher for those who are continually exposed to the environment compared to those who live indoors in protected surroundings. Most parents require their children to remain indoors, except for special outings.

Electric power production has quadrupled since 1970. Low-sulfur fossil fuel supplies have been exhausted, and most urban areas have high sulfur dioxide exposures. Utilities have switched heavily to nuclear energy, which has proved to be relatively safe, with only one catastrophic accident, which made the land and water unusable over a 10-mile area. But the nuclear hazard has proved preferable to the air pollution from fossil fuels, and most plants are now nuclear.

The automobile has been significantly improved with the recent development of low-cost gas turbine engines, but there are so many cars

[2] Herman Kahn, and Anthony J. Wiener, *The Year 2000,* Macmillan Co., New York, 1967, especially Chap. 4; also, Kurt Baier and Nicholas Rescher, *Values and the Future,* Free Press, New York, 1969; also, "Toward the Year 2000", *Daedalus,* Journal of the American Academy of Arts and Sciences, Summer 1967, Cambridge, Mass.

on the road, and still many old internal combustion engines, that air pollution has worsened. New mass transit systems have been installed in most cities, and people prefer them to automobiles because freeways are almost impassable. However, the urban sprawl of past generations has created such unmanageable city layouts, that mass transit cannot reach all the urban areas with thinner population densities. The result is that many people still have to use cars; but their congestion and emission are so severe that all vehicular movement is regulated to force car pooling and to reduce trips to a minimum.

The population densities and restrictions on transportation have caused people, on the one hand, to turn more inward in their interests, but, on the other, to demand more of the immediate city environment. Green walking areas and large pedestrian plazas, surrounded by restaurants, entertainment, and cultural outlets are common in the new urban developments. The parental generation in leadership positions in most institutions, who themselves were once the flower children of 1970, are so exasperated with youth that they seek more compulsory regulation over their behavior. It is not that the youth are aggressive or lawless, rather, too passive. Their indolence is particularly objectional to parents and compulsory work laws are before legislatures.

The youth regard themselves as the sensate precursors of the twenty-first century. The youth are given to lying on air beds and talking for hours to friends on the television-telephone. Others amuse themselves by projecting their own mental images on large wall screens with the newly invented mentalvision, which is a personal data retrieval and display for creating experienced or fanciful imagery. Also, youth are much given to rediscovering handicrafts and ceremonials of the past, almost living in an earlier age, with much fascination over mysticism and antiquities. The youth have very little interest in work, and rather seldom go out, except for evening gaieties on large pedestrian plazas.

When chided for thier indolence, the young people reply that they have been confined to their homes so long, left to their own devices, because the environment was too hazardous for them to play in as children, that they have no interest in work, affairs, or cities about them. Work is for parents, who like to change things; but the environment is oppressive and unchangeable, so the sensate youth would rather live in their own mental world, enlivened with emotions and imaginations from friends and the past.

2 *Contingencies and alternatives of the future*   By the year 2000, in this speculative scenario, youth have backed out of the world, because it is unlivable, to do their living in speculation. Their health has been protected by keeping them in an artificial environment with technological toys to keep them occupied indoors, in isolation from polluted surroundings, and in a protected state which has encouraged hyperimagination. The parental generation, never much interested in material progress in the first place, have let the institutional momentum of technology and economic growth proceed, somewhat checked of course by inflation and the declining role of the United States in the world economy. The parental generation has been more concerned about social change, preventing war, a somewhat more equal distribution of income, and a large amount of leisure and hedonism for themselves. They believe in the pleasures of the present world, and they feel left out of their children's pleasures in another world. Their own preference would be to continue a moderately productive, pleasurable world; and they resent youth wanting something more ephemeral. Still, technology is advancing sufficiently so that productivity could be maintained with fewer working hours and mental imagery could, technologically, be a more widely used media for conveying symbolic meanings. Technology could also be used to improve the environment, if one were willing to disperse the population over the countryside, and install even more costly pollution equipment. The costs of relocation and of pollution control would probably be so heavy, however, that material consumption would be reduced by as much as 10 to 20 percent to accomplish it. This reduction might not seem so bad, if people had not become accustomed to it, because the average family income is now over $25,000 a year, twice what it was in 1970 at the same prices. Even so, a reduction would be difficult to take for those acclimated to the higher consumption levels. Still, the ennui of youth and the confining environment are distressing, and three major alternatives are considered plausible:

a To continue the moderate rate of economic growth and pollution abatement, and to continue the pleasurable life, until something worse happens or the future generations change the mission.

b To help the youth hasten their escape from the real world by turning technological resources even more completely to imaginary living.

c To take drastic steps to check the burgeoning population, decentralize economic and urban activity and distribute the population more evenly over the land, reduce the production of residuals, recognizing that useful output will decline as well, turn technology almost wholly to ecological improvement, and try to restore a more natural living style consonant with ecosystem.

3 *Statement of criteria* The present state of the system (year 2000) is derived from the past criteria to emphasize economic growth and individuation. Moderate economic growth has been achieved (from 1970 to 2000), but individuation, originally conceived as pleasurable pursuits, has gone awry, to the extreme of imaginary living. The parental generation feels deep concern for their children, and one antidote to imaginary living is to return to natural living. The return to a more natural living state

has a beneficial aspect—that is, ecological quality will improve so that the environment will be bearable again; and people will not have to avoid their surroundings.

These thoughts suggest three major criteria for judging the alternatives. First, the highest priority will be given to try to restore the diversity, balance, and biological health of the ecosystem as it used to be. Secondly, individuation is to be realized in the natural state as well as in the imaginary state. And thirdly, economic and technological activity are to be regarded as constraints, not goals, which means that they will be used to fulfill environmental quality and natural life styles, rather than consumption as a first priority.

4 *Evaluation of alternatives against criteria* The criteria will apply two main measures to the alternatives. One criterion is to optimize the distribution of species populations in the ecosystem. The alternative which maximizes species distribution may be presumed to achieve diversity, balance, and biological well-being; for, if it did not, species would be maldistributed and depleted in populations. The second measure is the amount of interaction which individuals, particularly youth, have with each other and the ecosystem in the natural state. The measures to be applied to technoeconomic decisions will be the net gains over costs of environmental quality improvement (i.e., species population and distribution), without any special regard for increasing either output or profit. In fact, the presumption is that economic indicators and living standards may decline somewhat, at least initially.

5 *Selection of the best alternative* By these measures, alternative *c* would appear to be preferred over *b* or *a*, subject, of course, to examination of the costs and effectiveness of implementation means. Alternative *a* is an unlikely option because it aggravates pollution and does not achieve ecological diversity and balance. Alternative *b* is unlikely because it aggravates imaginary living and deviates even farther from a natural life style than the sequestered lives of the year 2000. Therefore, *c* appears to be the most likely alternative, but we must examine its technical feasibility and cost.

6 *Technical state of the art and costs* The technical alternatives for achieving better ecological balance and diversity exist in the year 2000 as they did in 1970. The application of higher capitalization to emission and effluent control, along with industrial dispersal, and diminishing the growth rate are all plausible. The costs would be to devote all productivity gains to environmental improvement, and let economic status remain stationary or decline. Living standards might still be regarded as rising in a qualitative sense, by abatement of pollution and dispersal of living to more natural environments, even though the actual materials consumption might not increase further. The question is really whether living standards are to be regarded quantitatively in goods, or qualitatively in the diversity and balance of one's surroundings. By the latter measure, there would be no costs but only gains; by the former measure the costs would be the consumption goods foregone to improve the environment.

7 *Specific outputs and implementation plan* Implementation would include decentralization of industry, dispersion of population over wider land areas, improvement of transit and circulation with urban areas, reduction of energy requirements, setting rigorous environmental quality standards, and specification of pollution control equipment to be used in manufacturing. A hypothetical implementation plan for mass transit is given in Chapter 22.

8 *Worth of the proposed mission* The worth of this mission is found in its disaggregation of populations into smaller urban areas, which produce less residuals, and in providing opportunity for living more naturally in a diverse and balanced environment. The improvement in biological quality and health of the environment is its main contribution to higher living standards; and these are measurable in reduced toxicity, pollutants, and health damage effects. The worth of the mission is also measurable, more abstractly, by counting the diversity and balance of species populations, on the assumption that the range and numbers of species generally are an indicator of the human habitability of the earth. The final measure of worth is the diversity of human experience available to youth and adults, which can be enumerated in the frequency of natural as well as imaginary life activities. While technological products tend to enrich human experience and ease, they also tend to move the individual into a more abstract and imaginary world, bereft of hands-on contact with real things. The mission does not diminish these technological enrichments, but restores the individual, and his innate state of interactions with nature, which has progressively been denied him in a technical, urbanized society.

A CRITERION FOR ENVIRONMENTAL QUALITY

The criterion for environmental quality, proposed in the scenario and utilized for much of the analysis elsewhere in this book, is to maintain the ecosystem in a state of diversity, balance, and biological well-being.

Diversity in the environment means that the varieties of species, plant and animal, in every ecological regime should be optimized. Conversely, an extinction or decline in species populations would be a matter of concern, to be rectified if possible. The decline or extinction of species populations is symptomatic of Liebig's law of the minimum, that is, minimal nutrient, energy, or climatic conditions are not present. Hence, the law of the minimum is a natural biological standard to apply to the environment. The deficiencies in nutrient, energy, or natural cycles which cause species populations to decline are often man-made alterations in the nutrient or chemical cycles, in energy utilization, in thermal, air, or water pollution. Therefore, the simplest and most workable of all environmental standards is the law of the minimum which, when applied, means regarding all species as indicator species. If any of them decline in population or vigor, then a scientific inquiry can be made into man-made disturbances of natural cycles which caused aberrations in the minimal conditions to species survival. If the disturbance is man-induced, then means could be found to rectify the problem.

The maintenance of ecological balance is a corollary derived from the objective of diversity, because ecological balance is the means to diversity. Ecological balance refers particularly to balance in the nutrient cycle, which in turn represents the entire food chain from the tiny producer organism through the herbivores and carnivores. The food chain itself is regulated by the solar energy, hydrologic, and meteorologic cycles. Therefore, the condition of the food chain, as seen in diversity of species, is a measure of ecological balance, and human beings depend upon that nutrient chain and ecological balance for their own survival and habitat.

The maintenance of biological well-being is another corollary, which says that health damage to any species is also an indicator and measure of ecological imbalance. Therefore, indicators like fish kills in streams are measures of environmental quality or its lack. So, too, are symptoms of respiratory ailments in human beings. Air pollution has been shown to cause contraction and narrowing of respiratory passages, and also is associated with elevated death rates for those with respiratory diseases, such as emphysema. The number of pollutants in the atmosphere is so numerous, and their interactions with the human body so complex, that medical science has not been able to trace exactly which pollutants are the cause of respiratory ailments, nor exactly how biological damage is caused. Under present economic criteria of using all means to produce more goods unless those means can be proven harmful, the burden of proof is on medical science or the individual to demonstrate that his ailment is caused by a specific pollutant from a specific source. Ecological interactions being myriad and complex, such proof is unavailable.

Under the proposed criteria for environmental quality, biological damage of any type is to be avoided at its first symptoms until its true gravity can be explored. This principle assumes that we know relatively little about the complexity of biological interactions, and, at the first symptom of biological damage, we should stop and investigate. This would mean operationally that the burden of proof would shift from the receptor to the polluter. That is, upon the first symptoms of contraction in respiratory tracts and elevated death rates among those with respiratory diseases, the polluting sources would be restrained from emission until they could prove that their emissions were not harmful. This places significantly different emphasis on environmental quality and pollution control than now prevails, because it throws the full effort and resources of the polluter into solving the problem, instead of making an adversary out of him and giving him an incentive to use his resources to justify current operations and deny environmental problems.

OPERATIONAL PRINCIPLES

Operational principles reflect the ethical implications of an accepted criterion. Thus we assume it is "good" to increase consumption, raise living standards, make a profit, and seek economic growth. These are ethical corollaries of the present economic criterion by which we live. The economic criterion of the present has little or nothing to say about biological damage or the ecosystem. Therefore, there is little or nothing in the mission analysis, scenario, or operational principles of today concerning the environment, except in recent environmental legislation. Moreover, our mores and culture have very few operational principles that admonish us to preserve nature. For the most part, we are conditioned to believe that it is not bad to destroy nature, because it is good to conquer it.

The operational principles derived from a criterion for environmental quality would be quite different. The scenario proposed in the mission analysis of this book is that good is to be found in individuation, maturation, and knowledge of a larger whole system; and this ethical concept of goodness is in keeping with the best thought of the Western tradition. The larger whole system, which is the test of the good in this proposal, is the ecosystem and the maintenance of its diversity, viability, and balance. That is to say, individual well-being and the process of maturation require that the human organism live in harmony with the energy-life-food chain and, failing this, irreparable biological damage is suffered, not only to physical well-being but also to the inner ability to associate with a larger whole. The test of progress, then, is in the individual's relation with the ecosystem, where he has his own individuated identity which is part of a diverse and balanced ecology.

The largest integrated whole of diverse parts which we can witness with our minds and sense is the ecosystem in which we live. For those reared and conditioned by a scientific tradition which says that reality is that which we can confirm with our senses, the ecosystem is the largest whole design which we can confirm sensately. Therefore, the ecosystem stands as the design and ethic for the whole system, which is confirmable by both scientific methods and traditional ethical philosophy. What is good for the ecosystem is good for man, and that, in essence, is the final measure of worth.

If we will assume that quality and progress may be defined as maintenance of the diversity, viability, and balance of the ecosystem, because only in this state can persons individuate and mature, then we must still examine what this assumption means operationally if it is to be used as the basis for a decision structure.

One operational guide to decision making, in keeping with the nature of individual and ecological well-being, is what Oliver Johnson has called the *principle of personal impartiality,* which can also be stated: One ought never to do an act having social or environmental consequences that discriminates among persons (or species) on the basis of their individual differences alone. One difference, of course, is between the self and all others; and so the principle says that one ought not do an act having social costs or damage effects, consequences which benefit oneself alone, or one's group alone, or some group versus another group. Thus, we ought not purchase our own happiness, even indirectly, at the expense of others. Hence, we should not purchase our personal transportation conveniences at the sacrifice of another's health caused by the air we polluted, nor purchase more consumption goods by chemicalizing the environment. To discriminate against the well-being of others, simply to act in favor of one's own happiness, is to act arbitrarily and unethically. Johnson derives this moral "ought" from the logical proposition that a person "ought" to act rationally. The rational "ought" is defensible on the grounds that reason is the source of commonality, or comparing thought and experience with others, which is how we seek to ascertain truth. The realm of moral action, in other words, is coextensive with the social significance of practical action to others.[3]

A second guide to action may be called the principle of equal rights, which is to say that every person has an equal right to well-being. The justification for this principle is that well-being is a universal object of men's desires, since to be "well" and to "be" constitute life itself. As long as men affirm life, well-being will be its general object. But well-being and happiness cannot be shared; they are individual possessions, individually felt, exclusively and privately one's own. Therefore, well-being can be evaluated only on a quantitative basis, as to the number of those who feel it, and not qualitatively because one cannot directly sense the feelings of another. If well-being is an individual possession, and if experiences of happiness are qualitatively indistinguishable, it follows that two experiences of happiness by two different individuals are equally desirable; and if one act of happiness should be incompatible and at the expense of the other, then to decide in favor of one's own well-being alone would be an arbitrary and immoral act.[4]

[3]Oliver A. Johnson, *The Moral Life*, George Allen and Unwin, Ltd., London, 1969, pp. 17, 37, and 46–49.

[4]Ibid., pp. 61–62.

A corollary, from the other two, is a third principle of equal well-being over time. That is, if a person should not exhibit partiality in the present, neither should he discriminate in the future on the basis of individual differences alone. If the difference is only the time span within which individuals live, those who live in the future have as equal rights to well-being as those who live in the present. The most obvious application of this principle in ecology, of course, is that environmental resources and quality should not be despoiled in the present, for contemporary benefit, at the sacrifice of well-being of future generations.

A fourth operational principle is that diversity should be prized and encouraged for itself, in the ecosystem or in the individual, because diversity in ecology is the means for adaptive survival, and diversity in the individual is his means of individuation and maturity.

A fifth principle is that, in environmental decision making, a choice favoring negative entropy is generally to be preferred over one conducive to entropy. That is, the life functions of storing and concentrating energy in biological cells is to be preferred to its mechanical dissipation because, by so doing, the ecology is more prolifically maintained, and thus its balance and viability are more assured. The normal energy losses are great, in any case, from reflection, respiration, and nonassimilation without augmenting the energy losses by decisions which dissipate it arbitrarily. The application of this principle would prefer conversions into food sources, for example, rather than into electric power.

A sixth operational principle is that, since the well-being of oneself and others is dependent upon complex and often little-understood inter-actions with the ecosystem, decisions are to be preferred which maintain viability and balance in the ecology even in the face of present personal wants. The application of this principle is that uncertain biological hazards are sufficient cause for denying certain personal desires, because of the inadequacy and humility of our knowledge of ecological interactions.

MEASURES OF WORTH

The discussion, so far, has attempted to identify the scope and ethics of the whole system. The criterion suggested is this: A good is that which conduces to a diverse, viable, and balanced ecosystem in which the individual person can achieve his own well-being and maturation. This moral "ought" is derived from the rationale "ought" that a person ought to use his reason to "be" and to be "well," i.e., to live and affirm life.

Secondly, some operational principles which derive from this alternative good have been stated which provide normative guidance to decision making.

Finally, then, we need to ask the question whether these operational principles can be formulated into a measure of worth. That is, in the scientific tradition, if we can define it, we should be able to measure it; and if we can measure, we can monitor its behavioral characteristics.

The answer is that the operational principles can be measured. The viability and balance of the ecosystem can be measured by the populations and survival rates of species. Entropy can be measured by energy consumption and losses. Well-being is a quantitative measure of the numbers who express a feeling of happiness, not the quality of happiness itself. Impartiality is measurable by the presence or absence of feelings of discrimination, and equality over time would be apparent from time-series data.

What we have established, then, as criteria and measures of worth are environmental qualities and human perceptions which are observable and quantifiable, as well as being derived from operational principles consistent with moral philosophy. These measures of worth can be incorporated into a decision structure for environmental administrators, both as goals of the mission analysis in justifying the basis for the decision and/or as objectives in a management system to establish control over operations.

SUMMARY

Any decision is inseparable from its contexts. The contexts are the surrounding events and problems of the time, plus the framework of thought or assumptions which determine the criteria. A new environmental decision structure needs to examine this framework, and to identify its own contexts and assumptions. One convenient way to examine context is through mission analysis.

Mission analysis is a rationale, a framework in which to describe the problems and state of the system, together with future alternatives and contingencies. These alternative futures are evaluated in the setting of criteria, which set forth the specific assumptions on which quality or worth of the outcome is to be identified. The technical state of the art to accomplish the alternatives, and the costs, are determined to select the most feasible solutions; and the best alternative is that which most closely fulfills the objectives of the criteria. The best alternative is then defined into the specific outputs and implementation steps needed to carry it out. Finally, a summary statement of the worth of the mission is summarized from the performance, costs, and criteria.

The mission analysis may next be converted into a scenario, which is a speculative account of the human activity implied in performance of the mission. A scenario of the present economic mission and criteria suggests that, despite environmental problems, the preferred solution is likely to be pollution abatement within the limits of achieving reasonable economic growth, even though the ultimate costs may be some additional environmental deterioration, inflation, and social unrest.

An alternative environmental mission analysis is suggested which is really the entire content of this book, Section One being the state of the system, Sections Two and Three the alternatives, and Section Four the criteria, mission, and implementation. A speculative environmental scenario for the year 2000 is hypothesized in which increased economic output has doubled material consumption but greatly restricted access to the natural environment, due to its biological hazards. In this scenario, three alternatives are: to continue a progress-pleasure syndrome, to intensify the technological realization of imaginary living, or to try to restore ecological balance and a more natural human estate.

The proposed environmental criterion, in this scenario, is to seek ecological diversity, balance, and biological well-being, in which the individual achieves maturation by more direct interaction with nature, in addition to his urban-technical experience. The argument for this criterion is that it establishes man in a sustainable natural habitat. The measure for diverstiy is in the range and count of species populations. The measure for balance is the law of the minimum, that species do not decline from man-made disruption of the environment. The measure of ecological well-being is the avoidance of biological damage in the form of rising mortality or morbidity rates for any species.

These criteria can be translated into operational principles which describe what is better or worse for the environment; and in this sense, the principles define progress, or, obversely, degradation. The operational principles are impartiality, equality, and a long-term view in environmental usage, as well as actions which favor diversity, negative entropy, and biological health. The environmental mission analysis has then established criteria and operational principles for administrative decisions which preserve the quality of the human habitat.

DISCUSSION QUESTIONS

1 What is your analysis of the present state of the system, and what alternatives would you currently pose as plausible for the future?
2 If you look at this book as a mission analysis, where does its emphasis seem to lie among the eight points in the content of a mission analysis? Would you change that emphasis if you were writing the book, or acting upon it as an environmental administrator? If so, why and how?
3 What changes or elaboration would you like to apply to the criteria for environmental quality for the future?

4 How would you interpret and apply the operational principles to your own behavior on a specific environmental issue which you select?

PROBLEM

Write your own scenario for the future, using the content of a mission analysis as the framework for posing alternatives.

Chapter 22

Environmental Program Organization and Control

An environmental problem becomes apparent and in need of corrective action, under the present practice, when environmental quality fails to meet governmental standards as, for example, when the amount of pollutants exceeds air or water quality standards. In single, specific cases, a court or administrative order may correct the deviation—but many times the failure to meet standards constitutes a general class of violations inherent in the performance of products or components of the system. For example, photochemical air pollution constitutes a broad class of deviations from air quality standards by automobile drivers, because the emissions are inherent in the design of the internal combustion engine and the form of transportation which the public uses. Similarly, water pollution by chemical plants may be intrinsic to the type of industrial processes and waste treatment plants which are available for use.

In such cases of broad class deviation from environmental quality standards, a governmental agency, such as the Environmental Protection

Agency, may need to develop a concerted program to bring a coordinated set of corrective events to bear upon the solution. For example, it may be necessary to experiment with the redesign of the automobile, the entire transportation system, or chemical processing procedures. In such cases, an environmental program needs to be developed with redesign and implementation functions to transform environmental quality, and the administrator will be faced with the problem of organization and control of the effort.

Before an administrator can begin to organize and control an environmental program, he needs to answer the questions: What is the system?; What is the measure of "good" in the system?; and, Who is the decision maker? The first two of these questions have been addressed in Chapters 5, 20, and 21. This chapter will concern itself with two issues: First, who is the decision maker? and, secondly, how can the tasks be organized for the "good" of the system?

These questions are dealt with under the following topical headings:

1 Who is the decision maker?
2 The public as decision maker.
3 The broadening of representation
4 An integrated framework for policy
5 Approach to administrative organization and control
6 Management-in-reverse
7 An environmental example of program implementation
8 Task and work assignments
9 Internal organizational structure
10 External organizational arrangements
11 Problems of control

WHO IS THE DECISION MAKER?

The question as to who the decision maker really is generally turns out to be deceptively simple. The assumption is usually made that someone upstairs in the hierarchy is the decision maker. Therefore, the simple answer is that the "boss" is the decision maker. However, the larger and more complex a problem becomes, the more overlapping are the jurisdictions and responsibilities, and the harder it is to find the boss.

The way society has historically organized itself is territorially or by specialized functions. So we have innumerable business firms engaged in manufacturing special products, trade, finance; and then there are township, county, city, district, regional, state, federal, and international governmental agencies, all based upon their historical territory or service. Yet who among all these is responsible for, say, law enforcement—the local police, sheriff, courts, district attorney; the highway patrol; state narcotic agents; FBI, T-men, the Department of Justice; the mayor, governor, President? Nobody? Everybody?

If there is a lack of law and order, who does the citizen go to for relief? Speeches ad nauseum are made on the subject of law and order at all political levels, while crime and violence get worse. It makes one suspect that no one is in charge here; and indeed, in a way, that is so. Law and order is a *mission* and a system, but it is administered by such segmented departments and jurisdictions that the effort is suboptimized and relatively ineffective.

The same thing is true in many corporations. Employees think the president is the "boss," and since business is a relatively simplistic and authoritarian affair, he often is. But even in business, if it becomes large and complex technically, the president is not really in charge because he is incapable of knowing enough about all the technologies and operations to make many of the decisions. The decisions are made, in this case, by what Kenneth Galbraith calls the *technostructure,* that is the structure of committees and communications by which specialists in various fields contribute to a group decision.

Ah! Now we have a logical difficulty. The groups are making decisions to solve problems based upon their specialties, but how do they know what the problem (whole system) really is? Surely their specialties do not qualify them to see the whole system; rather they prevent them from doing so. The lens or perspective of their specialty causes them to focus on part of the system, the part they understand or at least recognize.

Take the example of law and order again: Is law and order a police problem; an educational problem; a poverty problem; a community relations, parental, judicial, incentive, employment, racial, housing, urban planning, environmental, moral, or religious problem? If the specialized technostructures look at a broad mission-oriented problem like law and order, how does the administrator know that they have seen the whole system? They will see the whole system only if the sum of their specialties happens to coincide with the entire mission of the system, which indeed will be rare in most institutional organizations.

That brings us to a crucial conclusion, the jurisdiction and knowledge of the decision maker has to be coterminous with the boundaries of the system (problem) if the decision maker is to see the system whole and deal with it as a whole.

Now, let us ask the question: Where is the environmental decision maker whose jurisdiction, knowledge, and responsibility are coterminous with the ecosystem? It is not the Council on Environmental Quality because it deals in policy recommendations to the President and Congress and does no implementation. Not the President or the Congress because they exercise only the delegated powers of the Constitution and have no direct operational knowledge of or responsibility for the production processes causing pollution. Not the Environmental Protection Agency because, though it may take corrective actions to monitor deviations from quality standards, it does not make overall policy nor control the transformation (production) processes. Not the states because they are territorially limited and cannot control upstream or upwind pollution beyond their boundaries. Not the pollution control districts or local governments for the same reason. Not industry because it is selling products for which there is a demand regardless of their pollution or effects on the environment.

Is it any wonder that we have environmental problems? There is no "boss" in charge who can see the whole ecosystem and all the effects upon it—unless all the citizens can. All the citizens taken together do see the "whole" system, because the sum of their activity is the sum of the interaction with the ecosystem.

THE PUBLIC AS DECISION MAKER

The decision maker whose jurisdiction and knowledge is coterminous with the boundaries of the ecosystem is the public. The people have jurisdiction coterminous with the system, because they have reserved the rights of sovereignty under the constitution. Their knowledge is coterminous, because their activity is the sum total of interactions with the environment. As a result, the design of an organization and decision system for the environment should look to the public for key decisions as to value, worth, cost, performance, and preferred approaches to environmental improvement. However, there is no mechanism for such appeal to the public for key decisions at present, other than through attitude polls, consumer and conservation organizations, through the Congress. But the Congress does not see the whole ecosystem either because it is boggled with getting reelected, campaign funds, special interest lobbies, seniority, log-rolling, or seeing folks from home; this makes it see the ecosystem more as a voting constituency than as a set of natural laws whose jurisdiction takes precedence in the scheme of things over its own legislation.

Environmental administration, then, encounters an organizational difficulty in not having direct recourse to decision makers who can see the whole ecosystem. In such a situation, a top-level environmental administrator (such as the head of the Environmental Protection Agency) can build as direct and strong a link as institutional arrangements will allow to the real decision maker, the public. That is, he can make maximum reference to government legislators and private boards of directors, to the extent that their representativeness is confirmed by surveys or contacts with citizen organizations; but he may also be able to appeal to an environmental constituency of his own. A direct appeal to the public on environmental issues is, of course, a dangerous game, because that pits the environmental administrator as a politician and rival against elected representatives, who will of course take great umbrage upon the slightest implication that his actions may be more representative of the public interest (ecosystem) than theirs. Still, if there is to be any real progress in environmental quality, some environmentalists or administrators will have to take on the gamey role of challenging the political process, as well as the private decision process, which has, since the founding of this republic, been degrading the environment (see Chapter 4).

THE BROADENING OF REPRESENTATION

A first priority in environmental administration, in seeking to find the decision makers whose authority is coterminous with the ecosystem, is to try to expand the representation of the present institutions. This process of institutional change is undoubtedly long-term in its development, because it implies alteration of social rewards by legislation, persuasion, and public opinions, which are conducive to a more comprehensive set of goals by corporations or public agencies. Existing institutions need to recognize that they serve a multiplicity of interests (of the whole system), rather than the pursuance of narrow or exclusive goals as in the past.[1] In their study, of the role of a corporate board of directors, Adizes and Weston forecast that a broadening of representation will take place in all institutions in the future because rapid social and technical change is causing a goal-constraint displacement in the United States, as it shifts from an industrial to a postindustrial society.

The deterministic goals of productivity and economic growth, which have dominated the values and objectives of society in the past, are found wanting by a public which now has wider aspirations. New deterministic goals now appear to be social-political objectives of an improved quality of life, greater equality of opportunity and rewards, and further reductions in employee insecurities. The former economic goals and mechanisms have now become constraints, determining how fast or feasible the new goals may be achieved.

In considering how private corporations might adapt to the new

[1]Adizes and Weston, The Board of Directors—An Open Systems Analysis, Graduate School of Management, University of California, Los Angeles, research paper, 1971.

goal-constraint displacement, thinkers have suggested three main approaches to achieve the public interests. The first approach is basically to maintain the present business institutions and neoclassic market mechanisms, but to alter the incentives (through taxation) to modify the operation of the private economy. This school of thought, which includes Friedman, Hayek, Leavitt, Ruff, Solow, believes that incentives are the most effective means of redirecting effort. They also believe that the assumption of social responsibilities by private business would entail paternalism and eventually curtail individual freedom.

The second view is more behavioral and envisions changes in attitude by businessmen, in which a new breed of professional managers would be educated to orient the objectives of their corporation toward the values of society. Bowen and Frederic, who advance this view, see new internal rule making through reorientation of policies to be the key to change.

A third approach, suggested by the Project for Corporate Responsibility, would restructure the top organization of business, where policies are made, by making it representative of the consumer, workers, suppliers, and government.

Each of these approaches suggests a positive alternative which may be a necessary part of an ultimate solution, but none presents a sufficiently systematic framework to be sure that future institutions are responsive to changing social missions or ecological needs. The first approach does not fully address the question, because it does not resolve the issues of who is the decision maker who changes the incentive system, and how? The second approach looks at the corporation as a closed system, relying on internal rule making to accomplish change, but not incorporating the external or environmental influences acting upon boards of directors or executives. The third approach assumes that businessmen cannot change, and, if so, there is some possibility the addition of new viewpoints to the board might merely add to the factionalism of the decision process rather than its integration.

AN INTEGRATED FRAMEWORK FOR POLICY

What is needed, then, is a more integrated framework that relates resources and incentives in private corporations, which are the subsystems, to the mission and purposes of the whole social system. Certainly incentives, executive attitudes, and broad representation are a part of a new system, but the real issue is how to take a holistic view of the quality of life and environment desired by the people. This is basically a problem in mission analysis, criteria, and priority setting covered in the last chapter. The final arbiter of the quality of life has to be those who live that life. The relative role of business, government, or other pluralistic groups, will be determined by their ability to contribute and adapt to social development in the future. No social institution loses its power position in society without a struggle, but the future belongs to the institutions most adaptable and responsive to the change in life and quality.

This institutional responsiveness to the improvement in life quality pertains to the government as well as corporations. Indeed, Adizes and Weston point out that government may need to undergo the greatest adaptation in the future, but in fact may be the least adaptable of our institutions. If government is unadaptable, private and community forms of organization may tend to displace it. Among the difficulties which Adizes and Weston see with the government are these: (1) Government is seen in present value schemes as too big, something to be contained, and people feel that further power should not be centralized in it; (2) voting every two or four years does not provide either the participation or the continuity needed to determine social goals and missions in turbulent times; (3) the committee and seniority structure of Congress is an anachronism in the light of modern communication media; and (4) the educational level of the people has advanced, and is advancing, to the point where they are more able to resolve issues as to their own life quality than is a political elite. The latter is particularly true as environments become increasingly turbulent and intense, decisions more complex, and participative tradeoffs necessary to their resolution.

The implication of an open-systems approach to environmental decision making is that both governmental and private institutions will need more representative boards, who are constantly receiving value, goal, and incentive inputs from the participation of their constituencies. The problem of the environmental administrator today is where to start in creating such a participative, goal-setting mechanism. He can obviously start in at least three ways: (1) by presenting environmental mission analysis and alternatives to the public in a crisp and cogent manner himself, (2) by consultation and seeking the widest participation of the public himself, and (3) by administering regulation and control of the environment mainly through incentives which stimulate user-producer participation.

As to the latter point, which may not be as obvious as the first two, incentives for the control of air pollution, for example, might involve selling automobiles to users under a conditional sales contract as to their operational performance in emission control. Then the user would have a recourse, a participation whether through penalty or representation, to the producer for nonperformance or ecological damage. It is the unconditional nature of the sale, without any environmental warranty, which leaves the consumer helpless to seek redress for deterioration in his life's quality. The warranty of products against ecological hazard, with recourse through indemnification or representation in decision processes, might be the single most powerful incentive to improvement in the quality of life and the environment. If business could convince itself that such a warranty was in its long-run interest to survive as a participative institution in an open system, despite the trauma of unexpected liabilities, the private corporation could easily become the most responsive (and thus dominant) social institution of the future, displacing the government whose lack of adaptability may make it an intractable agency for the public interest in the future. If this should happen, it would not be an historic event, because historically centralized governments have continually been displaced by more responsive institutions.

APPROACH TO ADMINISTRATIVE ORGANIZATION AND CONTROL

Assume that an environmental administrator deals with the question of who is the decision maker in the three ways suggested: (1) by developing clear mission analysis and alternatives himself, (2) by seeking public participation himself, and (3) by administering incentives to cause user-producer participation. He would next concern himself with implementing his program of alternatives. We have seen that an administrator cannot really manage anything unless he knows the following things:

1 The design of the whole system and the criteria for determining the worth of the output
2 The constraints on the system, which are the forces in the environment beyond his control
3 Who the decision maker is and what is his jurisdiction
4 The processes of transformation in the system, which are the material-energy exchanges or the behavioral change potential of the human participants

If an administrator knows these characteristics of the system, which are very large concepts indeed to comprehend, he is then in a position to design and carry out a program by the arrangement of its managerial elements. That is, he can implement a program to carry out the mission (criteria) of the system by the following additional steps:

5 Mobilizing the resource inputs
6 Determining the performance and feasibility of components
7 Analyzing and controlling the costs

8   Developing an information system to ascertain actual performance and costs

9   Organizing tasks and work assignments sequentially, and motivating people to accomplish them

The latter five steps are management skills which are customarily regarded as all-important in the education or development of managers. In fact, however, all these managerial functions are secondary and subsumed in the first four steps, particularly in the decision criteria. As such, these managerial skills make up the work load of the organizational level (see Chapter 19) of administration; and they occupy most of the management literature, because they are the most easily learned, and because there are many middle-management jobs available in the organization level of institutions.

This observation is not to underestimate the role of managerial skills; the numbers of middle managers who use the skills are legion, and they are a powerful bureaucratic force in the technostructure of all modern institutions. The observation is made, rather, to point out that many managers, who are isolated within the institution, do not really understand the system which they are running; and they frequently try to perform their role in reverse.

MANAGEMENT-IN-REVERSE

That is, some managers have a narrow view of their mission and think that organization is the first problem to deal with, rather than among the last. But since they put it first, they start new activities with organizational structures which have hierarchical niches for themselves, often with a very heavy overhead cost structure.

The second step for these reverse-order managers is to develop a prospective information system, usually in the form of a pro forma balance sheet, income statement, and budget which show an early break-even analysis; this is substantiated by voluminous cost and performance data as proof.

There are many investors who accept such financial analyses without asking the really significant management question—what is the design and criteria of the whole system? The failure to ask this question, of course, is one of the reasons for overruns and failures.

Management-in-reverse is, then, a conspicuous style of industrial management, mainly because the incentives foster it. Management-in-reverse is the cause of many environmental and social difficulties, because actions are taken in an order and priority reverse to the public interest.

Let us return to the environmental administrator to see how he can proceed by starting with the public interest and ending with an organization plan, instead of the reverse. To play the game straight (i.e., not in reverse) the environmental administrator needs to know and deal with (1) the criteria of the common interest, (2) the constraints in the environment, (3) the scope of the decision maker, (4) the process of transformation, (5) resource inputs, (6) performance specifications, (7) costs, (8) an information system, and (9) organization structure.

AN ENVIRONMENTAL EXAMPLE OF PROGRAM IMPLEMENTATION

Perhaps the easiest way to see the approach of an environmental administrator in program implementation is to take an example. Indeed, the best example may well be one based upon drastic assumptions, because there are no good real cases which are not distorted by management-in-reverse conceptions. The drastic case will be to assume that public sentiment has been tested by referenda; and it was found that the people prefer the elimination of air pollution to former national priorities such as economic growth, going to the moon, armament, wars, or the inviolability of existing institutions. That is to say, the environmental administrator is given a clear mandate, at least through the paper planning stage, of making the United States atmospherically livable.

Let us proceed, now, with the same thought process of the environmental administrator to formulate the nine major implementation steps to develop an air quality improvement program.

1 The system design would be to develop the most productive industrial economy for satisfying human wants (recognizing all its demands upon air consumption for combustion and energy conversion processes), which is consistent with an air quality that will avoid deleterious biological effects on organisms within the ecosystem. Assume that the environmental administrator takes the federal air quality standards as one alternative, or working hypothesis, that photochemical oxidants should not exceed 0.08 ppm in the atmosphere or carbon monoxide 0.35 ppm for one hour, nor should sulfur dioxide exceed 0.14 ppm as a maximum twenty-four-hour concentration. He also defines as his measure of worth that the test of "good" in the system will be the diversity, balance, viability of organisms in the environment, including the well-being and maturation of human beings as individuals (see Chapter 21). This is his mission, the "ethics" of the whole system, and the measures of worth.

2 The constraints on the system design are the dispersion of residuals of combustion and human processes into the environment resulting in reactions which he cannot control. These natural reactions include meterological conditions, photochemical reactions in the atmosphere, and the interactions associated with atmospheric gases on minute particles.

3 The decision maker in the system is assumed to be the public generally, whose wants are reflected in part through polls and in part through representatives in the legislatures and environmental protection agencies.

4 The process of transformation in the system are basically two: (1) to improve combustion processes so there are fewer residuals from automobiles and stationary power sources, and (2) to alter human behavior patterns to lessen the need for or demand for energy uses, particularly for transportation.

5 The environmental administrator has mobilized the necessary funds for his program by legislative appropriations, in part, and by regulatory controls which require private industrial investment for the remaining part.

6 He has further examined the performance and feasibility of several alternative approaches to air quality and determined that two approaches are likely to be most effective: (1) development of an urban transit system as a long-run solution, and (2) used car retrofit with emission-control equipment as an interim measure. The trade-off analyses for these choices have previously been developed in Chapter 16.

7 The ultimate costs of the two implementation programs, i.e., transit and used car retrofit, are estimated at $37 billion (which is also derived from Chapter 16). This was an analytical cost estimate. The control of these costs, however, presents an operational problem, which means monitoring the performance of the contractors, firms, or agencies who will perform the assigned tasks in implementing the two systems. The balance of this chapter will be concerned with how the administrator can control the task assignments, costs, information system, and organizational structure to carry out his mission.

8 The informational system is the feedback reporting device which tells the environmental administrator how well contractors are carrying out their tasks in terms of system performance and costs.

9 The organizational structure consists of arranging the tasks assignments, work sequence, human motivation, reporting, and budgetary allocations to implement the system.

TASK AND WORK ASSIGNMENTS

In the brief description above for implementing an air quality program, the first six steps are reasonably well illustrated from analyses in previous chapters. But as an attempt is made to deal with cost control, information reporting, and organizational structure (i.e., steps 7, 8, 9), the environmental administrator clearly is in need of additional detail on the work assignments in order to carry out his system. This detailing of work assignments is basically a problem of technical assessment and technical design, which would ordinarily be performed by an engineering staff. The ultimate technical design of an urban transit system, or used car emission control devices, is beyond the scope of this book, but we can perhaps illustrate the main components sufficiently to demonstrate the management problems and role of the environmental administrator. Again, let us make some simplifying assumptions about the several functions to be performed to carry out the air quality mission. Perhaps this can best be illustrated by a block diagram which shows the main elements of work to be done (see Figure 22-1).

Let us assume also that the Environmental Protection Agency has set up a major program to improve air quality, which includes, not only its regular functions of monitoring air quality and determining used car emission controls, but also the planning of urban transit systems and urban redesign to mitigate air pollution by reducing dependence on automobiles. Perhaps the transit system and urban redesign work will be carried on in other departments, such as in Housing and Urban Development or the Department of Transportation. Still the entire project needs coordination and central direction. Therefore, a system project manager in the Environmental Protection Agency is assigned the direction of the entire program. This environmental project manager breaks down the air quality program into its main work functions and tasks for implementation. He will then delegate the tasks by work orders or subcontracts to whoever is most capable, in government or private business, of accomplishing the work.

The environmental project manager sees his mission, in the block diagram (Figure 22-1), as the achievement of the air quality standards, for example, that oxidants will not exceed 0.08 ppm. His trade-off studies have indicated to him that the most feasible way to achieve this standard is by a combination of used car emission-control devices and mass transit systems. Therefore, the desired air quality is shown on the right of the block diagram as the outcome. The outcome is to be produced by a series of work functions, which are also major task assignments: The design of (1) used car emission-control equipment, (2) a rapid transit system developed from the existing state of the art, (3) the conceptual study of a more ideal futuristic mass transit system called the self-taxi, (4) the study of future urban redesign configurations, and (5) an air monitoring system to determine the actual quality of the air which is being achieved.

The used car emission-control device is further broken down into a series of subsystems which are to perform the function of (1) an afterburner to combust unburned fuel elements, (2) a catalyst to react with the emissions from the afterburner to render them into inert gases, (3) a rack

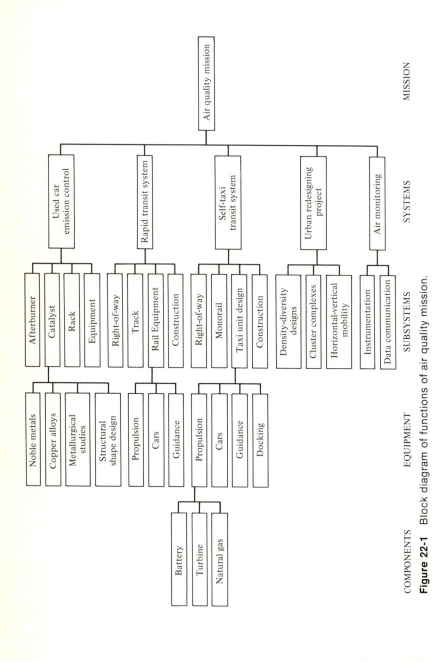

COMPONENTS   EQUIPMENT   SUBSYSTEMS   SYSTEMS   MISSION

Figure 22-1 Block diagram of functions of air quality mission.

or tray to hold and expose the catalytic materials to the gases while preventing undesired vibration, and (4) the complete catalytic afterburner assembly on existing cars. Let us assume that the environmental administrator contracts all these functions out, so that the afterburner is to be designed and built by a combustion engineering company, the catalysts by a metallurgical company, the rack by an auto equipment supplier, and the reactor equipment assembly by one of the major automobile manufacturers who would also test it.

The environmental administrator is also concerned, however, with technical studies about the cost and feasibility of various types of catalysts. The catalysts which have been tried and perform best are noble metals, gold, and platinum. While tests and designs will continue by the contractor with noble metals, a search is also to be undertaken to get lower-cost catalysts. The contracting metallurgical company thinks that some forms of copper alloys may be feasible, so they are also assigned that development task. The environmental administrator also sees a need to try to advance the state of the art in the catalyst field, and he contracts with two universities. One is to undertake metallurgical studies of what other catalytic materials might be conceivable, and the other to study the structural shapes of the catalytic material to see what structural forms function best for this purpose.

At the same time, the environmental administrator has contracted out a state-of-the-art rapid transit system, to be carried on concurrently with the used car emission-control project. A technical study indicates, let us assume, that San Francisco's new Bay Area Rapid Transit (BART) is high in performance among available systems. The environmental administrator makes grants to several major cities to have their planning departments and transit authorities begin selecting possible trunk-line routes with heavy enough traffic potential to justify a mass transit system. They are to study right-of-way acquisitions and costs and begin preparing specifications for construction contract bids. The administrator also lets a contract to a steel company to develop new track configurations and metals which will enable trains to operate smoothly at higher speeds than the BART system. He also goes out to bid on a contract to build transit cars similar to BART. At the same time, he specifies higher performance and speed for the propulsion unit, and lets a development contract for that purpose to a motor manufacturer. He also places a contract with an electronics company to develop a computer control which will operate trains at higher speeds than presently.

The traffic and revenue studies done for the environmental administrator suggest to him that the present form of rapid transit, such as BART, is applicable only where there are high-density populations and high-volume passenger movement. For the more spread-out urban areas, presently relying on freeways, a different form of mass transit may need to be provided. We shall assume that these areas cannot indefinitely be served by more and more freeways, because they would then be excessively paved over for living and commercial use. The objective is, then, to provide for convenience and independent driving of individuals on city streets to get to or from destinations, but major thoroughfares for longer transit would be moved on overhead rails with high-packing capacities of vehicles for traffic movement. One alternative proposed for study is a small and lightweight (under 800 pounds) commuter vehicle which would be rented per trip, leased for any time period, or sold to consumers. It would have a range of perhaps 50 miles; speeds up to 50 miles an hour; and operate on a battery, turbine, natural gas, or other low-emission propulsion unit. These small self-taxi units would be designed to enter a docking ramp where they would be picked up by an overhead conveyor or monorail and accelerated to high speeds, with a computer control to keep them properly grouped and spaced, and also to exit the car where the self-taxi commuter wanted to get off near his destination. Upon delivery to the undocking ramp, the commuter would drive his self-taxi under its own power to his work or shopping and park the vehicle. The environmental administrator has awarded a small study contract to a "think tank" research organization to test the feasibility of such a scheme, or to find an alternative which provides (1) high-density movement and (2) individual destination delivery.

The environmental administrator also has had some studies made which suggest that, by the year 2000, cities cannot be built as they are today, or all the inhabitants will be hopelessly snarled in traffic movement. Moreover, noise abatement and air quality will be hard to achieve. Therefore, he lets several conceptual design study contracts to architectural firms and university schools for urban design; their mission is to design urban forms which minimize human and material movement. In other words, given the population and materials transportation problems estimated for the year 2000, what urban structural designs would minimize the amount of movement of people to and from work, shopping, and recreation; and what design would minimize the intracity haulage of materials among factories and to retail distribution outlets? Speculatively, people would have to live near their work, shops, and recreations, which would imply higher densities than at present, perhaps in higher-rise structures. If that is one alternative, then what structural designs, both vertically and horizontally, would provide a sense of open space, and greenery, while still minimizing access and travel distances? Some mathematical models would show varieties of ways to minimize the travel distances, in either the vertical or the horizontal. Aesthetic architectural forms are then to be tried to see what groupings, clusters, shapes, and open areas are most pleasing. The relative density and diversity of these forms would then form the basis for recalculation and redesign to fit particular land areas and sites. Out of these studies would come a variety of horizontal and vertical grids, which would be the required travel corridors. New transit concepts would then be studied, such as vertical-horizontal elevators, which could travel the entire three-dimensional grid of the new urban area design.

A moment's reflection, regarding any of these functions, subsystems, equipment components, or research studies, suggests that any one of them can be subdivided further into an infinite variety of detailed tasks. In other words, each block on the diagram could be, itself, expanded into a network of events and tasks to be managed. Some illustrative networks will be expanded in the next chapter, where we deal more particularly with control and scheduling. For now, our interest is in how the environmental administrator integrates the many functional assignments which already exist, in broad delegations of work, on the block diagram. Clearly, he needs some internal organizational arrangement to supervise these several activities. Beyond that, he also needs external organizational ties or arrangements to supervise the many contractors and outside organizations upon whom he depends for the performance of the work and the mission.

INTERNAL ORGANIZATIONAL STRUCTURE

The management of a multibillion dollar program on air quality, such as the hypothetical example, would require an environmental administrator to have the normal departmental organizational units to deal with budgeting, financial accounting, contracting, engineering, personnel, and air quality instrumentation. The program might then be organized along the lines of Figure 22-2.

Each department has a variety of sections or activities under it, simply labeled as *A*, *B*, *C*, and *D*. For example, in finance, however, the sections might be payroll, accounts payable, accounts receivable, and general accounting. The engineering department might have a mechanical engineering unit, and also electronics engineering, power plants, systems engineering design, and a drafting section. Assuming that these are the engineering sections, then the mechanical engineering section might be concerned with the design of both the rapid transit train cars of the BART-type and also future self-taxi cars. But they do not have overall responsibility for delivering a transit system, and the environmental

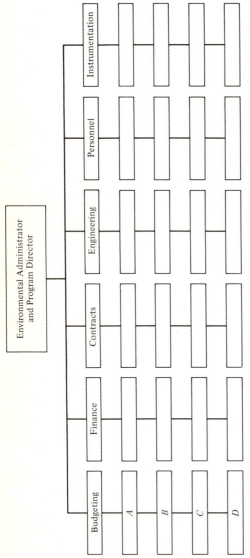

Figure 22-2 Air quality environmental program.

452

administrator himself cannot keep track of the details for all the systems and subsystems in his program.

Clearly, he needs someone responsible for the operational control of each project and all the contractors working together. That is the role of a system project manager. Hence, the environmental administrator overlays upon his departmental organization a set of project managers who can call upon the existing staff for the performance of work. That is, each project manager does not have to keep his own payroll and pay his own accounts payable to contractors. The finance office can do that for him. But the project manager must have control over those activities in the finance office which affect the performance of his project. The overlay structure which accomplishes this is frequently called a "matrix organization," and the matrix would look like Figure 22-3.

Project managers head up the several major functions to be performed, such as used car emission control, rapid transit, self-taxi transit, urban redesign, and monitoring; and these project managers report directly to the environmental administrator on their performance. In addition, the environmental administrator has departmental managers reporting to him on the major managerial activities to be performed such as budgeting, finance, engineering, and contracts. The project managers call upon these departmental services for the support of their projects. Thus, the used car emission-control manager would request the contracts department to advertise for bid, evaluate, and let the actual contract to the combustion engineering firm for the afterburner design; athough the project manager would have stipulated the performance characteristics as well as the general time frame and terms of the contract. In other words, the project manager determines the requirement, and then writes a work order to the contracts department of fulfill the contract as he has specified it. Similarly, the used car emission-control manager would request the finance department to audit the billings and make payment under the contract, and he would ask the engineering department to review and evaluate the performance of the contractor's design of the afterburner.

Clearly, then, what the matrix structure does is to place the specification, schedule, and output determination in the hands of the project manager, but delegates the specialized procedural tasks of management to existing departments. This provides the advantages of placing authority and responsibility for the conduct of the program in the hands of the project manager, while making available to him management services and expertise which he might not as effectively or economically mount for himself. That is, the departmental services are a common pool of skills available to all the projects. This is shown on the matrix organization charts by the broad arrows cutting across the departmental organization

454

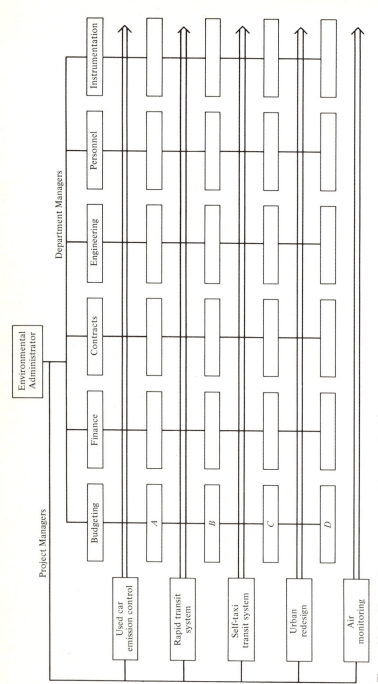

Figure 22-3 Air quality program—matrix organization.

structure that indicate that the project managers place work orders into the departmental organizations, across the board, to carry out as many of the task assignments as they can.

The internal organization then becomes a support and service activity for the project manager, while the project manager is really more concerned with the direction and coordination of *external* organizations. That is, the project manager is really directing and monitoring the performance of contractors, and in this sense he is more concerned with directing activities in other companies or institutions than in his own.

EXTERNAL ORGANIZATIONAL ARRANGEMENTS

The means by which the project manager directs the work performance in outside organizations is partly by contract authorization, but more precisely it is done by giving them performance specifications, task assignments, work authorizations, budgetary allotments, and information-reporting requirements. By spelling these details out carefully, and subsequently monitoring them, the project manager effectively controls the performance of external organizations. Now let us try to visualize the rather complex network of management relations in which the environmental administrator finds himself. Recall from Chapter 20 that the administrator in any environmental agency has many ties and relations with other governmental agencies, federal, state, and local. Assume that our illustrative air quality program is located organizationally in an environmental protection agency, then the internal and external relations of a project manager would appear as shown in Figure 22-4.

The diagram shows the project manager for the mass rapid transit system in a web of relationships, with a variety of informational or authority content. With respect to the performance of the external contracting companies for transit cars, track, propulsion, and guidance, he is the ultimate authority on the quality of their work performance on the transit project. With respect to the planning and transit departments of state and local governments, to whom he has made planning grants to develop transit systems, he provides general direction and guidance but not direct monitoring and control as he does over the contractors. His relations to the departmental service units within the environmental protection agency is authoritative as to work assignments, but not as to personnel or finance of the department. His relationships with other governmental agencies, such as the Department of Transportation is consultative. With citizen groups and the public, his role is informational, and his role is informational, too, with respect to the Council on Environmental Quality and the Congress.

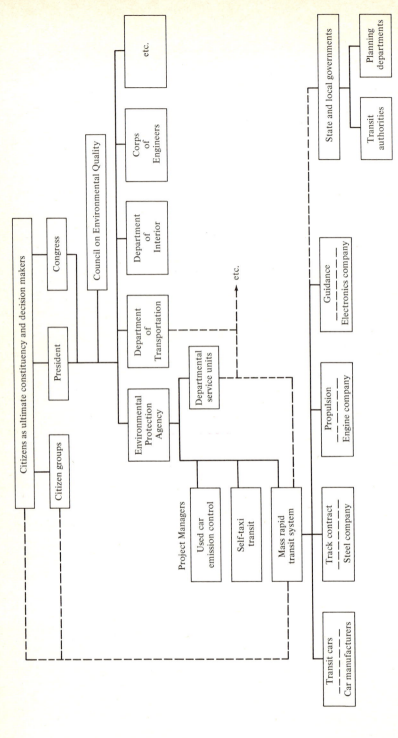

Figure 22-4 Schematic diagram of internal and external organizational relations of an air quality program manager.

The project manager has, therefore, a complex set of relationships which cut across institutional hierarchies and societal lines. He must play his role with considerable skill to obtain the results expected of him (i.e., the delivery of an emission-control system or a transit system) with the varying degrees of authority open to him. Much of his role needs to be persuasion. Indeed, the strange thing about his position is that the highest degree of authority which he exercises is over external organizations, while his internal authority is relatively weak. With respect to contractors, his authority is dominant, so long as he takes the care to plan thoroughly, specify work in detail, and develop performance specifications clearly.

If a project manager does a poor planning and specification job, his authority over external contracting organizations also becomes moot. In short, a strong project manager can exercise considerable authority, based on knowledge, over external organizations with respect to their final performance and output; but another person in the same job, who is less careful and persistent in planning details, might be quite a weak project manager. Perhaps this is another way of saying that project managers are not vested with the same kind of authority that business managers normally possess over their operations, because the project manager must exercise his authority externally, while the operational executive exercises it internally. There is a vast difference in the degree of authority which can be used in the two circumstances, due to the high dependence of internal employees upon their superiors for their advancement and livelihood; whereas the external relationship is contractual and interim which means that livelihood is not directly threatened.

A moment's reflection will also suggest how deeply the project manager's influence penetrates into the ramifications of an external organization. In any one of the contracting companies in the illustration, whether the propulsion or transit car manufacturer, several hundred employees would be engaged in the work of the contract. Within each company, specific task assignments and a network of events scheduling the work also must apply; and these records are usually part of the information system and progress reports required by the project manager. If performance and delivery under the contract falls behind schedule, the project manager would inquire into the cause and try to rectify it. Let us say, for example, that the pilot engines were not functioning properly in test runs and the difficulty appeared to be due to malfunctioning of very precisely machined parts, which had to fit to very close tolerances. The project manager might then direct the contractor to set up more numerous and precise inspection stations on the production line to check the tolerances in process of manufacture. That particular decision by direction of the project manager, with the concurrence of course of the contractor, substantively alters the work assignments of individuals in the inspection department. Similar redirection from the project manager could occur anywhere in the production process. Thus, one can see that the project manager has a very pervasive influence on work assignments down to the ramifications of an external organization.

PROBLEMS OF CONTROL

The authority of a project manager over an external organization is somewhat indirect and tenuous, but, at the same time, the project manager is responsible for obtaining a usable output from the external unit. Obviously, some rather interesting control problems can emerge from this situation. The project manager tries to establish his control over the obtaining of a usable product by a variety of planning measures, as we have seen. More particularly, his control measures include the determination or review of:

1   The several functions (work or energy transformation) which make up the system, together with their technical feasibility or uncertainty
2   The inputs of materials, equipment, skilled personnel, and ideas which are needed to make the functions work
3   The outputs of the process in terms of their standards, specification, and performance requirements
4   The resources or budgets which finance the system
5   The constraints, limitations, or what is not controllable
6   The informational feedback which measures the process
7   The sequence of events to accomplish the process
8   The rate of accomplishment
9   The state of the process and project in different modes or periods of time

If the project manager can define and keep track of these several elements of the system development, he is likely to obtain the result he wants from the contractor in terms of a usable product. The trouble arises when either (1) the project manager is not sufficiently precise in his definitions of the above specifications or (2) the contractor does not perceive or perform them as specified. If the trouble is from the first cause, the remedy is to reeducate or replace the project manager. If the trouble is from the contractor, the problem is to go over all the details of the requirement again with him, that is, to reeducate the contractor.

The redirection of contractors is, perhaps, the most frequent and painstaking of the project manager's duties. Contractors are prone to nonperformance on complex systems because of the difficulty of achieving complete communication or understanding on the part of the employees, and particularly the technical staff, who must do the work.

There is a strong tendency for technical bureaucracies to redefine performance specifications into terms of what they can do rather than what needs to be done from the project manager's viewpoint. This is an understandable tendency of all human beings, and indeed is one of the causes of environmental degradation. People continue to do what they know how to do. People know how to build cars, drive cars, and build highways. There is a strong inertia to continue to do the same despite noxious atmospheres, traffic jams, and paved-over cities. Perhaps one would not expect this human inertia to pertain so much among technical bureaucracies whose members are trained in the research and development of new products. But they, too, are limited by their past knowledge, and the project manager must be alert to their tendency to distort his specifications to their capability.

For example, let us assume that the project manager of the rapid urban transit system let the contract for the computerized guidance and control subsystem to an electronics company which had a high capability in semiconductor technology and a rather weak technology in microcircuitry. Semiconductors are discrete electrical devices made of materials which partially conduct or pass electricity, and thus serve as "gates," filters, or amplifiers in electric circuits. Microcircuits serve the same function but are many times smaller and are made by etching a miniature circuit on an inert background substrate, like glass, and then depositing a vapor or thin film of electrically conductive material on the substrate. Microcircuits were developed first to permit much higher density of parts, and therefore smaller equipment, in aerospace missions.

The project manager, in this case, has specified microcircuitry in the computer control, not because size and space is any problem on a transit train, but because of reliability and ease of repair. Semiconductors are usually soldered to a circuit board, while microcircuits are one integral part. The project manager feels that the train's vibration could loosen the solder joints, causing the part to fail. Moreover, in case of repair, microcircuits can be replaced by merely slipping out the whole part, while in the other case, the semiconductor that failed needs to be located by test instruments and a new part soldered in its place.

However, the electronics contractor, in this illustration, has mainly worked with semiconductors and has depth of knowledge in that field. The company's knowledge in microcircuitry is thin; the engineers have read the literature and done some design work with microcircuits. However, the contractor company does not have a microcircuit production capability, and this would be hard to acquire because the deposition of thin films on substrates is a bit of a "black art" in the electronics business.

In these circumstances, the most likely outcome of the design of the computer control is that it will be worked out to utilize semiconductors. That is, the project manager will find that his specifications for microcircuits have been rewritten by the technical bureaucracy of the contractor to require semiconductors. A lax project manager might not even catch the redefinition of the specifications until it is too late. If the project manager is alert and detects the change, then he is likely to be faced with arguments from the contractor that their design is "just as good," there is no need for high packing densities on a train, they will guarantee the reliability of their circuits, and so on. Perhaps they will even convince the project manager of their arguments, because he wants to believe them in order to get the job done on time.

Suppose the project manager is of firmer stuff, however, and is willing to put the project behind schedule to do it right. He sends the contractor back to do the job over again, insisting upon microcircuitry, but the contractor's technical staff does not really know how to do the job. They do not have the knowledge; they do not have the production facility; they cannot build test microcircuits to try out. What can the project manager then do? He can force the company to subcontract the microcircuitry out to another supplier which does have the competence. This will be a bitter and difficult thing to accept for the prime contractor, because the circuitry is the main production element of the job. It leaves the prime contractor as merely designer and assembler, while the microcircuit supplier does most of the production work where the money is to be made.

Perhaps this may seem like an extreme case, and perhaps the implication is that the electronics company should not have received the contract in the first place. But situations like this have happened frequently, especially in defense contracting, because the project manager may not always know in detail the capabilities and strengths of various contenders at the time the contract is let. After the contract is let, he is obliged to live with the contractor he has and make the best of it, or try to break the contract for nonperformance, which is a costly and time-consuming thing to do. The project manager seldom wants to lose the time and money involved in a nonperformance termination, unless it is a last resort.

Another similar, but more difficult case, is one in which there is technical uncertainty. That is, the state of the art has not developed to the point where the technical requirement can be met with certainty. For example, such a product may never have been made before. Literature and theory may suggest how the technical development might be done, but it has never been tried. The contractor may make optimistic technical plans on how he proposes to do it; but the system project manager is left with a probabilistic decision of whether the technical uncertainty is too great to proceed, or whether the technical problem has a sufficiently high probability of being solved to warrant the risk. Technical uncertainties, such as these, are among the most difficult project management problems, and they have been the cause of delays, overruns, or failures in defense or space efforts.

There is no simple answer as to how to deal with technical uncertainties. The two best approaches are to have: first, a very knowledgeable project manager with access to wide technical expertise, and secondly, to use a panel of scientists and technical experts to conduct a technology assessment.[2] A technology assessment is an orderly procedure for examining all the physical laws and experimental evidence to see if a technical advance is plausible, and if so, on what critical experiments the advance depends. The project manager would then require the contractor to conduct the critical analysis or experiments, before commiting funds to the general design. The depth of a technology assessment will depend upon the degree of risk and uncertainty involved. If the risk is very high, the project may be held in abeyance while basic research studies are contracted out to universities and research institutes.

The real issue which frequently comes before project managers, then, is how to live with technical uncertainty, and with contractors who do not quite know how to do their job and are therefore constantly trying to redefine the specifications to call for something which they understand. The management remedies for this condition are mainly in the realm of patience and reiteration along the following lines:

1   To maintain a close personal relation and dialogue with the technical staff regarding the final mission, the performance requirements, and the detailed specifications, so the project manager is sure that they understand. Personal discussion is much more effective in achieving understanding than relying only on written material.

2   To define the specifications very tightly in the first place so there is no contractual loophole that the contractor can slip through in case of misunderstanding. This means a very careful technical assessment and planning job by the project manager prior to the contracting.

3   To develop a frequent and adequate feedback of information so

[2]*A Study of Technology Assessment*, Committee on Science and Astronautics, U. S. House of Representatives, Washington, July 1969.

that the project manager can detect when the specifications are being rewritten. (The next chapter is concerned with such information systems.)

4 To motivate the contractor personnel with the pride and will to perform their mission well, and to get them to supplement their capability gracefully when they are incapable of handling certain requirements. The project manager will have to be adroit so that the contractor does not go on the defensive by feeling incompetent due to criticism. Somehow, the contractor has to be made to feel that he is doing well in most areas but should find or hire new employees of capability in a particularly difficult and specialized technical area. The contractor is not likely to feel so threatened if he believes his general competence is not under attack, but the criticism only applies to some specialized knowledge which he would not be presumed to possess.

The project manager is thus seen to be a person of very thorough interest in the planning of detailed specifications, a veritable sleuth in monitoring them, a patient educator to those who do not correctly interpret them, and a master psychologist in motivating technical bureaucracies whose sensitivities are easily offended by any allusions as to their competence. On top of these already idealized requirements, the project manager needs to be a semiphilosopher to think about the ethics of the whole system, and a semipolitician to develop adequate representation of public feelings in environmental needs. Obviously, not many project managers exist with such traits and abilities. When environmental administrators do not exist, if we know what we want in them, they can be developed. Most of the knowledge and skills of environmental administration are teachable, if we start with a person of broad perspective and some political sense.

SUMMARY

This chapter has shown that the environmental administrator has two urgent problems, once he has a basic mission.

The first is to identify the decision maker of the system, who he is, and exactly what he wants. In the case of environmental systems, we decided that the decision maker was the public interacting with the ecosystem.

The second problem is to determine the major functions of the system and arrange the internal and external assignments and organizations to carry them out. The organizational problem is by far the most tangible of the two and will undoubtedly appeal to many as the more solid part of this chapter.

In fact, the organizational and implementation steps are technicians' work and are subsumed in the criteria of the decision and the needs of the decision maker. The real policy issues lie in the value schemes of the users and the measure of worth as to the "good" of the system.

The environmental administrator faces a grave dilemma in that he has no existing mechanism to reach the decision makers, who are the public. He must look to and through existing representatives, in the form of legislators and boards of directors for some expression of the worth of environmental quality. As he tries to do this, he may well pit himself as a political rival against elected officials who presume to be representative. But representativeness is a doubtful claim in a world of rapid social and technical change, and, hence, the environmental administrator needs to exercise all his ingenuity to assure that he has some real and direct contact with public wishes and needs. The most difficult problem in environmental issues has been to determine what the public really wants, and in what priority.

Once the environmental administrator ascertains the public will, he is able to organize and implement the public interest, an approach which many managers approach in reverse. Management-in-reverse is induced by incentives which place the high rewards on organizational goals and thus put private interest ahead of the public.

The environmental administrator can avoid this pitfall of management-in-reverse by establishing a criterion in the public interest and then deriving his implementation steps from that ultimate ecological goal. He then proceeds to break the job down into specific tasks, work assignments, costs, and organizational structure. He may use systems analysis techniques to identify the functions of the system; a matrix organization to manage it; and controls over inputs, outputs, and resources to direct it. But, in the end, he is faced with the responsiveness and understanding of the external organizations, with whom he is contracting, as to whether they really have understood the communication of what is to be done.

All too often the technical bureaucracies of external organizations redefine the performance specifications to meet what they know how to do, rather than what ought to be done.

When this happens, the project manager needs to (1) exercise his patience and utmost skill to check on contractor performance, (2) define tight specifications, (3) keep in constant personal dialogue with the technical staff so he is sure they understand, and (4) motivate the external organization to acquire new capabilities which they do not have.

The project manager thus is faced with a broad spectrum of abilities which he must exercise, from political measures to ascertain the wants and values of the ultimate users (citizens), to the psychological motivation of employees in external organizations. While it is perhaps true that there are not many project managers with all these qualities now, most of the requirements are teachable once we (of the public) decide what we expect of a project manager and what decision system he should operate under.

DISCUSSION QUESTIONS

1   Suppose you were assigned the project of building a new rapid transit system for a metropolitan area, how would you go about finding the decision maker and defining the whole system?
2   What roles or incentives do you think might be created to broaden representation in all institutions, public and private, in order to see the whole system?
3   What are an administrator's principal problems of implementation and control? What methods does he have to deal with them?
4   How might a project manager deal with technological uncertainty?

PROBLEM

Select a project, with which you are familiar, and define the work functions and tasks needed to carry it out. Then create a block diagram, similar to Figure 22-1, and organizational charts, similar to Figures 22-3 and 22-4, to show how you would manage the project.

Chapter 23

Environmental Information Systems

An environmental information system consists of the data needed for monitoring; exception reporting; and control of schedule, cost, performance, and ecological effects. The information reported on schedule, cost, and performance is similar to the data requirements of any management information system, and, in terms of the environmental project manager, the reports would apply primarily to the internal and contractual arrangements discussed in the last chapter.

The ecological data are unique to environmental administration, and their content is similar to information discussed in Section Three. That is, the ecological data report actual experience compared to environmental quality standards. In addition, reporting covers the dispersion of pollution into the environment, and traces the secondary and tertiary effects to assess the extent of biological damage.

Perhaps there is a third kind of data network that the environmental manager needs, which derives from his semipolitical, representational problem of determining public wants. That is, an information system is needed to communicate to the public constituency the results of environ-mental improvement efforts. In fact, the data for such public information would come largely from ecological reports upon biological damage effects occurring in the environment.

The environmental administrator, then, has three types of data loops to construct in order to manage effectively: (1) the operational informa-tion system on cost, schedule, and performance; (2) the ecological moni-toring network on biological damage effects; and (3) the public informa-tional network which acquaints the constituency with the degree of biological hazard to which they may be exposed and the alternatives to cope with these hazards. The following discussion will cover the content of these three major information loops, under these headings:

1 The operational information system on cost, schedule, and per-formance
   a Decision trees
   b Task lists and time estimates
   c Networks
   d PERT and the critical path
2 Organizational accountability for task performance
3 The ecological monitoring network
4 The public informational network

THE OPERATIONAL INFORMATION SYSTEM ON COST, SCHEDULE, AND PERFORMANCE

Operational information systems reflect the work or tasks to accomplish the mission of a project. The information is concerned with physical or behavioral events which constitute the work assignments of the system. An operational manager pays close attention to the control of events, because time, cost, and performance depend upon how well the tasks are done and whether the events are accomplished. He is concerned with events, not only because they control performance, but also because they give an earlier indication of time and cost than do the usual financial reports.

Many, perhaps most, executives use financial reports to control their businesses or organizations on the assumption that the financial results are the measure of their own performance. While this is true, attention to financial reports, in lieu of controlling the physical events of the enter-prise, can result in serious lags and financial losses, because the physical events may precede their financial effects by several months. Consider, for example, the event of placing an order for a part, such as chrome trim, on an automobile model. Overordering or underordering that one part during a crucial time period near the end of a model run can cost the manufacturer several million dollars profit in a matter of days. Suppose a particular model is being closed out of the production run due to poor sales, but there is not close control or coordination between production and purchasing. Then the order for trim may be placed, although it will not be needed, but the financial effects will not show up until several months later on the income statement. In other words, control can be better achieved at the flow-of-events level than at the financial level.[1]

To control at the flow-of-events level, an operational manager must preplan or program the major actions and activities to take place in carrying out his project. Such preplanning of the implementation steps is detailed and takes time, which is one reason some executives shun doing the job; but the failure to do a good preplanning of work can result in costly mistakes and overruns later. That is, lack of preplanning is a frequent cause of the loss of control over operations.

Among the several useful tools for an effective preplanning of work are decision trees and networks. Indeed, these also form the inputs for the operational information system, and an illustration of their use might be helpful to see how the plan becomes input and then control.

Decision Trees

Decision trees are plans of events with some preliminary form of probabilities and payoffs assigned to them. The comparison of probability of payoff to cost shows the relative risk of the decision. To illustrate this point, let us return to the illustration of the last chapter, in which an environmental administrator had the mission of achieving the federal air quality standards and proceeded to develop a used car emission-control program plus alternative forms of mass transit. Among the problems for the used car emission-control was the development of a catalytic material which would have the reliability, product life, performance, and cost to be applied on all used cars. An appropriate catalytic material is presently not available, particularly one with long life and low cost. Suppose further the environmental administrator has completed a technical assessment which indicates that three different materials or alloys seem most promising as a suitable catalytic material. The costs and probability of success for materials A, B, and C are shown in Figure 23-1. Probability of success in this case means that the material will meet the performance requirements for removing emissions at the reliability, product life, and cost specified.

Material A is technically the most advanced idea, in this illustration,

---

[1]Stahrl Edmunds, "The Reach of an Executive," *Harvard Business Review*, January–February, 1959.

Figure 23-1   Calculated Risk of Loss on Catalyst Development

Alternatives	Probability		Cost, in dollars	Risk of loss, in dollars
	Success	Loss		
Material A	.80	.20	10,000,000	2,000,000
Material B	.70	.30	5,000,000	1,500,000
Material C	.40	.60	1,500,000	900,000

and thus costs the most to develop. Theoretically, from study and calculation, material A would appear to have the highest probability of meeting the performance requirements as to emission levels, life, and cost. Material B also has a high probability of success, but requires less technical development cost, since more is known about the material. Material C is relatively simpler as to its composition and properties, so it costs least for further development, but it also appears at the moment to have a low probability of meeting the performance specification. How should the environmental administrator decide among these three?

He is exposed to the largest calculated risk of loss on material A because it costs more to develop. On the basis of minimizing the risk of loss alone, he should decide to develop material C first. But suppose it takes two years to develop any one of the materials. Then, if material C should fail to develop into a workable catalyst, which is fairly likely, he could be four to six years from a usable result; and that is too long a time in the sequence of events specified in the last chapter. The catalyst is only one part of an equipment subsystem, which in turn is part of a $37 billion transportation system. It would be imprudent of him to impede a $37 billion program on a development effort costing $10 million or less.

Task Lists and Time Estimates

What the environmental administrator needs, in this case, is to break down the jobs of developing the three different materials into tasks and events, so he can begin running the work concurrently until he reduces the uncertainties enough to make a "go" decision. He decides to break the tasks down first into a "paper" or think-type study which will model the physical phenomena of the three materials, and secondly to detail the research and development tasks needed to take the three materials to the point of being producible. He also has the technical staff estimate the times to do each task. The task list looks like the one shown in Figure 23-2.

The modeling study is fairly low in cost compared to the research effort, and thus is a convenient way to reduce uncertainty with minimum

Figure 23-2   Task List, Cost, and Time to Develop Materials A, B, C

Task	Cost, dollars			Time, months	Event number
	C	B	A		
Modeling:					M
Physical analysis	$40	$50	$70	1	1
Formulate	20	30	30	1	2
Computer	60	60	60	1	3
	120	140	160	3	
Research:					R
Chemical reactions	200	360	1,840	6-8-9	4
Physical properties	180	500	1,000	4-5-7	5
Processing	300	1,300	2,000	9-12-16	6
Shape	100	300	1,000	3-4-5	7
Temperature	300	1,000	2,000	4-9-12	8
Density	200	800	1,000	7-8-9	9
Configuration	100	600	1,000	5-6-8	10
	$1,500	$5,000	$10,000		

expenditure of time or money. The study consists of a physical analysis of the properties of materials and their behavior when exposed to gaseous emission. These physical interactions are then formulated into mathematical expression to calculate the effects, and a computer model is constructed to process the data. Let us assume that by these calculations, the calculated risk of loss can be reduced by half. However, the modeling studies take three months to complete, and the environmental administrator may wish to consider starting some concurrent research activity to save time, provided he can minimize the amount of money committed (that is, keep his calculated loss below $900,000). In other words, he is trying to buy time while minimizing losses.

The research program begins with a series of chemical reaction experiments in a laboratory situation, as well as studies of the physics and properties of the material in laboratory experiments. These studies are intended to define exactly the catalytic performance characteristics of the material, and thus reduce the degree of uncertainty about its performance in an actual vehicle. The next research task is to develop the processing of the material for production, which will also provide additional information on technical feasibility and cost in a production process.

Networks

If the material can be produced in commercial quantities, then engineering development on the material's use is needed. This takes the form of determining the structural shapes of the catalyst, operating temperatures, density and quantity in relation to the gaseous emissions handled, and the configuration of the equipment within which the catalytic material will function. The costs of these various steps are shown for each material in the preceding table, as well as the time to accomplish each task. The time is shown in the form of three estimates, a minimum, average, and maximum time for the task. For example, the chemical experiments are estimated to take a minimum of six months, an average estimated time of eight months, and a maximum of nine months. The network of events for the modeling studies and the research on material C is shown in Figure 23-3 using the average time estimate.

The network shows that from the starting point S the plan is to analyze all materials, A, B, and C, in terms of a modeling study M. In three months all models will be complete and the probability of loss will be cut in half by the additional knowledge and calculations. This means that the probability of predicting success for material A will become 90 percent, for B, 85 percent, and C, 70 percent. In other words the calculated risk of loss will now become $1 million for A, $750,000 for B, and $450,000 for C. To reduce the uncertainty to this degree has cost $420,000 for the three studies and three months in time.

Meantime, the environmental administrator has also started, concurrently, the actual research program on material C in order to save or buy time. He has scheduled events 4, 5, and 6 which are three months under way. If the costs for these events can be prorated monthly, then by the third month he has spent $75,000 on event 4, $100,000 on event 5, and $50,000 on event 6. His total research cost of $225,000 and the modeling study costs of $420,000 make a total three-month expenditure of $645,000. What has he purchased with this expenditure? He has obtained a substantial reduction in his risks and bought three months of time to completion.

The reduction in risk, in the case of material C, is crucial to the decision process, because it is the least costly alternative and its original probability estimate was low. By improving the predictability of success of material C, the environmental administrator can either rule it out as infeasible or improve its chance of success sufficiently to make it a worthwhile risk. Suppose that the modeling study and the first three months of research on material C now make it seem reasonably feasible as the catalytic material with a 70 percent chance of success. This seems like a reasonable risk, and the administrator continues the research and development on material C, although he makes standby plans to pursue material B should material C fail at some point in further research. By the time the research has advanced to event 7 in the task list, the outcome would be virtually certain, because the remaining steps are mainly engineering. The engineering of a product is usually more tractable than the

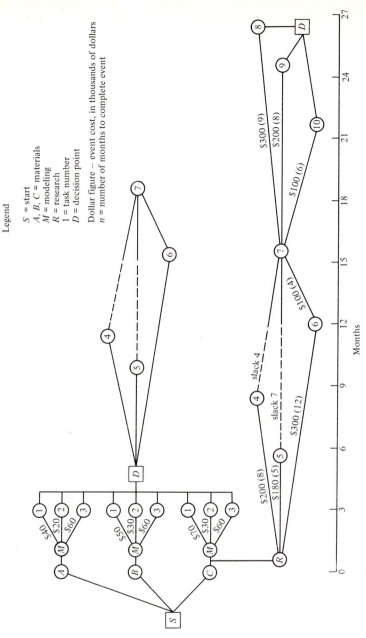

Legend

S = start
A, B, C = materials
M = modeling
R = research
1 = task number
D = decision point

Dollar figure – event cost, in thousands of dollars
n = number of months to complete event

Figure 23-3 Network of time and cost for initial modeling and research.

471

behavior of the physical materials; and the physical behavior of the materials will be virtually known by event 7 which is a second decision point thirteen months in the future from decision point *D.* The time of the several events is shown on the preceding network.

PERT and the Critical Path

The events in the research plan for material C are shown in PERT form in the network diagram. PERT (which stands for Performance Evaluation Review Technique) is a scheduling plan to control time in project management. The minimum, average, and maximum times are usually calculated in various combinations on a computer to show a complete PERT network. In the above example, only average times are used. Nevertheless, the average time does show the critical path.

The critical path is the longest time sequence of events to completion. In the example, the critical path is the line from the start of research on material C to event 6, then to event 7, and finally to event 8. These three events require twenty-five months to complete. Notice that there is four months of slack time (unused time) between events 4 and 7, and seven months slack between events 5 and 7. If events 6 and 7 could be shorted, the whole schedule could be shorted or collapsed. Then the managerial problem is to break these bottlenecks which can often be done by increasing the manpower or facilities to create a "crash" program to complete the event. Suppose that a 50 percent increase in expenditure would half the time needed to complete the event. Then, which events would the program manager seek to "crash"?

The first obvious choice would be to increase the effort and expenditure on events 6 and 7. By spending $200,000, he could save six months' time on the project. Then the critical path would run through events 4, 7, and 8. At that stage, he could cut out another two months by spending $100,000 on event 4, or cut off three months by spending $250,000 on events 9 and 8. It does not help much to decrease 9 without 8, because only one month can be reduced from the schedule (at a cost of $150,000). Perhaps the most effective decision for the project manager would be to expend the $300,000 to reduce the time on events 4, 6, and 7. This would bring him to a decision point of virtual certainty about material in eight months rather than fifteen.

His other option, as an insurance against failure, would be to start the research phase of material B concurrently with C in either the third or eighth month. This would increase his chances of solving the material problems in a minimal time span, albeit at increased cost.

The PERT network also makes it possible for the project manager to keep track of his costs on a current basis to see (1) whether he is staying on his budgetary targets, and (2) what level of increased costs he can afford to trade off to buy more time or greater certainty. The use of PERT for accounting control in this manner is sometimes referred to as a PERT cost system, to distinguish it from the usual PERT time, schedule, and event control which was illustrated first in the example above.

PERT cost makes it possible to accumulate obligations and expenditures by events for the operational information system. That is, the accumulated cost per event per time period (daily, weekly, or monthly) can be compared with the planned budget for that task, and this comparison of actual cost with budget can then become the means of exception reporting. Those tasks and events which are running over their budget can be singled out for attention, by flagging their overexpended condition in the information system reports.

In PERT cost networks, the budgetary planning is also prepared in terms of a range of estimates for each event: a minimum, average, and high level of expenditure corresponding to similar time estimates. This makes it possible for the program manager to ascertain his maximum liability or overrun condition, in a "worst case," where everything in the work performance goes wrong. If everything goes wrong, this indicates that a poor planning job was done in the work design in the first place, and the entire operating system must be replanned. The merit of PERT cost is that, if this happens, the environmental administrator knows it early while he can still do something about correcting the situation.

The absence of close cost control on tasks per time period can result in heavy overruns which, when discovered late in the implementation state, may have accumulated so many contractual or technical commitments that there is no turning back. That is, when a program has gone too far into its implementation stage and too much money has been spent, the options open to the manager are effectively gone. He has neither the time nor the money to make a major correction and start again. In effect, he is committed to try to make the best of a bad situation. This usually results in his trying to justify a bad program in terms of unexpected technical difficulties and the need for more money.

Once a manager has been forced, unwittingly perhaps by lack of timely information, into this defensive mode, he can scarcely retreat from it without loss of reputation as a manager. The point is that bad decisions tend to compound themselves into more bad decisions, with endless justifications as to who is to be blamed. The investigations into overruns on government contracts demonstrate this time and again, and the same type of argument appears repeatedly in corporate board rooms.

The way to avoid self-justifying failures is to catch the planning error early by close control over cost and time schedules for discrete tasks and events. Planning is always a chancy affair. The uncertainties of human behavior, technology, social change, or environment can always upset what appear to be carefully developed plans. Changing plans should be regarded as a routine and frequent adjustment to new circumstances and new information, but this requires that new information be frequently available.

One can almost posit the principle that the effectiveness of planning is directly related to its frequency of revision based upon continual feedback of information. That is, planning requires an accurate and continuous information system to provide correctional changes in the time and cost estimates for work assignments as actual operational experiences with the tasks unfold.

Planning must be experience corrected at short time intervals. If the time intervals become long, then the vested-interests in the mistakes tend to compound themselves to make bad decisions worse.

ORGANIZATION ACCOUNTABILITY FOR TASK PERFORMANCE

If the informational feedback and the replanning of work assignments are to be a frequent and routine role of management, then the responsibilities for work redesign must be clear so that an early and rapid redirection of effort from supervisor to worker is consumated. This means there must be a precise and direct relationship between the task lists, the network of events, the information system, and the organization structure. That is, a conversion table is needed to relate work, events, information, and organization; and this look-up table might be stored in a computer memory as part of the information system, or it can be a manual/visual table. One visual version of this conversion table is the linear responsibility chart.[2] The task list for developing a catalystic material has been converted into a linear responsibility chart in Figure 23-4.

The research department has been delegated responsibility for making a first approximation of the physical qualities and interactions among various catalytic materials, and this is shown in the linear responsibility chart by an entry (the number 1) opposite the task under research. The number 1 is the number of the event in the PERT network. The engineering department is responsible for event 2, the formulation of the reactions into a mathematical model; and the computer department is responsible for calculating the model. Similarly, other departments are given assignments for the rest of the events. Notice that there are two

[2]David I. Cleland and William R. King, *Systems Analysis and Project Management*, McGraw-Hill Book Company, New York, 1968, pp. 198ff.

Figure 23-4 Linear Responsibility Chart for Task in Developing Catalytic Material

Tasks	Departments							Contractors	
	Research	Engineering	Computer	Manufacturing	Marketing	Purchasing	Accounting	University contractor	Metallurgy contractor
Modeling:									
Physical analysis	1								
Formulate		2							
Computer			3						
Research:									
Chemical reaction								4	
Physical properties	5								
Processing				6					
Structural shape									7
Temperature									8
Density		9							
Configuration		10							
Management:									
Material						11			
Market research					12				
Consumer requirements					13				
Payroll							14		
Contract payments							15		

outside contractors, and their task assignments also appear in the linear responsibility chart. A university is doing the chemical reaction research, and a metallurgical contractor is responsible for the structural shape and temperature characteristics of the material.

The linear responsibility chart is a useful conversion table for a number of purposes: (1) to allocate budgets, (2) to set up the cost accounting system, and (3) to create the project management supervisory structure. The budgetary planning and allocations occur as the project manager writes a work order to specify the work to be done by each department. At the same time, he transfers the funds for them to do the work. This sets up a budgetary target and account.

The accounting system can then record the actual costs incurred as the work is done and accumulate them against the performing department. Each department then becomes a cost center for the work which it does on the project, and the project manager can establish accountability by reviewing the actual accumulated cost against the budgets which he allocated. That is to say, a cost accounting system with departments as cost centers can be derived from the task list and the linear responsibility chart.

The linear responsibility chart also makes possible the development of a matrix organization plan. The normal company organization chart is shown below (Figure 23-5), with departmental functions reporting to the president. Across these departmental lines is shown the project manager's allocation of events (by number) to the departments and contractors.

The definition of the work to be done is, then, the basic building block upon which the role of management rests. We have seen, in a series of steps, how the task (work) list became the basis first of the network of work flows, secondly of the information system (time and cost schedule reporting), thirdly of departmental assignments with budgetary and cost accounting identification, and fourthly of the organizational structure. These relations may be shown schematically in Figure 23-6.

Perhaps this schematic diagram demonstrates more clearly than any other illustration that organization is a dependent variable derived from the technical structure of the production process. If the tasks and work process are well-defined in the first place and a close control is placed over the network of time and cost scheduling, organizational arrangements can take a variety of forms, depending on the personalities and behavior of participants. When tasks, work design, and networks are tightly circumscribed by the information system, the organizational role is highly flexible and suited to the people concerned.

The preoccupation with organization structure as a first priority and independent variable represents a misunderstanding of management. Such organizational thinking is the road to management-in-reverse. The operational way to run an enterprise is to design the work process and set boundary conditions on it with time and cost schedules. Then the organizational structure conforms to the technology and people concerned.

THE ECOLOGICAL MONITORING NETWORK

The environmental administrator needs an internal, operational information system to determine the degree of progress in implementing his own managerial goals. The knowledge from the operating information system tells him the extent to which he has succeeded in carrying out his plans, where he has problems, and what resources he has to solve them. In short, the operational information system is the means by which the environmental administrator achieves direction and control over the internal organization and the performance of the environmental program.

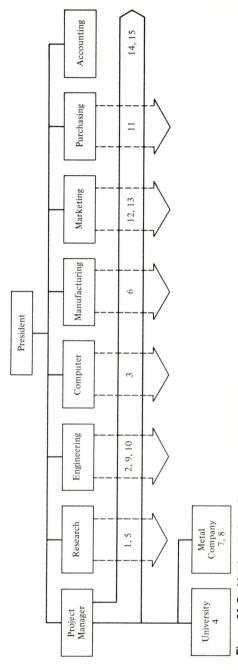

Figure 23-5 Matrix relation of project organization to company departments.

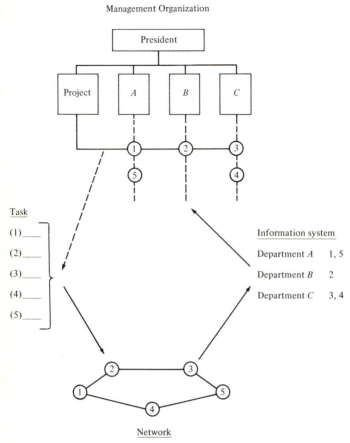

Figure 23-6 Schematic of the relation to tasks, information system, budgetary control, and organizational structure.

But even if the environmental administrator knows the internal effectiveness of his operations, he still needs to know something more to make decisions of future plans. That is, he needs to know whether the program he is implementing is doing anything to improve the environment. That is, he needs a measure of the effectiveness of his actions upon environmental quality. The whole purpose of his endeavor is to interact with the environment in a manner to bring about ecological improvement. If he has not improved environmental quality, his program is of little value no matter how internally efficient it may be. A measurement of environmental quality, therefore, is crucial to determine the worth of the program. The Council on Environmental Quality has said, on this subject:

Monitoring the environment is one of the keys to effective management of environmental quality. One cannot detect environmental changes, desirable or undesirable, natural or manmade, without established base lines and repeated observations. Such measurements are essential for the identification of environmental needs and the establishment of program priorities, as well as the evaluation of program effectiveness, and they provide an early warning system for environmental problems which allow corrective action to be taken before the problems become serious.[3]

The second report of the Council then describes some of the discrete efforts to monitor environmental quality, a few examples of which might indicate the nature of the measurements and the scope of the monitoring problem. Water quality, as we have seen in Chapter 11, is frequently measured by the biochemical oxygen demand of organic wastes disposed in the streams, and by toxic and chemical wastes which are exceedingly difficult to remove. The thousands of miles of waterways in the United States present a large moitoring problem; yet water quality is probably more completely measured, in terms of the number of instrumentation stations or samples, than any other environmental area. From these water measurements, the extent of pollution can be estimated. The Office of Water Quality, in the Environmental Protection Agency, estimates that 72 percent of the watersheds are predominantly or extensively polluted.[4] The breakdown of stream pollution by region is shown Figure 23-7.

The table indicates that the waters of the United States are uniformly polluted to a high degree with the exception of the Southeast, which has less pollution, and the Northeast, which is by far the worst.

Another form of monitoring environmental quality is the measurement of air pollution by selected cities. Air pollution monitoring is usually done by ground-based instruments. Los Angeles has had perhaps a score

[3]*Environmental Quality*, Second Annual Report of the Council on Environmental Quality, August 1971, Washington, pp. 209–210.
[4]Ibid., p. 220.

Figure 23-7

Region	Percentage of watersheds predominantly or extensively polluted
Pacific Coast	73.1
Northern Plains	70.8
Southern Plains	78.8
Southeast	54.4
Central	75.0
Northeast	86.1

or more of instrumented observation points in operation during the past decade, and this is one of the more highly instrumented air monitoring systems. But even in Los Angeles, there has been no way to tell what the actual air pollution or photochemistry interactions are in the atmosphere, at many points in the basin with no instrumentation, or at the human interface where the air is inhaled. Most of the data on air pollution, therefore, represent a few readings over time, which is something less than a close monitorship over air quality. An example of the kinds of measurements which are available is shown below in terms of the nitrogen oxide readings for Chicago and Washington.[5] Nitrogen oxides are emitted by both stationary power plants and automobiles, and they are a significant measure of the degree of air pollution because they are very reactive and form much of the oxidants and ozone which are deleterious to health.

The readings show that the degree of air pollution, in terms of nitrogen oxides, is high in Chicago and slowly becoming worse. Washington started early in the decade with relatively low air pollution, which has worsened very rapidly, to become about as bad as Chicago. Since Washington is not an industrial city like Chicago, which has many stationary power sources, the increase in air pollution in the nation's capital must be attributed almost wholly to the automobile.

The Environmental Protection Agency has also tried to translate air pollution data into health effects. The human health effects are estimated to incur costs of at least $2 billion, as shown in Figure 23-9.[6]

Other estimates have placed the health damage costs much higher, at $6 billion per year; and the total cost of air pollution damage to man, property, materials, and vegetation has been estimated at $16 billion annually.[7]

[5]Ibid., p. 212.
[6]Ibid., p. 106.
[7]*National Wildlife*. National Wildlife Federation, October–November 1971, p. 31, Washington.

Figure 23-8   Annual Levels of Nitrogen Oxides,
Milligrams per Square Meter

	Washington	Chicago
1962	56	81
1963	66	77
1964	68	87
1965	66	81
1966	66	105
1967	81	94
1968	88	90

Figure 23-9

	Health costs of air pollution, in millions of dollars
Respiratory diseases	1,220
Cancer	390
Cardiovascular disease	470

The several illustrations indicate that there are a number of discrete and separate measures of different aspects of environmental quality. The important managerial question is how these selected indicators can be aggregated into some useful measure of the quality of environment as a whole. The Council on Environmental Quality has commented on such an overall measure to this effect:

> This chapter has not answered the question of whether overall environmental quality is getting better or worse. . . the data are either not available or not reliable enough to give definite answers. . . . By next year the choice of appropriate environmental indices should be made. However, it will take a number of years before truly reliable data can be obtained for all the indices. Major changes probably will be necessary in such basic matters as selection or monitoring sites, instrumentation and frequency of samples. Implementation of these changes will then take several years.[8]

Besides the sheer instrumentation task to develop environmental indicators, a substantial effort and investment in developing a data handling and reporting system will be needed. The communication, computers, and management reports needed for an ecological information system are yet to be developed, though a number of conceptual models have been proposed.[9] These models are basically a systems analysis of what kind of data input would be needed to measure environmental quality for air, water, land use, or living space, together with the means of communicating, assembling, and reporting the data. Such conceptual models, while interesting and useful for planning purposes, await two crucial steps before they can be implemented: (1) the monitoring instruments to make the data input, and (2) the criteria as to what constitutes "quality."

The standards used for air and water quality today are largely chemical and biological, related to health effects. In addition, however, environmental quality also represents many aspects of group value judg-

---

[8]CEQ, Second Annual Report, op. cit., p. 241.
[9]*Scientific Manpower Utilization,* 1965–1966, Committee on Labor and Public Welfare, U.S. Senate Special Subcommittee on Utilization of Scientific Manpower, Washington, 1966.

ments relating to desired characteristics of diversity, privacy, convenience, amenities, cultural enrichment, or social order. That is, quality standards encompass those characteristics which give worth to living; and these are, in the end, qualitative judgments of human wants. The determination of these human wants and their conversion into environmental quality standards is theoretically possible through survey research methods and political participation.

One attempt to go beyond mere pollution measurements for air and water to a more general index of environmental quality has been attempted by the National Wildlife Federation. Their composite index of environmental quality includes measures of air, water, soil, timber, mineral, recycling, population, living space, and wildlife; but it does not cover aesthetic or cultural qualities. The two quality measures, as to human living space and wildlife do, however, begin to approach the issue of ecological balance, which certainly must be among the ultimate criteria for environmental quality. The Environmental Quality Index of the National Wildlife Federation has been estimated for three successive years, 1969, 1970, and 1971. During these three years the Environmental Quality Index has been gradually declining. The elements of the index are shown in Figure 23-10.

The overall environmental quality index declined by 1.5 points in 1971, and by a larger amount the previous year. The worst environmental quality problem is in air pollution, according to this index, and the next most serious is water pollution.

Not only is air quality the number one problem in the country, but it is getting worse. William Ruckelshaus, head of the Environmental Protection Agency, says that seven cities, New York, Chicago, St. Louis, Baltimore, Hartford, Buffalo, and Philadelphia, will have a hard time meeting the 1975 air quality standards. New York will have the most serious problem meeting the sulfur oxide standards; and New York,

Figure 23-10   Environmental Quality Index 1971[10]

Environmental Quality	Index
Air	34
Water	40
Minerals	48
Wildlife	53
Living Space	58
Timber	76
Soil	78
Overall environmental quality	55

[10]National Wildlife, op. cit., p. 40.

Chicago, Los Angeles, Denver, and Cincinnati will have difficulty meeting the carbon monoxide standards. The real problems are that clean fuels are getting scarcer for power plants, and automobile equipment makers are having difficulty reducing emissions to the control levels. The outlook is not promising, therefore, for turning around the decline in air quality by technical means, and politically there is little movement to find new means of urban transit which are less damaging to air quality.

Water quality is the next most serious problem, although the index of water quality is no longer declining. However, the present condition of much of the nation's drinking water is not tolerable, in that 36 percent of it contains bacteria or chemicals beyond standards or safe limits, 9 percent is potentially dangerous, and 79 percent is not inspected annually.[11]

Wildlife too is threatened by chemicals, as well as the loss of habitat. To the extent that wildlife is the indicator and precursor of both ecological balance and human health, the loss of bird populations is of considerable concern. Birds frequently live close to man, and in any case subsist from a food chain that has many parallels to man's. The osprey, canvasback duck, and Cooper's hawk have declined in population by 12 to 25 percent in recent years. Although there are thousands of brown pelicans on California's Pacific Coast, only one chick hatched in 1970. The number of endangered animal species has risen from 78 in 1968 to 101 in 1971.

The value of an environmental quality index to an administrator, of course, is that it gives him some indication of the results of his actions, whether there has been in fact an improvement in the environment, and where the significant problems are. The environmental indices available now undoubtedly need improvement by more complete and accurate data. But even now, the indicators are clear enough in showing that many aspects of our environment are in grave condition and getting worse, particularly in air pollution and wildlife.

To the extent that ecological balance and biological health are the desired objectives of an environmental program, the indicators demonstrate that there are serious hazards and imbalances in the hydologic cycle, atmospheric conditions, and the food chain. Since these cycles are so basic to the survival of man as well as the ecology, the future must be regarded as bearing serious human risks which are worth understanding and correcting. As the number of endangered species rises, the time span for remedial action becomes shorter before reaching a point of no return. Where that point is poses a serious enough question so that an adequate information system is essential if we are to understand the ecology and make intelligent decisions.

[11]Ibid., p. 29.

THE PUBLIC INFORMATIONAL NETWORK

A well-informed public is essential to solve ecological problems because environmental quality can be improved only by significant behavioral change on the part of human beings who are despoiling the environment. Behavioral change is required in population growth, transportation habits, urban densities, and chemical usage—perhaps as well in economic growth, power consumption, water, and land use. Some of these behaviors are related to basic biological functions, whose alteration depends upon depth of knowledge and the degree of peril in the environment. Therefore, environmental information, to reach the public with sufficient data and accuracy to convey the risks of biological damage inherent in present human practices, must be a very comprehensive and effective communication system. It is difficult to see how such extensive public information can reach popular levels without heavy reliance upon television; community groups, and informational aids, such as letters, posters, and educational pamphlets. The importance of television is already apparent in the significant coverage which newscasts have provided on ecological subjects.

The content of environmental data made available to the public is derived mainly from the ecological monitoring information system. That is, the key indicators of environmental quality and their meaning in terms of biological damage constitute the essential message which the public needs to know to make informed decisions about its own behavior. To the extent that declining wildlife populations and the deterioration in air and water quality convey peril to human health, such facts need to be known; for they are the informational feedback mechanism by which human decisions may be altered.

The informational loop for conveying ecological data to the public would consist of two parts: the outgoing messages, and the measurement of the returned response. The outgoing messages must be factual and accurate as to the quality of the air, water, land, and species survival, together with as objective a measure as can be developed on the health damage effects to human beings.

The health damage effects will always be subject to some differences of interpretation because the interdependencies and interactions of the environmental influences on the human system are difficult to isolate and measure. Epidemiological studies (i.e., general health statistics based upon the incidence and distribution of diseases in the population) are one reasonable way to resolve these objective difficulties. Epidemiological studies show that exposure to air pollution, for example, does correspond to higher rates of human cancer, respiratory diseases, and bodily resistance to infections. As an example of such a study, Dr. Bertram Carnow, chief of environmental health at the University of Illinois College of Medicine, recently conducted one of the most comprehensive studies on the health effects of air pollution. Dr. Carnow reported of his study, in the city of Chicago, that in ten days of high pollution there was a very sharp and significant rise in deaths of men over fifty-five. For respiratory disease, there was more than a doubling of deaths during the period. Taking only bronchitis and emphysema, Dr. Carnow found a quadrupling of deaths on high-pollution days. In cardiovascular diseases an average of eight excess deaths occurred each day from coronary heart disease.[12]

The number of careful epidemiological studies on health effects of environmental pollution are relatively few. A broad series of such studies, along with specific medical research into the mechanism of biological damage, would be of inestimable value in helping the public assess the degree of risk it wished to assume in being exposed to environmental hazards.

Information alone will not, of course, change behavior, witness the limited effect on smoking habits of the information about cancer being induced by cigarette smoking. A variety of incentives may need to be coupled with information, which is after all only the rationale for decision. The conditions of a decision are also influenced by costs, regulations, alternatives, or social disapprobation. Some effectuating measures, such as these, may be required along with information to bring about behavioral change.

In addition to adequate knowledge about biological damage in the environment, a public environmental information system needs a feedback mechanism by which the public can reflect its choices on how much effort and resources it would like to see allocated to solve the problem. This resource allocation may represent a personal sacrifice, in that the individual may be required to make expenditures of his own, say for equipment to reduce emissions on his car. It may also represent a public allocation of tax money for environmental improvement, in which case the individual would need to express the degree of sacrifice via taxation which he is prepared to bear.

In short, the public environmental information system is a two-way communication function: First, a transmission of knowledge about biological hazards, and secondly a feedback from the public of the appropriate response.

SUMMARY

The environmental administrator has need for three informational loops to manage an ecological program. This first is an operational information

[12] *Los Angeles Times*, Nov. 4, 1971.

system which is built upon the specific tasks and events which he must implement. These events become scheduled into a network of steps from which he can derive the data to control time, performance, and cost.

The organizational accountability for performance of task assignments is an important aspect of control, and the project manager can establish this control by creating a responsibility chart relating tasks to organizational units. With tasks, time, cost, and organizational responsibility assigned, an operational information system can monitor performace by cost center, and also identify the responsible organizational unit if performance slips.

The second information system needed by an environmental administrator is a monitoring network which measures the qualitative changes in the ecosystem. The indicators should measure the deviations from quality standards, which have been set to prevent biological damage to man or the ecology. Such a monitoring system takes a large instrumentation network. Water quality monitoring is perhaps most completely established, but even here 79 percent of the nation's drinking water is not tested annually. Air pollution monitoring exists only in major cities, and then at a few selected ground observation points. Little is known about pollution reactions in higher atmospheres. Until better instrumentation is available, one generalized indicator of ecological balance is the number of endangered species, which reflect the condition of the nutrient cycle upon which all depend. The number of endangered species increased from 78 in 1968 to 101 in 1971.

A third necessary network is a public environmental information system which would convey factual data on the degree of biological risk to which human beings are exposed, plus a feedback mechanism which indicates public response. Ecological information will, of course, have uncertainties due to the complexity of biological interactions. These uncertainties can be dealt with, in part, by epidemiological studies which show the incidence and distribution of diseases under varying or adverse environmental conditions. Several epidemiological studies have indicated elevated morbidity and mortality rates associated with chemical contaminations, air, and water pollution.

DISCUSSION QUESTIONS

1 How might the decisions on the catalytic development be altered, assuming different probabilities as the research progressed? Give examples.
2 What would the information system for the engineering department consist of, in the catalytic example, in terms of tasks, budgets, and time schedules? Suppose the engineering department fell behind in all its tasks, how would it affect the project and what would you do?

3 Given the present availability of instrumentation for monitoring environmental quality, what would you do, as an environmental administrator, to measure your own progress in improving environmental quality?
4 What steps would you take to try to make a public environmental network effective?

PROBLEM

Construct from Figure 23-4 an organizational chart for the catalytic material project, showing a statement of work for each department, and what a monthly information report would contain on the performance of each department.

Chapter 24

The Politics of Environmental Administration

The politics of environmental administration have their origin in three major issues: (1) What is adequate quality in the environment?, (2) How shall the choices of quality and technical alternatives be decided?, and (3) Who shall bear the costs of environmental improvement? These issues have been inherent in previous discussions, but a review might clarify the political controversies involved.

The quality issue is basically one of biological health and ecological balance, and it is usually resolved by a panel of government experts setting standards as to a safe level of air quality or water quality. However, since these standards are set by administrative hearing procedures, compromises are frequent with those who desire lenient standards for economic reasons. Then the citizen, who may feel that his health or satisfaction still suffers from poor environmental quality, has the burden placed upon him to prove that his ill-health is caused by pollution. The placing of the burden of proof on the citizen, in effect, permits the degraded environment to persist, because the citizen seldom has the scientific or financial resources to demonstrate conclusively the cause of his ailment, particularly when the biological reactions are complex and interdependent. This leaves the citizen with only two recourses: (1) to reconcile himself to poor environment, or (2) to get into the politics of how standards are set and how quality technical choices are made.

The second issue, how the choices are made on quality standards in relation to the technical alternatives, brings economic institutions into the political arena, because their equipment, investments, products of services are affected. That is, if tight emission or effluent standards are set, a company has to make heavy investments in new control equipment. Or, if a substitute form of product is proposed, such as mass transit in lieu of automobiles, the whole corporate future is at stake. In these circumstances, the corporations may be expected to bring to bear their financial and political resources, in order to prevent adverse economic effects upon themselves.

The third issue, who shall bear the cost, is usually a battle to shift the cost to someone else. The cost of environmental improvement may basically be shifted in three ways: (1) by raising prices, (2) by taxation, or (3) by doing nothing and placing the health-damage sacrifice on some other person or species. These several issues will be treated in the context of:

1 Why environmental politics are as they are
2 Participatory technology
3 Corruption of public interest
4 The public policy process
5 Public initiative in participation in administrative rulings
6 Problems of compliance
7 Political alignments
8 Crisis politics without crisis

WHY ENVIRONMENTAL POLITICS ARE
AS THEY ARE

The California air pollution case epitomizes the three major issues and why environmental politics are as they are. Two-thirds of the people of the state have regarded air pollution as a leading public problem, and less than one-sixth thought enough was being done to remedy it. This indicated clearly a frustration about government inactivity and nonresponsiveness; it resulted in an ennui concerning whether anything can be done. Yet a flurry of voter sentiment in favor of cleaning up air pollution in 1970 caused some legislative and administrative action. The results on the three basic political issues were:

1　Stringent air quality standards were set, but without sufficient implementation to see that they would be met. The consequence was a set of unrealizable standards and a program which did not provide a real solution.

2　A constitutional amendment was offered to divert part of the dedicated gas tax funds (worth $1 billion per year) to mass transit, as one technical solution to air pollution. A strong grass roots campaign by citizens nearly passed the amendment, but it was defeated by the highway lobby who spent about 10 times the amount of money which the citizens had, to defeat it.

3　The cost of smog was then transferred to two groups: (*a*) to persons with respiratory diseases as the cost of higher mortality rates, and (*b*) to new car buyers as the cost of higher prices for emission controls on new cars, even though the emission controls on new cars alone will not enable the community to achieve the air quality standards.

The series of nonsolutions in this case raise the question, "Why did this political outcome occur?" The citizens' desires were to improve air quality. What they got instead were unrealizable air quality standards, a rededication of funds to build more freeways to make more smog, higher car prices, and increased respiratory morbidity and mortality. As Kenneth Clark said of civilization in the past forty years, our institutions could hardly have done worse.

The reason the decision turned out as it did was that the wrong decision criterion was used. The decision criterion under which we operate is geared to foster economic growth and development. All the institutions are governed by that decision criterion, as are the rewards, incentives, organization structures, and financial resources. So when existing institutions are confronted with a choice between economic and environmental goals, their resources go into defeating environmental measures in order to achieve economic objectives. Since institutions have a resource advantage on specific issues relative to citizens, the outcome may be environmentally grievous but politically understandable.

Still, the grievous treatment of the environment in our present political economy is changing, according to Caldwell. As the social pressure on the environment becomes severe, and as man's relation to his milieu becomes hazardous, political change alters customary practices. Priorities and rationing of scarce environmental quality become necessary, and social choice begins to override self-interest decision making.[1]

Caldwell believes that at least three conditions must be realized for the citizenry to acquire political strength in environmental issues. First,

---

[1]Lynton K. Caldwell, *Environment: A Challenge for Modern Society,* American Museum of Natural History, Garden City, N. Y., 1970, p. 132.

the goals and tasks of environmental policy must be agreed upon by organized groups, which implies common values and shared beliefs. Secondly, the concept of environmental quality and its consequences must be more widely diffused, which means an environmental education and information system. Thirdly, the structure of public policy making must be adapted to permit consideration of alternative means of improving the environment.[2]

The alternative means of improving the environment are based on technical information. Obvious difficulties exist in trying to bring technological information and alternatives into the decision process. One is that relatively few people understand science and technology. Another is that those who do, the scientists, are trained to present factual findings but not to make judgments on what they mean to humanity. Presidential science advisor, Edward E. David, recommends that a science advisor should present options but not pass judgments. Most scientists, in an effort to preserve the objectivity of their research, deliberately avoid making any but technical judgments. The result is that they inadvertently fall into the role of advocate for the interests of their employers.[3]

PARTICIPATORY TECHNOLOGY

If scientists avoid value judgments, and if the public does not know enough about technology to make judgments of their own, what is clearly needed is some form of participatory technology, which involves public participation in the development and use of technology for the general welfare. The emergence of participatory technology has several origins: The first is that technological questions often embody significant political value choices which become binding upon the society. Secondly, technological alternatives are often political processes in which issues are posed and resolved in technical terms to which citizens do not have easy access. Thirdly, the public decision process of an industrial society is not well structured for identifying, publicizing, and resolving the political issues implicit in technology.[4]

The public order perpetuates obsolete values and perceptions which are derived from economic want and insecurity of past generations. The development of powerful technologies has alleviated the economic need and poverty for most; but the values in the decsion structure have not changed to encompass such vital new issues as environment, race, urban

[2]Ibid., p. 61.
[3]Constance Holden, "Public Interest: New Group Seeks Redefinition of Scientists Role," *Science,* July 9, 1971, vol. 173, p. 131.
[4]James D. Carroll, "Participatory Technology," *Science,* Feb. 19, 1971, vol. 171, p. 648.

development, population growth, educational opportunity, or the direction of technology.

Today, in the face of population growth, environmental degradation, and technological complexity, legislative bodies delegate the responsibility for developing and controlling technologies to administrative agencies. The objectives of these administrative agencies frequently mix value and technique in a way which furthers the interests of those who support their programs, mainly the economic groups who benefit from the agency.

The lack of an adequate public initiative and inquiry in administrative processes causes the responsibility for scrutinizing mixed questions of value and technique to pass, by default, to interest groups who are not representative nor objective in making such judgments. And indeed, the misdirection of technology by this process in recent years has denigrated science to its lowest ebb in public esteem for a century or more.

The reconstitution of science to its historic role as a powerful technique for improvement of the human condition awaits a redirection of research toward more socially acceptable purposes. The scientists cannot assume this role, because they have chosen to pursue judgments which are "value-free." The value judgments are made then by institutional users of technology.

Some attempts have been made toward the realignment of administrative decisions by measures to enable the public to participate in technological decisions. Three forms of participatory technology have been: private citizen litigation, technology assessment, and ad hoc advocacy groups. Private citizen litigation has been enlarged by the "private attorney general" concept under which courts have recently permitted citizens to present a case as an advocate of the public interest. These cases have covered such subjects as power plant placement, impairment of scenic views, pollution, and pesticides.

A second form of participatory technology is the process of technological assessment in which a panel of experts, under sponsorship of a public or community agency, undertakes to evaluate the impact of technical alternatives upon society. House Bill 6698 of March 7, 1967 defines technological assessment as "a method for identifying the potentials of applied research and technology and promoting ways and means to accomplish their transfer into practical use, and identifying the undesirable by-products and side effects of such applied research and technology in advance of their crystallization, and informing the public of their potential danger in order that appropriate steps may be taken to eliminate or minimize them."

The third form of participatory technology has been ad hoc activity by concerned citizen, scientific, and community groups who have attempted to publicize what they believe to be deleterious side effects of technological endeavors. Such groups have taken active stands on such issues as nuclear testing, population growth, sonic booms, new towns, air pollution, biological warfare, and power plant siting.

Despite these efforts to develop a participatory technology, the need for a participatory process itself has deep implications about the adequacy of the theory and practice of representative government.[5] Traditional political theory in America assumes that citizens should express their demands for public action through political representatives, and conflicting demands will be reconciled by legislative compromise. This theory of government does not correspond well with political realities or the administration of technical services. The political array is such that citizens have less influence than organized institutions; and secondly, the delegation of technical decisions to bureaucracies submerges political choices in administrative processes which have limited visibility, scrutiny, or public participation.

CORRUPTION OF PUBLIC INTEREST

Political decisions reside heavily in (1) those who are elected or appointed to public office, (2) those who finance or influence the selection of public officials, and (3) those who make value judgments on the use of technology. In the latter two respects, industry has a dominant role. The importance of business campaign contributions and lobbying is obvious. The technological influence of industry is also significant through its research and development expenditures.

Technological development is often associated with "pure" scientists in their laboratories pursuing their own intellectual interests, and this is true to a considerable extent of basic research in universities. Even here, however, the research is shaped by federal funding determined by administrative agencies.

At the more applied level, the purposive decisions in research are made by those who allocate research and development funds, and this is done principally by industrial executives in pursuit of their product line expansion. Therefore, the important decisions as to the use of technology lie primarily in private hands, where the decision process does not concern itself with side effects or public costs, either economic or biological. That is, the decision structure was conceived, in times past, to maximize output, without regard to public participation or public costs.

[5]Ibid., p. 652.

The guidelines of this decision structure make pollution, which is a public cost, the concern of someone else—not of the business-technological decision maker.

The industrial ability to foster or retard environmental improvement is enormous.[6] The power comes, not only from monetary resources and political sophistication, but more importantly from the fact that the ultimate decision to pollute or not pollute rests with the individual firm. Government may set and enforce standards, but without a considerable degree of voluntary compliance, pollution abatement cannot be achieved. In this sense, the private sector holds a veto power over environmental quality.

The veto power of the private sector over environmental quality is particularly significant in view of the "environmental backlash" which has been building in industrial circles. This backlash is apparent in trade journals and in legislative threats to weaken environmental control agencies.

John W. Gardner, former Secretary of Health, Education and Welfare, has pointed out that the political process, behind the scenes, has become a game of barter involving campaign contributions, appointments to high office, business favors, favorable legal decisions, favorable contracts. The soaring cost of political campaigns, $100 million or more for the Presidency, has increased the potential for influence and corruption. The nation is hurt when great decisions are made on the basis of payment of political obligation, private gain, or the consolidation of personal power. Sound public policy cannot be formulated, and the public process fails.[7]

THE PUBLIC POLICY PROCESS

The failure of the public policy process would, of course, strike at the very heart of democratic prodecures. The public policy process is a complex set of interrelationships, involving the legislature, the presidency, the bureaucracy, and those who seek to influence all three. Policy is frequently associated primarily with the legislature; but this form of policy making has become, in a technical society, increasingly general and permissive, rather than specific or mandatory. The detail of administrative actions to implement legislation, especially as to their cost and technical implications, has become so involved and minute that many administrative rulings have more force and effect than legislation. There-

[6]J. Clarence Davies III, *The Politics of Pollution*, Pegasus, New York, 1970, p. 91.
[7]John W. Gardner, *Corruption in Public Life*, address to American Association of Feature Editors, Portland, Ore., in *Los Angeles Times*, Oct. 24, 1971.

fore, policy making has gravitated away from the Congress toward the bureaucracy; and Congress has seen this as a growing power of the Presidency, which is, from the legislative view, to be eschewed. In this perception, Congress has mistaken its adversary, because the bureaucracy is quite able and willing to govern without the President as well;[8] and the President's influence on administrative detail is as removed, in specific knowledge, as that of Congress.

Political scientists have been concerned about how administrative plans and actions of the bureaucracy can be brought back into the cognizance of the Presidency and Congress. Reagan has proposed that the looseness of our national administrative style should be reoriented in the direction of presidential planning to strengthen the nation's capacity to govern itself.[9] In particular, he suggests that both the Congress and the Presidency establish national policy analysis offices, that of the President might be the Council of Economic Advisors. The three annual presidential messages on the budget, state of the union, and economic report might be combined into a single national economic budget plan. The framework of the overall plan might then be used to relate and integrate separate administrative plans of each bureau. By this linkage, some of the remoteness would be bridged, and a greater degree of direction and governance achieved.

Even with better planning, democratic procedure presumes some citizen input into the policy process. The policy process can be categorized into five steps, according to Jennings, that of (1) initiation of action, (2) fixing priorities, (3) mobilizing and using resources to gain acceptance of chosen alternatives, (4) legitimation, and (5) implementation.[10]

Policy is more difficult to initiate than it appears, especially in the environmental field. The appearance of ease in policy initiation is associated with the legislature where representatives can easily introduce bills. Policy in the form of administrative rulings is initiated in the bureaucracy. However, individual citizens find it difficult to initiate policy directly; and their access to policy initiation at either the legislative or the administrative level is cumbersome and difficult.

Fixing priorities is done partly through caucus or administrative review. The priorities fixed by administrative procedure sometimes involve hearings but most frequently are determined by an administrator's decision. Again, the individual's access to the priority process is

[8]Michael D. Reagan, *The Administration of Public Policy,* Scott, Foresman, and Company, Glenview, Ill., 1969, p. 279.

[9]Ibid., pp. 140–147.

[10]M. Kent Jennings, *Community Influentials,* Free Press, New York, 1964, pp. 107–109.

very limited. Institutional lobbies, which work with a governmental agency, frequently have some input.

Policy acceptance is the bargaining and conflict resolution in developing a workable alternative. The strategies for marshaling leadership, money, support, symbols, and information are the means of conflict resolution. Environmental proposals are very pervasive in their effects, and therefore clash with numerous and powerful economic groups. Considerable money, energy, and skill are needed to obtain a coalition large enough to support environmental proposals.

Policy legitimation takes place by legislation or by administrative rulings. Most environmental policy legislation is limited in scope, often narrow enough to invite specific opposition by economic groups affected, but too wide in public impact or interest to attract much support. The consequence is that many environmental proposals are easily defeated by specific opposition.

Policy implementation is carried out by an administrative agency, which often has the discretion to alter or repeal the policy by interpretation. The frustration of policy is particularly plausible when the government agency has a supporting clientele group whose economic interests would be adversely affected. That is, the agencies protect the status quo and use their discretion to maintain the stakes of those whom they regulate. Theodore Lowi observes that the rules of the game weigh heavily in favor of established interests.[11]

PUBLIC INITIATIVE IN PARTICIPATION IN ADMINISTRATIVE RULINGS

The difficulties of the public participation in the policy process, then, are those of initiative, access, and coalition formation. Initiative is needed to introduce policy, access to affect its priority and acceptance, and coalition to facilitate the formulation of opinion and social choice on an issue. The means to facilitate public initiatives, access, and coalition formation was explored in a study of the Forest Service by Charles Reich.[12] The people of the United States own in common two hundred million acres of land, rich in minerals, timber, and mountains. This vast domain of natural resources is administered by the Forest Service, the National Park Service, and the Bureau of Land Management. In this experiment in public ownership, the people might be expected to play a role in policy formation; but in fact that role is negligible. The Forest Service must

[11]Theodore Lowi, *The End of Liberalism*, W. W. Norton & Company, Inc., New York, 1969, p. 62.
[12]Reagan, op. cit., pp. 284–294.

decide among alternative uses of the land it administers. The principal economic use is for logging; but other uses include recreation, grazing, water rights, fishing, hunting, and tourism. How shall the decision be made between lumbering and scenery?

The decisions were made partly on the basis of hearings and administrative evaluation. Most forest management decisions depend upon technical information as to soil, water, timber, climate, and the affect of different use patterns on tree productivity. By and large the public is not knowledgeable on these subjects. To obtain informed opinion, the tendency was to invite expertise. The expertise was available largely from the lumbering companies. The result was that selective hearings and selective expertise tended to produce decisions favoring timber cutting over other uses. Reich suggests that one model to follow, in trying to increase public inputs into the administrative decisions, is the pattern of the legislative process, which provides a setting for adequate notice and debate. For example, citizen groups might be represented on technical advisory committees for government agencies, hearing notifications might be publicized well in advance, agenda and information made available. Then debate, opposition, deliberation, and a preparation of a report on the issues could be arranged, prior to decision. Finally a supporting statement on the facts, issues, and reasons for the ruling might be made. This would put important administrative decision making into the public forum, whereas selective hearings among experts have an inadvertant secrecy built into them. While procedural reforms such as this cannot alone solve environmental problems, they can at least ventilate the issues, bring broader vision, provide a sense of involvement, and bring a deeper relationship between man and his environment.

PROBLEMS OF COMPLIANCE

The policy formation aspects of environmental improvement are only the start of the problem, because even more difficulties lie in implementation and compliance. The making of government decision is not a majestic march of great majorities mobilizing behind grand policy issues; it is the steady bargaining and appeasement of small groups. That bargaining takes place as much, if not more, at the administrative level in the implementation stage as at the policy level. Indeed, the very act of bargaining has implied in it a mutual interest, as well as differences which conflict. The mutual interest is what makes the bargain possible, and this can have the effect of creating common cause between the pollution control agency and the polluter, as Ronald Loveridge has noted:

Repeated studies have documented that administrative agencies often become a reflection of the system of group pressures. And, in the case of air pollution control programs, the influence of administrative agencies depends especially on the good will and support of the groups they are set up to control. (Unfortunately, most pollution enforcement decisions are invisible and too complicated for the public-at-large.) Put briefly, the stakes of the pollution game can, in many ways, be won or lost in the politics of administrative control agencies.[13]

Without a strong independent constituency interested in environmental quality, control agencies face the prospect of offering the symbols of control, while in fact conducting a loose and ineffectual control process. Moreover, there have been few studies of the behavior of agencies on how to control effectively, a rather startling finding considering the substantial history of government regulation and intervention. Some illustrative examples of regulatory effectiveness can be brought to mind, of course, though systematic studies are few. The Federal Reserve System has been fairly effective in controlling the aggregate money supply and broad aspects of bank operations like reserve requirements and interest rates on savings. This is because the number of banks is relatively limited, and they deposit their reserves in the central bank. The Federal Reserve System has been reluctant, however, to administer Regulation W, a control over consumer credit terms and loan conditions, except in wartime or emergency. The reason is, of course, that the number of consumers and retail or financial establishments, from whom they can obtain credit, is very large; and the Federal Reserve has no organized liaison with these establishments upon which it can rely for monitoring. The result is that the majority of loans can be made without a source of information for routine audit.

The importance of information sources for routine audit is also illustrated by the Internal Revenue Service in income tax collection. The number of citizens and small establishments liable for income tax payments is very large, as in the Regulation W case; but the major sources of income payment lie in a finite number (a few thousand) of large institutions. By payroll deduction, reports on corporate income payments, and audits, the Internal Revenue Service can accumulate the information on most income sources. Beyond this, they are aided by a business milieu which gives the IRS auxiliary tools of examination and investigation. For example, the practice of a regular audit by a public accounting firm for all business with public shareholders, or seeking loans, creates accounting

[13]Ronald Loveridge, *Political Science and Air Pollution: A Review and Assessment of the Literature*, Project Clean Air, Task Force Assessment, vol. 3, University of California, Riverside, Calif., 1970, pp. 4–31.

documentation standards which make the records auditable for tax purposes as well. One of the principal differences between the tight income tax enforcement in the United States, and the substantial tax evasion in other countries, lies in the differences in accounting practices and documentation. Another powerful resource for analysis is the bank records of checking account transactions. The fact that most payments are by check, and that check transactions leave an audit trail, helps make income taxes as enforceable as they are.

Applied to environmental control, we may surmise that compliance and enforceability are directly proportional to the availability of source records and documentation on effluents or emissions.

The effectiveness of a control agency depends upon its information base, the ability to trace transactions from their source to destination, and the ability to audit them. Seen in this light, most pollution control agencies have little means for enforcement or compliance. There are no records of emissions, for example, by each automobile owner, nor a documented series of transactions of the emission through its photochemical interactions in the atmosphere to its final destination in the lungs of a receptor.

Air pollution control agencies are now seeking to establish tests on the emission levels of a sample of new cars as they come off of production lines, as a source record. Regular inspection would also add to the documentation. But a complete data base is far away in air pollution control; and, in the meantime, the control agency depends for its technical information about emission characteristics on the goodwill of the polluters, that is, upon the automobile and oil companies to give them information. It is this mutual requirement for information that makes the bargaining process one of mutual interest; and the dependence of the control agency on the polluter for the documentation to do even a symbolic job is what makes enforcement more of an accommodation than compliance.

Obviously the controller must be relieved of dependence upon the controlled if there is to be real enforcement. This is not a simple problem, because there is no milieu of documentation about the ecosystem, as there is for income taxes. The infrastructure of institutions, like banks and accounting firms, does not have a parallel in environmental control. The environmental administrator has few data sources, little systematic documentation, and no audit trails. He has to create his own control data base for himself. That is to say, environmental administration needs ecological indicators, instrumentation, and a monitoring network in order to have independence in enforcement. The Environmental Protection Agency and other control agencies are rapidly augmenting their instrumentation and monitoring networks, but no one pretends that this is an easy or rapid task. Accounting and banking practice took centuries to develop to the point of present controllability. In environmental monitoring, it is realistic to expect years or decades to build a data base for systematic enforcement.

The difficulty of enforcement without the data base has led to consideration of other avenues of compliance, and that is to rely on individuals to accumulate the data on damages from pollution. If such evidence of damage is available in individual hands, then there may be the basis for legal action of one individual against another in the courts as a means of compliance. However, the damages are only actionable if the court recognizes the liability of the polluter for injury to the plaintiff. This has led legal scholars to explore the alteration of liability rules to enable an injured receptor to show cause for damages from the polluter. The common theories for environmental litigation have been on grounds of negligence, nuisance, or trespass. Even when the court strains its interpretations of negligence (for example, under the doctrines of negligence per se, or *res ipsa loquitor*) the plaintiff must still offer proofs of cause and effect, which is difficult because there are multiple emission sources or complex intermediate interactions, which are common in biology.

Despite these difficulties, the redefinition of liability rules has promising potential, at least for avoiding most of the problems of enforcement by control agencies. Compliance by control agencies will always be a costly regime—to develop the data base, to staff the enforcement, to conduct the audits, and to prevent collusive interests among controller and controlled. The individual liability alternative presents the possibility of independent regulation through the market economy.

The market place now does not reflect environmental costs because they are not liabilities to the producer, nor are they actionable in court. If the proof of biological damage created the presumption of liability forcing the polluter to show cause that he did not initiate the injury, then the polluter's use of air or water for waste disposal would begin to assume market costs to him. That is the polluter would have to prove that he did not, in fact, emit pollutants. He could offer this proof by investing in pollution control equipment so there were in fact no emissions, or he would have to assume the liability for damage. Either way, he would incur a market cost for the use of air or water. That is, the redefinition of liability rules would have the effect of internalizing the costs of pollution control into the enterprise. Then the internalized costs would be treated and reflected in the market like any other price.

The objective of environmental litigation under strict liability rules, then, would be to internalize costs, reflect them in the market, and thus improve the process of public and private decision making. Private decision making would be improved because it would correct the misallocation of resources which occurs when resources like air and water are underpriced (see Chapters 13 and 14).

Environmental litigation can also serve an educational function. Every major piece of social legislation in the last fifty years has been preceded by a history of litigation which called to the attention of legislators the inadequacy of existing law. "Litigation can uncover administrative abuses, gather together hard evidence about previously unknown or poorly understood problems, pinpoint inadequacies in existing legislation and suggest the shape and direction of new laws."[14]

POLITICAL ALIGNMENTS

Governance consists of the advancement of group objectives and the reconciliation of conflicts among differing group objectives. In this sense, group interests are the motive force of politics and an essential part of conflict resolution and self-governance. In environmental politics, four kinds of group interests are most influential. They are the single-issue, conservation, professional, and economic groups.[15]

The single-issue interest group is on with a special concern for one problem, like air pollution, or banning DDT. These groups are often effective in initiating programs or supporting local activities, but they do not become broad popular movements. Their limited objective gives them focus, which often provides useful support for a control agency, but they are generally ignored by politicians seeking broader constituencies. Single-issue groups have a troublesome problem of sustained appeal to their membership, with the consequence that they often lack the concerted and continuous partisan influence to remain effective.

Citizen conservation groups represent broader appeals and interests than single issues, as their focus is more generally on wildlife, wilderness, or environmental problems. Their memberships represent, in a sense, a minority view in society, a position, a particular set of values with respect to nature. Both traditional conservationists and new environmentalists have enough breadth of appeal to sustain membership reasonably well, and they can be quite effective in winning litigation or legislation on a few, specific issues. However, they tend to be rather loose organizations, with diversity of interest, part-time leadership, moderate financing, and small

---

[14]James E. Krier, *Air Pollution and Legal Institutions,* Project Clean Air, University of California, Riverside, Calif., pp. 5–9.
[15]Loveridge, op. cit., pp. 4–10.

staffs. The two largest conservation organizations, for example, do not maintain full-time lobbyists in Washington. As a result, they are in no way equipped to take a broad range of environmental problems to the people, legislators, or administrators.

Professional, service, government, and even some social groups have, on occasion, taken up environmental issues. Among professionals, scientists, physicians, economists, and lawyers are likely to be exposed to environmental problems in the practice of their professions; and some portion of them become deeply concerned about what they find in their analysis and research. These concerned professionals tend to become splinter groups within their profession seeking environmental improvement; and they may, on occasion, reach across professional lines to become associated with colleagues in other disciplinary fields. Such interdisciplinary professionals have, potentially, an unsurpassed expertise on environmental issues, but they are also likely to be people who are more research- than action-oriented. They are not easily organized unless the issue becomes critical. The result is that coalitions are difficult to form for continuous impact.

Economic groups are the common basis for organization; and they are by far the most effective in terms of resources, skilled manpower, and sustained political pressures. The strength of economic groups politically lies in their capacity to wage intensive campaigns on specific issues which affect them, at the same time as they support a broad positional front that corresponds well with partisan politics. This is a posture which other interest groups cannot match. The result is that economic groups can almost always win on specific issues in the short run against other interest groups.

More generally, concentrations of interest have a short-run advantage over diffuse interest groups. Economic groups represent concentrations of both interests and resources, and these can be tactically massed to overwhelm opposition. The concentration of interest is partly possible because the group involves smaller numbers operating with traditional value constraints, and this is also the weakness of economic groups. Diffuse groups represent larger populations with wider value structures. They do not easily coalesce their wants on specific issues, but, once they do, they can generally win in the long run because of their larger voting power. The phenomenon of political coalescence is usually triggered by high levels of anxiety or aspiration, that is, from fear or hope. This is what gives the crisis proportions to political action. The fear of an enemy creates the crisis of war, or the hope for prosperity creates the crisis of economic reform.

Environmental problems have been below the threshold of crisis so far, and thus economic groups have had more sway in environmental compromise than the diffuse interest of other groups. With such uneven political weight on each side of the issues, society may be unable to redress its environmental ailments without a crisis; and of course this is dangerous politics because by then some ecological changes may be irreversible. One has to be an optimist to hope that incremental measures, such as internalizing cost, adjusting liability rules, and revising the decision structure, will be sufficient and timely enough to avoid environmental disaster.

The partisan alignment of interest groups presents no clear pattern. Economic groups tend somewhat to align with conservative party factions; and the conservation, single-interest, professional groups tend somewhat, perhaps, to liberal partisanship. But there are no clear party lines on environmental issues. All parties nominally favor environmental quality. Officials from both parties are vigorous environmentalists, and likewise some representatives of both parties consistently vote down environmental legislation in favor of economic priorities. Indeed, party seems to have relatively little to do with alignment on environmental issues.

A more fundamental distinction than party on environmental issues appears to be attitudinal, that is, the individual's faith in science. Many people, and the majority of politicians regardless of party, continue to act as though they believe that there are technological solutions to environmental problems. They continue to act like Bruno's Jove, they can operate outside the laws of nature. Here is the paradox: The scientific community is the source of scepticism about technical solutions to environmental problems; and politicians, who are the behaviorists without peer, are sceptical about behavioral solution. Or at least, the politicians continue to hope for a technical solution in preference to a behavioral one. One cannot spend very much time as an environmentalist talking to people without being impressed with the massive resistance, among public and politicians alike, to the idea that technical solutions are inadequate to meet the environmental crisis. This faith in technology is so culturally embedded that perhaps nothing short of ecological catastrophe will shake it.

The political alignments stemming from faith in technology have interesting historical roots, as well as current manifestations. The early stages of the industrial revolution, over a century and a half ago, were accompanied by vehement resistance to technology by both radicals and conservatives. The Luddites in England struck against the introduction of machinery, and radicals from Proudhon to Marx denounced the dehumanization and exploitation of labor which resulted from the industrial system. The conservatives, at the same time, decried the rise of technology for different reasons, that it changed the structure of society, increased conflicts among classes, and shattered the organic unity of traditional society. Thomas Carlyle, for example, looked upon competition and capitalism as barbaric, a setting of people against each other, and advocated return to traditional society.

The interesting thing is that radicals and conservatives have both said, from the beginning, that technology destroyed the emotional and collective life, not just of those caught up in it, but of the whole society. Today the left and the right see our present agony as a crisis of a technological society, but the liberals do not. Liberals then and now have seen technology as a tireless progenitor of progress, while overlooking the outlandish price paid for technology in the form of social control and poor environmental quality.[16]

The crossovers of interest groups against technological attitude produce some curious environmental bedfellows and alignments. The normal support for environmentalism would be expected from the liberal factions of the professional, conservation, and single-issue interest groups; but these liberals are also the persons with the most faith in technological solutions. The result is they are often unwilling or unable to see the need for underlying behavioral change.

Some of the strongest support on environmental issues comes from an unexpected source, the extreme right and the extreme left, because they have been opposed to technological change from the very beginning. Thus they are more ready to see its biological damage effects and its limited power to solve environmental problems.

Much of the support for environmental improvement then comes from antitechnologists on the left and the right, from splinter professionals immersed in the problem, from conservationists, from single-issue groups, and from a few liberals who have slipped over the line in their technological faith. These environmentalists represent a heterogeneous group of people, certainly a hodgepodge from which a coalition will not easily emerge. One could hardly create, if he purposefully tried, an interest group which cuts across more political, partisan, or social lines. It may be a long time, and several catastrophes away, before such an alignment will be a match for the economic groups which they oppose.

What is left, of course, is the populist hope that the good sense of the common people will prevail, and that they will see the environmental crisis in time to prevent it. In other words, democracy will again muddle through. But if the hope for averting the ecological disaster, of which the

[16]Edward Shorter, "Industrial Society in Trouble," *The American Scholar*, Spring 1971, pp. 330–345.

President warned, lies in good sense and democratic procedure, then the good sense must be informed with environmental knowledge and the democratic procedures must be made to work. What is needed for environmental quality is the politics of crisis without the crisis.

CRISIS POLITICS WITHOUT CRISIS

Is it possible to create the conditions of crisis politcs without the crisis? That is, can diffuse interest groups be brought to a state of awareness about a vital problem such as biological damage and environmental quality, so that their preferences coalesce into an environmental improvement program without an ecological disaster?

Kotler and Zaltman believe that social issues—such as pollution control, mass transit, private education, drug abuse, and public medicine—could benefit from marketing thinking and planning.[17] That is, continuous collection of information from the environment can be conducted by a change agency with research and planning functions. The research function would study needs, communication methods, channel distribution, and economic parameters of social (or environmental) issues. The planning function would determine media, personal contacts, and volunteer participation needed to reach primary and secondary audiences. A primary audience on ecological issues is the individual voting groups and voluntary conservation or environmental organizations. The personal contacts from volunteers to individual citizens could most readily be accomplished through the professional and conservation groups.

The success of such a policy communication mechanism depends heavily upon frequency of communication and face to face discussion. Studies of World War II bond drives, and fund raising in cancer and heart campaigns, indicate that the convenience of response is an important factor in success. The convenience of local banks or employer payroll deduction, for example, was a significant factor in the success of the war bond drives. Media saturation by itself is not effective unless coupled with a convenient, local link for responsive action.

With at least 2,500 local environmental organizations in the country plus hundreds of professional associations, the linkage to obtain responsive action on environmental issues should be feasible. This suggests that a response mechanism on environmental issues could function effectively in the framework of a policy communication system which had local linkages.

[17]Philip Kotler and Gerald Zaltman, "Social Marketing: An Approach to Planned Social Change," *Journal of Marketing*, July 1971, vol. 35, no. 3, pp. 3–12.

The counter argument is sometimes made that politics cannot be changed by procedures, because human nature will not change; and human nature is basically self-interested, motivated by the desire for goods and pleasure. The question then becomes what causes and constitutes pleasure? New behavioral research indicates that pleasure via consumption is only one, and not the most effective, stimulus to a pleasurable state. A series of experiments with men, animals, and fish demonstrate that electricity supplied to the limbic system of the brain, in charges similar to those normally developed by cellular activity, creates the pleasurable state of happiness or feeling good. This intercranial stimulation is so satisfying that organisms—men, fish, or animals—seek it in preference to food, even when they are very hungry.

Consumption too causes pleasurable sensations, by the same process of providing neural stimulation to the same limbic system of the brain, but the evolution of the nervous system is such that repeated stimulus from the same source (consumption) provides a diminishing sense of pleasure. While consumption provides a diminishing stimulus to the limbic system, direct forms of stimulation, like thinking, meditation, visual perception (or an electrode applied directly to the brain), provide a continuous and undiminished pleasurable state.

Distinctly human behavior causes activation of the limbic pleasure regions of the brain, not as a result of the sense organs, but primarily as a result of the brain's thinking regions.[18] This is powerful theory, because it has the potential to change the motivational structure of an industrial society and replace it with new motivations and new social structures. Stimulation by thinking, as a motivational force is not new, because contemplative or artistic people have been aware of it over the ages. What is new, in this age and no other, is that a whole generation of young people have learned to think. A whole generation of thinkers is truly portentous, because now millions of youth are capable of intercranial self-stimulation without reliance on consumption as their principle means of satisfaction. With alternative ways to achieve a pleasurable state, they can be more objective about the world around them, to consider the conditions of life quality and environmental quality, to feel released from the production-consumption syndrome which is an integral part of the environmental problem.

Given a population with a capacity to achieve satisfactions by thought as well as consumption, and given a policy communication mechanism on environmental problems with local response linkages,

[18]H. J. Campbell, "Pleasure-seeking Brains; Natural Joys of Thought," *Smithsonian*, October 1971, vol. 2, no. 7, pp. 14–23.

some hope, at least, exists that a state of awareness on vital issues can coalesce the preference of diffuse interest groups without the occurrence of a crisis or ecological disaster.

SUMMARY

Environmental politics are what they are because of the relative strength of interest groups. The main interest groups on environmental issues are the single-issue, conservation, professional, and economic groups. The economic groups have a concentrated set of objectives and resources which gives them a tactical advantage, in the short run, on most specific issues. The other groups, with diffuse interests, have loose organizations and more difficulty coalescing upon a preference. Once the preference formation and coalition begins to take place, however, the diffuse interest groups prevail politically through their greater numbers. This phenomenon of coalescence, on issues charged with anxiety or aspiration, is what gives politics crisis characteristics, and what creates policy which under-supplies or oversupplies public goods. Crisis politics is, therefore, a factor in the misallocation of resources, because the social choice mechanisms available are infrequent and inadequate to keep public policy aligned with public preferences (Chapters 18 and 23).

The public policy process can be categorized into five steps: (1) policy initiation, (2) fixing priorities, (3) use of resources to gain acceptance of alternatives, (4) legitimation, and (5) implementation. The public has some role in the legitimation process through representative government, but rather little input to the other policy steps. One of the means to improve the policy process would be to innovate ways the public can make input at all policy stages, and particularly on initiation and implementation.

A difficulty for the public in making policy inputs is that many of the issues involve technical alternatives, and the public has neither the background nor the knowledge to analyze technical problems. An approach to meet this problem is participatory technology in which panels of experts make technical assessments to identify the issues and test feasibility of alternative approaches. These technology assessments can then become the basis for public choice, advocacy, or litigation.

Policy is not effective without implementation and compliance. Compliance is difficult to achieve in environmental programs due to the lack of a source data base, audit trails, or collaborative institutions to effectuate enforcement. The establishment of an instrumented monitoring network is an important aid to enforcement, but long term in its realization. In the more immediate future, the redefinition of liability rules would internalize costs and decentralize compliance to the individual level.

The political alignments on environmental issues are basically nonpartisan; instead they are related primarily to attitudes toward nature and biological damage on one hand, and attitudes toward technology on the other. In consequence, the environmental interest group is a miscellany of otherwise incompatible interests, including the extreme right and left, single-issue groups, conservation groups, splinter professionals, and a few disenchanted liberals. The large liberal center, however, which is normally most receptive to change and improvement, social or environmental, retains its historic commitment to technology as a vehicle for social progress. The political alignments on environmental issues are so mixed with diverse interest groups that coalescence of a mainstream policy for environmental improvement seems far away, unless there is an ecological disaster or a significant change in environmental decision processes. The changes in environmental decision processes, which would improve environmental quality, and hopefully avert disaster, might be recapitulated briefly from the various sections of this book.

1   An analytic methodology and data base might be established to relate human and economic activity to its environmental consequences (Section Three).

2   Social choice-making mechanisms might be made more frequent. A timely indication of changing preferences is possible by applying present technology to direct referenda on environmental issues, by utilizing survey research methods and by more participative administrative processes (Chapter 18).

3   Environmental administrators can help formulate, clarify, and precipitate environmental choices by careful mission analysis, which demonstrates the purposes, biological effects, and alternatives in environmental decisions (Chapter 21).

4   The representativeness of private and public boards can be increased (Chapter 22).

5   An external environmental information system can be developed, using the data base described in Section Three, to inform the public more adequately about biological damage and alternatives for improving environmental quality (Chapter 23).

6   A public policy communication mechanism with local linkages can be created to help include the public in policy initiation (Chapter 24).

7   The public might be included in implementation by having administrative procedures follow the model of the legislative process. That is, administrative agencies might open their decisions to citizens by more frequent use of hearing notifications, agenda, background information, open degate, citizen representation, and a decision analysis with supporting rationale for the ruling made (Chapter 24).

8 Liability rules might be redefined to decentralize compliance with environmental quality standards (Chapter 24).

Surely alternatives, such as these, require debate; but just as surely a more adequate decision process must be found to make human activity consonant with ecological diversity, balance, and well-being. Surely, too, man has the intelligence to adapt to living in his own habitat. One would find it hard not to believe at least in that.

DISCUSSION QUESTIONS

1 What kinds of questions regarding environmental issues have occurred to you which might be assisted by technology assessment? How would you see the assessment functioning?
2 What are the various stages of the policy process, and how do you think that citizen inputs might be introduced into policy making?
3 Do you think the adaptation of administrative rulings to the legislative model would work? Why or why not?
4 Do you think there is any soltuion to crisis politics without crisis? If so, what?

PROBLEM

Select an environmental issue with which you have some familiarity, then analyze the interest groups in terms of their characteristics, strengths, and weaknesses, as a means of explaining the outcome of the issue.

INDEX

INDEX